ENCYCLOPEDIA OF AMERICAN DISABILITY HISTORY

VOLUME I

Edited by Susan Burch, Ph.D.
Foreword by Paul K. Longmore, Ph.D.

Facts On File
An imprint of Infobase Publishing

ENCYCLOPEDIA OF AMERICAN DISABILITY HISTORY

Copyright © 2009 Facts On File

Facts On File, Inc.
An imprint of Infobase Publishing
132 West 31st Street
New York NY 10001

Library of Congress Cataloging-in-Publication Data

Encyclopedia of American disability history / edited by Susan Burch ; foreword
by Paul K. Longmore.
p. cm.
Includes bibliographical references and index.
ISBN 978-0-8160-7030-5
1. Disabilities—United States—Encyclopedias.
2. Disabilities—United States—History. I. Burch, Susan.
HV1553.E523 2009
362.40973'03—dc22   2008030537

Facts On File books are available at special discounts when purchased in bulk
quantities for businesses, associations, institutions, or sales promotions.
Please call our Special Sales Department in New York
at (212) 967-8800 or (800) 322-8755.

You can find Facts On File on the World Wide Web at http://www.factsonfile.com

Text design by Erika K. Arroyo
Cover design by Takeshi Takahashi
Illustrations by Dale Williams

Printed in the United States of America

VB Hermitage 10 9 8 7 6 5 4 3 2 1

This book is printed on acid-free paper and contains 30 percent
postconsumer recycled content.

Contents

List of Entries

VOLUME I

VOLUME III

List of Documents

About the Editor

Susan Burch, Ph.D., is the author of *Signs of Resistance: American Deaf Cultural History, 1900 to World War II* (New York University Press, 2002), coeditor of *Double Visions: Multidisciplinary Approaches to Women and Deafness* (Gallaudet University Press, 2006), and coauthor of *Unspeakable: The Story of Junius Wilson* (University of North Carolina Press, 2007). She has written numerous articles and book chapters that have appeared in such publications as *The New Disability History*; *Sign Language Studies*; *Journal of Social History*; *Literacy and Deaf People: Contextual and Cultural Approaches*; *The Public Historian: Special Issue on Disability History*; *Literature and Medicine*; and the *Radical History Review*. She is cofounder and board member of the Disability History Association and has served on the Society for Disability Studies' board of directors. Her work has been acknowledged with several awards, including a Mellon Seminar Fellowship and a Fulbright lecturing award. Dr. Burch has taught at Gallaudet University in Washington, D.C.; Charles University in Prague, Czech Republic; King's College, University of Aberdeen, Scotland; and The Ohio State University. She also has worked with the Smithsonian National Museum of American History. Burch is currently an associate professor in the Department of American Studies at Middlebury College and director of the Center for the Comparative Study of Race and Ethnicity.

Acknowledgments

This distinctive encyclopedia is the product of more than 300 authors; we thank them all for their generous contributions of time and knowledge. Many activists, individuals, and scholars whose work has laid the foundation for this project deserve recognition as well. Thanks especially go to Jack Gannon, Paul Longmore, and Fred Pelka for their own encyclopedic knowledge of history. Brenda Jo Brueggemann, Grace Chang, Lee Craig, Phil Ferguson, Beth Haller, Marilyn Hamilton, John Kinder, Georgina Kleege, Cathy Kudlick, Neil Lerner, Josh Lukin, Ann Millett, Bob Osgood, Corbett O'Toole, Sue Schweik, J. David Smith, and Sunaura Taylor expanded the conceptual scope of this project and gave invaluable advice. The kind moderators and subscribers of various listservs answered our calls for help on numerous occasions. We are grateful especially to H-Disability, DS-Hum, and to the SDS listservs. Audra Jennings's diligent work on the chronology significantly enhanced the value of this reference tool.

Thankfully, there are various rich resources in American disability history. This project drew heavily from the materials and staff knowledge at Gallaudet University Archives and library, the Museum of disABILITY History, the Bancroft Oral History Archives, and the Disability History Museum. The Smithsonian National Museum of American History provided many primary sources, historical gems of lived experiences. Museum staff member Beth Ziebarth, intern Emily Holmes, and consultant Joel Snyder contributed their wisdom and support. Dr. James and Diane (Frampton) Bickford, Lilly Cleveland, Paul Leung, Colleen McHugh, Leroy Moore, Iris Frampton Muggenthaler, Tom Olin, Elaine Ostroff, Ken Stein, Karen Schneiderman, Dick Sobsey, Dale Swan, and Michael Welner kindly shared family and community histories and materials. David Gerber, Reid Dunlavery, and Vincent DiGirolamo located many of the quotations that appear throughout this work.

A special note of thanks goes to the people at Facts On File. Roxanna Krawczyk and Melissa Cullen-DuPont patiently endured torrents of e-mails and phone calls and often brought order out of chaos. Takeshi Takahashi and Dale Williams lent their talents to the cover and illustrations; we thank the many others who also helped produce this work. Executive Editor Andrew Gyory, whose delight in this project infused our collaboration, challenged and supported us to push the boundaries of historical inquiry.

The thoughtful, creative, and deeply committed advisers deserve special recognition: Kim Nielsen, Katherine Ott, Penny Richards, Julia Miele Rodas, Carrie Sandahl, Richard Scotch, Steve Taylor, Graham Warder, and Dan Wilson. Their essential contributions to this project included framing the encyclopedia's approach and content, gathering primary sources, editing drafts, and writing particularly challenging entries. Their good humor, collegiality, and brilliance were an additional blessing.

Disability history teaches us the powerful role of community. We appreciate the considerable encouragement our family, friends, and peers provided as this project unfolded. An ultimate measure of gratitude goes to Ian M. Sutherland for his devoted support.

Foreword

by Paul K. Longmore

This *Encyclopedia of American Disability History* is filled with surprises, small and large. As with all fresh approaches to history, it introduces us to people and things previously overlooked. More important, it reorients our perspectives on broad vistas of history, restructuring our understanding of experiences, ideologies, and processes we assumed we knew. When read in reference to one another, the articles that compose this encyclopedia contain four major themes: the importance of disability in American history despite its invisibility in historians' writings; the need to explain disability in historical terms rather than relegating it to the realm of medical pathology; the varieties and similarities of historical experiences among people with disabilities as well as their historical agency; and the necessity of comparing those histories of disability with one another.

Most obvious, this encyclopedia shows that "disability" has always been a key feature of American history. The plain demographic facts indicate its historical significance. Current estimates reckon that there are in the United States in the early 21st century, at a minimum, 51 million persons with disabilities that have a major impact on life activities. They represent one-sixth of the U.S. population. The numbers were surely proportionately as high or higher in the past. Disability's historical commonplaceness and importance also become apparent if we simply survey the topics covered in this encyclopedia and even more obvious if we peruse the articles. There it is in the histories of immigration, labor, and social reform, of politics, public policy, and war, of business, education, and popular culture, of America's various regions, races, and ethnic groups, of family and gender, of women's and men's experiences, and of virtually every other sphere of American life from movie theaters and sports arenas to Greyhound buses and school buses to schoolhouses and the White House. It appears not only in private lives but also in

the public arena as part of collective experience, as a social problem, as a cultural metaphor. Disability is historically pervasive and multifarious.

Yet, despite its historical ubiquitousness, disability and people with disabilities have typically gone unnoticed. In historical memory as in the writings of professional historians, these experiences, these themes, have been rendered invisible. What work historians have done has usually been inadvertent, peripheral to their primary concerns, and embedded in other subjects, such as the histories of aging, education, eugenics, medicine, social service professions, or social welfare policy. The entries that compose this encyclopedia not only examine the social history of people with disabilities in the United States and the intellectual and cultural history of disability as important in their own right; they also deepen comprehension of the many and varied historical fields in which disability and people with disabilities played an important but usually unrecognized part. They call our attention to disability as a subject of historical analysis. They compel recognition of it as a historical phenomenon we cannot ignore.

That a volume titled the *Encyclopedia of American Disability History* would prompt us to look at disability from a historical standpoint may seem obvious, but consider the far-reaching implications of a historical approach. It represents a major departure from the medical paradigm of disability and the medicalized interpersonal and public, institutional, and professional ways of regarding people with disabilities that, during the past several centuries, became deeply entrenched in every sphere of modern society. A view of disability and people with disabilities that considers them only in terms of medical pathology is not only nonhistorical; it completely removes them from the possibility of historical analysis. These collected articles take disability out of the realm of the simply and simplistically physiological and pathological. In considering disability as personal experience, identity, and social role, as social problem, public issue, and cultural metaphor, this encyclopedia significantly revises our understanding by explaining it as a historically contingent phenomenon.

Taken together, the articles in this volume demonstrate both the varieties of disability experiences throughout American history and their commonalities. In either case, the contributors again show the serious limitations of a medical pathology perspective that marginalizes these experiences to the realm of the private and individual by separating them from the cultural, social, and political. The contributors' approach explains disability as a historically evolving series of social identities and roles. Corollary to that finding is the recognition that, despite considerable differences in their physiological conditions, people with disabilities confronted a common set of stigmatizing social values embedded and expressed in social and institutional practices.

In addition, the various historical accounts gathered here show us that, again contrary to the medicalized and pathologized view dominant in the modern era, people with disabilities were never historically passive and inert. They were always historical agents. And—particularly important for our understanding of disability history—they often banded together and organized themselves to act collectively. Sometimes they provided one another with interpersonal support. Sometimes they built community among themselves. Sometimes they took political action to alter their standing and enhance their power in their society. Never mere victims of either impairment or society, they were always actors in their own histories.

Finally, this comprehensive encyclopedia of American disability history offers us many opportunities for comparative historical analysis. It helps us explore the ways in which the various disability histories laid before us were at times separate, at times parallel, at times intersecting. Notions of disability as both an organizing concept and a social problem operated in areas such as medicine, education, and social services, public policies, cultural representations, and social reform, but they did so only semi-autonomously. On a broader scale, they interacted with one another to uphold an underlying, culturewide modern ideology of disability. At the same time, people with disabilities, individually and collectively, defined themselves in multiple and varying ways, attempted to fashion social roles and identities in opposition to the dominant ideology, and sought to gain control of their lives, their social careers, and their collective destinies. We have in this encyclopedia fascinating possibilities for historical comparisons that are not only valuable but also absolutely necessary if we are to reconstruct fully and faithfully the general history of disability and people with disabilities in American history.

In recent decades, issues of disability have become central and pressing in every institution and sphere of American life, in education and health care, in social welfare policies and civil rights laws, in public spaces and public debates. Americans with disabilities of all sorts have moved into the public sphere as never before in our history. It is no exaggeration to say that we have been compelled to rethink all of our conventional wisdom about "disability," that it has become necessary for us to reexamine everything we have assumed about people with disabilities. As always, in order to understand our present situation, in order sensibly and responsibly to chart our shared future, we need to reconsider our past. We need to explain more clearly the history of disability and people with disabilities as an integral part of American history. This encyclopedia will aid us in that important and necessary task.

Introduction

When I teach disability history, I often first ask students to make a list of everything that comes to mind. Their lists are fairly consistent, often starting with objects: wheelchairs, hearing aids, and white canes. Iconic figures follow: Helen Keller, Franklin Roosevelt, and disabled veterans. Given more time to reflect, their examples frequently become more personal: relatives, friends, even themselves.

In recent decades, Americans in general also have come to recognize that issues and experiences of people with disabilities pervade every aspect of our society. This encyclopedia introduces readers to the history of America's largest minority—people with disabilities—and provides tools for understanding disability and America in new ways.

The field of disability history has its roots in the movement for disability civil rights, and, as advocates of the latter have worked to make society more inclusive, the related intellectual discipline has evolved to make Americans more aware of the historical role of disability in our culture. As with all historical approaches, disability history is complex, in part because its constituents infiltrate all of our institutions: social, legal, familial, medical, governmental, religious, and educational, to name just a few. By examining society broadly through the lens of disability, a new generation of historians is expanding and sometimes challenging the traditional interpretations of these institutions and reinterpreting fundamental concepts such as identity, community, citizenship, and "normalcy." We also confront factors that have determined the traditional meaning of disability. Disability scholars argue that disability is a social construction—that is, that disability is often less about physical or mental impairments than it is about how society responds to impairments. This is important for moving disability from the narrow, often stigmatizing, and ahistorical realms of medical facilities, charitable programs, and special education classrooms. The social model of disability in fact rejects the notion that

people with disabilities are inherently "defective" and solely in need of rehabilitation; rather, disability is seen as a common factor of life.

Demographics bear this out. According to the U.S. Census and other statistical studies, since 2000, nearly one out of every five Americans has qualified as disabled. That is 54 million people; 33 million people qualified as severely disabled. The numbers are probably much higher than this. And as Americans live longer, their chances of being at least temporarily disabled rise significantly. Among the readers of this encyclopedia, *all* of you either have or had some kind of disability yourselves, know someone who has a disability, or will become disabled at some point in your life. As many disability scholars have demonstrated, disability is everywhere, once you begin looking for it. Teachers, students, scholars, activists, policymakers, medical and health service professionals, community leaders, journalists, and parents and other family members will find this reference useful for explaining disability concepts and experiences, and will learn the central role disability has played in the formation of America's historical identity.

By including people with disabilities—and their families and communities—in American history, this encyclopedia offers a new conception of what it means to be in America and to be an American. In this way it differs significantly from traditional approaches, which often marginalize, institutionalize, and stigmatize individuals deemed "different."

Disability History

Recent scholarship in disability history has broadened the traditional scope of American society, illuminating individuals, issues, organizations, institutions, and movements that have made up significant components of our country throughout its history. In the colonial era, for example, strong familial, religious, and economic factors kept most individuals with disabilities in their homes and communities; informal support arrangements, some cruel, some caring, were guided by a diverse array of local standards and authorities, without any overarching organization or legal framework of rights. Significant changes in the 19th century, including industrialization, westward expansion, and political and social reform movements, altered the response to disability and people with disabilities: State-sponsored hospitals, asylums, and residential schools for blind, deaf, and cognitively disabled children emerged in the early 1800s and proliferated as the century wore on. For the first time many people with disabilities were actively segregated from their communities and mainstream society; some received education and special care, others were often "warehoused" and forgotten. In the late 19th century, a growing interest in scientific categories that defined human difference gave rise to eugenics, an ideology that soon permeated medical research and public policy and in the 20th century led to marriage bans and forced sterilizations of those deemed genetically "inferior."

Concurrent with these new trends in the 19th century, people with disabilities and their representatives often banded together and encouraged collective action. Deaf Americans, for example, used school newspapers to unite community members across states and the nation; in the 1850s a proposal to establish a deaf-only community in the western territories sparked fiery debates among deaf leaders and educators, and an increasingly galvanized deaf community founded formal local, state, and national associations to address social, educational, and economic issues. From 1851 to 1860, inhabitants of the Utica State Lunatic Asylum in Utica, New York, also gave voice to their collective experience through their monthly publication, *The Opal.* By the late 1800s, alumni from blind schools began founding organizations and producing newspapers to support their empowerment campaigns. In the wake of World War I, additional groups coalesced, such as the Disabled American Veterans and, in the 1930s, the New York–based League of the Physically Handicapped protested employment discrimination. Following World War II, disability activists, like other civil rights campaigners, challenged segregation and discrimination based on mental and bodily difference, demanding deinstitutionalization and educational reforms that closed the real and perceived gap between disabled and nondisabled citizens. The rise of the disability rights movement since that time has altered American society, literally and figuratively: from universally designed buildings, curb cuts, and handicapped parking spaces to antidiscrimination laws such as the Architectural Barriers Act of 1968 and the Americans with Disabilities Act of 1990, disability activism is fueled by an American dream of full access and inclusion of

all people everywhere. As the popular disability motto proclaims, "Nothing about us without us."

Responding to this call since the 1950s, scholars have shown an interest in these social, political, and cultural dimensions of disability, which forms the bedrock of disability studies and disability history. Particularly since the 1980s, when the term *disability studies* came into common use, work emanating from the field has taught us that while disability has existed throughout American history, it is neither a fixed nor a static concept but one whose definition and interpretation have changed markedly from era to era as America and notions of Americanism have changed. Disability is diverse and open-ended: The causes, types, and experiences with disability can vary widely. In this respect, disability embraces a broad, fluid group that is constantly changing and evolving, as are definitions of it. As many entries in this encyclopedia demonstrate, disability also transcends the institutions and categories that have marked it since our nation's earliest history. Thus, "daily life" experiences are included alongside the well-documented and often celebrated events in disability history.

Format and Features

Since this is the first historical encyclopedia of disability in the United States—and since disability itself is a dynamic discipline—organizing and composing this encyclopedia involved working through numerous challenges. For example, disability history does not unfold in a tidy, linear way. There is no single or canonical vocabulary because language and terminology vary with perspective. Gradual transitions and vague intersections outnumber precise definitions and clear boundaries. Sources of information vary in quantity and quality; some sources are nontraditional and opinions vary about what constitutes authority. Finally, for all of its involvement with institutions, disability history is also an intensely personal discipline: Its raw material is the individual, its crucible is the human body and mind, and its actors, with few exceptions, are people whose lives heretofore have attracted little, if any, attention. Apart from the occasional Barbara Jordan or Chang and Eng Bunker, many individuals included in this reference do not yet appear in the mainstream American pantheon. For all these reasons, a few words of guidance and explanation may assist the reader in taking advantage of this work.

The encyclopedia is generally organized around broad themes. Twelve anchor entries on these vital topics—activism and advocacy, community, daily life, disability art and artistic expression, disability culture, education, employment and labor, identity, language and terminology, law and policy, representation, and science and technology— discuss major issues that have been particularly relevant to understanding the meaning of disability from the colonial period to the present day. They are crafted to help the reader appreciate the complexity of disability history, and how it compares and contrasts with more traditional analyses of American civilization and society. The anchor entries also create a context that the other entries embellish with their detail and illustrative examples.

Many other entries reflect topics commonly included in the study of disability history. For example, readers will find entries on residential schools, "freak shows," organizations, court cases, and laws. Entries that examine specific sites, such as the American School for the Deaf, Perkins School for the Blind, and St. Elizabeths Hospital, as well as general locations, such as orthopedic hospitals; asylums and institutions; Martha's Vineyard, Massachusetts; and Berkeley, California, draw attention to the fact that places hold rich historical meaning. Individuals who shaped the history of disability also appear throughout, including physician Benjamin Rush, French deaf educator Laurent Clerc, performer Charles Stratton (better known as "General Tom Thumb"), author and reformer Randolph Bourne, vocational rehabilitation expert Mary Switzer, and activist Justin Dart.

Our contributors helped to extend the traditional boundaries of disability history, providing original studies of topics such as music, humor, sexuality, public history, poetry, ethnicity, films, drama, and violence. Those interested in popular culture can find a panoramic study of the subject as well as general articles on such topics as movies, television, comic books, the Internet, and numerous specific articles, such as *The Miracle Worker, Porgy and Bess, Mr. Magoo,* "What Is It?," *One Flew Over the Cuckoo's Nest, South Park, Star Trek,* and *X-Men.*

Historians rely extensively on primary source documents—the materials from the past. A wide array of these, including letters, interviews, newspaper clippings, pamphlets, speeches, laws, and literary works, complement many of our articles, highlighting key themes and features. In addition to their historical importance, primary sources commonly generate excitement because they close the distance between us and the past. The rich diversity of original documents collected in this encyclopedia are also intended to draw attention to different eras, topics, and perspectives in American disability history. For instance, an 1821 letter from 15-year-old Alice Cogswell captures the early years at America's first permanent residential school for the deaf, while Civil War ballads "When Johnny Comes Marching Home" and "Paddy's Lamentation" speak to the expectations and frustrations of disabled veterans. In the 1927 Supreme Court case *Buck v. Bell,* which upheld forced sterilization, Justice Oliver Wendell Holmes hauntingly argues that "three generations of imbeciles are enough," and public statements by famed actor and telethon host Jerry Lewis in "If I Had Muscular Dystrophy" (1990) invite us to consider our own beliefs about what it means to be disabled.

In addition to the more than 750 articles, the encyclopedia includes a comprehensive chronology of many significant events in American disability history. Stretching from the colonial era to the present, the chronology helps us understand that disability as a concept and lived experience has long historical roots. This tool also allows us to better grasp the wide scope and possibilities of studying disability. Because history does not unfold in a linear fashion, this chronology should be read more like a textual landscape painting. Taking in the events spread on these pages may reveal for you connections between topics and people, draw out the distinctive characteristics of different eras, and clarify the extent to which changes have occurred.

Language and terminology are a rich and complicated component of disability history. Labels applied to people with disabilities and descriptions of disabling conditions have changed significantly over time, and they continue to evolve. Consequently, terms are infused with deep and sometimes contentious meanings. The contributing authors vary in the expressions they employ. For example, some choose to capitalize words such as *Deaf* while others use *deaf,* noting different interpretations of the cultural and historical meaning of this term and community. We intentionally honored these diverse approaches to language and, wherever possible, clarify their specific connotation.

Article titles that commonly describe both people and conditions present the people first. For example, "mad people and madness" explores the history of those labeled "mad" and the meaning of "madness" across American history. The order demonstrates that individuals and their broad lived experiences receive priority over a consideration of the condition alone. Medical perspectives or explanations of medical conditions are contextualized in our entries as part of the many essential factors for understanding the full meaning of disability. It is impossible to cover all experiences of disability but major topics such as "deaf," "blind," "cognitive and intellectual disability," "polio," and "mental illness," among others, are highlighted. By providing extensive cross-references and the titles of related articles in each entry, this work seeks to enable readers from diverse backgrounds to understand both focused topics in disability history and the broader themes and contexts in which they exist.

This work addresses disability from various perspectives and on various interpretive levels. It covers basic factors, such as important events, laws, and biographies of people with disabilities. Entries on major historical experiences and concepts, including civil rights, war, public policy, family, media, institutions, education, and technology demonstrate the deeper meaning of the lived experience of disability. The explanations also make connections to race, class, and gender, as well as other critical categories, such as ethnicity, religion, and region. The broad entry on "stereotypes," for example, focuses not only on common representations of disability, but also shows the ways that various cultural examples reveal anxiety over various kinds of perceived differences that extend beyond disability. Likewise, "poverty" discusses the subject as a significant feature many disabled Americans have faced, but it also traces connections to broad policy, technological, and social trends.

As with all social histories, controversies reveal significant boundary points and highlight disparate views of disability and people with disabilities. This encyclopedia seeks to map out some of the central historical and contemporary conflicts, such as medical and social interpretations of disability, deaf and disability identities, oral and signed communication debates, organizational affiliations, Physician Assisted Suicide, and inclusion versus separatism. Our authors have attempted to show the broad spectrum of positions on these and other contested topics.

Biographical entries presented unique challenges. It is impossible to include all of the many prominent figures in American disability history. We primarily selected life stories that embodied themes we felt were important for understanding American disability history. It is significant to note that these also include profiles of some "common folk." These biographies demonstrate everyday experiences with disability throughout history while also presenting tangible evidence that people who lead "ordinary" lives have much to teach us. Biographies should be read in conjunction with broader conceptual entries. Just as the broader entries are enriched and made human by consulting the biographical entries, the individual's experience is explained and set in context by more general explanations of the conditions and currents at work in each life.

A guiding principle of inclusion also directly shapes another distinctive feature of this work: the highlighted quotes accompanying many of our conceptual entries. These short excerpts, taken from diverse and often obscure diaries, letters, interviews, and other sources from "rank-and-file" individuals with disabilities and their families, remind us that social history is, at its core, about people. They also serve as "snapshots" of the ways that the accompanying subject applies or relates to Americans' lives. (Sources for these highlighted quotes can be found on page 1048.)

Although this sizable work presents a strong foundation upon which more research may be pursued, it is also a "snapshot" of sorts. It reflects rigorous and creative research and our present understanding of disability. The latter is bound to evolve yet further. Practical issues also inherently limit the current scope and depth of the encyclopedia. For example, materials from the precolonial and colonial period are sparse in comparison to late 20th-century data, as is information on racial, ethnic, and gender minorities, economically marginalized people, specific disability populations, and certain geographical regions. We try to note known limits in the historical study whenever possible. And yet despite these limitations, the field of disability history has grown enormously in recent decades and has become a broad and fertile field of research and study. The bibliography at the end of Volume 3 includes hundreds of books, articles, and documents, all of which served as a basis for this encyclopedia. Separate sections on electronic resources covering CDs, DVDs, videorecordings, and Web sites are also included to help steer readers to other valuable sources of information.

A Multifaceted Approach

More than 350 authors contributed to this encyclopedia. They represent a richly diverse group of people interested in history and disability, including academic historians and scholars from various disciplines, medical researchers, community advocates, and students. We consider this range of talent and expertise to be among the work's strongest assets: a witness that history is—and should be—experienced, made, and interpreted by many. We hope this reference sparks broad interest in disability history, both informing readers of its fascinating and multifaceted components and acting as a springboard to further research.

By revisiting our history with an understanding of disability, new and more complex images appear. Ultimately, the analysis of disability may transform all of our comprehension of the past. It reveals, for instance, that society and scholars harbor a false assumption of commonality in our national history—through language, intellect, and cultural experience. By broadening the impact of multicultural approaches to history, a disability interpretation emphasizes that diversity is what we have most in common. Recognizing people with disabilities and society's response compels us toward greater and more creative inclusiveness in our work, in our history, and in our interactions with others.

List of Contributors

Emily K. Abel, University of California, Los Angeles

Deanna L. Adams, Syracuse University

Allyson Addams, CCAR Industries

Betty M. Adelson, Independent scholar

Neel Ahuja, University of North Carolina at Chapel Hill

Gary L. Albrecht, Professor Emeritus, University of Illinois, Chicago; Belgian Academy of Science and Arts and Leuven University (Belgium)

Ann Cooper Albright, Oberlin College

William P. Alford, Harvard Law School

Barbara M. Altman, Disability statistics consultant

Jeff Altman, National Blindness Professional Certification Board; Nebraska Commission for the Blind and Visually Impaired

Donalda Ammons, Deaflympics

Yerker Andersson, Independent scholar

Tal Araten-Bergman, Burton Blatt Institute, Syracuse University

Robert Archibald, Missouri Historical Society

David F. Armstrong, Gallaudet University

Adrienne Asch, Center for Ethics, Yeshiva University

Christine Ashby, Syracuse University

Jessica Bacon, Syracuse University

Stephen C. Baldwin, Texas Association of the Deaf

Jesse F. Ballenger, The Pennsylvania State University

Cherry Fletcher Bamberg, Independent scholar

Sharon N. Barnartt, Gallaudet University

Douglas C. Baynton, University of Iowa

Leslie M. Behm, Michigan State University Libraries

Chris Bell, Syracuse University

Liat Ben-Moshe, Syracuse University

Jean Lindquist Bergey, Gallaudet University

Edward D. Berkowitz, The George Washington University

Lauren S. Berliner, University of California at San Diego

Bob Bernotas, Journalist-author

Douglas Biklen, Syracuse University

Daniel Blackie, The Renvall Institute, University of Helsinki

Peter Blanck, Burton Blatt Institute, Syracuse University

Arthur Blaser, Chapman University

Robert Bogdan, Syracuse University

Virginia Borggaard, National Fraternal Society of the Deaf

Kathleen M. Brian, The George Washington University

Janice A. Brockley, Jackson State University

Priscilla C. Brown, Independent scholar

Steven E. Brown, Center on Disability Studies, University of Hawaii

Brenda Jo Brueggemann, The Ohio State University

Jeremy L. Brunson, Gallaudet University

Robert Buchanan, Goddard College

Jennifer Burek Pierce, The University of Iowa

Teresa Blankmeyer Burke, Gallaudet University

Elizabeth Bush, Westfield High School

Brad Byrom, MiraCosta College

Joe Caldwell, University of Illinois at Chicago

Anthony R. Candela, Independent scholar

Clifton F. Carbin, Independent Deaf history researcher and author

Allison C. Carey, Shippensburg University

Licia Carlson, Providence College

Cathryn Carroll, American University

Gretchen A. Case, Duke University/Northwestern University

Katherine L. Castles, Independent scholar

Ellen Castrone, Smithsonian's National Museum of American History

Patricia E. Cavanaugh, Holyoke V.N.A./Hospice Life Care

James Charlton, University of Illinois at Chicago; Access Living of Metropolitan Chicago

Michael Mark Chemers, Carnegie Mellon University

James L. Cherney, Wayne State University

John B. Christiansen, Gallaudet University

David Church, Indiana University

Laurel A. Clark, The George Washington University

Liza H. Colby, Antioch University New England

Diane Coleman, Not Dead Yet

Steven D. Collins, Gallaudet University

Aaron Cooley, University of North Carolina at Chapel Hill

G. Thomas Couser, Hofstra University

Nolan Crabb, The Ohio State University

Deborah Beth Creamer, Iliff School of Theology

Ethan Crough, Little People of America, Inc.
Susan Crutchfield, University of Wisconsin-La Crosse
Vickie D'Andrea-Penna, Frederick Community College
Michael Davidson, University of California, San Diego
Telory W. Davies, Missouri State University
Janet M. Davis, University of Texas at Austin
Lennard J. Davis, University of Illinois at Chicago
Megan V. Davis, The George Washington University
David de Lorenzo, University of California, Berkeley
John W. DenBoer, Arizona Neurological Institute
Samuel Di Rocco, II, The University of Toledo
Sherman Dorn, University of South Florida
Ian R. Dowbiggin, University of Prince Edward Island
Judith Felson Duchan, State University of New York at Buffalo
Reid Dunlavey, Museum of DisABILITY History
June Dwyer, Manhattan College
Linda Edwards, Syracuse University
R.A.R. Edwards, Rochester Institute of Technology
Kent D. Eilers, Huntington University
Jack El-Hai, Independent scholar
Meredith Eliassen, San Francisco State University
Julie Passanante Elman, The George Washington University
Judy Evans, American Foundation for the Blind
Pamela S. Fadem, Community Health Educator
Stefano Fait, Journalist and independent scholar
Mindy Farmer, University of Dayton
Mary Felstiner, Stanford University
Robin Feltman, Independent scholar and writer
Philip M. Ferguson, Chapman University
Beth A. Ferri, Syracuse University
Jim Ferris, The University of Toledo
Martha A. Field, Harvard Law School
Anne E. Figert, Loyola University Chicago
Ted Finlayson-Schueler, Syracuse University
Gail Fisher, University of Illinois at Chicago
Joseph P. Fisher, The George Washington University
Lakshmi Fjord, University of California, San Francisco
Doris Zames Fleischer, New Jersey Institute of Technology
Charlene Floreani, University of Chicago
Jean M. Flynn, Independent scholar
Brian M. Foster, Carleton University
Ann M. Fox, Davidson College
Hilary Franklin, Teachers College at Columbia University
Stephen Frantzich, U.S. Naval Academy
Tetsuya Fujiwara, University of Fukui
Susan L. Gabel, National College of Education, National-Louis University
Matthew Gambino, University of Illinois at Urbana-Champaign
Christine L. Gannon, Independent scholar
Jack R. Gannon, Gallaudet University/independent scholar
Carol Brooks Gardner, Indiana University-Purdue University, Indianapolis
Matthew J. Gaudet, Graduate Theological Union
David A. Gerber, University at Buffalo, State University of New York
Judith Gerber, Independent scholar

Darla Germeroth, University of Scranton
Mary E. Gibson, University of Virginia
Michael Gill, University of Illinois at Chicago
Elisabeth Gitter, Professor Emerita, John Jay College, CUNY
Kim A. Gorgens, University of Denver
Brian H. Greenwald, Gallaudet University
Nora Ellen Groce, University College London
Maureen Groden, Holyoke Visiting Nurse Association/Hospice Life Care
William P. Gronfein, Indiana University-Purdue University, Indianapolis
Brian R. Grossman, San Francisco State University; San Jose State University
Donald A. Grushkin, California State University-Sacramento
Alice Haisman, University of Illinois at Chicago
Kim Q. Hall, Appalachian State University
Beth Haller, Towson University
Beth R. Handler, University of Louisiana at Lafayette
Peter Harakas, Arizona State University
Wendy S. Harbour, Harvard University
Judy Harkins, Gallaudet University
Kristen Harmon, Gallaudet University
Ralph Hartsock, University of North Texas Libraries
Simon Hayhoe, On Blindness and the Arts
Kevin Hearle, Steinbeck Review Editorial Board
Malinda Hicks, University of Texas at Dallas
Laurel Iverson Hitchcock, University of Alabama
Arthur Holst, City of Philadelphia
Sigmund Hough, VA Boston Healthcare System, Harvard Medical School, Boston School of Medicine
Rob Imrie, King's College, London
Edward A. Janek, University of Wyoming
Michelle Jarman, University of Wyoming
Natalie N. Jean, Florida State University
Richard Jenkins, University of Sheffield
Audra Jennings, The Ohio State University
Stephanie Jensen-Moulton, Brooklyn College
Mary Johnson, The Advocado Press
Shersten R. Johnson, University of St. Thomas
Laura Jordan, University of Florida
Sandra Jowers-Bower, University of the District of Columbia
Hannah Joyner, Independent scholar
Bradley Kadel, Fayetteville State University
Alison Kafer, Southwestern University
Arlene S. Kanter, Syracuse University College of Law
John M. Kinder, Oklahoma State University
Corinne E. Kirchner, Columbia University; Emerita, American Foundation for the Blind
Anna Kirkland, University of Michigan
Anne Kish, University of Montana-Western
Mary Klages, University of Colorado
Georgina Kleege, University of California, Berkeley
Kanta Kochhar-Lindgren, University of Washington, Bothell
Jessica M. Kramer, University of Illinois at Chicago
Linda Hamilton Krieger, University of California, Berkeley, School of Law
Thilo Kroll, University of Dundee [United Kingdom]

Catherine Kudlick, University of California, Davis
Petra Kuppers, University of Michigan
Howard I. Kushner, Emory University
Emily Lane, Southern Illinois University Edwardsville
Harry G. Lang, National Technical Institute for the Deaf
Irene W. Leigh, Gallaudet University
Neil Lerner, Davidson College
Paul Leung, University of North Texas
Debra Levine, New York University
Merle R. Levy, Freelance journalist
Victoria Ann Lewis, University of Redlands/Other Voices
    Project
Rita M. Liberti, California State University, East Bay
Joseph Link, Xavier University
Beth Linker, University of Pennsylvania
Elizabeth McClain Lockwood, University of Illinois at Chicago
Larry M. Logue, Mississippi College
Paul A. Lombardo, Georgia State University
Paul K. Longmore, San Francisco State University
David de Lorenzo, University of California, Berkeley
Laura L. Lovett, University of Massachusetts
Jacqueline Lubin, Vieux-Fort Comprehensive Secondary
    School; Lynchburg College
Ceil Lucas, Gallaudet University
Josh Lukin, Temple University
Richard MacAleese, Independent scholar
Susan Magasi, Center for Outcomes, Research and Education
    at Evanston Northwestern
Myrna Magliulo, Independent scholar
Holly M. Manaseri, The College at Brockport, State
    University of New York
Elizabeth A. Marotta, Independent scholar
Charles E. McConnel, University of Texas Southwestern
    Medical Center
Brenda McCoy, University of North Texas
Aneri Mehta, United Cerebral Palsy
C. Michael Mellor, Independent scholar
Elizabeth E. Metcalf, Syracuse University
Melanie Metzger, Gallaudet University
Susan Gluck Mezey, Loyola University Chicago
Hélène Mialet, Harvard University
Jennifer Middlesworth, University of Virginia
Brian R. Miller, U.S. Department of Education
Ann Millet-Gallant, University of North Carolina at
    Greensboro
Mara Mills, Harvard University
Susannah B. Mintz, Skidmore College
Gene Mirus, Gallaudet University
Sheila C. Moeschen, Bentley University
Leila S. Monaghan, University of Wyoming
Nathan W. Moon, Georgia Institute of Technology
Leroy Moore, Jr., Independent scholar
Jeffrey J. Moyer, Independent writer and advocate
Kelly Munger, University of Illinois at Chicago
Peggy Munson, Independent author
Patricia A. Murphy, University of Toledo; independent scholar

William Norton Myhill, Burton Blatt Institute: Centers of
    Innovation on Disability at Syracuse University
Jessica Nassau, Independent scholar
Jennifer Nelson, Gallaudet University
Caryn E. Neumann, Miami University of Ohio
Sara Newman, Kent State University
Kim E. Nielson, University of Wisconsin-Green Bay
Anthony J. Nocella II, Syracuse University; SUNY Cortland
Steven Noll, University of Florida
Martin F. Norden, University of Massachusetts-Amherst
Gary Norman, Attorney and author
Jane Norman, Gallaudet University
David W. Oaks, MindFreedom International
Nancy Obermueller, Kirkwood Community College Library
Gerald O'Brien, Southern Illinois University Edwardsville
John O'Brien, Center on Human Policy, Syracuse University
Susan O'Hara, University of California, Berkeley
Marsha M. Olsen-Wiley, Kent State University
Beth Omansky, Disability Studies scholar
Colin Ong-Dean, University of California, San Diego
Rachel Oppenheim, Teachers College, Columbia University
John Morton Osborne, Dickinson College
Robert L. Osgood, Muskingum College
Lisa L. Ossian, Des Moines Area Community College
Noam Ostrander, DePaul University
Corbett Joan O'Toole, Independent scholar
Katherine Ott, Smithsonian's National Museum of American
    History
Mary Jane Owen, Disability Concepts In Action
Michael J. Paciorek, Eastern Michigan University
Carol Padden, University of California, San Diego
Cleo Pappas, University of Illinois at Chicago
Ryan C. Parrey, University of Illinois at Chicago
Manon Parry, University of Maryland
Lindsey Patterson, The Ohio State University
William Payne, Missoula 3:16 Rescue Mission; Bakke
    Graduate University of Ministry
William J. Peace, Independent scholar
Stephen Pemberton, New Jersey Institute of Technology
Ray Pence, University of Kansas
David Penna, Gallaudet University
Martin S. Pernick, University of Michigan
Kathy Peterson, Missouri Historical Society
Cynthia Pettie, Gallaudet University
Jessica Pliley, The Ohio State University
Lee S. Polansky, Independent scholar
Edward A. Polloway, Lynchburg College
Justin J.W. Powell, Social Science Research Center Berlin
    (WZB), Germany
Margaret Price, Spelman College
Bruce Quaglia, University of Utah
Katherine Randle, Independent scholar
Raphael Raphael, University of Oregon, Eugene
Geoffrey Reaume, York University & Psychiatric Survivor
    Archives, Toronto
Brian W. Refford, Indiana University of Pennsylvania

Jana Bouck Remy, University of California, Irvine
Mariela Gaeta Reyes, King's College London
Dave Reynolds, Inclusion Daily Express
Dawn Reynolds, University of Maryland
Kathleen Rice, Independent Scholar
Penny L. Richards, UCLA Center for the Study of Women
O. Robinson, The Ohio State University
Julia Miele Rodas, Bronx Community College of the City University of New York
Judy Rohrer, University of California, Santa Barbara; and Texas Women's University
Lisa Roney, University of Central Florida
Sarah F. Rose, University of Texas at Arlington
Zachary S. Rossetti, Providence College
Dana Rovang, The University of Chicago
Allen Rucker, Independent author
Catherine E. Rymph, University of Missouri
Philip L. Safford, Professor Emeritus, Kent State University
Ellen Samuels, University of Wisconsin–Madison
Carrie Sandahl, University of Illinois at Chicago
Steve Sandy, Independent researcher, Da-Cor Pictures
Marsha Saxton, World Institute on Disability; University of California, Berkeley
Walton O. Schalick, III, University of Wisconsin-Madison
Janet E. Schaller, Memphis Theological Seminary
Jerome D. Schein, Emeritus Professor, New York University; University of Alberta
Karen Schneiderman, Counselor, community activist
Kay Schriner, University of Arkansas
John S. Schuchman, Professor Emeritus, Gallaudet University
Stephanie Ricker Schulte, University of Arkansas
David G. Schuster, Indiana University-Purdue University, Fort Wayne
Richard K. Scotch, University of Texas at Dallas
Peter J. Seiler, National Fraternal Society of the Deaf
Steven Selden, University of Maryland-College Park
David Serlin, University of California, San Diego
Scott Sheidlower, York College, City University of New York
Mark Sherry, The University of Toledo
Bonnie Shoultz, Syracuse University
Kara Shultz, Bloomsburg University
Chloe Silverman, Penn State University
Anita Silvers, San Francisco State University
Murray Simpson, University of Dundee [United Kingdom]
Henry Slucki, University of Southern California; Access Unlimited
Cynthia A. Smith, Syracuse University
Dorsia Smith, University of Puerto Rico, Rio Piedras
J. David Smith, The University of North Carolina at Greensboro
Sarah Smith, The Ohio State University
Carrie Snow, Teachers College, Columbia University
Dick Sobsey, University of Alberta
Santiago Solis, Towson University
Sylvie Soulier, Independent scholar
Elizabeth T. Spiers, American Association of the Deaf-Blind

Michael Stein, Harvard Law School Project on Disability; William & Mary School of Law
Deborah Stienstra, University of Manitoba
Martha Stoddard Holmes, California State University, San Marcos
Alan Stoskopf, Northeastern University
Laurie Stras, University of Southampton
Karen Peltz Strauss, Coalition of Organizations for Accessible Technology
Chris Strickling, Actual Lives Performance Project
Zosha Stuckey, Syracuse University
Justin Suran, Malborough School
Ian M. Sutherland, Gallaudet University
Jennifer C. Swaim, St. Luke's Physical Medicine & Rehabilitation
Timothy N. Tansey, Michigan State University
Steven J. Taylor, Syracuse University
Sunaura C. Taylor, Independent scholar and artist
Heidi A. Temple, University of Maryland-College Park
Lauren J. Tenney, Human Rights Activist, The Opal Project
Empish J. Thomas, Writer and disability advocate
Allison Victoria Thompkins, Massachusetts Institute of Technology
Tim Thompson, Pacific University
Terri Lynne Thrower, The School of the Art Institute of Chicago
Anthony Todd, University of Chicago
Susan Tomlinson, University of Massachusetts, Boston
James W. Trent, Gordon College
David M. Turner, Swansea University
Lauri Umansky, Suffolk University
Janikke Solstad Vedeler, Burton Blatt Institute; Norwegian Social Research
John Vickrey Van Cleve, Professor Emeritus, Gallaudet University
Patricia Vertinsky, University of British Columbia
Sara Vogt, University of Illinois at Chicago
Edmund Vu, University of Texas-Dallas
Melanie Wakefield, University of Michigan
Graham Warder, Keene State College
Nick Watson, Strathclyde Centre for Disability Research, University of Glasgow
Alice Wexler, Writer
Julia M. White, University of Rochester
Parnel Wickham, Dowling College
Fred A. Wilcox, Ithaca College
Abby Wilkerson, The George Washington University
John Williams-Searle, The College of Saint Rose
Daniel J. Wilson, Muhlenberg College
Margret Winzer, Professor Emerita, University of Lethbridge
Gregor Wolbring, University of Calgary
John A. Woodcock, Indiana University
Brian Woods, The University of York
Katherine J. Worboys, University of Maryland
Richard LeMoine Wright, Georgia State University
Franklin K. Wyman, Kean University; Drew University
Kate Zoellner, Maureen and Mike Mansfield Library, The University of Montana

Chronology

1624

- John Burrows files a complaint with the general court of colonial Virginia, charging that his "very Dull" ward, Mara Buck, was the target of a kidnapping scheme; Buck, born in 1611 in Jamestown, is thus the first documented English child with developmental disabilities born in the American colonies.

1630s

- English colonists from the county of Kent settle on Martha's Vineyard; members' carrying a recessive gene for deafness intermarry, producing many deaf offspring over the next two centuries and fostering a community that significantly incorporated deaf people and sign language.

1641

- "Body of Liberties," an early draft of a Massachusetts law, is published; "Libertie 52" contains the provision that "Children, Idiots, Distracted persons, and all that are strangers, or new commers to our plantation, shall have such allowances and dispensations in any cause whether Criminall or other as reason require."

1664

- Boston establishes residential facilities to serve individuals considered economically dependent. By 1850 the state had 204 almshouses, and other states adopt similar means of housing. Many people with disabilities reside in almshouses, although specialized institutions replace many of them in the 19th century.

1699

- General Court of Connecticut passes "An Act for Relieving Idiots and Distracted Persons"—modeled on a similar act passed in Massachusetts in 1695.

1700

- The colonial government in Massachusetts passes a statute prohibiting immigration of people deemed "lame, impotent, or infirm persons, or those incapable of supporting themselves."

1736

- Bellevue Hospital in New York City opens. The city's largest municipal hospital, Bellevue gains notoriety in the 19th and 20th centuries for inhumane conditions in its psychiatric facilities.

1775–1783

- During the American Revolution, the Continental Congress promises pensions to disabled veterans, establishing a precedent for medical and financial support that increases significantly after the Civil War (1861–65). An estimated 8,500 to 25,000 members of the Continental armed forces are seriously injured or disabled during the conflict.

1803

- Francis Green, parent of a deaf son, collaborates with ministers to conduct a census of deaf people in Massachusetts. The results of this survey encourage advocates to seek a permanent school for deaf people in the region.

The chronologers wish to thank Jack R. Gannon, Fred Pelka, Paul Longmore, Penny Richards, and others whose reference works substantially contributed to this chronicle of events.

1805

- Benjamin Rush publishes *Medical Inquiries and Observations,* the first American attempt to scientifically outline natural causes for various mental disabilities.

1812

- Sponsored by Colonel William Bolling, oral educator John Braidwood tutors deaf pupils at the "Cobbs Manor" in Virginia. The school officially opens in 1815 but closes the following year.

1817

- *April 15*: Through the collaboration of Reverend Thomas Hopkins Gallaudet, Laurent Clerc, and Mason Fitch Cogswell, the American Asylum for the Education and Instruction of the Deaf, later the American School for the Deaf, opens in Hartford, Connecticut.
- *May 15*: Quakers open the Friends Asylum for people with mental illness, in Frankfort, Pennsylvania. Staff initially follow Benjamin Rush's moral treatment in their care of residents.

1823

- *April 10*: The Kentucky Asylum for the Tuition of the Deaf and Dumb, later the Kentucky School for the Deaf, is established in Danville.

1824

- French student Louis Braille invents a system based on raised dots that enables blind people to read and write. Many Americans use this code or variations on it by the late 19th and early 20th centuries.

1825–1850

- Most teachers of blind students are trained through apprenticeships at residential schools for the blind.

1825

- Eighteen-year-old Julia Brace enters the American School for the Deaf in Hartford, Connecticut. Deaf-blind from typhoid since the age of five, Brace is the first known woman with a disability to appear in popular juvenile literature when her teacher writes an essay about her for *Juvenile Miscellany,* in 1828.

1829

- *March 2*: The Massachusetts state legislature incorporates the New England Asylum for the Blind, later the Perkins School for the Blind.

1831

- The New York Institution for the Education of the Blind, later the New York Institution for Special Education, is established.
- Samuel Gridley Howe is named the first director of the New England Asylum for the Blind.

1832

- The first students arrive at both the New England Asylum for the Blind and the New York Institution for the Blind.
- Conjoined twins Chang and Eng (who adopt the last name Bunker in 1844) start their own business of managing themselves, which includes some work later with P. T. Barnum.

1837

- The New England Asylum for the Blind establishes a printing press, later named the Howe Memorial Press.
- Ohio establishes the first state-supported residential school for the blind.
- Laura Bridgman of Hanover, New Hampshire, the first deaf-blind child to be formally educated, is brought to the New England Asylum for the Blind by Samuel Gridley Howe.
- Massachusetts passes additional immigration restrictions to prevent people with various types of impairments from entering the ports.

1840

- Samuel Gridley Howe establishes a "separate work department," a prototype for a sheltered workshop, at the Perkins Institution in South Boston, Massachusetts.

1841

- Dorothea Dix begins advocating for people with mental disabilities confined in Massachusetts jails and poorhouses.
- P. T. Barnum obtains Scudder's American Museum in New York City and renames it Barnum's American Museum. Barnum exhibits numerous human "curiosities" at this museum. He sells his collection in 1855.

1842

- Charles Dickens publishes *American Notes,* including a description of the Perkins Institution and the education of Laura Bridgman there.
- The Georgia Lunatic Asylum opens near Milledgeville (changing its name in 1929 to Milledgeville State Hospital). Initially created in 1837 as the State Lunatic, Idiot, and Epileptic Asylum, Milledgeville becomes the subject of a Pulitzer Prize–winning newspaper exposé in 1959, drawing attention to the institution's appalling conditions.

- Four-year-old Charles Stratton is brought to P. T. Barnum's American Museum and is exhibited as "General Tom Thumb." Over subsequent decades, Stratton becomes internationally renowned.

1847
- *The American Annals of the Deaf* begins publication at the American School for the Deaf in Hartford, Connecticut.

1848
- Samuel Gridley Howe establishes the first residential school for people with developmental disabilities at the Perkins Institution in Boston.
- The story of Phineas Gage, a railroad worker who survives a penetrating injury to his brain, gains national attention. Changes in his personality emanating from the injury generate increased medical study on the relationship between the brain and behavior.

1850
- The state legislature establishes the Massachusetts School for Idiotic and Feeble-Minded Children.

1851
- *The Opal,* a monthly journal describing life at the Utica State Lunatic Asylum in Utica, New York, is first published by the men and women committed to the institution. The periodical runs until 1860.
- Deaf artist John Carlin produces the poem "The Mute's Lament," whose elegance impresses his peers. The painter-writer becomes a leading figure in the deaf community and in 1864 is the first recipient of an honorary degree from Columbia Institution for the Deaf (Gallaudet College).

1852
- Boston Line Type is the most common reading medium for blind Americans.
- In New York City, Reverend Thomas Gallaudet opens the first church for deaf people in America, St. Ann's Church for the Deaf.
- David Bartlett opens the Family School for Young Deaf-Mute Children, which educates hearing and deaf siblings together, in New York City.

1854
- The New England Gallaudet Association of the Deaf, the first organization of deaf people in the United States, is founded in Montpelier, Vermont.
- Thomas Kirkbride, superintendent of the Pennsylvania Hospital for the Insane, publishes his work, *On the Construction, Organization, and General Arrangements of Hospitals for the Insane with Some Remarks on Insanity and Its Treatment.* His "Kirkbride Plan" for asylum construction becomes a model that dozens of institutions follow over the next decades.

1855
- John J. Flournoy unsuccessfully advocates for a "Deaf-Mute Republic" in the western territories. Debates over this circulate in the *American Annals of the Deaf.*
- Ohio native Eli Bowen begins performing in Major Brown's Colliseum. The 13-year-old Bowen, who has phocomelia (a congenital condition that made him appear legless) works in freak shows until his death in 1924.

1856
- A poem on former president Zachary Taylor by Fanny Crosby is published. A graduate from and instructor at the New York Institution for the Blind, Crosby produces 9,000 hymns and many Civil War ballads in her lifetime.

1857
- Musical prodigy "Blind Tom" Wiggins Bethune performs piano at a concert hall in Columbus, Ohio. Bethune, a slave, is exhibited by promoter Perry Oliver for several years, earning thousands of dollars for his owner, James Bethune.

1858
- The Kentucky legislature creates the American Printing House for the Blind within the Kentucky Institution for the Education of the Blind in Louisville.

1859
- William Henry Johnson, an African-American man with microcephaly, begins working for P. T. Barnum, who commonly bills him as "What Is It?," the "missing link" between humans and apes. Johnson continues to perform in exhibitions until his death in 1926.

1860
- Dr. Simon Pollak brings Braille to the Missouri School for the Blind, the first institution in the United States to use the system.
- The *Gallaudet Guide and Deaf Mutes' Companion* begins publication.

1861–1865
- The Civil War results in the largest number of injured and disabled soldiers in American history. It also sparks new federal and state policies, pensions for disabled soldiers,

rehabilitation efforts, and prosthetic technology to address the needs of this vast population.

1862

- Anna Haining Swan, commonly known as the "Nova Scotia Giantess," joins P. T. Barnum's sideshow.
- Lavinia Warren is recruited by P. T. Barnum to join his American Museum. In the next year she marries Charles Stratton, and the dwarf couple is exhibited as "General Tom Thumb" and "Mrs. Tom Thumb," becoming popular cultural icons.

1863

- After gaining release from a state asylum in Illinois three years after her husband had her committed, and eventually declared sane by the courts, Elizabeth Ware Packard leads campaigns for asylum reform.

1864

- Congress authorizes the Columbia Institution for the Deaf and Dumb and Blind, later Gallaudet University, to issue college degrees. It is the first college in the world expressly established for people with disabilities.

1866

- Samuel Gridley Howe begins to question the value of a segregated residential education for students who are blind.
- Individuals with Hansen's disease (leprosy) are forcibly removed to the Molokai Leper Colony on the Hawaiian island of Kalaupapa. More than 8,000 people will be relocated to the colony by 1969.
- Doctors begin labeling specific conditions emerging after railroad disasters "railroad spine." This medical diagnosis embodies commonly held views of stress and the body, and also shows an important intersection between industrialization and health.

1867

- The prosthetic arm invented by Abner McOmber becomes the first employing interchangeable inserts.
- San Francisco passes the first known "ugly law." Chicago, Illinois, Columbus, Ohio, and other municipalities pass similar ordinances.
- *October 1*: The Clarke School for the Deaf opens in Northampton, Massachusetts. It becomes a leading oral program in America.

1868

- William B. Wait begins using the New York Point raised-dot system at the New York Institution for the Blind.

1869

- The first segregated state residential school serving African-American children with disabilities, the Institution for Colored Deaf and Dumb and Blind, is founded in Raleigh, North Carolina.
- Edwin Van Deusen and George Beard each independently claim to discover what comes to be called "neurasthenia" (meaning lack of nervous energy). The condition, which included a constellation of symptoms, is understood to be linked to stresses caused by modern, urban living, and doctors use this diagnosis widely, particularly with middle- and upper middle-class patients.

1871

- Braille music notation is established.
- The American Association of Instructors of the Blind is established and favors the use of New York Point.
- After the original cohort leaves the institution, Edward Miner Gallaudet blocks female students from enrolling at Gallaudet College. The ban is lifted in 1886.

1872

- Henry C. Rider creates the "Deaf Mute's Journal" as a column in New York's *Mexico Independent*. In 1874 he begins producing *Deaf-Mutes' Journal*, the first weekly newspaper for and by deaf people.

1876

- Edouard Séguin becomes the first president of the Association of Medical Officers of American Institutions for Idiotic and Feebleminded Persons, later renamed the American Association on Intellectual and Developmental Disabilities.

1877

- Thomas Edison lists "Books for Blind People" on his patent application for the tin foil phonograph.

1878

- The "War of the Dots" begins. Most blind advocates prefer Modified Braille, while most sighted teachers and administrators prefer New York Point.

1880

- Anne Sullivan leaves the Tewksbury State Almshouse and enrolls at the Perkins Institution.
- The National Convention of Deaf Mutes, later the National Association of the Deaf, first meets in Cincinnati, Ohio.

1882

- The Pennsylvania Institution for the Instruction of the Blind establishes a kindergarten.

- Congress passes a law specifically barring immigration to the United States of "any convict, lunatic, idiot or person unable to take care of himself or herself without becoming a public charge."

1883

- Sir Francis Galton in England uses the term *eugenics* for the first time.
- Alexander Graham Bell presents his *Memoir Upon the Formation of a Deaf Variety of the Human Race* to the National Academy of Sciences. Concerned by the evolution of a distinct deaf cultural community, he advocates measures to reduce its spread.
- Sophie B. Wright's Home Institute is chartered in New Orleans. The night school she opens serves 25,000 students before it closes in 1909. Commonly referred to by contemporaries as a "hopeless cripple," Wright is honored in 1988 with a statue in a New Orleans park named after her.

1886

- Caroline Yale ascends as principal of the Clarke School for the Deaf in Northampton, Massachusetts. She becomes a leading advocate of oral education and builds a significant teacher training program and network of female educators through this prominent deaf school.

1887

- Helen Keller of Tuscumbia, Alabama, age 7, acquires an understanding of language through the teaching of Anne Sullivan.
- The Perkins School for the Blind establishes a kindergarten.

1888

- The New Jersey Training School for Feebleminded Boys and Girls is established at Vineland, New Jersey. Starting in the 1890s, the school also serves as a central location for research on cognitive disabilities.
- Deaf baseball player William "Dummy" Hoy begins his major league career, playing centerfield for the Washington Nationals.

1890

- The American Association to Promote the Teaching of Speech to the Deaf, led by Alexander Graham Bell, is established in New York.

1891

- The Columbia Institution for the Instruction of the Deaf and Dumb and Blind in Washington, D.C. (later renamed Gallaudet College), initiates the first Normal Department for hearing educators of deaf students.

- "The Baseball Player," one of deaf artist Douglas Tilden's first bronze statues, is placed at Golden Gate State Park, in California. Tilden is considered the first California artist to receive critical acclaim outside the United States.

1892

- Charlotte Perkins Gilman publishes in the *New England Magazine* her semi-autobiographical short story, "The Yellow Wall-Paper" (later reprinted and published as *The Yellow Wallpaper*), which critically examines the impact of S. Weir Mitchell's rest cure.

1893

- *February 10:* A fire at the Stratford County Insane Asylum in Dover, New Hampshire, kills at least 40 inmates, most of them women. The watchman, the keeper, and the keeper's family escape before unlocking the cell doors. County asylums in New Hampshire are later abolished after an investigation recommends they be replaced with a state system.

1894

- The first documented epidemic of poliomyelitis in the United States occurs in Vermont.

1895

- A coalition of graduates from blind schools found the American Blind People's Higher Education and General Improvement Association (later the American Association of Workers for the Blind).
- Mabel Hubbard Bell publishes "Subtle Art of Speechreading," in *Atlantic Monthly*, which advocates for oral training for deaf people. Often seen as an exemplar of oralism, Hubbard Bell also writes elsewhere of her "lifelong struggle" to appear nondisabled.

1896

- Connecticut passes the first eugenic marriage law.

1898

- Edward Allen Fay's six-year study of deaf families culminates in *Marriages of the Deaf in America*, which challenges eugenicist Alexander Graham Bell's claims that deaf intermarriage and deaf culture foster a separate race of deaf people.

1899

- The first public school for "crippled children" opens in Chicago.

1900

- Deaf photographers Frances and Mary Allen join a group of female peers who are featured at the Universal Exposition in Paris. The Allen sisters gain considerable attention and support for their work from this event.

- The 1900 *Statistical Abstract of the United States* reports that between 1863 and 1900, 878,332 veterans filed for "invalid" pensions, or financial support payments for disabled veterans. Of these claimants, 586,521 individuals were approved to receive pensions.

1901

- Deaf members of the Coming Men of America in Flint, Michigan, found the National Fraternal Society of the Deaf to provide insurance protection for deaf Americans. By 1928 it claims 7,000 members and remains an important advocacy group through the 20th century.

1902

- While still a student at Radcliffe College in Cambridge, Massachusetts, Helen Keller, who would in 1904 become the first deaf-blind individual to graduate from college, begins publishing a serial autobiography in the *Ladies' Home Journal.* This autobiography, *The Story of My Life,* is later published as a book in 1903.
- Methodist Minister Edgar James Helms founds the charitable organization Goodwill Industries in Boston.
- Charles Bernstein becomes acting (and later official) superintendent of the Rome State Custodial Asylum for Unteachable Idiots in Rome, New York. Bernstein initiates colony and sheltered work programs.

1903

- The United States passes a ban against immigrants who have epilepsy.
- Baseball player "Three Finger Brown" Mordecai Brown joins the major leagues as a pitcher for the St. Louis Cardinals.
- Henry Ford opens the Ford Motor Company. Within a few years, the company will employ nearly 1,000 workers with disabilities. Particularly during the two world wars, Ford's factories recruit significant numbers of disabled laborers.

1905

- Originally founded by a group of well-educated blind individuals, the American Blind People's Higher Education and General Improvement Association is reorganized as the American Association of Workers for the Blind. Members work to professionalize services for blind Americans.
- Sisters Winifred and Edith Holt organize the New York Association for the Blind, which eventually becomes Lighthouse International. The organization works to prevent blindness and to collect information about visual impairments.

1906

- The amusement park Dreamland on Coney Island in Brooklyn, New York, opens Lilliputia, the first "Midget City." Modeled on earlier freak shows, "midget cities" become common features in world's fairs until the 1930s.

1907

- The first general interest magazine for blind readers of Braille, the *Matilda Ziegler Magazine for the Blind,* publishes its first issue. The magazine not only prints news in a format accessible to blind readers but also links its subscribers to a wider community of blind individuals.
- Indiana is the first state to pass a forced sterilization law. Over the next decades 33 other states will enact similar policies. By the 1970s more than 60,000 individuals are forcibly sterilized.
- *April:* The Massachusetts Association for Promoting the Interests of the Blind and founding editor Charles F. F. Campbell publish the first issue of *Outlook for the Blind,* a quarterly journal dedicated to publishing a "record of the progress and welfare" of blind individuals. The journal would later be published by the American Foundation for the Blind. In 1951 the journal is renamed the *New Outlook for the Blind,* and, in 1977, the journal's name changes again to the *Journal of Visual Impairment and Blindness.*

1908

- After a suicide attempt and three years spent in various psychiatric facilities, Clifford Beers publishes *A Mind That Found Itself.* In the book, Beers chronicles the terrible and inhumane conditions in both state and private institutions for people with mental illnesses.
- The federal government adopts a workers' compensation law, providing financial support to civilian employees of the federal government injured while at work. Within a few years, states begin to adopt workers' compensation laws to provide support and restitution to workers in a wide range of industries. By 1929 all but four states have adopted workers' compensation legislation.

1909

- After hearings to determine the type of Braille it would employ in its new day school program for blind students, the New York Public School System follows the advice of many advocates who emphasize the difficulty of reading New York Point and adopts American or Modified Braille.
- Clifford Beers organizes the National Committee for Mental Hygiene. He and other members of the committee, most of whom are mental health professionals, work to improve the quality and availability of care in mental health facilities.

- The first patent for a folding wheelchair is registered in the United States.

1910–1930

- Through its Motion Picture Committee, the National Association of the Deaf films a series of master signers to preserve and promote sign language.

1910

- There are 48 schools for blind children in the United States, enrolling 4,345 students.
- Across the nation, there are 58 residential schools for deaf students, serving 10,399 pupils. Additionally, there are 53 public day schools for deaf children that provide education for 1,508 students.
- There are 25 state institutions for "feebleminded" individuals that house 16,678 residents.
- Over half a million veterans are receiving "invalid" pensions.
- German psychiatrist Emil Kraepelin establishes a diagnosis for Alzheimer's disease, but understanding of the condition remains limited until research breakthroughs in the late 1960s.

1911

- Author Randolph Bourne publishes "The Handicapped," an essay that outlines the barriers caused by social discrimination. In this and other works he links his experiences as a person with disability to his radical vision for social reform.
- *Ethan Frome,* a novela by Edith Wharton that examines issues of mental illness, is published.

1912

- Educator and psychologist Henry H. Goddard publishes *The Kallikak Family: A Study in the Heredity of Feeble-Mindedness,* which traces the history and standing of two families—one a family of model citizens and one a family of immoral, criminal, and "feeble-minded" individuals. According to Goddard, these two families could both be linked to a single man and two very different women—one an upstanding woman and one a "feeble-minded" woman. Goddard used these two families to argue that "feeble-mindedness" was not only hereditary but also linked genetically to immorality and criminality. He and others used these findings to promote the eugenics agenda advocating the institutionalization and sterilization of people with disabilities, particularly individuals with cognitive, developmental, and psychiatric disabilities.
- The split hook hand, a terminal device for upper limb prosthetic users that improved dexterity, is introduced.

1913

- Minnesota establishes the first labor bureau for the deaf. By 1945 deaf leaders successfully convince a dozen states to follow Minnesota's example.

1915

- Chicago newspapers run front-page stories on Dr. Henry Haiselden, whose eugenically based campaign to promote euthanasia for significantly disabled infants sparks wide controversy.

1916

- Madison Grant's *The Passing of the Great Race* is published. Warning readers about the "menace" of hereditarily inferior stock, this eugenic work encourages greater immigration restrictions into the United States.
- The Stanford-Binet Test, formulated by psychologist Lewis Terman, is introduced. The test becomes the standard IQ test for school children and adults.
- *The Black Stork,* a film based on eugenic doctor Henry Haiselden and that advocates euthanizing significantly disabled infants, is released.

1917–1918

- The United States enters World War I. Many disabled civilians enter the workforce, and places such as Akron, Ohio, become deaf cultural hubs. The military officially discharges nearly 180,000 personnel because of disease or non-battle injuries, and over 300,000 soldiers experience physical and psychological disabilities.
- The whirlpool bath is invented in France and quickly adopted for rehabilitation treatment in the United States. The Jacuzzi Company popularized home models in the 1950s and 1960s.

1918

- The University of California establishes the first program to train individuals to teach blind students.
- An influenza pandemic (the "Spanish flu"), lasting until 1919, infects 28 percent of the American population and kills roughly 675,000 American soldiers and civilians. Many cities institute quarantines to contain the epidemic.
- Across the nation, there are 62 public schools for blind students that serve a total of 5,386 children.
- Sixty-eight state schools for deaf children educate 11,315 pupils. Additionally, nine public day schools teach 2,482 deaf children.
- There are 43 state institutions for "feebleminded" individuals that house 35,968 residents.
- *June 27*: Congress enacts the Vocational Rehabilitation Act of 1918, commonly referred to as the Smith-Sears Act, creating a federally funded program of rehabilitation for disabled soldiers.

1919

- Edgar F. Allen founds the Ohio Society for Crippled Children, which becomes the National Society for Crippled Children in 1921 and evolves into the National Easter Seal Society for Crippled Children and Adults in 1967.
- *Deliverance,* the semi-fictional film account of Helen Keller's life, is released. Keller and her teacher Anne Sullivan Macy play themselves in part of this silent movie.

1920s

- White Cane laws are passed. The laws protect pedestrians using the canes by making drivers of moving vehicles at fault in the case of accidents.

1920

- Disabled American Veterans, a nonprofit organization that advocates for disabled veterans and their families, is established.
- Deaf advocate Alice Terry is elected president of the California Association of the Deaf. Terry and Annie Lashbrook, president of New York's Empire State Association of the Deaf since 1919, are the only known female heads of state deaf organizations in the early decades of the 20th century.
- The 1930 *Statistical Abstract of the United States* estimates that, in 1920, there were 44,885 deaf Americans and 52,567 blind Americans. The leading causes of deafness in 1920 are congenital origins, scarlet fever, and meningitis. Blindness, however, is most often the result of injury or accident, cataracts, and congenital origins.
- *June 2*: With the enactment of the Industrial Rehabilitation Act of 1920, also known as the Smith-Fess Act, the federal government expands rehabilitation provisions to civilians with disabilities in an attempt to facilitate the return to the workforce of civilians disabled in industry.

1921

- Blindness service professionals organize the American Foundation for the Blind (AFB) to collect and provide information about vision loss and to stimulate discussions among professionals in the field. Helen Keller works for the organization for more than 40 years, lecturing, writing, and raising funds.

1922

- A group of teachers and administrators form the Council for Exceptional Children (CEC) at Teachers' College, Columbia University.
- Insulin is introduced as a treatment for diabetes.
- Wax or paraffin baths are used in Cleveland to treat arthritis in the hands. The treatment was first used in France and England during World War I and involves wrapping the hands in layers of soft, warm wax.

1923

- Universal Pictures releases the film *The Hunchback of Notre Dame,* whose representation of deaf and severely disabled bellringer Quasimodo reflects and reinforces the stereotype of disabled people as monsters.
- *March 8*: Pennsylvania bans deaf drivers. Over the next decades, other states prohibit deaf people from driving. Activists successfully get each of these bans repealed.

1924

- In conjunction with the American Radio Association, the American Foundation for the Blind distributes free or reduced-cost radios to Blind Americans.
- The International Committee of Sports for the Deaf is founded (later named Deaflympics), which fosters international sporting events among deaf people.

1927

- After personally benefiting from the hot mineral baths at Warm Springs, Georgia, as he recovered from polio, Franklin D. Roosevelt cofounds the Warm Springs Foundation, where polio survivors could benefit from mineral baths and community. The rehabilitation program there emphasizes the wisdom of experience and self-reliance.
- In the case *Buck v. Bell,* the U.S. Supreme Court upholds in an 8-1 decision the constitutionality of Virginia's sterilization law that allows state institutions to sterilize individuals with cognitive or psychiatric disabilities residing in state-funded institutions. While numerous states had passed similar laws, beginning in 1907, some 24 states would adopt sterilization laws by 1930. All told, eugenicists and state institutions use these laws to sterilize tens of thousands of Americans with disabilities without their consent.
- There are 78 state schools for blind students, serving 6,035 students.
- The states operate 68 residential schools for deaf children that serve 13,033 pupils. Eighty-three public day schools for deaf students serve 3,515 children.
- Across the country, 51 state institutions for "feebleminded" people house 49,791 residents.
- *October*: William "Blind Willie" McTell begins his recording career with Victor Records, in Atlanta, Georgia.

1928

- At Harvard University Philip Drinker and Louis Agassiz Shaw create the first successful tank respirator. A modified version of this "iron lung" is sold by John Emerson in 1931.
- Penicillin is discovered by Alexander Fleming. Penicillin is an antibiotic used to treat venereal disease and other infections. Its mass production in the 1940s marks the beginning of belief in and the search for antibiotics as miracle drugs.

1929

- In response to the success of Morris Frank and his guide dog Buddy who had been trained by Dorothy Harrison Eustis in Switzerland, Seeing Eye launches the first school to train guide dogs for blind people in the United States to increase the independence of blind Americans.
- Early Jazz pianist Art Tatum, who is blind, begins performing on the radio.
- *The Sound and the Fury,* William Faulkner's fourth novel, is released. The book receives praise and criticism for its complex structure; scholars continue to debate the meaning of Faulkner's character Benjy, who appears to have developmental disabilities.

1930s

- During the Great Depression, many federal relief programs discriminate against people with disabilities. Deaf workers challenge their exclusion from these programs, as do other disabled citizens.

1930

- The 1940 *Statistical Abstract of the United States* estimates that, in 1930, there are 63,503 blind Americans and 57,123 deaf Americans.

1931

- The film *City Lights,* starring Charlie Chaplin, is released. Granville Redmond, a deaf actor, is among the cast; the young blind woman depicted is one of few prominent representations of a disabled character in silent films.
- *March 3*: With the Pratt-Smoot Act, Congress authorizes the Library of Congress to provide books for adult blind citizens. The law provides the foundation for what would eventually become the National Library Service for the Blind and Physically Handicapped.

1932

- The efforts of British and American Braille users culminate in the Treaty of London, which standardizes Braille in the two countries, making it possible for Braille readers to use materials produced in either nation.
- Disabled American Veterans (DAV) is officially recognized by Congress as the representative agency for soldiers disabled in service. The organization works to improve federal programs and services for disabled veterans.
- The U.S. Public Health Service initiates the Tuskegee Syphilis Experiment, which continues until 1972. Nearly 400 African-American male subjects are denied treatment as part of the study.
- Engineers working for the American Foundation for the Blind (AFB) develop long-playing records and players.

These innovations make it possible for the AFB to establish studios to record "Talking Books."
- Tod Browning's horror film *Freaks* is released. Though this film portrays disabled people stereotypically as villainous avengers and freaks, it was the first to prominently feature actors with disabilities who were well known for their careers as sideshow and vaudeville performers.
- Harry Jennings creates the first tubular steel wheelchair that folds.

1933

- *March 4*: Franklin D. Roosevelt assumes the office of president of the United States. A polio survivor, Roosevelt is the first wheelchair user to hold the office of chief executive.

1934

- Three railroad companies allow blind individuals to ride with their guide dogs in day coaches.

1935

- In response to discrimination against people with disabilities in federal work relief programs, a group of New York City residents with disabilities organizes the League of the Physically Handicapped. Members of the league hold public protests in opposition to these discriminatory policies and meet with federal officials in Washington, D.C., to explain their grievances.
- President Franklin D. Roosevelt orders the Works Progress Administration, a national work relief program, to build 5,000 talking-book machines to supplement the Library of Congress's efforts to supply talking-books to blind Americans. These machines are to be loaned out to local libraries across the nation.
- American "folk opera" *Porgy and Bess* is produced in New York City. Based on a 1925 novel, this opera offers a complicated and at times contradictory representation of race and disability through its African-American character, Porgy.
- *August 14*: President Franklin D. Roosevelt signs the Social Security Act into law. Beyond providing pensions, unemployment insurance, and aid to dependent children, the law establishes programs to aid children with disabilities and needy blind citizens. Moreover, the act increases funding for the civilian vocational rehabilitation program first established in 1920.

1936

- The American Printing House for the Blind (APH) opens a recording studio to begin producing records for blind Americans.
- Neurologist Walter J. Freeman begins performing lobotomies, a psychosurgical procedure, as a treatment for peo-

ple with various mental illnesses. Over the next 30 years he lobotomizes 3,400 people.

- *June 20*: Congress passes the Randolph-Sheppard Act, allowing blind vendors to operate stands in federal buildings.

1937–1955

- Poliomyelitis epidemics sweep the nation. During these years, there are 415,624 reported cases of the disease. Thousands of children who contracted polio spent months, even years, in hospitals and rehabilitation centers during these epidemics. Some recovered use of limbs that had been paralyzed by the disease. In other cases, the disease caused permanent paralysis.

1937

- Blind workers strike for several weeks to protest salaries paid at a Pittsburgh sheltered workshop.
- Frances Bates organizes the National League for the Deaf-Blind. Originally conceived of as a correspondence club, the organization grows into a support and service organization. It is renamed the American Association of the Deaf-Blind in 1979.
- Disabled miner Herbert A. Everest and his friend Harry C. Jennings, an engineer, design and patent a folding wheelchair that can be loaded into the trunk of a car. From this design, the pair launches what will become the largest wheelchair manufacturing company in the nation, Everest & Jennings, or E & J.
- Ray Charles enters the St. Augustine (Florida) School for the Deaf and Blind. Charles, who had became blind from glaucoma two years earlier, receives musical training at the segregated blind school (a common form of vocational education for many southern African-American blind and low-vision children). Charles goes on to become a prominent figure on the American music scene.
- John Steinbeck publishes *Of Mice and Men*, which includes multiple characters with disabilities.

1938

- In an effort to raise money to combat poliomyelitis (polio), President Franklin D. Roosevelt establishes the National Foundation for Infantile Paralysis. The organization's fund-raising campaign would soon become popularly known as the "March of Dimes" because of its strategy to collect dimes from Americans across the nation. After shifting its focus from polio to "birth defects" in the early 1960s the organization officially adopts the name March of Dimes in 1979.
- Throughout the nation, 7,846 blind or vision impaired children, 10,848 deaf and hard of hearing children, 13,737 children with physical disabilities, and 103,637 children with intellectual or developmental disabilities receive spe-

cial instruction in public day school programs. Another 14,424 children with disabilities receive home or hospital instruction.

- Italian neuroscientists Ugo Cerletti and Lucio Bini first use electroconvulsive therapy, commonly called electric shock or electroshock therapy, to treat mental illness. Many American doctors advocate and use this technique in subsequent years although its popularity declines in the late 20th century.
- *June 25*: President Franklin D. Roosevelt signs the Fair Labor Standards Act, which establishes a minimum wage and limits working hours and child labor. By freeing sheltered workshops from many of the restrictions of the law, the Fair Labor Standards Act also leads to an expansion in the number of sheltered workshops in the nation. On the one hand, these workshops provide employment and training opportunities to people with disabilities, but, on the other hand, they offer workers low wages and virtually no benefits.

1939

- The film *Dark Victory* is released. Leading actress Bette Davis, who plays a wealthy socialite diagnosed with a brain tumor, is nominated for an Academy Award. The film reinforces various disability and gender stereotypes common at this time.
- There are 100,217 residents in state institutions for "mental defectives and epileptics."

1940

- A group of blind activists, including Jacobus tenBroek, meets in Wilkes-Barre, Pennsylvania, and they organize the National Federation of the Blind. The group works to improve services and laws for blind citizens and to give blind people a voice in shaping the programs designed to aid them.
- Carson McCullers's first novel, *The Heart Is a Lonely Hunter*, is published. The book includes numerous characters with disabilities and draws critical acclaim for its poignant condemnation of prejudices. In 1968 a film version of the story is produced.
- The National Association of the Physically Handicapped, a nonprofit social welfare group led by Paul Strachan, begins its work. The organization disbands in 1958.

1941–1945

- The United States joins the Allied powers during World War II. Mobilization sparks renewed economic opportunities for at least 200,000 Americans with disabilities, many of whom provide labor in factories. In addition to the many millions of Holocaust and battlefield victims, the war adds numbers to a new generation of disabled American veterans.

1941

- David Abraham of the Perkins School for the Blind develops the Perkins Brailler, a portable Braille typewriter. After World War II, Howe Press, a Braille printing house affiliated with the school, produces these machines for use by the wider public.
- Rosemary Kennedy, brother of future president John F. Kennedy, undergoes a lobotomy. The failed surgery limits Kennedy's physical and cognitive abilities.

1942–1944

- Henry Viscardi volunteers through the American Red Cross, training disabled soldiers in the use of their new prosthetic limbs at the Walter Reed Army Medical Center in Washington, D.C. He is dismissed by the Red Cross, but he continues to help veterans privately. He eventually meets Howard Rusk and Eleanor Roosevelt, and they work to push Congress to improve rehabilitation services for disabled soldiers.

1942

- Founded by Paul Strachan, a man with multiple disabilities, the American Federation of the Physically Handicapped is officially chartered in Washington, D.C. The organization works to improve employment opportunities for people with disabilities and demands federal antidiscrimination legislation. The group's efforts will eventually lead to the establishment of a permanent presidential committee dedicated to expanding the employment of people with disabilities.

1943

- In response to a widespread shortage of workers, Congress expands the national vocational rehabilitation program to provide some medical services to prepare people with disabilities for work during World War II. The Vocational Rehabilitation Amendments, commonly referred to as the Barden-LaFollette Act, also increase the types of educational and vocational assistance available to people with disabilities through the federal rehabilitation program.
- Katharine Butler Hathaway publishes *The Little Locksmith*. This memoir depicts the constraints Hathaway has faced because of her gender and physical disfigurements as a result of childhood tuberculosis.

1944

- During his World War II service in the U.S. Army Air Force, internal medicine specialist Howard Rusk is given the task of developing a convalescent program in Pawling, New York. Rusk institutes a program of rehabilitation, including physical therapy, exercise, recreation, and educational courses, for disabled airmen. Rehabilitation medicine is eventually adopted by all of the military hospitals and is recognized as a new medical specialty.
- Richard E. Hoover and others develop techniques using long canes to improve the mobility of blind people. Hoover begins teaching these techniques at the Valley Forge Army General Hospital. One student, Russell Williams, will improve on these techniques and teach them at the Hines Veterans Administration Hospital rehabilitation program for blind veterans.
- Tennessee Williams's play, *The Glass Menagerie,* is produced. His character Laura Wingfield becomes one of the best-known theatrical representations of disability.

1945

- The Blinded Veterans Association is founded by veterans who had been blinded during World War II at the Avon Old Farms Army Convalescent Hospital in Avon, Connecticut. The organization works to connect blind veterans to resources and services.
- The U.S. Office of Vocational Rehabilitation (OVR) hires Boyce R. Williams as a consultant on programs for deaf, hard of hearing, and speech impaired citizens. He works for the OVR for 38 years, developing and improving vocational and education programs for deaf Americans.
- The National Braille Club, which is later renamed the National Braille Association, is founded in New York City. It works to standardize Braille transcription and improve the quality and availability of materials available in Braille.
- John Howard Griffin begins to lose his vision as a result of war-related injuries. He writes extensively in his journals about his decade-long experience with blindness, which becomes the basis for his memoir, *Scattered Shadows,* posthumously released in 2004.
- *April 13*: The American Athletic Union of the Deaf is founded in Akron, Ohio (it is renamed the USA Deaf Sports Federation in 1997).
- *August 11*: President Harry S. Truman signs Joint Resolution 23 into law, establishing the first week in October as "National Employ the Physically Handicapped Week."

1946

- Parents of children with cerebral palsy organize the Cerebral Palsy Society of New York City. Members of the organization eventually work to form a state and then national organization, the United Cerebral Palsy Associations, Inc.
- Mary Jane Ward publishes her semiautobiographical novel *The Snake Pit,* which examines mental illness and treatment in institutions from the vantage point of someone labeled as ill.
- Conscientious objectors to World War II who had been assigned to work as attendants in state mental institutions organize the National Mental Health Foundation (becom-

ing Mental Health America in 2006). Members of the organization work to publicize the inhumane conditions at state institutions. Their work leads to funding increases for these facilities as well launching the beginnings of the deinstitutionalization movement.

- The March of Dimes selects Donald Anderson to be the organization's first poster child for its polio fund-raising campaign.
- The National Bituminous Coal Wage Agreement establishes its Welfare Fund, which eventually helps secure medical and rehabilitation services for disabled miners and their families.
- *The Beast with Five Fingers,* a Hollywood film about a pianist, reflects the anxiety many people feel about significant disabilities acquired from World War II.
- There are 54 state residential schools for blind children, teaching 5,150 students, while there are 79 state residential schools for deaf children that teach 12,971 students.
- *August 13*: Congress enacts the Hospital Survey and Construction Act, commonly referred to as the Hill-Burton Act, establishing federal grants to states to both survey the need for hospitals and construct them. States with lower per capita incomes and greater need for hospitals receive greater funding through the act.

1947

- Secretary of Labor Lewis B. Schwellenbach, under the direction of President Harry S. Truman, forms the President's Committee on National Employ the Physically Handicapped Week. With members drawn from federal agencies, disability activist organizations, and business, civic, labor, and women's groups, the committee works to promote "National Employ the Physically Handicapped Week."
- Veterans from numerous Veterans Administration hospitals across the nation meet together and organize the Paralyzed Veterans of America, an organization that works to improve accessibility and pushes for civil rights legislation for people with disabilities.
- For his portrayal of Homer Parish, a sailor returning home after a disabling injury during World War II, in the film *The Best Years of Our Lives,* Harold Russell, himself a disabled veteran, receives two Academy Awards—best supporting actor and a special award for his service to veterans.
- There are 530,255 patients in hospitals for "mental disease."
- State institutions for "mental defectives and epileptics" house 122,605 people with disabilities.

1948

- Congress amends the Civil Service Act to prohibit discrimination against people with disabilities in federal employment.

- Members of the Paralyzed Veterans of America form a civilian branch of their organization, the National Paraplegia Foundation, to advocate for civilians with spinal cord injuries. The organization works to improve accessibility and later to encourage research on spinal cord injuries.
- Timothy Nugent's program for students with disabilities at the University of Illinois at Galesburg gains official recognition from the university. The program works to integrate students with disabilities into all elements of campus life. The program is later moved to the Urbana-Champaign campus, which becomes a model for campus accessibility and independent living centers.
- Patients and former patients of the Rockland State Hospital in New York form the peer support group We Are Not Alone.
- *Johnny Belinda* wins the Academy Award for Best Actress (Jane Wyman), who plays the deaf heroine. It is the first major Hollywood film to portray sign language positively.
- Across the country, there are 6,335 hospitals with more than 1.4 million beds, representing a dramatic increase in the capacity and number of hospitals in the nation. In 1909 there were less than 5,000 hospitals with only 421,065 beds. This number continues to grow because of funding through the Hill-Burton Act of 1946.
- Throughout the nation, 8,216 blind or vision-impaired children, 13,977 deaf and hard of hearing children, 30,498 children with physical disabilities, and 87,067 children with intellectual or developmental disabilities receive special instruction in public day school programs.

1949

- Timothy Nugent, a pioneer in developing programs for college students with disabilities, organizes the National Wheelchair Basketball Association at Illinois University. Galesburg, Illinois, hosts the first Annual Wheelchair Basketball Tournament that same year. Nugent goes on to serve as the organization's commissioner for 25 years. Moreover, sports, such as wheelchair basketball, become an increasingly significant element of disability culture.
- Parents of children with cerebral palsy involved in the New York State Association for Cerebral Palsy organize the National Foundation for Cerebral Palsy, bringing together representatives of similar organizations across the country. In 1950 the organization is renamed the United Cerebral Palsy Associations, Inc. Along with the Association for Retarded Children, the organization becomes an important part of the parents' movement to improve educational opportunities and medical care for children with disabilities.
- Animated theatrical short, *Ragtime Bear* first presents the character with low vision, Mr. Magoo, who becomes a central figure in television cartoons and films. By the 1970s blind advocacy groups begin protesting this stereotypical object of humor.

1950

- Founded primarily by parents of children with cognitive disabilities who had been active in local and statewide support groups, the National Association for Retarded Children is organized at a meeting in Minneapolis. In its early years, the organization works to improve educational opportunities for children with cognitive disabilities. It eventually becomes the Association for Retarded Children and then later The Arc.
- The Federal Security Agency appoints Mary Switzer director of the U.S. Office of Vocational Rehabilitation, a position she will hold for 17 years. She later heads the new Social and Rehabilitation Service in the Department of Health, Education and Welfare.
- Parent advocates found the Muscular Dystrophy Association.
- *The Men,* a film about disabled veterans and starring Marlon Brando, offers a positive and empowered representation of people with disabilities, which is uncommon during this era.
- Pearl Buck publishes *The Child Who Never Grew,* which describes her experiences mothering her daughter, Carol, who has cognitive disabilities.
- Chlorpromazine (marketed under the brand name Thorazine) is first synthesized. This antipsychotic drug becomes a prominent form of treatment for various psychiatric conditions, often replacing electroconvulsive therapy and lobotomies. By 2008 more than 100 million people have been given Thorazine.
- The Korean War begins, lasting for three years. Tens of thousands of American soldiers return from war with permanent physical and mental impairments.
- *August 28:* Congress enacts the Social Security Amendments, extending provisions for public assistance payments to impoverished citizens with permanent and total disabilities. The original Social Security Act of 1935 had provided such funds as grants to states only for poor blind individuals and for the provision of services (but not direct benefits) to "crippled" children.

1951

- The New York University Medical Center and Howard Rusk launch the Institute of Rehabilitation Medicine. Rusk and the institute develop and encourage new technologies, such as better prostheses and adaptive aids, to enable people with disabilities to live more independently.
- Thadine Hedges Maytum begins publishing installments of her autobiographical novel, *Let the Day Perish,* which includes the social stigma associated with having cerebral palsy.
- The American Association of Instructors of the Blind launches the *International Journal for the Education of the Blind.* The journal will eventually become *Education of the Visually Handicapped* and then *RE:view.*

1952

- Reflecting an expanding mission, the President's Committee on National Employ the Physically Handicapped Week becomes the President's Committee on the Employment of the Physically Handicapped.
- Henry Viscardi founds Abilities, Inc., first a manufacturing business and later a jobs training and placement center for people with disabilities.
- The American Psychiatric Association begins publishing the *Diagnostic and Statistical Manual of Mental Disorders.* Its first edition describes 106 categories of mental disorder; the numbers of disorders expands over the next decades, from 182 in the 1968 second edition to 297 in the 2000 fourth edition.
- Hearing aids that use transistors rather than vacuum tubes are introduced. The devices are much smaller and more effective.

1953

- Abraham Nemeth establishes his system for mathematics coding for blind Americans, the Nemeth Braille Mathematics Code.
- Popular western performer Dale Evans writes *Angel Unaware,* which details her experiences with her daughter Robin, who has intellectual disabilities. Evans donates the royalties from the book (which total $40,000 in its first year) to the National Association for Retarded Children.
- There are 389,158 elementary students and 108,058 secondary students enrolled in "special" schools. Students in these schools have physical or intellectual disabilities, speech impairments, "health problems," and they include blind and deaf students.

1954

- In a unanimous decision, the U.S. Supreme Court issues the *Brown v. Board of Education of Topeka* decision, ruling that racially segregated school are inherently unequal and unconstitutional. The decision helps launch the civil rights movement and inspires the disability rights movement.
- Congress passes the Vocational Rehabilitation Amendments of 1954. These amendments alter the financing of the federal rehabilitation program, providing poorer states with additional federal assistance in maintaining the program. Additionally, the amendments provide federal funds for research and training grants. The Office of Vocational Rehabilitation uses these funds to support initiatives such as the University of Connecticut's Handicapped Homemaker Project. Further, the amendments require that each local office of the U.S. Employment Service employ at least

one staff person to assist people with disabilities in finding employment and training.

- Congress expands the Hill-Burton (Hospital Survey and Construction) Act to provide federal funds for the construction of hospitals for people with chronic illnesses, nursing care facilities, and rehabilitation centers.
- Andrew Foster becomes the first African-American graduate of Gallaudet College.

1955

- *April 12*: After field trials, Dr. Thomas Francis, Jr., of the University of Michigan concludes that Jonas Salk's polio vaccine is safe and effective. Over the next two years, application of the vaccine decreases the occurrence of polio by 85 to 90 percent.
- *June*: Carnegie Hall in New York City holds the first of what becomes the annual Muscular Dystrophy Association Jerry Lewis Telethon.

1956

- Congress expands Social Security coverage, making people with disabilities over the age of 50 eligible for Social Security payments through Social Security Disability Insurance.
- The first issue appears of *Accent on Living,* a quarterly magazine that promotes information sharing between people with disabilities about resources and strategies for daily life experiences. The periodical serves as a vehicle for activism in the disability rights movement.

1957

- Federal departments and agencies receive employment coordinators from the U.S. Civil Service Commission to encourage the hiring of people with disabilities.
- The first successful portable pacemaker is developed. The pacemaker is used to regulate the heart beat.
- Billy Barty establishes Little People of America in Reno, Nevada.
- The Association for Retarded Children names Gunnar Dybwad its executive director.
- Eugene O'Neil's play, *Long Day's Journey into Night,* is produced. Considered his masterwork, this play incorporates disability into its plot using nuanced representations of people with disabilities.
- There are 158,365 individuals institutionalized in state facilities for "mental defectives."
- *June 1*: Adelphi College in Garden City, New York, hosts the first National Wheelchair Games.

1958

- Gini Laurie becomes editor of the *Toomeyville Gazette,* later the *Rehabilitation Gazette,* at the Toomey Pavilion Respiratory Center in Cleveland, Ohio. The periodical becomes an early voice for disability rights and independent living.
- In Grand Rapids, Michigan, the American Federation of the Physically Handicapped is dissolved and the National Association of the Physically Handicapped, Inc., is formed.
- Kevadon (the brand name for Thalidomide) becomes available in sample form to American women as part of clinical trials. Controversy over the drug's impact on embryos contributes to more stringent Food and Drug Administration regulations.
- *August 28*: Congress amends the Social Security Act to provide Social Security Disability Insurance benefits to the dependents of disabled workers.
- *September 2*: Captioned Films for the Deaf, Public Law 85-905, is put into effect.

1959

- The American Optometric Association establishes its Committee on Aid to the Partially Sighted.
- Discoveries about cellular aspects of Down syndrome by French scientists Jerome Lejeune and Marthe Gauthier spark doctors' increased use of amniocentesis on pregnant women. Prenatal testing becomes widely used over the next decades, and disability activists challenge the ethical grounds of this procedure.
- The United States pays over $300 million in benefits to disabled workers through the Social Security Disability Insurance program.

1960s

- The deinstitutionalization movement grows. Broad disability rights initiatives gain momentum.
- Development of the myoelectric arm, the predecessor to micro-processor devices. The prosthetic is electrically powered and responds to muscle contractions relayed from an electrode placed on the skin.

1960

- The first Paralympic Games are held in Rome.
- *To Kill a Mockingbird,* a novel by Harper Lee, is published and wins the Pulitzer Prize the following year. In its critique of social prejudices, Lee also examines discrimination against people with disabilities. The film version, released in 1962, downplays most of these disability themes.
- The first university program for orientation and mobility is established at Boston College.
- There are approximately 175,000 people in institutions or schools for "mentally handicapped" individuals.
- *September 13*: The Social Security Act is amended to allow workers less than 50 years old to receive Social Security Disability Insurance benefits.

1961

- The American Council of the Blind is established.
- President John F. Kennedy appoints the President's Panel on Mental Retardation to improve the lives of people with mental retardation and to reform existing programs.
- *American Standard Specifications for Making Buildings Accessible to, and Usable by, the Physically Handicapped* is published by the American National Standards Institute, Inc. (ANSI).
- Erving Goffman publishes *Stigma: Notes on the Management of a Spoiled Identity,* which becomes a classic text on the social and physical dimensions of stigma.
- The first experimental cochlear implant surgeries are performed in the United States. By 2008 more than 100,000 Americans have undergone the procedure.

1962

- President John F. Kennedy issues an executive order, renaming the President's Committee on the Employment of the Physically Handicapped. To reflect both the president's and the committee's interest in creating opportunities for people with intellectual and psychiatric disabilities, the president strikes the word "physically" from the committee's name.
- The President's Committee on Employment of the Handicapped announces that more than 4 million people with disabilities had found jobs through the state employment services since the committee began its work in 1947.
- Ken Kesey publishes the novel *One Flew Over the Cuckoo's Nest,* which critically examines psychiatry and the medical model of disability. A film version of the book is produced in 1975.
- The film *Miracle Worker* is released, garnering two Academy Awards and solidifying a mythology of Helen Keller and Anne Sullivan Macy for a new generation of Americans.
- Edward V. Roberts enrolls at the University of California at Berkeley.
- Leo Jacobs helps found one of the first deaf-run agencies, Deaf Counseling, Advocacy, and Referral Agency, in the San Francisco Bay area.

1963

- President Kennedy calls for a reduction in the number of Americans institutionalized.
- South Carolina becomes the first state requiring public buildings physically accessible.
- Computers are first able to produce Braille.
- Ed Roberts, John Hessler, and other disabled students at the University of California at Berkeley form the Rolling Quads to advocate for disability rights.
- The Dialpak version of oral contraceptives is introduced by Ortho-Novum. Popularly known as "the Pill," it fuels the sexual revolution and alters perceptions about birth control.

- Blind singer, musician, and composer Stevie Wonder begins collaborating with Motown Records, launching his career as a recording artist.
- *September*: The *X-Men* comic book debuts. The series from Marvel Comics includes various central characters with atypical bodies. Television adaptations appear in the 1990s, and film versions of the superhero story are produced in the early 21st century.
- *October 31*: Congress passes the Mental Retardation Facilities and Community Health Centers Construction Act to provide federal funding for building community mental health centers.
- *December 18*: President Lyndon Johnson authorizes the Vocational Education Act, mandating that states use 10 percent of federal vocational education funding for services to students with disabilities.

1964–1965

- A rubella (German measles) epidemic among pregnant women causes disabilities, including deafness and blindness, in babies.

1964

- Registry of Interpreters for the Deaf, a national organization of professionals, is founded.
- Robert H. Weitbrecht invents the acoustic coupler to allow teletypewriter messages to be sent via standard telephone lines. This will give deaf people access to communication by telephone.
- The National Association of the Deaf racially desegregates; female members also gain the right to vote.
- The dark comedy *Dr. Strangelove or: How I Learned to Stop Worrying and Love the Bomb* is released. The film, which becomes a cult classic, showcases various stereotypes of people with disabilities.

1965–1975

- U.S. involvement in Vietnam escalates. The use of Agent Orange between 1961 and 1971 effects the development of embryos and causes significant health problems to others exposed to the herbicide. The war also sparks medical innovations, such as subcutaneous implants and bone grafts. Popular cultural representations of this war often emphasize physical and psychological disabilities sustained from the conflict.
- *July 2*: President Lyndon Johnson signs into law the Civil Rights Act to prohibit discrimination on the basis of race in public accommodations, employment, and federal education programs.

1965

- The Vocational Rehabilitation Amendments provide federal funding for rehabilitation facilities, for the expansion of existing programs, and for the establishment of the National Commission on Architectural Barriers to Rehabilitation of the Handicapped.

- William C. Stokoe, Carl Croneberg, and Dorothy Casterline publish *A Dictionary of American Sign Language on Linguistic Principles,* helping further establish the legitimacy of American Sign Language and supporting the move away from strict oralism.
- The Autism Society of America is founded by Dr. Bernard Rimland and Dr. Ruth Sullivan and many other parents of children with autism in response to the lack of services, discrimination against children with autism, and the prevailing view of medical "experts" that autism is a result of poor parenting, as opposed to neurological disability. The Autism Society of America becomes a leading source of information and research about autism.
- *June 8*: Congress establishes the National Technical Institute for the Deaf at the Rochester Institute of Technology in Rochester, New York, as the first and largest technical college in the world for students who are deaf or hard of hearing.
- *July 30*: With his signed approval, President Lyndon Johnson establishes Medicare and Medicaid to provide federally subsidized health care to disabled and elderly Americans covered by the Social Security program. Disability under the Social Security Disability Insurance program is redefined, from "of long-continued and indefinite duration" to "expected to last for . . . not less than 12 months."

1966

- Frederick C. Schreiber becomes the first paid executive secretary of the National Association of the Deaf.
- *Flowers for Algernon,* Daniel Keyes's novel about a man born with a low intelligence quotient, is published. The work critically examines representations of intellectual disability and medical practices. *Charly,* a film adaptation of the book, is produced in 1968.
- President Lyndon B. Johnson creates the President's Committee on Mental Retardation to provide advice regarding federal services, recommend new legislation, coordinate federal efforts, and promote public understanding about individuals with mental retardation.
- *Christmas in Purgatory,* by Burton Blatt and Fred Kaplan, is published, documenting, through photographs, the appalling conditions at state institutions for people with developmental disabilities. It adds to the movement for deinstitutionalization.
- The first episode of *Star Trek* appears on television. The popular series (and spin-off film adaptations) regularly include representations of people with disabilities, often reflecting changing notions of disability.

1967

- The National Theatre of the Deaf is founded by David Hays at the Eugene O'Neill Memorial Theatre Center in Waterford, Connecticut, with grants from the U.S. Department of Health, Education and Welfare and the Office of Education. It creates its Professional Training School and begins touring nationally.
- The President's Committee on Employment of the Handicapped releases estimates that five million people with disabilities had earned more than $4 billion at jobs acquired since 1947, paying taxes of more than $1 billion during that time.
- San Francisco State University and Florida State University establish the first programs to train mobility instructors of children with visual impairments.
- The Helen Keller National Center for Deaf-Blind Youth is established by the U.S. government to provide rehabilitation and training for the deaf-blind.
- Popular thriller film *Wait Until Dark* reinforces stereotypical images of the vulnerable blind woman, which is incorporated into many subsequent Hollywood productions.
- Anthropologist Robert Edgerton publishes *The Cloak of Competence: Stigma in the Lives of the Mentally Retarded,* which becomes an important study in the field of cognitive disability.

1968

- Building on a series of day camps started by Eunice Kennedy Shriver, the first ever International Special Olympics Games are held in July in Chicago, Illinois, to encourage athletic training and competition and physical activity among children and adults with intellectual disabilities.
- The National Technical Institute for the Deaf, part of Rochester Institute of Technology, opens.
- The American Association of Workers for the Blind begins to certify mobility instructors for the visually impaired.
- Samuel Genensky, a mathematician with low vision, and Paul Baron, along with colleagues at the Rand Corporation, demonstrate a prototype of closed-circuit television (CCTV) at a meeting of the American Academy of Optometry.
- There are 192,946 residents in public institutions for "mentally retarded" individuals.
- *August 12*: The Architectural Barriers Act is passed and signed into law by President Lyndon Johnson. The law requires that all buildings and other facilities designed, built, altered, or leased with federal funds be accessible to individuals with disabilities. It is one of the first laws to require access to buildings and other facilities.

1969

- Members of the National Rehabilitation Association initiate a protest to address issues of racial disparity. The protest results in the creation of the Council of Non-White Rehabilitation Workers; the council is renamed the National Association of Multicultural Rehabilitation Concerns in 1990.

- The International Committee on Technical Aids of Rehabilitation International selects the International Symbol of Access (a white outline of a wheelchair user within a blue square) intended to promote a consistent representation of access.
- At a conference sponsored by the President's Committee on Mental Retardation, Niels Erk Bank-Mikkelsen from Denmark and Bengt Nirje from Sweden introduce the concept of normalization to an American audience. Papers from the conference are published in *Changing Patterns in Residential Services for the Mentally Retarded* and help foster the movement for deinstitutionalization.
- Over 1.3 million disabled workers receive benefits through the Social Security Disability Insurance program.
- *January 1*: Julius and Harriet Wiggins begin publishing *Silent News,* which features reprinted and original articles about deafness.

1970

- The Insane Liberation Front is organized in Portland, Oregon, as one of the first psychiatric survivor organizations.
- The Developmental Disabilities Services and Facilities Construction Amendments to the Mental Retardation Facilities and Community Health Centers Construction Act of 1963 are passed by Congress. They contain the first legal definition of developmental disabilities and authorize grants for services and facilities for the rehabilitation of people with developmental disabilities including epilepsy and cerebral palsy and for the establishment of state "DD Councils."
- Max Starkloff, who was confined to a nursing home when he became quadriplegic following an accident, founds Paraquad in St. Louis. Paraquad is one of the first centers for independent living.
- Judith Heumann and other disability activists establish Disabled in Action in New York City. This follows her successful employment discrimination suit against the city's public school system. With chapters in several other cities, it organizes demonstrations and files litigation on behalf of disability rights.
- Ed Roberts, John Hessler, Hale Zukas, and others at the University of California at Berkeley establish the Physically Disabled Students Program (PDSP) at the university with an $80,000 grant from the U.S. Department of Education. With its provisions for community living, political advocacy, and personal assistance services, it becomes the nucleus for the first Center for Independent Living, founded two years later in the city of Berkeley that sparks the worldwide independent living movement.

- *October 15*: Congress passes the Urban Mass Transportation Assistance Act, which affirms that elderly and disabled individuals have an equal right to use mass transportation facilities and services.

1971

- The Mental Patients' Liberation Front is founded in Boston, and the Mental Patients' Liberation Project is founded in New York City as part of the growing psychiatric survivors movement.
- At Syracuse University, Burton Blatt establishes the Center on Human Policy, an advocacy, policy, and research institute.
- The National Center for Law and the Handicapped is founded at the University of Notre Dame in South Bend, Indiana, as the first legal advocacy center for people with disabilities in the United States.
- Judge Frank M. Johnson, Jr., of the U.S. District Court for the Middle District of Alabama hands down his decision in *Wyatt v. Stickney,* ruling that people in residential state schools and institutions have a constitutional right to appropriate treatment that can cure or improve their mental conditions. The ruling also requires a humane psychic and physical environment, adequate trained staff, individual treatment plans, and treatment in the least restrictive environment.
- The Caption Center is founded at WGBH Public Television in Boston as the world's first captioning center for providing captioned programming for deaf viewers.
- Deaf actress Linda Bove first appears on the public television program for children *Sesame Street,* a role she performs until 2003.
- The Fair Labor Standards Act of 1938 is amended to bring people with disabilities other than blindness into the sheltered workshop system. This measure leads to a significant expansion of the sheltered workshop system for people with cognitive and developmental disabilities.
- John Linvill and James C. Bliss develop the Optacon (OPtical TActile CONverter) reading machine to translate print into tactile vibrating images for the visually impaired.
- Shortly after his birth, David Vetter is placed in a sterile isolator. Commonly known as "David the Bubble Boy," Vetter spends virtually his entire life (12 years) inside the isolator. His medical treatment and personal experiences spark numerous debates and cultural representations.
- *October 8*: The U.S. District Court for the Eastern District of Pennsylvania, in a consent decree in *PARC v. Pennsylvania,* strikes down various state laws used to exclude disabled children from the public schools. Both this decision and *Mills v. Board of Education* in 1972 give rise to similar suits and encourage disability activists to use the courts to expand disability rights.

1972

- Ed Roberts and his associates establish a Center for Independent Living (CIL) in Berkeley, California, for the community at large. This helps foster the Independent Living Movement in the United States.
- The Institute for Rehabilitation and Research at the Texas Medical Center establishes the Houston Cooperative Living Residential Project in Houston, Texas. It becomes a model, along with the Center for Independent Living in Berkeley, California, for subsequent independent living programs.
- The Mental Health Law Center is founded in Washington, D.C., to provide legal representation and to advocate for the rights of people with mental illness. In 1993 it is renamed the Judge David L. Bazelon Center for Mental Health Law to honor a federal appeals court judge whose decisions did much to establish mental health law.
- Paralyzed Veterans of America, the national Paraplegia Foundation, and Richard Heddinger file suit to force the Washington Metropolitan Area Transit Authority to incorporate access into their design for a new, multibillion dollar subway system in Washington, D.C. Their eventual victory becomes a landmark in the struggle for accessible public mass transit.
- Wolf Wolfensberger and others publish *The Principle of Normalization in Human Services,* expanding the theory of normalization and bringing it to a wider American audience.
- The Network Against Psychiatric Assault is organized in San Francisco and focuses on the use of electroconvulsive therapy. Its efforts lead to a California law restricting and regulating the use of such therapy.
- The parents of residents at the Willowbrook State School in Staten Island, New York, file suit (*New York ARC v. Rockefeller*) to end the appalling conditions at that institution. A television report broadcast from the facility outrages the general public, who view the inhumane treatment endured by people with developmental disabilities. This exposure in the press together with the lawsuit and other advocacy efforts, eventually moves thousands of people from the institution into community-based living arrangements.
- Disabled activists, including those from Disabled in Action, Paralyzed Veterans of America, the National Paraplegia Foundation, and others hold demonstrations in Washington, D.C., and other cities to protest the veto of the rehabilitation act passed by Congress. A revised version becomes the Rehabilitation Act of 1973 signed by President Richard M. Nixon.
- *Madness Network News* begins publication in San Francisco as a newsletter, later a newspaper, covering the ex-patients' movement.
- Congress mandates that Head Start programs take a minimum of 10 percent children with disabilities and that these children be included in all programs.
- The beauty pageant Ms. Wheelchair America is founded in Ohio.
- The first Miss Deaf America pageant is held at a National Association of the Deaf convention in Miami, Florida; Ann Billington is crowned the winner.
- *August 1*: The U.S. District Court for the District of Columbia, in *Mills v. Board of Education,* rules that the District of Columbia cannot exclude disabled children from public schools.
- *October 30*: The passage of the Social Security Amendments of 1972 creates the Supplemental Security Income (SSI) program. This program extends Medicare benefits to individuals with disabilities and also extends childhood benefits to disabled individuals as adults allowing many to live more independently. It also consolidates existing federal programs providing assistance to those over 65 and to those who are blind and disabled effective January 1, 1974.

1973

- The Vera Institute of Justice establishes the Legal Action Center in New York City, and later in Washington, D.C., to advocate for the interests of people who are alcohol or drug dependent. In the early 21st century, it also works on behalf of people with HIV/AIDS.
- Washington, D.C., introduces the first handicap parking stickers.
- The first Conference on Human Rights and Psychiatric Oppression is held at the University of Detroit to discuss the philosophy and goals of mental patients' liberation.
- Congress passes the Federal-Aid Highway Act requiring that all pedestrian crosswalks constructed with federal funds include curb cuts.
- The Architectural and Transportation Barriers Compliance Board, later called the Access Board, is established under the Rehabilitation Act of 1973 to enforce the Architectural Barriers Act of 1968.
- The Consortium for Citizens with Disabilities is organized to advocate for people of all ages with physical and mental disabilities and their families.
- Fetal Alcohol Syndrome (FAS) first appears in American medical vocabulary. Identification and reporting of FAS increases rapidly in the 1970s.
- North Carolina passes a statewide building code with stringent access requirements drafted by access advocate Ronald Mace. This code becomes a model for effective architectural access legislation in other states. Mace later founds Barrier Free Environments to advocate for accessibility in buildings and products.

- *January 22*: In a 7-2 decision, the Supreme Court rules in *Roe v. Wade* that women have a constitutional right to abortion in the first three months of pregnancy.
- *September 26*: President Richard Nixon signs the Rehabilitation Act of 1973, marking the greatest legal achievement of the disability rights movement to date. The act—particularly Title V and, especially, Section 504—deals with discrimination against people with disabilities. Section 504 prohibits programs receiving federal funds from discriminating against "otherwise qualified handicapped" individuals and sparks the formation of "504 workshops" and numerous grassroots organizations. Disability rights activists seize on the act as a powerful tool and make the signing of regulations to implement Section 504 a top priority. Litigation arising out of Section 504 generates such central disability rights concepts as "reasonable modification," "reasonable accommodation," and "undue burden," which will form the framework for subsequent federal law, especially the Americans with Disabilities Act of 1990.

1974

- The first U.S. National Women's Wheelchair Basketball Tournament is held.
- The Boston Center for Independent Living is founded.
- The Housing and Community Development Act creates the Section 8 housing program for families with low incomes and individuals with disabilities.
- *Halderman v. Pennhurst* is filed in Pennsylvania on behalf of the residents of the Pennhurst State School and Hospital. The case highlights the horrific conditions at state "schools" for people with mental retardation. The lower courts rule that individuals have a right to adequate care and treatment.
- The first Client Assistance Projects are established under the provisions of the Rehabilitation Act of 1973 to ensure that clients receive all the benefits they are entitled to under the act.
- Ambassador Jean Kennedy Smith establishes Very Special Arts as an international, nonprofit organization to create opportunities for all persons with disabilities to learn through, participate in, and enjoy the arts. It is later renamed VSA arts.
- The American Coalition of Citizens with Disabilities is created by 150 disability activists attending a meeting of the President's Committee on Employment of the Handicapped.
- Disabled Women's Coalition is founded at the University of California at Berkeley by Susan Sygall and Deborah Kaplan. Other women involved include Kitty Cone, Corbett O'Toole, and Susan Schapiro. The coalition runs support groups and holds disabled women's retreats. Members write for feminist publications and lecture on women and disability.

- *January 1*: People First is established in Salem, Oregon. People First becomes the largest U.S. organization composed of and led by people with cognitive disabilities and holds its first convention in October 1974.

1975

- Congress passes the Developmental Disabilities Assistance and Bill of Rights Act, providing federal funds to programs serving people with developmental disabilities and outlining a series of rights for those who are institutionalized. The lack of an enforcement mechanism within the bill and subsequent court decisions will, however, limit the effectiveness of the act.
- The Atlantis Community is founded in Denver as a center for independent living to help severely disabled adults living in nursing homes move into independent housing with state-funded personal assistants.
- *Mainstream: Magazine of the Able-Disabled* begins publication in San Diego. *Mainstream* advocates for disability rights as well as providing news and information useful to individuals with disabilities. It suspends print publication in 1999, but it continues on the Internet.
- The first Parent and Training Information Centers are founded to help parents of disabled children to exercise their rights under the Education for All Handicapped Children Act of 1975.
- Ed Roberts becomes the director of the California Department of Rehabilitation. He moves to establish nine independent living centers all across that state, based on the model of the original Center for Independent Living in Berkeley. The success of these centers demonstrates that independent living can be replicated and eventually results in the founding of hundreds of independent living centers all over the world.
- The Western Center on Law and the Handicapped is founded in Los Angeles to provide legal advocacy for individuals with disabilities.
- Sylvia Walker helps establish the Center for the Study of Handicapped Children and Youth at Howard University in Washington, D.C.
- Congress passes the Age Discrimination Act, banning discrimination based on age in any program receiving federal funds.
- Raymond C. Kurzweil invents the Kurzweil Reader, the first print-to-speech reading machine for blind people. The machine uses existing technology combined with a new application developed by Kurzweil to translate print into synthesized speech.
- Roland Kirk's album for Atlantic Records, *The Case of the 3 Sided Dream in Audio Color*, is released, showcasing his distinct musical techniques with woodwind instruments. Kirk, who had faced considerable racism as a student at

the Ohio School for the Blind, incorporated his experiences into his music.

- *April 4*: The American Association for the Education of the Severely/Profoundly Handicapped is established to improve the lives of children with severe and profound disabilities. The organization becomes The Association for the Severely Handicapped in 1980.
- *June 26*: The U.S. Supreme Court unanimously rules in *O'Connor v. Donaldson* that people cannot be institutionalized against their will in a psychiatric hospital unless they are determined to be a threat to themselves or to others.
- *November 29*: The Education for All Handicapped Children Act is signed by President Gerald Ford, establishing the right of children with disabilities to a public school education in an integrated environment. The act is a cornerstone of federal disability rights legislation. In the next decades, millions of disabled children will be educated under its provisions, radically changing the lives of people in the disability community.

1976

- The National Exhibits by Blind Artists is incorporated.
- *Born on the Fourth of July,* a memoir by disabled veteran Ron Kovic, is published. A movie version of the story is released in 1989.
- Disabled fiction writer Stanley Elkins publishes *The Franchiser,* one of his many complicated works that prominently feature characters with disabilities.
- A major lawsuit, *Disabled in Action of Pennsylvania, Inc. v. Coleman,* seeks to expand wheelchair access to public transportation. A number of disability organizations, including Disabled in Action of Pennsylvania, the American Coalition of Citizens with Disabilities, and a number of United Cerebral Palsy associations, band together to form the Transbus group. With the representation of the Public Interest Law Center of Philadelphia, the Transbus group demands that buses purchased with federal funds must be wheelchair accessible.
- Activists from Disabled in Action protest at the United Cerebral Palsy telethon in New York City, charging that telethons are "demeaning and paternalistic shows which celebrate and encourage pity."
- Deborah Kaplan founds the Disability Rights Center in Washington, D.C., specializing in consumer protection for people with disabilities. With the support of consumer advocate Ralph Nader and his Center for the Study of Responsive Law, one of the earliest actions of the Disability Rights Center is to join the Justice Department in an antitrust action against the Everest & Jennings Company, a manufacturer of wheelchairs and other assistive devices.
- The first independent living center, the Westside Center for Independent Living, is officially opened at a storefront office in Los Angeles with E. Sherman Clarke, a blind quadriplegic Ph.D. candidate, as its first executive director. The Westside Center becomes the first of nine similar establishments launched by disability activist Ed Roberts and the California Department of Rehabilitation.
- With a grant from the U.S. Department of Health, Education and Welfare, the National Center for Law and the Deaf is founded at Gallaudet College in Washington, D.C. This organization later acquires the name National Association of the Deaf Legal Defense Fund. Agreeing to maintain the fund in 1996, the National Association of the Deaf renames it the National Association of the Deaf Law and Advocacy Center.
- Closed captioning of television takes a major leap forward when the Federal Communications Commission authorizes Line 21 (EIA-608) of broadcast information for the exclusive use of closed captions.
- Despite evident progress in the Independent Living Movement, more than 189,000 individuals continue to live in long-term care facilities for "mentally handicapped" individuals.
- *January 22*: The first meeting is held of the planning committee to form the Coalition of Provincial Organizations of the Handicapped. This organization, located in Winnipeg, Canada, later becomes the Council of Canadians with Disabilities.

1977

- Sociologist Irving Zola publishes "Healthism and Disabling Medicalization," an article in which he criticizes the dominant role of medicine and doctors in American society.
- National Theatre Workshop of the Handicapped is founded by Brother Rick Curry in New York City and Belfast, Maine. This nonprofit organization educates theater artists with disabilities, produces new work on the subject of disability, and advocates for disabled artists in the entertainment industry.
- As a comparable concept to sexism and racism, Tom Humphries coins the term *audism* to describe a belief system that values the ability to hear as superior.
- The Disabled Peoples Liberation Front is founded in Boston by Jean Wassell, James Brooks, and Richard Candelmo.
- Across the nation, 2.7 million Americans use a cane or walking stick, more than 645,000 use a wheelchair, and more than 205,000 have a prosthetic leg or foot.
- *January*: *Journal of Visual Impairment & Blindness,* or *JVIB,* acquires its present name, changing from *New Outlook for the Blind.* Founded in April 1907 as "a quarterly record of the progress and welfare of the blind," the journal is originally named *Outlook for the Blind,* is renamed once before (in February 1942) as *Outlook for the Blind and The Teachers Forum* when it chooses to publish jointly with the periodical of the Perkins School for the Blind.

- *March*: As the 10th administrator of Veterans Affairs, Max Cleland becomes the first severely disabled person to direct the federal agency. Serving under President Jimmy Carter, 34-year-old Cleland is also the youngest Veterans Affairs director in U.S. history and the first Vietnam veteran to serve in that position.
- *April 28*: Major protests by disability rights activists across the United States drive Joseph Califano, secretary of the U.S. Department of Health, Education and Welfare (HEW), to sign regulations implementing Section 504 of the Rehabilitation Act of 1973, legislation protecting qualified people with disabilities from employment discrimination. Protests are held in 10 cities and include occupations of HEW offices, most notably the nearly month-long occupation of HEW offices in San Francisco. While the legal outcome of the demonstrations is important, the actions are perhaps most significant for the way they bring disability activists into effective collective action, an experience that continues to benefit the community in the decades to come.
- *May 23*: President Jimmy Carter delivers his opening remarks at the White House Conference on Handicapped Individuals. A gathering of approximately 3,000 disabled citizens analyzes federal disability policy and develops recommendations. The meeting initiates significant grassroots activity in the arena of disability rights.
- *December 28*: Passage of the first Legal Services Corporation Act Amendment includes a clause making economically qualified "elderly and handicapped individuals" eligible for subsidized legal services, increasing the possibility of disabled self-advocacy.

1978

- Families and professionals band together to form Fiesta Educativa in Los Angeles. The organization serves Spanish-speaking people with disabilities and their families.
- Elaine Ostroff and Cora Beth Able found the Adaptive Environments Center in Boston. The organization is dedicated to actively promoting universal design, or what the center identifies as "human centered design."
- Throughout the year, the Atlantis Community coordinates multiple sit-in protests of Denver Regional Transit Authority buses to demand greater access, including buses with wheelchair lifts.
- The first federal funding for independent living is provided through the passage of Title VII of the Rehabilitation Act Amendments of 1978; the amended act also establishes an advisory board within the U.S. Department of Education, the National Council of the Handicapped (renamed in 1988 the National Council on Disability).
- One of the first Hollywood films to critique the Vietnam War, *Coming Home,* is released. It is remarkable also for its sensitive portrayal of daily life experiences, including access and sexuality, that disabled veterans face.
- Love Canal, a community near Niagara Falls, New York, comes under investigation and litigation when it is discovered that dozens of homes were built on top of an old municipal and industrial landfill. The toxic chemicals have contributed to illnesses and miscarriages and the location becomes a superfund site.
- Harper & Row publishes *Handicapping America: Barriers to Disabled People* by Frank Bowe. Clearly describing the framework that excludes Americans with disabilities from exercising full rights of citizenship, the book becomes an essential resource in the growing disability rights movement.
- Judi Chamberlin publishes *On Our Own: Patient-Controlled Alternatives to the Mental Health System.* This work becomes a vital text in the psychiatric survivor movement.
- Orientation and mobility (O&M) programs at the University of Wisconsin, Madison, are provided financial support by the U.S. Department of Education, Rehabilitation Services Administration. This funding is remarkable for including all disabilities ("Generic O&M") as opposed to the more usual O&M training offered exclusively for blind people. Federal funding is discontinued in 1983.
- The National Association of Sports for Cerebral Palsy (later renamed National Disability Sports Alliance) is founded.
- After living two years in a nursing home, 29-year-old Mark O'Brien, who uses an iron lung, gains admittance to the University of California, Berkeley, thus joining the Independent Living Movement.
- Over 30.3 million Americans have activity limitations because of some chronic condition.

1979

- Disabled athletes win a place in international competition as the U.S. Olympic Committee (USOC) organizes its Handicapped in Sports Committee, which will later become the USOC Committee on Sports for the Disabled.
- Mary Lou Breslin, Robert Funk, and Patrisha Wright cofound the Disability Rights and Education Defense Fund.
- Founded and directed by Rod Lathim, Access Theatre Company becomes one of the first theater groups in the United States to integrate disabled, deaf, and nondisabled performers.
- Marilyn Hamilton, Jim Okamoto, and Don Helman develop the first lightweight wheelchair, the "Quickie," using materials and technology from hang-glider design to produce an attractive, brightly colored product approximately half the weight of conventional wheelchairs. The quickie revolutionizes both wheelchair design and wheelchair sports. In 1983 the Quickie is introduced in a folding model and sales soar. Quickie is sold to Sunrise Medical in 1986.

- The Disability Rights Education and Defense Fund (DREDF) is founded in Berkeley, California, to advocate and provide legal services for disability rights. The organization quickly forges ties with other civil rights groups, opens an office in Washington, D.C., and successfully takes action to compel California to comply with existing special education legislation. DREDF subsequently participates in ongoing disability litigation and lobbying that brings about major civil rights in the 1980s and 1990s.
- The *Rehabilitation Gazette* begins receiving reports from polio survivors about emerging health concerns (referred to as post-polio syndrome), galvanizing members of the polio community to address these issues and sparking new medical research.
- The National Alliance for the Mentally Ill is founded in Madison, Wisconsin, by parents of persons with mental illness. Renamed National Alliance on Mental Illness, or NAMI, in 2004, the group emerges as the largest grassroots organization for people with mental illness and their families in the United States.
- Theater by the Blind, a theater group dedicated to providing legitimate performance opportunities for blind and vision-impaired actors, is founded by Ike Schambelan. In 2008 the group recognizes that its mission has expanded and is consequently renamed Theater Breaking Through Barriers.
- *June 11*: In the case of *Southeastern Community College v. Davis,* the Supreme Court rules unanimously that, under Section 504 of the Rehabilitation Act of 1973, the institution must make "reasonable modifications" to accommodate a hearing impaired nursing student, Frances B. Davis. The Supreme Court decision overturns a lower court ruling to uphold the language of Section 504 requiring that programs receiving federal funds must include otherwise qualified disabled individuals. As the Supreme Court's first ruling on Section 504, this finding asserts reasonable modification as a fundamental aspect of disability rights law.
- *November*: Howard E. "Rocky" Stone founds Self Help for Hard of Hearing People using the family room of his Potomac, Maryland, home as the corporation's first offices. The organization is renamed the Hearing Loss Association of America in 2005.

1980

- Amendments to the Social Security Act are adopted by Congress, including Section 1619, whose purpose is to overcome work disincentives for Social Security Disability Insurance and Supplemental Security Income beneficiaries. The amendments also require those receiving Social Security benefits as the result of disability to have their status periodically reviewed, with the result that hundreds of thousands lose their eligibility to receive cash payments.

- Richard L. Welsh and Bruce B. Blasch produce an edited volume called *Foundations of Orientation and Mobility.* Published by American Foundation for the Blind (AFB), the text is soon recognized as the most authoritative of its kind. A second edition is published by AFB in 1997 with the addition of a third editor, William R. Wiener.
- *The Empire Strikes Back,* the second film released in the Star Wars series, draws on disability and technology as hero Luke Skywalker loses his hand in battle with his father, Darth Vader. The film series continues to draw on disability and technology themes and symbolism in subsequent installments.
- Geri Jewell, an actress with cerebral palsy, first appears on the television show *Facts of Life* as the character Cousin Geri. Jewell was the first actor with a disability to be a network television regular on a situation comedy, ending her run on the series in 1984.
- Disability activists and advocates from the United States and Canada are instrumental in founding Singapore-based Disabled People's International, an international disability rights organization.
- The Womyn's Braille Press (WBP) is founded in Minneapolis. The goal of the organization is to make feminist literature accessible to visually impaired and nonprint readers. WBP shuts down in 1996 and its collection is now housed at the Florida Library for the Blind.
- Retail giant Sears, Roebuck begins sale of closed caption television (CCTV) decoders.
- More than 3 million people with disabilities receive benefits through Medicare.
- *January*: The first issue of the *Disability Rag & Resource,* the nation's premier disability activism periodical, is printed in Louisville, Kentucky. The first issue is a four-page photocopy distributed locally; within five years, the nationally distributed *Disability Rag* is featured on the cover of the *Wall Street Journal.* In 1997, the *Disability Rag* switches to electronic format and changes its name to *Ragged Edge.*
- *May 23*: President Jimmy Carter signs into law The Civil Rights of Institutionalized Persons Act, authorizing protection be given the rights of individuals with disabilities residing in institutions through civil suits filed by the U.S. Justice Department.

1981

- An unusually high incidence of Karposi's Sarcoma and PCP (Pneumocystis carinii pneumonia) alerts medical researchers and public health officials to the presence of a new threat to public health that will ultimately be identified as AIDS (Acquired Immune Deficiency Syndrome). In this early period, it is thought that the syndrome affects only gay men.

- Boston University establishes the first formal Deaf Studies program.
- Victoria Ann Lewis founds the Other Voices Project in Los Angeles, providing training in acting and playwriting for people with disabilities.
- Gini Laurie, editor of the *Rehabilitation Gazette,* helps organize in Chicago, Illinois, "Whatever Happened to the Polio Patient?" It is the first conference dedicated to issues facing polio survivors, including post-polio conditions.
- The dwarfism documentary film *The Little People* introduces the general public to the term "little people."
- *January*: The United Nations inaugurates the International Year of Disabled Persons. The international organization uses its influence to challenge governments around the world to create more inclusive and accessible systems. One important finding from the year's events is that social attitudes have a tremendous bearing on material quality of life for people with disabilities worldwide.
- *June 25–26*: Participants at the Black Deaf Conference in Washington, D.C., move to establish an advocacy organization. The National Black Deaf Advocates is founded the following year.
- *September*: The experiences of women with disabilities is given focused attention in the feminist work *Images of Ourselves: Women with Disabilities Talking* by Jo Campling.
- *September 3*: Publication of "Aiding the Disabled: No Pity, Please," Evan Kemp, Jr.'s groundbreaking *New York Times* op-ed piece challenging the value of the Muscular Dystrophy Association's Labor Day telethon.
- *December*: The publication of *All Things Are Possible* by Yvonne Duffy focuses on issues relating to disabled women.

1981–1983

- Shortly after Ronald Reagan is inaugurated president, the new administration threatens vital nondiscrimination legislation—Section 504 of the Rehabilitation Act of 1973 and the Education for All Handicapped Children Act of 1975. Led by Evan Kemp, Jr., of the Disability Rights Center and Patrisha Wright of the Disability Rights Education and Defense Fund, determined lobbying and vital grassroots efforts by disability rights activists result in the dispatch of more than 40,000 notes and letters of protest. In 1983 the administration concedes to the protesters, giving up its efforts to challenge the existing legislation.

1982

- National Black Deaf Advocates is established to advocate for greater access and equality for deaf and hard of hearing African-Americans.
- In a unanimous decision the Supreme Court rules in *Youngberg v. Romeo* that individuals with intellectual disabilities involuntarily held in state institutions have the constitu-

tional right to safe conditions, freedom from unreasonable bodily restraints, as well as minimally adequate habilitation training while residing in state facilities.
- A child known as "Baby Doe" is born in Bloomington, Indiana, with Down syndrome. Because she has Down syndrome, doctors advise the parents against a surgical procedure to unblock the baby's esophagus. Disability rights advocates try to intervene to prevent the baby from starving, but the baby dies before legal action can be taken. In response, the federal government issues regulations to safeguard the civil rights of newborns with disabilities.
- The Telecommunications for the Disabled Act passes Congress and is signed by President Ronald Reagan. It requires that important public places such as hospitals and police stations provide telephone access for deaf and hard of hearing individuals. It also requires that all coin-operated telephones become hearing aid compatible by January 1, 1985. It calls upon the states to subsidize the production and distribution of TTDs (telecommunication devices for the deaf), more commonly called TTYs. When implemented, this act enables deaf and hard of hearing individuals to access emergency services directly.
- The National Council on Independent Living is established as a national advocacy organization for state and local independent living centers and for the Independent Living Movement in general.
- The Section for the Study of Chronic Illness, Impairment, and Disability is founded as the first scholarly organization devoted to the academic study of disability in fields such as history, sociology, and literature. It is renamed the Society for Disability Studies in 1986.
- The Disabled Children's Computer Group is established in Berkeley, California, by parents, educators, and assistive technology specialists to help new computer technologies assist students with disabilities to speak, write, learn, and participate more fully in school and life. It is later renamed the Center for Accessible Technology.
- *June 28*: In a 6-3 decision, the Supreme Court rules in *Board of Education v. Rowley* that school boards are required to make individual decisions based on the unique needs of students with disabilities.
- *September*: AIDS (Acquired Immune Deficiency Syndrome) is first clearly defined by the Centers for Disease Control and Prevention in Atlanta.
- *October 13*: The Job Training Partnership Act is passed by Congress to provide individuals with disabilities and economically disadvantaged persons with training and placement through joint public and private initiatives.

1983

- Ed Roberts, Judy Heumann, and Joan Leon found the World Institute on Disability in Oakland, California, as a nonprofit organization to conduct research to shape public policy regarding disabilities and to conduct training to improve the lives of people with disabilities throughout the world.

- American Disabled for Accessible Public Transit (ADAPT) is established in Denver, Colorado, by Wade Blank and the Atlantis Community. From 1983 to 1990 it conducts demonstrations and civil disobedience campaigns against the American Public Transit Association (APTA) and local public transit authorities to protest the lack of accessible public transit. Following the passage of the Americans with Disabilities Act in 1990, ADAPT becomes the American Disabled for Attendant Programs Today and seeks adequate funding of programs for attendant care for individuals with disabilities.

- The National Council on the Handicapped calls on Congress to bring individuals with disabilities under the protection of the Civil Rights Act of 1964 as well as under other civil and voting rights laws and regulations so that they are guaranteed full participation in American life.

- The United Nations expands the International Year of Disabled Persons into the International Decade of Disabled Persons to last from 1983 to 1992.

- Medical researchers identify HIV, the virus that causes AIDS.

- Sharon Kowalski is disabled after her car is hit by a drunk driver in Onamia, Minnesota. After the accident, her parents discover that she is a lesbian and refuse to allow her to return to her home with her partner Karen Thompson. Instead, they place Kowalski in a nursing home. Thompson conducts an eight-year campaign to free Kowalski from the nursing home and to bring her home to care for her. Thompson is joined in her campaign by disabled rights and lesbian rights advocates, thus forging links between the two groups.

- The National Disabled Women's Educational Equity Project is established by Corbett O'Toole and based at the Disability Rights Education and Defense Fund. The project conducts the first national survey on disability and gender. The project also produces the book *No More Stares* and conducts training programs for younger disabled women at a number of sites.

- The association CODA (children of deaf adults) is founded. The group begins sponsoring annual conferences in 1986.

1984

- The Baby Jane Doe case, which involves a newborn with spina bifida, draws national attention in the media. On the doctors' recommendations the parents refused to approve an operation that could have improved the infant's condition. The case was litigated in *Bowen v. American Hospital Association* (June 9, 1986), in which justices rule 5-3 that the parents—not hospitals—make the decision and returns responsibility to the states. The case leads Congress to pass the Child Abuse Prevention and Treatment Act Amendments of 1984, which spell out a disabled infant's rights to medical care.

- George Murray is the first wheelchair athlete featured on the Wheaties cereal box as part of its Breakfast of Champions promotion.

- Numerous cases of an undetermined illness in Incline Village, Nevada, spark interest in chronic fatigue syndrome (the term coined in 1988). Controversies over the authenticity of this condition continue over the next decades.

- The National Council of the Handicapped becomes an independent federal agency giving disabled people a stronger voice in the federal government.

- The Networking Project on Disabled Women and Girls is established by Harilyn Rousso at the YWCA in New York City. The purpose is to help teenage girls and women with disabilities increase their educational and vocational goals.

- *July 5*: In a 6-3 decision, the Supreme Court rules in *Irving Independent School District v. Tatro* that school districts are required by the Education for All Handicapped Children Act of 1975 to provide some medical services, such as intermittent catheterization, so that children with disabilities can attend school.

- *September 28*: The Voting Accessibility for the Elderly and Handicapped Act is authorized by President Ronald Reagan; it requires that polling places be accessible or that reasonable ways be found to protect the right to vote among the elderly and disabled individuals.

- *October 9*: President Ronald Reagan signs the Social Security Disability Benefits Reform Act. This act seeks to correct the erroneous termination of Social Security disability benefits to hundreds of thousands of people during the previous three years by the Social Security Administration. The law requires that all benefits and health insurance coverage for individuals with disabilities continue until all appeals are exhausted. It also creates stricter guidelines for Social Security administrators to follow during the review to terminate recipients' benefits.

1985

- Wry Crips, a radical disability theater group, is founded by Cheryl Marie Wade in Oakland, California.

- The television series *Deaf Mosaic,* which is produced by deaf people and celebrates the cultural community, premieres on a public television station in Washington, D.C.

- Peter Bogdanovich's film *Mask* appears in theaters. Its depiction of a young man with significant facial deformity breaks from sentimental or monstrous stereotypes, making a trend toward more human and complex representations of people with disabilities in film.

- Vassar Miller edits *Despite This Flesh: The Disabled in Stories and Poems*, one of the first anthologies of literature about disability.
- Gini Laurie establishes the International Polio Network in St. Louis, Missouri. The network serves as a clearing house for information on post-polio syndrome and as an advocate for polio survivors.
- The National Association of Psychiatric Survivors is established to promote freedom of choice for those needing psychiatric treatment. It seeks to guarantee the rights of individuals with psychiatric disabilities and opposes involuntary hospitalization and treatment regimens.
- The DisAbled Women's Network (DAWN) is established in Ottawa, Ontario, Canada, to eliminate poverty, isolation, discrimination, and violence experienced by women with disabilities. Local groups are eventually begun in several Canadian provinces.
- *April 29*: In a unanimous decision, the Supreme Court rules in *Burlington School Committee v. Department of Education* that, under the Education for All Handicapped Children Act of 1975, the school district must pay the expenses of disabled children enrolled in private programs if the courts have ruled that such placement is necessary to provide the child with an appropriate education in the least restrictive environment.
- *July 1*: In a unanimous decision, the Supreme Court rules in *City of Cleburne v. Cleburne Living Center* that localities cannot use zoning laws to prohibit group homes for individuals with developmental disabilities in residential areas solely on the basis that the residents are disabled.

1986

- The Air Carrier Access Act is passed by Congress prohibiting airlines from discriminating against individuals with disabilities. The airlines may not refuse service on the basis of a disability, require advance notice, limit the number of disabled individuals per flight, or require a disabled individual to travel with an attendant except in limited circumstances. The airlines may not charge additional fees to individuals with disabilities except in certain circumstances.
- The National Council on Disability publishes *Toward Independence*. This report analyzes federal programs dealing with disability and proposes legislation to improve the effectiveness and efficiency of federal efforts to assist people with disability.
- Concrete Change is established in Atlanta, Georgia. Concrete Change advocates building accessible homes and ultimately adopts the philosophy of "visitability." The goal is to make every home accessible to individuals with a disability.

- Abused Deaf Women's Advocacy Services is established. In subsequent decades, 14 other cities will create similar advocacy service organizations, including Deaf Abused Women's Network, which is incorporated in Washington, D.C., in 1999.
- The Employment Opportunities for Disabled Americans Act passes Congress and provides that individuals with disabilities receiving Supplemental Security Income and Social Security Disability Insurance can retain their benefits, including Medicaid coverage, if they go back to work. The goal is to eliminate financial disincentives that keep people with disabilities from working.
- The Society for Disability Studies is established to foster and promote the academic study of disability in the humanities and social sciences. This is the successor organization to the Section for the Study of Chronic Illness, Impairment, and Disability established in 1982.
- *May 23*: The Protection and Advocacy for Mentally Ill Individuals Act passes Congress and receives presidential authorization. It establishes agencies to protect individuals with mental illness from abuse and neglect. It also advocates for the rights of individuals with mental illness.
- *October 21*: President Ronald Reagan signs the Rehabilitation Act Amendments of 1986 to increase employment opportunities for individuals with severe disabilities. They allow state rehabilitation agencies more flexibility in providing supported employment opportunities to individuals with severe disabilities.
- *November*: The radio show *Access Unlimited*, which focuses exclusively on issues relevant to people with disabilities, begins broadcasting on KPFK-FM in Los Angeles, California.

1987

- The Alliance for Technology Access (ATA) is established in California to increase technology use by individuals with disabilities. The ATA establishes a network of technology resource centers and engages in public education, information dissemination, and referral efforts to support increased technology use by children and adults with disabilities.
- Prozac, the brand name for fluoxetine (a selective serotonin reuptake inhibitor), is introduced by pharmaceutical giant Eli Lilly and Company. Intended for treating depression, Prozac receives popular support from many people, but controversies over its assets, limits, and widespread use increase significantly over subsequent decades.
- Marlee Matlin, an actress who is deaf, wins an Academy Award for best actress for her portrayal of a character who is deaf in the movie *Children of a Lesser God*.
- The AXIS Dance Troupe is established in Oakland, California, for dancers with and without disabilities. The group

is a pioneer in creating dance pieces that integrate dancers with and without disabilities.

- The Braille 'n Speak, a pocket note taker that is the equivalent of a scratch pad and address book, is introduced.
- In Chicago, Bill Graham establishes the Association of Late Deafened Adults (ALDA) to support and empower individuals who are deafened late in life.
- The Civil Rights Restoration Act of 1987 passes Congress. The act undoes the Supreme Court's 7-2 decision in *Grove City College v. Bell* (1984) that had limited the extent to which institutions receiving federal aid had to comply with antidiscrimination provisions of federal laws. It requires that all programs of an institution receiving federal aid, not just the program receiving aid, have to comply with antidiscrimination provisions regarding disability, race, gender, color, and religion. President Ronald Reagan vetoes the bill, but Congress successfully overrides this in 1988.
- *March 3*: In a 7-2 decision the Supreme Court rules in *School Board of Nassau County, Fla. v. Arline* that an individual with a contagious disease shall be considered to have an impairment that falls under the protection of the Rehabilitation Act of 1973. Institutions receiving federal funds may not discriminate against individuals with a contagious disease solely on the basis that it is contagious.

1988

- Neil Marcus's play *Storm Reading* premieres at the Lobero Theatre in Santa Barbara, California.
- *Rain Man,* a film starring Dustin Hoffman as Raymond Babbitt, a man viewed as autistic who had been institutionalized, and his brother Charles (played by Tom Cruise) appears in theaters. The film earns praise for its more humane depictions of disability but others criticize its use of nondisabled actors to portray disabled characters.
- *Deaf Life* begins publication in Rochester, New York, as a magazine written by individuals who are deaf for individuals with deafness. The magazine seeks to provide useful information to individuals who are deaf and to educate the hearing about deaf life and culture.
- Congress declares the second week of May as Stuttering Awareness Week.
- Congress amends the Fair Housing Act, extending the act's protections against housing discrimination to people with disabilities.
- President Ronald Reagan issues an executive order to rename the President's Committee on Employment of the Handicapped. Reflecting disability activists' desire to emphasize the individual over the disability, the committee's name is changed to the President's Committee on Employment of People with Disabilities.
- The National Council on the Handicapped issues *On the Threshold of Independence,* a report on the progress made on eliminating discrimination against people with disabilities and increasing access since the publication of *Toward Independence* in 1986. The report also makes recommendations for additional legislative and regulatory initiatives to eliminate discrimination and increase access.
- Senator Lowell Weicker and Representative Tony Coelho introduce the Americans with Disabilities Act in Congress.
- The Congressional Task Force on the Rights and Empowerment of Americans with Disabilities is created by Representative Major R. Owens (D-N.Y.) and co-chaired by Justin Dart, Jr., and Elizabeth Boggs. The task force is charged with conducting research on the extent of discrimination against persons with disabilities.
- The National Parent Network on Disabilities is established as an umbrella organization for the Parent Training and Information Centers. It provides information on how government activities affect individuals with disabilities and their families.
- More than 2.8 million disabled workers receive benefits through the Social Security Disability Insurance program.
- *January 20*: In a 6-2 decision, the Supreme Court reaffirms in *Honig v. Doe* the "stay put rule" established under the Education for All Handicapped Children Act of 1975. The Court rules that children may not be suspended for disabled-related behavior without a due process hearing, unless the child is an immediate danger to himself or others.
- *March 6–13*: In Washington, D.C., protesters calling for a "Deaf President Now" challenge the appointment of a nondeaf president of Gallaudet University. They shut down the university and occupy the campus for a week before the Board of Trustees reverses its original decision and appoints I. King Jordan as the university's first president who is deaf.
- *August 19*: The Technology-Related Assistance Act for Individuals with Disabilities is signed into law by President Ronald Reagan. The act provides assistance to states to develop programs to assist individuals with disabilities to acquire and use assistive technologies. It is reauthorized in 1994.
- *October*: Protesting discriminatory federal policies, scholar and activist Paul Longmore publicly burns his book, *The Invention of George Washington,* in front of the Social Security Administration's Los Angeles offices. The Longmore Amendment, which establishes publishing royalties as earned income for disabled authors and musicians, is subsequently passed.

1989

- Federal regulations that limit the amount public transit authorities have to spend on accessibility to 3 percent of their budget are overturned in a federal appeals court ruling.

- Revised versions of the Americans with Disabilities Act (ADA) are introduced in the U.S. House and Senate, following the original version's lack of progress in the previous year. An advocacy campaign to support the ADA's passage is launched by a national coalition of disability rights organizations, led by activists including Patrisha Wright, Marilyn Golden, Liz Savage, Justin Dart, Jr., and Elizabeth Boggs.
- The Center for Universal Design, created and led by Ronald Mace, opens in Raleigh, North Carolina.
- *Life Goes On* becomes the first television serial with a main character who has Down syndrome, played by actor Chris Burke.
- Reggie Showers, who is a double amputee, starts his career as a professional racer in the International Drag Bike Association, and is named Rookie of the Year.
- *July–September*: The advocacy organization ADAPT mounts a campaign to challenge the inaccessibility of Greyhound buses.

1990

- Howie the Harp, Gayle Bluebird, and others establish Altered States of the Arts.
- *Mouth: The Voice of Disability Rights,* a bimonthly magazine, releases its first issue.
- Using the motto "Social Justice for All Citizens with Autism," advocates establish the Autism National Committee.
- The U.S. military leads a multinational coalition against the Iraqi Army, which had invaded Kuwait. The Persian Gulf War ends a year later. Early observers point to technology and other factors for the comparatively low casualty rate for American troops, but over the next decade, thousands of soldiers report symptoms of what comes to be called "Gulf War Syndrome."
- Through Public Law 101-476, Congress amends the Education for All Handicapped Children Act, renaming the act the Individuals with Disabilities Education Act (IDEA). IDEA is reauthorized in 1997.
- The grassroots advocacy organization the Committee of Ten Thousand is created to support individuals with HIV and their communities. Especially supported by people with hemophilia, this organization emphasizes measures to ensure a safe and accessible national blood supply.
- The advocacy organization American Disabled for Accessible Public Transit (ADAPT) seeks to build on the enactment of the Americans with Disabilities Act by changing its focus from accessibility to ending Medicaid's bias toward nursing homes and supporting expanded community-based personal assistance services. ADAPT's name is changed to American Disabled for Attendant Programs Today.
- *March 12*: Protesting delays in passing the Americans with Disabilities Act, many hundreds of protestors in Washington, D.C., organized by American Disabled for Accessible Public Transit (ADAPT), participate in the Wheels of Justice campaign. This nonviolent demonstration, which continues for a week, includes a march from the White House to the Capitol steps, rallies and speeches, and the arrests of 104 protestors.
- *July 26*: After its passage by Congress with overwhelming majorities in the House and Senate, President George H. W. Bush signs the Americans with Disabilities Act (ADA) into law, a watershed event in civil rights for people with disabilities. The public signing ceremony takes place on the White House lawn in the presence of thousands of disability rights advocates. The ADA guarantees rights for people with disabilities in private employment and in public accommodations such as retail establishments, public transportation, state and local government facilities and programs, and telecommunications using a standard requiring "reasonable accommodations."
- *August 18*: Congress passes the Ryan White Comprehensive AIDS Resources Emergency Act, the largest HIV-specific federal grant program. It is reauthorized in 1996, 2000, and 2006.
- *October 15*: Signed into law by President George H. W. Bush, the Television Decoder Circuitry Act of 1990 requires that nearly all televisions sold in the United States include closed caption decoders in them. The law goes into effect in 1993.

1991

- Jerry's Orphans, including former "poster children" Cris Matthews and Mike Ervin, publicly picket Jerry Lewis and the Jerry Lewis Muscular Dystrophy Association Telethon. Other activists also stage regular protests against the telethon for its negative representation of people with disabilities.
- *June 20–23*: The first Deaf History International conference meets in Washington, D.C.
- *November 21*: President George H. W. Bush signs the Civil Rights Act of 1991, granting people with disabilities who experience discrimination in the workforce the right to sue for both punitive and compensatory damages.

1992

- The National Federation of the Blind launches its Newsline for the Blind, which offers news service over the phone lines 24 hours a day.
- *Passion Fish,* a Hollywood film about disability, friendship, gender, and race, opens in theaters.

- A news blitz fortifies the legal campaign to remove Junius Wilson from the locked wards at Cherry Hospital, in Goldsboro, North Carolina.
- *The Waterdance,* a film following the lives of three men who acquire significant disabilities, opens in theaters. It is distinctive for its generally authentic representations of people with disabilities.
- *October 29:* The Rehabilitation Act Amendments of 1992 are signed into law by President George H. W. Bush.

1993

- Douglas Biklen publishes *Communication Unbound,* which advocates Facilitated Communication for use with people with communication disabilities.
- Lucy Grealy's essay "Mirrorings," which describes her experiences with facial scarring and disfigurement, appears in *Harper's.* This work becomes the basis for her acclaimed memoir, *Autobiography of a Face,* which is published the following year.
- A criminal trial is held in Glen Ridge, New Jersey, following the rape of a 17-year-old woman with a mental disability. Three defendants are found guilty of sexual assault and conspiracy, and a fourth man is convicted of conspiracy. The trial publicly exposes an instance of sexual abuse of people with developmental disabilities, a common but often hidden occurrence.
- Inter-Sexed Society of North America is founded by activist Cheryl Chase. Its purpose is to educate physicians and the public about inter-sexed people, stop surgical interventions and arbitrary sex reassignments, and give inter-sexed people a voice in their care and in society.
- Barbara Waxman becomes the director of the California Family Health Council's Americans with Disabilities Act Project; throughout the 1990s she serves in various administrative roles advocating for reproductive rights of people with disabilities.
- Clayton Valli offers the first analysis of American Sign Language poetics in his dissertation, "Poetics of American Sign Language Poetry."
- Tony Kushner's landmark drama *Angels in America: A Gay Fantasia on National Themes* addresses the AIDS crisis. The first play, *Part One: Millennium Approaches,* is followed in 1994 with *Part Two: Perestroika.*
- *January 22:* The Consortia of Administrators for Native American Rehabilitation is created to advocate on behalf of American Indians and Alaska Natives.
- *June 10:* President Bill Clinton signs the Health Revitalization Act of 1993 (the "HIV Ban"), which prohibits any foreigner with HIV from entering the country.
- *August:* President Bill Clinton selects Robert Williams to head the Administration on Developmental Disabilities;

Williams is the first developmentally disabled commissioner of this organization.

1994

- The enforcement of the Individuals with Disabilities Education Act (IDEA) is upheld by a federal appeals court in *Holland v. Sacramento City Unified School District.* The case involves whether children with disabilities are entitled to attend classes in public schools alongside children who are not disabled as mandated by IDEA.
- Disabled in Action of Pennsylvania wins a legal settlement with Philadelphia; the city agrees that when streets are resurfaced it will install new and repaired curb cuts.
- Filmmaker Laurel Chiten's documentary *Twitch and Shout,* which explores lived experiences with Tourette syndrome, is released.
- The medical melodrama *ER* first airs on NBC. Over subsequent years disability studies scholars critique the popular show's varying representations of disability.
- National Center for Health Statistics reports 849,000 new cases of carpal tunnel syndrome.
- *September 17:* Heather Whitestone becomes the first Miss America winner identified as having a disability. Deaf community members soon protest Whitestone's public advocacy of oralism.

1995

- The Americans with Disabilities Act (ADA) is upheld in a ruling in *Helen L. v. Snider* by the Third Circuit federal appeals court. The case involved the use of public funds by the Commonwealth of Pennsylvania to maintain a disabled woman in a nursing home even though she did not require that level of skilled nursing care. The plaintiffs successfully argued that the ADA required the state to offer the alternative of community-based home care to people with disabilities for whom it is appropriate. The decision was considered by disability activists to be an important guarantee of the rights of people with disabilities to receive personal assistance services in their homes rather than be forced to live in nursing homes or other institutions.
- Justin Dart Jr., Mark Smith, Fred Fay, and Becky Ogle found Justice for All, in Washington, D.C.
- PBS stations air *When Billy Broke His Head . . . and Other Tales of Wonder,* a documentary by Billy Golfus and David E. Simpson. This film introduces many new viewers to the disability rights movement and a social interpretation of disability.
- Justin Dart Jr., Paul G. Hearne, I. King Jordan, John D. Kemp, and Sylvia Walker establish the American Association of People with Disabilities in Washington, D.C.
- A dispute occurs between disability rights activists and Stanford University's School of Medicine over whether

Sandra Jensen, a woman with Down syndrome and member of the self-advocacy organization People First, should receive a heart-lung transplant. After an initial denial based on Jensen's disability, the medical school reverses its decision in the face of the public controversy. Jensen receives the transplant in January 1996, a first for someone with Down syndrome.

- University of Michigan-Ann Arbor hosts This/Ability, an international conference on disability and the arts, coordinated by Joanne Leonard, Marcy Epstein, and Susan Crutchfield. The conference, brings together artists, academics, and activists, and galvanizes the disability arts and culture movement. It also serves as the basis for the anthology *Points of Contact: Disability, Art, and Culture* and the documentary film *Vital Signs: Crip Culture Talks Back.*
- Margaret Edson's play *Wit* opens at the South Coast Repertory Theater in Costa Mesa, California. The play offers a sympathetic, but at times stereotypical depiction of a woman facing ovarian cancer.

1996

- The Personal Responsibility and Work Opportunity Reconciliation Act restricts various public assistance options, including Supplemental Security Income and Medicaid, to immigrants (legal or illegal) until they become American citizens.
- Congress passes the Telecommunications Act, mandating that manufacturers of telecommunications equipment design and produce equipment that is accessible to people with disabilities.
- War veteran and Kansas senator Bob Dole wins the Republican nomination for president. During his unsuccessful bid for the White House, Dole acknowledges his physical disability.
- Disabled veteran Max Cleland is elected senator from Georgia.
- A U.S. Census Bureau report covering the first four years after Congress passed the 1990 Americans with Disabilities Act finds that 800,000 more Americans with severe disabilities have entered the workforce.
- Nancy Mairs's *Waist High in the World,* a memoir that details her experiences with multiple sclerosis, is published.
- Aimee Mullins becomes the first double below-the-knee athlete in Division I track sports.
- *April 27*: Opponents of physician assisted suicide advocate Jack Kevorkian form Not Dead Yet. The organization stages numerous protests against euthanasia, including sustained efforts over the Terri Schiavo case from 2003 to 2005.
- *August*: The animated television satire *South Park* first airs. The series becomes well known for its explicit treatment of disability.

- *August 21*: Authorized by President Bill Clinton, the Small Business Job Protection Act establishes the Work Opportunity Tax Credit that gives employers incentives to hire people from certain low-income groups, including people with disabilities.

1997

- The anthology *Staring Back: The Disability Experience from the Inside Out,* edited by Kenny Fries, is published. This collection brings together well-known and emerging disabled writers of poetry, fiction, nonfiction, and drama.
- *Ragged Edge Online,* originally called "Electric Edge," is launched.
- Fred Pelka's reference, *The Disability Rights Movement,* is published.
- Surveys show that 10 years after the passage of the Air Carrier Access Act, enforcement and accommodation remain significantly limited.
- The National Association of the Deaf Law Center, representing two young deaf clients and their families, sue Walt Disney World for lack of sign language interpreter accommodations. Disney agrees to add captioning, interpreters, and other aids on many of its rides and performances at its entertainment parks.
- The science fiction film *Gattaca* appears in theaters. The movie draws popular and scholarly attention for its critique of genetic engineering.
- *September*: Drawing on surveys conducted between 1994 and 1995, the Census Bureau reports that 54 million Americans (roughly 20% of the population) have an identifiable disability; 26 million (10% of the total population) have severe disabilities.

1998

- *The Poisonwood Bible,* a novel by Barbara Kingsolver, is published and becomes a finalist for the Faulkner and Pulitzer prizes. This richly told story examines the intersections of patriarchy, disability, and race.
- More than 5 million people with disabilities receive health care benefits through Medicare, and more than 6.6 million receive health care through Medicaid.
- In a 5-4 decision, the Supreme Court rules in *Bragdon v. Abbott* that HIV should be covered under the Americans with Disabilities Act. This is considered a significant victory by many AIDS and disability rights activists.
- James M. Boles opens the Museum of Disability History and People Inc. in Williamsville, New York.
- President Bill Clinton dedicates a memorial in Washington, D.C., to President Franklin D. Roosevelt. Activists protest the absence of an explicit representation of the 32nd president as disabled. In January 2001, a new bronze statue of Roosevelt in his wheelchair is added at the entrance to the memorial.

- Actor Christopher Reeve publishes his memoir, *Still Me,* which describes his struggles to overcome his paralysis, which resulted from an equestrian accident in 1995. Reeve becomes a highly controversial figure, especially among many disability activists and scholars, for his representations of disability and forms of advocacy to seek cures.
- Based on the 1989 John Irving novel *A Prayer for Owen Meany,* the film *Simon Birch* is released. Although some praise its casting of disabled actors, the film generally receives lukewarm reviews for its representation of people with disabilities.
- *May*: The Smithsonian's National Museum of American History hosts a national conference, *Disability and the Practice of Public History.* The conference brings together scholars and activists from around the country and leads to the exhibition, "The Disability Rights Movement," mounted two years later to commemorate the 10th anniversary of the ADA.

1999

- Over 54.8 million children and youths with disabilities receive benefits from IDEA programs.
- Over 4.8 million disabled workers receive benefits through the Social Security Disability Insurance program.
- *June 22*: In a 6-3 decision, the Supreme Court rules in *Olmstead v. L. C.* that unjustified isolation in an institution could be regarded as discrimination based on disability. This confirmed the right of people with disabilities to live in their communities.

2000

- Playwright and actor Lynn Manning premieres his autobiographical solo piece, *Weights,* which compares his experiences as a black man and as a blind man.
- Performance artist Bill Shannon premieres his work, *Spatial Theory.*
- Robert David Hall, an actor who uses prosthetic legs, becomes a series regular as Dr. Albert Robbins on the television show *CSI: Crime Scene Investigation.*
- Scholars attending the Summer Institute on Disability Studies in the Humanities at San Francisco State University begin discussing the creation of a disability history organization. By 2004, the Disability History Association is founded.
- *October*: Endowed with a five-year grant from the U.S. Department of Education's Rehabilitation Services Administration, the American Indian Disability Technical Assistance Center opens as a center serving American Indians and Alaska Natives with disabilities.

2001

- Laurie Block launches the Disability History Museum, an online resource in disability history.

- In a 5-4 decision in *Garrett v. University of Alabama,* the Supreme Court limits the options for people with disabilities to sue state governments for discrimination.
- The documentary film *King Gimp,* which chronicles the life of artist Dan Keplinger, wins an Academy Award.
- In a 7-2 decision, the Supreme Court affirms in *P.G.A. Tour, Inc. v. Martin* the concept of public accommodations outlined in the Americans with Disabilities Act.
- The first working draft of the human genome sequence is published. The Human Genome Project completes its genome sequencing work in 2003.
- John Belluso's play, *The Body of Bourne,* which chronicles the life of famed writer and reformer Randolph Bourne, opens at the Mark Taper Forum in Los Angeles.
- Greg Wolloch's documentary and performance video, *F**k the Disabled* (later renamed *Keeping It Real: The Adventures of Greg Walloch*) is produced.
- *January 28*: A Cingular ad featuring disabled artist Dan Keplinger appears during the Super Bowl, with a message about embracing new attitudes and self-expression.
- *March 25*: H-Disability, a scholarly discussion group through the listserv H-Net, is launched.
- *September 11*: Terrorists attack several American sites, including the World Trade Center in New York City and the Pentagon in Arlington, Virginia. In addition to their physical and psychological impact on many Americans, the attacks highlight limited rescue and support services available to people with disabilities. Advocacy and research sparked by these events produce new initiatives to enhance access and accommodation during emergencies.
- *December 21*: Following the events of September 11, more churches across the United States add annual "Blue Christmas" or "Darkest Night" services on the Winter Solstice, to honor the more somber, reflective mood of many Americans during that holiday season, and to meet the needs of congregants with depression, anxiety, post-traumatic stress, and other experiences.

2002

- The American Council of the Blind initiates a lawsuit against the U.S. Treasury to create accessible currency for blind users.
- *March*: Lawyer Harriet McBryde Johnson debates bioethicist Peter Singer over disability and personhood; the *New York Times Magazine* runs their exchange in a cover story.
- *July 16*: *Refrigerator Mothers,* a documentary by David Simpson, Gordon Quinn, and J. J. Hanley about autism theories and treatments in the 1950s, debuts on PBS.
- *December 2*: Oregon governor John Kitzhaber issues a formal apology for his state's forced sterilization program. Several other states, including California, North Carolina, and Virginia issue apologies over the next several years.

2003

- *March*: The U.S.-led invasion of Iraq begins. By 2008 the war produces more American casualties than any military conflict since the Vietnam War.
- *May 30*: The film *Finding Nemo* is released. The story of a young fish with a small fin and his overprotective father (and his father's forgetful friend) is embraced as disability-friendly children's fare.
- *October*: The national news focuses on the case of Terri Schiavo, raising significant questions about euthanasia; extensive intervention by government leaders sparks additional debate, which continues into 2004, when Schiavo dies.

2004

- In a 5-4 decision, the Supreme Court upholds in *Tennessee v. Lane* the constitutional right of people with disabilities to have access to the courts.
- The documentary film *Self-Preservation: The Art of Riva Lehrer* by David Mitchell and Sharon Snyder is released.
- *January 17*: "Lost Cases, Recovered Lives: Suitcases from a State Hospital Attic" exhibit opens at the New York State Museum in Albany and runs through September. It later tours to other venues, and it becomes the basis of a book and a video.
- *July 18*: The Inaugural International Disability Pride Parade is held in Chicago, with Yoshiko Dart as the parade marshall.
- *July 18*: ADAPT stages a protest at the National Governors Association meeting in Seattle; at the same meeting, Pennsylvania governor Ed Rendell introduces a resolution to reform the Medicaid long-term care system to provide more community supports.
- *July 23*: The U.S. Access Board publishes updated ADA Accessibility Guidelines, which set standards for building, sidewalk, restroom, parking, transportation design, and other areas of coverage. The new guidelines replace the 1991 guidelines and all earlier recommendations.
- *September 8*: The Disabled Peoples' International World Summit 2004, opens in Winnepeg, Canada; over a thousand participants gather from around the world.
- *September 14*: PBS airs *Freedom Machines*, a documentary by Jamie Stobie and Janet Cole, about cutting-edge assistive technology.
- *October 25*: President George W. Bush signs the Assistive Technology Act of 2004.
- *December 1*: The United Church of Christ launches an ad campaign highlighting the denomination's "extravagant welcome" of diverse families, including people with disabilities; CBS and NBC deem the campaign too controversial to broadcast.

2005

- *January 19*: Not Dead Yet and other activists rally at the Chicago Film Critics Association, protesting the support local critics gave the film *Million Dollar Baby*, which goes on to win an Academy Award for best picture.
- *January 25*: "Blind at the Museum," an exhibit and conference at the University of California-Berkeley Art Museum, opens to the public and runs through July 24.
- *January 29*: *Murderball*, the documentary about wheelchair rugby players, wins the Audience Award for best documentary at the Sundance Film Festival; later in the year, the documentary is successful in wide commercial release, and it is nominated for an Academy Award for best documentary in 2006.
- *February 7*: The Department of Education announces its plan to close regional offices of the Rehabilitation Services Administration (RSA); in protest, RSA commissioner Joanne Wilson announces her resignation the next day.
- *February 15*: The nationwide PBS broadcast of *On a Roll: Family, Disability, and the American Dream*, a documentary about talk-show host Greg Smith, debuts.
- *March 25*: Advocates at a public presentation in Madison, South Dakota, propose the creation in the same state of Laurent, a town (named after 19th-century deaf educator Laurent Clerc) that would use sign language as part of its goal of fostering an inclusive space for deaf people and their families and friends.
- *April 12*: "Whatever Happened to Polio," a social history exhibit, opens at the Smithsonian's National Museum of American History.
- *April 21*: The U.S. Court of Appeals for the Ninth District rules in the case of *Tchoukhrova v. Gonzales* that the parents of a disabled child are eligible to seek asylum along with the child, because the family incurred harm as a unit; on April 17, 2006, a summary order is issued by the Supreme Court, vacating this decision
- *May 22*: *Autism Is a World*, an Academy Award–nominated documentary, airs on CNN.
- *June 20*: ADAPT stages action in Tennessee to protest cuts to the state's TennCare program that will force many ventilator users to move into residential care; demonstrations at the governor's office and elsewhere continue for months.
- *July 16*: *Harry Potter and the Half-Blood Prince*, the sixth novel in the J. K. Rowling series, is released in the United States; that same day, a team of volunteers mounts a marathon recording session to ensure that an audio edition is quickly available to blind fans; a Braille version is also published within a week.
- *July 31*: To celebrate the 15th anniversary of the Americans with Disabilities Act, Familia Unida, a Spanish-language multiple sclerosis support organization in Los Angeles, sponsors their first annual "wheelchair wash," at which

chairs are cleaned and repaired and wheelchair users are treated to haircuts and manicures while booths provide food, information, and entertainment for the whole family.

- *August 11*: A probate judge refuses to grant the request of Vera Howse, who asked the Cook County courts to order an involuntary sterilization of her brain-injured niece, K. E. J., after she expressed a desire to have children. On April 18, an appellate court decision resolves the issue in favor of K. E. J.
- *August 29*: Hurricane Katrina makes landfall, decimating regions in Louisiana and Mississippi in subsequent days, and leaving many disabled residents of New Orleans without adequate means of evacuation or support. Subsequent studies of the disaster recovery efforts spark greater attention to issues of access and new policies to protect vulnerable populations during emergencies.
- *October 14–15*: "Art Beyond Sight: Multi-Modal Approaches to Learning," a conference cosponsored by the Metropolitan Museum of Art, the Art Association for the Blind, and the Museum Access Consortium, is held in New York City.
- *October 22*: The 1033 Group, a volunteer organization, holds a commemoration ceremony at the cemetery of the State Institution for the Disabled in Wassaic, New York, pledging to replace numbered tombstones with a plaque naming the residents buried there.

2006

- The Learning Channel airs *Little People, Big World,* which features dwarf couple Matt and Amy Roloff and their four children. The show runs for several seasons.
- *March 21*: Double-amputee Iraq War veteran Tammy Duckworth wins the Democratic primary to become her party's candidate for U.S. representative from Illinois's sixth congressional district; she loses in November, and she is appointed director of the Illinois Department of Veterans Affairs.
- *April 1*: "Humans Being: Disability in Contemporary Art," an exhibit at the Chicago Cultural Center, part of the city-wide "Bodies of Work" disability arts and culture festival, opens and runs through June 4.
- *April 3*: West Virginia enacts the first Disability History Week, which is celebrated during the third week in October.
- *April 17*: David M. Oshinsky wins the 2006 Pulitzer Prize for U.S. history for his book *Polio: An American Story.*
- *May 9*: Autism Speaks screens a video called "Autism Every Day" at a fund-raising event; in the video, a mother explains that she has thought of killing herself and her child, in front of the child in question. The video provokes widespread controversy in the autistic community.

- *May 13*: Three-year-old Katherine McCarron, who had an autism diagnosis, is suffocated by her mother, a medical doctor. (Dr. McCarron is found guilty of the crime in 2008.)
- *August 9*: Comedian Josh Blue wins the competition on *Last Comic Standing,* a popular television show. Blue, who has cerebral palsy, incorporates disability themes into his routine.
- *September 19*: The MacArthur Foundation recognizes several disability researchers with their "genius fellowships," including Jim Fruchterman, creator of Bookshare.org; and Anna Schuleit, an artist who creates commemorative installations and objects around defunct mental institutions.
- *October 24*: A Missouri congressional campaign ad about stem cell research featuring Michael J. Fox becomes controversial when radio commentator Rush Limbaugh accuses Fox of faking or exaggerating his Parkinsonian tremors for shock value.
- *October 29*: After months of protests, Gallaudet University's Board of Trustees rescinds its contract with president-select Jane Fernandes.
- *December 13*: In New York, the United Nations General Assembly adopts the International Convention on the Rights of Persons with Disabilities.

2007

- *January*: The case of "Ashley X," a Seattle-area child whose growth was stunted in 2004 with surgeries including a hysterectomy and hormone treatments, comes to public attention when her parents launch a blog to explain their decision; months later, the hospital where the treatment was performed admits that it had failed to follow legal procedures for the protection of the child's interests, and they agree to improve their protocols in the future.
- *March*: The documentary film *Through Deaf Eyes* is released on public television stations.
- *March 30*: More than 80 countries sign on to the International Convention on the Rights of Persons with Disabilities during the convention's opening day. The United States, arguing that national laws already protect citizens with disabilities, refuses to sign.
- *August 5*: American-born Pedro Guzman turns up in Calexico, at the U.S.-Mexican border, after three months missing. Guzman, who is cognitively disabled, was arrested on misdemeanor trespassing charges in April 2007, and turned over to Homeland Security when he mistakenly told officials he was from Mexico. He was deported.
- *December 1*: The New York University Child Study Center launches an awareness campaign called "Ransom Notes," in which autism, depression, attention-deficit hyperactivity disorder, and other disabilities are portrayed in advertisements and billboards as kidnappers, threatening the

lives and futures of children; public uproar about this depiction, spearheaded by disability groups, leads to the campaign's withdrawal within weeks of launch.

2008

- *January 29*: A sheriff's deputy in Hillsborough County, Florida, is captured on surveillance video "dumping" doctoral student Brian Sterner (who also is a quad rugby player and former director of the Florida Spinal Cord Injury Resource Center) from his wheelchair following a traffic stop, apparently to test whether Sterner was actually disabled.
- *February 1*: *Praying with Lior,* a documentary by Ilana Trachtman about the Bar Mitzvah experience of Lior Liebling, a boy with Down syndrome; is released commercially.
- *March 17*: New York lieutenant-governor David Paterson is sworn in as governor of New York. He is the first blind person of color to become a state governor.
- *April 28*: ADAPT initiates a protest and advocacy campaign at the Capitol in Washington, D.C., as part of its 30-year anniversary. The protest continues through May 2, and some of the protesters are arrested.
- *May 20*: A federal court of appeals in the District of Columbia upholds in a 2-1 decision that the U.S. Treasury is in violation of the Rehabilitation Act of 1973 because it has not issued currency that is accessible to blind users.
- *May 21*: A teacher in Port St. Lucie, Florida, leads a class of kindergarteners in "voting out" Alex Barton, a child under evaluation for autism. After the story receives national attention, the district removes the teacher from the classroom, and the boy's mother brings a lawsuit against the district.
- *July*: Radio talk show host Michael Savage draws widespread criticism for his assertion that autism is a "fraud" and that "in 99 percent of the cases, it's a brat who hasn't been told to cut the act out."
- *July 31–August 3*: An international disability history conference, sponsored by San Francisco State University, the Disability History Association, and the British Disability History Group, is held in California.
- *August 12*: Disability advocates protest the premier of the film *Tropic Thunder* for its negative depiction of people with cognitive and developmental disabilities.
- *September 25*: President George W. Bush signs into law the Americans with Disabilities Amendment Act of 2008,

which is intended to restore the 1990 act's original intent and purpose.
- *November 4*: In his acceptance speech in Chicago, Illinois, president-elect Barack Obama refers to "disabled and not disabled" Americans. Many interpret this positive recognition of people with disabilities as a momentous shift in the national understanding of disability.
- *November 20*: As part of Pittsburgh's 250th anniversary, the Allegheny County Department of Human Services launches "Voices of Our Region," an oral history project about disability experiences in the greater Pittsburgh area. Interviews with more than 75 people were recorded, transcribed, and published on CDs and online.
- *December 22*: The Inaugural Committee for president-elect Barack Obama invites a contingent of Special Olympics athletes, volunteers, and supporters from across the United States to participate in the Inaugural Parade.

2009

- *January 20*: The inauguration of President Barack Obama is accompanied by concerns about accessibility in the capital, as crowding overwhelms public transit and other infrastructure. The inauguration coverage is available with live description and closed captioning on television and in an online feed, provided by WGBH's Media Access Group.
- *February 7–13*: The Special Olympics World Winter Games take place in Boise, Idaho.
- *February 20–22*: Responding to the announcement of the Academy of Motion Picture Arts and Sciences (AMPAS) in December 2008 that Jerry Lewis would receive the Jean Hersholt Humanitarian Award at the next Academy Award ceremony, a coalition of disability rights activists called "The Trouble with Jerry" initiate protests that include a petition, letter, online videos, Web site, demonstrations at the AMPAS offices, and street theater outside the Kodak Theater, where the ceremony is held on February 22.
- *March 1*: The Supreme Court dismisses without comment the Vietnamese Victims Association's class action lawsuit that was brought on behalf of millions of Vietnamese victims of Agent Orange. The lawsuit had charged the chemical manufacturers of Agent Orange with war crimes.
- *March 31*: Date designated by members of the Special Olympics for "Spread the Word to End the Word," an awareness effort against the widespread use of "retarded" as a casual insult.

Entries A–E

Abbott, Jim (James Anthony) (1967–) *baseball player*

Born without a right hand, pitcher Jim Abbott, during 10 seasons in the major leagues, was the most successful disabled athlete in the history of professional SPORTS.

James Anthony Abbott was born on September 10, 1967, in Flint, Michigan, where he spent his childhood. Growing up, he loved, played, and excelled at all sports, showing a particular talent for pitching a baseball. At a young age Abbott, with his father's help, learned to throw and catch using just his left hand by balancing his glove on the end of his right arm as he pitched the ball, slipping the glove onto his left hand as the ball was being thrown or hit back to him, and then cradling the glove in the crook of his right arm to remove it quickly and take out the ball so he could throw it again. In time Abbott's "glove-hand switch" became so smooth and effortless that it was barely noticeable.

As a star pitcher for the University of Michigan, Abbott was selected to Team USA and played in the 1988 Pan-American Games, World Amateur Baseball Championships, and Summer Olympics, where he pitched and won the gold medal game. He was honored with the 1988 Sullivan Award as the nation's top amateur athlete, and he was chosen in the first round of Major League Baseball's amateur draft by the California Angels. Abbott began the 1989 season with the Angels without spending any time in the minor leagues, a very rare accomplishment, and in four seasons as a starting pitcher for the team posted a respectable 47–52 won-lost record. After the 1992 season he was traded to the New York Yankees, where he played for two years, pitching a no-hitter in September 1993.

Before the 1995 season Abbott signed as a free agent with the Chicago White Sox, but was traded to the California Angels in July. That year he received the Hutch Award, presented annually to the player who best exemplifies a fighting spirit and competitive desire to win. Abbott was released by the Angels before the 1997 season and did not play baseball that year, but he returned to the majors in September 1998, winning five consecutive games for the White Sox. He joined the Milwaukee Brewers in 1999, but Abbott was ineffec-

tive on the mound and his comeback ended when the team released him in July. He retired from baseball with a lifetime record of 87 wins and 108 losses, and began a new career as a motivational speaker.

As a successful ballplayer Jim Abbott served as role model for disabled men, women, and especially children, although reluctantly at first. A naturally humble and self-effacing person, he would tell reporters that he pitched to win, not to be courageous. Still, Abbott responded personally to letters from disabled CHILDREN, and often met with them to offer advice and encouragement, always emphasizing to them that their disabilities need not limit their personal achievements.

Bob Bernotas

Further Reading:

Berkow, Ira. "A Most Extraordinary Fella." *New York Times,* 12 December 1992, p. B7.

Bernotas, Bob. *Nothing to Prove: The Jim Abbott Story.* New York: Kodansha America, 1995.

Kroichick, Ron. "No Longer a Novelty . . . Jim Abbott." *Sport* 82, no. 7 (July 1991): 56.

Lichtblau, Eric. "Abbott Helps Kids Explore Potential of Inner Strength." *Los Angeles Times,* 4 August 1989, section 3, p. 8.

Official Jim Abbott Web site. URL: http://www.jimabbott.info/biography.html.

ableism

Ableism (sometimes spelled "ablism") is a term for discrimination against, and subordination and oppression of, people with disabilities. Ableism exists at all levels of American society—ideas, attitudes, practices, institutions, social relations, and culture. Its "ism" suffix is used to highlight institutional or systematic forms of oppression in the United States, putting ableism in the same family with sexism, racism, heterosexism, ageism, and other systematic forms of oppression. As with these other forms of bias, ableism also names unfair or unearned advantages—in this case, the privileges given to those perceived to be able-bodied. In the United

Kingdom, the term "disablism" is also used to name the same phenomenon.

Examples of ableism are everywhere, from the steps and stairs that exclude people with mobility impairments to preventing alternative methods of test-taking for students with learning disabilities. Other forms of institutionalized ableism include the lack of captioning or sign language interpretation (which excludes people with hearing impairments), asking a person with a disability "what happened?" (an invasion of privacy that assumes disability is abnormal or tragic), and the medically encouraged selective abortion of fetuses that show the possibility of IMPAIRMENT.

The term ableism came into use in the early 1980s among feminists in the United States. It seems first to have appeared in print in a May 1981 special issue of the newspaper *Off Our Backs* on feminism and disability. In 1985 the term showed up again in *With the Power of Each Breath,* one of the first anthologies by women with disabilities. In the early 1990s the term gained more widespread academic and public attention, with both positive and negative consequences. Prominent feminist scholars, including Iris Marion Young and Martha Minow, included "ableism" in their theorizing of social difference. Looking back, many have noted how the passage of the 1990 AMERICANS WITH DISABILITIES ACT, unlike other major civil rights legislation, preceded widespread public awareness of disability rights. In the wake of its passage, some media sources made efforts toward public education, and terms like "ableism" were useful. However, this awareness coincided with a period of conservative backlash against "politically correct" speech and "ableism" was heavily targeted for derision.

One reason these attacks gained ground is that many Americans have difficulty believing ableism exists, which, ironically, allows this form of discrimination to persist. The general disbelief regarding the oppression of those with disabilities is one of several components of ableism. Other elements include an unexamined belief in the normalcy of the NONDISABLED, fear and denigration of disability, understanding disability as a tragedy or social burden, medicalizing and pathologizing disability, and pervasive paternalism, disrespect, pity, infantilization, and VIOLENCE against people with disabilities. Although estimates place the number of disabled Americans at between 15 and 19 percent—making people with disabilities the largest "minority" group in the country—disability remains largely unconsidered and unrecognized, much less appreciated, as a valuable form of social difference.

As a concept, the understanding of ableism lags far behind public knowledge of sexism or racism. While some people try to argue that sexism and racism are "in the past," the majority of Americans are at least familiar with what these terms mean. That is not the case with ableism. Students

> *"The only thing a society that thrives upon perfection, upon production, can do is to reject somebody who appears to be 'different.' By the very fact that I am 'different,' I am a threat to them because if I can do the job, and do it as well, and maybe even better, I'm a threat to their position. So they keep shoving it off in the corner because they don't know what else to do."*
>
> —Tom Teggatz, a 26-year-old graduate student at the University of Wisconsin, Milwaukee, to a reporter for the *Wisconsin State Journal,* in 1971

learn in school about the civil rights and women's rights movements, but they are rarely educated about the DISABILITY RIGHTS MOVEMENT. Furthermore, there are few positive REPRESENTATIONS of disability in POPULAR CULTURE.

Until the late 20th century, most disabling conditions were shrouded in shame, silence, condemnation, and isolation. Exceptions to these attitudes include the approach to physically disabled war VETERANS as heroic, also an objectifying gesture; as well as the dehumanizing hypervisibility of disabled people who worked in circuses or "FREAK SHOWS." More generally, those who could conceal their disability did so; visibly disabled people were typically hidden from public view. In the 1970s the INDEPENDENT LIVING MOVEMENT began to change this practice, encouraging all people with disabilities to fight for self-determination and independence.

Ableism is deeply connected to the culturally ingrained notion of nondisabled bodies as the norm. Society encourages people to think about able-bodiedness as a "natural" proposition rather than one that is constructed or political. Robert McRuer and other scholars discuss this in terms of "compulsory able-bodiedness," which borrows from the idea of "compulsory heterosexuality" articulated by Adrienne Rich. According to this idea, people are presumed to be able-bodied and all people, disabled or not, are compelled to cultivate the appearance of "normalcy" because that is what is culturally valued. In order to disrupt this, many disability activists use the term "TEMPORARILY ABLE-BODIED" to identify the nondisabled. This label highlights one difference between disability and other identity groups, the fact that anyone could become disabled at any time and that most people do eventually become disabled as they age. Rather than foster identification, this potential emergence into disability often creates fear and disavowal, reinforcing the fictional line between a nondisabled "us" and a disabled "them."

One of the ways that society promotes and fosters ableism is by medicalizing and pathologizing disability. According to this idea, disabled lives are thought of as inherently bad, full of suffering, and burdensome to both families and the larger society. Rather than understanding disabled people as a politically oppressed group, the dominant ableist culture sees people with disabilities as "sick" and requiring a "cure," attributing exclusion to physical rather than social factors. This representation is strongly influenced by eugenics, which considers disabilities "undesirable traits" to be bred out of the gene pool.

Contemporary analysis demonstrates that ableism is inseparably interwoven with all other systems of oppression. Fighting against this form of subjugation requires a continual struggle against other forms of oppression as well.

See also IMPAIRMENT/IMPAIRED; LANGUAGE AND TERMINOLOGY; MEDICAL MODEL OF DISABILITY; NORMAL AND NORMALCY; SOCIAL CONSTRUCTION OF DISABILITY.

Judy Rohrer

Further Reading:

Davis, Lennard J., ed. *The Disability Studies Reader.* New York: Routledge, 1997.

Johnson, Mary. "'Disablism': A Closer Look." *Ragged Edge* (2006). Available online. URL: http://www.raggededgemagazine.com. Accessed June 20, 2008.

Linton, Simi. *Claiming Disability: Knowledge and Identity.* New York: New York University Press, 1998.

abuse

Abuse may be defined as behavior that deliberately and wrongfully inflicts physical or emotional injury upon a person. Abuse can take many forms, including physical, sexual, emotional, and financial, as well as neglect. Disabled people seem to be particularly susceptible to a wide variety of abuse, and there are specific forms of disability abuse. For instance, taking a person's WHEELCHAIR, HEARING AIDS, CRUTCHES, cane, medication, or other disability-related equipment is a form of abuse because it involves an attack on the individual's quality of life and sense of independence.

What is understood by the term "abuse" has changed over time. Many "treatments" for people with disabilities that were implemented in the past are now recognized as abusive. For instance, one history of the Pennsylvania Hospital for the Insane describes the following treatments, which were widely used in colonial America: being drenched with cold or warm water; taking large quantities of blood from a patient until they lost consciousness, and chaining people to the walls of their "cells." These techniques often were resisted (sometimes violently) by the patients receiving them, but they were widely considered the most effective treatments for MENTAL ILLNESS at the time. Nevertheless, by standards in the 21st century, such "treatments" are certainly considered abusive. Arguably, the resistance by people with mental illness at that time might also have reflected their feelings that such actions did more harm than good.

In 19th-century America, what was called "IDIOCY" (and what is now called "intellectual disability") was considered hereditary, incurable, and untreatable and was cloaked in public shame and humiliation. People with this disability were placed in large residential institutions because they were seen as a threat to the social order and were often regarded as an embarrassment to their families. Conditions in these residential institutions were often very harsh, and they were characterized by overcrowding, lack of hygiene, and punitive responses to the behavior of patients. Although many families believed that they were ill-equipped to deal with the problems of a family member who experienced "idiocy" and hoped that a residential institution would be able to best look after that person, the conditions in these institutions were often deplorable and by modern-day standards would certainly be regarded as abusive. Even by the standards of the day, the excessive use of force by people in positions of authority was regarded as abusive. However, such abuse was rarely made public.

Early practices of hydrotherapy for people with psychiatric illnesses in the late 19th century included strapping patients into hammocks suspended in a bathtub for hours or days at a time and leaving patients wrapped in wet sheets and blankets that would shrink as they dried so that the patients felt like they were being suffocated or were burning up. In the 20th century Metrazol convulsive therapy (chemically induced convulsions), used on over 35,000 psychiatric patients in American HOSPITALS in the period between 1936 and 1941, often caused spinal fractures and other broken bones. At the time, however, such therapy was not seen as abusive—it was considered state-of-the-art "treatment." Electroshock therapies (see ELECTROCONVULSIVE THERAPY), used on over 1 million Americans, also had disastrous effects: approximately 40 percent of such treatments caused bone fractures, and the brain damage caused by such treatment has also been regarded as abusive. Lobotomies (see LOBOTOMY) a psycho-surgical procedure that gained prominence between the 1930s and 1950s, often resulted in damaging emotional and personality changes, seizures, incontinence, and a small number of deaths. Once again, however, such responses to psychiatric illness were not seen as "abuse" at the time; they were the standard treatment in many hospitals.

Various accounts of abuse in public institutions gained media and public attention throughout the 20th century. One of the early influential criticisms of public psychiatric institutions was *A Mind That Found Itself,* written by CLIFFORD BEERS (a man who had been hospitalized for three years in various psychiatric institutions). Beers's tales of VIOLENCE, abuse, and hostility from staff at psychiatric hospitals led to the establishment of the Connecticut Society for Mental Hygiene in 1908.

Complaints about the treatment of people with psychiatric disabilities were not limited to former patients. Between 1907 and 1930, a leading American psychiatrist, Dr. Henry Cotton, the medical director of the New Jersey State Hospital at Trenton, adopted a method for treating psychosis that involved extracting the teeth (and sometimes, the colons) of his patients. Even though Cotton was highly regarded at the time, and his treatments were considered "cutting edge" by some colleagues, there were widespread concerns by former patients, staff, and other professionals. Indeed, the perception that Cotton's treatment approach was abusive was so widespread that the New Jersey State Senate launched an inquiry into practices at the hospital.

It should not be assumed that the abuse of disabled people has been limited to those with psychiatric disabilities. There have been a number of nationwide investigations into abuse at schools for the DEAF. In 1988 the superintendent at the Mississippi school, for example, was fired after widespread sexual and physical abuse of students at the school was revealed; five years later, two former employees of the South Carolina state school plead guilty to sexual assault of students. A 2001 special report by the *Seattle Post Intelligencer* into sexual abuse, molestations, rape, and other sexual assaults at deaf schools suggests that almost half of the 50 state-run RESIDENTIAL SCHOOLS for the deaf in the United States have been investigated for sexual and physical abuse of students.

One of the most well known examples of the abuse of people with intellectual disabilities (see COGNITIVE AND INTELLECTUAL DISABILITY) in the 20th century involved the Willowbrook State School on Staten Island in New York City in the 1960s and 1970s. Initially, negative attention was drawn to Willowbrook because of the practice of injecting healthy CHILDREN with the hepatitis virus in order to study the virus and vaccinations for it—a practice carried out from 1966 to 1969. Later criticisms were much stronger—focusing on the terrible living conditions at Willowbrook. These inhumane conditions were exposed in 1972 in nationally broadcast television reports by journalist Geraldo Rivera as well as in other media reports. Forms of abuse exposed by these reports included people being neglected and left in unclean and overcrowded conditions without appropriate food, clothes, or medical care. Images of naked people lying in their own feces had a great impact on the public, and Willowbrook State School was eventually closed down, with the last child leaving the school in 1987.

The INVOLUNTARY STERILIZATION of disabled people, a key element of the EUGENIC program to rid the nation of the "unfit," is also now recognized as a widespread form of abuse that was perpetrated against disabled people. Such sterilizations were widely accepted in America and were practiced in 33 states. An estimated 35,000 people were sterilized in the United States alone from the first decade of the 1900s to the 1950s, with thousands more in other countries.

The profound maltreatment of people with intellectual disabilities in institutions is another form of abuse that has been recognized only relatively recently. However, histories of such institutions have consistently revealed a great deal of sexual, physical, emotional, and financial abuse, as well as neglect. For instance, *Lest We Forget: Spoken Histories,* an oral history of Ohio institutions for people with cognitive disabilities conducted by the disability activist Jeff Moyer and published in 2005, recorded widespread and extensive abuse in such institutions.

For various reasons, including social STIGMA, isolation, and communication barriers, scholars know comparatively little about many cases of abuse of disabled individuals outside of institutions. Anecdotal evidence, court cases, and occasional media reports shed some light into the ways people with disabilities have experienced abuse from FAMILY members, co-workers, or teachers in mainstream schools. Research that specifically examines abuse and disabled people has grown, especially since the passage of the AMERICANS WITH DISABILITIES ACT in 1990. Advocacy groups such as THE ARC, for example, have promoted conferences, workshops, and studies especially on abuse issues and people with developmental and cognitive disabilities. Scholars who specialize in this area of research, such as Dick Sobsey, have asserted that disabled women in the late 20th century were considerably more likely to be raped or sexually abused than their NONDISABLED peers, and evidence from ORGANIZATIONS such as DEAF ABUSED WOMEN'S NETWORK and DISABLED WOMEN'S NETWORK suggests that this trend has continued into the 21st century. In addition, a study in 2000 concluded that CHILDREN with any type of disability are more than three times as likely to experience a form of abuse (such as neglect, physical abuse, or sexual abuse) than are NONDISABLED children.

The history of abuse and disability in the United States presents a vivid marker of the continuous, marginal, and vulnerable place of people with disabilities. It also draws attention to the changing attitudes about the meaning of disability and the evolving status of disabled citizens that have contributed to new interpretations of past treatments and current policies that affect the daily lives of disabled Americans. Addressing the historic impact of abuse on people with disabilities also matters, not only because it presents a more accurate representation of the past but also because it may promote greater empathy, EMPOWERMENT, and inclusion of individuals in society.

See also ASYLUMS AND INSTITUTIONS; SLAVERY.

Mark Sherry

Further Reading:

Braddock, David L., and Susan L. Parish. "An Institutional History of Disability." In *Handbook of Disability Studies,* edited by Gary L. Albrecht, Katherine D. Seelman, and Michael Bury, 11–68. Thousand Oaks, Calif.: Sage, 2001.

Moyer, Jeff. *Lest We Forget: Spoken Histories.* Highland Heights, Ohio: Music from the Heart and Partners for Community Living, 2005.

Sobsey, Dick. *Violence and Abuse in the Lives of People with Disabilities.* Baltimore: Paul H. Brookes Publishers, 1994.

Teichroeb, Ruth. "Abuse and Silence—Examining America's Schools for the Deaf: Sex Abuse Plagues Schools for the Deaf Nationwide," *Seattle Post-Intelligencer Reporter.* (27 November 2001). Available online. URL: http://seattlepi.nwsource.com/national/48233_deaf27.shtml. Accessed April 13, 2008.

Whitaker, Robert. *Mad in America: Bad Science, Bad Medicine, and the Enduring Mistreatment of the Mentally Ill.* Cambridge, Mass.: Perseus Publishing, 2002.

Wickham, Parnel. "Idiocy in Virginia, 1616–1860." *Bulletin of the History of Medicine* 80 (2006): 677–701.

access and accessibility

Access has been a pivotal concept used in the formulating of histories of disability and in understanding the daily experiences of disabled people in America. The term has multiple meanings that combine to form a complex, yet well-defined and very useful metaphor. The metaphor builds upon one's everyday experience of traveling along a road or pathway to a destination. If the pathway is clear, the destination is said to be accessible. Pathways for people with disabilities are often blocked, however. These blocks are referred to as "barriers" or "obstacles" by those using the access metaphor. One key way to improve disability access is to remove the barriers or to change the situation to accommodate the person's difference. Curbs are barriers, CURB CUTS are a means for removing the barriers, and ramps are a way to accommodate or circumvent the barrier. The aim is to get around the barriers to make destinations accessible.

Accessibility can involve different pathways. For example, success in school requires a physical pathway—a means for getting to school and the classroom and getting around once you are there; a communication pathway—a means for accessing information in the curriculum; and a social pathway—a means for being part of the social activities and having positive relationships with others in the classroom. A child may be able to access the classroom physically but have trouble accessing the curriculum or social network. Similarly, a building, such as a museum, may have ramps and handrails, but unintelligible signage. In order to understand

In the 1970s when this photograph was taken, people in wheelchairs found limited access on streets and in buildings. Curbs and ramps were among the first areas activists focused on for accessibility. *(Smithsonian National Museum of American History, Division of Medicine and Science)*

historical events, examine the impact of disability legislation, and work to improve access to specific situations, one needs to attend to the various types of barriers and pathways that are involved. Disability activists have focused their efforts since at least the early 19th century on attaining access to different realms of society, including EDUCATION, work, the arts, TRANSPORTATION, housing, and politics, as well as to forms of entertainment and communication.

Prejudice toward people with disabilities represents an especially formidable historic access barrier for those with disabilities. Disability histories are replete with people's stories of their being regarded as frightening, inferior, and incompetent—prejudices that have resulted in people being ostracized, bullied, demeaned, and legally excluded. For example, DEAF Americans since the colonial period technically could testify in court but until the 20th century there were no laws that required qualified SIGN LANGUAGE INTERPRETERS to facilitate communication, making it difficult to assure equal access to the legal system for generations in the deaf COMMUNITY. Similarly, VOTING areas historically were inaccessible to people with MOBILITY impairments, resulting in the exclusion of disabled citizens from suffrage and the democratic process. In addition, late 19th-century UGLY LAWS, which appeared in various American cities, prohibited people with visible deformities (see DEFORMITY) from being seen in public, thereby denying certain disabled citizens access to daily activities that others enjoyed.

As scholars commonly have noted, EDUCATION represents a significant example that reflects and reinforced issues of access. Beginning in the early 1800s, segregated RESIDENTIAL SCHOOLS, for example, were established for the deaf and BLIND, and ASYLUMS were built for those with intellectual impairment and MENTAL ILLNESS. These schools offered disabled CHILDREN greater access to education by making available materials in BRAILLE for blind students and by providing contexts for the use of sign language for deaf children. Similarly, asylums frequently improved some disabled people's access to HEALTH CARE and shelter. Yet these same institutions, because they were segregated from mainstream society, also thwarted access to social events outside the institution, to gainful EMPLOYMENT, and to independent living.

The access metaphor, in addition to offering disabled people a way to understand the world, offers a way to understand disability itself. Members of the LEAGUE OF THE PHYSICALLY HANDICAPPED in the 1930s, for instance, organized PROTESTS to draw attention to inaccessible workplaces and discriminatory hiring policies, arguing that as citizens they deserved equal opportunities to gainful employment. Four decades later, the organized DISABILITY RIGHTS MOVEMENT expanded on these ideas, presenting disability as a problem of attaining access rather than a deficiency of one's own body. A prominent example of ACTIVISM shaped by this model and focused on access was the DEINSTITUTIONALIZATION movement, which gained momentum in the 1960s and 1970s; its primary goal was to provide disabled people with access to social, educational, and political institutions outside the residential schools or asylums. Likewise, the theory of UNIVERSAL DESIGN, also emerging in the 1960s, promotes accessible buildings as part of a broader effort to include all people in constructed spaces. This 20th-century shift from the strict medical interpretation of disability (see MEDICAL MODEL OF DISABILITY) to a social model of disability has served the movement well, leading to dramatic positive changes in attitudes, opportunities, and political climates.

"My deafness hadn't bothered me in the past but now I thought of so many things—the way I was politely passed over when someone in the church wanted something done, the quick snicker when I misunderstood something said to me, and other little things. If it was like that among people who knew me, what would it be like without Mama or someone here at school to make me feel like I was a person too?"

—Mary Herring Wright, recalling her concerns as a graduating student from the North Carolina School for the Negro Blind and the Deaf, in 1942

Especially since the 1960s, a strategy of disability activists has been to promote legislation to assure equal access. These efforts have resulted in new disability legislation that mandates the removal of physical barriers to public buildings and public transport, including the ARCHITECTURAL BARRIERS ACT of 1968 and the AMERICANS WITH DISABILITIES ACT of 1990, and of communication and social barriers to education and the workplace, such as the INDIVIDUAL WITH DISABILITIES EDUCATION ACT of 1975. Activists have also successfully lobbied for legislation to eliminate discrimination in housing and employment resulting from attitudinal prejudices and social barriers, such as the Fair Housing Amendments Act of 1988.

ASSISTIVE TECHNOLOGIES AND ADAPTIVE DEVICES represent another enduring feature of the struggle for greater access. In basic ways, the creation of devices such as WHEELCHAIRS, telecommunications devices for the deaf (TTYs), FACILITATED COMMUNICATION, and OPTICAL RECOGNITION SCANNERS have enhanced access for various disability populations to travel, communicate, and work. At the same time, technological developments can result in new barriers. For example, the creation of "talking" motion pictures in the 1930s marginalized deaf people until captions became available, while many INTERNET Web sites since the late 1990s have remained inaccessible to low vision users, as well as to many economically disadvantaged citizens.

In the 21st century, access remains a defining feature and goal in the daily lives of many disabled Americans. Activists continue to address its many dimensions, including educational, political, employment, technological, and social. The history of access as metaphor, application, and goal demonstrates both the significant progress made by and for Americans with disabilities, as well as the limitations to full inclusion and citizenship.

See also IMPAIRMENT/IMPAIRED; LAW AND POLICY.

Judith Felson Duchan

Further Reading:

Access-Able Travel Source (2007). Available online. URL: http://access-able.com/graphical_index.html. Accessed December 4, 2007.

Morris, J. "Community Care or Independent Living?" *Critical Social Policy* 14 (1994): 24–45.

Rubin, S. "A Conversation with Leo Kanner." In *Autism and the Myth of the Person Alone,* edited by D. Biklen, 82–109. New York: New York University Press, 2005.

Shapiro, Joseph. *No Pity: People with Disabilities Forging a New Civil Rights Movement.* New York: Times Books, 1993.

Stroman, D. *The Disability Rights Movement: From Deinstitutionalization to Self-Determination.* New York: University Press of America, 2003.

Swain, J., S. French, C. Barnes, and C. Thomas, eds. *Disabling Barriers—Enabling Environments.* 2d ed. London: Sage, 2005.

Fleischer, Doris Zames, and Frieda Zames. *The Disability Rights Movement: From Charity to Confrontation.* Philadelphia: Temple University Press, 2001.

Access Board

The Access Board, originally named the Architectural and Transportation Barriers Compliance Board, was created within Section 502 of the Rehabilitation Act of 1973. Established to enforce the 1968 ARCHITECTURAL BARRIERS ACT (ABA) and to provide technical assistance to facilitate compliance, the board emerged following the stipulation of the ABA that all federal facilities had to be accessible. Progress in making that a reality proved very slow. So little was being done that Congress created an agency, the Access Board, to oversee implementation and create standards for ACCESS. The board reviews access issues related to federal facilities and communications, and public TRANSPORTATION, playgrounds, and outdoor environments.

The Access Board comprises members from federal agencies and 12 members from the general public, half of whom must have a disability. All members are appointed by the president of the United States. The first public members were added in 1979, appointed by President Jimmy Carter; Georgia state senator and disabled veteran MAX CLELAND was named chair.

In 1978 review of communications was added to its authority. Under this category of oversight, one of its most important duties has been implementation of accessibility requirements for Web sites, information technology (IT) hardware, and software and telecommunications products used or created by the federal government. The accessibility standards for IT were finally released in 2000. The standards were authorized under Section 508 of the Rehabilitation Act of 1973 (as amended in 1998 to ensure electronic accessibility).

The Access Board also played a crucial role in determining the content of the AMERICANS WITH DISABILITIES ACT and its implementation. Its work throughout the 1980s in analyzing and formulating the details of accessibility, as well as through testimony and ACTIVISM, was embodied in the law. Consequently, the Access Board has been a powerful influence on the configuration of public space both on the INTERNET and in real time.

See also ACCESS AND ACCESSIBILITY.

Katherine Ott

Further Reading:

Access Board Web site. URL: www.access.board.com.
"Electronic and Information Technology Accessibility Standards (Section 508)." *Federal Register* 65, no. 246 (December 21, 2000): 80500–80528.

Accessible Pedestrian Signal

People with visual impairments historically have utilized a range of skills to cross the streets. Since the early 20th century these have consisted of the white cane (see LONG CANES), partnership with a GUIDE DOG, and reliance on auditory queues about the environment. With the advent of new and quieter AUTOMOBILES and the increasing complexity of intersections, some have proposed external accommodations to ensure the safe travel of BLIND and visually impaired people. One external adaptation to the environment that enhances independent MOBILITY is the Accessible Pedestrian Signal (APS). APS communicates information about the intersection in a nonvisual format, such as by means of audible tones, verbal messages, or vibrating surfaces. Known by additional names such as Audible Traffic Lights or Acoustic Signals, these devices provide nonvisual information to users, such as whether or not and where a pushbutton is available or the timing of pedestrian lights and Beginning of the Walk interval.

During the 1920s, William L. Potts, a police officer in Detroit, adapted railroad signals to address increased street traffic. Using, red, amber, and green railroad lights and about $37.00 in wire and electrical controls, he made the world's first four-way three-color traffic light system. In 1975 the first microcomputer was developed. With the miniaturization of computer chips, the first APS were installed at intersections during the 1970s.

This ASSISTIVE TECHNOLOGY has drawn debates between blind advocates. For example, the AMERICAN COUNCIL OF THE BLIND (ACB) advocates for APS, arguing that civil rights laws require that the same or near to same type of information furnished to a sighted person be provided to visually impaired citizens. Generally opposing APS, the NATIONAL FEDERATION OF THE BLIND (NFB) emphasizes that blind people primarily rely on the long white cane and listening skills to navigate street crossings. Although NFB members admit that the efficacy of these techniques can be reduced by several factors, they believe that APS constitutes a danger to visually impaired users by covering the sounds of traffic and the general environment that are essential to independent travel. In recent years, various disability advocacy groups and scholars have been funding and sponsoring research on issues relating to APS, such as the conditions and locations that make these adaptive devices most appropriate and effective.

The rise of disability civil rights legislation (see LAW AND POLICY) generally supports APS. For example, the 1998 Transportation Equity Act for the 21st Century directs that pedestrian safety considerations, including the installation of APS where appropriate, be included in new TRANSPORTATION plans and projects. In June 2007 representatives of the ACB and the city of San Francisco publicly celebrated a comprehensive agreement to commit at least $1.6 million to install APS at no fewer than 80 intersections. Demonstrating what can be accomplished by cross-disability collaboration, other parties to the agreement included the Lighthouse for the Blind and Visually Impaired and the Independent Living Resource Center of San Francisco.

ACCESS constitutes a central theme in the DISABILITY RIGHTS MOVEMENT. The history of APS demonstrates the challenges and changing meaning of gaining access. It also highlights ways that advocacy, public policy, and technology can ensure greater access to basic activities such as crossing the street.

Gary Norman

Further Reading:

Ashmead, Daniel H., Robert Wall, Billie Louise Bentzen, and Janet M. Barlow. "Which Crosswalk?: Effects of Accessible Pedestrian Signal Characteristics." *ITE* [Institute of Transportation Engineers] 74, no. 9 *Journal* (Sept. 2004): 26–30.

Barlow, J. M., Louise Billy Bentsen, and Lee S. Tabor. *Accessible Pedestrian Signals and Travel by Pedestrians Who Are Blind or Visually Impaired.* Report Prepared for National Cooperative Highway Research Program, Transportation Research Board, National Research Council. May 2003.

Bentsen, Louise Billie. *Accessible Pedestrian Signals.* U.S. Access Board, August 1998.

Grubb, Debbie, ed. *Pedestrian Safety Handbook: A Handbook for Advocates Dedicated to Improving the Pedestrian Environment Guaranteeing People Who Are Blind or Visually Impaired Access to Intersection Identification and Traffic Control.* 2d ed. American Council of the Blind, April 2000.

"Resolutions of the National Federation of the Blind, 2002." Available online. URL: http://projectaction.easterseals.com/site/DocServer/04APS.pdf?docID=7543

Smith, Donna, and Susan Clark. "Accessible Pedestrian Signals: Making Your Community Safer and More Accessible for Everyone." Easter Seals Project Action, August 2004.

access symbol   See INTERNATIONAL SYMBOL OF ACCESS.

Access Unlimited

Access Unlimited is a radio program dedicated exclusively to issues and concerns of people with disabilities. It began broadcasting on KPFK-FM in Los Angeles, California, in November 1986. For its first 10 years the program was titled *"Challenge!"* It serves as a forum for individuals in Los Angeles who are disabled, as well as for NONDISABLED individuals who may be caregivers, professionals, or relatives, or friends of people with disabilities.

KPFK-FM is the Los Angeles station of the Pacifica Foundation, a progressive listener-supported network that is an alternative to commercial radio. Pacifica radio stations seek to advance progressive causes, including ending oppression and VIOLENCE against minorities. The movement for disability rights that seeks to ensure equal rights and opportunities for individuals with disabilities fits nicely within the broader objectives of the Pacifica Foundation.

Programming on *Access Unlimited* seeks to inform, educate, and raise the awareness of the listening audience regarding disabilities of all types and among all ages. The programs stress political, educational, EMPLOYMENT, consumer, HEALTH CARE, and human welfare concerns as they affect individuals with disabilities. In addition, the weekly programs incorporate information on artistic and recreational activities as well as moral and ethical concerns. Some programs address current issues, while others present a more historical perspective. Topics may include specific disabilities, such as blindness, or broader concepts of a chronic disorder, including CANCER.

Guests on the program have come from the ranks of both the disabled and the nondisabled, from all races and backgrounds, and have included all ages from childhood to the elderly. Guests and co-hosts have had a wide variety of disabilities, including speech impediments, such as STUTTERING, and hearing and SPEECH DISORDERS, including deafness. Other guests have had neurological and psychiatric disorders, learning disabilities, and other behavioral disabilities. The co-hosts have interviewed artists and performers, academicians, professionals in many fields, politicians, legislators, advocates for people with disabilities, and FAMILY members.

Since its inception, *Access Unlimited* has been run by a three-person team that has co-hosted and co-produced the program. The team has always integrated people with disabilities with one nondisabled person and at least one woman. The team has also sought to include diverse ethnic and cultural representatives. The initial co-hosts and co-producers in November 1986 were Mario Casetta, KPFK folk music programmer who had recently experienced a stroke; Dr. Carol Gill, a clinical psychologist and POLIO survivor who used a motorized wheelchair; and Dr. Henry Slucki, a behavioral scientist on the faculty of the University of Southern California. Slucki, who is not disabled, is the only member of the original team still associated with the program. Subsequent teams have sought to maintain a similar diversity of viewpoints and experiences.

Access Unlimited has received several awards for its programming. In 1988, when it was still called *Challenge!*, it received an award for outstanding programming from the

Southern California Rehabilitation Association. In January 2008 *Access Unlimited* was recognized by the Workmen's Circle, a secular Jewish organization, and by the California State Assembly for its work on behalf of human rights and humanitarian issues.

Henry Slucki

Further Reading:
Access Unlimited Web site. URL: www.kpfk.org.

activism and advocacy

Activism and advocacy represent two related and fundamental features of disability history in America. They are particularly important for understanding the engaged, intentional, and sometimes contested actions by NONDISABLED and disabled people. Forms of activism and advocacy, as well as issues motivating these actions, demonstrate the complex and evolving notions of disability as well as the changing status of people with disabilities in the United States.

ADVOCACY

Advocacy generally refers to actions aimed at producing change that fall within the realm of those expected by the political system. Actions such as writing editorial opinions, voting, law suits, political campaigning, and lobbying—which could include testifying before a legislative body or personally meeting with a legislator—attempt to communicate support for a position and thereby to convince a policymaker to support that position. Some of these forms of advocacy occur on an informal basis by people with disabilities and their allies and may occur without organizational involvement.

Many of the earliest examples of disability advocacy were conducted by people who had personal connections to individuals with disabilities, and they were based on religious and moral convictions. For example, Colonel William Bolling of Virginia and other NONDISABLED parents of CHILDREN with disabilities sought private schools to educate their offspring during the late 18th and early 19th centuries. MASON FITCH COGSWELL, whose daughter ALICE COGSWELL became DEAF as a child, joined with minister THOMAS HOPKINS GALLAUDET and French deaf educator LAURENT CLERC, to advocate for a more generally accessible means of educating deaf Americans. Their efforts resulted in the first government-supported residential school for deaf children in 1817. Other 19th-century social reformers, such as DOROTHEA DIX and SAMUEL GRIDLEY HOWE, worked to establish ASYLUMS AND INSTITUTIONS to serve BLIND, mentally ill, and "FEEBLEMINDED" citizens. Some, like ELIZABETH PACKARD, became advocates after experiencing discrimination firsthand. In Packard's case, false charges by her husband led to her incarceration in an insane asylum in the 1860s. When she gained her release, Packard successfully campaigned for laws to protect individuals facing forced commitment to psychiatric HOSPITALS.

Individual cases of self-advocacy by disabled Americans occasionally occurred during the 19th century. For example, in a letter to the editor published in the *Washington Post* in 1878, "A True Union Maimed Soldier" asked for a job with the "Republican Senate." While pointing out how few "maimed" soldiers worked there, he offered to work for "two thirds, if not half" of what able-bodied ex-soldiers were being paid. In the process of advocating for himself, this disabled VETERAN also raised larger social issues of STIGMA and discrimination.

ACTIVISM

Advocacy can cross the line into activism. Activism can be defined as actions that are not expected by, or acceptable to, the political system and that are aimed at producing social change. These can include either individual or group/collective actions, but they are always disruptive either because they are not part of the everyday political processes or because they intend to be disruptive.

What causes activism? There are many situations that participants or observers may think are abusive, discriminatory, outrageous, immoral, or otherwise objectionable but which do not lead to collective action; collective actions require more than the mere presence of stigma, inequities, or injustices. Rather, social, economic, political, and cultural conditions must support the expression of the grievance in order for group actions to occur. One social condition that is an extremely important precursor for collective action is the existence of formal organizations or informal groups. Because such joining together tended not to occur when individuals with disabilities were isolated within their family homes, group advocacy or activism by disabled people was slow to assert itself in American history.

DEVELOPMENT OF ORGANIZED ACTIVISM AND ADVOCACY

There were few if any conditions during colonial times or even after the War of 1812 and the Mexican War of 1846–48 that would have been conducive to the development of group PROTESTS or any other forms of collective action, despite the numbers of disabled soldiers each war produced. However, this began to change in the early to mid-1800s as formal institutions such as schools for blind or deaf children were founded. In large part because of these schools, ORGANIZATIONS run by disabled adults began to be established, beginning with the NATIONAL ASSOCIATION OF THE DEAF in 1880. Associations for (but usually not run by) adults with other types of disabilities were also established in the 1870s and 1880s, including the Friedlander Union and the New York

Blind Aid Association for blind adults and the Anti-Insane Asylum Society for adults with mental illness. These organizations set the stage for the types of interactions among people with disabilities that would be necessary for the development of the collective and oppositional consciousnesses necessary for disruptive activism.

Group advocacy based upon an oppositional consciousness and conducted by disabled people emerged during the late 1800s. America's deaf community was particularly visible in this regard. For example, in 1890, a group of "deaf-mutes" (a term commonly used then) met formally to object to the EUGENIC and oralist theories (see ORALISM) of ALEXANDER GRAHAM BELL. In 1897 other groups of deaf people gathered to protest the selection of a hearing sculptor for the contract to erect a statue of Thomas Hopkins Gallaudet. Leaders as well as rank-and-file deaf community members also demonstrated organized activism in their challenges to employment bans from the Civil Service Commission in the early 1900s and against driving rights bans (see AUTOMOBILES) beginning in the 1920s. In these latter efforts, activists engaged in letter writing campaigns, testified in court and before legislative bodies, attended conferences, and exploited newspaper and other media outlets as part of public relations campaigns.

Organized activism *by* disabled people, which used disruptive tactics and which aimed at producing social change for disabled people, became more apparent in the 1930s. For example, in 1935 in New York City, members of the LEAGUE OF THE PHYSICALLY HANDICAPPED formed picket lines and protested employment discrimination. Two years later, over 80 blind workers in Pittsburgh participated in a series of sit-down strikes that lasted several days; these protestors sought public redress of meager wages.

There was also activism *for* disabled people, especially for children. Parents of children with MENTAL RETARDATION began to organize in the 1930s, forming groups such as the Cuyahoga County Council for the Retarded Child in Ohio in 1932, the Washington state's Children's Benevolent League in 1934, and the New York Welfare League for Retarded Children in 1939. Many groups initially focused on enhancing children's experiences within segregated schools such as the Willowbrook State School. These groups generally worked in isolation from one another until collaboration with and through professional associations sparked a national effort in 1952 by parents to create the association then called the National Association for Retarded Children (now known as THE ARC of the United States).

LITIGATION AND LEGISLATION

A common form of activism by such parents groups was lawsuits. One of the most important cases was the 1971 *PARC v. COMMONWEALTH OF PENNSYLVANIA*, whose decision affirmed the right of children to free and equal public educa-

tion. Advocates in this lawsuit successfully argued that the paucity of educational services for children with cognitive disabilities violated their constitutional rights. Numerous lawsuits involving mental health and mental retardation institutions reached state and federal courts over the next two decades. Some have sued airlines and other transportation providers to improve access options and eliminate other forms of discrimination.

Goals and forms of advocacy and activism expanded after WORLD WAR II as new generations of people with disabilities and their allies built on the examples of other social activists fighting prejudice, such as African Americans and women. Many advocates, including disabled VETERANS particularly, sought greater ACCESS—into buildings, workplaces, and public spaces—as a practical means of achieving fuller citizenship. The "barrier free" movement, which gained momentum in the 1950s, resulted in laws such as the 1968 ARCHITECTURAL BARRIERS ACT, the 1978 REHABILITATION ACT, the 1986 AIR CARRIER ACCESS ACT, and the 1990 AMERICANS WITH DISABILITIES ACT. Others interpreted access differently. For example, deaf people and their allies during the 1960s and 1970s petitioned for captioning in FILMS and TELEVISION programs as an issue of access, while PSYCHIATRIC SURVIVORS and mental health consumers initiated campaigns to deinstitutionalize (see DEINSTITUTIONAL-IZATION) the many thousands of people forcibly committed to psychiatric facilities. During this era, some parents groups and disability organizations also joined campaigns to promote more inclusive educational opportunities for people with disabilities, sparking the rise of MAINSTREAMING by the late 1960s and propelling the move toward INCLUSIVE EDUCATION in the 1980s.

Some disability activism has taken the very traditional form of testifying before the U.S. Congress or a state legislature. An especially well publicized example of this occurred over the passage of the Americans with Disabilities Act, when individuals such as JUDY HEUMANN and Perry Tillman testified about personal experiences of disability discrimination. Many other individuals have provided testimony to local and state representatives, and sometimes this has been combined with political protests.

NEW AVENUES FOR ACTIVISM AND ADVOCACY

Additional forms of advocacy have emphasized COMMUNITY pride and self-EMPOWERMENT. Performance groups, such as the NATIONAL THEATRE OF THE DEAF, established in 1967 and the Wry Crips (created in the mid 1980s) offered positive cultural role models and actively challenged pervasive STE-REOTYPES about people with disabilities. Similarly, the rise of the field of DISABILITY STUDIES since the 1970s reflects an intentional fusion of activist aspirations with scholarly work.

Many contributors to this interdisciplinary field have sought social change through their research.

Contentious, disruptive activism conducted by large groups of disabled people became more common after 1970. Several of the larger and more well-known protests include the 1977 section 504 SIT-IN PROTEST AT THE DEPARTMENT OF HEALTH, EDUCATION AND WELFARE in San Francisco, the 1988 DEAF PRESIDENT NOW! protest, and the 1990 WHEELS OF JUSTICE protest. One important factor that contributed to this activism was the presence of formal organizations that had the resources needed to mobilize, promote, and support activist work within the disability community. An additional factor was a change in the type of organization.

Many of the early organizations run by disabled people themselves, such as the National Association of the Deaf, the NATIONAL FEDERATION OF THE BLIND, the AMERICAN COUNCIL FOR THE BLIND, and Support Coalition International (SCI), were disability-specific organizations. These organizations addressed multiple issues, but they are of interest primarily to people with one type of impairment. Cross-disability organizations were present before World War II but had little overall impact. By the 1970s, cross-disability groups, such as DISABLED IN ACTION and the DISABLED PEOPLES LIBERATION FRONT, became more popular. These types of organizations conducted a majority of the protests in the 1970s. Their actions drew attention to and built on the common issues many people with disabilities have faced.

In the 21st century new avenues for advocacy and activism have carried forward the lessons of past protests and successes. New advocacy groups have emerged, some in response to new definitions and diagnoses. The growing neurodiversity movement is one example: the Autism Self-Advocacy Network and similar organizations counter the messages of cure-focused groups such as Autism Speaks, and in 2007 they led a successful call for the withdrawal of offensive advertising by the New York University Child Study Center. New groups also formed at the intersections of disability and other causes. For example, Feminist Response in Disability Activism (FRIDA) began in Chicago in 2005 to organize action on the many ways disabled women's REPRODUCTIVE RIGHTS are violated.

Along with new organizations and directions for activism, new technologies are changing activist strategies and possibly increasing their chances for success. Web sites, blogs, podcasts, and video content can mobilize a wider population by presenting experiences and opinions to wider audiences (including international audiences). E-mail alerts and text messages can bring together participants more quickly for demonstrations or the work that supports more visible actions. Small cameras, cell phones, and other portable recording devices can transmit front-line documentation of protests and their reception. Even the traditional movement standbys—newsletters, posters, t-shirts, bumper stickers, and buttons—can be produced more quickly and inexpensively today.

CONCLUSION

The history of disability cannot be fully understood without considering the many dimensions and changes in activism and advocacy. These related themes demonstrate the complex social conditions and expectations that have largely shaped the daily lives of generations of people with disabilities and those who know, love, and work with them. Scholars in disability history have drawn attention to activism and advocacy in part because they reflect larger American values of citizenship while also challenging stereotypes of disabled people as helpless or insignificant. Because many forms of activism and advocacy have yet to be fully studied, scholars and activists likely will continue to examine the historical meaning of these issues in shaping lives, policies, and notions of disability.

See also COMMUNITY; IMPAIRMENT/IMPAIRED; LAW AND POLICY.

Sharon N. Barnartt

Further Reading:
Barnartt, Sharon N., Kay Schriner, and Richard Scotch. "Advocacy and Political Action." In *Handbook of Disability Studies,* edited by Gary L. Albrecht, Katherine D. Seelman, and Michael Bury, 430–449. Thousand Oaks, Calif.: Sage Publications, 2001.

Barnartt, Sharon N., and Richard Scotch. *Disability Protests: Contentious Politics 1970–1999.* Washington, D.C.: Gallaudet University Press, 2001.

Charlton, James. *Nothing About Us Without Us: Disability Oppression and Empowerment.* Berkeley: University of California Press, 1998.

Longmore, Paul. *Why I Burned My Book and Other Essays on Disability.* Philadelphia: Temple University Press, 2003.

Shapiro, Joseph P. *No Pity: People with Disabilities Forging a New Civil Rights Movement.* New York: Times Books, 1994.

actors

The term *actor* usually refers to a person who represents through his or her body and voice a character other than him or herself as part of a DRAMA performed in the THEATER, on TELEVISION, or in a FILM. In this traditional sense of an actor, DEAF and disabled actors have only begun to achieve recognition and EMPLOYMENT only since the expanded opportunities achieved by the DISABILITY RIGHTS MOVEMENT. Exceptions include actors who acquired their disabilities after their careers were established, such as early 20th-century film star Lionel Barrymore, who had rheumatoid arthritis and used a WHEELCHAIR in his later films. However, skilled disabled performers—acrobats, musicians, and comedians—have been part of POPULAR CULTURE for centuries, working in carnivals, vaudeville, and variety acts. Though many of these performers took pride in their craft, more often than not their employment was seldom due to their talent alone. Their enduring attraction for the spectator was tied to the strangeness and excitement of viewing a taboo, a disability, while at the same time confirming one's own "normality." Though recent research has done much to recover the stories of performers involved in side-show exhibits, very little progress has been made in identifying disabled stage actors in the 19th century. Initial findings suggest that a deeper investigation will uncover a hidden history of performers with disabilities, such as the discovery that the inspiration for the controversial minstrel character Jim Crow was an African-American song and dance man, Jim Crow or Jim Cuff, who supposedly had EPILEPSY as well as MOBILITY.

By the mid-20th century disabled actors created landmark roles on the Broadway stage. Broadway itself was changing as it was influenced by alternative movements in the theater that questioned what kind of body had the right to be on the stage. Theater pioneers such as Megan Terry and Joe Chaikin (himself disabled by a heart condition) threw out conventional ideas of the desired physical traits and created new roles that pushed beyond conventional character types of leading lady, ingénue, and character actor. A landmark in recognition of disabled actors during this period was Michael Dunn's Tony nomination for the role of Cousin Lymon in Edward Albee's *Ballad of the Sad Cafe* (1964). Dunn was a DWARF who went on to television fame in his role as Miguelito Loveless on the 1960s television drama *The Wild Wild West*. Other stage actors who received critical and popular fame on the legitimate stage as the century progressed included deaf actors PHYLLIS FRELICH as Sarah Norman in CHILDREN OF A LESSER GOD (1979) and Howie Seago as Ajax in Sophocles' *Ajax* (directed by Peter Sellars, 1986) as well as Mark Povinelli, a dwarf, who played Torvald Helmer in the Mabou Mines's adaptation of Henrik Ibsen's *A Doll House* (2003). Other notable stage actors include Peter Dinklage, Anita Hollander, Linda Hunt, Lewis Merkin, Clark Middleton, David Rappaport, and Ann Stocking.

The 1980s marked major advocacy efforts that fused the profession of acting to disability rights. Disabled and deaf actors organized a Performers with Disabilities Committee across the three performing unions—Screen Actors Guild (SAG), Actors Equity Association (AEA), and the American Federation of Television and Radio Artists (AFTRA)—to advocate for inclusion in diversity and affirmative action initiatives in theater, film, and television. The issue centered on the addition of disabled actors to the historic 1963 agreement between the performing unions and producers that explicitly stated that mass media must reflect "the American scene," and

that discrimination by color, RACE, or creed was prohibited. Persons with disabilities were added to the composite picture of the "American scene" that had already been expanded since its first articulation in 1963 to include women in 1972.

Television has provided the most opportunities for showcasing disabled talent, given the amount of product required by the medium. Thousands of minor and major roles have been played by disabled actors since the 1980s, including many so-called nontraditional roles in which the actor's impairment is irrelevant to the role, for example, a disabled judge or a deaf social worker. Groundbreaking roles and series include GERI JEWELL as Cousin Geri on *Facts of Life* (1980–84), LINDA BOVE on *Sesame Street* (1971–2003), CHRIS BURKE as Corky Thatcher on LIFE GOES ON (1989–93), Deanne Bray as Sue Thomas on *Sue Thomas FBEye* (2002–05) and Robert David Hall as Dr. Albert Robbins on *C.S.I. Crime Scene Investigations* (2001–07). There is some evidence that deaf and BLIND characters most often were female, a pattern going back into the early days of drama. The addition of a sensory disability to a female character intensifies the vulnerability of the female character, as depicted in works like *Orphans of the Storm* (1921), JOHNNY BELINDA (1948), and WAIT UNTIL DARK (1967), A complementary pattern of creating male, orthopedically disabled characters was also established early on, prime examples being THE MEN (1950), COMING HOME (1978), and BORN ON THE FOURTH OF JULY (1989).

Since the advent of moving pictures in the early 20th century, very few major American films provided starring vehicles for disabled actors, with the exception of two outstanding, Academy Award-winning performances separated by 40 years: WORLD WAR II veteran HAROLD RUSSELL as double-AMPUTEE Homer Parish in THE BEST YEARS OF OUR LIVES (1946) and MARLEE MATLIN as Sarah Norman in the movie version of *Children of a Lesser God* (1986). More often disabled characters with leading roles are cast with NONDISABLED actors: Some independent films have featured disabled talent in lead roles—Michael Anderson in Julie Taymor's *The Fool's Fire* (1992) and Peter Dinklage in *The Station Agent* (2003). Both of these actors are short-statured.

Actors of short stature represent a subset of disabled actors, one with a long and complex lineage of stage and film performance. The majority of roles for actors of short stature call for male performers. Female actors of small stature are rarely employed, though some females have taken on "suit" work, for example, Shari Weiser in her masked performance of Hoggle in Jim Hanson's *Labyrinth* (1986).

There is historical precedent for disabled artists taking control of media into their own hands. During the era from WORLD WAR I through the 1920s and the advent of sound films, deaf people created their own cinema. These films were often documentary in nature but some were structured around dramatic interpretations and fictional stories populated by deaf characters. Although many disability-driven projects have occurred on stage since the 1970s, the economics of 21st-century filmmaking have made it difficult for disabled artists to create their own media. A 2005 study commissioned by the Screen Actors Guild revealed that less than 2 percent of television show characters display a disability and only 0.5 percent have speaking roles. In a profession notorious for rejection and financial instability—the average SAG actor made $5,000 in 2005—disabled actors are at a further disadvantage because an erratic income pattern can endanger Social Security and health benefits.

Given these challenges, most disabled performers, like nondisabled performers before them, often choose to find support in collective, mutual aid ORGANIZATIONS. Union membership among disabled actors is growing. In 2005 SAG reported that 1,237 members self-identified as having a disability or using adaptive equipment, almost double the 1999 figure of 650. In addition to educational initiatives designed to dispel industry fears about working with disabled actors, the tri-union committee investigates discrimination practices and employment concerns that an actor with a disability encounters. Two prominent nonprofit organizations that advocate for performers with disabilities are the Media Access Office of the California Governor's Committee on Employment of People with Disabilities (MAO) and the Alliance for Inclusion in the Arts (formerly the Non-Traditional Casting Project). Since 1980 the Media Access Office has functioned as a liaison between the disability COMMUNITY and the entertainment industry promoting the accurate portrayal of persons with disabilities and a recognition of disability as part of diversity initiatives in the performing arts. Projects include a casting clearinghouse for union and nonunion disabled talent, acting workshops, and the annual Media Access Awards. The Alliance for Inclusion in the Arts (AIA), founded in 1986, administers Artist Files/Online (AFO), a database of disabled and deaf performers as well as actors of color available to casting directors throughout the world. Both MAO and AIA advocate reform in casting practices: the casting of disabled actors for disability-specific roles (i.e., a deaf actor for a character who is deaf) and "color-blind" casting that encourages the use of disabled actors in non-disability specific roles, such as a physically disabled lawyer or mothers.

As a particularly public embodiment of social values and expectations, actors represent an important symbol of the status and understanding of the deaf and disabled person in American society. Despite discrimination against the impaired from the beginning of the country's founding and even taking into account the considerable financial success that many of the carnival sideshow exhibits garnered, the post–civil rights performer represents a dignity and agency

not available to past generations. As beneficiaries of important civil rights legislation, the performing artist with disabilities now has the capability and opportunity to imagine a new social identity for Americans with disabilities, an identity that, in turn, can become a reality of daily living.

See also REPRESENTATION.

Victoria Ann Lewis

Further Reading:
Adelson, Betty M. "Theatre, Film and Television." In *The Lives of Dwarfs: Their Journey from Public Curiosity toward Social Liberation.* New Brunswick, N.J.: Rutgers University Press, 2005.

Bogdan, Robert. *Freak Show: Presenting Human Oddities for Amusement and Profit.* Chicago: University of Chicago Press, 1988.

Lewis, Victoria Ann. "Afterword: The Casting Question." In *Beyond Victims and Villains: Contemporary Plays by Disabled Playwrights.* New York: Theatre Communications Group, 2006.

Norden, Martin F. *The Cinema of Isolation: A History of Physical Disability in the Movies.* New Brunswick, N.J.: Rutgers University Press, 1995.

Pointon, Ann, ed., with Chris Davies. *Framed: Interrogating Disability in the Media.* London: British Film Institute Publishing, 1997.

Schuchman, John S. *Hollywood Speaks: Deafness and the Film Entertainment Industry.* Urbana: University of Illinois Press, 1988.

Tolan, Kathleen. "'We Are Not a Metaphor': A Conversation about Representation." *American Theatre* (April 2001): 17–21, 57–59.

ACT UP

ACT UP, an acronym for the AIDS Coalition to Unleash Power, is a grassroots direct action political movement that formed in 1987 as a response to AIDS activist Larry Kramer's challenge to New York City's gay and lesbian community to take responsibility for ending the AIDS crisis. Already decimated by more than five years of the epidemic, the gay community in New York City created several community-based organizations—the Gay Men's Health Crisis (GMHC) and the PWA Coalition (PWAC) among others—to provide services for people with AIDS (PWA). Although they developed an ethics of care, these ORGANIZATIONS had not articulated an inclusive or radical political analysis regarding the conditions that led to the state of crisis; they had not publicly denounced the structural inequities and discriminatory practices many perceived within the public HEALTH CARE system, nor did they express a vision of how to contain the burgeoning epidemic.

Empowered by the PWAC's implementation of the 1982 Denver principles that asserted the primacy of each individual with AIDS in determining the course of his or her treatment, a coalition of people with AIDS, gay activists, and radical graphic artists carried out the first civil disobedience under the name of ACT UP. This "action," as ACT UP's large demonstrations involving civil disobedience were named, effectively blockaded New York City's Wall Street on March 24, 1987, calling on pharmaceutical giant Burroughs Wellcome to reduce the prohibitive price of AZT, which at that time was the only retroviral treatment approved by the U.S. Food and Drug Administration (FDA). ACT UP protestors also demanded that the federal government increase ACCESS to experimental and ethically designed pharmaceutical drug studies; provide affordable health care for all; coordinate a massive initiative on AIDS prevention education; and end racist, sexist, homophobic, and xenophobic public health-care policies.

Beginning in April 1987, ACT UP met weekly at New York City's Lesbian and Gay Community Center. Modeling participatory democracy, ACT UP was an umbrella organization that united a variety of committees and affinity groups and demonstrated against the conditions that created and exacerbated the AIDS crisis. ACT UP's Treatment and Data Committee meticulously researched and analyzed current scientific and medical data on AIDS and HIV infection and distributed its findings and recommendations to the entire group. Those recommendations provided the basis for many of ACT UP's actions, such as the 1988 protest against the FDA to demand speedier development of more AIDS treatments and access to experimental drugs for all patients who might benefit from them.

ACT UP was notorious for its theatricalized demonstrations, innovative tactics, stark graphic visual displays, and sophisticated use of both mainstream and independent media to convey its message. Members used a variety of outrageous interventionist tactics to occupy spaces of power such as chaining themselves in the offices of pharmaceutical executives and on the trading floor of the New York Stock Exchange. ACT UP's media committee and visual collectives assisted affinity groups by providing posters and placards of images and text that summarized the message of each action, and its many video collectives used their recordings of those events as video ACTIVISM, producing and distributing programming based on those events that also documented the history of ACT UP's ACTIVISM.

As the most visible and radical AIDS activist organization in the late 1980s and early 1990s, ACT UP was instrumental in lowering the price of AZT, expanding the definition of AIDS used by the Center for Disease Control and Prevention to include infections that presented in women and CHILDREN, increasing access to clinical trials, and setting the federal research agenda for greater availability of treatments for both opportunistic infections and underlying HIV infections. ACT UP also collaborated with other grassroots advocacy organizations to create needle exchange programs and AIDS prevention programs for at-risk youth, to support prisoners in forming their own peer education and counseling programs, and with immigration advocates to repeal immigration policies (see IMMIGRATION POLICY) that discriminated against HIV-positive individuals. Still active today, but no longer as large or influential as it had been in the past, ACT UP's greatest accomplishment lay in its success in changing how people conceived their ability to transform the conditions surrounding their disease. ACT UP provided an example of how social and medical policy could be changed by those most affected and how people living with AIDS, not just doctors, scientists and politicians, could alter the course and the discourse of the epidemic.

ACT UP's highly developed critique of medical and social stigmatization derived from its members' experience of being cast as sexual and gender "deviants." Although ACT UP never overtly articulated its connection with the DISABILITY RIGHTS MOVEMENT, ACT UP members, like DISABILITY studies scholars, critically challenged forms of oppressions based on GENDER, RACE, class, sex, and ability in their efforts to identify and eradicate the socially constructed biases that pathologized the lives of people with AIDS and their affected communities.

Debra Levine

Further Reading:

Jennings, M. Kent, and Ellen Ann Andersen. "The Importance of Social and Political Context: The Case of AIDS Activism." *Political Behavior* 25, no. 2 (2003): 177–199.

McRuer, Robert. "Disability and the NAMES Project." *The Public Historian* 27, no. 2 (Spring 2005): 53–61.

Wolfe, Maxine, and Sommella, Laraine. "This Is about People Dying: The Tactics of Early ACT UP and Lesbian Avengers in New York City." In *Queers in Space: Communities, Public Places, Sites of Resistance,* edited by Gordon Brent Ingram, Anne-Marie Bouthillette, and Yolanda Retter, 407–438. Seattle: Bay Press, 1997.

ADA   See AMERICANS WITH DISABILITIES ACT.

ADAPT   See AMERICAN DISABLED FOR ATTENDANT PROGRAMS TODAY.

ADD   See ATTENTION DEFICIT HYPERACTIVITY DISORDER.

addiction

Addiction is a condition defined by an individual's intense need to consume a particular substance, usually an illicit drug or alcohol. Typically regarded as a disease or medical condition, addiction is seen by many as a form of disability. Addiction is generally diagnosed based on the following criteria: tolerance, withdrawal, and craving. Tolerance refers to the body's ability to metabolize, or tolerate, a certain quantity of a substance prior to reaching the point of intoxication. Withdrawal refers to the agitated behavior, ranging from mild irritability to severe physical illness, that many habitual substance users display when they cannot consume their desired substances. Finally, craving refers to a user's physical, and frequently psychological, need to consume a substance in order to offset withdrawal symptoms. People are believed to be addicts when they habitually consume drugs or alcohol, often to the point of intoxication, and when they display signs of withdrawal and craving in the absence of those substances. Recently some scholarship has examined how many behaviors like gambling, sex, and exercise can also be addictive based on these criteria.

Although the temperance movement of the 19th century introduced addiction as a concept, it was not until early in the 20th century that the current paradigm emerged. Individuals no doubt exhibited addictive behaviors long before that time but they were not likely to be considered addicts, nor were they said to be experiencing addiction because such terms did not exist. In the early 1900s public concern over drug use, particularly about opium and heroin consumption, increased as the drug trade began to spread throughout Europe and America. Consequently, medical and legal authorities coined the terms "addiction" and "addict" to describe forms of substance use considered excessive, abnormal, and dangerous to individual users and to the general public. As the century progressed addiction came to be diagnosed as a DISEASE from which addicts could only recover but never be cured. This particular understanding of addiction has its roots primarily in the recovery movement, specifically in the ideology of Alcoholics Anonymous (founded in 1935), rather than in the field of medicine.

Employing theories developed within the arena of DISABILITY STUDIES, scholars in the academic field of cultural studies have proposed that addiction be understood outside the framework of medical terminology, arguing that the term addiction emerged primarily from cultural concerns, rather than strictly medical ones. Contemporary cultural scholarship has begun to examine how the term is often used in a derogatory manner to marginalize substance users—generally labeled "addicts"—who are viewed as abnormal. Seeing addiction within the context of disability studies concepts that seek to question and critique the social construction of concepts such as "normalcy" and "deviant behavior," some contemporary addiction critics have pointed out that the distinction between necessary, healthy drug use and excessive, addictive drug use has become unclear in a time when most people regularly consume substances such as aspirin, caffeine, and vitamin supplements. Likewise, some critics have interpreted the construction of addiction as disease as symptomatic of a larger discourse of pathology that negatively defines addicts and others as culturally deviant or inferior.

See also NORMAL AND NORMALCY; SOCIAL CONSTRUCTION OF DISABILITY.

Joseph P. Fisher

Further Reading:
Derrida, Jacques. "The Rhetoric of Drugs." Translated by Michael Israel. *Differences: A Journal of Feminist Cultural Studies* 5, no. 1 (1993): 1–25.
Levine, Harry G. "The Discovery of Addiction: Changing Conceptions of Habitual Drunkenness in America." *Journal of Studies on Alcohol* 15 (1979): 493–506.
Peele, Stanton. *Love and Addiction.* New York: Taplinger, 1975.
———. *The Meaning of Addiction: Compulsive Experience and Its Interpretation.* Lexington, Mass.: Lexington Books, 1985.
Redfield, Marc, and Janet Farrell Brodie, eds. *High Anxieties: Cultural Studies in Addiction.* Berkeley: University of California Press, 2002.
Sedgwick, Eve Kosofsky. "Epidemics of the Will." In *Tendencies,* edited by Michèle Aina Barale, Jonathan Goldberg, Michael Moon, and Eve Kosofsy Sedgwick, 130–142. Durham: Duke University Press, 1993.

"She is mortified and miserable she says, because she is compelled to do it. She cried bitterly about it a few days ago, and declared that she could never do without it. That she was an opium eater for life. They were her words."

—Lucy Plummer Battle in a letter to her husband, about their adult daughter Susan, April 1833

ADHD See ATTENTION DEFICIT HYPERACTIVITY DISORDER.

adoption See FOSTER CARE.

advertising

The history of advertising offers important insights into the changing meaning and perception of disability in America. Images of disability consistently appeared in American print advertising in the 19th and early 20th centuries. These images most typically advertised a disability-related product or people with disabilities who worked as "freaks" in carnivals or CIRCUSES. For example, beginning in 1843, P. T. BARNUM used images of CHARLES SHERWOOD STRATTON, the famous little person known as General Tom Thumb, to promote international appearances by the three-foot-tall performer. An advertisement in the *Brooklyn Eagle* newspaper in 1848 stated: "Every afternoon at 3 o'clock, the little General will appear on the stage in the Lecture Room, in his CITIZEN'S DRESS, in which he will relate his history, travels, &c., and exhibit his Extraordinary Performances and Imitations, including Napoleon, Frederick the Great, Songs and Dances, Grecian Statues." In 1860 Stratton began managing his own performances and placed newspaper ads to promote himself. Some people used their fame to sell products other than themselves. Three-quarters of a century later, Robert Wadlow, 8 foot, 4 ½ inches tall, appeared in a display ad to sell Peters All Leather Shoes in 1936. The ad said that Wadlow wore the largest pair of shoes for the human foot, size 35. In these examples advertisers presented those with a disability or different body type as exotic and "freakish."

Several well-known disability charities began in the early 20th century and promoted themselves using images of CHILDREN with disabilities, linking CHARITY to pity. EASTER SEALS (which began in 1919 as the National Society for Crippled Children), MARCH OF DIMES (1938), and the MUSCULAR DYSTROPHY ASSOCIATION (1950) used children with disabilities in their promotional materials. This method raised money by inspiring pity for the children and a desire for them to be CURED.

After WORLD WAR II, TELEVISION became an important venue for advertising, and some charities took their fund-raising to the new medium in the form of TELETHONS.

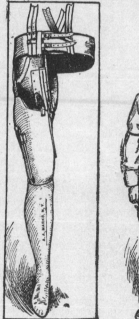

MARKS ARTIFICIAL LIMBS
Designed for all Amputations and Deformities

THE MOST DIFFICULT problem in adapting artificial legs to amputations is presented in the hip joint disarticulation; Furneaux-Jordan and other methods.

The pelvic socket artificial leg here illustrated is the most recent creation of the A. A. Marks' establishment. The socket is constructed to receive one-third of the pelvis. An artificial leg is attached to this socket so that it will articulate on the same axis as the hip on the opposite side. The leg is constructed with knee-lock, spring mattress rubber foot, and other improvements.

LEGS and ARMS

Persons walk acceptably, stand with safety, stoop and sit in a very natural way with one of these legs, although there is no stump to control the leg movements.

For particulars regarding artificial legs and arms adaptable to the most difficult and complex cases, read a

"Manual of Artificial Limbs"

just published. A cloth bound copy (worthy of any library) will be sent, free of all charges, on application by mail or person.

A. A. MARKS, 701 Broadway, NEW YORK CITY
Established Over Half a Century

Prosthetic devices such as artificial limbs were among the most common 19th-century products marketed to people with disabilities. This A. A. Marks advertisement, using a direct and unsentimental approach, was typical.   *(John Williams-Seale)*

Telethons gave numerous hours of televised publicity to a charity, drew viewers to the event through the use of celebrity hosts and performers, and had viewers call in to donate to "help find a cure." Telethons and the television advertising they used heightened the cultural link between pity and disability.

In recent decades, disability rights advocates have increasingly challenged advertisements that invoke pity and thus stigmatize disability. In particular, telethons have fallen in numbers due to the criticism. Other charity organizations have retooled their promotions to present disabled people in more positive ways.

The growing influence of disability rights advocates contributed to other changes in imagery, primarily a move from invisibility in general print and television ads to gradual inclusion in advertisements. Early disability rights successes, such as the Rehabilitation Act of 1973 (see VOCATIONAL REHABILITATION ACT) and the INDEPENDENT LIVING MOVEMENT, enhanced the visibility of people with disabilities in mainstream society.

The 1980s represented an important era in advertising in disability history. In 1980 CLOSED CAPTIONING became a more common feature in televised programs, enabling DEAF and other viewers to ACCESS this medium more fully. Disability ACTIVISM and increased rights stemming from new federal legislation motivated the general business community to recognize people with disabilities as consumers. Consequently, in the 1980s ads began to be directed at the disability community through the use of actors and models with disabilities. A 1984 Levi's ad, in which a WHEELCHAIR user "popped a wheelie," generally is considered the first commercial to feature a person with a disability.

Since the late 1980s, commercials with disabled people were intended to reach broader society. For example, chain store giant Target initiated a print ad campaign that included adults and children with disabilities in its sales circulars that went to 30 million households in 32 states. Target officials boasted about the success of this disability-related initiative, pointing to specific sales results as proof of its effectiveness.

After 1990 most advertisements featuring disabled people were accepted and considered nonstigmatizing. Still, controversies occasionally arose. In 1993 Dow Chemical's TV ad for Spray 'N Wash Stain Stick used a child with DOWN SYNDROME and her real mother. The nonactors were found through the National Down Syndrome Congress. The organization applauded the final ad and even gave it a media award, but an *Advertising Age* writer called the ad exploitative, "appalling," and "the most crassly contrived slice-of-life in advertising history," according to the *Wall Street Journal*. But consumer response contradicted this opinion: Dow's toll-free telephone line received 700 calls about the ad, virtually all of which were positive. Nike, in contrast, upset disability rights advocates in 2000 when it ran magazine ads for its new running shoe that called people with disabilities "drooling and misshapen." After complaints, Nike quickly withdrew the ads and issued a formal apology.

Advertising has shaped not only economic features of American life but also the way consumers view products and people. The changing depiction of disability and people with disabilities in advertisements reflect important social and political changes over the past two centuries.

See also REPRESENTATION; STEREOTYPES; STIGMA.

Beth Haller

Further Reading:

Disability History Museum Library. "Visual still collection." Available online. URL: http://www.disabilitymuseum.org/lib/. Accessed June 30, 2008.

Haller, Beth, and Sue Ralph. "Profitability, Diversity, and Disability in Advertising in the UK and United States." *Disability Studies Quarterly* 21, no. 2 (Spring 2001). Available online. URL: http://www.dsq-sds.org. Accessed June 30, 2008.

Longmore, Paul K. "Screening Stereotypes: Images of Disabled People in Television and Motion Pictures." In *Images of the Disabled, Disability Images,* edited by Alan Garner and T. Joe, 65–78. New York: Praeger, 1987.

Shapiro, Joseph P. *No Pity: People with Disabilities Forging a New Civil Rights Movement.* New York: Times Books, 1993.

AFB   See AMERICAN FOUNDATION FOR THE BLIND.

affirmative action

As with many other underrepresented groups, Americans with disabilities have been strongly influenced by affirmative action. At a 1965 commencement speech at Howard University, President Lyndon Johnson explained affirmative action in the context of civil rights by using the image of the individual who "for years has been hobbled by chains," and then, after being liberated, is unfairly considered "free to compete [in a race] with all the others." Thus, Johnson continued, "it is not enough to open the gates of opportunity. All our citizens must have the ability to walk through." Given the accessibility issues with which the disability population has had to contend, Johnson's image is especially apt.

When first introduced, affirmation action programs designed to promote equal EMPLOYMENT opportunities and eliminate employment discrimination included people with disabilities. Section 503 of the Rehabilitation Act of 1973 (see VOCATIONAL REHABILITATION ACT), as amended, and Section 402 of the Vietnam era Veterans' Readjustment Assistance Act of 1974, as amended, mandated that "federal contractors and subcontractors . . . take affirmative action to ensure that all individuals have an equal opportunity for employment, without regard to disability or status." In the 1970s, however, the concept of affirmative action changed from establishing a "level playing field" for those who had been subjected to discrimination to forging diversity in schools and in workplaces. While both approaches are pivotal to affirmative action in a disability context, the idea, embedded in disability civil rights legislation, that, in order to be competitive, a prospective worker with a disability must be able to perform "the essential function of the job," is in harmony with the latter approach.

While the Rehabilitation Act of 1973 requires affirmative action in federal employment and federal contracts, the omission of an affirmative action requirement in the 1990 AMERICANS WITH DISABILITIES ACT (ADA) has resulted in failure of the private sector to seriously pursue qualified workers with disabilities. This development is ironic since the primary purpose of the ADA, which extended the civil rights protection of people with disabilities to the private sector where over 85 percent of the jobs are found, was to increase employment opportunities for this population.

Partially because of this ADA omission people with disabilities continue to experience employment discrimination. Eight years after the passage of the ADA, a study by the Louis Harris Association for the NATIONAL ORGANIZATION ON DISABILITY noted that 79 percent of the NONDISABLED population of working age were employed while only 29 percent of those with disabilities of working age were employed. This is despite the fact that people with disabilities have many skills to bring to the workforce. A 1993 Standard and Poor's study revealed that "companies that achieved some threshold level of diversity had stock market records that were almost two and one-half times better than similarly situated companies," and "that diverse work force includes individuals with disabilities." The growing disability population has added pressure to the debates over affirmative action, highlighting the many dimensions of disability in American society.

See also ACCESS AND ACCESSIBILITY; DISABILITY RIGHTS MOVEMENT; EMPLOYMENT; LAW AND POLICY.

Doris Zames Fleischer

Further Reading:
Americans with Disabilities Act of 1990 (Title 42, United States Code).
Fleischer, Doris Zames, and Frieda Zames. *The Disability Rights Movement: From Charity to Confrontation.* Philadelphia: Temple University Press, 2001.
National Council on Disability. *National Disability Policy: A Progress Report (December 2004–December 2005)* November 9, 2006.
National Council on Disability. *Social Security Administration's Efforts to Promote Employment for People with Disabilities,* November 30, 2005.
U.S. Equal Employment Opportunity Commission Meeting. *Proceedings.* March 12, 1996.

age and ageism

AGING has always posed a challenge to humanity, but the experience of old age has varied dramatically in different historical contexts. The history of aging and ageism in the United States can usefully be divided into three periods—the preindustrial, industrial, and post–WORLD WAR II eras.

In the preindustrial era during the colonial and early national periods, the elderly typically lived in households with adult CHILDREN over whom they continued to exercise authority to the degree that they retained legal control over farmland, the most important economic resource of the era. Retirement did not formally exist, and the elderly typically worked until their deaths unless interrupted by debilitating illness. The position of older slaves (see SLAVERY) and women was much more precarious since slaves were forbidden to own land and a woman's status derived from her husband, thus opening windows to drastic changes of fortune. But old age was broadly revered in preindustrial America. Sermons and medical and legal treatises stressed that the elderly's links to FAMILY, COMMUNITY, and church forged over long years of experience made them extraordinary assets to bind society together even if declining physical and mental abilities rendered the aged economically unproductive.

In the second half of the 19th century, INDUSTRIALIZATION and the emergence of a modern liberal social order significantly changed the experience of aging. The widespread introduction of mechanized production meant that skilled labor could more readily be replaced with unskilled labor, and consequently, older workers' relative incomes and employment prospects fell. The declining value of farmland in all but the most productive regions of the country and the propensity of children to leave home to find work in growing urban centers caused a dramatic shift in traditional family structures, undermining the position of the elderly within families. Retirement became an expected and dreaded stage of life, carrying the real threat of poverty and poor house. In an increasingly loose, cosmopolitan society that celebrated the ability of individuals to rise and fall according to their own efforts, anxiety about what seemed the inevitable physical and mental decline associated with old age markedly increased. Foundational texts in the emerging fields of geriatrics and gerontology, such as Ignatz Leo Nascher's *Geriatrics* (1914) and G. Stanley Hall's *Senescence* (1922), reinforced this anxiety and the expectation that old age would normally be marked by a steady and inevitable decline in physical and mental ability. Passage of the SOCIAL SECURITY ACT in 1935 marked the first national effort to provide financial assistance to the elderly.

After World War II, recognition that the elderly were destined to become an increasingly large part of the U.S. population led to a reexamination of assumptions about aging throughout American society. Mandatory retirement was prohibited for most occupations, while Social Security and private pension benefits were systematically increased through the 1950s and 1960s to the point where retirement became less a source of anxiety than an entitlement. The passage of MEDICARE and the Older Americans Act in 1965, and the creation of the National Institute on Aging in 1974, solidified the commitment of the federal government to funding services and research into the problems of aging. Meanwhile, the burgeoning academic field of social gerontology began to show that much of the mental and physical disability associated with aging was the result either of DISEASE processes distinct from aging or "excess disability" produced by social STIGMA and learned helplessness.

In 1969 gerontologist Robert N. Butler coined the term "ageism" to describe what he saw as systematic discrimination against and stereotyping of older people. To combat ageism, social gerontologists accentuated the positive aspects of aging; older people, they stressed, could normally expect to remain healthy, active, and fully engaged with life. Although gerontology's elevation of "successful aging" as the norm for older people clearly did much good in dispelling ageist stereotypes, critics argued that it reflected an intolerance for disability and dependence, potentially further marginalizing those elderly who did not meet the conventional standards of ability.

By the early 21st century, research into the biology of aging even appears to be at the threshold of mastering basic mechanisms of aging so that the human lifespan could be dramatically increased, though bioethicists worry about what such a development would mean. Meanwhile the retirement of the baby boom generation is widely seen as threatening the solvency of Social Security. Rising HEALTH CARE costs coupled with the fact that the relatively sick 85 and older age group constitute the most rapidly growing segment of the population lead many observers to worry that both Medicare and the health care system could be overwhelmed.

See also AGE DISCRIMINATION ACT.

Jesse F. Ballenger

Further Reading:
Butler, Robert N. *Why Survive? Being Old in America.* New York: Harper & Row, 1975.
Cole, Thomas R. *The Journey of Life: A Cultural History of Aging in America.* Cambridge: Cambridge University Press, 1992.
Haber, Carole, and Brian Gratton. *Old Age and the Search for Security: An American Social History.* Bloomington: Indiana University Press, 1994.
Nelson, Todd D., ed. *Ageism: Stereotyping and Prejudice against Older Persons.* Cambridge, Mass.: MIT Press, 2002.

Age Discrimination Act

The Age Discrimination Act of 1975 was introduced to prohibit age-related discrimination in programs and activities that receive federal assistance. The primary sponsor of the legislation was Senator Jacob K. Javits (R-N.Y.). Modeled on the regulations issued under Title VI of the Civil Rights Act of 1964, the act was introduced in November 1975 as part of the amendments to the Older Americans Act of 1965. Although congressional debate and advocacy groups focused on discrimination against elderly people, the act applies to people of all ages (see AGE AND AGEISM). The act is enforced by the Office for Civil Rights (OCR) of the U.S. Department of Health and Human Services. Legislative recognition of the discrimination that older Americans experience had occurred through the passage of the 1967 Age Discrimination in Employment Act. This earlier legislation had recognized the pervasive experience of discrimination against older people in the labor market. The passage of the 1975 Age Discrimination Act occurred in the context of the federal government's intention to expand civil rights protection more generally. For instance, the Race Discrimination Act was also passed in 1975.

Under the Age Discrimination Act, recipients of federal funds are prohibited from denying services, limiting services, or otherwise discriminating on the basis of age. The act does permit certain exceptions, where age distinctions are allowed, and factors that may have a disproportionate effect on the basis of age are permitted. The act does not apply to federal, state, and local laws that provide benefits to people based on age, nor does it apply to laws that establish criteria for participation in age-related terms. Also, the act does not apply to laws that identify the intended beneficiaries in age-related terms. Similarly, the act does not apply to EMPLOYMENT. The Age Discrimination in Employment Act covers employment matters and applies only to people over 40 years of age.

Congress required the Commission on Civil Rights to conduct a study on the extent of age discrimination in federally funded programs prior to the development of regulations for the Age Discrimination Act. Initial results of this study were provided in January 1978, with a follow-up report published in 1979. Federal agencies that were affected by this study were required to respond to the results of this study. The regulations required that any complaint go through mediation through the Federal Mediation and Conciliation Service. These regulations permit claims to the federal court in two circumstances: if the OCR has not given an order and 180 days have passed since the complaint was filed; or if the OCR has ordered in favor of the recipient.

The Age Discrimination Act does not specifically address the issue of disability. However, some of the age-related discrimination that people experience attributes certain disabilities to them (for instance, to suggest that older people are losing their mental faculties or are mentally incompetent in some ways). Discriminating against older people on the basis of such STEREOTYPES is unlawful under the Age Discrimination Act of 1975.

In some ways, the spirit of expanding civil rights legislation throughout the 1960s and 1970s not only helped to fuel support for the Age Discrimination Act of 1975 but also specific disability rights legislation. The passage of the Rehabilitation Act of 1973 reflected the preparedness of Congress to pass wider civil rights legislation and acknowledge that disabled people needed protection from patterns of discrimination that were quite pervasive in society. Arguably, the passage of the AMERICANS WITH DISABILITIES ACT of 1990 also reflected this concern with redressing pervasive patterns of discrimination against disabled people.

See also LAW AND POLICY.

Mark Sherry

Further Reading:

Barnartt, Sharon N., and Katherine Seelman. "A Comparison of Federal Laws toward Disabled and Racial/Ethnic Groups in the USA." *Disability and Society* 3, no.1 (1998): 37–48.

Gliedman, John, and William Roth. *The Unexpected Minority: Handicapped Children in America.* New York: Harcourt Brace Jovanovich, 1980.

U.S. Department of Health and Human Services. "Nondiscrimination on the Basis of Age in Programs or Activities Receiving Federal Financial Assistance From HHS." Available online. URL: http://www.hhs.gov/ocr/agereg.html. Accessed July 10, 2007.

Agent Orange

Agent Orange, named after the color-coded stripe painted around the 55-gallon barrels in which it was stored, was a 50/50 combination of two commercial herbicides, 2-4-D and 2,4,5-T. Designed to kill triple canopy jungles, Agent Orange was tested in Vietnam in 1961 in the early stages of the VIETNAM WAR. It worked so well that by 1962 the military commenced a program of systematically defoliating millions of acres of Vietnam's jungles, mangrove forests, and croplands. The South Vietnamese government cooperated fully with the defoliation campaign. Scientists familiar with the massive destruction of Vietnam's natural habitat call the damage "ecocide."

Agent Orange contained TCDD-dioxin, one of the most deadly chemicals in existence. At the height of the defoliation campaign in Vietnam, scientists at Bionetics Laboratories of Bethesda, Maryland, discovered that even in the lowest doses given, 2,4,5-T, the herbicide contaminated with TCDD-dioxin, causes cleft palates, missing and deformed eyes, cystic kidneys, and enlarged livers in the offspring of laboratory animals. This study was instrumental in convincing the military to stop using Agent Orange in Vietnam in 1970. By then, the U.S. Air Force had already sprayed 12 million gallons of Agent Orange over 5 million acres, an area about the size of Massachusetts.

As early as 1967 Vietnamese peasants living near spray missions were complaining of miscarriages, skin rashes, sick and dying farm animals, and the sudden death of weak and elderly people. More than 35 years after the Air Force flew its last spray mission in Vietnam ex-soldiers from Vietnam, the United States, South Korea, New Zealand, and Canada continue to suffer from a wide variety of debilitating illnesses, including CANCERS, kidney failure, and heart problems, related to their exposure to Agent Orange.

The DEPARTMENT OF VETERANS AFFAIRS now recognizes a number of illnesses as grounds for service-connected disability. However, there are no accurate records of the number of men and women who are permanently disabled from exposure to Agent Orange. Approximately 220,000 Vietnam VETERANS, suspecting their illnesses are related to Agent Orange, have applied to the Veterans Administration for physical examinations.

In 1978 a 28-year-old Vietnam veteran who had been exposed to Agent Orange shocked the nation by announcing: "I died in Vietnam but I didn't even know it." Before he succumbed that same year to cancer of the colon, liver, and abdomen, Paul Reuthersahn initiated a lawsuit against Dow

"In my case I'm sure it was in the water that we used, and I presume it was on the foliage and in the dirt. Yeah, it was just there, and it was a lot of chemicals. . . . A few times when I was in the field, I could actually smell what I thought was diesel fuel, and I never had any idea what that was all about. It was very faint, but it was very clear. It smelled like being around the pumps at a gas station with diesel fuel."

—Vietnam War veteran Jim Fiebke, describing in an interview how he acquired multiple myeloma from exposure to Agent Orange in the early 1970s

Chemical and other wartime manufacturers of Agent Orange. At the time, the Agent Orange class action was the largest class action and product liability lawsuit in U.S. history. It was settled out of court on May 7, 1984, for $180 million. Under the terms of the agreement, a totally disabled veteran would receive $12,000 spread out over 10 years. The average expected payout was $5,700, and the maximum death benefit was set at $34,000.

In February 1979 the Environmental Protection Agency issued an order of emergency suspension for 2,4,5-T. In 2004 Vietnamese Agent Orange victims launched a class action suit charging chemical manufacturers of Agent Orange with war crimes. The industrialized world remains inundated with dioxin and other deadly chemicals that attack the human immune system, disabling, crippling, and killing untold numbers of people. The history of Agent Orange offers a stark example of the connection between WAR, toxic chemicals, and disability.

Fred A. Wilcox

Further Reading:

Brown, Michael. *Laying Waste: The Poisoning of America by Toxic Chemicals.* New York: Pantheon, 1980.

Linedecker, Clifford. *Kerry: Agent Orange and an American Family.* New York: St. Martin's Press, 1982.

Wilcox, Fred A. *Waiting for an Army to Die: The Tragedy of Agent Orange.* New York: Random House, 1983.

aging

Concepts of aging and old age, like disability, have varied throughout history. While many Americans never reached older ages in colonial America, those who did typically held valued roles within society. To a large extent, life expectancy and the general status of older Americans were linked to with property ownership. While there is debate among scholars concerning societal attitudes toward older Americans over time, a significant shift seemed to occur during the INDUSTRIALIZATION period of the late 19th and early 20th centuries. The conventional view, known as modernization theory, argues that industrialization contributed to the diminished status of older Americans due to the rise of capitalism and labor markets, which led to exclusion of older individuals from the labor force and devalued in society. In recent years, however, historians David Hackett Fisher, W. Andrew Achenbaum, and others have shown that little change in economic and social status for the vast majority of older Americans occurred during this period. They assert that older Americans continued to work and reside within intergenerational FAMILY arrangements.

Most scholars agree, however, that societal issues increasingly became categorized during the late 19th century and

> *"Even if it is the wreck of my old physical body, I am not abandoning it until I have to."*
>
> —Fannie Hardy Eckstorm (1865–1946) in a letter to fellow Maine writer Joanna Colcord, January 7, 1945

that, for the first time, old age was designated as a social policy category. Some historians believe this categorization was intimately linked to the rise of ASYLUMS AND INSTITUTIONS, as older Americans with disabilities who lacked assistance from family were often warehoused in ALMSHOUSES, which were the precursor of a variety of modern-day institutions, including nursing homes. As Americans established institutions for individuals with psychiatric and cognitive disabilities, the population of older disabled individuals left in the almshouses became more noticeable. Professional organizations rallied behind passage of old age pensions through the SOCIAL SECURITY ACT of 1935, which solidified old age as a social category, led to the demise of the almshouse, and reduced competition between younger and older workers in the labor market. Furthermore, the category of old age was placed among the "deserving poor," a key distinction that has driven the evolution of American disability policy.

Many professional organizations devoted to aging proliferated during the 20th century, which further influenced policy development and, arguably, promoted a further divide between aging and disability. In 1939, the National Institute on Aging was established to promote aging research and in 1945 the Gerontological Society of America was founded. The AARP (originally known as the American Association of Retired Persons) was founded in 1958 to promote the needs of retired teachers for health insurance. The first White House Conference on Aging was held in 1961, which led to the enactment of many key federal social programs in 1965, including MEDICARE, MEDICAID, and the Older Americans Act. Medicare extended universal HEALTH CARE to eligible individuals age 65 and older, while Medicaid extended health care to several other categories of "deserving poor," including younger individuals with disabilities, pregnant women, and children. The Older Americans Act established the Federal Administration on Aging and a network of local Area Agencies on Aging.

Aging and disability share important connections, including the overlap caused by the increased likelihood of acquiring IMPAIRMENTS with age. Society's response to both reflects other common traits. For example, early gerontological work viewed aging in strictly biological and negative terms, often portraying advanced age as a period of natural "decline and loss" and "disengagement," an approach that closely resembles how medical professionals have depicted disability. In other ways, approaches to aging and disability highlight important philosophical divides. In the 1980s, for instance, the paradigm of "successful aging" emerged within the field of aging. While this paradigm catalyzed advances in preventative health care, health promotion, and active engagement, it also marginalized older disabled individuals as not "aging well." Various feminist and DISABILITY STUDIES scholars have critically assessed this paradigm, calling for greater focus on removing environmental barriers and promoting social justice.

The United States and other industrialized countries are witnessing a dramatic increase in their aging populations. Since 1900 overall life expectancy in the United States has risen from approximately 49 to 78 years of age. Increased life expectancy and aging of the baby boom generation (individuals born between 1946 and 1964) are factors driving significant demographic shifts. Between 2010 and 2050, the population of Americans over 65 is projected to grow from 39 to 80 million, representing from 13 percent to 21 percent of the overall U.S. population. The population of individuals over 85 will increase even more rapidly from 6 to 21 million, from 2 percent to 5 percent of the overall U.S. population. These demographic shifts will fundamentally challenge the U.S. welfare state and social contract with older Americans to provide sufficient income and health care through such programs as Social Security and Medicare. Moreover, America faces significant challenges in financing long-term care services and supports. The current system often forces people into impoverishment, is fraught with an institutional bias, can place strain on family and informal caregivers (see CAREGIVING) and is unable to meet current needs, let alone significant future needs of an aging population. In recent years, aging and disability communities have forged new alliances, particularly in the area of long-term services, in which cherished ideals from the INDEPENDENT LIVING MOVEMENT have become increasingly embraced by seniors. As the United States faces new challenges posed by demographic shifts, collaborative advocacy efforts will prove essential in protecting rights and expanding opportunities for all disabled Americans, regardless of age.

See also AGE AND AGEISM.

Joe Caldwell

Further Reading:

Administration on Aging. U.S. Department of Health and Human Services. Available online. URL: http://www.aoa.gov/. Accessed December 18, 2006.

Estes, Caroll L. *Social Policy and Aging: A Critical Perspective.* Thousand Oaks, Calif.: Sage Publications, 2001.

Feder, J., H. Komisar, and R. Friedland. *Long-Term Care Financing: Policy Options for the Future.* Washington, D.C.: Georgetown University, Long-Term Care Financing Project, 2007.

Haber, Carole, and Brian Gratton. *Old Age and the Search for Security: An American Social History.* Bloomington: Indiana University Press, 1994.

Hooyman, Nancy R., and H. Asuman Kiyak. *Social Gerontology: A Multidisciplinary Perspective.* 7th ed. Boston: Allyn & Bacon, 2004.

Minkler, M., and P. Fadem. "Successful Aging: A Disability Perspective." *Journal of Disability Policy Studies* 12 (2002): 229–235.

AIDS

The term *AIDS* (Acquired Immune Deficiency Syndrome) appeared in 1982 to describe opportunistic infections that occur in a person who has contracted HIV (*Human Immunodeficiency Virus*). The term *AIDS* also designates the public health crisis, first recognized in the early 1980s in which public HEALTH CARE institutions were slow to provide HIV prevention information to people at risk for contracting the DISEASE and affordable treatment options for those already infected.

The first clinically recognizable symptoms of HIV disease were reported in 1981. Initially named GRID (Gay Related Immunodeficiency Disease) because symptoms were observed primarily among gay men in urban areas such as San Francisco and New York City, the cause of the illness was not determined until 1984 and not officially renamed HIV until 1987. Because the media frequently portrayed communities with a large number of people with AIDS as an "infected" community, anyone identified as gay or lesbian, Haitian, hemophiliac, or using intravenous drugs often suffered job, housing, and medical discrimination as well as acts of physical VIOLENCE. Mainstream media exacerbated public fear and widened the divide between "infected" groups and "general populations."

People with AIDS (PWA) refused to be portrayed as victims of this disease. Instead, many organized themselves into activist and advocacy groups, such as the PWA Coalition, Body Positive, ACT UP (AIDS Coalition to Unleash Power), WARN (Women and AIDS Resource Network), and the Gay Men's Health Crisis, to obtain the services and support necessary to live with and manage their own disease. These self-advocacy organizations worked to change prevention and treatment efforts and to end discrimination. They advocated minimizing unsafe behaviors rather than stigmatizing certain people or groups.

In 1988 AIDS activists pressured Surgeon General Everett Koop to send out a detailed pamphlet to every household in the United States, which gave detailed accurate information regarding the practices that enabled HIV transmission. This began to transform the public idea of AIDS from an unstoppable plague to a type of chronic disease. Koop worked with AIDS advocates to shift the dialogue that had emphasized the morality of certain identities to focus instead on real public health policy: the ways in which the epidemic could be contained through behavioral changes—safe sex and safe injecting practices—and how increased efforts would be undertaken to research the causes of the disease and develop treatments for the infections. Activists also educated the public and the media on the need to support medical and economic assistance for those infected and to respect their civil rights.

Discovered in 1995, a "cocktail" of protease inhibitors, which are a combination of drugs that suppress the replication of the HIV virus in the blood system, allowed AIDS to become a "manageable" disease for those able to afford and tolerate those medications. These medications are very expensive, however, and people in many countries around the world cannot afford them. A pandemic with an estimated 25 million deaths worldwide continues.

The complex relationship between people with AIDS and the broad COMMUNITY of disability activists reflects diverse understandings of disability, issues of STIGMA and status, as well as strategies for EMPOWERMENT. For example, some disability activists were initially divided over advocacy for people with AIDS, in part because they did not consider AIDS a disability. At the same time, concerns over the stigma associated with disability motivated some people with AIDS and their allies to resist alliances with disability activists. Still, lawyers involved in communities affected by AIDS worked with disability activists to ensure that an enforceable prohibition on discrimination against people with AIDS was included in the 1990 AMERICANS WITH DISABILITIES ACT. Members of both communities came together to support this vote.

As some scholars have noted, people with AIDS and people with disabilities share other common features. For example, AIDS and disability activists have fought the prejudices against their communities. AIDS is still referred to as a "gay disease," and divisions between contaminated and uncontaminated populations continue to exist. In addition, the rise of disability and AIDS advocacy organizations that empower community members and demand accommodations marks an expansive understanding of civil rights; forms of public PROTEST demonstrate similar movement strategies as well. At the same time, tensions remain, and scholars and activists continue to critique the distinctive characteristics of AIDS and people with AIDS and the complications they pose to concepts of disability and disability IDENTITY.

AIDS and people living with AIDS have been an important and complicated part of American disability history. According to the Centers for Disease Control, in 2008,

roughly 1 million Americans currently live with HIV or AIDS. In addition to its significant demographic presence, the treatment, REPRESENTATION, and changing meaning of AIDS highlight many of the social, political, and economic factors that have shaped American history and the lives of disabled citizens in the United States.

See also ACTIVISM AND ADVOCACY.

Debra Levine

Further Reading:

Chambré, Susan Maizel. *Fighting for Our Lives: New York's AIDS Community and the Politics of Disease.* New Brunswick, N.J.: Rutgers University Press, 2006.

Cohen, Cathy. *The Boundaries of Blackness: AIDS and the Breakdown of Black Politics.* Chicago: University of Chicago Press, 1999.

Crimp, Douglas. *AIDS: Cultural Analysis/Cultural Activism,* Cambridge, Mass.: MIT Press, 1988.

Fee, Elizabeth, and Daniel M. Fox. *AIDS: The Making of a Chronic Disease.* Berkeley: University of California Press, 1992.

Grmek, Mirko D. *History of AIDS: Emergence and Origin of a Modern Pandemic.* Princeton, N.J.: Princeton University Press, 1990.

Sontag, Susan. "AIDS and Its Metaphors." In *The Disability Studies Reader,* edited by Lenny Davis, 153–160. New York: Routledge, 2006.

Air Carrier Access Act

People with disabilities have faced many challenges in efforts to travel by air. Legislation, such as the Federal Aviation Act of 1958 and the Rehabilitation Act of 1973, technically protected people with disabilities in any federally assisted programs but in reality these laws had little effect in protecting the civil rights of disabled passengers. Lobbying groups such as the PARALYZED VETERANS OF AMERICA sought protection under these acts, arguing that since all airlines and airports indirectly receive federal support, they should comply with federal civil rights legislation. After the Supreme Court rejected this argument in *Department of Transportation v. Paralyzed Veterans of America,* 477 U.S. 597, in 1986, Congress passed the Air Carrier Access Act later that year. Under this act the Department of Transportation developed consistent regulations regarding air travel for disabled passengers.

Since the passage of this act, an airline may not deny TRANSPORTATION on the basis of the person's impairment or limit the number of disabled passengers on a flight unless transportation of the person violates the Federal Aviation Administration's safety rules. In the case of a carrier that holds 30 or fewer passengers, transportation may be refused if the aircraft lacks a lift, boarding chair, or any other device required to enable access for disabled travelers. All carriers must be equipped with a Complaint Resolution Official (CRO) to address conflicts between the carrier and disabled travelers. If resolution is not attained, the passenger may file a complaint with the Department of Transportation (DOT).

Upon request, a disabled traveler must be provided with information regarding the carrier and the services available to them. An airline requires advance notice only in certain situations: if dangerous materials are needed for an assistive device (see ASSISTIVE TECHNOLOGY AND ADAPTIVE DEVICES), if the traveler needs an electric WHEELCHAIR on an aircraft with 60 or fewer seats, or if 10 or more disabled travelers need accommodation.

An airline may require that a traveler be accompanied by a flight attendant in the following cases: a person traveling on a stretcher or with the assistance of an incubator, a person who is unable to comprehend safety instructions, a person who would be in need of assistance in the case of evacuation due to a MOBILITY disability, and a person with severe hearing or sight who is in need of assistance if faced with evacuation.

The Air Carrier Access Act also extends to regulating an airport's service, accessibility, and assistance for disabled travelers. Under these regulations, airports are required to provide parking near the terminal and signs indicating these spots, accessible lounges, accessible water fountains, accessible baggage areas, accessible telephone stations, accessible ticketing stations, accessible medical stations, accessible lavatories, ramps, and lifts, and information systems made understandable for disabled passengers. Disabled travelers must undergo the same security measures as other travelers. The Air Carrier Access has greatly improved ACCESS to transportation. More accommodations are available for air travelers with disabilities today than at any time in history. Yet the availability of accommodations is inconsistent, and discriminatory treatment continues.

The Air Carrier Access Act has produced mixed results. Although airports became much more accessible to people with disabilities in the 1990s as a result of the law, reports of mistreated passengers continue to be registered. In the late 20th century, the National Council on Disability wrote numerous reports regarding continuing problems, lack of or poor employee assistance, and civil rights discrimination. In the face of these and other complaints, the DOT, in 2000, raised the penalty for airlines failing to meet regulations from $1,100 up to $10,000 for each infraction. Despite these higher fines, some airlines still fell short of meeting their obligations. In 2003 alone Southwest Airlines was penalized $500,000, U.S. Airways $400,000, and America West $150,000. The DOT allowed these airlines to allocate the money toward resolving the problems of their flawed systems.

Because it embodies economic, social, and political factors, activism on behalf of travelers with disabilities remains an important feature of the DISABILITY RIGHTS MOVEMENT.

See also AIRPLANES; IMPAIRMENT/IMPAIRED.

Arthur Holst

Further Reading:

Huber, Joe, and Jaime MacKool. "Turbulence in the Airline Industry Remains for Travelers with Disabilities." Available online. URL: http://proquest.umi.com.ezproxy.library.drexel.edu/pqdweb?index=2&did=646699271&SrchMode=1&sid=6&Fmt=4&VInst=PROD&VType=PQD&RQT=309&VName=PQD&TS=1150831847&clientId=18133. Accessed July 25, 2006.

National Council on Disability. "Enforcing the Civil Rights of Air Travelers with Disabilities: Recommendations for the Department of Transportation and Congress." Available online. URL: http://www.ncd.gov/newsroom/publications/1999/acaa.htm. Accessed July 25, 2006.

———. "Position Paper on Amending the Air Carrier Access Act to Allow for Private Right of Action." Available online. URL: http://www.ncd.gov/newsroom/publications/pdf/aircarrier.pdf#search='Air%20Carrier%20Access%20Act%20legislative%20history'. Accessed date?

Norrbom, C. E. *Mobility & Transport for Elderly & Disabled Persons.* New York: Gordon & Breach Publishing Group, 1991.

"Position Paper on Amending the Air Carrier Access Act to Allow for Private Right of Action." Available online. URL: http://www.ncd.gov/newsroom/publications/2004/aircarrier.hm. Accessed July 13, 2006.

Air Carrier Access Act (1986)

In 1986, Congress passed the Air Carrier Access Act, which authorized the Department of Transportation to develop regulations that protected airline travelers with disabilities. With some exceptions, the act prohibits airlines and airports from denying their services to disabled passengers and from limiting the number of disabled travelers allowed on individual planes. Although many people with disabilities continue to experience problems when traveling by air, this act represents an important move toward greater accessibility and inclusion.

**Air Carrier Access Act of 1986
TITLE 49, SUBTITLE VII, PART A,
subpart ii, CHAPTER 417, SUBCHAPTER I,
§ 41705**

§ 41705. Discrimination against handicapped individuals

(a) In General.— In providing air transportation, an air carrier, including (subject to section

40105 (b)) any foreign air carrier, may not discriminate against an otherwise qualified individual on the following grounds:

(1) the individual has a physical or mental impairment that substantially limits one or more major life activities.

(2) the individual has a record of such an impairment.

(3) the individual is regarded as having such an impairment.

(b) Each Act Constitutes Separate Offense.— For purposes of section 46301, a separate violation occurs under this section for each individual act of discrimination prohibited by subsection (a).

(c) Investigation of Complaints.—

(1) In general.— The Secretary shall investigate each complaint of a violation of subsection (a).

(2) Publication of data.— The Secretary shall publish disability-related complaint data in a manner comparable to other consumer complaint data.

(3) Review and report.— The Secretary shall regularly review all complaints received by air carriers alleging discrimination on the basis of disability and shall report annually to Congress on the results of such review.

(4) Technical assistance.— Not later than 180 days after the date of the enactment of this subsection, the Secretary shall—

(A) implement a plan, in consultation with the Department of Justice, the United States Architectural and Transportation Barriers Compliance Board, and the National Council on Disability, to provide technical assistance to air carriers and individuals with disabilities in understanding the rights and responsibilities set forth in this section; and

(B) ensure the availability and provision of appropriate technical assistance manuals to individuals and entities with rights or responsibilities under this section.

Source: Excerpted from the U.S. Department of Transportation Web site at http://airconsumer.ost.dot.gov/rules/382short.doc.

airplanes

Airplanes represent one of the most significant TRANSPORTATION innovations of the 20th century, but the relationship between disability and this new mode of travel has been largely overlooked by scholars. Examining several aspects of this complicated relationship reveals contests over accessibility, compliance, and EMPOWERMENT and points to rich possibilities for future research.

The first successful airplane was built in 1903 by Wilbur and Orville Wright. Since that time, planes evolved quickly, expanding seating space, flight longevity, control, and purpose. During the early decades of the 20th century, some people believed that plane rides could "CURE" forms of deafness, and pilots such as Charles Lindbergh charged special fees to take DEAF passengers on flights intended to regain their hearing. Eventually this dangerous and unsuccessful "cure" fell out of favor. Airplane manufacture, like other assembly-line industries, also provided economic opportunities for many disabled workers, particularly during WORLD WAR I and WORLD WAR II when many able-bodied laborers left for the battlefields.

Individuals with disabilities who have wanted to fly planes commonly faced both attitudinal and technological challenges. Deaf people particularly drew attention to pilots from their COMMUNITY, such as Nellie Zabel Whillhite, who, after her solo flight on January 13, 1928, was acknowledged by many to be the first deaf pilot in the world. Deaf flying clubs and community newspaper accounts of "successful" deaf pilots celebrated their achievements and cast these pilots as evidence that deaf people were completely "NORMAL." More rare were cases of pilots with multiple disabilities, such as Jack Calveard of Louisville, Kentucky. Deaf since birth and partially paralyzed, Calveard in 1954 became the first pilot with those impairments to fly in America. Calveard used the media attention he garnered to challenge stigmatizing REPRESENTATIONS of people with disabilities in general. In subsequent decades, local, national, and international ORGANIZATIONS for deaf and disabled pilots have been established, including the International Wheelchair Aviators (founded in 1972), the International Deaf Pilot Association (founded in 1994), and the Deaf Pilots Association (since 2001). In the 21st century some flight schools, such as the Anglo-American Training, USA, offer specialized training for disabled pilots. Funding opportunities, such as the Able Flight Scholarship (established in 2006), enable people with disabilities to learn how to fly as well as offering opportunities for pilots who have been disabled to train as sports pilots.

Although the increase in training opportunities for pilots has signaled important progress, accessibility has continued to be a problem for passengers with physical impairments and limited MOBILITY. The airline industry expanded rapidly during the second half of the 20th century, becoming for many Americans an increasingly popular mode of transportation. For citizens with mobility and other impairments, however, airplanes represented a strikingly inaccessible feature of American life. Steep steps to enter planes, narrow aisles, inaccessible toilets, tight seats, and policies that block disabled travelers from sitting in emergency exits, represent some of the many features that activists have criticized over the decades. Anecdotal evidence suggests widespread discriminatory attitudes toward disabled travelers by members of the airline industry, including reservation staff, flight attendants, customer service agents, disability service representatives, and managers. Disability activists particularly since the 1970s have fought to eliminate these barriers. The 1986 AIR CARRIERS ACCESS ACT, which prohibits airlines from denying transportation because of a person's disability, and the 1990 AMERICANS WITH DISABILITIES ACT (ADA), which addresses antidiscrimination policies in EMPLOYMENT, transportation, and accommodations, reflect activist efforts to create more inclusive travel options for Americans. Since March 1990 the Department of Transportation has published these approved ADA guidelines and regulations. Still, anecdotal evidence and subsequent lawsuits reveal that many airlines continue to discriminate against disabled travelers in numerous ways, such as refusing to allow them to sit in emergency exit rows, not providing accessible means to enter and exit airplanes, requiring that disabled passengers sign legal indemnity forms, and speaking to disabled individuals in hostile and degrading ways.

Travel by airplanes thus continues to embody complex and contradictory meanings in the history of disability in America. As a vocation and hobby, flying has enriched the lives of many disabled citizens; however, for many others airplanes represent a mode of transportation and a major symbol of American culture that remains inaccessible. In this way, airplanes and air travel also reflect the diverse and complicated position of America's broad disability community.

Sylvie Soulier
Susan Burch

Further Reading:
Department of Transportation. URL: www.DOT.org.
"Disabled Pilot Plans to Pass Along 'Fantastic Gift' to Others." EEA Org News (6 February 2008). Available online. URL: http://64.233.169.104/search?q=cache:41z5scrFxIAJ:www.eaa.org/news/2008/2008-02-06_ableflight.asp. Accessed February 6, 2008.
Gannon, Jack. *Deaf Heritage.* Silver Spring, Md.: National Association of the Deaf, 1980. Available online. URL: www.disabilitytravel.org. Accessed March 10, 2008.

Alexander Graham Bell Association for the Deaf

Originally named the American Association to Promote the Teaching of Speech to the Deaf, the Alexander Graham Bell Association for the Deaf (AGBAD) has been a driving force behind the oralist movement in the United States for over a century.

Established in 1890 at the New York conference of the Convention of American Instructors of the Deaf, the AGBAD has focused on one objective: to promote speech and lipreading to DEAF individuals. The organization was renamed in 1956 to honor its founder and first president, ALEXANDER GRAHAM BELL, inventor of the telephone and a devoted advocate of ORALISM.

Although oral training historically occurred mostly in schools, the ORGANIZATION has sought to recruit allies beyond the traditional membership of deaf educators by connecting with the parents of deaf CHILDREN. An important means for sharing the organization's vision is its journal, which began in 1899 as the *Association Review*, ; it was renamed the *Volta Review* in 1910. The *Volta Review* primarily has addressed issues in deaf education but included parenting advice and other issues that appealed to a broader audience. A new bimonthly journal, *Volta Voices,* has been available since 1994. It includes news of technological advances, legislative updates, as well as professional networking and support.

The organization's headquarters are housed in the Volta Bureau in Washington, D.C. Built as a research site for Bell in 1893 with the funds the French government awarded him for his invention of the telephone, the bureau now includes a reference library and an archival center open to the public for research on deaf-related topics.

Since the early 1900s the organization has expanded to include over 5,000 members, international affiliates, and representative chapters across the United States. To support its diverse membership, the AGBAD manages three separate sectors within the organization. The International Parents' Organization, established in 1958, provides resources for families with deaf children, including workshops and outreach programs, as well as scholarships for oral education of deaf children. In 1964 the Oral Deaf Adults Section was formed to serve deaf adults and families of deaf children, particularly promoting speech and lipreading through social gatherings and vocational education. The International Organization for the Education of the Hearing Impaired, established in 1967, represents a global network initiative to promote oralism. Through this section, chapters of the organization have been formed in every state as well as in more than 38 countries.

The AGBAD has also exerted its influence in launching major campaigns outside the realm of education. From the 1920s to the 1940s the AGBAD Board of Directors collaborated with the Deaf cultural community to denounce various state bans against deaf drivers (see AUTOMOBILES). Over the past 20 years the AGBAD has focused advocacy efforts on such issues as the AMERICANS WITH DISABILITIES ACT in 1990 and CLOSED CAPTIONING laws.

Backed by influential leaders and supporters, such as CAROLINE YALE and former U.S. president Calvin Coolidge, the AGBAD has formed powerful networks to disseminate its oral philosophy worldwide. Its mission to provide deaf people with skills to assimilate successfully into mainstream society has resonated with generations of Americans; close links to parents, the medical profession, and policymakers has enabled the organization to remain a powerful and influential force in the education of deaf people. Today, the AGBAD is at the forefront of exploring new technologies, such as COCHLEAR IMPLANTS and genetic testing, to find a CURE for deafness.

Long-standing conflicts also define the group's history. Many deaf cultural advocates have opposed the AGBAD and its mission. Insisting that deaf people deserve to learn their "natural" language—AMERICAN SIGN LANGUAGE—and pointing to the limited success of oralism, these advocates question the values and rationale for promoting linguistic and cultural assimilation of deaf people.

Understanding the history of the AGBAD enhances the meaning of broader American and disability history, demonstrating additional ways that educational activism and policies reflect social values and expectations. The conflicts arising from such expectations also reveal changing notions of citizenship, normalcy (see NORMAL AND NORMALCY), and culture.

Lindsey Patterson

Further Reading:

Abel, Emily K. "Like Ordinary Hearing Children: Mothers Raising Offspring According to Oralist Dictates." In *Women and Deafness: Double Visions,* edited by Brenda Jo Brueggemann and Susan Burch, 130–146. Washington, D.C.: Gallaudet University Press, 2006.

"Alexander Graham Bell Association for the Deaf." Subject File. Washington, D.C.: Gallaudet University Archives.

Alexander Graham Bell Association for the Deaf Web site. URL: www.agbell.org.

Bruce, Robert V. *Alexander Graham Bell and the Conquest of Solitude.* Boston: Little Brown, 1973.

Van Cleve, John Vickrey, and Barry Crouch. *A Place of Their Own: Creating the Deaf Community in America.* Washington, D.C.: Gallaudet University Press, 1989.

Allen, Frances (1854–1941) and Mary (1858–1941) *photographers*

Frances and Mary Allen, or "The Misses Allen" as they were most often called, became internationally recognized photographers in the early 20th century. Their personal and professional experiences highlight the importance of FAMILY, artistic expression, and GENDER.

The sisters were born to a successful farmer, Josiah Allen, and his wife, Mary Stebbins, in the town of Deerfield,

Massachusetts. Frances Stebbins Allen, the elder, was born August 10, 1854, and Mary Electa Allen was born May 14, 1858. In the fall of 1874, both Frances and Mary began attending a two-year program at the State Normal School teacher's college in Westfield, Massachusetts. The two entered the teaching profession in 1876, but by 1886 both had experienced significant hearing loss, which ultimately contributed to their decision to leave the field. The specific source of the loss is unknown but did not seem to have surfaced as a significant problem until they were in their late 20s and early 30s.

In 1893 the two sisters traveled to Boston to be examined at the Massachusetts Eye and Ear Infirmary, where it was determined that Frances would not benefit from surgery on her ears but that Mary might. Thus, surgery was performed on Mary but it proved unsuccessful and she apparently made use of an ear trumpet for some time.

Frances and Mary Allen had apparently first been exposed to PHOTOGRAPHY by their brother, Edmund Allen, who often took photographs for his job as a civil engineer in the 1880s, as the sisters were going DEAF and leaving their careers as teachers. By at least 1884, while they were still teaching, Frances and Mary were photographing with the use of a view camera and creating albumen prints. By the turn of the 20th century the sisters turned to photography as a means of creative expression as well as EMPLOYMENT.

Mary Allen repeatedly described their work as a cross between "art" and "craft." She may have designated it so because photography served as both artistic expression and basic income for the sisters via portrait photography and through the photographic illustration of magazine articles that they were often commissioned to complete when this new technique began to replace engravings. They typically worked within four subjects or themes: re-creating posed scenes of colonial life; capturing the natural and posed interactions of children; documenting natural scenes around Deerfield and also on several trips to the western United States and abroad; and illustrating the vibrant arts and crafts movement, including pageants and performances, in the Deerfield area.

In 1900 their work, together with that of 30 other American women photographers, was featured in the Universal Exposition in Paris. The Allen sisters found themselves the center of considerable attention when the exhibition organizer, Frances Benjamin Johnston—herself a well-known photographer and critic—declared the sisters two of "the Foremost Women Photographers in America" in a July 1901 issue of *Ladies Home Journal*.

Following on this fame, they opened their own formal studio in 1901 by converting an upstairs bedroom in their home into their darkroom while the parlor downstairs became the salesroom. In 1904 the Allen Sisters began publishing catalogs of their images. Their last catalog was published in 1920. Mary Allen apparently continued to work

Titled "How d'y do?" this picture taken by Deerfield, Massachusetts, photographer Frances Allen around 1900 shows two women dressed in 19th-century attire greeting each other. Frances and her sister Mary Allen, both of whom were deaf, were leading American photographers in the early 20th century.   *(Library of Congress)*

throughout the 1920s but Frances's sight began to deteriorate considerably during that decade. Scholars know little of their daily lives for the years following the end of their published photography in 1920 until their deaths in 1941, except that Frances, now also BLIND, continued to garden and would walk the equivalent of a mile on their front porch most days. Their FAMILY resources had left them with a house they had occupied most of their lives, and they lived and worked within a vibrant community of craftspeople and artisans, as well as good neighbors, who most likely helped take care of them in these last years.

Frances Allen died on February 14, 1941. Mary Allen died four days later on February 18, 1941. Their work is archived and on exhibit at the Memorial Hall Museum in Deerfield, Massachusetts, and a collection of their photography has traveled to many cities and galleries across the United States. An "Allen Sisters Retrospective" was first created in 1984 and 1985, and there were a few traveling exhibits beginning in 1997 before the 2002 "The Allen Sisters: Pictorial Photographers 1885–1920" opened at Memorial Hall Museum. This exhibit traveled from 2003 to 2006 with the exhibit at Gallaudet University in spring 2006 as the last venue.

Although they did not themselves associate with other members of the American deaf COMMUNITY at this time, the "deaf eyes" of the Allen sisters and their turn to, and skill at, photography did stem from the loss of their hearing. Their deafness and their gender also seems to have mattered in their collaborative techniques, their mutual support of each other in art and life, and their conversion of their home's primary social space into their studio.

Brenda Jo Brueggemann

Further Reading:

Flynt, Suzanne L. *The Allen Sisters: Pictorial Photographers, 1885–1920.* Foreword by Naomi Rosenblum. Deerfield, Mass.: Pocumtuck Valley Memorial Association and University Press of New England, 2002.

Griffith, Bronwyn A. E., ed. *Ambassadors of Progress: American Women Photographers in Paris, 1900–1901.* Giverny, France: Musée d'Art américan, 2001.

almshouses

For much of the history of the United States, the almshouse was one of the main governmental responses to the needs of poor, elderly, and disabled people and their families. The facilities existed under different names from state to state—almshouse, poorhouse, workhouse, poor farm—but they shared a common function of serving as the disposal site for all of those deemed "surplus" population (i.e., unproductive and dependent). They also shared a common administrative location with their operation and oversight handled primarily by county governments.

By the end of the colonial period, and using the Elizabethan Poor Laws as the model, a number of large cities in the Northeast, such as Boston in 1664 and New York City in 1736, had established a facility for "indoor relief," or, in other words, residential facilities for those who were, for various reasons, found to be economically dependent. By the middle of the 19th century, almost every county in the states of the Northeast and Midwest had at least one almshouse. Between 1824 and 1850 the number of almshouses in Massachusetts more than doubled from 83 to 204. Indeed, unlike most states, Massachusetts actually established three state-run almshouses in addition to expanding the county system. Other states showed a similar pattern of rapid growth.

While most almshouses paid little attention to the emerging diagnostic categories of disability, they did often make a basic distinction between the "able-bodied poor" and the "truly needy." The truly needy included not only the elderly and "infirm" but also those identified with various types of psychological or cognitive disabilities. The treatment of many of these "insane" and "idiotic" individuals was usually primitive and cruel, with many houses using what was often called the "crazy cellar" as the place of confinement for those seen as most incapable of any work. A few crusaders such as DOROTHEA DIX mounted very public campaigns to expose the squalid conditions in which many of these disabled individuals were confined. It was partially in reaction to these exposés that states began to establish the network of specialized ASYLUMS AND INSTITUTIONS that still exist today. The combination of these schools, HOSPITALS, and other residential settings, along with a slow expansion of "in home" FAMILY support, and a growing wave of child-protection legislation, led to a gradual shift of the population of disabled poor away from the local almshouse either back to the family or to the growing network of state-managed facilities. Some almshouses themselves became specialized state mental hospitals or otherwise specialized institutions. By 1900 the almshouses had, in most states, become "old age homes" for the elderly poor, a public precursor to today's network of privately run nursing homes.

See also POVERTY.

Philip M. Ferguson

Further Reading:

Ferguson, Philip M. "The Legacy of the Almshouse." In *Mental Retardation in America: A Historical Reader,* edited by Noll Trent and J. W. Trent, Jr., 40–64. New York: New York University Press, 2004.

Katz, M. B. *In the Shadow of the Poorhouse: A Social History of Welfare in America.* New York: Basic Books, 1986.

Rothman, David J. *The Discovery of the Asylum: Social Order and Disorder in the New Republic.* Boston: Little, Brown, 1971.

Alzheimer's disease

Alzheimer's disease (AD) was established as a diagnosis in 1910 by German psychiatrist Emil Kraepelin, but it remained little known for the next 70 years. Kraepelin named the condition for his protégé, Alois Alzheimer, who a few years earlier had published a detailed description of the brain pathology and clinical symptoms of a 51-year-old woman with DEMENTIA. Both the pathology—senile plaques and neurofibrillary tangles (an abnormal and dense collection of twisted fibers that collect in the brain)—and clinical symptoms had previously been described in the psychiatric literature on senile dementia. What seemed novel about the case was the relatively young AGE of the patient. This seemed to Kraepelin to warrant a separate DISEASE category, and he thus called AD a pre-senile dementia that occurred in people under the age of 65, in contrast to the much more common senile dementia that often affected older people. Alzheimer himself questioned the significance of the age distinction, and although AD was recognized in subsequent decades, it was widely believed that AD and senile dementia were essentially identical.

Apart from this confusion over classification, from the 1930s through the 1950s American psychiatrists, led by David Rothschild, argued that both AD and senile dementia were better thought of as psychodynamic disorders rather than brain diseases. Since correlations between the amount of brain pathology found at autopsy and the degree of dementia in life were far from perfect, they argued that social and psychological factors could best explain any particular case of dementia. This psychodynamic model seemed to bring dementia into mainstream psychiatry in America, but the age-associated dementias still did not attract a great deal of attention from American psychiatry as a whole. A series of studies done by a British team from the late 1960s through the 1970s established the pathological basis of these disorders.

AD became a major public issue in the late 1970s through the efforts of a coalition of caregivers (see CAREGIVING) and family members, biomedical researchers, and government officials intent on winning greater public attention and support for the condition. They claimed that chronic dementia in the elderly is a disease process rather than a normal part of AGING, thereby agreeing with people within gerontology and geriatrics who argued that aging itself should not normally be accompanied by disease and disability. Neurologist Robert Katzman argued in an influential 1976 article that AD and senile dementia ought to be seen as a unified entity and that this entity should be called AD rather than senile dementia. The problem was large. Katzman claimed that AD was the fourth or fifth leading cause of death in the United States, and with the eventual aging of the baby-boom generation in the 21st century, it would soon become enormous. Calling the unified category AD made it a disease entity with a well-established pathological basis in the brain, a disease that was "real" and thus worthy of a massive research effort into its cause and CURE.

Two other developments were crucial to the rising prominence of AD: the creation in 1974 of the National Institute on Aging (NIA), which focused on AD, and the creation in 1980 of the Alzheimer's Disease and Related Disorders Association—later shortened to the Alzheimer's Association—which provided support for family caregivers and lobbied for federal money for research. Second, gerontologist Robert Butler, founding director of the NIA, believed that the agency needed a disease-specific focus to successfully compete for funding with the other National Institutes of Health and that AD as reconceptualized by Katzman was a perfect fit for the fledgling institute. With the combined efforts of the NIA and Alzheimer's Association, federal funding for AD research grew dramatically, from less than $1 million in 1976 to $700 million in 2005.

Thus, nearly a century after it was named, AD became the dominant approach to chronic, age-associated dementia. Nonetheless, critics questioned the value of the construct and the strategy used to make it a prominent public problem. Some pointed out that insisting that AD be regarded as a disease distinct from aging was somewhat arbitrary. Since the incidence of AD rises steadily with age, and all of the markers for AD can typically be found in the brains of older people, it seemed plausible to view AD as an extreme point on a spectrum of normal cognitive aging. Others argued that the effort to promote AD has in fact been too successful. The "Alzheimerization" of the federal budget makes it difficult to win support for broader research on aging. Still others decried the overwhelming focus on biomedical mechanisms to the exclusion of social and psychological aspects of the problem. Today, increasing numbers of people diagnosed with dementia and their families struggle to find more meaningful frameworks for dealing with their experience of dementia.

Jesse F. Ballenger

Further Reading:

Ballenger, Jesse F. *Self, Senility and Alzheimer's Disease in Modern America: A History.* Baltimore: Johns Hopkins University Press, 2006.

Beach, Thomas G. "The History of Alzheimer's Disease: Three Debates." *Journal of the History of Medicine and Allied Sciences* 42 (1987): 327–349, 987.

Katzman, Robert, and Katherine L. Bick, eds. *Alzheimer Disease: The Changing View.* San Diego, Calif.: Academic, 2000.

Leibing, Annette, and Lawrence Cohen, eds. *Thinking about Dementia: Culture, Loss and the Anthropology of Senility.* New Brunswick, N.J.: Rutgers University Press, 2006.

Whitehouse, Peter J., Konrad Maurer, and Jesse F. Ballenger, eds. *Concepts of Alzheimer Disease: Biological, Clinical and Cultural Perspectives.* Baltimore: Johns Hopkins University Press, 2000.

American Annals of the Deaf

Established in 1847 by the faculty of the AMERICAN SCHOOL FOR THE DEAF in Hartford, Connecticut, the *American Annals of the Deaf* is the oldest educational journal still in production today. Thirty years after the founding of the American School for the Deaf in 1817, teachers Luzerne Rae and Samuel Porter recognized the rising interest in EDUCATION and pedagogy. They envisaged the *Annals* as a means to promote the field of DEAF education and teacher training. Rae served as its first editor, from 1848 to 1854.

The journal grew unevenly at the outset but solidified as the field of deaf EDUCATION took root in America. In 1850 the newly created Convention of Instructors of the Deaf (CAID) made the *Annals* its official journal. Afterward, the *Annals* included papers presented at the biannual CAID conferences as well as articles written specifically for the periodical. As its scope and subscriber base broadened, the journal increasingly presented national perspectives on deaf educational issues. The CIVIL WAR (1861–65) disrupted production of the *Annals,* but the publication resumed in 1868.

The *Annals* generally espoused moderate and conservative views on deaf education. For example, during the late 19th century and much of the 20th century, it tended to support ORALISM (speech and lipreading) over signed communication. Deaf cultural advocates, then and now, attempted to offer alternative perspectives to oralism with varying success. White, male hearing editors and contributors dominated the periodical since its inception. In more than 160 years of publication, the *Annals* has yet to have a deaf or a female editor. In spite of these limitations, the *Annals* has served as an important venue for pedagogical debates as well as for discussion of broader issues facing the deaf community. Particularly before the advent of accessible telecommunications such as the TTY and the INTERNET, the journal provided a crucial forum for intellectual exchanges. Heated debates over JOHN FLOURNOY's proposal to establish a deaf-only state in the 1850s, for example, played out extensively in the *Annals,* as did discussions of racial segregation, EUGENIC ideology, and the feminization of deaf education in the late 19th century. From early on, contributors have presented articles based on scientific research, often addressing ways to eliminate or "CURE" deafness. Since the late 19th century, the journal has included international perspectives, particularly from Europe but increasingly from other regions.

In the mid-20th century, the *Annals* became the official journal of both CAID and its partner organization, the Conference of Educational Administrators Serving the Deaf (CEASD), which was founded in 1868. The Joint Administrators Committee, which consists of presidents and executive members from each organization, oversees production.

The *American Annals of the Deaf* provides a rich source for understanding both deaf history and American history more generally. As a repository of discussions and debates within the field of education it offers clear evidence of the attitudes and aspirations of leading figures in education. In addition, the evolution of the *Annals* highlights changing ideas about language and related concepts of citizenship, IDENTITY, and community.

See also PRINT MEDIA; RESIDENTIAL SCHOOLS; SPECIAL EDUCATION; TTY.

Lindsey Patterson

Further Reading:

Gannon, Jack. *Deaf Heritage.* Silver Spring, Md.: National Association of the Deaf, 1981.

Schein, Jerome D. "American Annals of the Deaf." In *Gallaudet Encyclopedia on Deaf People and Deafness,* edited by John Vickrey Van Cleve, 15–17. New York: McGraw-Hill, 1987.

Winzer, Margaret A. *The History of Special Education: From Isolation to Integration.* Washington, D.C.: Gallaudet University Press, 1993.

American Association of the Deaf-Blind

The American Association of the Deaf-Blind (AADB) was founded in 1937 as the National League for the Deaf-Blind. Over several decades the ORGANIZATION expanded its mission, shifting from a service-oriented to a membership agency. Reflecting its changing character and goals, the AADB underwent several name changes from the National League of the Deaf-Blind to the National Association of the Deaf-Blind to the National Association of the Deaf-Blind of America, ultimately adopting in 1979 its present name, the American Association of the Deaf-Blind.

The AADB is distinguished as a national consumer-based ORGANIZATION in which people who are DEAF-BLIND direct, guide, and supervise its programs. The purpose of the AADB is to empower all deaf-blind people by promoting options that foster individuals' independence and full inclusion in society; the term "deaf-blind" is not always a complete inability to hear and see but includes all levels of hearing and vision loss. The association serves as an informational resource for members of the deaf-blind community, and its close collaboration with the American Red Cross and sign language interpreting organizations encourages improved ACCESS and support. In addition, the AADB hosts national conferences and provides a listserv group where deaf-blind people can interact, build relationships, and share information.

As part of its advocacy for increasing deaf-blind people's access and independence, the AADB in recent years has drawn attention to the need for more qualified support service providers (SSPs). These are specially trained individuals who provide visual, auditory, and environmental information to a deaf-blind consumer. SSPs provide sign language interpretation as well as transportation and assistance in daily activities, such as grocery shopping, transacting business at the bank, or attending events.

In the early 21st century the AADB counted 1,250 members, including deaf-blind individuals, their FAMILY members, SIGN LANGUAGE INTERPRETERS, and other professionals working with the deaf-blind COMMUNITY. New AADB initiatives have focused on assisting individuals who have lost their sight or hearing later in life and who may not identify as deaf-blind. Greater recognition of multiculturalism has motivated the AADB to consider new forms of outreach to the larger community. For example, the group established a committee to reach the Latino population and is examining ways to provide Spanish language options on their Web site.

The struggle to achieve civil rights and to empower marginalized people remains an enduring theme in American history. The evolution of advocacy organizations such as the AADB embody these themes, revealing new ways of understanding disability and citizenship.

See also ACTIVISM AND ADVOCACY; EMPOWERMENT.

Empish J. Thomas

Further Reading:

Boggs-Qualls, Rosezelle. *Walking Free: The Nellie Zimmerman Story.* Richmond, Iowa: Densmore Reid Publications, 2002.

Charlton, James. *Nothing About Us Without Us: Disability Oppression and Empowerment.* Berkeley: University of California Press, 1998.

Lawhorn, Geraldine. *On Different Roads.* New York: Vantage Press, 1991.

American Association of People with Disabilities

The American Association of People with Disabilities (AAPD) is a cross-disability advocacy group with headquarters in Washington, D.C. It is a nonprofit agency, founded in 1995. Its primary focus is to bring about full inclusion of people with disabilities throughout American life and cul-

ture. Members of AAPD are especially active in cases in which they perceive the AMERICANS WITH DISABILITIES ACT (ADA) and the Rehabilitation Act of 1973 (see VOCATIONAL REHABILITATION ACT) are under attack.

AAPD was created by several powerful leaders of the DISABILITY RIGHTS MOVEMENT as a vehicle for exerting national pressure: JUSTIN DART, who had been chair of the President's Committee on Employment of People with Disabilities; PAUL G. HEARNE, president of the Dole Foundation; I. KING JORDAN, president of GALLAUDET UNIVERSITY; John D. Kemp, president and CEO of Very Special Arts (now called VSA ARTS); and SYLVIA WALKER of Howard University.

Members of AAPD work closely with other disability groups, including ADAPT, Justice for All, and PARALYZED VETERANS OF AMERICA. The organization produces action alerts when important legislation, votes, and hearings arise; sponsors forums on disability issues; and provides services, such as group health insurance. Since 1999 AAPD has hosted Disability Mentoring Day. The event, originally supported by the White House, involves several thousand students from around the United States who visit Washington, D.C., to learn about careers and government operations and to meet national leaders and each other.

In 2000 AAPD began sponsoring the annual Paul G. Hearne Leadership Award, honoring the businessman and cofounder of AAPD. This $10,000 award is given to a young person who has shown leadership potential in disability rights. Another one of AAPD's high-profile activities is awarding the annual Betts Award to people who have contributed to furthering disability rights. The award, which includes a prize of $50,000, was created in 1989 by the Prince Charitable Trust and the Rehabilitation Institution of Chicago (RIC), and it is named in honor of Henry B. Betts, a Chicago specialist in rehabilitation medicine. In 2001 AAPD joined with RIC to oversee this award.

AAPD is significant because of its cross-disability success. Few advocacy groups that serve the community as a whole have survived for long periods of time. It is also important for its vigilance about the ADA. It has identified powerful allies and corporate sponsors that support its mission and have ensured its existence.

See also ACTIVISM AND ADVOCACY; ORGANIZATIONS.

Katherine Ott

Further Reading:

Barnartt, Sharon, and Richard Scotch. *Disability Protests: Contentious Politics, 1970–1999.* Washington, D.C.: Gallaudet University Press, 2001.

Charlton, James I. *Nothing About Us Without Us: Disability Oppression and Empowerment.* Berkeley: University of California Press, 1998.

American Association on Intellectual and Developmental Disabilities

Originally named the Association of Medical Officers of American Institutions for Idiotic and Feeble-Minded Persons in 1876, the American Association on Intellectual and Developmental Disabilities (AAIDD) is one of the oldest professional groups focusing on the prevention and treatment of MENTAL RETARDATION and developmental disabilities. During its century and a third of existence, the AAIDD has undergone numerous transformations, serving as a reflection of American society's changing attitudes toward individuals with intellectual and developmental disabilities.

During its first 30 years, the association represented small group of medical professionals associated with institutions and ASYLUMS. Its first president was EDOUARD SÉGUIN, a French immigrant and leading researcher on "IDIOCY." In 1906 the association changed its name to the American Association for the Study of the Feeble-Minded (AASFM) to allow nonphysicians such as educators and administrators to join. This would be the first of many name changes for the association, mostly based on the diversification of its professional membership but also accompanying changes in attitudes and terminology (see LANGUAGE AND TERMINOLOGY) related to the care and treatment of individuals with intellectual disabilities.

Early publications from the organization's first journal, *The Journal of Psycho-Asthenics* (1896–1918), focused on the importance of institutions in the care of "FEEBLEMINDED" persons, the alleged need for their segregation from society, and the promotion of EUGENICS (the use of selective breeding techniques to control and improve the human race). In the era of WORLD WAR I, data from the U.S. Army and other INTELLIGENCE TESTS suggested that a significant number of Americans qualified as feebleminded. Members of the association concluded that if so many individuals were diagnosed with sub-NORMAL intelligence, community-based services were needed to meet the demand. Consequently, in 1917, the association publicly reversed its original position on treatment options and began advocating for a more open, tolerant view of mental retardation. Four years later, hoping to standardize clinical practice and research efforts, the AASFM published the first official manual on the definition and classification system of mental retardation.

In 1933 the AASFM membership voted for another name change to the American Association on Mental Deficiency (AAMD). At the time, professionals considered terms such as "mental deficiency" and "mental sub-normality" more medically appropriate and less stigmatizing than feebleminded and idiot. The association became incorporated in 1938 and its membership grew to include psychologists, social workers, and prison officials among professionals who had begun to provide services to individuals with mental retardation in the community and in other institutional settings. In 1918 the association ceased publishing the *Journal of Psycho-Asthenics* and for the next 21 years published proceedings of its annual meetings. In 1940 the association began publication of a new quarterly journal, the *American Journal of Mental Deficiency (AJMD)*.

The association's first executive director, Glenn E. Milligan, was hired in 1960 and a second serial publication, *Mental Retardation (MR)*, was launched in 1963 to accommodate the growing number of submissions to the *AJMD*. This new journal served as the official organ of the AAMD, but, over time, it developed into an influential scientific research journal. During the 1960s the association became more involved in federal legislation and advocacy efforts, such as President JOHN F. KENNEDY's Panel on Mental Retardation (see PRESIDENT'S COMMITTEE FOR PEOPLE WITH INTELLECTUAL DISABILITIES), members also testified in judicial hearings, encouraging increased legal rights for mentally retarded individuals.

The emergence of the parents' advocacy and the DISABILITY RIGHTS MOVEMENTS during the 1960s and 1970s encouraged the association to open its membership to individuals with mental retardation and their FAMILY members; by 1975, the AAMD had 11,000 members, including community representatives. Since 1980 the AAMD's membership has grown to more than 50,000 individuals across 55 countries and its research efforts on behalf of individuals from the disability COMMUNITY and their families has increased significantly.

During the 1980s and 1990s the association responded to new broad interest in multiculturalism, publishing numerous family-related studies that focused on the needs and coping skills of culturally diverse and nontraditional family environments. In 1987 AAMD adopted a new name, the American Association on Mental Retardation (AAMR), and the *AJMD* was changed to the *American Journal on Mental Retardation*. Discussions to remove the term "mental retardation" from the association's name and journal titles began in the late 1990s, and, in 2007, the organization became the American Association on Intellectual and Developmental Disabilities (AAIDD). Many consumers and advocates applauded the association's new approach because they considered "mental retardation" both stigmatizing and inaccurate; others, however, criticized the group, noting that these changes were overdue.

In the 21st century the association's membership consists of faculty members, researchers, and service professionals as well as consumers and family members who participate in various levels of the association's activities.

Pressing legal issues for some people with intellectual disabilities has drawn the organization's attention since 2000. For example, in 2001, the AAMR, along with other groups, successfully petitioned the U.S. Supreme Court to stop executing individuals with intellectual disabilities who are convicted of serious crimes. The association's current mission is to promote progressive policies, sound research, effective practices, and universal rights for people with intellectual disabilities. This reflects the association's evolution from a small group of physicians focused on institutional care to an interdisciplinary organization of professionals, consumers, and family members interested in the physical, intellectual, social, and improvement of the legal status of persons with intellectual and developmental disabilities.

See also ACTIVISM AND ADVOCACY; COGNITIVE AND INTELLECTUAL DISABILITY; DEVELOPMENTAL DISABILITY.

Laurel Iverson Hitchcock

Further Reading:

American Association on Mental Retardation. *Mental Retardation: Definitions, Classification, and Systems of Support.* 10th ed. Washington, D.C.: American Association on Mental Retardation, 2002.

Blacher, Jan, and Bruce L. Baker. *The Best of the AAMR, Families and Mental Retardation: A Collection of Notable AAMR Journal Articles across the 20th Century.* Washington, D.C.: American Association on Mental Retardation, 2002.

Braddock, David. *Disability at the Dawn of the 21st Century and the State of the States.* Washington, D.C.: American Association on Mental Retardation, 2002.

Trent, James W., Jr. *Inventing the Feeble Mind: A History of Mental Retardation in the United States.* Berkeley: University of California Press, 1995.

American Association on Mental Retardation

See AMERICAN ASSOCIATION ON INTELLECTUAL AND DEVELOPMENTAL DISABILITIES.

American Association to Promote the Teaching of Speech to the Deaf   See ALEXANDER GRAHAM BELL ASSOCIATION FOR THE DEAF.

American Athletic Association of the Deaf

See USA DEAF SPORTS FEDERATION.

American Coalition of Citizens with Disabilities

Founded in 1974 by MAX STARKLOFF, JUDY HEUMANN, FRED FAY, and ED ROBERTS, the American Coalition of Citizens with Disabilities (ACCD) represented a confederation of ORGANIZATIONS dedicated to advancing the civil rights of people with disabilities. At the 1974 meeting of the PRESIDENT'S COMMISSION ON EMPLOYMENT OF THE HANDICAPPED, a group of disability rights activists, each representing an organization for people with disabilities, met informally and identified common goals. They committed their organizations to forming a coalition, which they named the ACCD.

Prior to this time, NONDISABLED people led most organizations dedicated to people with disabilities, but the cofounders of ACCD all had disabilities. They decided that their organization should exemplify belief in the abilities of people with disabilities by requiring that individuals with disabilities maintain leadership roles. The cofounders recruited activists with a wide range of physical disabilities to play key roles in the ACCD. These subsequent leaders included Anna Fay, Lex Frieden, Pat Pound, Eunice Fiorioto, Roger Petersen, FREDERICK SCHREIBER, and Deborah Kaplan. Organizations representing people with developmental disabilities, such as People First (see SELF ADVOCATES BECOMING EMPOWERED), joined the ACCD, but their members did not hold leadership positions.

A widespread lack of compliance to SECTION 504 of the Rehabilitation Act of 1973 (see VOCATIONAL REHABILITATION ACT) prompted the founding of this cross-disability coalition. Section 504 guaranteed that qualified people with disabilities were eligible to participate in any program or activity funded by the federal government. Organizations such as the NATIONAL ASSOCIATION OF THE DEAF, the AMERICAN COUNCIL OF THE BLIND, the PARALYZED VETERANS OF AMERICA, and the NATIONAL SPINAL CORD INJURY ASSOCIATION joined the ACCD to demonstrate a united front on the issue.

In the first three years of ACCD, its leaders and member organizations bore all expenses themselves. In 1976 they began receiving grants for their community coalition-building and civil rights efforts. The cofounders hired FRANK BOWE, a disabilities activist interested in coalition building, as the paid director of ACCD and the organization continued to rely on grant funding until 1983. Board members often disagreed on the prioritization of ACCD goals and on the allotment of funds to meet those goals. Board members often pursued individual projects without reaching consensus on the funding for those projects. And when civil rights grant opportunities decreased, the organization disbanded in 1983 due to lack of funds.

The crowning achievement of the ACCD was its role in securing the implementation of Section 504. In 1977, after the ACCD led lobbying and civil disobedience efforts, the Carter administration created and implemented specific regulations detailing the exact requirements of Section 504. The ACCD also lobbied successfully for the passage of the 1978 amendments to the Rehabilitation Act of 1973. The amendments provided funding for states to develop Independent Living

Centers where people with disabilities could receive services including VOCATIONAL TRAINING, housing referrals, and self-advocacy training. The ACCD helped to procure equitable education for children with disabilities. The coalition lobbied for WHEELCHAIR ACCESS to buses, AIRPLANES, and trains. And ACCD director Frank Bowe assisted Congress in drafting the Education of all Handicapped Children Act of 1975.

Despite its disbanding, the successes of the ACCD comprised an integral step toward the 1990 passage of the landmark AMERICANS WITH DISABILITIES ACT (ADA). The ACCD armed a generation of youthful activists with the skills and experiences needed to achieve social change. All ACCD leaders continued to participate actively in the disability rights movement. For example, board member Lex Frieden contributed to drafting the ADA. In 1974 then vice president Gerald Ford recognized the efforts of disability activism in his speech to the President's Commission on Employment of the Handicapped, claiming: "We are coming into a new day in which handicapped people are expressing themselves, are making their voices heard, are arriving at their own decisions." The ACCD afforded people with disabilities a forum to make themselves heard and to serve as leaders in their own movement for civil rights.

See also DISABILITY RIGHTS MOVEMENT; SELF-ADVOCATES AND SELF-ADVOCACY.

Anne Kish

Further Reading:

"Rights of the Handicapped." *The CQ Researcher* (November 26, 1974). Available online. URL: http://library.cqpress.com/ index.php. Accessed August 10, 2006.

University of California Berkeley Archives. "The Disability Rights and Independent Living Movement." 2004. Available online. URL: http://bancroft.berkeley.edu/collections/ drilm/index.html. Accessed August 1, 2006.

U.S. Department of Justice. "A Guide to Disability Rights Laws." 2005. Available online. URL: http://www.usdoj.gov/crt/ada/ cguide.htm. Accessed August 10, 2006.

American Council of the Blind

The American Council of the Blind (ACB) is one of the largest advocacy groups for the BLIND in the United States.

Its origins are closely linked to the NATIONAL FEDERATION OF THE BLIND (NFB), a civil rights ORGANIZATION founded in 1941 by JACOBUS TENBROEK. The ACB was founded on July 6, 1961, in Kansas City, Missouri, when several dozen NFB members walked out of an NFB convention and elected Ned Freeman as the ACB's first president. The early leaders of the ACB believed that tenBroek had too much control over the NFB, and that state affiliates did not have autonomy to control their resources and set policies. This split within the organized blind movement would eventually be referred to as the "civil war," and it would shape the character of both the NFB and ACB for decades.

The ACB spent much of the 1960s and 1970s organizing state affiliates, and, in many cases, battling with NFB affiliates for membership and financial resources. Over the course of its first two decades, the organization fashioned a separate IDENTITY that was more than merely oppositional to the NFB and its leaders. The ACB proved more willing to seek compromise and reconciliation with the public institutions charged with providing services to the blind. For example, it became more closely allied with the SHELTERED WORKSHOPS, which employed the blind and the associations that accredited them.

Throughout the 1980s the ACB focused on issues the membership identified as most salient: assisting blind individuals to secure or retain EMPLOYMENT. Several resolutions passed by the ACB membership addressed the subminimum wage paid blind employees in "sheltered workshops." The ACB called for legislation that would ensure that the blind were paid at least 75 percent of the federal minimum wage in all employment settings.

In the 1990s the ACB focused its attention on the decline of BRAILLE literacy among the blind. There were fewer teachers of Braille, and many schools believed that Braille was obsolete due to the advent of the personal computer and recorded books on tape. In 2002 the ACB brought suit against the U.S. Treasury Department claiming that the lack of accessible currency created a substantial barrier to the ability of blind people to engage in commercial activities. This suit is still pending in the federal appeals court following an initial favorable ruling on the part of a federal district judge.

Today the ACB counts tens of thousands of members and 71 affiliated groups, including at least one affiliate in each of the 50 states. Its board includes a president, vice president, second vice president, secretary, treasurer, and eight board members. All officers, except the secretary and treasurer, are required by ACB bylaws to be blind.

The two major organizations representing the blind, NFB and ACB, have never reconciled, despite a short-lived effort in 1985. The ACB emphasizes its democratic procedures and focuses on inclusiveness and diversity of voices. This commitment to diversity often means that ACB avoids establishing a single philosophy that governs all its policies, preferring to allow the democratic process within the organization to determine the organization's position. Against charges that the organization is less than effective at influencing national trends in the field of blindness, the ACB asserts the benefits of a diversity of voices about blindness and the blind in the world.

The continued existence of two consumer-driven advocacy organizations for the blind is explained by competing philosophies and approaches to effecting change and the long memories of the leadership of both organizations of the history of bitter rivalry. Some advocates compare the two organizations to political parties with differing policy platforms, each with its own view on what the blind need to achieve to secure the goals of independence and integration into society. Other advocates chafe against the fracturing of the voice of the blind into competing camps, and they see the existence of two organizations as a barrier to effecting change as there is no one single voice for the nation's blind. There seems to be little immediate prospect of comprehensive cooperation between ACB and NFB, however, as each organization focuses on growing its membership, increasing its revenues, and expanding its influence at the local, state, and federal levels.

Brian R. Miller

Further Reading:

Koestler, Francis. *The Unseen Minority: A Social History of Blindness in America.* New York: David McKay, 1976.

Matson, Floyd. *Walking Alone, Marching Together: A History of the Organized Blind.* Baltimore: NFB Press, 1990.

Megivern, James J., and Margorie L. Megivern. *People of Vision: A History of the American Council of the Blind.* Washington, D.C.: American Council of the Blind, 2003.

American Disabled for Accessible Public Transit

See AMERICAN DISABLED FOR ATTENDANT PROGRAMS TODAY.

American Disabled for Attendant Programs Today

American Disabled for Attendant Programs Today (ADAPT) is an important activist group in American DISABILITY RIGHTS MOVEMENTS for nearly three decades. Founded in 1978 with the name American Disabled for Accessible Public Transit, ADAPT has conducted street protests favoring accessible public TRANSPORTATION and expansion of personal attendant services for people with disabilities.

ADAPT grew out of the Atlantis Community, an independent living center in Denver, Colorado. In 1978 disabled activists in WHEELCHAIRS led by WADE BLANK, a NONDISABLED minister and activist, protested the lack of accessible public transportation by surrounding two buses in Denver. For four years, the demonstrators continued their PROTESTS, engaging in "crawl-ins," in which wheelchair users would attempt to crawl up the steps of a bus, and the disruption of Regional Transit District (RTD) board meetings. In 1982

the RTD conceded and ordered 89 new accessible buses and subsequently agreed to retrofit all of its existing buses with wheelchair lifts.

ADAPT became a national organization in 1983 and invited 40 disability activists from around the country to Denver to train them in protest tactics for the upcoming annual conference of the American Public Transit Association (APTA), the trade association for public transportation providers. For the next six years, ADAPT mobilized protests at APTA conventions, chaining themselves to inaccessible buses and blocking access to convention sites.

In 1990 ADAPT organized protests in support of the passage of the AMERICANS WITH DISABILITIES ACT (ADA). ADAPT's WHEELS OF JUSTICE March, held in Washington, D.C., in support of the ADA, attracted between 500 and 1,000 demonstrators. After listening to speakers, dozens of wheelchair users abandoned their chairs and began to crawl up the front steps of the Capitol building, each carrying a scroll with the opening words from the Declaration of Independence. The next day, 150 ADAPT demonstrators conducted a sit-in in the rotunda. Three months after the ADAPT protests, Congress passed the ADA and it was signed into LAW by President George H. W. Bush.

After the passage of the ADA in 1990, ADAPT changed its name (although it maintained the same acronym) and its primary focus, seeking redirection of MEDICAID'S LONG-TERM CARE funds to pay for personal assistance services that would permit people with impairments to live independently instead of within nursing homes. Attendant services include help with activities of daily living (e.g., eating, dressing, toileting, etc.) and other types of household assistance such as meal preparation, shopping, and management of finances.

ADAPT, with slogans of "free our people" and "stolen lives," has conducted numerous protests against the unnecessary INSTITUTIONALIZATION of people with disabilities in nursing homes. One notable demonstration involved the country's largest nursing home, Laguna Honda, in San Francisco. In 2001 the announcement of plans to renovate the city-owned facility, at a cost of over $400 million, outraged disability activists who believed the money would be better spent for COMMUNITY-based services that provided more independence to those being served. Over 600 members of ADAPT and other disability ORGANIZATIONS gathered on the grounds of the 1,200-bed facility to call for its closure.

When the Medicaid Community-Based Attendant Services and Supports Act (MiCASSA) was introduced in Congress in 2001, over 500 ADAPT members gathered in Washington to support the legislation, blocking traffic for seven hours and picketing the White House. In 2003, ADAPT organized a 144-mile "Free Our People" march by 250 protesters, many using wheelchairs, from Philadelphia to Washington, D.C. ADAPT activists have continued to advocate for expanded attendant services to improve the autonomy and quality of life for people with disabilities.

See also ACTIVISM AND ADVOCACY.

Richard K. Scotch

Further Reading:

Shapiro, Joseph P. *No Pity: People with Disabilities Forging a New Civil Rights Movement.* New York: Times Books, 1993.

Switzer, Jacqueline Vaughn. *Disabled Rights: American Disability Policy and the Fight for Equality.* Washington, D.C.: Georgetown University Press, 2003.

American Federation of the Physically Handicapped

From 1942 to 1958 the American Federation of the Physically Handicapped (AFPH) served as a leading ORGANIZATION advocating greater ACCESS and opportunity for people with physical disabilities. With strong connections to the labor movement, the AFPH lobbied Congress, promoted legislative policies that would increase EMPLOYMENT opportunities for people with disabilities, and sponsored dances, parties, and other social events for its members. After 16 years, the organization folded under financial pressures and a dispute over the leadership of the organization's founder PAUL STRACHAN and was replaced by a new organization, the NATIONAL ASSOCIATION OF THE PHYSICALLY HANDICAPPED.

In 1942, after two years of organizational work, Paul Strachan chartered the AFPH, a national pan-disability activist organization. The goals of the young group were succinctly articulated in 1944 by Agnes Schnaus, a national AFPH vice president who testified before a U.S. House of Representatives subcommittee investigating the problems faced by people with disabilities. Schnaus and the AFPH called for the establishment of a federal agency for people with disabilities that would provide them with medical care and aids such as eyeglasses or WHEELCHAIRS, EDUCATION, training, and, most importantly, job placement. Additionally, the AFPH sought greater access to public buildings as well as monthly pension and educational opportunities for individuals deemed unfeasible for rehabilitation. Fundamentally, AFPH members wanted equal access to job opportunities. According to Schnaus, the AFPH demanded an end to "all unfair discrimination against the employment of otherwise qualified but physically HANDICAPPED applicants."

The AFPH grew rapidly and, by 1946, the organization had branches across the nation. Membership was particularly heavy in urban and industrial areas in states such as Michigan, Pennsylvania, and New York, and, by 1947, the organization counted some 17,000 members. On the local level, lodges sponsored dances, holiday parties, athletic teams, and picnics, providing members with a space to socialize with other people with disabilities. Lodges also allowed members the opportunity to address local concerns. For example, members of the Carville, Louisiana, lodge who had all been diagnosed with Hansen's disease (also known as LEPROSY) used their membership in the AFPH to raise awareness of their condition.

AFPH founder Paul Strachan had been a labor organizer and had close ties to major unions, including the American Federation of Labor, the Congress of Industrial Organizations, the UNITED MINE WORKERS OF AMERICA, and the International Association of Machinists. On the national level, the AFPH pushed for numerous initiatives, including increased medical research and rehabilitation reform. Dissatisfied with what they perceived as the patronizing attitude of rehabilitation professionals in the Federal Security Agency's (FSA) Office of Vocational Rehabilitation and the limited range of services offered, AFPH activists and their allies in the labor movement sought to move federal-state rehabilitation services from the FSA to the Department of Labor, where the emphasis would be on job training and placement rather than on medical supervision. In 1945 the AFPH won approval for its initiative to make the first week in October "NATIONAL EMPLOY THE PHYSICALLY HANDICAPPED WEEK." The AFPH also successfully pushed for the establishment of the President's Committee on National Employ the Physically Handicapped Week, which launched a year-round effort to promote the employment of people with disabilities.

WORLD WAR II played a significant role in the success of the AFPH. As the nation's factories began to produce the implements of WAR in the early 1940s and while the federal government recruited able-bodied men to serve in the armed forces, employers increasingly hired workers with disabilities. Some 83 percent of the nation's factories hired people with disabilities during the war. Awareness of disability issues also increased after the war because the nation and its leaders felt they owed a great debt to the country's disabled soldiers. The AFPH promoted this view, arguing that people with disabilities had played a major role in winning the war; but, as the war faded from the nation's memory in the 1950s, this consciousness of disability waned. Additionally, Strachan made plans for the AFPH to build the Institute for Human Engineering, a massive residential facility in Florida where people with disabilities could receive medical treatment, education, training, and job placement. Strachan's obsession with the institute caused him to turn his attention away from national legislation and created continued pressures to raise additional funds, and, as a result, he lost supporters. Furthermore, Strachan alienated former allies in the labor movement by his constant appeals for additional money to support both the AFPH's legislative agenda and the institute. As national politics became more conservative in the 1950s and Strachan's influence waned, he became caustic, bitter, and, worst of all, critical of his strongest supporters. In 1958 the organization dissolved, and many members launched a new organization, the National Association of the Physically Handicapped. Although much of the group's legislative agenda had failed, the AFPH succeeded in forcing the federal government to reexamine its disability policies, and this pressure created real results. For example, in 1940, only about 11,890 disabled citizens benefited from the federal rehabilitation program, however, and by 1959, the number had grow dramatically to 80,739.

See also LABOR UNIONS; VOCATIONAL REHABILITATION.

Audra Jennings

Further Reading:

Jennings, Audra. "'The Greatest Numbers . . . Will Be Wage Earners': Organized Labor and Disability Activism, 1945–1953." *Labor: Studies in Working-Class History of the Americas* 4, no. 4 (November 2007): 55–82.

"Paul A. Strachan." Biographical file. Washington, D.C.: Gallaudet University Archives.

American Foundation for the Blind

The American Foundation for the Blind (AFB) was founded in 1921 by a group of professionals providing services for BLIND people. Represented publicly for many years by the renowned DEAF-BLIND figure Helen KELLER, AFB is dedicated primarily to the dissemination of information to the blind and vision-impaired.

In the early 20th century, the return of a significant number of WORLD WAR I–blinded VETERANS heightened interest in rehabilitation services and programs for blind youth and adults. Blindness professionals, however, disagreed on the best methods to address the EDUCATION, EMPLOYMENT, and negative depictions of blind people in society.

In 1921, at their biennial convention in Vinton, Iowa, members of the American Association of Workers for the Blind, an advocacy group dedicated to promoting a unified code for blind readers, passed a resolution to create an independent ORGANIZATION to meet the needs of the blind people and professionals in the field on a national level. The new organization was named the American Foundation for the Blind. In 1922 M. C. Migel, a philanthropist and president of the New York Commission for the Blind, was elected president of AFB. He held this position until 1945, when he moved to the newly created post of chairman of the board.

In its earliest days, AFB focused on improving access to information for people who were blind. One early notable accomplishment included AFB's successful effort to standardize the English BRAILLE CODE at a time when there were many different styles of raised print technology competing for primacy. AFB also worked to improve the capabilities of the Braille stereotyper, a machine that could print two-sided Braille in large quantities, making Braille production less costly and more widespread. In 1931 AFB helped draft the Pratt-Smoot bill, which established the NATIONAL LIBRARY SERVICE FOR THE BLIND AND PHYSICALLY HANDICAPPED (NLS) at the Library of Congress. In 1933 AFB engineers developed the first long-playing TALKING BOOKS record and player and began recording audio books for NLS.

In 1924 AFB gained a popular and influential spokesperson in Helen Keller. At a time when blindness was even more widely viewed with suspicion, fear, or as a social liability, Keller became a model of what a person who was not only blind but also DEAF could achieve. Keller and her teacher ANNE SULLIVAN (MACY) were AFB's chief spokespersons between 1924 and 1929. Keller was named a trustee and AFB's ambassador and counselor on national and international relations, a job she held until her death in 1968.

Throughout the decades that followed, AFB's work focused on meeting the predominant needs of the blind and visually impaired population in the United States. AFB's devotion to blind veterans and the vision rehabilitation of newly blinded adults continued through WORLD WAR II. In the 1950s and 1960s disease outbreaks led to an increasing number of blind and deaf-blind CHILDREN, and AFB devoted its resources to the development of model early childhood education programs for blind children. It also spearheaded a growing movement to establish standards for schools that trained professionals and agencies providing services to blind children and adults. While AFB discontinued its activities to develop and market new products and technology in the 1990s, it continues to work with developers and manufacturers to ensure that blind or visually impaired people are guaranteed ACCESS to rapidly advancing technologies. AFB has also continued its advocacy for national legislation, playing a key role in the passage of the AMERICANS WITH DISABILITIES ACT in 1990. In the early 21st century AFB has turned its focus to the graying population and the growing epidemic of age-related eye diseases in the United States. At the same time, AFB is increasingly using INTERNET technology to continue its primary mission, distributing information on blindness to people with vision loss, their families, and professionals in the field.

See also ACTIVISM AND ADVOCACY.

Judy Evans

Further Reading:

American Foundation for the Blind. "75 Years of AFB and Talking Books." American Foundation for the Blind Web site. Available online. URL: http://www.afb.org/section. asp?sectionID=69. Accessed December 17, 2007.

———. "Helen Keller." American Foundation for the Blind Web site. Available online. URL: http://www.afb.org/Section.asp?SectionID=1. Accessed December 17, 2007.

Koestler, Frances A. *The Unseen Minority: A Social History of Blindness in the United States.* 2d ed. New York: AFB Press, 2004.

American Indian Disability Technical Assistance Center

The American Indian Disability Technical Assistance Center (AIDTAC) was established in October 2000 to help American Indians and Alaska Natives with disabilities reach their EMPLOYMENT goals and lead productive lives. According to the 2000 UNITED STATES CENSUS, nearly 2.5 million Americans identify themselves exclusively as "American Indian or Alaska Native." The same census listed 4.1 million people identifying themselves either as Indian only or as Indian in combination with another RACE. Approximately 22 percent of the American Indian and Alaska Native population has one or more disabilities. An important goal of AIDTAC is to provide assistance in a culturally sensitive manner. The work has expanded to include Native Hawaiians, a third group of indigenous people who comprise the Native American population. AIDTAC is located at the University of Montana Rural Institute, and the center addresses disability-related issues such as employment, TRANSPORTATION, health, independent living, voter participation, and EDUCATION.

A Rural Institute project (1993–2000), titled the American Indian Disability Legislation (AIDL), formed the foundation for AIDTAC. The project, funded by the NATIONAL INSTITUTE ON DISABILITY AND REHABILITATION RESEARCH, conducted research among federally recognized tribes to determine the necessary accommodations for tribal members with disabilities. Although federally recognized tribes are exempt from the AMERICAN WITH DISABILITIES ACT (ADA), the project assisted several tribes to develop policies similar to the ADA while at the same time respecting tribal sovereignty and culture diversity. Traditionally, American Indians and Alaska Natives have no concept of disability parallel to Western understanding, but disabilities constitute accepted parts of their Creator's design. The AIDL project used a consultation method called the Tribal Disability Actualization Process (TDAP) to initiate group discussions concerning disability topics on Indian reservations. The TDAP is based on the long-held Indian tradition known as "talking circles," which requires respectful listening to group members. The project resulted in several tribal governments' resolutions related to employment and other accommodations for tribal members with disabilities, demonstrating that tribes can develop disability legislation consistent with the ADA without U.S. government intervention.

In 2000 AIDTAC was formally created through a five-year grant from the Department of Education, Rehabilitation Services Administration. The project trained tribal and urban vocational counselors, helping them to provide culturally sensitive employment consultation for Native American Social Security Administration beneficiaries with disabilities. AIDTAC staff and contracted trainers conducted TDAP workshops and self-employment seminars in tribal lands across America as well as modified sessions in urban areas.

A project titled the Technical Assistance on Native American Culture (TANAC) began in 2005 with funding from the SSA. In accordance with AIDTAC objectives, TANAC provides training and technical assistance on Native American culture to Community Work Incentive Coordinators who are employed by nonprofit ORGANIZATIONS in every state and contracted to advise SSA beneficiaries with disabilities on their employment options.

In 2006 AIDTAC was funded by the Administration for Developmental Disabilities under a grant through the Help American Vote Act to provide cultural training for Protection and Advocacy (P&A) representatives who work in every state, assisting people with disabilities on a variety of legal and advocacy issues. The Native American Considerations on the Electoral Participation project trains P&A staff working to increase electoral participation by Native Americans with disabilities.

AIDTAC continues to serve organizations and individuals to create equal opportunities for Native Americans with disabilities. Awareness of unique traditions, values, and communication styles is essential for respectful interaction within the diverse mixture of cultures found in the United States.

See also ACTIVISM AND ADVOCACY; ETHNICITY; LAW AND POLICY; ORGANIZATIONS; VOTING.

William Payne

Further Reading:

Dwyer, K., L. Fowler, T. Seekins, C. Locust, and J. Clay. "Community Development by American Indian Tribes: Five Case Studies of Establishing Policy for Tribal Members with Disabilities." *Journal of the Community Development Society* 31, no. 2 (2001): 196–215.

"Special Issue on American Indians and Disabilities." *Common Thread . . . from the RTC Rural* (Summer 1999). RTC: Rural, the University of Montana Rural Institute. Available online. URL: http://rtc.ruralinstitute.umt.edu/Indian/AmICT.htm#In_this_Issue. Accessed November 15, 2007.

Stromnes-Elias, Katja. *A Field Guide for Community Work Incentives Coordinators: How to Improve Services to Native American Social Security Beneficiaries with Disabilities.* Missoula, Mt.: American Indian Disability Technical Assistance Center, 2007.

Understanding Disabilities in American Indian and Alaska Native Communities: Toolkit Guide. Washington, D.C., National Council on Disabilities, 2003. Available online. URL: http://www.ncd.gov/newsroom/publications/2003/native_toolkit.htm. Accessed November 15, 2007.

American National Standards Institute   See ANSI.

American Printing House for the Blind

The American Printing House for the Blind (APHB) is America's oldest agency dedicated to providing textual services and materials to BLIND citizens. The APHB began with the efforts of two blind men, Morrison Heady and Dempsey B. Sherrod. In 1854 Heady solicited private donations for mass production of John Milton's *Paradise Lost* in embossed text. In 1856 Sherrod successfully lobbied states to collaborate in the establishment and funding of a national publishing house for the blind. In 1858, with promised funding from multiple states and agreement on the Louisville site, the General Assembly of Kentucky passed "An Act to Establish the American Printing House for the Blind."

In 1860 the APHB operations began in the basement of the Kentucky Institution for the Education of the Blind, but they were soon interrupted by the CIVIL WAR (1861–65) as the facility was converted into a military hospital and funds promised from Southern states were redirected to war efforts. After the WAR, however, Sherrod, Heady, superintendents from a number of blind schools, and the APHB trustees were able to once again secure funds and to resume operations. In 1866 the APHB published *Fables and Tales for Children,* the first mass-produced book in raised text. *Fables and Tales for Children,* a shortened version of John Gay's *Fables,* a popular book of poems written to appeal to CHILDREN published in 1727, was published in the raised letter font called Boston Line Letter.

Although the APHB quickly became the provider of embossed materials to the nation's schools for the blind, its status as the national publishing house was not established until 1879 with passage of the 1879 Act to Promote the Education of the Blind. Passage of this legislation was the direct result of the combined efforts of national leaders, including the American Association of Instructors of the Blind (AAIB), educators, and grassroots advocates.

As the national publishing house for books and materials for the blind, the APHB played an important role in debates over embossed type. Prior to the APHB, schools for the blind produced their own embossed books, and there were a number of unique type styles employed, rather than a single universal standard. Because schools wanted materials in their preferred type, creating raised print texts became quite costly. The APHB took the lead in calling for a type standard. But the "type question" was not easily or quickly settled. Each type system had passionate advocates campaigning for its adoption as the standard. Trustees on the APHB board, many of whom were also superintendents of schools for the blind and advocates of a particular type, employed their influence to control publication at APHB. Some, including the superintendent of the APHB, resorted to subterfuge to influence the outcomes of votes within the AAIB. This long, bitter, and contentious debate raged for more than 60 years and became known as the "WAR OF THE DOTS" or the "typefight." The "war" finally ended in 1932 with the adoption of Standard English Braille as the uniform system of type for all publications for the blind in the United States. This change eliminated the need to support multiple tactile systems and freed APHB funds and time for development of large type and recorded books.

Originally incorporated as a nonprofit institution that manufactured embossed books and appliances for students enrolled in the schools for the blind, the APHB has grown be the largest, private, nonprofit producer of materials for blind and visually impaired persons in the United States. In 1985 the APHB produced "Echo Commander" and "Talking Apple Literacy," the first publicly available talking computer programs. Today, the APHB catalog is quite extensive and includes digital recordings and computer software. Among the other services it offers, the APHB creates customized BRAILLE, audio, or tactile graphic forms and documents and assistive technology development that facilitate inclusion, access, and ADA compliance. The field services department works with external organizations to provide training and information about blindness and visual impairments as well as about APBH products and services.

The APBH is unique among American organizations having been started by and continuing to be run by blind people. In the tradition of its founders, blind and visually impaired people serve on advisory committees and on the Board of Trustees and they work as employees or volunteers. Just as in the past, determination of offerings, operations, and future directions are driven by input of the APBH's blind and visually impaired clientele. As such, the APBH is an organization run for and by people who make up the DISABILITY CULTURE and possess the experience necessary to best respond to the needs of its constituency.

See also ACCESS AND ACCESSIBILITY; TALKING BOOKS.

Beth R. Handler

Further Reading:

American Printing House for the Blind. "APH: What Is the American Printing House for the Blind?" *About APH.*

Available online. URL: http://www.aph.org/about /hist. html. Accessed October 10, 2006.

Thompson, Ken D. *Beyond the Double Night.* Taylorsville, Ky.: Buggy Whip Press, 1996.

Zahl, Paul A., ed. *Blindness: Modern Approaches to the Unseen Environment.* New York: Hafner Press, 1973.

American Revolution (1775–1783)

The foremost result of the American Revolution, fought between the 13 colonies and Great Britain from 1775 to 1783, was American independence. As the term *revolution* makes clear, historians have characterized the period as one of profound change in which not only the political but also the social and cultural fabric of North America was dramatically altered. How that change affected the lives of Americans with physical or mental impairments (see IMPAIRED/IMPAIRMENTS) is difficult to ascertain, as the disability history of the Revolutionary period has yet to be studied adequately.

The research that has been done suggests that, on the whole, the Revolution did not constitute a radical break with the colonial American past. For the remainder of the late 18th century, and a large part of the 19th, Americans with impairments continued to live and work in their local communities just as they had in pre-Revolutionary times. Moreover, those requiring care or assistance did not usually receive such attention in an institutional setting at the hands of a self-conscious, professional class of medical practitioners or rehabilitation specialists. Instead, they were treated or supported in their own homes by their families, friends, or neighbors. HOSPITALS and SPECIAL EDUCATION facilities for the "disabled" would not emerge on a large scale until well into the 19th century.

The ideological conditions that allowed INSTITUTIONALIZATION to be seen as an acceptable response to "disability" can be traced back to the late 18th century. It is hard, however, to establish a categorical link between this development and the Revolution. Lennard Davis, a leading scholar in DISABILITY STUDIES, has persuasively argued that the emergence of "disability" as a distinct social category was also occurring in Britain at about the same time. It seems, therefore, that any transformation in attitudes toward impairment in the United States constituted part of a much wider cultural trend occurring throughout the Atlantic world rather than a direct product of the Revolution.

The one area in which the Revolution can be seen to have had a decisive impact on American disability history concerns the relationship between the nation-state and its "disabled" citizens. Almost immediately after it came into existence, the federal government involved itself directly in disability issues. Beginning in the early 1790s, Congress passed a series of military pension acts aimed at compensat-

"ORDERED, That the case of Margaret Corbin, who was wounded and utterly disabled at Fort Washington, while she heroically filled the post of her husband, who was killed by her side serving a piece of Artillery, be recommended to a further consideration of the Board of War, This Council being of the opinion that notwithstanding the rations which have been allowed her, she is not Provided for as her helpless situation really requires."

—from Minutes of the Supreme Executive Council of Pennsylvania, in 1779

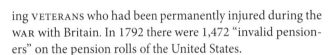

ing VETERANS who had been permanently injured during the WAR with Britain. In 1792 there were 1,472 "invalid pensioners" on the pension rolls of the United States.

The most significant of the early pension laws was the "Act to regulate the Claims to Invalid Pensions" passed on February 28, 1793. Under this act, claimants had to "prove decisive disability to have been the effect of known wounds" received during the Revolutionary War. "Disability" was understood in terms of an inability to labor for a living and was to be assessed by "two physicians or surgeons." The definition of disability as an inability to work because of physical impairment had been made by Congress before, but the involvement of doctors as medical specialists in the certification process marked a new development. To a large extent, then, the 1793 act can be seen as evidence of an increasing "medicalization" in the legislative construction of disability. This process would intensify in the next century and affect the lives of an ever-growing number of Americans classified by the state as "disabled." The law of 1793 should, therefore, be considered one of the foundations upon which all other subsequent national disability policies were built.

Daniel Blackie

Further Reading:

Davis, Lennard J. "Dr. Johnson, Amelia, and the Discourse of Disability in the Eighteenth Century." In *"Defects": Engendering the Modern Body,* edited by Helen Deutsch and Felicity Nussbaum, 54–74. Ann Arbor: University of Michigan Press, 2000.

Library of Congress. *A Century of Lawmaking for a New Nation: U.S. Congressional Documents and Debates, 1774–1875.* Available online. URL: http://memory.loc.gov/ammem/amlaw/lawhome.html. Accessed August 29, 2006.

Mutschler, Ben. "The Province of Affliction: Illness in New England, 1690–1820." Ph.D. diss., Columbia University, 2000. Available online. URL: http://wwwlib.umi.com/dissertations/fullcit/9985926. Accessed February 15, 2005.

American School for the Deaf

One of the most significant institutions in American DEAF history is the American School for the Deaf (ASD), founded in Hartford, Connecticut, in 1817 as the Connecticut Asylum for the Education and Instruction of the Deaf and Dumb Persons. As the original place where Deaf people gathered in sizable numbers and learned a common language—sign language—ASD embodies distinctive features that have defined the DEAF COMMUNITY for almost 200 years.

PARENT ADVOCACY GROUPS and individual aspirations, along with the rise of missionary spirit and democratic activism in early 19th-century America, provided the necessary means to establish the residential school. Before 1815 affluent families occasionally sent their deaf CHILDREN to Braidwood Academy in Scotland to gain an EDUCATION. Geographic distance, cost, and political strains between the United States and Britain during and after the War of 1812 made this option increasingly unappealing. Hartford physician MASON FITCH COGSWELL encountered these same issues as he hoped to educate his deaf daughter, Alice. A neighbor of the Cogswell family and recent graduate of Yale University and Andover Theological Seminary, THOMAS HOPKINS GALLAUDET met the deaf girl in 1814. Their interaction inspired him to collaborate with Cogswell and others to educate deaf people in America. In 1815 Cogswell helped raise funds for Gallaudet to study the teaching methodologies for the deaf in Europe.

First arriving in Great Britain, Gallaudet encountered obstacles at the Braidwood Academy because of the proprietors' commitment to keep their techniques private. An exhibition in London by representatives from the National Institute, originally a free school for the deaf founded in Paris by Abbé de l'Epée, ultimately led Gallaudet to France. Teachers at the school welcomed the American minister's quest to study and apply their educational methods in the United States. At the institute, Gallaudet met LAURENT CLERC, a deaf teacher and former pupil of the school.

The first permanent residential school for the deaf, the American School for the Deaf was founded in Hartford, Connecticut, in 1817. This photograph shows the original hub of American deaf culture before school buildings were moved to a new location in 1921. *(Gallaudet University Archives)*

After working together for a few months, Gallaudet invited Clerc to return with him to establish a residential school in Connecticut.

After returning to the United States in 1816, Gallaudet and Clerc traveled widely, holding public EXHIBITIONS to raise awareness and funds for the institution. The idea of public education had begun spreading in the northern part of the country, and the Connecticut legislature set an important precedent of government support in special education when it agreed to fund the deaf school. The plan for ASD included free tuition to deaf pupils aged seven to 50 years from all over New England; it also enrolled African Americans and females. The residential institution enabled pupils to live and study together for most of each year. These features promoted the gathering together of a comparatively diverse population.

On April 15, 1817, the Connecticut Asylum for the Education and Instruction of the Deaf and Dumb Persons opened. (It was renamed the American School for the Deaf in 1895.) Gallaudet became the principal while Clerc served as a head teacher. Seven students enrolled in the first class and 24 would join them by the end of the academic year. The first pupils included Cogswell's daughter Alice. Sophia Fowler who would later marry Gallaudet, and Eliza Boardman, who became Clerc's wife after attending the institution for two years, were also among the original cohorts. ASD was a pioneering school in numerous ways, admitting the first African-American student in 1825, and it remained an integrated institution thereafter.

The ASD became a model for other institutions. Deaf members at ASD developed folklore and visual HUMOR, produced a rich and vivid storytelling tradition, and commonly intermarried, creating cultural traits that would flourish at the many state RESIDENTIAL SCHOOLS based on ASD founded during the next six decades. Alumni often remained nearby, creating alumni associations and expanding ties within the community. The American school no longer provided only classroom instruction but also fostered the growth of a distinct cultural community. Even as ORALISM gained prominence in deaf schools in the late 19th and 20th centuries, ASD continued to offer signed communication inside and outside the classroom. The institution produced many leaders within the Deaf community, including EDMUND BOOTH and JOHN HOTCHKISS.

In 1925 a replica of the Thomas Hopkins Gallaudet and ALICE COGSWELL statue (the original was installed in 1889 at GALLAUDET UNIVERSITY) was erected on ASD's campus in honor of the founder and first pupil. Since WORLD WAR I the institution has continued to produce leaders in the Deaf community, such as actor and community activist Gil Eastman, Deaf minister HENRY WINTER SYLES, and SOPHIA FOWLER GALLAUDET. It was not until the 21st century that ASD had its first deaf superintendent, Harvey Jay Corson, who served from 2001 until 2006.

The American School for the Deaf holds a significant place in deaf history as the first permanent residential school and the birthplace of an American deaf cultural community. It serves an important role in American history, too, because it represents a tangible example of the reform movements of early 19th-century America and the nation's enduring interest in EDUCATION.

Lindsey Patterson

Further Reading:

American School for the Deaf Residential Schools File, Gallaudet University Archives.

Gannon, Jack. *Deaf Heritage.* Silver Spring, Md.: National Association of the Deaf, 1981.

Van Cleve, John Vickrey, and Barry Crouch. *A Place of Their Own: Creating the Deaf Community in America.* Washington, D.C.: Gallaudet University Press, 1989.

Contract between Thomas Gallaudet and Laurent Clerc (1816)

As cofounders of the first permanent school for the deaf in the United States, Protestant minister Thomas Hopkins Gallaudet (1787–1851) and Laurent Clerc (1785–1869) often are cast as "founding fathers" in the history of the American deaf community. On June 13, 1816, they signed a contract in Paris in which Clerc agreed to direct the institution that would later become known as the American School for the Deaf. The obligations listed in this original contract for the French deaf educator Clerc mark clear directives for administering and protecting the school. Religious concerns also dominate, as evidenced by the emphasis placed on religious training and the protections afforded to Clerc, who was Catholic.

Contract between Thomas Gallaudet and Laurent Clerc
June 13, 1816

The undersigned, Thomas H. Gallaudet, a citizen of the United States of America, of the first part, and Laurent Clerc, professor in the Royal Institution for Deaf-Mutes, situated at Paris, where he resides, of the second part, do make the following contract:

ARTICLE 1. Mr. Clerc engages to take up his residence during the space of three years, to date from the day of his arrival at Hartford, in the Institution for Deaf-Mutes which Mr. Gallaudet proposes to establish in the United States of America.

ART. 2. Under the direction of the head of the Institution, Mr. Clerc shall be employed in the instruction of deaf-mutes for six hours of each day except Saturday, on which day the time shall be but for three hours. He shall be entirely at liberty on Sundays and on holidays, and he shall have, moreover, six weeks of vacation annually. All these exceptions shall be made without any deduction in the pecuniary compensation below specified.

ART. 3. He shall be present and assist at all the public lectures, as well at Hartford as in other cities of the United States, always being under the direction of the head of the Institution; and, in case of removal, every expense whatever to which the change may give rise is to be at Mr. Gallaudet's charge without appeal.

ART. 4. Mr. Clerc shall have no connection whatever with any other establishment, and shall give no instruction or public lectures, (this stipulation not conflicting with that contained in Art. 5,) except under the direction of Mr. Gallaudet. This restriction shall remain in force only for the duration of three years; which limit having expired, Mr. Clerc shall no longer be bound by these engagements, and shall have the right, according to his own judgment and wherever he shall desire it, to continue the work of deaf-mute instruction, publicly or privately, under his own direction or in any other manner; this being a particular and indispensable condition of the present agreement.

ART. 5. Mr. Clerc shall have the privilege of giving private lessons, in his own room or in the town, during the hours that he is not occupied with his class.

ART. 6. Mr. Gallaudet pledges himself to defray all Mr. Clerc's travelling expenses from Paris to Hartford, viz., for food, lodging, washing, and transportation for himself and his effects, by land and water; and this to the same extent and in the same manner as Mr. Gallaudet's own expenses.

ART. 7. From the day of his arrival in Hartford, Mr. Clerc shall be given apartments near the Institution until further arrangements are made. He shall take his meals at the table of Mr. Gallaudet; and shall also have provision made for his washing, fires, lights, and attendance.

ART. 8. In consideration of the engagements above stipulated, Mr. Gallaudet promises and binds himself to pay to Mr. Clerc at Hartford, as his annual salary, two thousand five hundred francs (*argent de France*) in quarterly instalments; the first quarter to date from the day of his arrival in Hartford.

ART. 9. At the expiration of three years, if Mr. Clerc desires to return to France, Mr. Gallaudet shall pay to him before his departure, to indemnify him for the expense of going back, the sum of one thousand five hundred francs, in addition to what has already been promised.

ART. 10. It is agreed, moreover, that in case Mr. Clerc is obliged, by circumstances beyond his own control, to leave America, and in consequence to give up the work of instruction there, these articles of agreement are to be considered void and of no effect. But Mr. Clerc shall still have a legal right—1st, to the indemnity of fifteen hundred francs above stipulated, even though the period of three years shall not have expired; 2nd, to the promised compensation at the rate of twenty-five hundred francs per year for whatever time may have already elapsed.

ART. 11. Mr. Clerc shall endeavor to give his pupils a knowledge of grammar, language, arithmetic, the globe, geography, history; of the Old Testament as contained in the Bible, and the New Testament, including the life of Jesus Christ, the Acts of the Apostles, the Epistles of St. Paul, St. John, St. Peter, and St. Jude. He is not to be called upon to teach anything contrary to the Roman Catholic religion which he professes, and in which faith he desires to live and die. Mr. Gallaudet, as head of the Institution, will take charge of all matters of religious teaching which may not be in accordance with this faith.

To these presents bear witness Messrs. Jean Conrad Hottinguer, banker, No. 20 Rue du Sentier, Paris, and Sampson Vryling Stoddard Wilder, an American merchant, now in Paris, No. 1 Rue du Sentier; who, after having acquainted themselves with the articles of agreement above stipulated, have voluntarily declared that they each and jointly constitute themselves sureties of Mr. Gallaudet on account of his engagements to Mr. Clerc as stated in the above contract; and in case of failure by Mr. Gallaudet to fulfil them punctually, they pledge themselves, singly and conjointly, to pay to Mr. Clerc at his new place of residence the promised amounts in the sums and at the times previously fixed upon.

Thus contracted, finished, and signed at Paris, the thirteenth day of June, one thousand eight hundred and sixteen.

[Signed and sealed]
THOMAS H. GALLAUDET,
LAURENT CLERC,
S. V. S. WILDER,
J. C. HOTTINGUER.

Source: "Contract between Thomas Gallaudet and Laurent Clerc (June 13, 1816)." American Annals of the Deaf and Dumb. Available online. URL: http://www.disabilitymuseum.org/lib/docs/689.htm?page=print. Accessed June 20, 2008.

American Sign Language

American Sign Language (ASL, also previously known as Ameslan) is used primarily by members of the DEAF cultural COMMUNITY in the United States and parts of Canada. Many people referring to ASL have used the general term *signs* or *sign language,* but this does not capture its unique linguistic features. Some scholars have argued that the use of signs for communication has likely existed longer than spoken language. The roots of ASL stretch back at least to 16th-century Europe, and its evolution highlights major issues in deaf and American history.

Some individuals have suggested several contributing factors to early American Sign Language, including American Indian sign systems and a form of British and community-created sign language found in colonial MARTHA'S VINEYARD. The most accepted interpretation ties ASL's origins and early features mostly to the sign language used in 18th- and 19th-century France. Broad trends in America and Europe, as well as individual activists and educators, contributed to this form of signs taking root in the United States.

The early 19th century was an era of educational and social reform, as well as missionary spirit. In 1815 a group of Connecticut philanthropists, headed by Dr. MASON FITCH COGSWELL (whose daughter ALICE COGSWELL was deaf), paid for Reverend THOMAS HOPKINS GALLAUDET to go to Europe to ascertain how best to educate deaf students. Gallaudet first visited the Braidwood school in Great Britain but was put off by the secrecy surrounding the school's oral program. Gallaudet next visited the French school in Paris, the Royal Institution of Deaf and Mutes. There he cultivated a friendship with LAURENT CLERC, teacher and graduate of the school, who advocated the use of "the natural language of signs," which became known as French Sign Language. Clerc was persuaded to come to America with Gallaudet and together, with assistance from Cogswell and other allies, they successfully petitioned legislators to fund a RESIDENTIAL SCHOOL for the deaf. Their efforts resulted in the 1817 establishment of Hartford's Connecticut Asylum for the Education and Instruction of Deaf and Dumb Persons, now known as AMERICAN SCHOOL FOR THE DEAF (ASD). Many culturally deaf people view ASD as the birthplace of a distinctly American sign language. Throughout this campus, and then at other schools modeled on ASD, generations of deaf people would learn, share, and shape a system of signs based originally on Clerc's French Sign Language and the students' locally created signs, called homesigns.

Clerc's historical and linguistic impact was profound; he personally trained many of the school's hearing teachers in the use of "manual French adopted to English." The spread of state-sponsored residential schools for the deaf in the mid 19th century fortified and standardized early American Sign Language, as graduates of ASD and other schools influenced by Clerc became teachers in the new institutions. New generations of deaf people would foster this emerging American Sign Language through everyday use, in social gatherings with other signers, and by sharing it with their CHILDREN.

Challenges to signed communication in schools for the deaf gained force in America by the latter half of the 19th century. Already predominant in Europe, ORALISM (the teaching of speech and lipreading) became the primary official pedagogy in most schools for the deaf by the 1890s. Since that time, schools often have been viewed as battlegrounds over language and IDENTITY. As several historians have shown, efforts to eliminate deaf culture as well as physical deafness often focused especially on eradicating sign language use by young deaf people. One of the leading opponents of signed communication in deaf schools was ALEXANDER GRAHAM BELL. Throughout the 20th century battles over communication methods (see COMMUNICATION DEBATES) in the classroom would strongly shape deaf people's experiences.

Much of deaf peoples' activism in the late 19th and 20th centuries focused on preserving ASL. Some individuals, such as J. W. Michaels, created dictionaries to further codify the language; others chose to join deaf ORGANIZATIONS where signing was a common link. In the early 20th century, technological changes provided a new means to protect and transmit this "language of the eye."

In 1910 the NATIONAL ASSOCIATION OF THE DEAF (NAD) initiated a campaign to use moving pictures to capture masterful signers demonstrating the beauty and richness of ASL. NAD president GEORGE VEDITZ's "Preservation of the Sign Language" remains one of the most important visual documents depicting 20th century ASL. Other deaf people at the time and since, such as filmmaker Ernest Marshall, have produced entertainment as well as instructional FILMS in American Sign Language.

Although these efforts helped unify a distinct deaf cultural community, RACE and GENDER, among other factors, complicated the meaning and transmission of ASL. In the era of racial segregation, for example, many African-American deaf students, while educated to varying degrees in residential schools, did not always learn formalized ASL. Female students often had less access to teachers who signed and only one deaf woman was filmed in the NAD preservation series. In pre–WORLD WAR II America, deaf women and girls commonly were encouraged to perform feminine, dramatic interpretations in signs at public gatherings, while men and boys demonstrated their signing skills in debates and speeches. Social and cultural differences between and among minorities in America's signing communities continues today, although scholars have only recently begun to study this in earnest.

The 1960s marked an important watershed moment in the history of ASL. In 1960 Gallaudet College (later renamed GALLAUDET UNIVERSITY) professor WILLIAM C. STOKOE produced the first authentic, linguistic study of ASL in Sign Language Structure. Five years later, Stokoe, along with deaf colleagues Carl Croneberg and Dorothy Casterline published the first true sign language dictionary that listed signs based not on their English equivalency but on their handshape, location, and movement; it was entitled *A Dictionary of American Sign Language on Linguistic Principles*. Using standard linguistic criteria, they showed that ASL was an authentic language and not merely an inferior and gestural form of English. This dictionary sparked a new generation of sign language research. This comparative linguistic research of "the sign language" contributed to the term "American Sign Language" to describe this distinct language.

Initially, this new label caused a firestorm of controversy inside the deaf community. Many deaf people rejected the formal recognition of ASL, considering it a new kind of STIGMA, a marker that emphasized deaf people as different in yet another respect. Still adhering to the historic representation of ASL, others were reluctant to accept the new interpretation that ASL was an authentic language.

With emerging linguistic studies of ASL came new questions about language training and deaf education. Throughout the 1960s and 1970s, teachers, community members, and others debated ways to enhance or improve ASL. "Artificial" sign systems, such as "SEE" (Signed Exact English), were created to match signs with standard English more closely.

Other advances in the 1960s and 1970s brought ASL more fully into the public domain. For example, in 1964, the REGISTRY OF INTERPRETERS FOR THE DEAF (RID), the first formal organization overseeing and promoting the emerging field of sign language interpreting, was founded. Three years later the NATIONAL THEATER OF THE DEAF (NTD) was established; NTD included both hearing and deaf actors who performed using ASL and spoken English. The expansion of both the RID and NTD has helped legitimize and "normalize" ASL in mainstream society, as did deaf actress LINDA BOVE's long-term work on *Sesame Street* (from 1971 to 2003). Increased interest in American Sign Language sparked formal courses in the language at community colleges and elsewhere since the 1970s. This widespread interest in ASL helped de-stigmatize signing, and deaf people became more comfortable signing in public places. The changing status of ASL both fueled and was sparked by increasing deaf cultural pride and EMPOWERMENT.

Building on a long tradition of ASL POETRY within the deaf world, and echoing Stokoe's linguistic research, CLAYTON VALLI and others in the 1980s and 1990s offered compelling evidence that ASL poetry marked a distinct and authentic literary form. The proliferation of ASL poetry since the 1990s further demonstrates the linguistic capabilities of this language. Today many people now study ASL poetry; specific genres, such as "ABC poems," which employ alphabet handshapes, have become a popular tool for teaching American Sign Language.

As with all living languages, ASL has evolved throughout history. For instance, signers in the past tended to use greater space when communicating, extending arms further out from their bodies. Common signs now tend to be located closer to the head and upper body. The influence of manually coded English in the 1960s and 1970s promoted initialized signs, meaning signs that incorporated handshapes for alphabetical letters, which specifically linked signed communication to written English. One example of this was the sign for "dinner," which included the letter "d" handshape near the mouth. By the late 20th century, many of these initialized signs had changed to reflect the concept of the word rather than the written English equivalent. As with spoken and written English, new terms continue to enter the ASL lexicon. In recent years, for instance, ASL users have adopted signs for "Internet," "pagers," and "transgender." Even the demographics of sign users have shifted in the past few decades. Traditionally, most signers were deaf or had close personal or professional ties to deaf people. Today ASL represents the third most used language in America and the most popular foreign language offered in many high schools and colleges. Increasingly, hearing people study ASL even if they are not drawn to the deaf cultural world. This suggests that the social meaning of ASL—for deaf and nondeaf Americans—will expand in new directions in the future.

Greater recognition of multicultural America and linguistic diversity has opened the concept of what being "American" means. The treasured place of American Sign Language in the deaf cultural world marks boundaries of equality, EDUCATION, ACCESS, IDENTITY, and community.

See also NATIONAL ASSOCIATION OF THE DEAF SIGN LANGUAGE FILM PRESERVATION CAMPAIGN; SIGN LANGUAGE INTERPRETERS AND INTERPRETING.

Steven D. Collins

Further Reading:

Baynton, Douglas. *Forbidden Signs: American Culture and the Campaign against Sign Language.* Chicago: University of Chicago Press, 1996.

Burch, Susan. *Signs of Resistance: American Deaf Cultural History, 1900 to World War II.* New York: New York University Press, 2002.

Maher, Jane. *Seeing in Sign Language: The Work of William C. Stokoe.* Washington, D.C.: Gallaudet University Press, 1996.

Padden, Carol, and Tom Humphries. *Deaf in America: Voices from a Culture.* Cambridge, Mass.: Harvard University Press, 1990.

Van Cleve, John Vickrey, and Barry Crouch. *A Place of Their Own: Creating the Deaf Community in America.* Washington, D.C.: Gallaudet University Press, 1989.

Americans with Disabilities Act (1990)

The Americans with Disabilities Act (ADA) of 1990 represents the latest and most comprehensive effort to fight discrimination on the basis of disability in the United States. The first major civil rights LAW passed since the Civil Rights Act of 1964, the ADA was estimated to affect the lives of 43 million Americans at the time of its passage. In enacting the law, Congress sought, as its purpose, to send a straightforward message to society that discriminating against people with disabilities was unacceptable and unlawful. Moreover, it specified that the aim of the law was to "provide clear, strong, consistent, enforceable standards addressing discrimination against individuals with disabilities [and] to ensure that the Federal government plays a central role in enforcing the standards established in this Act." In 2000, a decade after its passage, the UNITED STATES CENSUS Bureau reported that almost 50 million people aged five and over had a disability, which constituted nearly 20 percent of the over-five population. In *GARRETT V. BOARD OF TRUSTEES OF THE UNIVERSITY OF ALABAMA,* decided in 2001, the Supreme Court characterized the ADA as "a milestone on the path to a more decent, tolerant, progressive society."

At the time of the ADA's passage, laws banning discrimination against people with disabilities were not novel. However, earlier laws related to disability generally emphasized vocational rehabilitation of people with disabilities, rather than establishing prohibitions on discriminatory treatment. By the 1960s the focus of the laws had changed as the government attempted to bar social and economic discrimination against people with disabilities in a wide range of policy areas such as health, housing, TRANSPORTATION, and EDUCATION. One example of this was the ARCHITECTURAL BARRIERS ACT of 1968, which required that buildings and transportation facilities constructed, altered, or financed with federal funds after 1969 comply with federal accessibility standards for people with MOBILITY, visual, and hearing disabilities.

During the 1970s congressional support for ending discrimination against people with disabilities continued to grow, in part because of the disability COMMUNITY's success in associating its rhetoric and ideology with the earlier civil rights movements of African-Americans and women. Demanding equality, people with disabilities gave persuasive accounts of the effect of discrimination against them that were reminiscent of the hardships endured by individuals in the civil rights movements. Their efforts proved successful as laws were enacted such as the Urban Mass Transportation Act of 1970; the Rehabilitation Act of 1973; the 1975 DEVELOPMENTALLY DISABLED ASSISTANCE AND BILL OF RIGHTS ACT; the Education of All Handicapped Children Act of 1975, later called the INDIVIDUALS WITH DISABILITIES EDUCATION ACT; the AIR CARRIER ACCESS ACT of 1986; and the Fair Housing Act Amendments of 1988. Although each was aimed at combating discrimination against people with disabilities, they focused on specific disabilities or social spheres and none reflected a comprehensive approach to address discrimination that became the hallmark of the ADA.

PASSAGE OF THE ADA

The ADA was first introduced in 1988 in the 100th Congress by Senator Lowell Weicker (R-Conn.) and Representative TONY COELHO (D-Calif.). The proposed bill passed in the Senate but died in subcommittee in the House of Representatives. Despite its failure to pass that year, the bill drew attention to the issue of discrimination against people with disabilities and its sponsors hoped that it would gain the support of the candidates in the 1988 presidential election campaign and pass the next year. After George H. W. Bush became president, a new version of the bill was introduced in the 101st Congress in May 1989 by its prime sponsors, Representative Steny Hoyer (D-Md.), and Senators Ted Kennedy (D-Mass.) and Tom Harkin (D-Iowa).

In lobbying Congress to enact the law, members of the disability community argued that it must transform the status of people with disabilities. During debate over

On July 26, 1990, President George H. W. Bush signed the Americans with Disabilities Act into law, an event celebrated as a watershed moment in disability rights history. Witnessing the signing were disability advocates Evan Kemp *(seated left)*, of the Equal Employment Opportunity Commission; Justin Dart *(seated right)*, from the President's Committee on Employment of People with Disabilities; and Rev. Harold Wilke and Sandra Swift Parrino, from the National Council on Disability.   *(Smithsonian National Museum of American History, Division of Medicine and Science)*

its passage, Congress made it clear that the law sought to advance the aim of guaranteeing the civil rights of people with disabilities by broadly stating that the purpose of the act was to establish a "national mandate" to end discrimination against people with disabilities and to guarantee that the federal government would play a key role in enforcing the law. To place it within the context of earlier civil rights laws, most notably the 1964 Civil Rights Act, a House committee report compared the discriminatory experiences suffered by people with disabilities to those suffered by members of the African-American community. In keeping with this theme, Congress characterized people with disabilities as "politically powerless" and declared that discrimination against them was "a serious and pervasive social problem." The ADA broadly proclaimed that the act was intended "to provide a clear and comprehensive national mandate for the elimination of discrimination against individuals with disabilities."

The final version of the bill was overwhelmingly approved by the House of Representatives on July 12, 1990, with a 377 to 28 vote and by the Senate on July 13 in a 91 to 6 vote. Thirteen days later, on July 26, 1990, President George H. W. Bush signed the ADA into law.

In remarks in a signing ceremony on the White House lawn that day, President Bush compared the event to the fall of the Berlin Wall eight months earlier, declaring that "every man, woman, and child with a disability can now pass through once closed doors into a bright new era of equality, independence, and freedom." Presidents Bill Clinton and George W. Bush later proclaimed the importance of the law and expressed their commitment to furthering the dignity of people with disabilities by allowing them to participate more fully in society, particularly by fostering EMPLOYMENT opportunities. Since its passage, other public officials have spoken eloquently about the ADA and its aims of eliminating discrimination against people with disabilities.

PROVISIONS OF THE ADA

The ADA defines an individual with a disability as a person with "a physical or mental IMPAIRMENT that substantially limits one or more of the major life activities"; a person with "a record of such an impairment"; or an individual who "is regarded as," that is, perceived by others as, "having such impairment." Consisting of five titles, or sections, the heart of the ADA is contained in the first three provisions. Title I prohibits discrimination against "qualified people with disabilities" in hiring, firing, and promotion by private employers with at least 15 employees, state and local governments, employment agencies, and labor unions. Title II bars discrimination in the delivery of state and local government services; it applies to these government entities and the National Railroad Passenger Corporation (Amtrak), requiring them to accord persons with disabilities an equal opportunity to receive or participate in programs, services, and activities, including recreation, social services, transportation, HEALTH CARE, and VOTING, to name just a few areas. Title III bans discrimination by private entities in places of public accommodations. Modeled in part after Title II of the 1964 Civil Rights Act, the provision that bans discrimination in accommodations on the basis of race and national origin, Title III of the ADA includes a wide range of privately owned retail and service establishments as well as commercial facilities, such as factories and warehouses, within its reach. Of the remaining sections of the law, Title IV pertains to telecommunications and Title V consists of miscellaneous provisions, including the availability of attorneys' fees, alternative dispute resolution, claims for retaliation, consistency with state laws, and insurance underwriting. The provision regarding insurance underwriting has produced considerable litigation in the lower federal courts, with plaintiffs filing lawsuits against insurance companies and employers, claiming they are being denied equality in health or life insurance benefits.

ADA ENFORCEMENT

During debate over the bill, members of Congress had raised objections to portions of the law, predicting that it would prove costly to owners of small businesses and that, by arousing sympathy in court, litigants would prevail in frivolous lawsuits. Some feared that the rights language of the statute would lead to expensive and unnecessary litigation and far-reaching judicial interpretation of the mandate against discrimination. Despite these concerns, Congress relied on well-established principles of civil rights laws by placing primary enforcement authority in the federal courts; it also assigned lesser roles to the Equal Employment Opportunity Commission and the Department of Justice. Thus, the judiciary was given primary responsibility for establishing the parameters of disability rights policy in both the public and the private sector.

Following in the path of civil rights groups that had preceded them, the disability community turned to the federal courts, arguing that Congress had manifested its intent that the judiciary interpret the law broadly to eradicate discrimination against people with disabilities. Disability rights advocates hoped that the courts would follow the traditional approach to civil rights laws by effectuating the remedial purpose of the statute. In part, however, because the ADA contains many vague terms, such as "disability," "reasonable accommodations," "readily achievable," "undue hardship," and "undue burden," the courts have discretion in implementing the ADA. In the ensuing litigation, many members of the disability community were disappointed by the judiciary's approach to enforcing the law. They believed that the ADA has failed to achieve many of the goals they envisioned because, despite congressional intent, the Supreme Court has interpreted the statute narrowly in such cases as *Sutton v. United Airlines,* 527 U.S. 471 (1999), *Murphy v. United Parcel Service,* 527 U.S. 516 (1999), and *Toyota Motor Manufacturing v. Williams,* 584 U.S. 184 (2002). These cases restricted the definition of who qualified as disabled and thus limited the law's application.

Although the ADA constituted a monumental step forward in extending civil rights guarantees to people with disabilities, the law also sought to allay the fears of members of Congress about the cost of the bill to the business community. The fear that litigants would unreasonably prevail in ADA suits has largely proved groundless because of the federal judiciary's narrow interpretations in adjudicating ADA cases, particularly in employment discrimination actions. To the disappointment of the disability community, the courts have interpreted the law to exclude many claimants, such as those with hypertension and severe myopia, from its reach, despite Congress's stated intent that the courts interpret the act broadly to aid victims of discrimination on the basis of disabilities.

As a civil rights statute, the ADA borrowed heavily from prior civil rights laws, but it differs from earlier civil rights statutes in several ways. First, unlike the traditional civil rights laws, it permits only people with disabilities to file lawsuits, allowing the courts wide latitude in deciding whether they are persons that Congress intended to include within the reach of the act. Known as the "definition of disability" stage, this stipulation has been the subject of much dispute, raising concerns within the disability community that the courts are blocking the courthouse entrance to people with disabilities by raising the bar higher than Congress wished. Indeed, this provision has proven to be an obstacle to large numbers of people who claim they are disabled yet are unable to satisfy the courts that they are within the class of people with disabilities that Congress intended to protect.

Second, unlike the civil rights laws of the 1960s and 1970s, the ADA explicitly allows defendants to argue that the expense of providing an accommodation is unreasonable and excuses their failure to adopt them. As a result, the rights guaranteed in the ADA are balanced against cost so that discrimination is justifiable if the price to remedy it is too high. Additionally, unlike the traditional civil rights laws, the ADA is based on a principle of equality that differs from laws guaranteeing equality on the basis of RACE, sex, or AGE. In these laws, persons found guilty of discrimination are ordered to stop the discriminatory behavior; in ADA cases, defendants who violate the law may also be ordered to modify the environment to enable persons with disabilities to achieve equality with other members of society.

RESULTS OF ADA LITIGATION

In assessing the results of ADA litigation, the law has proven to be most beneficial to persons seeking to make sidewalks, buildings, and transportation systems more accessible to people with disabilities. This is not surprising as Congress had intended the ADA to play an important role in removing physical obstacles to mobility and, for the most part, the courts have been sympathetic to persons seeking to remove such physical barriers.

In its first decade after the ADA's passage, the Supreme Court issued 12 Title I rulings, with only three decided in favor of the plaintiff. The high court has ruled on seven Title II cases through 2008, with five decided in favor of the plaintiff and on two Title III cases, the plaintiff prevailing in both. Consistent with these results, analysis of lower federal court rulings since the act was passed shows that ADA litigants are more likely to prevail in Title III suits, with Title II suits next, and least likely to win in Title I lawsuits. Indeed, Title I plaintiffs overwhelmingly lose their cases in the lower federal courts, having a success rate of only about 5 percent, with employers prevailing in at least 90 percent of the cases brought against them.

A review of ADA litigation shows that federal court rulings in ADA suits have constricted the parameters of disability rights and excluded large numbers of disabled individuals from the protection of the law, especially in the employment context. Thus, although the ADA was greeted with great enthusiasm by members of the disability community, many became disappointed in the implementation of the law. Many disability rights advocates believe that the federal judiciary's narrow interpretation of the statute—in contradiction of Congress's intent—has led to the ADA's failure to achieve the goals they envisioned.

In an effort to counter this trend, advocates lobbied Congress to approve the Americans with Disabilities Act Amendments Act of 2008. Rejecting the Supreme Court's interpretation in a number of key ADA cases, the law clarifies and broadens the definition of disability; it also expands the population eligible for protections under the ADA. President George W. Bush signed the amendments into law on September 25, 2008, and they are effective as of January 1, 2009.

See also ACCESS AND ACCESSIBILITY; ACTIVISM AND ADVOCACY; BACKLASH; CLOSED CAPTIONING; DART, JUSTIN, JR.; DISABILITY RIGHTS MOVEMENT; EMPOWERMENT; FAY, FRED; KEMP, EVAN, JR.; PROTEST; SIGN LANGUAGE INTERPRETERS AND INTERPRETING; WHEELS OF JUSTICE.

Susan Mezey

Further Reading:

Blanck, Peter David, ed. *Employment, Disability, and the Americans with Disabilities Act: Issues in Law, Public Policy, and Research.* Evanston, Ill.: Northwestern University Press, 2000.

Colker, Ruth. "The Americans with Disabilities Act: A Windfall for Defendants." *Harvard Civil Rights–Civil Liberties Law Review* 34 (1999): 99–162.

Krieger, Linda Hamilton, ed. *Backlash against the ADA: Reinterpreting Disability Rights.* Ann Arbor: University of Michigan Press, 2003.

Mezey, Susan Gluck. *Disabling Interpretations: Judicial Implementation of the Americans with Disabilities Act.* Pittsburgh: University of Pittsburgh Press, 2005.

O'Brien, Ruth. *Crippled Justice: The History of Modern Disability Policy in the Workplace.* Chicago: University of Chicago Press, 2001.

Shapiro, Joseph A. *No Pity: People with Disabilities Forging a New Civil Rights Movement.* New York: Random House, 1994.

Switzer, Jacqueline Vaughn. *Disabled Rights: American Disability Policy and the Fight for Equality.* Washington, D.C.: Georgetown University Press, 2003.

Americans with Disabilities Act

Signed into law by President George H.W. Bush on July 26, 1990, the Americans with Disabilities Act of 1990 (ADA) generally is considered the most significant piece of disability civil rights legislation in American history. Based in large part on the 1964 Civil Rights Act, the ADA prohibits discrimination against individuals or groups based on their disabilities. Although the law has significant limitations, including scope of protection and enforcement measures, it reflects a considerable recognition of people with disabilities as full citizens and seeks to promote a more inclusive society. These selections from the ADA offer central definitions of relevant terms such as "disability" as well as some of the primary aspects of society that the law addresses, including employment, public transportation, and public accommodations.

Americans with Disabilities Act of 1990
Public Law 101-36
An Act

To establish a clear and comprehensive prohibition of discrimination on the basis of disability. July 26, 1990

. . . (b) Purpose

It is the purpose of this chapter

(1) to provide a clear and comprehensive national mandate for the elimination of discrimination against individuals with disabilities;

(2) to provide clear, strong, consistent, enforceable standards addressing discrimination against individuals with disabilities;

(3) to ensure that the Federal Government plays a central role in enforcing the standards established in this chapter on behalf of individuals with disabilities; and

(4) to invoke the sweep of congressional authority, including the power to enforce the fourteenth amendment and to regulate commerce, in order to address the major areas of discrimination faced day-to-day by people with disabilities.

. . . (2) Disability

The term "disability" means, with respect to an individual

(A) a physical or mental impairment that substantially limits one or more of the major life activities of such individual;

(B) a record of such an impairment; or

(C) being regarded as having such impairment.

. . . (9) Reasonable accommodation

The term "reasonable accommodation" may include

(A) making existing facilities used by employees readily accessible to and usable by individuals with disabilities; and

(B) job restructuring, part-time or modified work schedules, reassignment to a vacant position, acquisition or modification of equipment or devices, appropriate adjustment or modifications of examinations, training materials or policies, the provision of qualified readers or interpreters, and other similar accommodations for individuals with disabilities.

. . . Sec. 12112. Discrimination

(a) General rule

No covered entity shall discriminate against a qualified individual with a disability because of the disability of such individual in regard to job application procedures, the hiring, advancement, or discharge of employees, employee compensation, job training, and other terms, conditions, and privileges of employment.

(b) Construction

As used in subsection (a) of this section, the term "discriminate" includes

(1) limiting, segregating, or classifying a job applicant or employee in a way that adversely affects the opportunities or status of such applicant or employee because of the disability of such applicant or employee;

(2) participating in a contractual or other arrangement or relationship that has the effect of subjecting a covered entity's qualified applicant or employee with a disability to the discrimination prohibited by this subchapter (such relationship includes a relationship with an employment or referral agency, labor union, an organization providing fringe benefits to an employee of the covered entity, or an organization providing training and apprenticeship programs);

(3) utilizing standards, criteria, or methods of administration

(A) that have the effect of discrimination on the basis of disability;

(B) that perpetuates the discrimination of others who are subject to common administrative control;

(4) excluding or otherwise denying equal jobs or benefits to a qualified individual because of the known disability of an individual with whom the qualified individual is known to have a relationship or association;

(5)

(A) not making reasonable accommodations to the known physical or mental limitations of an otherwise qualified individual with a disability who is an applicant or employee, unless such covered entity can demonstrate that the accommodation would impose an undue hardship on the operation of the business of such covered entity; or

(B) denying employment opportunities to a job applicant or employee who is an otherwise qualified individual with a disability, if such denial is based on the need of such covered entity to make reasonable accommodation to the physical or mental impairments of the employee or applicant;

(6) using qualification standards, employment tests or other selection criteria that screen out or tend to screen out an individual with a disability or a class of individuals with disabilities unless the standard, test or other selection criteria, as used by the covered entity, is shown to be job-related for the position in question and is consistent with business necessity; and

(7) failing to select and administer tests concerning employment in the most effective manner to ensure that, when such test is administered to a job applicant or employee who has a disability that impairs sensory, manual, or speaking skills, such test results accurately reflect the skills, aptitude, or whatever other factor of such applicant or employee that such test purports to measure, rather than reflecting the impaired sensory, manual, or speaking skills of such employee or applicant (except where such skills are the factors that the test purports to measure).

... SUBCHAPTER II – PUBLIC SERVICES
Part A – Prohibition Against Discrimination and Other Generally Applicable Provisions
... (1) Public entity
The term "public entity" means
(A) any State or local government;
(B) any department, agency, special purpose district, or other instrumentality of a State or States or local government; and
(C) the National Railroad Passenger Corporation, and any commuter authority (as defined in section 24102(4) of title 49).

... Sec. 12132. Discrimination
Subject to the provisions of this subchapter, no qualified individual with a disability shall, by reason of such disability, be excluded from participation in or be denied the benefits of services, programs, or activities of a public entity, or be subjected to discrimination by any such entity.

... (2) Designated public transportation
The term "designated public transportation" means transportation (other than public school transportation) by bus, rail, or any other conveyance (other than transportation by aircraft or intercity or commuter rail transportation (as defined in section 12161 of this title)) that provides the general public with general or special service (including charter service) on a regular and continuing basis.

... It shall be considered discrimination for purposes of section which operates a fixed route system to purchase or lease a new bus, a new rapid rail vehicle, a new light rail vehicle, or any other new vehicle to be used on such system, if the solicitation for such purchase or lease is made after the 30th day following July 26, 1990, and if such bus, rail vehicle, or other vehicle is not readily accessible to and usable by individuals with disabilities, including individuals who use wheelchairs.

... It shall be considered discrimination for purposes of section 12132 of this title and section 794 of title 29 for a public entity which operates a fixed route system (other than a system which provides solely commuter bus service) to fail to provide with respect to the operations of its fixed route system, in accordance with this section, paratransit and other special transportation services to individuals with disabilities, including individuals who use wheelchairs that are sufficient to provide to such individuals a level of service

... (1) Eligible recipients of service
The regulations issued under this section shall require each public entity which operates a fixed route system to provide the paratransit and other special transportation services required under this section
(A)
(i) to any individual with a disability who is unable, as a result of a physical or mental impairment (including a vision impairment) and without the assistance of another individual (except an operator of a wheelchair lift or other boarding assistance device), to board, ride, or disembark from any vehicle on the system which is readily accessible to and usable by individuals with disabilities;
(ii) to any individual with a disability who needs the assistance of a wheelchair lift or other boarding assistance device (and is able with such assistance) to board, ride, and disembark from any vehicle which is readily accessible to and usable by individuals with disabilities if the individual wants to travel on a route on the system during the hours of operation of the system at a time (or within a reasonable period of such time) when such a vehicle is not being used to provide designated public transportation on the route; and

(iii) to any individual with a disability who has a specific impairment-related condition which prevents such individual from traveling to a boarding location or from a disembarking location on such system;

(B) to one other individual accompanying the individual with the disability; and

(C) to other individuals, in addition to the one individual described in subparagraph (a), accompanying the individual with a disability provided that space for these additional individuals are available on the paratransit vehicle carrying the individual with a disability and that the transportation of such additional individuals will not result in a denial of service to individuals with disabilities.

. . . Sec. 12146. New facilities

For purposes of section 12132 of this title and section 794 of title 29, it shall be considered discrimination for a public entity to construct a new facility to be used in the provision of designated public transportation services unless such facility is readily accessible to and usable by individuals with disabilities, including individuals who use wheelchairs.

Sec. 12147. Alterations of existing facilities

(a) General rule

With respect to alterations of an existing facility or part thereof used in the provision of designated public transportation services that affect or could affect the usability of the facility or part thereof, it shall be considered discrimination, for purposes of section 12132 of this title and section 794 of title 29, for a public entity to fail to make such alterations (or to ensure that the alterations are made) in such a manner that, to the maximum extent feasible, the altered portions of the facility are readily accessible to and usable by individuals with disabilities, including individuals who use wheelchairs, upon the completion of such alterations. Where the public entity is undertaking an alteration that affects or could affect usability of or access to an area of the facility containing a primary function, the entity shall also make the alterations in such a manner that, to the maximum extent feasible, the path of travel to the altered area and the bathrooms, telephones, and drinking fountains serving the altered area, are readily accessible to and usable by individuals with disabilities, including individuals who use wheelchairs, upon completion of such alterations,

where such alterations to the path of travel or the bathrooms, telephones, and drinking fountains serving the altered area are not disproportionate to the overall alterations in terms of cost and scope (as determined under criteria established by the Attorney General).

. . . (7) Public accommodation

The following private entities are considered public accommodations for purposes of this subchapter, if the operations of such entities affect commerce

(A) an inn, hotel, motel, or other place of lodging, except for an establishment located within a building that contains not more than five rooms for rent or hire and that is actually occupied by the proprietor of such establishment as the residence of such proprietor;

(B) a restaurant, bar, or other establishment serving food or drink;

(C) a motion picture house, theater, concert hall, stadium, or other place of exhibition entertainment;

(D) an auditorium, convention center, lecture hall, or other place of public gathering;

(E) a bakery, grocery store, clothing store, hardware store, shopping center, or other sales or rental establishment;

(F) a laundromat, dry-cleaner, bank, barber shop, beauty shop, travel service, shoe repair service, funeral parlor, gas station, office of an accountant or lawyer, pharmacy, insurance office, professional office of a health care provider, hospital, or other service establishment;

(G) a terminal, depot, or other station used for specified public transportation;

(H) a museum, library, gallery, or other place of public display or collection;

(I) a park, zoo, amusement park, or other place of recreation;

(J) a nursery, elementary, secondary, undergraduate, or postgraduate private school, or other place of education;

(K) a day care center, senior citizen center, homeless shelter, food bank, adoption agency, or other social service center establishment; and

(L) a gymnasium, health spa, bowling alley, golf course, or other place of exercise or recreation.

. . . (1) General prohibition

(A) Activities

(i) Denial of participation

It shall be discriminatory to subject an individual or class of individuals on the basis of a disability or disabilities of such individual or class, directly, or through contractual, licensing, or other arrangements, to a denial of the opportunity of the individual or class to participate in or benefit from the goods, services, facilities, privileges, advantages, or accommodations of an entity.

(ii) Participation in unequal benefit

It shall be discriminatory to afford an individual or class of individuals, on the basis of a disability or disabilities of such individual or class, directly, or through contractual, licensing, or other arrangements with the opportunity to participate in or benefit from a good, service, facility, privilege, advantage, or accommodation that is not equal to that afforded to other individuals.

(iii) Separate benefit

It shall be discriminatory to provide an individual or class of individuals, on the basis of a disability or disabilities of such individual or class, directly, or through contractual, licensing, or other arrangements with a good, service, facility, privilege, advantage, or accommodation that is different or separate from that provided to other individuals, unless such action is necessary to provide the individual or class of individuals with a good, service, facility, privilege, advantage, or accommodation, or other opportunity that is as effective as that provided to others.

(iv) Individual or class of individuals

For purposes of clauses (i) through (iii) of this subparagraph, the term "individual or class of individuals" refers to the clients or customers of the covered public accommodation that enters into the contractual, licensing or other arrangement.

(B) Integrated settings

Goods, services, facilities, privileges, advantages, and accommodations shall be afforded to an individual with a disability in the most integrated setting appropriate to the needs of the individual.

(C) Opportunity to participate

Notwithstanding the existence of separate or different programs or activities provided in accordance with this section, an individual with a disability shall not be denied the opportunity to participate in such programs or activities that are not separate or different.

(D) Administrative methods

An individual or entity shall not, directly or through contractual or other arrangements, utilize standards or criteria or methods of administration

(i) that have the effect of discriminating on the basis of disability; or

(ii) that perpetuate the discrimination of others who are subject to common administrative control.

(E) Association

It shall be discriminatory to exclude or otherwise deny equal goods, services, facilities, privileges, advantages, accommodations, or other opportunities to an individual or entity because of the known disability of an individual with whom the individual or entity is known to have a relationship or association.

Source: Excerpted from the Web site of the United States Access Board at http://www.access-board.gov/about/laws/ADA.htm.

amniocentesis

Amniocentesis is one method of prenatal testing. In amniocentesis, a medical professional inserts a thin needle through the abdomen of a pregnant woman in order to take a sample of the fluid in the amniotic sac that surrounds the fetus. Sampling of amniotic fluid was first performed in Germany in 1882, and in the 1950s American doctors widely used the technique both to relieve abnormally high fluid pressure and to determine the sex of the fetus in cases where they suspected that the fetus might have a hereditary sex-linked condition. Historically, mainstream society viewed prenatal tests as a positive scientific advancement since many doctors and lay people have long hoped to eliminate birth defects and hereditary disabilities.

Prenatal testing became an important feature in disability history starting in the late 1950s. In 1958 French scientists Jerome Lejeune and Marthe Gauthier examined tissue samples from several persons with DOWN SYNDROME and discovered that their cells contained 47 chromosomes instead of the usual 46. Scientists in Scotland soon confirmed their findings. By 1967 amniocentesis, followed by microscopic chromosome analysis, was in widespread use in the United States to test for Down syndrome. Because the chances of bearing an infant with Down syndrome increases with the age of the mother, most medical authorities recommend amniocentesis for all pregnant women who will be 35 years of age or older at the time of delivery. Amniocentesis slightly increases the risk of harm to the mother, the fetus, or both, through spontaneous abortion and other causes. Many pregnant women whose fetuses tested positive for the syndrome have chosen "therapeutic" abortions.

Many disability rights activists oppose prenatal tests precisely because test results that show significant risk of disability often motivate parents to abort the fetus. These advocates view the elimination of "birth defects" as the elimination or further marginalization of disabled people. They argue, first, that if society at large places a negative value on fetuses with a particular impairment, less respect will be given to persons with the same impairment who are already born. Society usually ignores the good qualities of the IMPAIRED fetus or person, noticing only the impairment. Second, they fear that as fewer CHILDREN are born with a particular impairment there will be less incentive to provide services to persons living with that impairment. They thus fear that what society does not value and will not support, it may eliminate, as demonstrated by the EUGENIC practices of the early and mid 20th century in both Germany and the United States. As science and medicine discover genes linked to a given disease or disability, new forms of testing arise that can be applied to the amniocentesis sample, and disability advocates express concern about the potential impact of each newly developed test.

Other forms of prenatal testing are also controversial. For example, ultrasound, developed during WORLD WAR I, was based upon the principles of navy sonar. While it does not test genetic material, ultrasound was first used to examine fetuses in 1957, chiefly to determine the sex of the fetus; it is also used to detect larger scale physical abnormalities, such as a missing arm or leg. Chorionic villus sampling, developed in the late 1960s, is used very early in pregnancy to sample a small portion of the tissue that will develop into the placenta. Risks to both mother and fetus are greater with this procedure than with amniocentesis. For this reason, some nations, particularly Denmark and Sweden, have banned this technique.

In the early 1970s researchers tested amniotic fluid for alpha-fetoprotein (AFP), and found it a good indication of the presence or absence of neural tube impairments in the fetus, including spina bifida and anencephaly. Shortly thereafter, it appeared that AFP levels might be sampled in the mother's blood. This method of testing became widespread in the United States in the 1980s and 1990s.

Amniocentesis and other forms of prenatal testing may be considered either medical miracles or threats to disabled people as a group. Their contested place in American society reveals changing judgments of disability as well as SCIENCE.

See also REPRODUCTIVE RIGHTS.

Franklin K. Wyman

Further Reading:
Asch, Adrienne, and David Wasserman. "Where Is the Sin in Synecdoche? Prenatal Testing and the Parent-Child Relationship." In *Quality of Life and Human Difference: Genetic Testing, Health Care, and Disability,* edited by David Wasserman, Jerome Bickenbach, and Robert Wachbroit, 172–216. New York: Cambridge University Press, 2005.

Burleigh, Michael. *Death and Deliverance: "Euthanasia" in Germany 1900–1945.* Cambridge and New York: Cambridge University Press, 1994.

Powell, Cynthia M. "The Current State of Genetic Testing in the United States." In *Prenatal Testing and Disability Rights,* edited by Erik Parens and Adrienne Asch, 44–53. Washington, D.C.: Georgetown University Press, 2000.

Rapp, Rayna. *Testing Women, Testing the Fetus: The Social Impact of Amniocentesis in America.* New York and London: Routledge, 2000.

Rosenthal, M. "The Prenatal Exam and Prenatal Testing" WebMD. Available online. URL: http://www.webmd.com/content/article/4/1680_51789.htm. Accessed July 21, 2006.

amputees and amputation

Amputation, the removal of a body part by surgery or injury, often results in a readily visible sign of bodily difference or lack of "whole-ness." American amputees have to cope with mobility differences as well as misunderstandings about their health and physical capabilities. Though amputations occur for a variety of reasons, depictions of amputees in the media are frequently emblematic of wartime trauma. In American fiction, amputees are typically portrayed as villainous characters. There are approximately 160,000 amputations each year in the United States, half of which are due to vascular or circulatory DISEASE. Eighty percent of amputees are age 50 or older.

Though any removal of bodily tissue is an amputation, typically the loss of a limb or digit is called an amputation, whereas the loss of organ tissue, such as an eye or a breast, is referred to using more specific terminology such as enucleation or mastectomy. Similarly, the term amputee is generally used in reference to a person missing one or more limbs, fingers, or toes. Some amputees use PROSTHETIC devices to replace the amputated body part. Prosthetics may disguise the lack of a particular body part or imitate the functionality of a missing limb.

Well-known amputees include Ted Kennedy, Jr., son of U.S. senator Ted Kennedy (D-Mass.), who lost his leg as part of the treatment for bone cancer during his teens. Mountaineer Aaron Ralston gained fame in 2003 after amputating his own arm with a pocketknife to free himself from a fallen boulder. Athlete and double leg amputee AIMEE MULLINS was featured multiple times in *Sports Illustrated* and is also a model and an actress.

Since the CIVIL WAR (1861–65), the image of the amputee VETERAN has symbolized the heroism and physical sacrifices of soldiers during battle. Because of innovations in military technology, such as bone-shattering bullets, there were more than 45,000 limb amputees from the Civil War. Photographers such as Matthew Brady documented field site surgical procedures as well as new amputees on CRUTCHES, showing the empty sleeves and pants legs of their uniforms neatly folded and pinned to accommodate their limb loss. In response to this large pool of new amputees, prosthetic manufacturers developed and aggressively marketed artificial limbs to veterans. Amputee soldiers received funds from the federal government to purchase their prosthetic devices.

While the press lauded Civil War veterans for their efforts and sacrifices, postbellum society was not accepting of amputees and other disabled soldiers. The manhood of veterans was questioned, as many were unable to return to former occupations or became "burdens" on society—begging for food and requesting remuneration for their WAR-related injuries. To care for Union veterans who were unable to earn a living wage, the federal government paid monthly pensions and established a network of Veterans' Homes to house them. Confederate states established similar homes for their veteran soldiers and also offered commutation payments for amputee soldiers.

Throughout the 20th century and continuing today, portrayals of military-related amputees evoke the enduring costs of WAR. Such images are particularly prevalent during times of strong antiwar fervor, such as in the Vietnam era; amputee veterans often lead antiwar PROTESTS or are depicted in media to personalize the sacrifices of combat. Popular movies, such as THE BEST YEARS OF OUR LIVES, *Home of the Brave,* and *FORREST GUMP,* show soldier amputees experiencing barriers to adapting to civilian life after their rehabilitation process, including emotional trauma and social marginalization. In the case of the IRAQ WAR, much media attention has focused on amputee soldiers as

> "As I sat restlessly in the coach of a fast moving train, many thoughts were flashing through my bewildered mind. It was going to be my first trip home since being wounded overseas. I was very sensitive over the loss of my arm, and I was wondering how my family felt about it. What would be my sweetheart's reaction? Would she still love me the same?"
>
> —Richard A. Frazee, a soldier who lost his arm during World War II, contemplating his return home

an expression of the physical costs paid by U.S. soldiers. However, unlike the earlier imagery from the 19th and early 20th centuries that portrayed the physical inabilities of amputee veterans, recent media accounts often emphasize the nascent technology of computer-driven prosthetic limbs and underscore the ability of the amputee to transition smoothly back into civilian life.

Following an amputation there are two main challenges in adapting to daily life, the first being the process of relearning to do daily tasks to accommodate the limb loss or to use a prosthetic device, and the second being the social barriers that accompany amputation. Often a new amputee will undergo rehabilitation therapy to learn how to safely and efficiently perform daily activities. Additionally, such therapy can teach a new amputee exercises to strengthen their body in ways that will help to compensate for limb loss. If choosing to use a prosthesis, an amputee will often engage in physical therapy to learn how to use the device.

STIGMA often causes significant social and economic barriers for people with amputations who are discriminated against because of their obvious physical difference. Additionally, amputees may encounter difficulty in garnering medical insurance coverage to pay for their prosthetic limbs, which can cost tens of thousands of dollars. Organizations that provide support and advocacy for amputees include the Amputee Coalition of America, the National Amputee Foundation, and the National Limb Loss Information Center. Such organizations provide peer counseling for amputees and may lobby at the state and federal level for policy changes such as better insurance coverage for necessary medical equipment and prosthetics. Many amputees have turned to INTERNET blogs as a way to share support and information with each other. For example, Sara at "Moving Right Along" writes about practical issues such as bathing, biking, and footwear for amputees. TheAmpuT, writing at the blog "Amputeehee" shares HUMOR and vignettes from her life as an amputee dancer (see DANCE).

There are numerous depictions of amputees in American LITERATURE and FILM. Fictional amputees are often antagonistic characters, with personality flaws that are signaled by their missing limb. For example, Captain Ahab from Herman Melville's novel *Moby-Dick* (1851) loses his leg in pursuit of his nemesis, the whale Moby-Dick. The amputation of his limb inflames his single-minded drive to kill the whale. In the Disney film *Peter Pan,* based on the early 20th-century play and novel by J. M. Barrie, Captain Hook, the villain, loses his arm to a crocodile and uses a hook-style arm prosthesis. The murderer from the 1960s TELEVISION program and 1993 film *The Fugitive* is a one-armed man. In the case of all three of these movies, the absence of a limb accentuates the character's malign intentions—as they seem less human because of their amputation.

More recent literary and film examples suggest changes in the way society perceives and represents disability. For example, a 1989 novel, *Geek Love,* depicts a cult movement called Arturism in which followers undergo elective amputation surgeries as a ritual of spiritual progression. In many ways, this work presages current trends in body modification practices that can include the elective amputations of body parts, including digits and genitals. FILMS such as *Forrest Gump* (1994), which features a secondary character who is a bilateral leg amputee, and *The Horse Whisperer* (1998), a story about a young girl who loses her leg in a traumatic horse-riding accident, use digital techniques to "remove" the legs from nonamputee ACTORS. In these films the amputee characters struggle to assimilate back to "normalcy" following their limb loss, though the war veteran is shown to be more bitter than the young girl who loses her leg through an accident. Both stories highlight the humanity and complexity of the characters' experiences.

The history of amputation brings together a number of important and complex themes in American and disability history, including technology, war, and stigma. Equally, its changing meaning and representation show the powerful role individuals and organizations play in shaping the cultural and economic experience of amputees.

See also ACTIVISM AND ADVOCACY; ASSISTIVE TECHNOLOGY AND ADAPTIVE DEVICES; FETISHISM; HANGER, JAMES EDWARD; NORMAL AND NORMALCY; POPULAR CULTURE; STEREOTYPES.

Jana Bouck Remy

Further Reading:

Figg, Laurann, and Jane Farrell-Beck. "Amputation and the Civil War: Physical and Social Dimensions." *Journal of the History of Medicine and Allied Sciences* 48, no. 4 (1993): 454–475.

Goler, Robert I. "Loss and Persistence of Memory: 'The Case of George Dedlow' and the Disabled Civil War Veterans." *Literature and Medicine* 23, no. 1 (2004): 160–183.

Klatzker, Izzy "Socket." "The New Wartime Body." *Clamor* (Fall 2006).

O'Connor, Erin. "Fractions of Men: Engendering Amputation in Victorian Culture." *Comparative Studies in Society and History* 39, no. 4 (1997): 742–777.

Ott, Katherine, David Harley Serlin, and Stephen Mihm. *Artificial Parts, Practical Lives: Modern Histories of Prosthetics.* New York: New York University Press, 2002.

Serlin, David Harley. *Replaceable You: Engineering the Body in Postwar America.* Chicago: University of Chicago Press, 2004.

Smith, Julian. "Between Vermont and Violence: Film Portraits of Vietnam Veterans." *Film Quarterly* 26, no. 4 (1973): 10–17.

Andersson, Yerker (Jerker) (1929–   ) *activist and educator*

As a leader during the formative years of international cooperation among DEAF ORGANIZATIONS, Yerker Andersson has guided the world to view deaf people as a distinct cultural-linguistic group rather than merely as people with a sensory impairment. His global advocacy work and collaboration with cross-disability campaigns highlight complex interpretations of ACCESS, IDENTITY, and COMMUNITY in disability history.

Jerker Andersson (he would later change his first name to Yerker) was born deaf on November 29, 1929, in Vallentuna, a small village north of Stockholm, Sweden. His father was a school superintendent and his mother was a teacher. Andersson and his younger brother, Svante, who was also deaf, attended the Manilla School (Manillaskolan) for the Deaf in Stockholm. Following graduation in 1945, Andersson continued his studies via correspondence.

As a young man Andersson held positions at the Stockholm Dovas Forening (Deaf Club) as vice secretary and secretary, and was its adult education director. Early community work included roles as foreign news editor and club news reporter for the deaf Swedish magazine *SDR-Kontakt* (1950–55) and cofounder and coeditor of the Newsletter *Techentydaren* (*The Sign Reader*) (1952–55).

In 1955 Andersson immigrated to the United States to study at Gallaudet College (later renamed GALLAUDET UNIVERSITY) in Washington, D.C. Four years later he married Gallaudet student Ann Marie "Nancy" Timko. In 1960 he earned his bachelor's degree in sociology. Upon becoming a naturalized U.S. citizen in 1962, he changed his first name from the Swedish Jerker to Yerker. In the same year Andersson earned a master's degree in rehabilitation counseling and a professional diploma in counseling from Teachers College, Columbia University. In 1981 he earned a doctorate in sociology at the University of Maryland, where he completed a comparative study of organizations of the deaf in Sweden and the United States.

Joining the Sociology Department at Gallaudet College in 1964, Andersson taught at his alma mater for over three decades; he also held administrative positions, serving from 1980 until 1982 as special assistant to the dean of the College of Arts and Sciences. Deaf teachers of the deaf have long played a central role in the community's history; Andersson's far-reaching career as an educator has particular historical importance because he represents a generation of teacher-leaders who adopted civil rights ideology to empower his community, a strategy that fundamentally altered relations between deaf people and mainstream society.

Within America's deaf community, Andersson gained a reputation as a world leader on issues related to deaf life, cultural studies, disability rights, and access. Responding to the growing interest in the academic-activist study of deaf and disability issues emanating with and from movements for civil rights, he helped found the DEAF STUDIES Department at Gallaudet in 1993 and served as chairperson of the program from 1994 until 1996. In 1995 President Bill Clinton selected Andersson to serve on the National Council on Disability (NCD), and Andersson led the NCD International Watch from 1997 until 2001.

Andersson's decades of work with the World Federation of the Deaf (WFD) reflect his commitment to global activism. First elected to the WFD Bureau in 1975, Andersson served the organization for 20 years, including eight as vice president (1975–83), and 12 as president (1983–95). As president of the WFD he was the first deaf person to address the United Nations (UN) General Assembly. Andersson has served as a consultant or participant for multiple UN meetings related to the rights of people with disabilities, including the UN Global Project Policy meeting (1991), the UN Seminar on the Measurement of Disability (2001), and the INTERNATIONAL CONVENTION ON THE RIGHTS OF PERSONS WITH DISABILITIES (2007).

The author of numerous published articles on topics related to leadership, language use, and disability, Andersson also holds many honors, including the WFD International Solidarity Merit Award (1983), Gallaudet University Alumni Association Edward Miner Gallaudet Memorial Award (1986), Gallaudet University's Powrie Vaux Doctor Medallion (1989), and Distinguished Faculty Member at Gallaudet (1992). America's NATIONAL ASSOCIATION OF THE DEAF recognized him with its Distinguished Service Award in 1994. From Gallaudet University, Andersson was awarded professor emeritus status (1996) and an honorary doctorate (1998).

Yerker Andersson's academic and advocacy work has broadened the definitions of deaf identity by recognizing the cultural factors that profoundly shape peoples' lives inside and outside of the American context. Many scholars and members of America's deaf cultural community resist labels of disability and collaboration with disability advocates; Andersson's active and exceptional role in pan-disability and global deaf movements reveals diverse views of community and strategies of EMPOWERMENT.

Yerker and Nancy Andersson currently live in Frederick, Maryland.

See also ACTIVISM AND ADVOCACY.

Jean Lindquist Bergey

Further Reading:

"Upward Mobility—Yerker Andersson." NTID Life Histories Project: A Collection of Life Stories of Deaf People. Available online. URL: http://www.rit.edu/~468www/DeafHist/andersson.htm. Accessed August 4, 2008.

"Who Are Our Actual Leaders?" *The Deaf American Monograph* 46 (1996).

Angels in America

Tony Kushner's epic 1990s DRAMA, *Angels in America: A Gay Fantasia on National Themes,* holds considerable artistic and political importance in disability history. It was a landmark American drama in its thematic, symbolic, and theatrical innovation. It also marked a significant culmination in playwriting about the AIDS crisis, creating a theatrical space for COMMUNITY and ACTIVISM in the face of homophobia and the fear of AIDS. It is not typically defined as a "disability play" per se by critics or scholars, and yet its significance to American disability history is no less palpable, given its depiction of the AIDS crisis in the mid 1980s. As character Roy Cohn so bitingly observes, "The worst thing about being sick in America, Ethel, is that you are booted out of the parade. Americans have no use for the sick."

The drama is divided into two plays, *Part One: Millennium Approaches* (1993) and *Part Two: Perestroika* (1994). The plot follows two couples living in New York: Joe and Harper, and Louis and Prior. When Prior is diagnosed with AIDS, he is abandoned by his longtime lover, Louis; Louis then takes up with Joe, who decides—at least for a time—to stop fighting the dictate of his Mormonism that homosexuality is a sin. Joe in turn abandons his wife Harper, who experiences DEPRESSION and drug ADDICTION in the face of the longtime isolation in her marriage. Over the course of the play, each of these main characters must take a journey toward self-determination. And in the tradition of such epic literary journeys, they encounter a wide and fantastical set of characters (some drawn from real-life historical counterparts), such as Roy Cohn, Ethel Rosenberg, the AIDS nurse Belize, Joe's Mormon mother Hannah, and an angel. Over the course of the play, those characters who have been abandoned begin to heal: Harper begins to reclaim her life, emerging from the fantasy and illusion that has been her refuge in the face of overwhelming despair, while Prior accepts his role as a "prophet" who insists on "more life" for himself and other gay men who had previously been cast as pariahs because of AIDS. Louis learns what it means to take responsibility for others, and shapes a new kind of FAMILY with Prior, Belize, and Hannah. Only Joe remains adrift by the end of the plays: having looked out only for his own self-interest, he, and the individualist model he represents, is isolated, and therefore, defeated. Through exploring the fates of these characters, then, the play asks viewers to contemplate a series of important ideas: the importance of compassion for those with AIDS; the tragic consequences of oppression and homophobia; that American independence and fortitude cannot ultimately be based on victimizing those seen as different, for whatever reason; and the necessity of envisioning a future in which there are no silenced victims, one where citizenry is based on forgiveness but also on fairness.

The form of this play, as complex as it is, makes it particularly important to disability history. Building on Brechtian devices of THEATER (meant to disrupt the play's realism and remind the audience they are seeing a performed event), gay culture, and the aesthetics of camp (a kind of ironic theatricality), Kushner creates a fantastical world that rejects traditional dramatic realism. The body of the play, therefore, is itself not "NORMAL" in the context of the usual presumption that realism is the form of traditional American theater. That the play also creates a testament to the historical reality of the AIDS crisis—and how that crisis was long denied by the Reagan administration in the 1980s—is also of central significance. Furthermore, *Angels* is also quite complex in how it negotiates the REPRESENTATION of the AIDS crisis—and by extension, the dramatic representation of disability. For instance, part of its dramatic project is to place this crisis in context, asking how the "othering" of minority communities, whether enslaved African, immigrant, female, Mormon, gay, or disabled, has long been a part of American history. It shows how queer and disabled identities are intertwined in being subject to STIGMA and persecution because they lie outside the heteronormative ideal; they serve, Kushner shows, as the unwitting and unwilling site onto which dominant society projects its fears (including boundary-crossing of any kind). The play's depiction of the stress of living with AIDS in an uncaring society is moving, as is the nuanced portrayal of individuals who both fail and flourish when called on to become empathetic caregivers. Finally, that the central character of the play is Prior, a man living with AIDS who is by turns terrified, resolved, resilient, frightened, and powerful, significantly trumps both the moral and medical models of disability. Prior, as prophet, may be flawed, but his epic journey and complex struggle constitute the play's heart: He is neither tragic victim nor mere pathology.

The play is important, finally, not only because it sidesteps many of the familiar traps of disability representation, but indeed, because it replaces them with nuanced depictions of disabled characters and the disability experience. This is in the interest of a more expansive, and hopefully, essentially American vision; as Prior says directly to the audience at the play's end: "The world only spins forward. We will be citizens. The time has come." The "Great Work" Prior is called to, and calls each of us to, is not just to have hope and compassion but to claim a real place for gay and disabled members of society in the American landscape: one that honors their worth as citizens, recognizes their struggles, and accords them justice.

See also LGBT.

Ann M. Fox

Further Reading:

Geis, Deborah, and Steven F. Kruger. *Approaching the Millennium: Essays on* Angels in America. Ann Arbor: University of Michigan Press, 1997.

Roman, David. "November 1, 1992: AIDS/*Angels in America.*" *Acts of Intervention: Performance, Gay Culture, and AIDS.* Bloomington: Indiana University Press, 1998.

ANSI

The American National Standards Institute, Inc., or ANSI, is a private, nonprofit ORGANIZATION established in 1918 that supervises the voluntary setting of standards related to products, services, personnel, and consumer and manufacturing entities. In the history of disability, ANSI usually is synonymous with ANSI's Project A-117. Established in 1959, Project A-117's purpose was to create architectural standards that could be used in building construction.

The need for Project A-117 originated in the 1940s and 1950s. Thousands of VETERANS who had been disabled by WORLD WAR II–related injuries as well as people who had muscle weakness as a result of poliomyelitis (POLIO) were excluded from public spaces, buildings, and TRANSPORTATION. For people with MOBILITY impairments who used WHEELCHAIRS, CRUTCHES, and other assistive devices, the ARCHITECTURE and organization of public spaces of that era made getting around nearly impossible. There were no CURB CUTS, ramps, kneeling buses, grab bars, or other aids. ANSI initiated Project A-117 to examine the problems and create standards for designers, builders, and engineers.

Project A-117 was directed by TIMOTHY NUGENT. Nugent had been director of the Rehabilitation Education Center at the University of Illinois and a pioneer in creating ACCESS for students with disabilities. Project A-117 included architects, government representatives, rehabilitation specialists, builders, and activists. They published their report in 1961, called *American Standard Specifications for Making Buildings Accessible to, and Usable by, the Physically Handicapped.* It explained such things as the necessary width of doorways and the angle for ramps so that people who use wheelchairs would have full access. The report became the basis for most of the legislation related to architectural barriers for the next several decades, including the ARCHITECTURAL BARRIERS ACT of 1968 and the AMERICANS WITH DISABILITIES ACT of 1990.

ANSI A-117 is a living document and is regularly updated. Building codes and architectural standards are a reflection of the ongoing struggles for inclusion as well as the importance of new technology and materials in shaping culture.

See also ASSISTIVE TECHNOLOGY AND ADAPTIVE DEVICES.

Katherine Ott

Further Reading:

ANSI. *American Standard Specifications for Making Buildings Accessible to, and Usable by, the Physically Handicapped.* Washington, D.C.: ANSI, 1961.

antidepressants

Antidepressants are medications used to treat DEPRESSION, a condition in which a person experiences feelings of sadness that last two weeks or more, and that interfere with daily tasks and enjoyment of activities. It is not known exactly what causes depression, although it is believed that a combination of genetics, life circumstances, and chemical imbalances plays a central role.

Antidepressants are thought to work by slowing the removal of certain neurotransmitters (hormones that regulate mood) such as serotonin, norepinephrine, and dopamine from the brain, making more of these key chemicals available. Antidepressants have a slow onset of action and are typically taken several weeks before full therapeutic effects are experienced. Side effects associated with antidepressants are usually mild and temporary. Common side effects of the most popular antidepressants, selective serotonin reuptake inhibitors, are headache, nausea, nervousness, and sexual dysfunction.

In the 1950s the first antidepressants were introduced. Named for their chemical structure, tricyclic antidepressants (TCAs) were thought to increase levels of serotonin and norepinephrine. An example of these medications is amitriptyline, known by its brand names Elavil® and Endep®. Another type of antidepressants, monoamine oxidase inhibitors (MAOIs), were also introduced at this time. These drugs were mainly recommended for people with depression whose condition did not improve with other antidepressants.

During the 1960s and 1970s TCAs dominated the antidepressant market in the United States. However, severe side effects, which included dizziness and hypotension, continued to be a concern. As a result, in the 1980s several new antidepressants were marketed to be as effective as older ones, but with fewer side effects. These included mirtazepine (Remeron®), a tetracyclic antidepressant, and bupropion (Wellbutrin®). By the late 1990s marketing campaigns aggressively promoted use of selective serotonin reuptake inhibitors (SSRIs). Today, SSRIs, which specifically target serotonin, are most physicians' treatment of choice for depression. They include fluoxetine (PROZAC®), sertraline (Zoloft®), and paroxetine (Paxil®). Since 2000 additional antidepressants, such as Lexapro® and Cymbalta®, which target serotonin and norepinephrine, came on to the market. Drug makers continue to research new ways to medically address depression and to minimize treatment side effects.

Many Americans have found antidepressants to be helpful, and society at large generally has supported this form of treatment. However, some disability advocates strongly challenge the widespread use of these medications. They question these pharmaceutical treatments since the exact mechanism of action and longer term effects of these agents—particularly in CHILDREN—are still not fully understood. Critics also have challenged the antidepressant industry for creating a "Prozac Nation" of overmedicated children and adults.

In support of this criticism, several clinical trials of antidepressants in recent years have shown virtually no improvement in depression when people taking antidepressants were compared to people taking a placebo (sugar pill). In 2004 the U.S. Food and Drug Administration (FDA) issued a Black Box warning (the most serious warning label for prescription drugs) for all antidepressant medications. The FDA cautioned consumers about the potential increased risk of suicidal thoughts or suicide attempts in children and adolescents taking antidepressants. In 2007 the warning was extended to include young adults up to age 25.

Proponents of antidepressants continue to praise the so-called miracle drugs for vastly improving quality of life for many people. They point to other recent studies that have shown antidepressants to have positive effects in reducing depression in children and adolescents, as well as in adults. Complicated factors, including contradictory research results, financial and medical investments in pharmaceutical treatment, as well as advocacy efforts by proponents and opponents of antidepressant medications make this an important and changing feature in American life.

See also MENTAL ILLNESS; PROZAC.

Dawn Reynolds

Further Reading:

Ables, Adrienne Z., and Otis L. Baughman III. "Antidepressants: Update on New Agents and Indications." *American Family Physician* 67, no. 3 (February 2003): 547–554.

Elliott, Carl. *Prozac as a Way of Life.* Chapel Hill: University of North Carolina Press, 2004.

Healy, David. *The Antidepressant Era.* Cambridge, Mass.: Harvard University Press, 1999.

National Institute of Mental Health. "Medications. With Addendum January 2007." National Institute of Mental Health, National Institutes of Health, U.S. Department of Health and Human Services, Bethesda, Md., September 2002. (NIH Publication No. 02-3929). Available online. URL: http://www.nimh.nih.gov/publicat/NIMHmedicate.pdf. Accessed April 2, 2007.

National Mental Health Association. Web site. URL: www.mentalhealth.org.

Wurtzel, Elizabeth. *Prozac Nation.* New York: Riverhead Trade, 1995.

antipsychotic drugs

Initially developed in the 1950s to treat SCHIZOPHRENIA, antipsychotic drugs, or neuroleptics, were intended as a less intrusive alternative to earlier interventions such as electroshock (see ELECTROCONVULSIVE THERAPY), surgical lobotomies (see LOBOTOMY), and physical restraints, including straight jackets. Antipsychotics consist of two categories: the early generation of "typical" antipsychotics, some of which are considered major tranquilizers because of their sedating effects, and a later generation of "atypicals" heralded as less sedating and with fewer unwanted effects. Drugs such as haloperidol (Haldol) and THORAZINE (chlorpromazine) often were seen as a breakthrough allowing people otherwise incapable of surviving on their own to live outside institutions. Some consider these drugs a medical advancement as significant as the advent of antibiotics, while others view them as a form of chemical restraint producing extreme sluggishness and a range of intolerable side effects, as noted by patients and psychiatrists from the drugs' first use.

For some patient advocacy groups access to these drugs is a high priority. Yet other groups representing patients and ex-patients oppose the drugs' widespread use. Some advocates contend, for example, that hearing voices—considered a hallmark of psychosis—calls for attention to what the voices say, processing their content rather than attempting to quiet or eradicate them with antipsychotics. Others charge that the drugs frequently cause damaging and often irreversible motor effects, cognitive dysfunction, and other physiological harms; are likely to exacerbate rather than diminish symptoms; and have too often been administered in ways that violate human rights through less than fully informed consent or through harmful involuntary treatment. Some critics also question the "brain imbalance" theory of MENTAL ILLNESS upon which these drugs are predicated, seeing antipsychotics as symptomatic of PSYCHIATRY's increasing turn to pharmaceutical solutions at the expense of insight-based treatment and attention to the role of social environments in individual suffering. Additional controversies include the increasing numbers of children prescribed these drugs, overprescription, and disproportionate prescription to African Americans and poor people.

The first antipsychotics were derived from compounds used to kill insects and swine parasites, which were then researched as a numbing agent and found effective for physical sedation. Thorazine, still in widespread use, blocks dopamine reception in the brain, and it soon became standard treatment in state mental hospitals. It was not thought to alter the content of atypical mental states but rather to produce emotional detachment from them and from environmental stimuli. Although Thorazine often triggered an extreme lethargy and Parkinson's-like symptoms, researchers tended to perceive these as preferable to unmedicated symptoms. Thorazine, first presented as a "chemical lobotomy" (advantageously nonsurgical), was eventually promoted as a drug allowing people to function in society again.

Haloperidol, a far more potent drug than Thorazine, was introduced to the market in the 1960s. Many psychiatrists preferred it over Thorazine because of its more effective blocking of dopamine transmission, believed in turn to control psychosis. Many patients found its side effects difficult to tolerate. These effects relate so closely to Parkinson's disease that Haldol has been used to induce the disease in order to study it. The Soviets used Haldol, as well as the antipsychotic Aminazine, to punish dissident political prisoners.

Many factors, including the public expense of high psychiatric in-patient rates, increasing public demand for community treatment, and favorable business conditions for pharmaceutical companies, led to the development of less sedating antipsychotics. Introduced in the 1990s, these so-called atypicals, such as risperidone and clozapine, targeted multiple neurotransmitters. Believed to normalize the brain chemistry imbalance thought to foster psychosis, some patients using atypicals return to behavior described as normal functioning—a visible improvement over the older generation of drugs, whose side effects include not only extreme sedation but also various involuntary movements. Through fostering an appearance of NORMALCY and furthering a sense of mental illness as chemical imbalance, atypicals have been said to contribute significantly to lifting the STIGMA of mental illness. This apparent advantage in terms of side effects still awaits verification, since the new drugs may not have been in use long enough to produce the side effects that in the older drugs often emerge only after a decade or more of use. Though atypicals are widely used, evidence of their superiority over the older drugs remains inconclusive; many studies touting these drugs' effectiveness were funded by pharmaceutical companies, and there is increasing concern over their emerging metabolic side effects, as well as their specific risks for particular groups of patients, such as children and the elderly.

Antipsychotics raise important historical, philosophical, and political questions about what kinds of mental and emotional states are intrinsic to the self, the social norms used to evaluate them, and the appropriate basis for social intervention into individuals' behavior and mental states.

See also MAD PEOPLE AND MADNESS.

Abby Wilkerson

Further Reading:
Hearing Voices Network, Manchester, England. Available online. URL: http://www.hearing-voices.org/index.htm. Accessed December 21, 2006.

Whitaker, Robert. *Mad in America: Bad Science, Bad Medicine, and the Enduring Mistreatment of the Mentally Ill.* Cambridge, Mass.: Perseus Publishing, 2002.

Arbus, Diane (1923–1971) *photographer*

Photographer Diane Arbus is best known for her trademark portraits of eccentric subjects. Among celebrities, burlesque performers, conventioneers, transvestites, nudists, and individuals in quirky finery, Arbus photographed many people with disabilities, displaying their corporeal and behavioral differences from the norm: *Jewish Giant at Home with His Parents in the Bronx, NY* (1970); *Mexican Dwarf (a.k.a Cha Cha) in His Hotel Room* (1970); *Masked Woman in a Wheelchair* (1970); and *Untitled* (1970–71), a series photographed in institutions for the developmentally disabled. These portraits of disabled subjects are among her best-known photographs today; however, all of Arbus's photographs accentuate the idiosyncratic and eye-catching characteristics of her subjects, disabled and NONDISABLED. Arbus indeed plays an important role in the visual REPRESENTATION of disability as social spectacle.

Arbus was born on March 14, 1923, into a family of Jewish storeowners in New York City. Her older brother, Howard Nemerov, became a prominent poet. She later married photographer Allan Arbus, with whom she had two daughters, Doon and Amy, and a successful commercial career. She ended the collaboration with her husband in the early 1960s to pursue creative "street photography," a style that documented urban subjects and turned away from "formalism," a movement in art PHOTOGRAPHY that aimed to create aesthetically pleasing compositions, toward a more grainy or gritty aesthetic. Arbus strategically employed a Rolleiflex camera for its square-frame format, intense details, and exaggerated distortion of image edges. She uniquely practiced hand-printing techniques to create striking contrasts, palpable textures, and bold borders. These visual characteristics call attention to Arbus's photographic manipulation and nature of the photographs *as* artistic representations, as they contradict the assumed objectivity of photography. Arbus's specific developing and framing techniques made even the ordinary subject extraordinary.

Arbus was always drawn to various offbeat subcultures, which operated by rules and social norms separate from the mainstream and which she found refreshingly liberated. She frequented Hubert's Museum and Coney Island, revival side show venues, and befriended and photographed many of the performers (*Russian Midget Friends in a Living Room on 100th St., NYC*) (1963). Arbus's personal and professional affinity for the so-called freakish has been associated by many critics with her self-image as a social outcast and ongoing struggle with depression, which intensified in the last years of her life and led to her suicide on July 26, 1971. However, these opinions may reveal viewers' stereotypical assumptions about her distinctive subjects, rather than reflect the real identities of those featured in the photographs. Arbus achieved professional and financial success, causing critics to question her motivations for representing disabled people and accusing Arbus of exploitation. Her portraits of disabled individuals invite viewers to stare (see STARING), an act that DISABILITY STUDIES scholars have said exploits and degrades disabled people. Yet many of Arbus's compositions may also implicate the viewer in this act, causing viewers to question their desires to stare and their classifications of disabled people as freakish. Further, many subjects actively perform and consciously pose before Arbus's camera, acknowledging and even soliciting the stare. Many of her subjects, such as Eddie Carmel (the subject of *Jewish Giant*) and Andrew Ratoucheff (featured in *Russian Midget Friends*) were already actors and subcultural entertainers, professions in which they placed themselves on public display. Ironically, Arbus's photographs feature them in their familiar living spaces to show them as "NORMAL" folk—the people of our own neighborhoods. Arbus's compositional arrangements and her affection for her subjects, which is often revealed in the photographs, blur distinctions between the so-called normal versus abnormal or freakish. Finally, the photographs uniquely juxtapose aesthetics and conventions drawn from FAMILY and personal images, social documentary, fine art portraiture, FREAK SHOWS, and medical photographs, making them deeply historical and layered representations of disability. Viewing Arbus's photographs through the lens of disability themes adds dimensions to them.

See also FREAKERY; REPRESENTATION.

Ann Millett-Gallant

Further Reading:

Garland Thomson, Rosemarie. "Seeing the Disabled: Visual Rhetorics of Disability in Popular Photography." In *The New Disability History: American Perspectives,* edited by Paul K. Longmore and Lauri Umansky, 335–374. New York: New York University Press, 2001.

Hevey, David. *The Creatures Time Forgot: Photography and Disability Imagery.* New York: Routledge, 1992.

Millett, Ann. "Exceeding the Frame: The Photography of Diane Arbus." *Disability Studies Quarterly* 24, no. 4 (Fall 2004).

ARC, The

The ARC of the United States is a nonprofit ORGANIZATION advocating for people with intellectual disabilities (see COGNITIVE AND INTELLECTUAL DISABILITY). Established in Minneapolis in 1950 as the National Association of Parents and Friends of Mentally Retarded Children by a committee of local parent associations, its first president was Alan Sampson. The organization has undergone several name changes since, including the National Association for Retarded Citizens (1973–81) and the Association for Retarded Citizens (1981–92). Its current name was adopted in 1992. Members initially focused on the lack of educational opportunities for their CHILDREN, the difficulty of getting people into state institutions, and the quality of care provided.

Two incidents raised public awareness about intellectual disabilities in the organization's early years. In 1950 PEARL BUCK published *The Child Who Never Grew* about her daughter with an intellectual disability and, in 1953, DALE EVANS ROGERS published *Angel Unaware* about her daughter born with DOWN SYNDROME, and donated royalties from the book to the organization. By 1964 the group counted more than 100,000 members, making it one of the largest disability organizations in the country. The ARC had grown by 2008 to more than 140,000 members and claimed to be the largest COMMUNITY-based organization of and for people with intellectual disabilities.

A review of the ARC's early programs indicates that the focus lay on issues related to children and families, including school admission, access to and improvement of state institutions, and research into prevention of MENTAL RETARDATION. Responding to changes in disability ACTIVISM, the organization in recent years has broadened its mission statement and opened its leadership to include adults with intellectual disabilities.

By the 1970s the organization became involved in lawsuits aimed at ending mistreatment in institutions. It supported the movement toward DEINSTITUTIONALIZATION of people with intellectual disabilities. During this time, the organization used insider tactics to influence policy, namely testimony, research, and lobbying rather than PROTEST or demonstration. It used a similar approach in 1990 in lobbying for the AMERICANS WITH DISABILITIES ACT.

Three areas are emphasized nationally now: public policy advocacy, research into the prevention of intellectual and developmental disabilities (see DEVELOPMENTAL DISABILITY) and integration of people with disabilities into society, and raising public awareness of these issues. It supports Social Security payments to people with intellectual disabilities and expansion of the 1973 VOCATIONAL REHABILITATION ACT. At the state level, member units have been active in the development of plans promoting EMPLOYMENT and EDUCATION.

The ARC's relationship with the broader DISABILITY RIGHTS MOVEMENT has been complex. Founded as a parent organization, its viewpoint generally reflected this population more than those it served. Critics also point to its lackluster response to reports of conditions inside institutions during the 1960s. The ARC encouraged only better oversight and improved programs for people in residential care during that decade; not until the 1970s did it advocate broader deinstitutionalization. Still, the organization was an early advocate of community living for people with intellectual disabilities, a position embraced by disability activists in the INDEPENDENT LIVING MOVEMENT.

Strategies for promoting employment represents another area of contention. The ARC strongly advocated for employment of people with developmental disabilities, but early efforts resulted in inappropriate placements in repetitive, low-skill jobs providing little fulfillment and income. The organization continues to counter this criticism, noting that it was one of the sole advocates for people with intellectual disabilities before the 1980s, bringing attention to issues such as housing and appropriate education and employment for people with intellectual disabilities.

The ARC has been active recently in supporting policies providing respite care and removing discrimination against people with disabilities (such as a law proposed in Hawaii to remove the bar on voter registration for people with mental retardation). The organization has also supported federal bills requiring the inclusion of people with disabilities in emergency management and disaster relief planning (see DISASTERS AND DISASTER RECOVERY) and an appropriation supporting housing programs for people with disabilities. The ARC has taken an active role in advocating protection of the rights of criminal suspects with intellectual disabilities, arguing against the death penalty and for safeguards for people with intellectual disabilities as suspects, defendants, or witnesses in criminal proceedings. The ARC issued position statements in 2004 opposing PHYSICIAN-ASSISTED SUICIDE in alignment with the mainstream disability movement.

The ARC's role in disability history demonstrates the importance of families and activists, as well as the evolving understanding of citizenship, rights, and IDENTITY.

See also FAMILY; PARENT ADVOCACY GROUPS; VOTING.

David Penna
Vickie D'Andrea-Penna

Further Reading:

Jackson, Laura. "Serving the Housing Needs of the Disabled." *Journal of Housing and Community Development* 58, no. 6 (2001): 32.

Segal, Robert. "The National Association for Retarded Citizens." Available online. URL: http://www.thearc.org/history/segal. htm. Accessed February 22, 2007.

Williams, Paul, and Bonnie Shoultz. *We Can Speak for Ourselves: Self-Advocacy for Mentally Handicapped People*. Bloomington: Indiana University Press, 1982.

Architectural Barriers Act

The Architectural Barriers Act (ABA) of 1968 is generally considered the first piece of federal disability rights legislation. It was also the first attempt by the U.S. government to make buildings accessible to people with disabilities. The ABA was the brainchild of HUGH GREGORY GALLAGHER. A POLIO quadriplegic and longtime Democratic Party political aide, Gallagher worked as a legislative assistant to President Lyndon B. Johnson in 1968. He conceived and wrote the ABA, framing the legislation as a civil rights issue.

The ABA required that all buildings constructed, altered, or financed by the federal government after 1969 be made accessible. The law made the same stipulation for buildings leased or purchased by the federal government after that date and authorized the General Services Administration to establish standards for accessibility. The ABA covered not only federal office buildings but also recreational, medical, and educational facilities run or financed by the federal government. Specifically excluded were buildings intended primarily for NONDISABLED military personnel.

The ABA contained other significant weaknesses that dramatically diminished its value. The ABA did not apply to most buildings, government or private. A disabled person also had no way of determining accessibility or the degree of accessibility without testing a particular site. Moreover, it had no provision for enforcement or compliance. Disability activists and their allies campaigned to rectify this point and, in 1973, Congress created the Architectural and Transportation Barriers Compliance Board (ATBCB) to enforce the original act. Chronically underfunded, the board chose to focus on mediation and persuasion rather than enforcement. It quickly earned a reputation for granting waivers to those who sought exemptions to the ABA's requirements. When the administration of President Ronald Reagan attempted to abolish the ATBCB in the 1980s, pressure by disability activists kept it alive. Over time, the ATBCB subsequently devoted more attention to enforcement, possibly because of changing societal views toward disabilities. As a result of weaknesses in the ABA, the AMERICANS WITH DISABILITIES ACT (ADA) of 1990 covered accessibility in all public accommodations.

The U.S. ACCESS BOARD, a federal agency created in 1973 and committed to accessible design, periodically issues updated guidelines to serve as the baseline for standards used to enforce the ABA and ADA. The guidelines address access in new construction and alterations. They contain scoping provisions, which indicate what has to comply, and technical specifications, which spells out how compliance is to be achieved. The standards, which are maintained by other federal agencies such as the Department of Justice, are the ones that building designers and owners must follow. The revisions reflect technological innovations, such as the provision that ATM machines include audible output so that people with vision impairments are provided equal access.

The Architectural Barriers Act of 1968 set the stage for more substantial legislation, such as the ADA. The passage of the legislation demonstrated the power of activism and the ability to produce policy change, as well as the slow but general forward movement of accommodation for people with disabilities.

See also ACCESS AND ACCESSIBILITY; LAW AND POLICY.

Caryn E. Neumann

Further Reading:

Bowe, Frank G. *Handicapping America: Barriers to Disabled People.* New York: Harper & Row, 1978.

Frechette, Leon A. *Accessible Housing.* New York: McGraw-Hill, 1996.

U.S. Access Board. *Americans with Disabilities Act and Architectural Barriers Act Accessibility Guidelines.* Washington, D.C.: U.S. Access Board, 2004.

Architectural Barriers Act (1968)

In 1968 President Lyndon B. Johnson's legislative assistant, Hugh Gregory Gallagher (1932–2004), proposed that all buildings erected, renovated, or financed by the federal government should be made accessible. Gallagher's proposal led to the Architectural Barriers Act of 1968 (ABA), one of America's first disability rights laws, that President Johnson signed on August 12, 1968. Although the act applied to a comparatively limited range of buildings and specified no mechanism for enforcing its mandates, the ABA served as an important move toward full inclusion of people with disabilities in society.

Architectural Barriers Act of 1968, as amended
42 U.S.C. §§ 4151 et seq.
Public Law 90-480

§ 4151. "Building" defined
As used in this chapter, the term "building" means any building or facility (other than (A) a privately owned residential structure not leased by the Government for subsidized housing programs and (B) any building or facility on a military installation designed and constructed primarily for use by able bodied military personnel) the intended use for which either will require that such building or facility be accessible to the public, or may result in the employment or residence therein of physically handicapped persons, which building or facility is—

(1) to be constructed or altered by or on behalf of the United States;

(2) to be leased in whole or in part by the United States after August 12, 1968;[1]

[1] A 1976 amendment deleted the following words from the end of paragraph (2): "after construction or alteration in accordance with plans and specifications of the United States." That amendment applied to "every lease entered into on or after January 1, 1977, including any renewal of a lease entered into before such a date which renewal is on or after such date." (Pub. L. 94-541)

(3) to be financed in whole or in part by a grant or a loan made by the United States after August 12, 1968, if such building or facility is subject to standards for design, construction, or alteration issued under authority of the law authorizing such grant or loan; or

(4) to be constructed under authority of the National Capital Transportation Act of 1960, the National Capital Transportation Act of 1965, or title III of the Washington Metropolitan Area Transit Regulation Compact.

§ 4152. Standards for design, construction, and alteration of buildings; Administrator of General Services

The Administrator of General Services, in consultation with the Secretary of Health and Human Services, shall prescribe standards for the design, construction, and alteration of buildings (other than residential structures subject to this chapter and buildings, structures, and facilities of the Department of Defense and of the United States Postal Service subject to this chapter) to insure whenever possible that physically handicapped persons will have ready access to, and use of, such buildings.

§ 4153. Standards for design, construction, and alteration of buildings; Secretary of Housing and Urban Development

The Secretary of Housing and Urban Development, in consultation with the Secretary of Health and Human Services, shall prescribe standards for the design, construction, and alteration of buildings which are residential structures subject to this chapter to insure whenever possible that physically handicapped persons will have ready access to, and use of, such buildings.

§ 4154. Standards for design, construction, and alteration of buildings; Secretary of Defense

The Secretary of Defense, in consultation with the Secretary of Health and Human Services, shall prescribe standards for the design, construction, and alteration of buildings, structures, and facilities of the Department of Defense subject to this chapter to insure whenever possible that physically handicapped persons will have ready access to, and use of, such buildings.

§ 4154a. Standards for design, construction, and alteration of buildings; United States Postal Service

The United States Postal Service, in consultation with the Secretary of Health and Human Services, shall prescribe such standards for the design, construction, and alteration of its buildings to insure whenever possible that physically handicapped persons will have ready access to, and use of, such buildings.

§ 4155. Effective date of standards

Every building designed, constructed, or altered after the effective date of a standard issued under this chapter which is applicable to such building, shall be designed, constructed, or altered in accordance with such standard.

§ 4156. Waiver and modification of standards

The Administrator of General Services, with respect to standards issued under section 4152 of this title, and the Secretary of Housing and Urban Development, with respect to standards issued under section 4153 of this title, and the Secretary of Defense with respect to standards issued under section 4154 of this title, and the United States Postal Service with respect to standards issued under section 4154a of this title—

(1) is authorized to modify or waive any such standard, on a case-by-case basis, upon application made by the head of the department, agency, or instrumentality of the United States concerned, and upon a determination by the Administrator or Secretary, as the case may be, that such modification or waiver is clearly necessary, and

(2) shall establish a system of continuing surveys and investigations to insure compliance with such standards.

§ 4157. Reports to Congress and Congressional committees

(a) The Administrator of General Services shall report to Congress during the first week of January of each year on his activities and those of other departments, agencies, and instrumentalities of the Federal Government under this chapter during the preceding fiscal year including, but not limited to, standards issued, revised, amended, or repealed under this chapter and all case-by-case modifications, and waivers of such standards during such year.

(b) The Architectural and Transportation Barriers Compliance Board established by section 792 of Title 29 shall report to Public Works and Transportation Committee of the House of

Representatives and the Environment and Public Works Committee of the Senate during the first week of January of each year on its activities and actions to insure compliance with the standards prescribed under this chapter.

⬥

Source: Excerpted from the Web site of the United States Access Board at http://www.access-board.gov/about/laws/ABA.htm.

architecture

Architecture may be the issue that best reminds the general public that, when dealing with disability, there is no us/them dichotomy. Because all people deal with the vicissitudes of chance, change, and advancing age, in themselves and in those with whom they share their lives, an accessible built environment is required, not only by those individuals included in the 1990 AMERICANS WITH DISABILITIES ACT definition of disability but also by all human beings. Historically, the need for an accessible built environment was so unappreciated that, for example, after the 1945 death of President FRANKLIN D. ROOSEVELT, the accessibility that had been provided in Washington, D.C., to serve the MOBILITY needs of the WHEELCHAIR-using president were dismantled just as the VETERANS with disabilities were returning from WORLD WAR II.

There has been little research with respect to most 19th-century buildings accommodating people with sensory or mobility impairments. For example, while an institution built in Pennsylvania to serve DEAF students in the early 19th century (now part of the Philadelphia University of the Arts) achieved architectural prominence in the 19th century, there is no indication that there was consideration of accessibility in the structure. Architecture did, however, play a key role in the design of "insane asylums," hundreds of which were built across the United States in the 19th century. Flawed as they were in treating people with psychiatric and cognitive disabilities, they were nonetheless "an improvement," historian Carla Yanni has written, "over dark, wet cellars, holes in the ground, or cages." In 1854 THOMAS KIRKBRIDE, superintendent of the Pennsylvania Hospital for the Insane, laid out a plan for asylum design in his book, *On the Construction, Organization, and General Arrangements of Hospitals for the Insane with Some Remarks on Insanity and its Treatment*. Kirkbride recommended a group of connected pavilions built in a V-shaped pattern with separate areas for work and recreation. The "Kirkbride Plan," as it became known, also included parlors to help forge a comforting, homelike atmosphere. There were separate wings for men and women, and, in many southern asylums, separate floors for whites and blacks, with the latter often housed in the basement. Later in the century prominent American architects, such as Henry Hobson Richardson, designed monumental stone buildings for people with MENTAL ILLNESS, such as the Buffalo State Hospital in Buffalo, New York. Many of these massive structures still exist.

One of the most important examples of architecture influenced by disability issues was created in Georgia. At ROOSEVELT WARM SPRINGS INSTITUTE FOR REHABILITATION, a rehabilitation center for POLIO survivors established in the 1920s by Roosevelt before his presidency, "accessibility" was determined to be a major goal. This facility included such amenities as ramps between buildings with slopes suitable for wheelchair users, "electric eyes" to open doors, incline elevators for negotiating stairs, and wheelchair-accessible bathrooms. As pioneering as Warm Springs was, the nation was unprepared to deal with the overwhelming number of World War II veterans who, because of the advent of antibiotics and improved medical and surgical techniques, returned, in unprecedented numbers, as PARAPLEGICS and quadriplegics. By 1948, to serve these disabled veterans, the University of Illinois established a wheelchair accessible campus that, however, was not generally used as a model by other major universities until the 1970s. By the 1970s BERKELEY, CALIFORNIA, became the "mecca" for those with mobility disabilities because of its implementation of the principles of "UNIVERSAL DESIGN," designs that create environments that serve the broadest public, including those with disabilities.

Descriptions of the requirements for "wheelchair accessibility" in the homes of disabled veterans of World War II frequently were evident in their monthly publication, *Paraplegia News*, in the late 1940s. By 1950 they revealed, in this publication, their concern with the inequality of accessibility available to civilian paraplegics and quadriplegics as compared to disabled veterans who shared the same issues. For example, "References to the need that mobility-impaired veterans had for 'houses fitted with special equipment' or 'remodeling conventional dwellings to wheelchair living'" appeared in the same publication. There was little recognition of a similar need, nor provision of such accessibility, for mobility-impaired civilians. However, many of the emerging independent living centers that began in the 1970s, especially Access Living of Chicago, Illinois (founded in 1980), begun to focus on ensuring that housing developers complied with the Fair Housing Amendments Act of 1988, mandating that these developers conform to the principles of "adaptable design," which enables all people to remain in their homes as their physical conditions change as a consequence of age or disability.

Incorporating specific fixed-access features while allowing others to be added to existing structures as they are needed, "adaptable design" was developed in the mid 1980s by the disability community in conjunction with architects.

Adaptable design features include the following: at least one building entrance must be on an accessible route; all doors into and within all premises must be wide enough to allow passage by wheelchair users; all premises must contain an accessible route into and through the dwelling unit; all light switches, electrical outlets, thermostats, and environmental controls must be in an accessible location; reinforcements in the bathroom walls for later installation of grab bars around toilet, tub, and shower must be provided; and usable kitchens and bathrooms must be provided so that wheelchair users can maneuver about the space.

"Visitability" expanded and built on the principles of "adaptable design." Developed by Eleanor Smith of Concrete Change, an Atlanta, Georgia, disability rights ORGANIZA-TION, "visitability" is a grassroots movement to ensure that all new housing, not just the specific homes of people with disabilities, is accessible to all people for visiting. While the Fair Housing Amendments Act of 1988 set out designs and guidelines for multidwelling residences, "visitability" focuses on the accessibility of all homes with three, purposefully simple, basic essentials: one zero-step entrance, all main floor interior doors—including bathrooms—with 32 inches of clear passage space, and at least a half bath (though preferably a full bath) on the main floor. These low-tech features for "adaptable design" or for "visitability" add no or minimal expense if included in the design phase of a structure rather than if that structure requires retrofitting for accessibility.

The widespread recognition of the relevance of accessibility to the general public became increasingly evident as three *New York Times* articles, the first two in the real estate section published in the late 1990s, revealed. The first referred to "the new militant attitude among many of the disabled." The second observed, "Advocates of barrier-free environments are pursuing the . . . ambitious goal of what they call universally accessible buildings; comfortable, usable and safe for anyone whose physical capabilities differ from those of an able-bodied, average-sized adult. As baby boomers go grey, the thinking goes there will be more need than ever for environments that are easy to get around." Ten months later, a front-page *Times* article noted that the necessity for accessibility had become strikingly apparent to retirees in Florida condominiums in their eighties who could no longer negotiate the flight of steps that they scarcely noticed in their sixties.

The "militant" approach of activists in the disability COMMUNITY is exemplified by two actions of the mid 1990s, each spearheaded by disability rights organizations: the first by DISABLED IN ACTION of New York City, the second by ADAPT of Denver, Colorado. The former, the "one-step" campaign, was an effective reaction to edifices built with a single step in front of the entrances, an architectural tradition in New York City. Disabled in Action invoked the "readily achievable" mandate in the 1990 Americans with Disabilities

Act requiring that such structures be accompanied by a ramp that would render them accessible to those with motor disabilities. In the second example, ADAPT protested the refusal of the proprietor of an elegant Denver restaurant to comply with the law requiring that he provide accessibility to his establishment. Demonstrating their wit and determination, members of the organization set up tables and chairs in front of the restaurant, served cheap wine and canned food, and displayed a sign reading, "accessible seating."

Since World War II the activism and needs of people with disabilities have profoundly affected architecture in the United States. As the *New York Times* declared in the 1997 article "Architecture in the Age of Accessibility," "it [accessibility] is reshaping the entire built environment. And it is defining architecture of the 1990s as much as any other stylistic impulse." This "impulse" of accessibility has continued to shape architecture in the 21st century.

See also ACTIVISM AND ADVOCACY; AMERICAN DISABLED FOR ATTENDANT PROGRAMS TODAY; ASYLUMS AND INSTITUTIONS.

Doris Zames Fleischer

Further Reading:
Americans with Disabilities Act of 1990 (Title 42, United States Code).
Dunlap, David W. "Architecture in the Age of Accessibility," *New York Times,* 1 June 1997, sec. 9, p. 1.
Fair Housing Amendments Act of 1988 (Title 42, United States Code).
Fleischer, Doris Zames, and Frieda Zames. *The Disability Rights Movement: From Charity to Confrontation.* Philadelphia: Temple University Press, 2001.
Martin, Douglas. "Disability Culture: Eager to Bite the Hand That Would Feed Them," *New York Times,* 1 June 1997, sec. 4, pp. 1, 6.
Rimer, Sara. "New Needs for Retirement Complexes' Oldest," *New York Times,* 23 March 1998, p. A1.
Yanni, Carla. *The Architecture of Madness: Insane Asylums in the United States.* Minneapolis: University of Minnesota Press, 2007.

archives See DISABILITY HISTORY ARCHIVES.

art See DISABILITY ART AND ARTISTIC EXPRESSION.

arthritis

Arthritis, deriving from the Greek roots, arth- (joint) and -itis (inflammation), is a common DISEASE attacking connective tissues such as joints, muscles, and tendons. Many sources call arthritis the primary source of disability and the most prevalent health problem in the United States, limiting the activities of about 70 million Americans—one in three adults, along with many CHILDREN.

There are roughly 100 forms of arthritis, known as rheumatic diseases, some of them caused by immune disorders, all of them hindering mobility and causing PAIN. The extraordinary prevalence of arthritis as both a disease and a disability has not raised its profile in public consciousness as much as might be expected, possibly because arthritis is associated with elderly people (though this is untrue of many forms), because it is often considered shameful, and because it strikes twice as many women as men.

Although some forms of arthritis have been found in bones since the time of the dinosaurs, its causes have remained elusive, and as yet there is no cure. In the United States, where the disease was long known, its prevalence first became evident during WORLD WAR I, when 92,000 American soldiers were diagnosed with chronic arthritis, either osteoarthritis, rheumatoid arthritis, or rheumatic fever. Today arthritis persists as a difficult disability, affecting the bodily connectors essential for full participation in living. The most common form, osteoarthritis, wears down cartilage between the bones in hips, knees, and fingers; ankylosing spondylitis stiffens the spine; rheumatoid arthritis, an autoimmune disease in which the immune system attacks the organs it is supposed to protect, causes damage throughout the body. All forms of arthritis tend to be chronic, that is, they stay in the connective tissues for years.

Many treatments have been tried, some deadly, some fraudulent, others extremely helpful. Since the mid 20th century, drugs such as cortisone, developed specifically for rheumatoid arthritis, have transformed the situation of many sufferers. By the 1990s new pharmaceutical remedies (so-called biologics) produced significant advances, allowing less pain and more mobility. Worldwide access to these new and expensive drugs remains limited. However, medical breakthroughs hold great promise, regimens of exercise as well as drugs have proven effective, and advocacy ORGANIZA-TIONS such as the Arthritis Foundation reach more patients and politicians than ever before.

The DISABILITY RIGHTS MOVEMENT and the broad spectrum of arthritis sufferers have only begun to make use of each other's potential. On the one hand, people with disabilities may wish to avoid being considered diseased, which could invite quarantine or rejection. On the other hand, people with arthritis may hope for alleviation or keep their pain under wraps, so as not to jeopardize their jobs. In some cases, those with illness and those with disabilities argue over issues at the beginning and end of life, such as AMNIOCEN-TESIS (prenatal genetic screening) and assisted choices to die. However, arthritis proves that actual bodies get disabled from being sick and sick from being disabled.

In fact, the history of arthritis validates one of the indispensable concepts of the DISABILITY RIGHTS MOVEMENT, namely, that addressing the problems of disabled people addresses universal human concerns. Innovations such as the Jacuzzi, Good Grip implements, and speech recognition computer programs, which were developed to help people with IMPAIRED joints, have improved the physical functioning of all people. Likewise, several of our most effective drugs—aspirin, cortisone—originated specifically to remedy arthritis inflammation, and they ended up benefiting human health at large.

Mary Felstiner

Further Reading:

Felstiner, Mary. *Out of Joint: A Private & Public Story of Arthritis.* Lincoln: University of Nebraska Press, 2005.

Flynn, John A., and Timothy Johnson. *Arthritis 2006.* Baltimore: Johns Hopkins White Papers, 2006.

Fries, James F. *Arthritis: A Take Care of Yourself Health Guide for Understanding Your Arthritis.* New York: Perseus, 1999.

artists   See DISABILITY ART AND ARTISTIC EXPRESSION.

ASL   See AMERICAN SIGN LANGUAGE.

Asperger's syndrome

Asperger's syndrome (also referred to as Asperger syndrome) is a neurodevelopmental disorder characterized by narrowly circumscribed interests and difficulties with social interactions. In most instances, people with Asperger's syndrome have typical or even above-average measurable intelligence and language skills, although they may have trouble using language to communicate their thoughts and feelings. Asperger's syndrome is often described as a "mild form of AUTISM" or Autism Spectrum Disorder. Although Asperger's syndrome is not universally recognized as a disability, diagnoses increased markedly during the 1990s, leading to the formation of support and advocacy groups.

The syndrome was first identified by Hans Asperger in 1944, a year after LEO KANNER published his findings on infantile autism. Working at a psychiatric clinic in Vienna, Asperger observed CHILDREN who seemed uninterested in human relationships but fascinated by seemingly arcane topics. Asperger borrowed language used by Kanner, applying the term "Autistic Psychopathy" to the children he observed. Even though Asperger used the term "psychopathy," he did not view the children he observed as psychotic and believed that the disorder was biologically based and heritable. Perhaps because he was writing in the shadow of the devastating Nazi EUGENICS programs, Asperger did not describe the syndrome as a disability but as an "abnormal personality structure." Rather, he argued that these children showed great originality of thought and could go on to achieve professional success.

Asperger's work was largely ignored in the English-speaking world, although it was known and referred to in Europe and Japan. In 1981 Englishwoman Lorna Wing realized that many psychiatric inpatients might actually have undiagnosed Asperger's syndrome and argued for the utility of the diagnosis; a decade later, Uta Frith published a full translation of Asperger's original article. Following this translation and republication, rates of diagnosis of Asperger's syndrome rose dramatically in the United States as mental health professionals learned to recognize the disorder and many adults began to diagnose themselves.

The DISABILITY RIGHTS MOVEMENT has had a powerful impact on the lives of people with Asperger's syndrome. In keeping with the values of the movement, Michael John Carley founded the Global and Regional Asperger's Syndrome Partnership (GRASP) in 2003; the by-laws of the ORGANIZATION require that much of its leadership be composed of people on the autism spectrum. Some activists have also argued that Asperger's syndrome should be viewed not as a disability, but simply as a variant in cognitive processing, or a form of "neurodiversity," undervalued in a world that is predominantly "neurotypical."

Autism and Asperger's syndrome advocates such as Stephen Shore and Temple Grandin emphasize how important it is that people on the autism spectrum find careers that suit their unique interests.

Many other researchers and advocates concur, urging that a social model analysis can do much to improve the lives of those with Asperger's syndrome. They argue that educational accommodations emphasizing the strengths associated with Asperger's syndrome and workplace environments that accommodate sensory and social differences can enable fuller participation by people with Asperger's syndrome.

See also ACTIVISM AND ADVOCACY; SOCIAL CONSTRUCTION OF DISABILITY.

Chloe Silverman

Further Reading:

Asperger, Hans. "'Autistic Psychopathy' in Childhood." In *Autism and Asperger Syndrome*, edited by Uta Frith, 37–92. Cambridge: Cambridge University Press, 1991.

Baron-Cohen, Simon. *The Essential Difference: The Truth about the Male and Female Brain*. New York: Perseus Books Group, 2003.

Carley, Michael John. "The Origins of GRASP," *Autism Perspective Magazine,* Spring 2006. Available online. URL: http://www.grasp.org/ab_hist.htm. Accessed January 3, 2007.

Grandin, Temple. *Developing Talents: Careers for Individuals with Asperger Syndrome and High-Functioning Autism.* Shawnee Mission, Kans.: Autism Asperger Publishing Company, 2004.

Osborne, Lawrence. *American Normal: The Hidden World of Asperger Syndrome.* New York: Copernicus Books, 2002.

assistive technology and adaptive devices

The evolution of assistive technology (AT) and adaptive devices is important for understanding disability in America because it offers insights into the challenges and efforts to create a more inclusive society. AT is basically a solution to a barrier. It is a tool that increases a person's independence. These tools relate to daily activities, such as domestic chores and MOBILITY aids, as well as urban-scale ACCESS systems, such as bus lifts and elevators. Medical or physiological AT assists anatomical functions and includes such things as IRON LUNGS, HEARING AIDS, eyeglasses, and CRUTCHES. Similarly, canes, walkers, and WHEELCHAIRS represent important devices that have assisted people with mobility impairments. Adaptive devices, which modify the environment or assist people with altering the environment, also encompass a wide range of innovative examples, including ramps, benches, lifts, grab bars, one-handed can openers, specialized light switches, and AUDIBLE PEDESTRIAN SIGNALS.

Prosthetic devices (see PROSTHETICS), such as artificial legs and arms, have been used since at least the colonial period. Early forms were made from wood or metal and crafted by local artisans and most served strictly functional purposes, enabling people to better perform daily living tasks. Particularly since the CIVIL WAR, prosthetic devices have changed dramatically, employing new materials and produced in mass quantities. Some forms of prosthetic devices reflect changing social expectations, such as the "Cheetahs," carbon-fiber J-shaped blades (legs) developed in the 1980s,

"Not being able to hear the doorbell ring when someone calls, deaf couples have invented contraptions of their own to take the place of the ear. . . . It consists of a toy hoe-handle, a gimlet, part of a door latch, piece of iron pipe and two nails, yet it works perfectly. It is not patented, so any of our readers are at liberty to try it in their own homes."

—notice by anonymous author in a deaf newspaper, December 1921

One of the main purposes of assistive devices, such as prosthetic limbs, is restoration of function, which, in turn, assists in independence. This man is using a split-hook hand to steer an automobile. *(Smithsonian National Museum of American History, Division of Medicine and Science)*

which have made it possible for elite athletes with disabilities to perform at times far beyond their NONDISABLED peers.

Hearing aids represent another historic assistive device. Examples of mechanical devices intended to enhance hearing were present in early American history, but the first electronic hearing aids appeared during the first decades of the 20th century. Over the century, innovations in hearing aids produced smaller and more powerful devices. As some scholars have noted, the proliferation of hearing aids embodies important cultural values. For example, many early 20th-century devices were "masked" as earrings or other gendered accessories in order to downplay women's and men's impairment; the external material's coloring, intended also to blend with the users' body, presumed that only white consumers

needed or used hearing aids. Hearing aids—symbolically and sometimes literally—mark the differences between DEAF, HARD OF HEARING, and hearing people. As such, hearing aids, and to a greater extent COCHLEAR IMPLANTS, are controversial, sparking debates over the rationales for and against technologically changing a person's hearing.

In the 1960s the successful creation of TTYs (telecommunication devices for the deaf) provided deaf and hard of hearing people with a means to communicate across phone lines independently of others. Innovations in communications technology, such as the creation of video phones in the 1990s, which enables people to see one another while communicating across phone lines, has further expanded options for sign language users.

For the millions of people who have found speech difficult or impossible, Augmentative Alternative Communication (AAC) devices have been particularly useful. Although examples of AAC existed earlier in American history, the formal concept of AAC emerged in the 1950s and 1960s and was recognized as an independent field by the 1970s. Its active evolution was linked to disability rights ACTIVISM and broad educational and vocational efforts to empower people with significant disabilities. A prominent example of an ACC is communication boards, which may include pictures, letters, numbers, symbols, and words that users can point to as a means of communication. An early electronic device called the Auto-Com, which was developed in the 1970s, printed messages on paper or showed them on screens. In subsequent decades, the rise of microcomputers and other advanced technology has sparked new AT options, including artificial or synthesized speech with words and phrases chosen by the user.

One of the largest categories of AT relates to blindness and low vision. Among the first examples of this was a typewriter invented to assist BLIND people in writing print in 1808. In 1848 the Fairbanks typewriter was invented and, in 1856, the Beach Typewriter was patented by Alfred Ely Beach. In 1892 Frank Haven Hall, superintendent of the Illinois Institution for Education of the Blind, had his students demonstrate a BRAILLE writing machine, which gained national acceptance and became known as the Hall Brailler. In 1951 David Abraham designed a braillewriter known as the Perkins Brailler, named after the PERKINS SCHOOL FOR THE BLIND in Watertown, Massachusetts. Blind students and adults alike still use the Perkins Brailler in the 21st century, and its design has undergone only minor cosmetic changes since it was originally introduced.

Other forms of assistive technology have played an important role in the lives of blind and low vision consumers. In the late 1960s, for example, Sam Genensky developed the first closed circuit TV or CCTV magnification system, which was used by people with limited sight to read documents. Genensky's original design was improved upon and marketed by such assistive technology giants as Apollo Lasers, VisualTek, and TeleSensory Systems, Inc. Smaller CCTVs with additional features are still in use in the 21st century.

In the early 1970s the Optacon (Optical to Tactile Converter) enabled totally blind people to read the printed word. This machine included a small camera that sent an image of a character or graphic to a series of vibrating pins that would form the shape of the character or image seen by the camera. The blind user would slide the camera across the printed page or whatever surface he needed to read; with the other hand, he could feel the shape of the character or image vibrating against his index finger. Unlike scanners connected to computers, the Optacon could read even curved surfaces such as cans so that the blind user could read anything from labels to whole novels. The Optacon was difficult to use, and within two decades of its introduction, its use was in sharp decline. The device is no longer being manufactured or marketed, but it retains a small cadre of dedicated users.

The ability to create Braille documents using a computer has evolved significantly over the years as well. The earliest software that translated printed mathematic information into Braille was created by IBM in partnership with the American Printing House for the Blind in 1960. The first commercially available Braille translation software debuted in late 1969, and was known as DOTSYS III. DOTSYS III was the predecessor to a program known as the Duxbury Braille Translator. The Duxbury Braille Translator has become the industry standard where braille translation is concerned. There are other programs available, at least one of them at no cost, but the Duxbury Braille Translator commands the vast majority of installations of Braille translation software in the English-speaking world. The first version of that program was installed in July 1976.

Because far fewer people use Braille, most of the advances in the arena of assistive technology have come from computers that talk and from the introduction of software that allows people to talk to computers. In the early 1980s Maryland Computer Services introduced the Total Talk, a terminal that, when connected to computer mainframes, could voice the words appearing on the screen. One of the early users of Total Talk was a blind programmer named Ted Henter. He ultimately formed a company with an investor that would create a screen reader called JAWS (Job Access With Speech). In the early 21st century JAWS has become an industry standard. Along with Window-Eyes (available from GW Micro) and System Access to Go (available from Serotek Corp.), it represents the three leading screen readers available to blind computer users.

The rise of VOICE RECOGNITION SOFTWARE, particularly since the 1990s, has made it feasible for many people with disabilities as well as nondisabled people to operate computers. Voice or speech recognition allows someone to talk to the computer and either dictate documents to it or give it commands equivalent to clicking a mouse or pressing keys. Research into speech recognition began as early as 1936 by AT&T BELL LABORATORIES in partnership with universities and the U.S. Department of Defense. The first commercially available software for speech recognition was released in 1982 and worked on IBM systems and on the Commodore 64. Dragon Systems, Inc., which was founded in 1982, has since become the leader in speech recognition technologies for a variety of uses.

As technology experienced greater miniaturization and as computing processor power grew, these communications aids have become increasingly important in the lives of millions of children and adults. The most complex of these devices actually speak for the nonverbal user. These devices have followed closely the development of screen reading technologies for blind and visually impaired people. In their formative stages, voice synthesizers had a cold, mechanical, robotic sound. Many of the same voice chips that were used by blind computer users to read their screen also went into devices that allowed nonverbal people to verbally communicate with others. In the early 21st century synthesizers have become much more humanlike in their tone and inflection, and both male and female voices are available.

In recognition of the important role technology plays in promoting access and equality for people with disabilities, laws and policies were established in the late 20th century. By mandating technology services and options for disabled CHILDREN, the Education of the Handicapped Act Amendments of 1986 set an important precedent for AT support. Two years later, the Technology-Related Assistance for Individuals with Disabilities Act of 1988 provided a formal, legal definition of AT. In the next year, the Technology-Related Assistance for Individuals with Disabilities act (P.L. 100-407) was passed; this act required that all states seek to provide AT to their constituents with disabilities.

Assistive technology and adaptive devices continue to play a central role in the efforts to promote accessibility and inclusion of disabled Americans in society. Their evolution demonstrates the impact of activism and advocacy on the expectations of what people with disabilities can and should be able to do. As such, assistive technology and adaptive devices present a rich area for further research in disability history.

See also AUDIO DESCRIPTION; CLOSED CAPTIONING; DAILY LIFE; EMPLOYMENT AND LABOR; LAW AND POLICY; NEWSLINE FOR THE BLIND; OPTICAL CHARACTER RECOGNITION; SCIENCE AND TECHNOLOGY; TALKING BOOKS.

Nolan Crabb

Further Reading:

Fein, Judith. "A History of Legislative Support for Assistive Technology." *Journal of Special Education Technology* 13, no. 1 (Spring 1996): 1–3.

Hourcade, Jack, Tami Everhart Pilotte, Elizabeth West, and Phil Parette. "A History of Augmentative and Alternative Communication for Individuals with Severe and Profound Disabilities." *Focus on Autism & Other Developmental Disabilities* 19, no. 4 (Winter 2004): 235–244.

Lang, Harry G. *A Phone of Our Own: The Deaf Insurrection Against Ma Bell.* Washington, D.C.: Gallaudet University Press, 2000.

Ott, Katherine, David Serlin, and Stephen Mihm, eds. *Artificial Parts, Practical Lives: Modern Histories of Prosthetics.* New York: New York University Press, 2002.

Woods, Brian, and Nick Watson. "A Glimpse at the Social and Technological History of Wheelchairs." *International Journal of Therapy and Rehabilitation* 11, no. 9 (2004): 407–410.

Association for Retarded Citizens   See ARC, THE.

Association of People with Severe Handicaps, The   See TASH.

asylums and institutions

Before the first decade of the 19th century, most Americans with disabilities lived with their families. A few, especially those with MENTAL ILLNESS and from well-to-do families, lived in rural retreats, and others became patients in one of the specialized urban HOSPITALS. Still other disabled people found themselves in local ALMSHOUSES, including many BLIND and DEAF persons, as well as people with intellectual and developmental disabilities and mentally ill persons, particularly if their families were poor and could not care for them. In 1810 physicians in Boston called for a medical facility for "lunatics" (then a medical term for people with mental illness), resulting in the opening of Mclean Hospital in 1818. A year earlier a similar facility had been opened near Philadelphia by members of the Society of Friends, or Quakers. Both of these institutions based their methods on a therapeutic philosophy called MORAL TREATMENT that influenced asylum development throughout the pre–CIVIL WAR period. Based on Philippe Pinel's reforms at the Bicêtre Hospital in Paris and William Tuke's treatment methods at the York Retreat in England, moral treatment held that, with rational and kindly care given away from the pressures of the world, distressed people could regain their reason and their membership in the larger society.

From these early beginnings, institutions and asylums in the United States grew in number and size, dedicated to providing not only for people with mental illness but also for people with a variety of needs. In 1817 THOMAS HOPKINS GALLAUDET opened the Hartford Asylum for the deaf. By the end of the decade his facility was providing DEAF EDUCATION for more than 60 students from 10 different states. In 1832 residential institutions in Boston and Philadelphia opened for the blind. Inspired by the traveling lectures of philanthropists and educational reformers such as Gallaudet and SAMUEL GRIDLEY HOWE, institutions for the deaf and BLIND opened all across the United States in the 1840s and 1850s. Like asylums for people with mental illness, these facilities stressed moral treatment, but, unlike

Since the early 19th century, asylums and institutions became a common response to treating people with, or perceived to have, disabilities. By the 20th century, disability advocates began to challenge institutions, using testimony and exposés such as this 1966 photograph of dismal conditions in a hospital day room. *(The Center on Human Policy at Syracuse University)*

the former, they also emphasized EDUCATION and the learning of life skills.

With the growth of this institutional culture, some reformers began to discover that many people with disabilities were wrongly housed in PRISONS and penitentiaries. In the spring of 1841 Unitarian reformer DOROTHEA DIX (1802–87), began visiting the women's jail in East Cambridge, Massachusetts, as a part of her Unitarian outreach. Dix's visits revealed that many prisoners were guilty only of poverty and INSANITY. After state newspapers presented nearly two years of persistent coverage of Dix's findings, the Massachusetts General Court in 1843 passed legislation providing funds for the institutional treatment of the state's indigent people with mental illness. Dix spent the next decade advocating to state lawmakers across the nation for better treatment of mentally ill people in public institutions. A saint to her supporters, a rigid authoritarian to her detractors, Dix more than any other figure expanded and solidified American confidence in the antebellum asylum.

With the success of asylums for the blind, the deaf, and people with mental illness, reformers and lawmakers looked finally to the situation of intellectually disabled children (called "idiots"), many of whom, before 1850, were placed in almshouses if FAMILY members could not care for them after they became adults. The American effort to found institutions for the cognitively developmentally disabled followed reports from France in the mid 1840s that teachers had developed successful programs for the education of "idiots." In 1848 Howe persuaded Massachusetts officials to fund an

experimental school for idiots at his existing institution, the PERKINS SCHOOL FOR THE BLIND. Within a decade, other northern states also began to use public funds to open facilities for cognitively disabled children.

Before the Civil War (1861–65), the people of the United States saw the asylum as a place of treatment, education, rehabilitation, and care. Rejecting prerevolutionary Calvinist attitudes that tended to blame people for what were seen as personal failings, the nation after 1810 took a more optimistic approach to disability. The rational stance of the 18th-century Enlightenment philosophers and the feeling of communality popularized by the Romantics from the turn of the 19th century inspired American belief in institutional change. A free republic, it was thought, could create reasonable, humane institutions to achieve cures, changes, and improved character in all its citizens—even those who had disabilities. The successful development and operation of institutions in the United States lasted for about 50 years.

The four decades after the Civil War, however, saw dramatic changes in American society. From the growth of industrial capitalism, immigration from Europe and Asia, and urbanization to a national ethos of racial segregation and SOCIAL DARWINISM (which rationalized the dominance of those who were most socially and financially successful), the country moved from a nation of rural and small town life where extended families cared for their members and participated in community decision making toward one of urban anonymity. For nearly 100 years, from 1870 to 1970, residential institutions grew in number and size, but they lost their sense of "asylum," the faith that the institution would provide a place of care, change, and growth.

By the beginning of the 20th century asylums had become places for controlling social problems. Throughout the nation, state-operated institutions increasingly defined their mentally and intellectually disabled residents as chronically sick and their deaf and blind residents as unemployable. Complicating these attitudes was the nation's growing interest in EUGENICS and concern among authorities over disabled people's reproduction. The "survival of the fittest" rhetoric of late 19th-century Social Darwinists joined with

"We would like to have her home as we are getting old and need her help."

—Mr. and Mrs. Burner to Virginia governor Harry Byrd, requesting their daughter's release from the state colony at Lynchburg, February 1928 the eugenics movement of the 1910s and 1920s to call for incarcerating the insane and the FEEBLEMINDED in institutions. By segregating these groups, state authorities believed they could protect the genetic purity of "healthy" American communities.

With economic and social stresses caused by the Great Depression of the 1930s followed by the demands of WORLD WAR II (1941–45), state funding for residential institutions remained stable or diminished even though institutional populations continued to increase rapidly. By the late 1940s state investigations commonly referred to these facilities as "snake pits" (see SNAKE PIT, THE). The 1950s and 1960s saw an increase of state funding for the construction and maintenance of institutions, especially for people with mental illness and intellectual disabilities. But states in the late 1960s found that, despite new facilities, client treatment remained poor and costs grew. Besides poor treatment and high costs, authorities from several fields began to question the idea of the institution itself. Was the residential institution, where people are segregated from regular social interaction, the best setting for the treatment and education of people with disabilities? By the mid-1970s doubts about institutions had reached a high point. A combination of federal judicial and legislative action, along with changes in state policy and federal funding, saw the end of the state residential institution as a force in American treatment, care, and control. By the end of the 20th century, the asylum, which had once embodied the hopes of a new nation, had become a source of shame. In its place came an old, if renewed, reliance on integrated community institutions, now called MAINSTREAMING.

See also COGNITIVE AND INTELLECTUAL DISABILITY; DEINSTITUTIONALIZATION; DEVELOPMENTAL DISABILITY; HOSPITALS; INSTITUTIONALIZATION; RESIDENTIAL SCHOOLS.

James W. Trent

Further Reading:

D'Antonio, Patricia. *Founding Friends: Families, Staff, and Patients in the Friends Asylum in Early Nineteenth-Century Philadelphia.* Bethlehem, Pa.: Lehigh University Press, 2006.

Grob, Gerald N. *From Asylum to Community: Mental Health Policy in Modern America.* Princeton, N.J.: Princeton University Press, 1991.

Rothman, David J. *The Discovery of the Asylum: Social Order and Disorder in the New Republic.* Boston: Little, Brown, 1971.

Trent, James W., Jr. *Inventing the Feeble Mind: A History of Mental Retardation in the United States.* Berkeley: University of California Press, 1994.

Astounding Disclosures! Three Years in a Mad House by Isaac H. Hunt (1851)

In 1844 Isaac H. Hunt was committed to the Maine Insane Hospital in Augusta, where he stayed for three years. In 1851 he published an account of his experiences, detailing abuse by staff and forced medications that caused him considerable distress. Exposés, such as presented in this excerpt, reflect a long history of institutionalized people protesting their treatment and challenge many official histories of asylums.

Astounding Disclosures! Three Years in a Mad House by Isaac H. Hunt 1851

The author of this little work, was, on the 21st of September, 1844, taken to the Maine Insane Hospital, in the city of Augusta, State of Maine, a wild maniac. The Hospital at that time was under the superintendance of Dr. Isaac Ray, now of the Butler Insane Asylum, of Providence, R.I. In this institution I remained nearly three years, and I shall endeavor to give a vivid description of each and every circumstance connected with my confinement, treatment, torture of body and mind, and the malpractice performed on me. These facts will enable the reader to judge of the extent of my madness. It is of no use for me to deny, (for of that fact there is abundant proof,) that when I was taken to the Hospital I was a perfectly deranged man, laboring under a strong fever of the brain, or great and uncontrollable mental excitement, of which, under humane treatment, I should have recovered, and no doubt returned to my business in full possession of my mental and physical faculties. But the moment I entered the Hospital a fear came over me—a deep state of mental depression was followed by that of horror and fear, and of course what little consciousness I had at the time was put to flight, for I knew not, but dreaded what was to follow. I entered the Hospital on Saturday evening; the first assay they made was to have me swallow some Pills. I refused, but was forced to submit, and took them. This operation was under the direction and personal assistance of Dr. Ray, and the attendant, Alvin S. Babcock. The next day I felt the necessity of a shower bath, and expressed my feelings to Dr. Ray. But, in language, you will doubtless think very cold and vulgar in so learned a gentleman, he thus addressed me:—"*We're very short on't for water,* and I can't let you have it; there has'nt been no rain lately, and I can't let you have it." I then said: "Sir, if you will tell me where you get your water, I will go and get some myself, as a gallon will be sufficient." He then said that he could not let me have it; to which I replied:—"Sir, I think that I need it, and if you cannot let me have it here, will you permit me to go to my own house, or some other place, where I can have such remedies as my case requires." To this he replied:— "You can't go; you have been brought here by your friends, and you must stay until you get well." I was hereupon plied with medicine, the effect of which was to cause me to travel the gallery for hours and hours, perfectly wild and uncontrolable, as patients often are in almost any Insane Hospital. But I trust to God that in no other case have those walks been caused in mad men, as was mine, by horrid draughts of, to me, a nameless medicine. This state of my mind and physical prostration, through the effect of that medicine, was continued for several days without intermission, until about the close of the next week, or sometime in the week following, when I was given medicine which threw me upon my bed, followed by the most horrid chills, that shook me, body and soul and made my very bones rattle,—my teeth chattered and my bones rattled like the dry bones of a skeleton; I gave up all hope of life with such composure as I could muster; but my hour had not come, for at this juncture, Babcock, the attendant, came and gave me a bowl of hot ginger tea, saying in a jocular manner:—"Die! oh, no, not you—you'll not die yet—you're worth a dozen dead men." The tea and the application of a pyramid of blankets and comforters, warmed the system—the chills retreated, and I kept my bed for some days. About the ninth day after I went there, I was again subjected to the horrid wild-fire medicine, which was followed by the same terrible and strange sensations and wanderings over the gallery. I refused peremtorily to suffer this treatment; I refused to take the medicine. The attendant insisted that I should, and harsh words followed. I told him the medicine was destroying me and I would not take it. He then commanded me in a tone of authority, to take the medicine. I did take it. I took it from his hand and dashed it out of the window! In a moment this stalwart, muscular man struck me a violent blow upon my head which either knocked me down, or he instantly seized me and crushed

me to the floor. I struggled, when he siezed me by the throat and choked me. I began to have fear that he had my death in view, and would murder me upon the spot. I begged for my life, when he harshly exclaimed. "I will learn you not to throw away your medicine when I give it to you!" I begged for mercy, and promised if my life was spared to take anything he might give me. Upon this he released me, and I continued my usual dull routine of the previous days. The next morning, Babcock entered my room, as usual, with medicine. From the treatment I had already received, of course I dared not refuse to swallow the terrible draught, though it should instantly cause death. I took the pills, and some liquid contained in a mug. These compounds had the effect to destroy my bodily health for the residue of my earthly existence. There is a penalty for such malpractice, and if I had it in my power to bring Dr. Isaac Ray and Dr. Horatio S. Smith before the legal tribunals of my country, I should not possibly find any difficulty in sending them to the State Penitentiary for the full term of twenty years for malpractice, and three years additional for conspiracy.

Source: Isaac H. Hunt. *Astounding Disclosures! Three Years in a Mad House, by a Victim. A True Account of the Barbarous, Inhuman and Cruel Treatment of Isaac H. Hunt, in the Maine Insane Hospital, in the Years 1844, '45, '46 and '47, by Drs. Isaac Ray, James Bates, and Their Assistants and Attendants.* Skowhegan, Me.: The Author, 1851. Available online. URL: http://www. disabilitymuseum.org/lib/docs/736.htm. Accessed June 26, 2008.

attention-deficit/hyperactivity disorder

Attention-deficit/hyperactivity disorder (ADHD) is generally characterized by hyperactivity, inattentiveness, and impulsiveness. The symptoms of ADHD are considered clinically meaningful, however, only when they measurably exceed the behaviors of other individuals within a particular age group. ADHD is most commonly associated with CHILDREN and adolescents. Research suggests that about 5 percent of school-age children in the United States have the disorder; however, ADHD is also increasingly diagnosed in adults, many of whom went undiagnosed as children.

ADHD gained widespread recognition in the United States during the late 1980s and early 1990s, although medical experts described its features much earlier. The work of

American pediatrician Charles Bradley during the 1930s is a primary starting point for understanding ADHD and its management. Bradley was the director of the Emma Pendleton Bradley Home in East Providence, Rhode Island, which opened in 1931 as the nation's first psychiatric hospital devoted to children. Six years later, Bradley made the discovery that the amphetamine medication Benzedrine had a distinctive calming effect on children with "behavior problems" ranging from learning disabilities to EPILEPSY. Bradley continued to seek explanations for his own paradoxical observation that a drug known to be a stimulant produced subdued behavior in children.

On the basis of Bradley's research, the term minimal brain damage (MBD), later to become known as minimal brain dysfunction, was proposed in the 1950s to describe symptoms in children ranging from excessive restlessness to aimless wandering to poor appetite. The driving theoretical force behind MBD was a belief that such behaviors in children were the result of damage or defects in the central nervous system. However, lacking any proof of brain damage in these children, not to mention the STIGMA associated with such a diagnosis, the concept of MBD began to fade during the 1960s. The emergence of a new idea to describe the same symptoms hastened the decline of MBD diagnoses. In 1957 Maurice Lauffer, the new director of the Bradley Home, coined the term "hyperkinetic disorder of childhood," which focused on hyperactivity in children.

During the 1970s hyperkinesis, as it became known, was more strongly linked with other symptoms, including distractibility and inattention. Researchers at this time found that hyperkinetic children were not merely hyperactive, but that they experienced greater difficulty sustaining attention and controlling impulses. This new view was formalized in 1980 with the introduction of the term "attention deficit disorder" (ADD) in the third edition of the *DIAGNOSTIC AND STATISTICAL MANUAL OF MENTAL DISORDERS (DSM-III)* to describe what had been formerly called hyperkinesis or hyperactive child syndrome. In response to concerns that hyperactive behavior had been disregarded, the name ADD was officially changed to ADHD in 1987.

Just as important as the medical history of ADHD is its social history. ADHD and its antecedents have long been associated with boys rather than girls. Although there is now a growing awareness that school-age girls, as well as adults, experience the disorder, a gendered view (see GENDER) of ADHD is an integral part of its social history, and may be seen in the observation that "emotional disturbance" was the most commonly noted mental health problem affecting young boys during the 1950s and mid 1960s. The symptoms of emotional disturbance bore a close relationship to the modern ADHD diagnosis and included such behaviors as hyperactivity, inattention, moodiness,

delinquency, and impulsiveness. A 1956 social guidance film, *Helping Johnny Remember,* about a selfish, uncooperative, and domineering boy rejected by his classmates, suggests one possible cultural REPRESENTATION of ADHD's antecedents. Many popular women's magazines from the 1950s and early 1960s discussed mothers' anxieties regarding emotional disturbance in their sons, as well as the roles that mothers might play in preventing and managing such symptoms through "proper" child-rearing techniques. During the 1960s hyperkinesis became viewed less as a social condition and more as a medical disorder with a physiological origin that could be treated with medications. By 1971 the U.S. Department of Health, Education, and Welfare estimated that 3 percent of school-age children suffered from hyperkinesis. In a well-publicized incident from 1970, the *Washington Post* reported that Ritalin or other behavior modifying drugs were being prescribed for between 5 and 10 percent of children in the Omaha Public Schools district in Nebraska. Though a subsequent federal investigation found these claims to have been somewhat exaggerated, the use of drugs for the treatment of hyperkinesis years before ADHD became widely known to the American public suggests a rich social history behind the contemporary diagnosis.

ADHD is commonly managed with stimulant drugs. The medication most associated with ADHD is methylphenidate, introduced as Ritalin in 1955. During the past half-century, Ritalin has remained the most popular drug for the management of ADHD, with estimates of up to 5 million children using the medication in 2000. One of the main controversies surrounding ADHD is the use of such powerful drugs for treatment or therapy, many of which, including Ritalin, are tightly controlled by the U.S. Drug Enforcement Administration because they have a high potential for dependence.

Moreover, despite wide recognition within the medical and education communities, ADHD remains a somewhat controversial diagnosis. Some opponents contend that the disorder is a socially constructed condition, not a medical one. Others believe that medicating children for behavioral issues is ethically questionable. Even among those who acknowledge that ADHD is a genuine disorder, some criticize the lack of rigorous diagnostic procedures and the use of potent drugs for its management.

People with ADHD have responded to these debates over diagnosis and treatment in a multitude of ways. Many have been active in ORGANIZATIONS that seek to raise awareness about ADHD and to promote research into the causes and treatment of ADHD. Other groups have accepted the diagnosis but contend that there are viable alternatives to drug therapy, such as dietary modification and behavioral therapies. A small but distinct minority of individuals have rejected the diagnosis outright as a social construction, as well as the need for treatment with medications. As more Americans have been diagnosed over the past two decades, ADHD has been increasingly recognized as a disability and some disability activists have argued that information on ADHD is scarce because the disorder was not categorized as a disability in SPECIAL EDUCATION until recently, which limited the amount of funding provided for research. These activists contend that educators have had to rely on treatments for learning or behavioral disabilities that may not address the particular needs of students with ADHD.

Individuals with ADHD have gained disability rights in the United States as part of two major laws. First, SECTION 504 of the Rehabilitation Act of 1973, a civil rights law, requires that schools and any other program receiving federal assistance not discriminate against anyone with a physical or mental impairment that limits a "major life activity." Second, the INDIVIDUALS WITH DISABILITIES EDUCATION ACT (IDEA) of 1990 mandates that eligible children receive access to special education and related services through individualized programs. In 1991 the Department of Education issued an official memorandum designating ADHD as a covered disability under both Section 504 and IDEA, recognizing that those diagnosed with ADHD are entitled to reasonable accommodations under the LAW. The labeling of ADHD remains a contentious issue. Leading experts contend that ADHD is best understood as a DEVELOPMENTAL DISABILITY. While ADHD is studied in conjunction with learning disabilities, most definitions of the disorder consider it distinct from learning disabilities, as defined by the National Joint Committee on Learning Disabilities. However, studies indicate that as many as 50 percent of children with ADHD also have learning disabilities. While some criticize that labeling the disorder as a disability may increase stigmatization of affected individuals, other experts contend that a precise categorization allows access to government resources and services. However, limited government resources for research and provision of services have occasionally placed ADHD and learning disability stakeholders at odds with those representing better established physical disabilities, such as MOBILITY and sensory impairments. Nevertheless, ADHD remains covered as an eligible condition under the AMERICANS WITH DISABILITIES ACT (ADA).

Nathan W. Moon

Further Reading:

Diller, Lawrence. *Running on Ritalin: A Physician Reflects on Children, Society, and Performance in a Pill.* New York: Bantam Books, 1998.

Singh, Ilina. "Bad Boys, Good Mothers, and the 'Miracle' of Ritalin." *Science in Context* 15, no. 4 (2002): 577–603.

audio books See TALKING BOOKS.

audio description

Audio description, also called video description, descriptive video, or descriptive video service (DVS), has been around as long as there have been sighted persons describing their surroundings for people who are BLIND or who have low vision. It is a narration service that attempts to describe the visual elements of THEATER, TELEVISION, FILMS, museum EXHIBITIONS, and other art forms for people who are unable to ACCESS visual materials. This process allows individuals to receive content that is not accessible simply by listening to the audio. In audio description, narrators typically use pictorially descriptive language to describe actions, gestures, scene changes, props, and other visual information. They also describe titles, speaker names, and other text that may appear on a screen or in the text on display. This information is usually given to the listener in between portions of dialogue or songs or as supplemental text.

Audio description is carefully scripted and typically written by trained professionals. The language is concise and objective. Audio describers only "say what they see." Ideally, there is no subjectivity in audio description. Describers do not interpret what they see or distract from the performance being described.

Although the profession of audio describing is of recent origin, no one knows exactly where or when it began. In 1964 Chet Avery began agitating for something for blind people that was parallel to the captioning being proposed for people who were DEAF or HARD OF HEARING. Avery, a blind man, lived in Alexandria, Virginia, and worked for the Department of Education. In the late 1970s Gregory Frazier in San Francisco became inspired by a blind friend as they watched a Hollywood movie together. Frazier founded Audiovision in order to produce descriptive audio, delivered through radio-controlled headphones. He won an Emmy in 1990 for his work.

Margaret Pfanstiehl and her husband Cody, of Silver Spring, Maryland, were the first to develop a practical, workable program and training methods for audio description. They trained hundreds of audio describers, who in turn trained others. Pfanstiehl, who has had limited vision for most of her life, founded the Metropolitan Washington Ear, the first radio reading service on the East Coast for the visually impaired, in 1974. As a result of her work, she was contacted by Washington's Arena Stage, along with Chet Avery, in 1980 to aid in improving accessibility at their performances. Pfanstiehl assisted them, utilizing ideas from her past work in adapting plays from the stage for radio performance. The first official theatrical use of audio description is believed to have been in 1981 for

George Bernard Shaw's *Major Barbara,* at the Arena Stage in Washington, D.C.

In 1985 the Public Broadcasting System (PBS) Boston affiliate WGBH began to explore the possible applications of the separate audio program (SAP) that was included on stereo television sets. One of their ideas was to develop a descriptive video system utilizing the SAP. The national description service on PBS was officially formed and funded in 1987, taking on the official name Descriptive Video Service (DVS). Working with the Pfanstiehls and Metropolitan Washington Ear, in 1988 PBS's "The American Playhouse" was the first national test for a show written and produced in an audio description format. During the 1990 season premier of *American Playhouse,* the DVS format was launched as a permanent national service. To hear the DVS, listeners press the SAP button on their stereo TV, VCR, or adapter and hear description in addition to the regular audio. If a television does not have stereo capabilities, an FM tuner can be purchased to receive the SAP channel. By 1992 more than 60 PBS stations around the country carried the service. By 1994 a number of other venues nationwide were offering audio description to their patrons: the John F. Kennedy Center for the Performing Arts, the Smithsonian's National Air and Space Museum, various IMAX theater performances across the country, and the National Park Service.

The Federal Communications Commission (FCC) created a requirement in 2000 that television stations in the top markets must supply a minimum of four hours of described programming each day. The ruling was struck down as falling outside of the FCC's authority. Similar legislation is reintroduced from time to time but has yet to prove successful.

Although there are no laws requiring description and the professional level of the service is inconsistent, the service is now widely available for cultural events and many broadcasters voluntarily supply programming that is described. Audio description is an important aspect of equality of access to information and will no doubt increase as disability rights gain support.

Heidi A. Temple

Further Reading:
Axel, Elizabeth, and Nina Levant, eds. *Art Beyond Sight: A Resource Guide to Art, Creativity and Visual Impairment.* Baltimore: American Federation for the Blind, 2002.

Audio Description: Tour of Elephant Diorama at the National Museum of Natural History (2009)

For those who cannot access visual information, audio description provides verbal narration of various events, including television shows, theatrical performances, films, and museum exhibits. Audio description commonly describes nonspoken aspects of events, such as actions or movements, settings, gestures, and other visual cues. Audio description also includes titles, names of individuals speaking, and text that is displayed but not spoken during the event. It thus represents an important example of access and accommodation for people with disabilities. In this sample from the National Museum of Natural History, the audio description offers the user an orientation of the exhibit, a narration of the written text displayed, details about the artifacts, and verbal guidance for navigating the space of the exhibit. This material, like most audio description, serves to supplement the exhibit's visual display, enabling the user to enjoy the museum experience more fully.

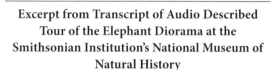

Excerpt from Transcript of Audio Described Tour of the Elephant Diorama at the Smithsonian Institution's National Museum of Natural History 2009

(Courtesy of Susan Burch)

You are now facing the information desk, near the Mall entrance to the Museum. Turn around 180 degrees and walk twenty-five feet toward the center of the rotunda. You've reached the elephant diorama. Directly in front of you is the diorama's sand-colored base. On your left, the base is about five feet high. On your right, it slopes down to an 18-inch-tall sandy bank. Standing atop the diorama is the largest mounted specimen of the world's largest living land animal—an African elephant. It measures 4 m (13.2 ft) tall at the shoulder, and, in life, weighed nearly 12 tons. The tusks project over seven feet from its body.

Listen—those are the sounds of the African savanna and its inhabitants.

Now move clockwise around the diorama and feel its coarse, sandy surface on your right. About 22 feet along, you will encounter the first of two welcome panels featuring a bronze, raised or bas-relief sculpture of the elephant in profile. Reach out and trace its trunk with your hands.

The panel reads:
"Welcome to the Elephant's World
"Trunk raised . . . ears fanned . . . this elephant is on the alert. Something has caught his attention, and he's off to investigate.

"In this Museum, we also investigate the natural world, using our rich collections to unravel the mysteries of nature and culture.
"Come join this investigation. Listen. Explore this small slice of African savanna . . . and the many exhibits beyond."

Now, continue clockwise around the diorama about twenty feet to the next textrail. You will pass the rear of our grand elephant, his wispy gray tail suspended above his right rear leg, a limb that is almost ten feet long and two feet in circumference. The leg is raised slightly off the ground, as though in motion. This elephant looks like it is moving at a fast trot. Near his feet, leather and hide beetles feed on the remains of a white cattle egret.
The next textrail focuses on the insects in the diorama. Attached to the seven-foot rail are four bronze models of dung beetles rolling elephant dung balls. Reach out and feel them.

The text reads:
"Tiny Animals Perform a Huge Service

"Here comes the savanna's clean-up crew! The insects in this diorama break down dung and dead animals and plants into tiny bits that bacteria and fungi decompose even further. Their combined efforts hasten the return of essential nutrients to the soil."

Listen for the low buzz of dung beetles and the louder buzz of flies swarming around dung.

On the left side of the rail, a graphic illustration features a richly textured dung pile containing undigested seeds, husks, and fibers.

The next section reads:
"Dung Beetles Go For Elephant Waste

"The instant elephant dung hits the ground, dung beetles zoom in. Within hours, they can eat or cart away much of a 6.3-kg (14-lb) heap like this!

"Some species roll the dung away, other bury it beneath the pile or even steal it from other dung beetles—then lay their eggs in it.

"As they dig, dung beetles turn over and fertilize the earth, greatly enriching the savanna soil."

Source: Elephant Diorama Audio Description at the Smithsonian Institution's National Museum of Natural History in Washington, D.C. Available online. URL: http://www.astc.org/resource/access/medadexc.htm. Accessed June 20, 2008.

audism

The word *audism,* coined by disabilities scholar Tom Humphries in 1977, began with a simple mock dictionary definition: the notion that one is superior based on one's ability to hear or behave in the manner of one who hears. Its creation and changing meaning mark important shifts in the understanding of DEAF people and deafness in America.

For generations deaf and HARD OF HEARING citizens had experienced various forms of discrimination but had no specific term to describe this unique system of oppression. In part influenced by other flourishing social movements in the 1970s, Deaf people in the United States began to assert their cultural and COMMUNITY identity in more public ways. Audism as a concept emerged initially as a critique of the ideology of the superiority of a state of being hearing, or the embodiment of the essence of hearing-ness. Like racism and sexism, audism reveals belief systems that shape the identity of all people by dividing and judging their bodies. Some scholars have defined audism as a specialized form of ableism (discrimination or prejudice that favors able-bodied people and able-bodiedness).

Although the term *audism* did not reach mainstream recognition until the 1990s, seminal events such as the 1988 DEAF PRESIDENT NOW! movement at GALLAUDET UNIVERSITY represent greater awareness and collective responses to oppressive attitudes and unwritten policies regarding deaf people. Two particularly visible responses to audism include protection of and demands for the use of AMERICAN SIGN LANGUAGE, and the clear expectation that community members participate directly in policy decisions affecting their society.

As with other "ism" concepts that interpret broad and pervasive systems, audism has expanded to encompass more complex meaning as community members and scholars apply, incorporate, and question its place in America. DEAF STUDIES scholars in the past two decades, such as Harlan Lane, have used audism to describe deaf peoples' distinct experiences with EXPLOITATION, oppression, discrimination, paternalism, and ethnocentrism. As deaf cultural experts have demonstrated, audism has been embedded within cultural practices and coded into social and cultural institutions, often appearing in the form of treatments, therapies, and interventions connected to a psychology of deficit.

By the 1990s Deaf people were more widely using audism to expose and name forces that suppressed both their cultural IDENTITY and their individual advancement. Since that time scholars have begun to identify diverse forms of audism and discussions on the interplay between audism and broader societal factors point to greater awareness of global implications. Recent studies of Deaf experiences in nations and regions outside the United States additionally highlight the ways that cultural context shapes the understanding and application of audist ideas. Workplace discrimination, undereducation, and stigmatizing STEREOTYPES of Deaf individuals represent some examples of audism that are drawing greater attention.

Although FILMS, blogs, and articles increasingly include the term *audism*, little historical study of the concept has yet been produced. In addition, debates continue over ways of defining audism or applying it as a critical framework. For example, some people assert that audism may emanate only from hearing people and applies only to Deaf bodies; others interpret the concept more broadly, noting multidimensional qualities of the concept. Still, by providing a name and framework for critiquing oppression, audism continues to play an important theoretical role in the expanding field of Deaf studies.

The concept of audism originally responded to a specific theory of humanness; bodies that hear are judged as ideal human bodies. It also sought to address the historic struggle of Deaf people to maintain a sense of identity in the context of an oppressive world. Over the past three decades, responses to audism both as a term and as an interpretive lens have brought identities into question among Deaf people. Activists have adopted this term to shape a movement of cultural EMPOWERMENT while others have used it to enhance the theoretical and academic study of Deaf communities. Its changing meaning and use mark the important role LANGUAGE plays in constructing communities, academic disciplines, and history itself.

Further Reading:

Audism Unveiled (2005). [DVD]. Produced by D. Bauman, B. Bahan, and F. Montenegro. Down Sign. USA.

Bauman, Dirksen. "Audism: Exploring the Metaphysics of Oppression." *Journal of Deaf Studies and Education* 9, no. 2 (2004): 239–246.

Humphries, Tom. "Communicating Across Cultures (Deaf-Hearing) and Language Learning." Ph.D. diss., The Union Institute, 1977.

Lane, Harlan. *The Mask of Benevolence: Disabling the Deaf Community.* New York: Alfred A. Knopf, 1992.

"When I am in the presence of, say, two other persons and one turns to me to explain or repeat whatever they may have been laughing about, if I fail to understand at once, he may dismiss me with a wave of the hand and a 'never mind!' and make no further attempt to talk to me. This has the effect of a slap in the face—it leaves me feeling very flat. . . . [T]o be given an opportunity to be brought into the conversation, only to fail and be dropped, leaves one feeling disappointed, stupid and unsatisfied."

—Catherine A. Hood, a hard of hearing, orally trained woman from New Haven, in a 1941 commentary

---

autism

Autism is a DEVELOPMENTAL DISABILITY, diagnosable in the first three years of life, and described as a neurological condition that is thought to impair social interaction, communication, and imagination, and to be associated with repetitive and restricted behaviors. People on the autism spectrum frequently have difficulty communicating, especially in spoken language, and often exhibit unusual habitual behaviors such as hand flapping, rocking of the body, humming, biting of the hand, and head banging.

Autism was first identified in 1943 with the publication of "Autistic Disturbances of Affective Contact" by Johns Hopkins University professor LEO KANNER. Kanner described autism from his clinical notes and parent reports of 11 individuals whom he had seen as patients. He determined that they shared certain qualities that he declared were evidence of a "unique syndrome," different not only from what was seen as the norm but also from existing classifications of FEEBLEMINDEDNESS and SCHIZOPHRENIA. Less than a year after

Kanner's publication, Viennese doctor Hans Asperger also published an article identifying a new disability called autism. Asperger described his patients as sharing a single principal characteristic: disturbed social interaction. Asperger argued that the person with autism was uninfluenced by others and basically lacked the ability to relate to the world.

Diagnoses and interpretations of autism often reveal broader social attitudes. For example, during the 1960s, psychiatrist Bruno Bettleheim proposed that inadequate maternal affect was the root cause of autism, that mothers brought on symptoms by being "cold" toward their CHILDREN, giving rise to the pejorative term, "refrigerator mothers." The practice of blaming mothers for their children's autism went out of favor in the 1970s, in part perhaps because of the appearance of alternative explanations, but also undoubtedly as a consequence of the growing feminist movement. Another common view of autism linked the condition to MENTAL RETARDATION; experts conflated intellectual disability with difficulties in communication and test-taking and saw the unusual tics and physical behaviors of persons with autism as being connected to those with lower intelligence. Neither Kanner nor Asperger viewed autism as a type of mental retardation, but a number of leading researchers in the 1990s argued that up to 75 percent of those labeled autistic should be considered intellectually disabled. Indeed, school officials, diagnosticians, and researchers routinely continue to identify more than 50 percent of those classified as autistic as retarded. Disability activists, including many who self-identify as autistic, now vehemently challenge the retardation label, arguing that the problem lies not in any defect inherent in the autistic individual but in the biased perspective of the "neurotypical" mainstream society.

REPRESENTATIONS of autism in POPULAR CULTURE also commonly reinforce limiting STEREOTYPES of autism. In the movie RAIN MAN (1988), for example, the main character, Raymond, is seen as simultaneously savant, aloof, compulsive, bumbling, innocent, vulnerable, and endearing, but these features stress his place as a character rather than showing him as a person. (More recent films, such as WHAT'S EATING GILBERT GRAPE (1993) and Mozart and the Whale (2005), offer more complicated and sensitive depictions.) News magazines and TELEVISION programs, too, often depict autism as a wholly tragic condition that imposes excessive hardship on parents, destroys marriages, and ruins the opportunity for siblings to experience "NORMAL" lives.

This interpretation of autism as a tragedy fails to explore the extent to which disability is a social construct, meaning that the failure of social policy to provide FAMILY support and quality INCLUSIVE EDUCATION may be seen as disabling certain people by creating an environment that does not allow them to grow and develop. Limiting views of autism were effectively challenged beginning in the mid 1980s as

> *"Took Jojo to Dr. Jamieson's at Seagirt for school. Beautiful place but it was hard on the poor little darling and me too."*
>
> —Dawn Powell, writing in her journal about her nine-year-old son Joseph, who was diagnosed autistic as an adult, November 2, 1930

people classified as autistic began to publish autobiographies in which they contest many assumptions about autism. In one of the first such accounts, *Emergence: Labeled Autistic* (1986), TEMPLE GRANDIN describes how she learned to read, how she could understand conversations long before she could enter into them, and how she has been affected by a variety of sensory differences, including touch. Another well-known autism activist and author is Donna Williams, who has written such internationally popular memoirs as *Nobody Nowhere* (1994) and *Somebody Somewhere* (1995). Other autobiographical accounts paint rich pictures of autism as a life experience rather than as a disorder or defect in need of a CURE. Sue Rubin, the subject writer of the Academy Award–nominated film *Autism Is a World* (2004), explains how she thought of herself as mentally retarded and autistic until she developed a means of independent communication, whereupon her opportunities to interact with peers and family were transformed. These and other autobiographical accounts challenge the conventional notion that autism is a tragic deficit.

The struggle to define autism helps to offer insight into two contesting views of disability: the medical model, which seeks to define, classify, and cure; and the social construct model, which defines disability as society's failure to accommodate difference. The emerging activist movement by and for people with autism thus reflects not only the larger DISABILITY RIGHTS MOVEMENT but also Americans' abiding interest in civil rights. Autism remains an important topic for understanding American history and cultural IDENTITY.

See also ASPERGER'S SYNDROME; COGNITIVE AND INTELLECTUAL DISABILITY; MEDICAL MODEL OF DISABILITY; SOCIAL CONSTRUCTION OF DISABILITY.

Douglas Biklen

Further Reading:

Biklen, Douglas (with Richard Attfield, Larry Bissonnette, Lucy Blackman, Jamie Burke, Alberto Frugone, Tito R. Mukhopadhyay, and Sue Rubin). *Autism and the Myth of the Person Alone*. New York: Teachers College Press, 2005.

Kanner, Leo. "Autistic Disturbances of Affective Contact." In *Classic Readings in Autism,* edited by Anne M. Donnellan, 11–49. New York: Teachers College Press, 1988. Originally published 1943.

Williams, Donna. *Autism: An Inside-Out Approach.* London: Jessica Kingsley Publishers, 1996.

Autism Society of America

The Autism Society of America (ASA) is the oldest AUTISM advocacy ORGANIZATION in the United States. Initially called the National Society for Autistic Children, the ASA was founded in 1965 by Bernard Rimland and other parents who had grown concerned about the impoverished state of educational services for their CHILDREN. Ruth Christ Sullivan became the first president elected by the organization membership in 1968. The organization continues to focus on advocacy, services, and support for children and adults with autism and their families.

Prior to the late 1960s many medical professionals believed that autism was a "psychogenic" disorder, meaning that the psychological problems of parents were responsible for their child's disability. This belief stigmatized parents of children with autism and made it difficult for people with autism to obtain educational services, support, or effective treatment. Members of the organization successfully lobbied the U.S. Department of Education to reclassify autism from a "Severe Emotional Disorder," a classification based on the psychogenic theory of autism, to a developmental disorder, a term that reflected research indicating that the disorder had an organic cause. This new classification suggested that their children could learn if they were given the appropriate educational accommodations. The founding members of the society believed that their children could be educated successfully, and they sought to promote the therapeutic technique of Applied Behavior Analysis (ABA), developed as a treatment for autism by O. Ivar Lovaas at the University of California, Los Angeles, during the late 1960s and early 1970s. The organization combined these specific aims with a more general program of public awareness and political and educational advocacy.

Through the 1980s and 1990s the ASA maintained a strong focus on legislation and educational issues. Local chapters functioned as support groups and as sources of information for the parents of children who had been recently diagnosed. The ASA, currently a community of nearly 200 chapters nationwide, has moved in new directions under the leadership of Lee Grossman, who became president and CEO in 2005. In addition to public awareness campaigns and other advocacy work, the organization promotes an "options" policy, which emphasizes several key points. These include supporting parental choice in treatments for children with autism, recognizing the importance of the input of the person with autism, and accepting the fact that no treatment is guaranteed to be effective for all individuals. Reflecting the movement for self-determination in disability communities, the ASA during the 1990s began to include SELF-ADVOCATES with autism diagnoses in the organization leadership and policies. Two board members in the 21st century, Stephen Shore and Ruth Elaine Hane, have had diagnoses on the autism spectrum.

In addition to the active inclusion of self-advocates, the ASA has also begun to focus more actively on the neglected area of services for adults with autism, who are often left with few supports when they reach an age at which they no longer qualify for educational services. The organization has also begun to sponsor conferences and research on environmental factors in autism after parents raised concerns over the potential links between autism and childhood exposures to lead, mercury, and pesticides, as well as vaccines and antibiotic overuse. Some adults with autism view the ASA with some wariness because of this interest in a search for a CURE for autism, which they resist because—like many disability advocates—they consider social attitudes rather than their diagnosis to be the main source of their difficulties.

The Autism Society of America reflects many historical trends in parent advocacy for children with disabilities. Its success in influencing educational policy and treatment methods demonstrates the effectiveness of parent advocacy and the ability of members of a COMMUNITY to alter the social meaning of a disability. Its evolution from an organization *for* people with autism to a group *with* autistic members likewise reflects the influence of the DISABILITY RIGHTS MOVEMENT on many advocacy organizations in the United States and the move toward greater social and political inclusion.

See also ACTIVISM AND ADVOCACY; PARENT ADVOCACY GROUPS.

Chloe Silverman

Further Reading:

Autism Society of America Web site. URL: http://www.autism-society.org/site/PageServer.

Charlton, James I. *Nothing About Us Without Us: Disability Oppression and Empowerment.* Berkeley: University of California Press, 2000.

Hart, Charles. *Without Reason: A Family Copes with Two Generations of Autism.* Arlington, Tex.: Future Horizons, 1989.

Trent, James W., Jr. *Inventing the Feeble Mind: A History of Mental Retardation in the United States.* Berkeley: University of California Press, 1995.

automobiles

An American cultural icon, automobiles have played a central role in the nation's history, particularly since the early

20th century with the emergence of their mass production. Although numerous books, articles, and documentaries celebrate and study the history of cars, few have taken into consideration the intersection of automobiles and people with disabilities.

A particularly important contribution cars have made in the history of disability involves EMPLOYMENT. The emergence of automobile factories in the early 1900s created numerous job opportunities. Historian Robert Buchanan has shown that the FORD MOTOR COMPANY promoted a policy of nondiscrimination toward DEAF and disabled workers, often specifically recruiting them. Goodyear and Firestone tire factories likewise hired many deaf and disabled workers, particularly during WORLD WAR I and WORLD WAR II.

Social dimensions of automotive history matter as well. Many people with disabilities, like NONDISABLED Americans, have enjoyed the freedom and fun of cars. However, in addition to causing thousands of disabling conditions, particularly from collisions and assembly-line injuries, cars have represented new forms of STIGMA or marginalization. For example, the rise of safety tests and driving laws, particularly since the 1920s, encouraged eye exams as a standard feature for obtaining a license, which has excluded and stigmatized many Americans with low vision. In addition, both formal and informal bans have prohibited many people with EPILEPSY, developmental disabilities (see DEVELOPMENTAL DISABILITY), or with various MOBILITY impairments from driving. Anecdotal evidence suggests considerable variation in the support of or opposi-

"The truth of the matter—in my opinion—is that hearing is of little or no value in driving. Just how much is hearing worth to a driver when he has his windows closed and a blaring radio giving out red hot swing music?"

—an unnamed deaf driver bemoaning the rise of deaf driving bans, quoted in an article, September 1939

tion to disabled drivers throughout the 20th century, partly because states individually oversee driver licensing and testing occurs at the local level.

One particularly vivid campaign against driving bans involved deaf Americans. During the 1920s and 1930s, numerous states, including Maryland, New York, California, Pennsylvania, and Ohio, prohibited deaf people from driving. Sophisticated collaborations between schools, ORGANIZATIONS, employers, and individuals resulted in the reversal of deaf driving bans by the 1940s, although individual cases of discrimination against deaf drivers have been reported.

Adaptive devices for vehicles also represent an important feature of this history. Especially since disabled World War I VETERANS returned home, innovators have been developing various types of devices, such as hand controls, to assist AMPUTEES, PARAPLEGICS, and other disabled drivers. In the 1930s President FRANKLIN D. ROOSEVELT's automobile was altered with such extension devices and hand controls.

Since the 1940s the industry for adaptive devices for cars has grown, and more recent legislation has acknowledged the importance of ACCESS for disabled travelers. For example, handicap parking stickers were introduced in 1973 in Washington, D.C. Over the next decade various states adopted Handicap Parking Programs, reserving spaces near buildings for drivers and travelers with mobility impairments in order to promote greater access. In 1988 Congress enacted legislation forcing the U.S. Department of Transportation to develop the "Uniform System for Parking for Persons with Disabilities." Although states still govern parking privileges, this federal system provides models based on accessible design. These federal guidelines have expanded since the passage of the AMERICANS WITH DISABILITIES ACT in 1990.

In POPULAR CULTURE, disability and cars share an important history. For example, throughout the 20th century comedians, such as Eddie Murphy, and entertainment FILMS, such as SCENT OF A WOMAN (1992), have played on images of BLIND drivers as objects of humor. Since the 1990s vari-

Automobiles revolutionized transportation in the 20th century, transforming notions of freedom and independence. Cars have represented opportunity as well as challenge for people with disabilities, such as this World War II veteran whose prosthetic limb and adaptive devices enable him to drive.   *(Smithsonian National Museum of American History, Division of Medicine and Science)*

ous professional race car drivers who are PARAPLEGIC have gained popularity in America, including Lance Magin (the first such driver licensed to compete in NASCAR), Carol Hollfelder, and Tim Totherow.

Understanding the evolution of automobiles in relation to people with disabilities changes the typical interpretation of this technology by showing the ways it has enhanced and limited diverse people over time. It also shifts the REPRESENTATION of disability by showing economic, social, and legal dimensions of the disability lived experience.

See also ACTIVISM AND ADVOCACY; ASSISTIVE TECHNOLOGY AND ADAPTIVE DEVICES; FORD, HENRY; NATIONAL ASSOCIATION OF THE DEAF; TRANSPORTATION.

Sylvie Soulier
Susan Burch

Further Reading:

Buchanan, Robert. *Illusions of Equality: Deaf Americans in School and Factory.* Washington, D.C.: Gallaudet University Press, 1999.

Burch, Susan. *Signs of Resistance: Deaf Cultural History, 1900 to World War II.* New York: New York University Press, 2002.

Bush, Elizabeth. "The Deaf Community and the Automobile: 1900–1940." Master's thesis, Gallaudet University, Washington: D.C., 2007.

Henning, Anna. "CRS Report for Congress: Federal Law on Parking Privileges for Persons with Disabilities." (July 23, 2007). Available online. URL: http://assets.openers.com/rpts/RS22697_20070723.pdf. Accessed November 1, 2008.

Koppa, Rodger. "Automotive Adaptive Equipment and Vehicle Modifications" United States National Highway Traffic Safety Administration, National Reseach Council. *Transportation in an Aging Society: A Decade of Experience, Technical Papers, and Reports from a Conference, November 7–9, 1999, Bethesda, Maryland.* Transportation Research Board, 2004.

Avila, Homer (1955–2004) *dancer*

Disability directly shaped accomplished dancer Homer Avila's repertoire as well as the field of DANCE in the early 21st century.

Born in 1955 and raised in New Orleans, Avila studied at the University of Tennessee, Knoxville. There he began a lifelong fascination with dance. Avila trained early in gymnastics, which aided his interest in dance and body movement. In 1976 he moved to New York City to pursue dance. He worked and danced with several different dance troupes, including Twyla Tharp, Bill T. Jones/Arnie Zane, Mark Morris, Ralph Lemon, and Momix. Eventually he formed the Avila/Weeks Dance Company with Edisa Weeks. Avila and Weeks danced and choreographed together for nine years.

In early 2001 Avila was diagnosed with chondrosarcoma, a rare form of CANCER. He continued dancing, but on April 12, 2001, he underwent surgery to amputate his right hip and leg because of the cancer. Like many artists with limited income, Avila was often unable to afford health insurance, and because of this lack of medical coverage, he may have delayed seeking medical attention.

Avila accepted help from the dance community, which allowed him to pursue his artistic life. At the same time he voiced strong opinions on the bleak financial circumstances of many artists, including writing an article in the *Village Voice* in spring 2001. The following fall, One Step Forward, a fund of the New York Foundation for the Arts, held a benefit for Avila, which spurred discussion resulting in the development of further resources to help artists with disabilities. The Actor's Fund, a nonprofit organization that serves members of the entertainment industry, also now makes resources available to New York dancers.

On the night before surgery, Avila told a *Village Voice* reporter: "All I knew was that dancing let me live larger than I thought possible." The surgery marked a monumental change to his body, the instrument of his expression, but it did not prevent him from dancing or from enjoying a full and enriched life. He returned to dancing in September 2002, with performances in Vermont and at the Kennedy Center for the Performing Arts in Washington, D.C.

Avila saw the loss of his leg as an opportunity. He used his disability to continue to explore movement through his body. As Avila remarked in 2001, he had a chance to "apply the lessons I've learned in art: what you do with what you are given." He learned to use his body in a new way, perfecting balance both with other dancers and by himself.

Avila danced solo performances using small movements and jumps with his one leg, often balancing with his arm. The 2006 documentary film by Karina Epperlein, *Phoenix Dance*, showed Avila dancing alone. One dance review of Avila noted: "He moves with such fluidity and power that your eyes can be tricked into thinking he is dancing with three legs rather than one." His collaboration with other dancers sparked new, creative movements to balance together. He also enjoyed working with other prominent choreographers, such as Alonzo King, Victoria Marks, and Dana Casperson.

Avila continued his pursuit of dance until the end of his life. The last weekend before his death he attended a class on Friday and a concert on Saturday evening, then checked himself into the hospital. He died there the next day on April 25, 2004, from the spread of the chondrosarcoma to his lungs.

Avila always considered himself an artist, and he lived that vision with renewed passion as a disabled dancer. While he certainly was an example of mastery in teaching and choreography, Avila continued to use his instrument—his body—through dance itself. His uniquely creative response encompassed and reflected the exploration of truly human concerns—ability, strength, and balance.

See also AMPUTEES AND AMPUTATION; DISABILITY; ART AND ARTISTIC EXPRESSION.

Nancy Obermueller

Further Reading:

Artists with Disabilities Oral History Project. "Homer Avila, In Memoriam." Regional Oral History Office. Available online. URL: http://bancroft.berkeley.edu/ROHO/projects/artistsdis/homer_avila.html. Accessed December 13, 2006.

Avila, Homer. "Between a Rock and a Hard Place," *Village Voice*, 25 April 1–May 2001. Available online. URL: http://www.villagevoice.com/generic/show_print.php?id=24147&page=avila&issue=0117&printcde=Mz. Accessed August 21, 2006.

Dance Magazine. "Up from the Ashes," *Dance Magazine.* Available online. URL: http://galenet.galegroup.com/servlet/BioRC?vrsn=149&OP=contains&locID=waterpl_main&srchtp=name&c=6&tbst=prp&tab=8&n=10&docNum=A155615623&bConts=8. Accessed December 13, 2006.

Linton, Simi. *My Body Politic: A Memoir.* Ann Arbor: University of Michigan Press, 2005.

Marcotty, Fiona, et al. "Flash Memorial, 4–30: Funeral for a Friend, Homer's Odyssey." The Dance Insider. Available online. URL: http://www.danceinsider.com/f2004/f0430_2.html. Accessed August 21, 2006.

Suki, John. "Homer Avila: Fresh Steps," NYFA Quarterly—Fall 2001. Available online. URL: http://www.nyfa.org/archive_detail_q.asp?type=4&qid=51&fid=6&year+2001&s=Fall. Accessed August 21, 2006.

Sygoda, Ivan. "Remembering Homer (1955–2004)," *Dance Magazine.* Available online. URL: www.dancemagazine.com. Accessed December 13, 2006.

Awakenings   See SACKS, OLIVER.

AXIS Dance Company

Founded in 1987, the AXIS Dance Company of Oakland, California, challenges canonical DANCE forms through an alternative approach to modern dance and mixed-ability dancers. From its inception, AXIS has built its troupe with dancers of varying MOBILITY levels. Some are standing dancers, some are dancers with orthopedic physical impairments who use WHEELCHAIRS, and some move with canes. With the aid of such technology and changing concepts of what constitutes "dance bodies," disabled dancers offer alternatives to conventional ideas of the body, aesthetics, GENDER, and dance itself.

Under the artistic direction of Judith Smith, this company has a portfolio that includes more than 30 repertory works, two evening length pieces, and two works for young audiences. Among other venues, they have performed at the Olympic Arts Festival in Salt Lake City, the Dance Umbrella's International Festival in Boston, Central Park Summerstage in New York City, the University of Cologne in Germany, and the Railroad Theater in Novosibirsk, Russia. Nominated for numerous honors and awards, AXIS won Isadora Duncan Dance Awards in 2000 and 2002.

For the AXIS dancers, it took some time to establish an internal system of checks and balances that allowed members to invite external artists and know when limits were being pushed too far. Their strongest choreographers reimagined accommodation: dancers with disabilities have had to adapt to new movement as much as choreographers have adjusted to their impairments. In the first two years of the 21st century the AXIS Dance Company commissioned mainstream choreographers, such as Bill T. Jones and Stephen Petronio, to choreograph for their mixed-ability ensemble. Jones's *Fantasy in C Major* (2000) and Petronio's *Secret Ponies* (2001) invite spectators to look with a difference, changing conventional notions of the body: its limits, its capabilities, and its borders. In choosing these prominent choreographers, the company makes the statement that mixed-ability dancers deserve equal respect and acclaim; at the same time, this choice shows other choreographers that bodies with a physical difference can alter stage dynamics in exciting ways.

Artists debate whether disability in the performing arts changes the way people see the body in social space, asking how disability necessitates changes in perception, action, and interpersonal relations. In disability dance, difference may be seen as a creative potential rather than as a reason for exclusion. Difference and movement accommodation are acknowledged and respected as part of what each dancer brings to the creation process. For dancers in wheelchairs, for example, arms become the primary means of expression. Dance acts as an aesthetic model for social change when disabled and NONDISABLED dancers use accommodation techniques: different physical needs require alternative interactions that reinvent stage dynamics. In AXIS's mixed-ability dance, the choreographers and the NONDISABLED dancers put a large amount of energy into making a physical connection with the disabled dancers in the company so that the work avoids a total division between performers. This focus on integration can open up new possibilities. With choreographers who are willing to work with and from the company's movement potential to build movement that both challenges physical limits and pushes audience perceptions, mixed-ability dance can be productive and informative for all involved.

Disability is a major part of the company's practice and aesthetic but not necessarily the thrust of its content. The AXIS Dance Company claims to make work whose content is not necessarily about disability, but rather includes disabled bodies as a source for movement. Still, the presence of wheelchair and cane-assisted bodies in dance calls for new ways of looking at dance as a social, spatial art form that challenges audience perception. Mixed-ability dance fosters new ways of looking that redefine the aesthetic process.

See also DISABILITY CULTURE.

Telory W. Davies

Further Reading:

Guter, Bob. "'Dancing toward the Light': An Interview with Tom Metz and Michael Perrault on Their Collaboration with AXIS Dance Company in 1996." *BENT* (July 2000). Available online. URL: http://www.bentvoices.org/. Accessed August 4, 2008.

Richter, Nicole. "Changing the Moves: The Emergence of Dancers with Physical Disability in the Professional Dance Realm." Master's thesis, Laban Centre for Movement and Dance, London, 1996.

B

Baby Doe cases

"Baby Doe" is a phrase used to refer to public controversies surrounding the provision of life-sustaining care and treatment to infants born with disabilities in the 1980s. Infants and families at the heart of the controversies went unnamed in the media and court cases. The first case to receive widespread public attention in the decade involved an infant born in 1982 in Indiana with DOWN SYNDROME and a defective esophagus that made it impossible for him to receive nutrition or fluids. On the advice of one of the family's physicians who believed that the infant would not be able to maintain a minimally adequate quality of life because of his Down syndrome, the infant's parents decided not to authorize routine surgery to correct his esophagus. A pediatrician and the family physician disagreed with the decision to withhold surgery. The hospital's attorney and other lawyers asked a state court to intervene in the case based on child neglect. The judge refused to order life-saving surgery on the infant. The infant died of dehydration and pneumonia six days after he was born. U.S. Surgeon General C. Everett Koop followed the Indiana Baby Doe case very carefully. Koop stated that he had performed over 400 surgeries on infants with similar conditions and claimed that the operation had become 100 percent successful.

Another controversy involving an infant born in 1983 in Long Island, New York, with SPINA BIFIDA, an opening of the spine, erupted a little over a year after the death of Indiana's Baby Doe. Physicians involved in the case, which became known as Baby Jane Doe, gave conflicting advice to the infant's parents on her long-term prospects. The parents decided not to permit surgery on the infant to correct the opening in her spine. Surgeon General Koop unsuccessfully tried to intervene in the case. The infant was left untreated while the controversy played out legally and publicly. Although the infant lived, she came down with an infection in her spine and inflammation of her brain, resulting in brain damage.

In the aftermath of the Baby Doe controversies, the U.S. Department of Health and Human Services in President Ronald Reagan's administration acted to prevent the withholding of life-sustaining care and treatment to infants born with disabilities. It issued new regulations under SECTION 504 of the Rehabilitation Act, which outlawed discrimination against people with disabilities by recipients of federal funds. The new regulations made it a violation of the law to deny routine medical treatment to infants born with disabilities. In 1986 the U.S. Supreme Court struck down the regulations and ruled that Section 504 did not protect infants whose parents had decided to forego medical treatment. In the meantime, Congress amended the definition of child ABUSE under federal law to include the withholding of food, fluids, and appropriate medical treatment from infants with disabilities.

The Baby Doe cases focused public, legal, and political attention on a long-standard practice at some, and perhaps many, HOSPITALS. The withholding of nutrition, hydration, and routine medical care from infants born with disabilities was not new. In his book THE BLACK STORK, historian Martin Pernick documented a national controversy in 1915 involving a physician who regularly withheld medical treatment from infants born with disabilities. In the 1970s and 1980s, articles were published in medical journals in which physicians described their practice of withholding treatment from infants with disabilities. Physicians Raymond Duff and A.G.M. Campbell wrote a 1973 article in the *New England Journal of Medicine* stating that they had denied surgery or medical treatment to over 40 infants with Down syndrome or other disabilities at Yale–New Haven Hospital during a two-and-one-half-year period. Then, in 1983, Richard Gross, Alan Cox, Ruth Tatyrek, Michael Pollay, and William Barnes published an article in *Pediatrics* reporting on an experiment on infants with SPINA BIFIDA at the University of Oklahoma Health Sciences Center. Based on the infants' presumed future quality of life, the physicians divided the infants into two groups, one receiving active medical treatment and one receiving supportive care with no surgery or medications. Of those receiving supportive care only, all 24 infants died. In the group receiving vigorous medical treatment, 35 of 36 infants lived, and the one death that occurred was due to an unrelated accident.

The Baby Doe controversies stirred up political passions unrelated to disability issues. Many of those supporting government restrictions on the withholding of life-sustaining care and treatment were identified with anti-abortion, "right-to-life" causes. Medical, civil liberties, and women's groups tended to oppose what they saw as government intrusion on the privacy of parents and the decision making of physicians. The Baby Doe controversy became a stand-in for the "pro-life" versus "pro-choice" debate.

Most disability rights activists and groups supported a government role in protecting infants from the denial of food, fluids, and regular medical care. For most of these advocates, the Baby Doe controversy was unrelated to the abortion debate. The denial of care and treatment to infants with disabilities reflected long-standing prejudice and discrimination against people with disabilities. The level of treatment required by the Baby Does was no different from that routinely provided to NONDISABLED infants, with or without parental approval. Assessments of the future quality of life of infants with Down syndrome, spina bifida, and other disabilities were flawed.

The Baby Doe controversy soon faded from the media spotlight, although it has flared up occasionally in ethical debates about the personhood and humanity of persons with disabilities. Some advocates and groups regard PHYSICIAN-ASSISTED SUICIDE and the denial of life-sustaining care and treatment for adults with severe intellectual, physical, or cognitive disabilities as reflecting the same views that led to the denial of fluids, food, and routine medical care to the infants in the Baby Doe cases.

Steven J. Taylor

Further Reading:

Biklen D. P., and P. M. Ferguson. "In the Matter of Baby Jane Doe: Does Reagan Really Agree with Us?" *Social Policy* (Summer 1984): 5–8.

Hentoff, Nat. "The Awful Privacy of Baby Doe." *Atlantic Monthly* (January 1985): 54–62.

Pernick, M. S. *The Black Stork: Eugenics and the Death of "Defective" Babies in American Medicine and Motion Pictures since 1915.* New York: Oxford University Press, 1996.

Profiles in Science, U.S. National Library of Medicine. The C. Everett Koop Papers: Congenital Birth Defects and the Medical Rights of Children: The "Baby Doe" Controversy. Available online. URL: http://profiles.nlm.nih.gov/QQ/Views/Exhibit/narrative/babydoe.html. Accessed December 20, 2007.

backlash

The AMERICANS WITH DISABILITIES ACT (ADA), passed by huge majorities in Congress in 1990, seemed an unlikely trigger for backlash against the DISABILITY RIGHTS MOVEMENT. The ease with which the ADA passed was remarkable, given its broad coverage, its endorsement of a flexible, expansive minority group model of disability, and its incorporation of structural theories of discrimination. Between 1990, when the ADA was passed, and 1994, when its provisions became fully effective, expectations for its transformative potential ran high.

By 1996, however, as decisions in ADA cases began to accumulate, it became increasingly clear that federal judges were not interpreting the ADA as its supporters had anticipated. Law review articles written by many of the statute's drafters described a powerful narrowing trend in the courts, particularly on the foundational question of who was a "person with a disability" within the meaning of the statute.

During the same period, media coverage of the ADA turned increasingly negative, portraying the ADA, its enforcers, and its beneficiaries as opportunists or fools run wildly amuck, providing windfalls to unworthy rent-seekers and imposing unbearable hardships on businesses. Article headlines such as "The Disabilities Act Parade of Absurdities" and "Late for Work: Plead Insanity" were accompanied by TELEVISION shows, including *The Simpsons* and *King of the Hill,* which mocked the ADA, its enforcers, and its beneficiaries in episodes with titles such as "King Size Homer" and "Junkie Business." Articles and shows such as these regularly depicted patently NONDISABLED workers exploiting the statute's flexible definition of disability and reasonable accommodation provisions to legitimize their own narcissism or to dodge the reasonable consequences of their own bad behavior.

Soon, supporters of the ADA began using the term "backlash" to describe what they were seeing in the courts of law and public opinion. In 1998 and 1999, two empirical studies of ADA employment case outcomes reinforced the impression that something significant and negative was occurring in the courts. These studies showed that between 92 and 95 percent of plaintiffs whose ADA cases went to judgment were losing (a much higher loss rate than in other civil rights cases), and that the losses largely turned on the foundational question of whether the plaintiff was a "person with a disability" and, if so, whether they were "qualified." In three cases decided in 1999, the U.S. Supreme Court followed suit, interpreting the ADA's coverage and qualification provisions in an extremely narrow way, effectively denying the act's protection to large classes of disabled people and reasserting the old impairment model of disability that the statute's drafters had intended to displace.

Attempts in the late 1990s and early 2000s to understand "what went wrong" with interpretations of the ADA in the courts of law and public opinion generated an analysis of change and retrenchment that can be applied to public, judicial, and media reactions to the ADA and more generally to social justice movements such as that for disability rights. This model views the ADA as an example of transformative law, that is, law designed not to reinforce established social norms and institutions, but to destabilize and transform them. Absent continued efforts for social change, however, transformative laws are always subject to capture by preexisting ideologies, practices, and norms. Transformative law is captured when it is reinterpreted and applied in ways that reinforce the very preexisting norms and social meanings that the law was intended by its drafters to displace.

Backlash represents a subtype of capture. Capture can be subtle and can occur even if legal and social actors do not deliberately set out to undermine the goals of the transformative law. In backlash, however, opponents of transformative law explicitly reject one or more of its key elements, and they ground that rejection in an open and aggressive assertion of the superiority of the preexisting social and legal order. Backlash included explicit attacks on the morality and intentions of the transformative law's beneficiaries, often accompanied by attempts to limit the benefiting group, or by vivid anecdotes designed to convince the public that the new legal rules result in unfair or absurd outcomes. Backlash is most likely to occur in situations characterized by sharp disparities.

Because the ADA was not preceded or followed by a broadly based, well-publicized social change movement successful at spreading a social constructionist model of disability, it was particularly vulnerable to both ordinary capture and backlash effects.

See also LAW AND POLICY; SOCIAL CONSTRUCTION OF DISABILITY.

Linda Hamilton Krieger

Further Reading:

Diller, Matthew. "Judicial Backlash, the ADA, and the Civil Rights Model of Disability." In *Backlash against the ADA: Reinterpreting Disability Rights,* edited by Linda Hamilton Krieger, 62–97. Ann Arbor: University of Michigan Press (Corporealities), 2003.

Hahn, Harlan. "Accommodations and the ADA: Unreasonable Bias or Biased Reasoning?" In *Backlash against the ADA: Reinterpreting Disability Rights,* edited by Linda Hamilton Krieger, 26–61. Ann Arbor: University of Michigan Press (Corporealities), 2003.

Krieger, Linda Hamilton. Foreword: "Backlash against the Americans with Disabilities Act: Interdisciplinary Perspectives and Implications for Social Justice Strategies." *Berkeley Journal of Employment and Labor Law* 21 (2000): 1.

———. "Socio-Legal Backlash." In *Backlash against the ADA: Reinterpreting Disability Rights,* edited by Linda Hamilton Krieger, 340–394. Ann Arbor: University of Michigan Press (Corporealities), 2003.

Barden-LaFollette Act

Signed by President FRANKLIN D. ROOSEVELT in 1943, the Barden-LaFollette Act was a major piece of VOCATIONAL REHABILITATION legislation with very significant effects for people with disabilities. The Barden-LaFollette Act significantly amended the previous vocational rehabilitation legislation, the SMITH-FESS ACT, which restricted the types of services offered by vocational rehabilitation providers. By 1943 large numbers of disabled VETERANS from WORLD WAR II, coupled with major changes in medical and rehabilitation practices, necessitated an update in vocational rehabilitation laws. The desire to enable disabled workers to be involved in WAR production constituted another impetus for the Barden-LaFollette Act.

Named for its sponsors Representative Graham Barden (D-N.C.) and Senator Robert LaFollette, Jr. (Progressive-Wisc.), the Barden-LaFollette Act massively expanded vocational rehabilitation programs. It did so by including people with MENTAL ILLNESS and those labeled with "MENTAL RETARDATION" in rehabilitation programs, increasing physical rehabilitation and restoration services for people with physical disabilities, recognizing the need for separate agencies administering vocational rehabilitation for BLIND people, and increasing financial assistance for HEALTH CARE. The inclusion of mental illness in this act was driven partly by the large numbers of disabled veterans who were diagnosed with "shell shock" (now known as post-traumatic stress disorder), which had shown the need for expanded vocational rehabilitation services. The act also required states to develop their own plans for vocational rehabilitation that would be submitted to the federal government.

Blindness organizations regard the Barden-LaFollette Act as a major legislative development because it contained provisions specifically giving blind people a wider range of options for vocational rehabilitation services. It enabled state agencies, commissions, and private agencies for BLIND people to administer state-federal vocational rehabilitation programs. Members of the NATIONAL FEDERATION OF THE BLIND, for instance, welcomed this development because they felt it fostered partnerships between the federal government and agencies that had specific expertise in the blindness area. They also applauded the financial stability and security provided by the act, because they believed that it enabled such ORGANIZATIONS to plan and organize their services more effectively. Indeed, the act was called "The Magna Carta of the Blind" by some National Federation of the Blind members.

The Barden-LaFollette Act set a precedent for broadening vocational rehabilitation programs, a trend that continued with the Vocational Rehabilitation Amendments of 1954 and 1968.

Mark Sherry

Further Reading:
Cavenaugh, Brenda S., and Steven J. Pierce. "Characteristics, Services, and Outcomes of Rehabilitation Consumers Who Are Blind or Visually Impaired Served in Separate and General Agencies." Where in Mississippi, Mississippi, Rehabilitation Research and Training Center on Blindness and Low Vision, Mississippi State, 1998. Available online: URL: http://www.blind.msstate.edu/mono.html. Accessed December 15, 2006.
Rumer, Thomas A. *The American Legion: An Official History, 1919–1989.* New York: M. Evans, 1990.
Scotch, Richard K. *From Good Will to Civil Rights: Transforming Federal Disability Policy.* Philadelphia: Temple University Press, 2001.

Barnum, P. T. (Phineas Taylor) (1810–1891)
showman and circus promoter

Phineas Taylor (P. T.) Barnum, the best-known huckster and CIRCUS operator in American history, gained fame and wealth in the mid 19th century by exhibiting people. Although not the first showman to display people with disabilities as "freaks," no one else possessed Barnum's flair for capturing publicity and the imagination of the public. He and his employees simultaneously exploited the public while portraying disability as a spectacle for the entertainment of the masses.

Barnum was born in Bethel, Connecticut, on July 5, 1810. Barnum's father died bankrupt in 1825, and Barnum clerked in general stores before opening his own successful confectionary store in Bethel. In 1835 he moved to New York City and purchased a blind African-American slave woman named Joice Heth, purportedly the 161-year-old ex-nurse of George Washington. Heth's public appearances brought Barnum $750 weekly. Upon her death, Barnum hired a juggler. When audiences shrank, Barnum hired a heckler who swore he could outdo the juggler. The subsequent duels brought customers flocking. In 1835 Barnum led a small traveling circus through the South. He spent the next few years in and out of show business.

In 1841 Barnum took over Scudder's American Museum in New York City and renamed it Barnum's American Museum. His policy was to spend lavishly on "curiosities," which included trained fleas, living statuary, and mechanical figures as well as "freaks," and to then profit from their exhibition. Barnum was responsible for showing the best-known human exhibits of his day. Among these were the CONJOINED TWINS, CHANG BUNKER and ENG BUNKER. The Lucasies, a family of albinos, also drew large crowds. In 1842 Barnum employed CHARLES SHERWOOD STRATTON, a two-foot-tall 10-year-old whom Barnum billed as "General Tom Thumb." Tom Thumb quickly became a public favorite and Barnum toured England with him in 1844 to considerable acclaim.

Thumb, very different from the DWARF exhibits frequently displayed in Europe, was an engaging, well-dressed boy who sang, danced, and carried on enlightened conversation. He became one of Barnum's biggest stars, collaborating with the showman to exploit the public for financial gain. Yet Barnum also included—for a considerable profit—Jane Campbell, "the largest Mountain of Human Flesh ever seen in the form of a woman"; R. O. Wickware, "the Living Phantom" (so labeled because of his thinness); ANNA SWAN, the "Nova Scotia Giantess"; and "Leopard-Spotted" blacks with the pigmentation illness, vitiligo. Scholars like Rosemarie Garland Thomson have since noted that such EXHIBITIONS conflated racist, sexist, xenophobic, and ableist beliefs.

Between 1851 and 1856 Barnum operated the Great Asiatic Caravan, Museum, and Menagerie, which featured Stratton, elephants, and other wild animals. In the circus as well as the earlier museum, Barnum always exhibited some "WHAT IS IT?" The most famous of this type of display was a cone-headed African-American dwarf (the term then used for LITTLE PEOPLE), William Henry Johnson, also known as "Zip" to generations of Americans. Johnson typically crouched with legs spayed outward. Barnum described him as the connecting link between Africans and animals, a description that particularly satisfied whites by supporting the notion that blacks were an inferior RACE. Barnum sold the American Museum's collection in 1855. He merged with a British circus run by James Bailey in 1881 and effectively retired from the ring. He spent his final days lecturing before dying of heart failure.

Barnum's relationship to people with disabilities—perceived and real—has received considerable attention from disability scholars. His success depended heavily on his marketing of disability and difference, and his life story raises important questions about the important themes in disability history, including EXPLOITATION, EMPOWERMENT, STEREOTYPES, and EMPLOYMENT.

See also FREAK SHOWS; POPULAR CULTURE.

Caryn E. Neumann

Further Reading:
Adams, Bluford. *E Pluribus Barnum: The Great Showman and the Making of U.S. Popular Culture.* Minneapolis: University of Minnesota Press, 1997.
Bogdan, Robert. *Freak Show: Presenting Human Oddities for Amusement and Profit.* Chicago: University of Chicago Press, 1988.
Harris, Neil. *Humbug: The Art of P. T. Barnum.* Boston: Little, Brown, 1973.
Reiss, Benjamin. *The Showman and the Slave: Race, Death, and Memory in Barnum's America.* Cambridge, Mass.: Harvard University Press, 2001.
Saxon, A. H. *P. T. Barnum: The Legend and the Man.* New York: Columbia University Press, 1989.

The Life of P. T. Barnum by P. T. Barnum (1855)

Flamboyant showman and exhibitor P. T. Barnum remains an American cultural icon. His popular "freak shows" during the 19th century drew national and international attention. As these selections from his 1855 memoir attest, he delighted in his business success and considered the recruitments of individuals such as Charles Stratton, whom he renamed General Tom Thumb, a stroke of genius. Disability studies scholars since the 1990s have focused extensively on Barnum's career, raising critical questions about the exploitation and agency of his performers, as well as the meaning of Barnum's representation of the extraordinary bodies he displayed.

The Life of P. T. Barnum
by Phineas T. Barnum
1855

There has been a gradual change in these, and the transient attractions of the Museum have been greatly diversified. Industrious fleas, educated dogs, jugglers, automatons, ventriloquists, living statuary, tableaux, gipsies, albinoes, fat boys, giants, dwarfs, rope-dancers, caricatures of phrenology, and "live Yankees," pantoming instrumental music, singing and dancing in great variety, (including Ethiopians,) etc. Dioramas, panoramas, models of Dublin, Paris, Niagara, Jerusalem, etc., mechanical figures, fancy glass-blowing, knitting machines and other triumphs in the mechanical arts, dissolving views, American Indians, including their warlike and religious ceremonies enacted on the stage, etc., etc.

. . . Apart from the merit and interest of these performances, and apart from every thing connected with the stage, my permanent collection of curiosities is, without doubt, abundantly worth the uniform charge of admission to all the entertainments of the establishment, and I can therefore afford to be accused of "humbug" when I add such transient novelties as increase its attractions. If I have exhibited a questionable dead mermaid in my Museum, it should not be overlooked that I have also exhibited cameleopards, a rhinoceros, grisly bears, orang-outangs, great serpents, etc., about which there could be no mistake because they were alive; and I should hope that a little "clap-trap" occasionally, in the way of transparencies, flags, exaggerated pictures, and puffing advertisements, might find an offset in a wilderness of wonderful, instructive, and amusing realities. Indeed I cannot doubt that the sort of "clap-trap" here referred to, is allowable, and that the public like a little of it mixed up with the great realities which I provide. The titles of "humbug," and the "prince of humbugs," were first applied to me by myself. I made these titles a part of my "stock in trade[.]"

. . . I had heard of a remarkably small child in Bridgeport; and by my request my brother brought him to the hotel. He was the smallest child I ever saw that could walk alone. He was not two feet in height, and weighed less than sixteen pounds. He was a bright-eyed little fellow, with light hair and ruddy cheeks, was perfectly healthy, and as symmetrical as an Apollo. He was exceedingly bashful, but after some coaxing he was induced to converse with me, and informed me that his name was CHARLES S. STRATTON, son of Sherwood E. Stratton.

. . . They arrived in New-York on Thanksgiving Day, Dec. 8, 1842, and Mrs. Stratton was greatly astonished to find her son heralded in my Museum bills as Gen. TOM THUMB, a dwarf of eleven years of age, just arrived from England!

This announcement contained two deceptions. I shall not attempt to justify them, but may be allowed to plead the circumstances in extenuation. The boy was undoubtedly a dwarf and I had the most reliable evidence that he had grown little, if any, since he was six months old; but had I announced him as only five years of age, it would have been impossible to excite the interest or awaken the curiosity of the public. The thing I aimed at was, to assure them that he was *really a dwarf*—and in *this,* at least, they were not deceived.

It was of no consequence, in reality, where he was born or where he came from, and if the announcement that he was *a foreigner* answered my purpose, the people had only themselves to blame if they did not get their money's worth when they visited the exhibition. I had observed (and sometimes, as in the case of Vivalla, had taken advantage of) the American fancy for European exotics; and if the deception, practised for a season in my dwarf experiment, has done any thing towards checking our disgraceful preference for foreigners, I may readily be pardoned for the offence I here acknowledge.

I took great pains to train my diminutive prodigy, devoting many hours to that purpose, by day and by night, and succeeded, because he had native talent and an intense love of the ludicrous.

He became very fond of me. I was, and yet am, sincerely attached to him, and I candidly believe him at this moment to be the most interesting and extraordinary natural curiosity of which the world has any knowledge.

Four weeks expired, and I re-engaged him for a year at seven dollars per week, (and a gratuity of fifty dollars at the end of the agreement,) with privilege of exhibition in any section of the United States. His parents were to accompany him, and I was to pay all travelling expenses. Long before the year was out, I voluntarily increased his weekly salary to $25—and he fairly earned it, for he speedily became a public favorite. I frequently exhibited him for successive weeks in my Museum, and when I wished to introduce fresh novelties there, I sent him to numerous cities and towns in many of the States, accompanied by my friend Fordyce Hitchcock.

In the mean time, I had entirely paid for the American Museum, and entered into an agreement with Gen. TOM THUMB for his services another year, at fifty dollars per week and all expenses, with the privilege of exhibition in Europe.

Source: Phineas T. Barnum. *The Life of P. T. Barnum.* New York: Redfield, 1855. Available online. URL: http://www.disabilitymuseum.org/lib/docs/1248.htm. Accessed June 30, 2008.

Bazelon Center for Mental Health Law

The Bazelon Center for Mental Health Law is a national legal-advocacy ORGANIZATION, founded in 1972 as the Mental Health Law Project. It changed its name in 1993 to honor the legacy of the late chief judge David L. Bazelon of the District of Columbia. The center works to protect and expand the rights of children and adults with mental disabilities through litigation, public education, and federal policy advocacy. Its pioneering work in the *Wyatt v. Stickney* case in 1970 in Alabama and the Willowbrook case in New York in 1972 set minimum standards for living conditions, staffing, and safeguards of human rights in psychiatric and mental retardation institutions, which was one of the catalysts for the DEINSTITUTIONALIZATION movement. The organization's precedent-setting cases also established the right of children with disabilities to attend public school, and the rights of adults and CHILDREN to live in the community, to be free from misuse of seclusion and restraint for punishment or administrative convenience in institutions, and to receive treatment and services in the least restrictive and most integrated setting.

The organization often works with attorneys from Protection and Advocacy organizations, as it did in *City of Cleburne v. Cleburne Living Center* (1985), in which the Supreme Court invalidated a local zoning scheme that prevented a group home for adults with mental retardation from locating in a residential neighborhood. This case laid the groundwork for the 1988 Federal Fair Housing Amendments Act that prohibits discrimination against people with disabilities in housing. In the area of Social Security, the center successfully challenged standards denying mental disability claims, and worked with the Social Security Administration to draft new standards for evaluating such claims, resulting in hundreds of thousands of adults and children securing economic support and access to MEDICAID. The center also helped to establish the right of people with disabilities to receive public services in the most integrated setting consistent with their needs under the AMERICANS WITH DISABILITIES ACT, in *Olmstead v. L. C.* Today, the center continues to engage in litigation, public education, and federal policy advocacy, working with Congress and administrative agencies, to ensure that people with mental disabilities are included within the protections of federal laws, to resist cutbacks in federal benefits, and to promote self-determination and self-sufficiency so that people with various labels related to mental health and cognitive disabilities can enjoy the social, recreational, political, educational, and cultural benefits of community living, and receive equal treatment within the criminal justice, family court, and mental health systems. The center also is a partner in the newly established National Resource Center on Psychiatric Advance Directives, which offers resources to support consumer self-determination and quality mental HEALTH CARE. The center's court cases and advocacy initiatives exemplify the organization's commitment to promoting COMMUNITY membership of people with mental disabilities and protecting them from ABUSE, while also working with them to assure their equal rights under the LAW and dignity of choice.

Arlene S. Kanter

Further Reading:

Bazelon Center for Mental Health Law Web site. URL: www.bazelon. org.

Charlton, James I. *Nothing About Us Without Us: Disability Oppression and Empowerment.* Berkeley: University of California Press, 2000.

Rothman, David J., and Shelia M. Rothman. *The Willowbrook Wars: Bringing the Mentally Disabled into the Community.* New Brunswick, N.J.: Aldine Transaction, 2005.

Beast with Five Fingers, The

Based on a 1919 short story by William Fryer Harvey, the 1946 FILM *The Beast with Five Fingers* offered audiences images of a pianist paralyzed by a stroke. Appearing right after WORLD WAR II, the film reflects and amplifies widespread anxieties over people who had become paralyzed or lost limbs during the WAR. Focusing as it does on a concert pianist, *The Beast with Five Fingers* draws attention to the implied social expectations governing the performance of concert-hall MUSIC, namely, that pianists must have two hands to be considered normal.

After Warner Brothers studio purchased the rights to Harvey's story, several screenwriters adapted the story into a feature-length film. Screenwriter Curt Siodmak did a considerable amount of the work and received the screen credit. While the original story centered around a blind naturalist, Siodmak changed the character into a concert pianist paralyzed by a stroke. Studio documents reveal that Siodmak originally wanted to name the film "Concerto for the Left Hand," intending to use the Ravel work (*Concerto pour la main gauche*) that had been commissioned by Paul Wittgenstein, a famous concert pianist who lost an arm during WORLD WAR I and who enjoyed success as a performer of music for one hand in the United States after World War II. Permission to use the Ravel work proved difficult and expensive, however, so a one-handed arrangement of J. S. Bach's Chaconne in D minor for violin, as arranged by Johannes Brahms, was employed instead.

The one-handed pianist in the film dies relatively early in the film, whereupon another character (named Hilary and performed to a campy extreme by Peter Lorre) begins to see a disembodied hand that also plays the Bach work on the piano; soon after, a character is found dead by strangling, presumably a victim of the disembodied hand. Ultimately the independently mobile disembodied hand is shown to be a hallucination by Hilary. Set within the genre of a horror film, *The Beast with Five Fingers* positions the one-handed pianist as something potentially monstrous. Set against a post–World War II milieu sadly full of those injured by war, the film participates in the negative stereotyping of persons with disabilities while also highlighting the strict norms of classical music.

See also POPULAR CULTURE; REPRESENTATION; STEREOTYPES.

Neil Lerner

Further Reading:

Edel, Theodore. *Piano Music for One Hand.* Bloomington: Indiana University Press, 1994.

Lerner, Neil. "The Horrors of One-Handed Pianism: Music and Disability in *The Beast with Five Fingers.*" In *Sounding Off: Theorizing Disability and Music,* edited by Neil Lerner and Joseph N. Straus, 75–90. New York: Routledge, 2006.

Norden, Martin F. *The Cinema of Isolation: A History of Physical Disability in the Movies.* New Brunswick, N.J.: Rutgers University Press, 1994.

Taves, Brian. "Whose Hand? Correcting a Buquel Myth." *Sight & Sound* LVI/3 (Summer 1987): 210–211.

beauty pageants   See MISS DEAF AMERICA; MS. WHEELCHAIR AMERICA; WHITESTONE, HEATHER.

Beecher, Catharine (1800–1878) *health advocate and reformer*

Catharine Beecher was one of several female health reformers in the 19th century who believed that the health of American women had deteriorated to the point of a national crisis. Plagued periodically during her adult life with physical and emotional problems that stemmed apparently from both spiritual turmoil and personal troubles, she came to rely on healthful exercise as an important remedy. Through a series of successful entrepreneurial and educational activities Beecher promoted health and fitness as a means for middle-class women to combat myths about female frailty and disability, improve their functional efficiency, and expand their influence in the home and society at large.

Born on Long Island, New York, on September 6, 1800, Beecher was the eldest child of the influential evangelical minister Lyman Beecher and sister to abolitionist Harriet Beecher Stowe and congregational ministers Henry Ward Beecher and Charles Beecher. Her later childhood years at Litchfield Academy in Connecticut persuaded her of the importance of female education and a healthy body. It also provided her with a model for incorporating physical training into women's schools when she embarked upon her own career as an educator. The death of her fiancé in a drowning accident in 1822 further stimulated her to dedicate her life to public service, initially through founding and running Hartford Female Seminary. Focusing on domestic EDUCATION, health, and calisthenics, the curriculum was designed to prepare women for their presumed profession as housewives and family caretakers and constituted one of the most significant advances made in early 19th-century education for women.

Beecher did not confine her activities to the classroom. Despite the fact that her health problems periodically sabotaged her efforts to promote the new women's professions of teaching and domestic economy, she enthusiastically assigned herself the task of designing techniques to mold, from early childhood, the new American woman—whose devotion and self-sacrifice would aid the creation of a perfect society. Among her books and pamphlets she viewed *Letters to the People on Health and Happiness* (1856) as the pivotal piece in her campaign to improve women's health. Although written as a physiology primer, her outrage at the ways American women neglected their bodies through lack of exercise and how they became disabled through poor health habits and slavish attention to fashion was quite apparent. In *Physiology and Calisthenics for Schools and Families* (1856) she described for women the structure of their own bodies and discussed the importance of female exercise to wife and motherhood.

In using calisthenics Beecher insinuated strict GENDER definition and capabilities into a gymnastic system that became increasingly popular throughout the 19th century. Her system of calisthenics was designed neither to cultivate muscles nor to enable women to realize outdoor recreation, but to provide appropriate physical discipline to fit women better for traditionally defined women's work. Rejecting the push for gender equity begun by early feminists, she favored the more socially acceptable image of a healthy woman in the home. By placing in their hands the means for their own self-improvement and raising the status of domestic work, she showed women how to combat poor health and contribute more usefully and knowledgeably to the life of the nation. In her continuing effort to combat her own ill health, she retired to the Thomas Beecher Home and its neighboring water cure in Elmira, New York, in 1877 and died of a stroke a year later on May 12, 1878.

Beecher's efforts to improve women's health and domestic life to "relieve the disabilities and sufferings of their sex" reveal the vulnerable place of women in her era. Her health reforms and educational prescriptions, while potentially helpful to many women, also reveal the common anxiety felt toward issues of disability and people with disabilities. Frequently experiencing physical and emotional challenges, Beecher exercised and sought out health CURES popular in that time period. Her life story thus offers multiple examples of the complex connections between gender, disability, and domestic reform.

Patricia Vertinsky

Further Reading:

Boydston, Jeanne, Mary Kelley, and Anne Margolis. *The Limits of Sisterhood: The Beecher Sisters on Women's Rights and Woman's Sphere.* Chapel Hill: University of North Carolina Press, 1988.

Sklar, Katherine Kish. *Catharine Beecher: A Study in American Domesticity.* New York: W. W. Norton, 1973.

Todd, Jan. *Physical Culture and the Body Beautiful: Purposive Exercise in the Lives of American Women, 1800–1873.* Macon, Ga.: Mercer University Press, 1998.

Vertinsky, Patricia. "Sexual Equality and the Legacy of Catharine Beecher." *Journal of Sport History* 6 (Spring 1979): 38–49.

Letters to the People on Health and Happiness by Catharine E. Beecher (1856)

Born on Long Island, New York, in 1800, Catharine E. Beecher challenged 19th-century notions of women's inherent biological and civic limitations by advocating health and fitness. In these letters and in her general campaign to empower women, Beecher called for an end to clothing that restricted breathing and movement, greater balance between work and leisure, and healthy exercise for mind and body. Linking healthy female bodies to domestic functionality and good citizenship, Beecher sought ways to enhance women's lives; at the same time, her ideas supported traditional notions of gender and anxiety over disability.

Letters to the People on Health and Happiness by Catharine E. Beecher 1856

My Friends:

. . . I have facts to communicate, that will prove that the American people are pursuing a course, in their own habits and practices, which is destroying health and happiness to an extent that is perfectly appalling. Nay more, I think I shall be able to show, that the majority of parents in this nation are systematically educating the rising generation to be feeble, deformed, homely, sickly, and miserable; as much so as if it were their express aim to commit so monstrous a folly.

I think I can show also, that if a plan for *destroying female health,* in all the ways in which it could be most effectively done, were drawn up, it would be exactly the course which is now pursued by a large portion of this nation, especially in the more wealthy classes.

. . . A large majority of the mothers and daughters of the nation adopt a style of dress that is exactly calculated to produce disease and deformity.

In the first place, they dress the upper portion of the body so thin [sic], that the spine and chest are exposed to sudden and severe changes of temperature in passing from warm to cold rooms, and this tends to weaken that portion. Then they accumulate such loads of clothing around the lower parts of the body, as debilitates the spine and pelvic organs by excess of heat. At the same time, they bind the ribs so tight, that there is constant lateral pressure against one side of the spine, tending to produce a curvature that distorts one shoulder and one hip. At the same time the weight of clothing on the hips and abdomen presses down on the most delicate and important organs of life to move them from their proper positions, while pointed bodices, with whalebone pressure, co-operate as a lever in front, to accomplish the same shocking operation.

. . . To add to the mischief of vitiated air, young women are generally girt so tight around the body, that the lower part of the lungs, where the air-cells most abound, are rarely used. *Abdominal breathing* has ceased among probably a *majority* of American women. The ribs are also girt so tight, in many cases, that even the *full* inspiration at the *top* of the lungs is impossible. And this custom has operated so, from parent to child, that a large portion of the female children now born have a deformed thorax, that has room only for imperfectly formed lungs.

. . . The man of study or of business sleeps all night in bad air; then he goes to his office, store, or shop, with uncleansed skin to breathe bad air all day; then at his meals he takes meat, which is the most stimulating food, and condiments to stimulate appetite. These make him eat more than he needs, or he has such a variety as tempts to an overloaded stomach. Then he drinks tea, coffee, and perhaps alcohol, to stimulate the brain and nerves to increased action. Then he keeps tobacco in his mouth, to stimulate another portion of his brain. Then he stimulates the brain with anxiety, or business cares, or study, or deep thought all day long, without the relaxation of amusement or the refreshment of muscular exercise. And then at night he returns, exhausted, to sleep again in bad air, and next day renews the same exhausting process. Thus it is *stimulate, stimulate, stimulate the brain,* from year's end to year's end, till disease interrupts or death ends the career. Or, in other cases, the man becomes a pale, delicate, infirm being, every function and organ ministering feebly to a half-living man. Thus it is that an active, vigorous, well-formed, healthy manhood is so rarely seen in this nation.

At the same time, a vast portion of the women of our nation are pursuing a course equally abusive of the brain and nervous system. As a general rule, woman originally is organized more delicately than the other sex, have a constitution that can not bear either labor or long or strong mental excitement as can the more vigorous sex. Then all her physical training is less invigorating than that of man. Then her pursuits, as a wife, mother, and housekeeper, are more complicated, less systematized, and less provided with well-trained assistants than the professions of men.

. . . The great majority of American women have their brain and nervous system exhausted by too much care and too much mental excitement

in their daily duties; while another class, who live to be waited on and amused, are as great sufferers for want of some worthy object in life, or from excesses in seeking amusement.

. . . A "perfectly healthy" or "a vigorous and healthy woman" . . . is one who can through the whole day be actively employed on her feet in all kinds of domestic duties without injury, and constantly and habitually has a feeling of perfect health and perfect freedom from pain. Not that she never has a fit of sickness, or takes a cold that interrupts the feeling of health, but that these are out of her ordinary experience.

A woman is marked "well" who usually has good health, but can not bear exposures, or long and great fatigue, without consequent illness.

A woman is marked "delicate" who, though she may be about and attend to most of her domestic employments, has a frail constitution that either has been undermined by ill health, or which easily and frequently yields to fatigue, or exposure, or excitement.

Source: Catharine E. Beecher. *Letters to the People on Health and Happiness.* New York: Harper & Brothers, 1856. Available online. URL: http://www.assumption.edu/whw/Hatch/Beecher/BeecherLettersonHealth.html. Accessed June 30, 2008.

Beers, Clifford (1876–1943) *founder of the mental hygiene movement*

In 1908 Clifford Beers published his autobiographical account of three years in mental HOSPITALS, *A Mind That Found Itself.* Beers recounted his nervous breakdown and subsequent brutal and harsh treatment at three Connecticut mental institutions. From the outset, Beers sought not just to tell his story but also to lead a reform movement: "As I have noted in the preceding pages, this book was neither conceived nor written merely as an entertaining story; it was intended to serve as the opening gun in a permanent campaign for improvement in the care and treatment of mental sufferers, and the prevention, whenever possible, of MENTAL ILLNESS itself." Taking inspiration from the transformative effect *Uncle Tom's Cabin* had on alerting northerners to the horrors of slavery in the 1850s, Beers hoped his exposé would reveal the dark side of INSTITUTIONALIZATION, sparking reform in the United States and around the world.

Beers was born in New Haven, Connecticut, on March 30, 1876. He received his high school diploma and entered Yale University in 1894. That same year, his older brother was affected with what was thought to be EPILEPSY and subsequently died in 1900. Beers reported experiencing attacks of nervousness and anxiety at the time, but he graduated from Yale in 1897. He then held jobs as a clerk in the office of collector of taxes in New Haven and at a life insurance company in New York City. Then, in June 1900, believing that he was destined to become epileptic like his brother, Beers unsuccessfully attempted suicide by jumping out of the fourth floor of his family's home; he received treatment at a general hospital for broken bones in his feet and a sprained spine. Beer's mental condition deteriorated and his FAMILY placed him at the first of two private institutions. He was later committed to Connecticut Hospital for the Insane. He was released from Connecticut Hospital in 1903 and committed himself to writing a book about his experiences.

Prior to publishing *A Mind That Found Itself,* Beers circulated his manuscript to prominent psychologists, physicians, and civic leaders and obtained their endorsements not just of his book, but of his plans for a national movement as well. The prominent Harvard psychologist and author William James wrote a letter to Beers that was published as an introduction to the book: "You have handled a difficult theme with great skill, and produced a narrative of absorbing interest to scientist as well as layman. It reads like fiction, but it is not fiction; and this I state emphatically, knowing how prone the uninitiated are to doubt the truthfulness of descriptions of abnormal mental processes." When the book was finally published, it received widespread attention and rave reviews in both the popular press and scientific publications.

In 1908 Beers convened a small group of 13 supporters, including his father and younger brother, to form the Connecticut Society for Mental Hygiene. The phrase "mental hygiene" was suggested by Adolf Meyer, a leading psychiatrist at the time and early supporter of Beers. The NATIONAL COMMITTEE FOR MENTAL HYGIENE (NCMH) was founded by 12 charter members one year later. The national society sought numerous reforms for people with mental illness, including improved research, treatment, and prevention, as well as expanded federal and state support to create agencies that would link to the Society for Mental Hygiene. Beers envisioned the NCMH to be an auxiliary ORGANIZATION to the psychiatric profession.

Until 1912 Beers paid for most expenses associated with the National Committee through borrowed money. Then late in 1911, he received donations of $50,000 for the committee and $5,000 to pay off debts and for his personal use from Henry Phipps, a wealthy benefactor. Beers was paid a salary of $3,000 to serve as secretary of the NCMH. The committee also hired Dr. William Stanton, who later became its first medical director. One of Stanton's first tasks was to conduct visits to ASYLUMS and other institutions during which he documented the widespread presence of brutality and substandard conditions reported by Beers.

By 1918 Beers had founded an International Committee on Mental Hygiene. When the first International Congress of Mental Hygiene was held in Washington, D.C., in 1930, mental hygiene societies representing 25 countries were in attendance. Beers established the American Foundation for Mental Hygiene to fund mental hygiene activities in 1928.

From the founding of the NCMH, Beers cultivated relationships with medical professionals and psychiatrists. They embraced his cause, and he embraced theirs. He was one of the few lay persons ever given an honorary membership in the American Psychiatric Association. Beers did not attempt to involve other former mental patients in the committee or the movement he initiated.

Beers retired as secretary of the NCMH in 1939 when he experienced a reported relapse of his mental illness. He spent his final years at Butler Hospital in Providence, Rhode Island, and died there on July 9, 1943.

The NCMH remained influential in mental health after Beers's death in 1943 and merged with other organizations in 1950 to form what is now known as MENTAL HEALTH AMERICA. The National Committee advocated for the National Mental Health Act, which was passed by Congress in 1946 and led to the development of the National Institute on Mental Health in 1949. The National Institute provided grants for research, training, and community services. By 1963 *A Mind That Found Itself* was in its 35th printing. The last edition of the book was published in 1981.

Steven J. Taylor

Further Reading:
Beers, Clifford W. *A Mind That Found Itself: An Autobiography.* 7th ed. Garden City, N.Y.: Doubleday, 1956.

Deutsch, Albert. *The Mentally Ill in America: A History of Their Care and Treatment from Colonial Times.* 2d ed. New York: Columbia University Press, 1949.

Grob, Gerald N. *Mental Illness and American Society, 1875–1940.* Princeton, N.J.: Princeton University Press, 1983.

Ridenour, N. "The Mental Health Movement." In *The Encyclopedia of Mental Health,* edited by A. Deutsch and H. Fishman, 1,091–1,102. Vol. 3. New York: Franklin Watts, 1963.

A Mind That Found Itself by Clifford Beers (1908)

After struggling with mental health conditions, Clifford Beers (1876–1943) was committed to the Connecticut Hospital for the Insane from 1900 to 1903. Five years after his release he wrote A Mind That Found Itself *(1908), an autobiography describing his nervous breakdown as well as the brutal treatment he received at the hospital and other institutions. The exposé drew national attention and contributed to Beers's effort to form a national movement for mental hygiene. These sections reflect some of the harsh treatments Beers experienced and his call for action.*

A Mind That Found Itself: An Autobiography
by Clifford Beers
1908

The last week of June, 1894, was an important one in my life. An event then occurred which undoubtedly changed my career completely. It was the direct cause of my mental collapse six years later, and of the distressing and, in some instances, strange and delightful experiences on which this book is based. . . . My brother had enjoyed perfect health up to the time he was stricken; and, as there had never been a suggestion of epilepsy, or any like disease, in either branch of the family, the affliction came as a bolt from a clear sky. Everything possible was done to effect a cure, but without avail. On July 4th, 1900, he died at the City Hospital, in Hartford, Connecticut. . . .

. . . Now, if a brother who had enjoyed perfect health all his life could be stricken with epilepsy, what was to prevent my being similarly afflicted? This was the thought that soon got possession of my mind. The more I considered it and him, the more nervous I became; and the more nervous, the more convinced that my own breakdown was only a question of time. Doomed to what I then considered a living death, I thought of epilepsy, I dreamed epilepsy, until thousands of times during the six years that this disquieting idea persisted, my overwrought imagination seemed to drag me to the very verge of an attack.

. . . AFTER remaining at home for about a month, during which time I showed no improvement mentally, though I did gain physically, I was taken to a private sanatorium.

. . . Soon after I reached my room in the sanatorium, the supervisor entered. Drawing a table close to the bed he placed upon it a slip of paper which he asked me to sign. I looked upon this as a trick of the detectives to get a specimen of my handwriting. I now know that the signing of the slip is a legal requirement, with which every patient is supposed to comply upon entering such an institution—private in character—unless he has been committed by some court. The exact wording of this "voluntary commitment" I do not now recall; but, in substance, it was an agreement to abide by the rules of the institution—whatever *they* were—and to submit to such restraint as might be deemed necessary.

. . . FOR the first few weeks after my arrival at the sanatorium, I was cared for by two attendants, one by day and one by night. . . . The earliest possible dismissal of one of my two attendants was expedient for the family purse; for the charges at this, as at all other sanatoriums operated for private gain, are nothing less than extortionate. . . . No sooner was the number of attendants thus reduced than I was subjected to a detestable form of restraint which amounted to torture. To guard me against myself while my remaining attendant slept, my hands were imprisoned in what is known as a "muff." A "muff," innocent enough to the eyes of those who have never worn one, is in reality a relic of the Inquisition. It is an instrument of restraint which has been in use for centuries among ignorant practitioners, and even in many of our public and private institutions is still in use. Such an incident as I am about to recount cannot occur in a properly conducted institution, and that fact made its occurrence a crime, though perhaps an unintentional one; for good motives born of professional ignorance are little, if at all, better than deliberate bad intention. The muff I wore was made of canvas, and differed in construction from a muff designed for the hands of fashion only in the inner partition, also of canvas, which separated my hands but allowed them to overlap. At either end was a strap which buckled tightly around the wrist and was locked.

. . . The putting on of the muff was the most humiliating incident of my life. The shaving of my legs and the wearing on my brow of the court-plaster brand of infamy had been humiliating, but those experiences had not overwhelmed my very heart as did this bitter ordeal. I resisted weakly, and, after the muff was adjusted and locked, for the first time since my mental collapse, I wept.

. . . Many times was I roughly overpowered by two attendants who locked my hands and coerced me to do whatever I had refused to do.

. . . Let those in charge of such institutions, who have a stubborn patient to deal with, remember what I say. In the strict sense of the word there is no such thing as a genuinely stubborn insane person. The stubborn men and women in the world are sane; and the fortunate prevalence of sanity may be approximately estimated by the preponderance of stubbornness in society at large. When one possessed of the blessed means of resolving his own errors continues to cherish an unreasonable belief—that is stubbornness. But for a man bereft of reason to adhere to an idea which to him seems absolutely correct and true because he has been deprived of the means of detecting his error—that is not stubbornness. It is a symptom of his disease, and merits the indulgence of forbearance, if not genuine sympathy. Certainly the afflicted one deserves no punishment. As well punish with a slap the cheek that is disfigured by the mumps.

. . . A camisole, or, as I prefer to stigmatize it, a strait-jacket, is really a tight-fitting coat of heavy canvas, reaching from neck to waist, constructed, however, on no ordinary pattern. There is not a button on it. The sleeves are closed at the ends, and the jacket, having no opening in front, is adjusted and tightly laced behind. To the end of each blind sleeve is attached a strong cord. The cord on the right sleeve is carried to the left of the body, and the cord on the left sleeve is carried to the right of the body. Both are then drawn tightly behind, thus bringing the arms of the victim into a folded position across his chest. These cords are then securely tied.

After many nights of torture, this jacket, at my urgent and repeated request, was finally adjusted in such manner that had it been so adjusted at first, I need not have suffered any *torture* at all. This I knew at the time, for I had not failed to discuss the matter with a patient who on several occasions had been restrained in this same jacket. It is the abuse rather than the use of such instruments of restraint against which I inveigh. Yet it is hardly worth while to distinguish between "use" and "abuse," for it is a fact that where the use of mechanical restraint is permitted, abuse is bound to follow.

. . . He said nothing, but, unhappily for me, he expressed his pent-up feelings in something more effectual than words. After he had laced the jacket, and drawn my arms across my chest so snugly that I could not move them a fraction of an inch, I asked him to loosen the strait-jacket enough to enable me at least to take a full breath. I also requested him to give me a chance to disentangle my fingers which had been caught in an unnatural and uncomfortable position.

. . . Instead of loosening the strait-jacket as agreed, this doctor, now livid with rage, drew the cords in such a way that I found myself more securely and cruelly held than before. This breach of faith threw me into a frenzy.

. . . No one incident of my whole life has ever impressed itself more indelibly on my memory. Within one hour's time I was suffering pain as intense as any I ever endured, and before the night had passed that pain had become almost unbearable. My right hand was so held that the tip of one of my fingers was all but cut by the nail of another, and soon knife-like pains began to shoot through my right arm as far as the shoulder. If there be any so curious as to wish to get a slight idea of my agony, let him bite a finger tip as hard as he can without drawing blood. Let him continue the operation for two or three minutes. Then let him multiply that effect, if he can, by two or three hundred.

. . . After fifteen interminable hours the strait-jacket was removed. Whereas just prior to its putting on I had been in a vigorous enough condition to offer stout resistance when assaulted, now, on coming out of it, I was helpless. When my arms were released from their restricted position the pain was intense. Each and every joint had been racked. I had no control over the fingers of either hand, and could not have dressed myself had I been promised my freedom for doing so. And this, bear in mind, was the effect of a camisole, which form of restraint hospital officials, when called upon to testify, so often describe as being harmless and not very uncomfortable.

. . . AFTER again becoming a free man, my mind would not abandon the miserable ones whom I had left behind. I thought with horror that my reason had been threatened and baffled at every turn. Without malice toward those who had had me in charge, I yet looked with contempt upon the system by which I had been treated.

Source: Clifford Whittingham Beers. *A Mind That Found Itself: An Autobiography*. New York: Longmans, Green, and Co., 1910. Available online. URL: http://www.disabilitymuseum.org/lib/docs/1672.htm?page=16. Accessed June 30, 2008.

beggars and begging

The image of the person with disabilities as a street corner beggar is one of the most historically consistent images of disability. This link shows up in the literature of ancient Greece and Rome, in biblical allegory, and in medieval morality plays, and it occupies an especially pertinent place in American history and culture.

Whether the image is a historical reality or simply a convenient literary convention, there is little doubt that it effectively inspired the passage of a variety of reform laws, particularly in late 19th- and early 20th-century urban America. Among the types of legislation at least partially inspired by the image of the disabled beggar are WORKERS' COMPENSATION laws, VOCATIONAL REHABILITATION programs (both state and federal), and state-funded ORTHOPEDIC HOSPITALS.

Charitable ORGANIZATIONS, including the MARCH OF DIMES and the Shriners' Crippled Children's HOSPITALS, have used the offensive prospect of disabled beggars crowding city streets to raise funds. The methods used to convince leading citizens of New York City to fund the creation of the nation's first orthopedic hospital in 1863 provide an early example of the use of this image. Supporters of the New York Hospital for the Ruptured and Crippled cited the growing number of disabled beggars as justification for the new institution. Fenwick Beekman, an orthopedist employed by the hospital in 1939, claimed that: "The streets were filled with unfortunates who sought alms and, to make their pleas more forceful, exposed their bodily deformities to the passerby. Persons afflicted with ruptures, ulcerated legs, varicose veins, etc., became beggars by profession. Poor families having crippled children, suffering from spinal and paralytic affections, thronged our streets, dwellings and places of business, making revolting displays of their infirmities and misfortunes." HELEN KELLER also appears to have understood the importance of the image in her fund-raising activities, once referring to herself as an "international beggar."

It has frequently been assumed that legislative and charitable efforts at eradicating the disabled beggar were motivated by altruism. However, primary sources related to these efforts suggest less charitable factors. Concerns over the "revolting displays" of disabled mendicants not only played a major factor in motivating New Yorkers to act in 1863 but also contributed to so-called unsightly beggar ordinances aimed at controlling those who became "beggars by profession." Although these laws appear to have been present in only a handful of cities and were most likely only rarely enforced,

such laws suggest that many Americans found the presence of disabled beggars more of a nuisance than a humanitarian concern. Even DEAF activists, who were commonly seen as disabled by mainstream society, seemed to adopt similar approaches to the issue. Campaigns between 1900 and the 1950s by the NATIONAL ASSOCIATION OF THE DEAF, for example, proclaimed that "the deaf do not beg." The desire to eliminate the stigmatizing STEREOTYPE of deaf beggars generally drew greater attention than policies or efforts to eradicate economic and other factors that contributed to begging.

Whether viewed as an annoyance or as an object of pity, the perception of disabled persons as frequent beggars has had an impact on American history in significant ways, shaping policy, status, and daily interactions between people and communities. What all of this means within the broader historical context of both American and disability history has yet to be resolved but clearly suggests an important avenue for further historical inquiry.

See also CHARITY; REPRESENTATION; STIGMA; UGLY LAWS.

Brad Byrom

Further Reading:
Baynton, Douglas C. "Disability and the Justification of Inequality in American History." In *The New Disability History: American Perspectives,* edited by Paul Longmore and Lauri Umansky, 33–57. New York: New York University Press, 2001.

Beekman, Fenwick. *Hospital for the Ruptured and Crippled: A Historical Sketch Written on the Occasion of the Seventy-Fifth Anniversary of the Hospital.* New York: privately printed, 1939.

Burch, Susan. *Signs of Resistance: American Deaf Cultural History, 1900 to World War II.* New York: New York University Press, 2004.

Byrom, Brad. "A Pupil and a Patient: Hospital-Schools in Progressive America." In *The New Disability History: American Perspectives,* edited by Paul Longmore and Lauri Umansky, 133–157. New York: New York University Press, 2001.

Schweik, Susan M. "Begging the Question: Disability, Mendicancy, Speech and the Law." *Narrative* 15 (January 2007): 58–70.

"*A single, able-bodied, deaf mute tramp or beggar, casts odium upon all deaf-mutes. A single hearing tramp or beggar would not be looked upon as a sample of the average hearing person, but would be correctly judged as a freak or a loafer, far removed from the ordinary citizen.*"

—anonymous author in a deaf newspaper, January 1907

Bell, Alexander Graham (1847–1922) *inventor, eugenicist, and teacher of the deaf*

Alexander Graham Bell is best known to the world as an inventor and scientist and is particularly renowned for his invention of the telephone, which launched profound changes in telecommunications worldwide. From a disability perspective, however, Bell's involvement in DEAF EDUCATION and his advocacy of ORALISM, the teaching of speech and lipreading for deaf students, are equally significant. Likewise, Bell's interest in GENETICS, and later, EUGENICS, a pseudoscientific movement that sought to "improve" America's genetic stock, are crucial to the way Bell is viewed by disability scholars and advocates.

Bell was born in Edinburgh, Scotland, on March 3, 1847. The middle child of three boys, his two brothers died of TUBERCULOSIS as adolescents. He took the middle name "Graham" in his youth in honor of family friend Alexander Graham. Bell's parents, Eliza and Alexander Melville Bell, were both involved in the oralist movement. Eliza Bell, who was deaf, was a user of spoken language and Bell's father was the pioneer of "visible speech," a system of symbols corresponding to tongue placement that made it possible for deaf CHILDREN to learn speech. He trained all three of his sons in this system. Deafness and disability directly and indirectly shaped Bell's life. His mother's deafness provided him with both a model for deaf education and a sense of the social possibilities available to deaf people.

Bell's father moved the FAMILY to Brantford, Ontario, in 1870 and, during the early 1870s, Alexander Graham Bell relocated from Canada to Boston, where he became a teacher for deaf children. During this time he pursued research that he hoped would result in ASSISTIVE TECHNOLOGY for the deaf; ironically, this research resulted in his 1876 patent for the telephone, a device that, despite its great utility, did much to underscore the isolation of deaf people. At the same time, the royalties generated from the Bell telephone allowed him to pursue private interests in eugenic research, including studies of hereditary deafness. Bell also advocated for the broad application of oralism in schools for the deaf throughout the United States. His revered status lent credence, power, and attention to his work in these areas.

In 1877, after a two-year courtship, Bell married his former student, Mabel Hubbard, the daughter of a prominent Boston entrepreneur. She, like Bell's mother, was a successful oral deaf person. The presence of MABEL HUBBARD BELL in his life likely informed his ideas about the rights of deaf people as well as reinforcing his abiding interest in oralism.

In 1880 Bell won the Volta Prize from the French government for his invention of the telephone; Bell used the money to establish the Volta Bureau. Located in Washington, D.C., the Volta Bureau became a leading clearinghouse for the dissemination and promotion of oralism, which was becoming increasingly popular in deaf education. A decade later, Bell would help found the American Association to Promote the Teaching of Speech to the Deaf, a leading educational organization that fostered oral communication.

At his induction to the National Academy of Sciences in 1883, Bell introduced his paper *Memoir Upon the Formation of a Deaf Variety of the Human Race*. In this address, Bell outlined the growth of Deaf culture, which he considered both socially and genetically degenerative. He particularly scorned signed communication, which he felt fostered clannishness among deaf people, and the high rate of intermarriage among deaf people, a trend resulting in large part from RESIDENTIAL SCHOOL education for deaf people across America. Bell feared that cultural separatism and intermarriage would produce an entire race of deaf offspring. He proposed a number of options to halt this trend: dismiss Deaf teachers from residential schools (when possible, replacing RESIDENTIAL SCHOOLS with mainstream day schools), remove signed communication from schools and replace this with strict oral training, and strongly discourage the intermarriage of deaf people.

The *Memoir*, and much of Bell's subsequent work and advocacy, fused his interest in deaf education, deaf people, and eugenics. Bell supported what is now characterized as "positive eugenics," an effort to improve the human race by encouraging people with "good" genetic qualities to reproduce. Most eugenicists considered deaf people—by their very impairment—unfit, but Bell disagreed. He felt that deaf people should be able to marry, but he preferred that they choose hearing partners to halt the "deaf variety of the human race." It is probable that Bell's advocacy and expertise on deafness influenced other eugenicists to focus their attention elsewhere. Still, Bell's interest in eugenics reflected common values of many intellectuals and reformers in the late 19th century. His role in promoting eugenic research and policy offers a window into the issues surrounding deaf people and others deemed "DEFECTIVE" and disabled at that time.

Bell's close ties to the eugenics movement make him an especially important figure for understanding disability in the United States. His views on national identity and genetic worth, for example, motivated him to call for disallowing the admission of certain immigrants to the United States during the late 19th and early 20th centuries. Bell seemed generally less interested in applying common eugenic principles to other Americans with disabilities and rejected radical efforts such as the INVOLUNTARY STERILIZATION of those deemed "unfit." The inventor-educator maintained close working and personal relationships with a number of people with disabilities, which may account for his moderate eugenic position.

One of the most recognized relationships Bell enjoyed was with HELEN KELLER, the famous DEAF-BLIND author and activist. Bell also supported deaf artists such as Albert Ballin and kept close ties with one of his former deaf pupils, George Sanders. Ballin and others later complimented Bell for his sign language skills and for his willingness to use signed communication with those who could not use speech. In the last five years before his death, Bell seemed to turn away from eugenics but he remained committed to oral advocacy.

Bell died on August 2, 1922, at his estate, Beinn Bhreagh (Gaelic for "Beautiful Mountain"), near Baddeck, Nova Scotia.

Mainstream society has long celebrated Bell as an American icon, praising him for his ingenuity and scientific prowess. In contrast, Bell holds a more complicated and largely negative place in deaf and disability history because of his advocacy of eugenics and because of his opposition to the use of sign language in deaf schools. Deaf leaders such as George Veditz (1861–1937) and Jay Cooke Howard (1872–1946) strongly criticized Bell for his oral advocacy and many deaf cultural activists today perceive Bell as an enemy of their cultural community. Excessively positive and negative perceptions, however, likely overlook the complexity of Bell's actions and ideals. His life story is relevant for those interested in disability and American history because it demonstrates important yet often unchallenged assumptions about language and education, citizenship, and the close link between scientific research and public policies for people with disabilities.

See also Alexander Graham Bell Association for the Deaf; communication debates; reproductive rights.

Brian H. Greenwald

Further Reading:

Bruce, Robert V. *Bell: Alexander Graham Bell and the Conquest of Solitude.* Boston: Little, Brown, 1973.

Greenwald, Brian H. "The Real 'Toll' of A. G. Bell: Lessons about Eugenics." In *Genetics, Disability, and Deafness,* edited by John Vickrey Van Cleve, 35–42. Washington, D.C.: Gallaudet University Press, 2004.

———. "Alexander Graham Bell through the Lens of Eugenics, 1883–1922." Ph.D. diss., George Washington University, January 2006.

Grosvenor, Edwin, and Morgan Wesson. *Alexander Graham Bell: The Life and Times of the Man Who Invented the Telephone.* New York: Harry N. Abrams, 1997.

Winefield, Richard. *Never the Twain Shall Meet: The Communications Debate.* Washington, D.C.: Gallaudet University Press, 1987.

Memoir Upon the Formation of a Deaf Variety of the Human Race by Alexander Graham Bell (1883)

Telephone inventor Alexander Graham Bell held a life-long interest in deaf people and deaf education. Both his mother and wife were deaf. In the 1880s he also was drawn to eugenic research in heredity aimed at improving living species. These interests were deeply connected, as evidence by his 1883 paper Memoir Upon the Formation of a Deaf Variety of the Human Race. Presented to the National Academy of Sciences, the memoir warned researchers that increased deaf intermarriage might produce many deaf offspring. As these portions of Bell's paper show, his solution included strict oralist training (speech and lipreading) rather than signed communication and the elimination of other prominent features of deaf culture. Scholars and activists debate Bell's impact on deaf people, but the memoir remains an important example of eugenic attitudes toward this community.

Memoir Upon the Formation of a Deaf Variety of the Human Race
by Alexander Graham Bell
1883

I think all will agree that the evidence shows a tendency to the formation of a deaf variety of the human race in America. What remedial measures can be taken to lessen or check this tendency? We shall consider the subject under two heads: (1) repressive, (2) preventive measures.

(1.) *Repressive measures.*—The first thought that occurs in this connection is that the intermarriage of deaf-mutes might be forbidden by legislative enactment. So long, however, as deaf-mutes of both sexes continue to associate together in adult life, legislative interference with marriage might only promote immorality. But, without entirely prohibiting intermarriage, might not the marriages of the deaf be so regulated as to reduce the probabilities of the production of deaf offspring to a minimum? For instance, a law forbidding congenitally deaf persons from intermarrying would go a long way towards checking the evil. Such a law might, however, become inoperative on account of the impossibility of proving that a person had been born deaf.

. . . A due consideration of all the objections renders it doubtful whether legislative interference with the marriage of the deaf would be advisable.

(2.) *Preventive measures.*—The most promising method of lessening the evil appears to lie in the adoption of preventive measures. In our search for such measures we should be guided by the following principle: (1.) *Determine the causes that promote intermarriage among the deaf and the dumb; and* (2.) *remove them.*

The immediate cause is undoubtedly the preference that adult deaf-mutes exhibit for the companionship of deaf-mutes rather than that of hearing persons. Among the causes that contribute to bring about this preference we may note: (1) segregation for the purposes of education, and (2) the use, as a means of communication, of a language which is different from that of the people. These, then, are two of the points that should be avoided in the adoption of preventive measures. Nearly all the other causes I have investigated are ultimately referable to these.

Segregation really lies at the root of the whole matter; for from this the other causes have themselves been evolved by the operation of the natural law of adaptation to the environment.

We commence our efforts on behalf of the deaf-mute by changing his social environment. The tendency is then towards accommodation to the new conditions. In process of time the adaptation becomes complete; and when, at last, we restore him to the world as an adult, he finds that the social conditions to which he has become accustomed do not exist outside of his school life. His efforts are then directed to the restoration of these conditions, with the result of intermarriage and a tendency to the formation of a deaf-mute community.

The grand central principle that should guide us, then, in our search for preventive measures should be *the retention of the normal environment during the period of education.* The natural tendency towards adaptation would then co-operate with instruction to produce accommodation to the *permanent* conditions of life.

. . . Segregation during education has not only favored the tendency towards the formation of a race of deaf-mutes, but has led to the evolution of a special language adapted for the use of such a race—"the sign-language of the deaf and the dumb." This is especially true in America where the sign-language is employed by a large majority of the teachers in instructing their pupils. In foreign countries the vast majority employ, for this purpose, the ordinary language of the people. . . .

The lack of articulate speech should also be noted as an indirect cause of segregation in adult life, operating to separate deaf-mutes from hearing persons. Hence, instruction in articulation and speech-reading should be given to every pupil.

This is done in Germany. Indeed, in 1882, more than 65 per cent. of all the deaf and dumb in foreign schools were being taught to speak and understand the speech of others, whereas in America less than 9 per cent. were to be found in oral schools.

According to more recent statistics compiled by the Clarke Institution we find that in May,

1883, about 14 per cent. of the deaf and dumb in American institutions were using speech in the school-room as the language of communication with their teachers; 18 per cent. were taught to speak as an accomplishment, and 68 per cent. received no instruction whatever in articulation.

Nearly one-third of the teachers of the deaf and the dumb in America are themselves deaf, and this must be considered as another element favorable to the formation of a deaf race—to be therefore avoided.

The segregation of deaf-mutes, the use of the sign-language, and the employment of deaf teachers produce an environment that is unfavorable to the cultivation of articulation and speech-reading, and that sometimes causes the disuse of speech by speaking pupils who are only deaf.

Having shown the tendency to the formation of a deaf variety of the human race in America and some of the means that should be taken to counteract it, I commend the whole subject to the attention of scientific men.

<hr>

Source: Alexander Graham Bell. *Memoir Upon the Formation of a Deaf Variety of the Human Race.* A paper presented to the National Academy of Sciences, November 13, 1883.

Bell, Mabel (Mabel Gardiner Hubbard) (1859–1923) *deaf philanthropist, wife, and mother*

As the DEAF wife of telephone inventor ALEXANDER GRAHAM BELL, who was once his student, Mabel Gardiner Hubbard Bell influenced her husband's life and work in many ways while she also achieved many things in her own right.

Born on November 25, 1859, in Cambridge, Massachusetts, to lawyer and philanthropist Gardiner Green Hubbard (first president of the National Geographic Society and benefactor and president of the CLARKE SCHOOL FOR THE DEAF) and Gertrude Mercer McCurdy, Mabel contracted scarlet fever at age 3 and became DEAF. At age 15, after some years of EDUCATION at the Clarke School for the Deaf and abroad in Germany, she became a student of deaf educator Alexander Graham Bell. The two eventually married, in 1877, when she was 17 and he was 29. They had two daughters: Elsie May Bell (1878–1964) and Marian ("Daisy") Hubbard Bell (1880–1962); and two sons: Edward (1881) and Robert (1883), neither of whom lived past early infancy.

In the summer of 1886, the Bells discovered a special place on their way to Newfoundland—Baddeck on Cape

Breton Island (of Lake Bras d'Or) in Nova Scotia. Here they built an estate on a cliff overlooking the lake, Beinn Bhreagh ("Beautiful Mountain") that they occupied largely between the months of May through November, returning to social and work commitments in Washington, D.C., during the winter and spring. For the next 38 years, until her death there in 1923, Mabel Bell clearly preferred life at the Baddeck estate and thrived there. She arranged grand dinners and themed banquets for both locals and visitors who were often working with her husband on his experiments and projects. In this location she became more of a partner in her husband's scientific experiments with sheep, kites, and aviation, and in ways in which she had never been engaged with him, either with his invention of the telephone or his work on behalf of the deaf.

Since there was very little of the "learned society" with whom she was acquainted in the United States, she created her own at Beinn Bhreagh. For example, in 1891 she helped found Baddeck's first public library, set up the "Home Industries of Baddeck" to display and sell the handiwork of the local women, and established the Young Ladies Club of Baddeck (modeled on the Washington Club of which she was a member) that brought women—and men—together to discuss books, art, travel, and local and world events. In 1895 she formed the Canadian Home and School Association, which was essentially the first Canadian parent-teacher educational association, and about 1898–99, she helped bring the first Victorian Order of Nurses to Baddeck to improve health care in the area. She also founded the Children's Laboratory at Beinn Bhreagh Estate, which was Canada's first Montessori school (1912). It was her interest in and partnership with her husband's work on flight and with tetrahedral kites on the grounds of this estate—and with her financial backing of $35,000—that the Aerial Experiment Association was formed in 1907. In this sense she might be thought of as the first lady of aviation.

Mabel Bell chose not to associate with other deaf people during her lifetime. For example, in a letter to a family friend in 1922, a few months after her husband's death and a few months before her own, she wrote that, "I shrink from any reference to my disability and won't be seen in public with another deaf person." She also did not approve of her husband's work related to deaf education or EUGENIC-influenced studies of the marriage and progeny of deaf people, calling it, with some disdain, his "deaf-mute business." Although her husband had a lifelong relationship with HELEN KELLER, Mabel Bell seems to have had little communication or connection with the DEAF-BLIND icon. It is possible that the STIGMA of disability and deafness at this time, which commonly motivated individuals to distance themselves from other disabled and deaf people, also influenced Mabel Bell's interaction with Helen Keller.

Few DEAF STUDIES scholars have examined Mabel Hubbard Bell's life, but her approach to ORALISM (the teaching of speech and lipreading), among other issues, offers rich insights into the complexity of communication modes in her lifetime. For example, in 1895, she published an essay about the "Subtle Art of Speechreading" in *Atlantic Monthly,* which argued for the importance of deaf people learning "speechreading" while she documented her own skills at it. Although there are numerous accounts indicating that she managed to lipread "so well that none of the family thought of her as deaf" there are also references throughout the voluminous letters she wrote during her lifetime of her "lifelong struggle" to "pass" as hearing and her animosity toward oral educators, including her own husband, whom she believed condescended to deaf people.

Mabel Hubbard Bell died on January 3, 1923, at Beinn Bhreagh.

Brenda Jo Brueggemann

Further Reading:

Bruce, Robert V. *Bell: Alexander Graham Bell and the Conquest of Solitude.* Ithaca, N.Y.: Cornell University Press, 1990.

Eber, Dorothy Harley. *Genius at Work: Images of Alexander Graham Bell.* New York: Viking, 1982.

Tulloch, Judith. *The Bell Family in Baddeck: Alexander Graham Bell and Mabel Bell in Cape Breton.* Halifax, Canada: Formac Publishing, 2006.

Waite, Helen Elmira. *Make a Joyful Sound: The Romance of Mabel Hubbard and Alexander Graham Bell.* Philadelphia: Macrae Smith, 1961.

Bellevue Hospital

Bellevue Hospital in New York City is the oldest existing public hospital in the United States and the biggest in the city's municipal system. Begun in 1736 as a six-bed infirmary within New York's "Publick Workhouse and House of Correction," or ALMSHOUSE, Bellevue's origins lie in a desperate and humanitarian effort to deal with the increasing numbers of poor and indigent in the rapidly growing city. Accordingly, in the 18th and 19th centuries, Bellevue dealt with devastating epidemics of flu, cholera, typhus, smallpox, and yellow fever. These efforts, undertaken without modern medicine or sanitation, could not prevent great suffering or a high death rate. Thus, Bellevue earned a notoriety that it has never entirely outlived. Nonetheless, even a century ago, the majority of Bellevue's patients were poor and treated without charge by volunteer physicians. Moreover, since its founding, Bellevue has been at the forefront of contemporary practices and perspectives on disability and mental health.

Bellevue's contributions to medicine include many notable achievements, among them the first American maternity ward (1799); the first ambulance service in the world (1868), the first American children's clinic (1874), the first American emergency room (1876), and the first American nursing college for men (1888). Having also established the world's first hospital catastrophe unit (1939), Bellevue has more recently been known for its work in triage, the latter in the aftermath of SEPTEMBER 11, 2001. Today, Bellevue is comprised of three HOSPITALS, the General Hospital, the Tuberculosis Hospital, and the Psychiatric Hospital, making it among the world's most comprehensive municipal hospitals.

Of its three hospitals, the psychiatric one is perhaps Bellevue's best and most sensationally known. This hospital has contributed most notably to disability awareness and reform and other mental health issues. In the 19th and early 20th centuries, it was fashionable for patients to write exposés characterizing Bellevue as a dark and overcrowded "madhouse." Indeed, at that time this unit of Bellevue was subject to the same overcrowding that affected the entire hospital. In particular, prisoners were often sent there for observation as were individuals deemed insane on the basis of now outmoded approaches to psychiatry. As a result, many individuals ended up in Bellevue who would perhaps have been better treated elsewhere, if they needed psychological treatment at all. Fortunately, penal and medical reforms since the mid-20th century have allowed Bellevue's psychiatric facilities to become involved in state-of-the-art work in the diagnosis and treatment of MENTAL ILLNESS and in educating mental health professionals. Until recently, too, Bellevue provided the only psychiatric facilities to the indigent in New York. Though generally considered a residential facility, it is primarily a diagnostic center that treats individuals in transition from unhealthy living circumstances to healthier lives. Today, Bellevue's psychiatric facility remains at the forefront of research on and treatment of disability and mental health issues.

See also ASYLUMS AND INSTITUTIONS; INSANITY; INSTITUTIONALIZATION.

Sara Newman

Further Reading:
Barry, Anne. *Bellevue Is a State of Mind.* New York: Harcourt Brace Jovanovich, 1971.
Covan, Frederick L., and Carol Kahn. *Crazy All the Time: On the Psych Ward of Bellevue Hospital.* New York: Fawcett, 1995.
Cutolo, Salvatore R. *Bellevue Is My Home.* New York: Doubleday, 1956.
Opdycke, Sandra. *No One Was Turned Away: The Role of Public Hospitals in New York City since 1900.* New York: Oxford University Press, 1999.

Bell Laboratories

As the longtime research and development unit for American Telephone and Telegraph (AT&T), Bell Laboratories has been at the forefront of many innovations in telecommunications technologies since its establishment in 1925. A number of inventions credited to Bell Labs have benefited users with hearing, vision, and speech impairments, allowing these individuals to participate more fully in the revolutions created by the telephone and modem.

The origins of Bell Labs dates to 1884, when the American Bell Telephone Company, later to become AT&T, established a "mechanical department" by acquiring the machine shop of independent Boston machinist Charles Williams. It was in this same shop that Thomas Edison and ALEXANDER GRAHAM BELL performed some of their most famous experiments and constructed models of their inventions. Two-and-a-half decades later, AT&T chief engineer John J. Carty organized a Research Branch at the company in 1911. In 1925 AT&T established Bell Laboratories in Murray Hill, New Jersey, as an independent research unit that took over the activities formerly done by the Research Branch, as well as research done by Western Electric, the engineering and manufacturing firm that supplied AT&T with its telephones. Carty's former assistant, Frank Jewett, served as the first president of Bell Labs.

During its initial decades in existence, Bell Labs contributed important innovations in the areas of long distance telephone service, sound recording, and facsimile (fax) service. In the 1920s, as part of its sound research, researchers at Bell Labs collaborated with otologist Edmund Prince Fowler to develop the audiometer, the first scientific instrument to measure hearing acuity. The audiometer rapidly became an important tool for the measurement of hearing loss. Harvey Fletcher, who directed acoustical research at Bell Labs beginning in 1928, collaborated with the New York League for the Hard of Hearing to test the hearing of New York City schoolchildren in 1929. Fletcher later served as president of the American Federation of Organizations for the Hard of Hearing.

As well as making contributions to diagnostic technologies for hearing loss, Bell Labs also made important advances in HEARING AID technologies. AT&T was one of the first companies to develop and manufacture amplified hearing aids, and the first AT&T Western Electric Audiphones were marketed in 1923. Weighing 11 pounds, however, the hearing aids were hardly wearable. Subsequent improvements helped make the hearing aids more portable, and especially important was the invention at Bell Labs of the transistor in 1947, allowing further reduction in hearing aid size and weight. Bell Labs offered hearing aid manufacturers royalty free licenses, and, in 1954, transistorized hearing aids became the first nonmilitary application of solid state electronics developed at the Labs.

Another important invention of Bell Labs was the development of the first artificial larynx in 1929. The device consisted of a tube in which air from the user's stoma (an artificial opening) moved across a metallic reed to create voice for an individual otherwise unable to speak. One of the drawbacks of the mechanical larynx was that it produced a rather weak voice, but, in 1960, Bell Labs introduced an electronic version that was more powerful and required no stoma to use. Since that time, Bell Labs has made important contributions in other areas, such as radio astronomy, the invention of transistor and laser technologies, and the development of the UNIX operating system and C programming language. Eleven Nobel prizes have been awarded for the work done in Bell Labs.

In 1996 Lucent Technologies was created from AT&T as an independent company. As part of the spin-off, Bell Labs became part of Lucent (later renamed Alcatel-Lucent), while a small number of researchers stayed with the mother company as part of AT&T Laboratories. Recent highlights of Bell Labs have been its development of a closed captioning system for high definition television (HDTV) and advanced teletypewriter (TTY) devices for DEAF and HEARING IMPAIRED users. Meanwhile, AT&T Laboratories has pioneered text-to-speech technologies employed in screen reader programs for the visually impaired.

While Bell Labs has made numerous contributions to ASSISTIVE TECHNOLOGY AND ADAPTIVE DEVICES for people with disabilities, there have also been some notable criticisms raised about work at the Labs. First, the work done at Bell Labs for deaf and hearing impaired people often served only to launch or advertise new technologies. Harriet Green, who worked on the sound spectrograph at the Labs in the 1940s, noted that the Labs had underfunded and then abandoned the project of applying spectrography—the study and analysis of spectra—to deaf EDUCATION. Second, Bell Labs may have shown a certain level of discrimination in its EMPLOYMENT of people with hearing impairments. For example, Edgar Bloom—perhaps the first deaf employee of Bell Labs—unsuccessfully applied twice for employment as a chemist, but was only later employed as a "guinea pig" for the sound spectrograph and Picturephone projects. However, the major complaint among people who are culturally Deaf has been the apparent commitment to ORALISM, a focus on spoken language skills, by researchers at Bell Labs. Such an orientation may be evidenced by the emphasis at the Labs on the development of hearing aids, artificial larynxes, and speech synthesizers.

In spite of such criticisms, however, many employees associated with Bell Labs have shown a commitment to education, social needs, and environmental issues through their participation in the AT&T Pioneers, a division of the international association Telecom Pioneers (formerly the Telephone Pioneers of America), founded in 1911. The AT&T Pioneers are a group composed mainly of retired AT&T employees, including Bell Labs researchers and associates, whose primary focus is community service work. The volunteers participate in activities that include disaster assistance, literacy, beach cleanups, food distribution programs, special athletic competitions for people with physical impairments, and even building talking dolls for BLIND children.

Though no longer a division of AT&T, where it resided for much of its history, Bell Laboratories continues as a leader in telecommunications research, as well as in other scientific and technological fields. Its innovations have sometimes had profound implications for people with disabilities and have helped them to participate more fully in telephone and INTERNET communications.

Nathan W. Moon
Mara Mills

Further Reading:
Hughes, Thomas. *American Genesis: A History of the American Genius for Invention.* New York: Penguin Books, 1989.
Potter, Ralph, George Kopp, and Harriet Green Kopp. *Visible Speech.* 2d ed. New York: Dover, 1966.
Reich, Leonard. *The Making of American Industrial Research: Science and Business at GE and Bell, 1876–1926.* Cambridge: Cambridge University Press, 1985.

Belluso, John (1969–2006) *playwright*

John Belluso was a disabled PLAYWRIGHT who achieved great success in the American THEATER writing from and about the lived experience of disability, bringing new complex disabled characters and stories to the modern stage. Belluso was among the first disabled writers to both make a living in the theater and embrace his IDENTITY as a disabled person who was part of a larger disability COMMUNITY.

Belluso was born in Warwick, Rhode Island, on November 13, 1969, in a working-class, single-parent home. He began using a WHEELCHAIR when he was 11 due to a rare bone condition called Engleman-Camudrie Syndrome. Although bright and a voracious reader, Belluso dropped out of Warwick Veterans Memorial High School in 11th grade, as he was disengaged from his schooling and distanced from his classmates. In 1989, when he was 20, he saw a production of William Shakespeare's *Julius Caesar* at the Trinity Repertory Theatre in Providence, Rhode Island. Directed by famed American stage director Oskar Eustis, who would later become one of Belluso's closest friends and artistic collaborators, the play was set in modern Washington, D.C., and drew parallels between the political worlds of ancient Rome and contemporary America. Watching the play, Belluso made the decision to find a life in the theater. He applied to New York University (NYU) initially as a journalism student because at that time the Rhode Island Department of Rehabilitation, which funded his EDUCATION, did not consider theater a realistic career choice for a young disabled man.

On arriving his freshman year, Belluso went to the NYU library hoping to research disabled playwrights in the past and to find inspiration and direction. When he could not find any records of disabled playwrights, he began to doubt his career choice and the wisdom of dealing with disability openly in his work. However, one of his teachers was the Pulitzer Prize–winning playwright Tony Kushner, (see ANGELS IN AMERICA) who affirmed the importance of writing from and to the disability experience. Belluso ultimately earned a B.F.A. and, in 1996, an M.F.A. in playwriting from the Tisch School of the Arts at New York University.

The playwright used a dark HUMOR and historical perspective to study American DISABILITY CULTURE. Set in the 1950s, his play *Gretty Good Time* (1998) depicts medical caregivers who threaten Gretty, a character who had had polio as a child, with permanent INSTITUTIONALIZATION more because of her POVERTY than her impairment. *The Body of Bourne* (2001), an historical epic, chronicles the life of radical, turn-of-the last century essayist and thinker RANDOLPH BOURNE. In the romance *Pyretown* (2003), a single mother and a disabled community college student meet in an emergency room, fall in love, and eventually separate because of personal limitations and POVERTY, particularly substandard HEALTH CARE. Belluso's last, unfinished play, *The Poor Itch,* tells the story of a young disabled VETERAN returning home from the IRAQ WAR. On February 10, 2006, Belluso died in New York City from complications related to his disability.

Other plays Belluso wrote include *The Rules of Charity* (1999), *Henry Flamethrowa (2001), A Nervous Smile* (2006), and *bodySONGS* (2001), created with theater director Joseph Chaikin as part of the Disability Project at the Public Theater. He also wrote for TELEVISION, including the series *Ghost Whisperer* (CBS) and *Deadwood* (HBO).

As codirector (1999–2002) and director (2002–05) of the Mark Taper Forum's OTHER VOICES project, one of the few professional programs for disabled theater artists, Belluso mentored other artists and worked to remove the architectural and attitudinal barriers that keep disabled people from participating in the performing arts. He also was affiliated with New Dramatists, Playwrights Horizons, and the Ensemble Studio Theatre. Numerous prominent professional theaters commissioned, supported, and produced his work.

John Belluso wrote a new kind of story about disability, one that turned the traditional model of tragic illness, loss, and isolation, into one of shared identity, history, and COMMUNITY. He stated that although he was too young to have participated in it, he saw himself as a writer born of the contemporary DISABILITY RIGHTS MOVEMENT of the 1970s. Without the civil rights laws they fought for and the history

they changed, he said, he doubted he would have been able to seek out training and create a life in the American theater.
See also ANGELS IN AMERICA.

Victoria Ann Lewis

Further Reading:
Belluso, John. "Artist Statement" and "Gretty Good Time." In *Beyond Victims and Villains: Contemporary Plays by Disabled Playwrights,* edited by Victoria Ann Lewis, ed. New York: Theatre Communications Group, 2006.
———. *Henry Flamethrowa, A Nervous Smile, Pyretown, Rules of Charity.* Dramatists Play Service, 2006.
Lewis, Victoria. "Radical Optimist: Interview with Playwright John Belluso." *American Theatre,* 21, no. 4. April 2004, 40.

Berkeley, California

Berkeley, California, has played an important role in American disability history. Formed from three major entities in the mid- to late 19th century—the post–gold rush transplants and immigrants who lived in West Berkeley; the forerunner to the California School for the Deaf; and the University of California, founded in 1873—the city of Berkeley incorporated on April 1, 1878. It is located in Alameda County on San Francisco Bay and borders Oakland, Emeryville, and Albany.

Originally founded in 1860 in San Francisco as the Society for the Instruction and Maintenance of the Indigent Deaf and Dumb, and the Blind in California, the institution moved to Berkeley in 1867 where it attracted students with a thirst for learning. The school underwent several name changes, including the California School for the Deaf and Blind, and it is known today as the California School for the Deaf (CSD). When the newly formed University of California at Berkeley (UCB) began classes two DEAF students enrolled: Theophilus d'Estrella (1851–1929), and Charles T. Smith (1879–1900). D'Estrella left school after two years to teach at the CSD in Berkeley. Smith also left, citing problems with finances and sign language ACCESS to courses. Sign language support for both students seems to have come from Superintendent Warring Wilkinson, head of CSD. In 1883 Theodore Grady became the first deaf student to receive a degree from the university.

The California School for the Deaf and Blind in Berkeley also produced important leaders, such as NEWEL PERRY (ca. 1873–1961). Perry came to the BLIND school in 1883 at the age of 10 and graduated from UCB with a degree in mathematics in 1896. After traveling and teaching internationally, he returned to Berkeley and taught at the blind school. Like many other disabled COMMUNITY leaders, he believed in mentoring and financed needed accommodations for blind students attending UCB. Perry created the California Council of the Blind, a founding organization for the NATIONAL FEDERATION OF THE BLIND spearheaded later by UCB law graduate JACOBUS TENBROEK (1911–68).

The huge earthquake of 1906 brought masses of refugees to Berkeley, many of whom stayed after San Francisco was rebuilt. Since San Francisco's Chinatown was completely destroyed, a number of the new Berkeley residents were Chinese. Berkeley grew from 13,000 residents in 1900 to 56,000 in 1920. During the early decades of the 1900s Berkeley survived a massive fire, which burned nearly 600 buildings, created a new water and transit infrastructure, and residents elected the first socialist mayor in the United States and the first female police chief. Berkeley's African-American population grew from 66 in 1900 to 12,000 by 1945. Activists, including Frances Albrier, who, in 1939, became the first African-American to run for the city council, staged demonstrations to protest discrimination based on race. In 1948 William Byron Rumford became the first African-American from northern California to serve in the state legislature. His success resulted from a coalition of union activists, white liberals, and African-American voters.

In the second half of the 20th century, massive campus demonstrations and community PROTESTS for the civil rights of oppressed people brought a national focus to Berkeley. The GI Bill had brought many new students to UCB and between 1945 and 1948 enrollment more than doubled to over 25,000. Over the next decade, new political coalitions within the state reflected increasing support of minorities and civil rights issues.

It is with this backdrop that, in 1962, ED ROBERTS (1939–95) became the first quadriplegic to attend UCB. Due to the lack of accessible housing, the university designated a wing of the on-campus Cowell Hospital as a dormitory for Roberts and a dozen subsequent students. This arrangement provided a critical transition from home- and family-based personal care to paid employees. The group, nicknamed "THE ROLLING QUADS," shared resources and developed strategies to create needed services.

In 1969 UCB student Ruth Grimes surveyed disabled students to identify priority intersections for the first CURB CUTS, which became the basis for city policy. By 1970 the corners of Telegraph Avenue nearest the university received the first city curb cuts. This allowed students who used wheelchairs to visit local stores for the first time. With this new freedom, the Rolling Quads applied for a grant to establish campuswide resources for students with disabilities. In 1970 the federal Department of Health, Education and Welfare granted the university funds for the Physically Disabled Students' Program (PDSP), which became a national prototype. PDSP facilitated campus access, created resources for blind students, including a tactile campus map, trained professors in academic accommodations, and provided direct

services. Now renamed the Disabled Students' Program it continues to serve university students.

The increasing visibility of students with disabilities on campus spurred members of the faculty to address disability issues. In 1971 Professor Frederick Collignon, Department of City and Regional Planning, set up a disability research "studio" to teach disabled students to research and document critical issues.

In the same year a group of former UCB students created the Center for Independent Living (CIL) in Berkeley. In an era without accessible TRANSPORTATION or buildings, CIL initially focused on creating a community response to rampant inaccessibility. Direct services, such as wheelchair repair and housing referral, allowed disabled people to live throughout Berkeley. CIL organized public education campaigns, legislative action, and public protests to create opportunities for change.

In 1973 Ed Roberts became CIL's second director and invited JUDY HEUMANN to join the ground-breaking Berkeley work. With a diverse activist staff and community, CIL became the base for the 1977 SECTION 504 protest that occupied the Region IX Health, Education and Welfare regional director's offices in San Francisco for nearly a month. The dedication of nearly 150 people with disabilities and their allies to live in an office building created an enduring national image of a disability civil rights struggle. The resulting political and community victory shaped the 1980s generation of disability rights activists, many of whom went on to create unique, and often repeated, models of disability EMPOWERMENT in LAW, EMPLOYMENT, recreation, and public policy.

The city of Berkeley became a primary location for disability-related organizations as well. Throughout the 1970s and beyond, buoyed by successful disability rights campaigns, many people, Deaf, disabled, as well as allies began to create responses to emerging needs, such as Berkeley Planning Associates, founded by Frederick Collignon in 1972 to address public policy; Computer Technologies Program, created by CIL and IBM in 1975 for employment issues; the DISABILITY RIGHTS EDUCATION AND DEFENSE FUND, Inc., founded by Robert Funk and MARY LOU BRESLIN in 1979 to address legal rights; and the parenting ORGANIZATION, Through the Looking Glass, founded by Megan and Hal Kirschbaum in 1982. These community-based organizations and others that followed emerged with support and resources from both the university and the city.

Drawing from and as part of this ACTIVISM, UCB faculty played pivotal roles in developing a new academic field, DISABILITY STUDIES. Following academic models laid down by ethnic studies, women's studies, and queer studies, they worked with American and international colleagues to create resources for students interested in studying disability. In addition to increasing support for a broad Disability Studies

Program at the turn of the 21st century, in 2005 the university approved a proposal to initiate a disability studies minor.

Spurred by people with disabilities who fought many battles for fuller access and inclusion, both the city and the university have for more than a century blazed new trails for people with disabilities. Recognition by others of Berkeley's unique character and inclusive approach to people with disabilities is evident in its colloquial designation as the place where "the INDEPENDENT LIVING MOVEMENT began." In 2003 Berkeley won second place in "American Foundation for the Blind Livable Community Award" and in 2007 Berkeley was named the "Most Accessible City in the U.S." by the NATIONAL ORGANIZATION ON DISABILITY.

The history of people with disabilities in Berkeley provides a peek into the struggles and possibilities of full inclusion and acceptance in both university and community life.

Corbett Joan O'Toole

Further Reading:

"Builders and Sustainers of the Independent Living Movement in Berkeley." Regional Oral History Office, the Bancroft Library, University of California, Berkeley, 2000.

Charlton, James. *Nothing About Us Without Us: Disability Oppression and Empowerment*. Berkeley: University of California Press, 1998.

Longmore, Paul. *Why I Burned My Book and Other Essays on Disability*. Philadelphia: Temple University Press, 2003.

"History of UCB's Disabled Students' Program and Residence Program." URL: http://dsp.berkeley.edu/history.html.

Shapiro, Joseph A. *No Pity: People with Disabilities Forging a New Civil Rights Movement*. New York: Random House, 1994.

Bernstein, Charles (1872–1942) *superintendent of the Rome State Custodial Asylum*

As the longtime superintendent of the Rome State Custodial Asylum in New York State during the first half of the 20th century, Charles Bernstein, M.D., pioneered community support and transition services that helped his "FEEBLEMINDED" charges to learn to live outside an institution. His insistence on using inmate work programs to defray costs and enforce discipline reflected contemporary views of work as a moral good and a citizenship obligation, even for institutionalized people with disabilities. Yet Bernstein also became one of the few superintendents of institutions for the feebleminded to challenge the EUGENIC orthodoxies of his day, such as INVOLUNTARY STERILIZATION and permanent incarceration.

Charles Bernstein was born on December 21, 1872, in Carlisle, New York. After his parents died, his stern and often angry uncle took in the nine-year-old Bernstein and his siblings. As a child, Bernstein vowed that "If ever I have the care of children, I shall be fair to them and let kindness rule my acts."

After graduating from the Albany Medical College in 1894, Bernstein joined the staff of the new Rome State Custodial Asylum for Unteachable Idiots in Rome, New York, as an assistant physician. Following the pioneering efforts of earlier superintendents such as HERVEY WILBUR, Bernstein would establish work programs to provide the inmates of the bleak institution with at least some form of occupation to instill discipline, and to help defray institutional costs.

In 1902 Bernstein became the acting superintendent; one year later he assumed the official leadership role. In his new capacity Bernstein quickly began extending work programs and VOCATIONAL TRAINING to nearly all inmates, including the multiply disabled men and women whom most ASYLUM superintendents assumed could never be productive. He reclassified inmates by their ability to labor rather than by medical categories.

His interest in labor as a form of rehabilitation motivated Bernstein to establish a system of colonies and supervised parole for "high-grade inmates" (obedient inmates with mild cognitive disabilities). In these sheltered environments, parolees could gradually learn to live independently and provide for themselves in a supportive COMMUNITY. The colonies plan also relieved population pressure at the main asylum and helped reduce overall institutional expenses. By 1909 inmate labor had defrayed more than 25 percent of annual maintenance costs at Rome, with inmates doing most of the sewing, laundering, and farming, among other tasks. By 1925 the colonies housed 30 percent of the asylum's population (parolees composed another 15 percent); the system proved highly profitable, returning 100 percent to 200 percent of the money invested.

By the mid-1920s Bernstein's programs had been adopted nationwide, partly because of their substantial financial and administrative benefits. The Great Depression of the 1930s, however, drastically reduced EMPLOYMENT among colony residents and parolees at the same time that the main asylum began admitting delinquent and severely disabled inmates who were ineligible for colony life. When Charles Bernstein died on June 13, 1942, at the age of 70, few of Rome's 51 colonies were still profitable; most closed within a few years.

Despite the mixed results of his colony and parole programs, Bernstein challenged the dominant eugenic ideas of his day, serving as a key early advocate of community living for disabled people. Bernstein was the first superintendent to implement successful work programs as a means of reintegrating people labeled "idiotic" and "feebleminded" into society. Additionally, Bernstein's colonies and parole programs foreshadowed the GROUP HOMES and transition services used to integrate former institutional inmates into their communities during the DEINSTITUTIONALIZATION movement of the 1950s and 1960s. At the same time, his inmate labor programs reflected contemporary views of work as a citizenship obligation and colonies provided a powerful model of SHELTERED WORKSHOPS for the burgeoning vocational rehabilitation movement.

See also COGNITIVE AND INTELLECTUAL DISABILITY.

Sarah Rose

Further Reading:

Ferguson, Philip M. *Abandoned to Their Fate: Social Policy and Practice toward Severely Retarded People in America, 1820–1920.* Philadelphia: Temple University Press, 1994.

Riggs, James G. *Hello Doctor: A Brief Biography of Charles Bernstein, M.D.* Oswego, N.Y.: James Riggs, 1936.

Trent, James W., Jr. *Inventing the Feeble Mind: A History of Mental Retardation in the United States.* Berkeley: University of California Press, 1994.

Best Years of Our Lives, The

An abiding audience favorite and one of the technical masterpieces of American realist filmmaking, director William Wyler's 1946 movie *The Best Years of Our Lives* remains a stunning cinematic achievement, with high production values, and consistently excellent acting from its stellar lead cast and those in several vividly portrayed lesser roles. The FILM, which won seven Academy Awards and continues to be a moneymaking staple of cable TELEVISION film networks, offered its contemporary audience an emotional summation of the experience of the sacrifices made by ordinary Americans during WORLD WAR II, just at the moment when the nation began to look hopefully and anxiously to the restoration of a NORMAL, peacetime social order. Its perspective on WAR is not the battlefield, but rather the soldier's return to the home he had left behind when called to do the fighting. In no small measure, the film's success was based on its portrayal of the burdens, especially the physical and emotional injuries, caused by war.

The film originated with the intuition of Hollywood producer Samuel Goldwyn that, when the war ended, American society would face profound challenges in reintegrating the 16 million men whose lives had been disrupted by military service. Goldwyn commissioned journalist and screenwriter MacKinlay Kantor to do a screenplay based on the readjustment of recently demobilized VETERANS. Overwhelmed by the classical provenance of his theme, Kantor created a 268-page novel written in Homeric verse about three variously troubled men, whose intricately connected homecomings in the fictional all-American metropolis of Boone City are filled with difficulties, mostly reflected in relationships with wives, daughters, and girlfriends. The characters are all disaffected from the emerging postwar society and unable to eas-

ily resume their personal lives, for which Kantor blamed the social order, not the inadequacies of his characters or their wartime experience.

Much of Kantor's original scenario was rejected because it was too political in Goldwyn's eyes, and because one of the three veterans suffered from a devastating brain injury, which, Goldwyn believed, would frighten the audience. Wyler and screen writer, novelist, and presidential speechwriter Robert Sherwood, however, preserved the basic structure of Kantor's story. The movie follows the homecoming of three combat veterans, whose stories become intertwined: Al Stevenson (Frederic March), a middle-aged banker with a sometime drinking problem, whose children have grown up in his absence; Fred Derry (Dana Andrews), a decorated Air Force officer haunted by combat experiences who returns to a dead-end proletarian existence and an unfaithful wife; and Homer Parrish (HAROLD RUSSELL), a young sailor who lost both of his hands and wears PROSTHETIC metal hooks, which he manipulates with great skill, but which fail to provide the confidence required to resume his relationship with his fiancé, Wilma. The film focuses alternately on the problems of each of the three men with reintegration into the civilian workforce and with resumption of a marriage or sustaining a romantic relationship. While the look of the film is realistic, in the end the plot is resolved conventionally through the device of these heterosexual relationships. While powerful in the evocation of the difficulties faced by the three men, the film does not seriously engage the problems of disabled veterans as a group. Each man's problems are ultimately personal and individual, and each man is redeemed by the love of an unselfish, faithful, and strong woman, not through solidarity with other veterans, disabled or able-bodied.

Russell, a veteran who had never acted before and was himself a bilateral hand AMPUTEE as a consequence of a World War II demolition accident, proved a convincing performer. The treatment of his efforts to come to terms with this injury, as he seeks a way to resolve the impasse in his relationship with Wilma, provides the viewer with moments that constitute some of the most vivid visualizations of disability in the history of American film. For his portrayal of Homer, Russell won two Academy Awards, one for Best Supporting Actor and an honorary award for humanitarian service.

See also GENDER; POPULAR CULTURE; REPRESENTATION.

David A. Gerber

Further Reading:

Gerber, David A. "Anger and Affability: The Rise and Representation of a Repertory of Self-Presentation Skills in a World War II Disabled Veteran." *Journal of Social History* 27, no. 1 (Fall 1993): 1–27.

———. "Heroes and Misfits: Conflicting Representations of Disabled Veterans of World War II in *The Best Years of Our*

Lives." *American Quarterly* 46, no. 4 (December 1994): 545–574.

Jackson, Martin A. "The Uncertain Peace: *The Best Years of Our Lives.*" In *American History/ American Film: Interpreting the Hollywood Image,* edited by John E. O'Connor and Martin A. Jackson, 147–166. New York: Routledge, 1992.

Bethune, Thomas "Blind Tom" (Thomas Greene Wiggins) (1849–1908) *composer and pianist*

Thomas Greene "Blind Tom" Wiggins was a leading American pianist and composer in the late 19th and early 20th centuries. On May 25, 1849, in Columbus, Georgia, Thomas Greene Wiggins, the 14th child of African-American slaves Charity Greene and Mungo Wiggins, was born BLIND. Less than a year later, the Wiggins FAMILY was sold to the Bethunes, also of Columbus. Wiggins's legendary career as a pianist began at age four, when he played one of the Bethune daughters' most difficult piano pieces without prior instruction. General James N. Bethune brought Wiggins to the concert stage by age eight. A review in the *Columbus Enquirer* of Blind Tom's first performance notes that he was an "eight year old genius, without benefit of instruction, yet capable of performing the most difficult works by Beethoven, Mozart, Herz, and others of equal reputation." Wiggins would also sing, pace around the stage, and make circular motions with his hands while he performed. In addition to playing parlor songs that he had written and piano works by Chopin and Gottschalk, Wiggins would take requests from the audience and play them backward, simultaneously, or with his back turned to the piano. Bethune, who served as master of ceremonies for "Blind Tom," prevented Wiggins's family from having any involvement in the performances. General Bethune soon sold Wiggins's "show," but not Tom himself, to manager Perry Oliver for $15,000; Oliver then earned over $50,000 exhibiting Wiggins. "Blind Tom" would provide income for his plantation masters and their descendents for the duration of his life. As a result of post–Civil War loopholes, Wiggins was never actually or legally freed from slave status.

Three trials concerning Wiggins's custody occurred between 1865 and 1886. Each trial revolved around three issues: Wiggins's legal status (slave or free), his mental state (competent or incompetent), and his potential as an income-earner for the appointed guardian. Custody in the first two trials was granted to Bethune, with whom Wiggins toured extensively in the United States, Europe, and Canada. Wiggins continued to tour after his custody was granted to Bethune's estranged daughter-in-law, Eliza Stutzback. Wiggins commanded large audiences throughout his life, up until just three years before his death on June 13, 1908.

Understanding "Blind Tom" Wiggins and his role in 19th-century American musical life requires an acknowledg-ment of the full spectrum of his disabilities, both physical and cognitive. Contemporary accounts universally acknowledge his blindness, but his COGNITIVE DISABILITY is either disputed or difficult to quantify. A merely uneducated or undisciplined individual, even if blind, might not require full-time care into middle age, suggesting that Wiggins was not just blind but also an autistic savant (see AUTISM). Compositional techniques that reflect Wiggins's autistic behaviors include awkwardness of transitional moments in his MUSIC, the tendency to repeat tunes and figures in a way that set him apart from his contemporaries, and the imitation of everyday sounds Wiggins employed in his compositions.

Wiggins's compositions mirror the style of the pieces he studied with teachers such as Joseph Poznansky, and they are steeped in 19th-century European pianistic practices. More than 100 piano pieces (some published) and a handful of songs bear the name "Blind Tom" or one of his noms de plume such as "François Sexalise" and "Professor W. F. Raymond." Compositions include "Oliver Galop" (1861), Improvisation on "When this cruel war is over" (1865), "Battle of Manassas" (1866), "March Timpani" (1880), "Sewing Song: Imitation of a Sewing Machine" (1888), "Water in the Moonlight" (1894), and "Grand March Resurrection" (1901).

See also MUSIC; SLAVERY.

Stephanie Jensen-Moulton

Further Reading:

Davis, Rebecca Harding. "Blind Tom," *Atlantic Monthly,* November 1862, pp. 580–585.

Jensen-Moulton, Stephanie. "Finding Autism in the Compositions of a 19th-Century Prodigy: Reconsidering 'Blind Tom' Wiggins." In *Sounding Off: Theorizing Music and Disability,* edited by Neil Lerner and Joseph N. Straus, 199–215. New York: Routledge, 2006.

Robinson, Norbonne T. N., III. "Blind Tom, Musical Prodigy." *Georgia Historical Society Quarterly* (Spring 1967): 336–396.

Sacks, Oliver. *An Anthropologist on Mars: Seven Paradoxical Tales.* New York: Alfred A. Knopf, 1995.

Southall, Geneva H. *Blind Tom, the Black Pianist-Composer (1849–1908): Continually Enslaved.* Oxford: Scarecrow Press, 1999.

Southern, Eileen. "Thomas Greene Bethune (1849–1908)." *The Black Perspective in Music* 4, no. 2 (1976): 177–183.

Binet, Alfred (1857–1911) *French psychologist and creator of the modern intelligence test*

French psychologist Alfred Binet is best known as the "father" of the modern INTELLIGENCE TEST. Elements of his original tests can still be found in psychology tests used today. Binet's association with intelligence testing, however, has overshadowed his wide research interests and his belief in the diversity of individual intelligence.

Binet was born in Nice, France, on July 11,1857, to wealthy but unhappily married parents. The influences of his artist mother and physician father may have stimulated his own wide-ranging interests. As a young man, he studied law, medicine, and natural science, but he never formally studied psychology.

In 1891 Binet found a permanent position at the Sorbonne's new Laboratory of Physiological Psychology. Despite periodic failed attempts to find a position as a university professor, Binet remained at the laboratory for the rest of his life, becoming the laboratory director in 1894. Binet published prolifically on a wide range of topics and was one of the founders of France's first psychology journal, *Année psychologique,* as well as the author of four plays. He was particularly fascinated by individual differences in mental performance and dedicated to making psychology useful to educators. These two interests merged in his development of the Binet-Simon mental test.

Appointed to the 1904 government Commission on the Education of Retarded Children, Binet and his collaborator, physician Theodore Simon (1873–1961), decided to develop a test to identify which CHILDREN required SPECIAL EDUCATION. Binet feared that teachers might relegate their troublemakers to the new classes, rather than students who needed the alternative education. In order to accurately measure intelligence Binet believed that a test must measure multiple specific mental competencies, such as attention, memory, and comprehension, unlike previous mental tests that focused on easily measured traits like hand-eye coordination. Finally Binet and Simon arranged their tests according to age, creating a scale of tasks from the simple to the complex. Children, they believed, developed skills over time so a NORMAL infant could grasp objects while an older child could detect contradictions in spoken sentences. A disabled child would develop the same skills but at a slower rate. A child who tested at two years or more behind what they determined was the normal mental level required special education.

The 1905 Binet-Simon test and its subsequent revisions were quickly adopted in the United States and other nations while being mostly ignored in France. Binet believed that intelligence could be improved through training (within limits) and that social and cultural circumstances shaped mental development. He saw the tests as a tool to guide educators and emphasized the importance of studying students' performances on individual items as much as their overall scores. American psychologists and educators, however, embraced the test as a way to measure an individual's intellectual potential and the most enthusiastic proponents of the test generally regarded an individual's intelligence level as fixed. Even before Binet's early death on October 18, 1911,

in Paris eugenicists and others were using his tests to justify a wide array of social programs Binet would probably have deplored, including immigration restriction and state-sponsored sterilization.

See also EUGENICS; IMMIGRATION POLICY; INVOLUNTARY STERILIZATION.

Janice A. Brockley

Further Reading:

Fancher, Raymond E. *The Intelligence Man: Makers of the IQ Controversy.* New York: W. W. Norton, 1985.

Foschi, Renato, and Elisabetta Cicciola. "Politics and Naturalism in the 20th Century Psychology of Alfred Binet." *History of Psychology* 9 (2006): 267–289.

Siegler, Robert S. "The Other Alfred Binet." *Developmental Psychology* 28 (1992): 179–190.

Sokal, Michel M. *Psychological Testing and American Society, 1890–1930.* New Brunswick, N.J.: Rutgers University Press, 1987.

Wolf, Theta H. *Alfred Binet.* Chicago: University of Chicago Press, 1973.

Zenderland, Leila. *Measuring Minds: Henry Herbert Goddard and the Origins of American Intelligence Testing.* New York: Cambridge University Press, 1998.

Bisexual   See LGBT.

Bishop, Elizabeth (1911–1979) *poet, short story writer, essayist*

One of the premier American poets of the mid-20th century, Elizabeth Bishop is known for a spare, technically precise, emotionally restrained style that explores the effects of psychological trauma and physical impairment. Scholars have attributed Bishop's unsentimental view of nature and of human experience to the combined influence of her father's early death, her mother's MENTAL ILLNESS, and Bishop's own recurring physical ailments.

Bishop was born in Worcester, Massachusetts, on February 8, 1911, to Canadian parents. When her father Thomas Bishop died suddenly in Elizabeth's infancy, her mother suffered a breakdown and remained institutionalized for the rest of her life. Elizabeth, just eight months old at the time of her father's death, was sent to live with her maternal grandparents in Nova Scotia and never saw her mother again. When Bishop was six, she returned to the United States to live with her paternal grandparents; there, a series of severe chronic conditions, including bronchitis, asthma, and eczema, prevented her from attending school regularly. Bishop later lived in Boston with an aunt, attended boarding school and then Vassar College, and in 1952 moved to Brazil, where she lived for 15 years with Lota de Macedo Soares. Bishop died on October 6, 1979.

Among writers of her generation—including "confessional" poets Anne Sexton, Sylvia Plath, Randall Jarrell, and perhaps most notably longtime friend Robert Lowell, all of whom wrote explicitly of their own DEPRESSION and MENTAL ILLNESS—Bishop has the reputation of tending to avoid direct reference to her personal life, although instances of autobiographical writing can be found in her body of work. Nonetheless, themes of psychological fragility and the isolating effect of physical difference can be discerned in much of Bishop's work. Her attitude toward both mental and physical impairments anticipates a later disability rights consciousness in that it blurs the distinction between the "NORMAL" and the strange.

The hybrid title creature of the poem "The Man-Moth" (from *North & South,* 1946), for example, represents both the inherent ambiguity of human embodiment and the oppression that banishes to the underworld anyone who travels, metaphorically, "facing the wrong way." The renowned poem "In the Waiting Room" (*Geography III,* 1976) dramatizes the realization that there is "nothing stranger" than discovering one's "similarities" to people who are, in certain obvious ways, very different. Here, a young American girl reads the *National Geographic* while waiting for her aunt in a dentist's office and becomes frightened by a photograph of "black naked women" with "awful hanging breasts." The encounter stimulates not repudiation of difference but rather recognition: to be "an *I*," "an *Elizabeth*," is also, however "unlikely" it might seem, to be "one of *them*." Though not overtly concerned with matters of disability, "In the Waiting Room" exemplifies Bishop's denial of stereotypical biases toward physical and cultural difference.

Similar concerns are featured in two of Bishop's short stories. In the autobiographical piece "In the Village" (1953), a mentally ill widow has not, "in spite of the doctors, . . . got any better." The widow's daughter watches as her mother is fitted for a new dress, her first since coming out of mourning. But the dress is "all wrong," and the mother screams. This haunting scream, which "hangs over that Nova Scotian village" like a dark cloud, suggests that madness is a frightening and unpredictable threat, but also that madness is natural, its sound no more strange, finally, than that of the "elements speaking: earth, air, fire, water."

The bedridden narrator of "Gwendolyn" (1952), who has been "sick with bronchitis for a long time," plays with a doll named for her dead friend Gwendolyn Appletree, a diabetic whose parents had "not obey[ed] the doctor's orders and gave her whatever she wanted to eat." Illness, in this story, manifests the loneliness and vulnerability of childhood, but it is not simply metaphorical: like mental illness, physical disease happens naturally in the course of life, a reality empha-

sized by the doubling of illness in the narrator and her friend. Bishop also underscores the fact that illness and impairment take place in communities; how disability is experienced depends in large part on the way in which the social network responds to the need for care.

Unlike many of her contemporaries, Bishop preferred emotional reticence to direct revelation of the author's own experience. Nonetheless, Bishop shares with those poets (in particular Sexton) an interest in challenging firm distinctions between crazy and sane, and—very much like the poet Karl Shapiro, also a contemporary—she was keenly attuned to the kinds of social hierarchies that arbitrarily designate some individuals as the invalid or the freak.

See also IMPAIRMENT/IMPAIRED; LITERATURE; MAD PEOPLE AND MADNESS; POETRY.

Susannah B. Mintz

Further Reading:
Bishop, Elizabeth. *The Collected Prose.* New York: Farrar, Straus & Giroux, 1984.
———. *The Complete Poems, 1927–1979.* New York: Farrar, Straus & Giroux, 1983.
Costello, Bonnie. *Elizabeth Bishop: Questions of Mastery.* Cambridge, Mass.: Harvard University Press, 1991.
Fountain, Gary, and Peter Brazeau. *Remembering Elizabeth Bishop: An Oral Biography.* Amherst: University of Massachusetts Press, 1994.
Giroux, Robert, ed. *Elizabeth Bishop: One Art.* New York: Farrar, Straus & Giroux, 1994.
Goldensohn, Lorrie. *Elizabeth Bishop: The Biography of a Poetry.* New York: Columbia University Press, 1991.

black lung

Black lung (coal workers' pneumoconiosis), a chronic, irreversible, disabling respiratory DISEASE, which often results in or at least contributes to death, is an occupational illness that results from inhaling coal dust over prolonged periods. Deposits of coal dust in the lungs can block airways into the lungs, scar lung tissue, or damage blood vessels. People with the disease experience coughing, shortness of breath, and an inability to fight off other infections. For many, the condition directly affected their EMPLOYMENT options as well as their daily living. In the late 1960s, after decades of medical research, union intervention, and an explosion of activism among coal miners, black lung, a common 19th- and 20th-century ailment among coal miners, finally captured the nation's attention as a serious threat to worker safety and as a deplorable side effect of American INDUSTRIALIZATION. The history of black lung demonstrates how the physical realities of disease and disability do not always coincide with medical opinions and how public awareness and the economic concerns of industry leaders can shape medical and government health and safety programs in positive and negative ways.

During the Great Depression in the 1930s, silicosis, another occupational respiratory disease caused by inhaling silica dust in the dusty work environments of mines, factories, mills, and construction sites, gained national attention as a serious threat to the health of the nation's workers. Whereas nearly every state's workers' compensation laws provided benefits for sufferers of silicosis by the 1940s, only a handful compensated for black lung in the late 1960s. The silicosis crisis of the 1930s obscured the importance of other occupational respiratory diseases such as black lung, effectively prolonging the battle for recognition of and compensation for the disease. As silicosis gained recognition by the medical profession, government, and insurance providers, professionals still refused to recognize the existence of other occupational respiratory diseases, believing occupational dust disease had been eliminated.

Dust diseases, however, had not been conquered, and black lung had yet to be widely recognized. In the 1940s the United Mine Workers of America (UMWA) remained one of the few groups that continued to be concerned with dust diseases. It was clear that miners suffered from some type of respiratory disease that could not be attributed to silicosis, but physicians and workers' compensation laws did not recognize this condition. Even after British researchers identified coal workers' pneumoconiosis as a distinct disease, for which Great Britain provided compensation beginning in 1943, the UMWA achieved little progress in gaining recognition of the disease.

Officials within the UNITED MINE WORKERS OF AMERICA WELFARE AND RETIREMENT FUND worked through the 1950s and 1960s to raise awareness about black lung. In 1951 Alabama added black lung to the state's workers' compensation laws as disabled miners increasingly won damage awards from their employers in lawsuits sponsored by the UMWA. Frustrated at union officials' failure to alter compensation laws in West Virginia, local UMWA leaders and miners formed the West Virginia Black Lung Association (BLA) in January 1969. The BLA held rallies, meetings, and protests in the state and even hired a lobbyist to push for recognition of black lung in the state's workers' compensation LAWS. A wildcat strike, a strike not officially sanctioned and planned by union leadership, broke out on February 18, 1969, near Beckley, West Virginia. By March 2 the strike had spread throughout the state, and more than 40,000 miners refused to work. The BLA won the fight for reformed workers' compensation laws on March 11. Miners throughout the coalfields seemed invigorated by the victory, and Congress passed the Federal Coal Mine Health and Safety Act in December of that same year. The law forced coal operators to control the amount of dust in the mines and established the

Black Lung Benefits Program, which provided compensation for miners with black lung.

Unfortunately, black lung continues to plague coal miners today. In April 1998, the Louisville *Courier-Journal* ran a five-day exposé on the continued, widespread significance of black lung. More than two decades after Congress passed the 1969 Federal Coal Mine Health and Safety Act, which officials hoped would virtually wipe out black lung, some 1,500 miners still died each year of black lung. The *Courier-Journal* also exposed widespread corporate cheating on air quality tests in the mines and the inability of Kentucky miners to obtain compensation for the disease after the state's workers' compensation laws were revised in 1996. The new state law governing compensation of black lung set stricter standards for diagnosing compensable black lung so that even miners who have been diagnosed by a physician and show evidence of the disease on chest X rays do not always qualify for benefits. In the three years before the 1996 Kentucky legislation, about 80 percent of miners who applied for black lung compensation won benefits, but in 1997, under the new law, less than 1 percent won benefits.

Audra Jennings

Further Reading:
Derickson, Alan. *Black Lung: Anatomy of a Public Health Disaster.* Ithaca, N.Y.: Cornell University Press, 1998.
"Dust, Deception and Death: Why Black Lung Hasn't Been Wiped Out." Available online. URL: http://www.courier-journal.com/dust/. Accessed December 15, 2006.

Black Panther Party

The Black Panther Party was an African-American socialist revolutionary organization that existed from 1966 until 1982. Active on a national level for the first six years of its existence, the party confined most of its later activity to Oakland, California, and the surrounding area. The Panthers advocated self-determination for all oppressed peoples, pioneered the fight against class-based health disparities, and sought "intercommunal" alliances with liberation movements of all colors and nationalities. The party's authoritarian organization, its uneasy mix of ideologies and classes, and the U.S. government's aggressive campaign against its members led to its decline and ultimate extinction; however, it had lasting effects upon public awareness of black communities' needs and upon other minority movements, among them the DISABILITY RIGHTS MOVEMENT.

Party founders Huey P. Newton and Bobby Seale met when student-activists in Oakland. Inspired by the writings of Malcolm X, Frantz Fanon's anticolonial classic, *The Wretched of the Earth,* and many conversations with the poor residents of Oakland, they drafted a party platform that called for full EMPLOYMENT, fair treatment by police, and "land, bread, housing, education, clothing, justice, and peace" as well as self-determination for the "colonized" black American population. Among its many activist efforts, several directly intersected with issues of disability, including the Sickle Cell Anemia Research Foundation and its support for the "SECTION 504" demonstrators in 1977.

Although styled a "Research Foundation," the Panthers' sickle-cell anemia program focused chiefly on diagnosis and public awareness of the disease, which mainly affected African-Americans. In 1970 there were no foundations devoted to sickle cell anemia; medical textbooks generally used it as an example of a genetic principle, rather than addressing its diagnosis and treatment. The Panther newspaper in January 1971 characterized official neglect of the disease as "Black Genocide," calling attention to the fact that genetic diseases prevalent among white Americans received comparatively greater funding and attention. The Panthers' health clinic workers added sickle cell to the list of diseases—such as hypertension and lead poisoning—that they offered testing for and education on to black communities. The party took credit for having brought the disease into the public eye, which in turn prompted President Nixon to promise support for its treatment and research.

In April 1977 the Panthers proved indispensable allies to the disability movement during the Section 504 demonstration in California, when over 120 disability activists occupied the San Francisco offices of the federal Department of Health, Education and Welfare (HEW) to demand enforcement of the Rehabilitation Act of 1973. In other cities, the government had successfully starved the demonstrators out; the Panthers thwarted the government's attempts to use that tactic in San Francisco, bringing in dinners donated by local businesses every day of the four-week-long protest. The Panthers' willingness to defy the government by threatening armed confrontation and media exposure enabled them to enter the HEW building unmolested. Seeing the 504 demonstrators fighting for self-sufficiency and exposing the federal government's failure to abide by its own laws, the Panthers had recognized a movement analogous to their own and promptly effected a powerful coalition.

From their first public appearance, the Panthers' ACTIVISM, their confrontational tactics, and their violent, communist-inspired rhetoric had alarmed the law-enforcement community. Between 1967 and 1977, the FBI facilitated the police assassination of activists, repeatedly arrested groups of Panthers on trumped-up charges, and sought—using forged letters and infiltrators—to estrange party leaders from one another. One of their main targets was leader Huey Newton, and disability issues played a key role in government strategies.

Bullied as a child because of his social anxiety, high voice, and delicate "pretty" features, Newton had developed a volatile "Crazy Huey" persona to compensate for his constant self-doubt and fear; he would become enraged at the first sign that he was dealing with a potential challenger. Imprisoned from late 1968 to mid-1971 for crimes of which he was then acquitted, Newton intensified his battle against fear, as he was subjected to psychological tortures, such as being stripped and confined for 325 hours to a six-by-four-foot cell with no light, sound, or working drain for human waste. FBI memos from 1971 and earlier reveal that the government eagerly promoted his "paranoid-like responses" and "hysterical reaction" to feeling threatened, in the hope of eliciting a "mental collapse." The campaign to exploit and intensify Newton's emotional disabilities succeeded, as after his release from PRISON he began to see disloyalty everywhere, expelling many party chapters. By the late 1970s Newton relied heavily on the use of cocaine and alcohol. Weakened by his maladministration subsequent to 1977, the party closed its sole remaining program—Oakland's Liberation School—in 1982. Newton, dominated by shame over his drug ADDICTIONS, came to regard himself as a failure. He was shot and killed by an Oakland crack dealer in 1989.

Historically, scholars have tended to focus on the Black Panther Party's radical RACE politics, but the important relationship between the party and disability highlights both vital collaboration between activists and the common challenges oppressed people have faced. The party's successes in changing public perception and discussion of a besieged minority, and its continued invocation as a symbol of group pride, exemplify ways of facing those challenges.

See also SICKLE-CELL DISEASE; SIT-IN PROTEST AT THE DEPARTMENT OF HEALTH, EDUCATION AND WELFARE.

Josh Lukin

Further Reading:
Abu-Jamal, Mumia. *We Want Freedom: A Life in the Black Panther Party.* Cambridge, Mass.: South End, 2004.

Brown, Elaine. *A Taste of Power: A Black Woman's Story.* New York: Pantheon, 1992.

Foner, Philip S., ed. *The Black Panthers Speak.* Cambridge, Mass.: Da Capo, 1995.

Jones, Charles E., ed. *The Black Panther Party [Reconsidered].* Baltimore: Black Classic Press, 1998.

Moore, Gilbert. *Rage.* With a new introduction and afterword by Michael Thelwell. New York: Carroll & Graf, 1993.

Shapiro, Joseph P. *No Pity: People with Disabilities Forging a New Civil Rights Movement.* New York: Times Books, 1993.

Black Stork, The

The Black Stork, a feature-length motion picture shown commercially in several editions from 1916 to at least 1948, urged physicians and parents to withhold treatment from infants born with disabilities. The FILM dramatized the actual cases of a prominent Chicago surgeon, HARRY J. HAISELDEN, and Haiselden himself starred in it as the doctor.

In the film, a man with an unnamed inherited disease ignores repeated graphic warnings from his doctor and marries his sweetheart. As the doctor had predicted, their baby is born "DEFECTIVE." The baby requires immediate surgery to save its life, but the doctor concludes the child will have incurable hereditary physical and mental impairments, and he refuses to operate. The mother prays to God for guidance, and when God shows her a vision of the child's future of misery and crime, including his brood of "defective" future offspring, she agrees to withhold surgery. The baby's soul leaps into the open arms of Jesus.

The film is filled with images that portray people with disabilities, actual patients and actors, as repulsive, expensive to treat and care for, and dangerous. Yet it also appealed to audience sympathy with the disabled characters, to depict EUTHANASIA as an expression of both love and hatred. These conflicting emotional responses were united by the supposedly objective science of EUGENICS. The film was produced by Wharton Brothers, an Ithaca, New York, studio under contract to William Randolph Hearst's International Film Service, with a script by the well-known Hearst columnist Jack Lait. It opened in New York in late 1916, and was officially released state by state in April 1917. After 1918 it was renamed, *Are You Fit to Marry?* and in 1927 was reissued under that title, with a newly updated prologue. Initially shown in major commercial movie palaces, the film continued to appear in small theaters and traveling road shows for decades. The *Los Angeles Times* listed a number of different neighborhood theater showings in the 1940s, the latest from April 20 to April 29, 1948, at the Pico Theater.

After 1918, however, the film increasingly ran afoul of movie censors. Ironically, while *The Black Stork* sought to portray people with disabilities as repulsive, many viewers found such scenes made the film itself disgusting and upsetting. Such responses were one important reason that films about eugenics and about disability were banned from mainstream commercial theaters. *The Black Stork* played a key role in provoking, and became one of the first victims of, a growing movement to censor films on aesthetic grounds. By the 1920s film regulators expanded far beyond policing sexual morality to include what can be termed "aesthetic censorship," much of which aimed at eliminating unpleasant medical conditions from entertainment theaters, much as earlier vagrancy laws had been used to protect the public from their discomfort at having to see actual people with disabilities on the street.

See also POPULAR CULTURE; STEREOTYPES.

Martin S. Pernick

Further Reading:

Pernick, Martin S. *The Black Stork: Eugenics and the Death of "Defective" Babies in American Medicine and Motion Pictures since 1915.* New York: Oxford University Press, 1996.

———. "Medical Films." In *Censorship: A World Encyclopedia*, edited by Derek Jones, Vol. 2, 815–816. London: Fitzroy Dearborn, 2001.

Blank, Wade (1940–1993) *activist and disability rights leader*

Wade Blank is best known within the disability COMMUNITY for his role in founding and leading American Disabled for Accessible Public Transportation (ADAPT), one of the most influential American disability rights PROTEST groups.

Blank was born on December 4, 1940, in Pittsburgh, Pennsylvania. While attending college, he joined Reverend Martin Luther King, Jr., and others in 1965 on the historic voting rights march and demonstration in Selma, Alabama. A graduate of McCormick Theological Seminary and an ordained Presbyterian minister, Blank was pastor of a church near Kent, Ohio, in 1971 that became a meeting place for the Kent State University chapter of Students for a Democratic Society (SDS), and he was involved in helping students who opposed the VIETNAM WAR to avoid the draft by leaving for Canada.

In 1971 Blank went to Denver, Colorado, where he worked as an attendant at the Heritage House nursing home for four years. Blank was increasingly disturbed by the conditions in which the nursing home residents with disabilities lived, and ultimately he was discharged for encouraging residents to leave the facility for independent apartments in the community. Blank went on to found the Atlantis Community in 1975, a Denver collective and independent living center that included a number of former Heritage house residents.

Blank and other Atlantis Community members began to work for more accessible buses in the Denver Regional Transportation District (RTD) in 1975, engaging in legal advocacy and, by July 1978, street PROTESTS in which 19 activists, known as the "Gang of Nineteen," surrounded two buses at a downtown intersection. The Gang of Nineteen became the nucleus for ADAPT, which, after four years of protests in Denver, were successful in committing RTD to completely accessible buses.

In 1983 ADAPT organized a gathering of disability rights activists from around the United States to protest inaccessible public TRANSPORTATION at the national convention of the American Public Transit Association (APTA), and Blank and ADAPT continued to lead protests at APTA conventions for eight years, until the AMERICANS WITH DISABILITIES ACT OF 1990 (ADA) guaranteed transit accessibility across the nation. Blank and ADAPT were also active in advocacy for passage of the ADA, and subsequently for redirecting federal MEDICAID funding from nursing homes to personal attendant services that would enable disabled people to live independently in their communities.

In 1993 Blank and his family were vacationing in Mexico, and Blank's son Lincoln became caught in an ocean undertow. In an effort to save him, Blank and his son both drowned. He was survived by his wife Molly and daughters Heather and Caitlin. His memorial service in Denver was attended by over 1,100 people. While he did not have a disability himself, Wade Blank was revered throughout the DISABILITY RIGHTS MOVEMENT for applying lessons from the civil rights movement to support rights and independence for Americans with disabilities.

See also ACTIVISM AND ADVOCACY; AMERICAN DISABLED FOR ATTENDANT PROGRAMS TODAY; INDEPENDENT LIVING MOVEMENT.

Richard K. Scotch

Further Reading:

Tari, Susan Hartman. "If Heaven Isn't Accessible, God Is in Trouble." *Incitement* 9, no. 1, January/February 1993. Available online. URL: http://www.geocities.com/Area51/Shire/8897/USS_Adapt/Wade_Blank.html). Accessed May 21, 2008.

Thomas, Stephanie, Mary Johnson, Barrett Shaw, and Tom Olin. *To Ride the Public's Buses: The Fight That Built a Movement (Disability Rag Reader)*. Louisville, Ky.: Advocado Press, 2001.

Blatt, Burton   See CHRISTMAS IN PURGATORY.

blind

There have always been blind people on the North American continent, but there is little historical evidence about the specifics of their lives before 1800. The leading causes of blindness, including injury, ILLNESS, AGING, and genetic predisposition, were as prevalent in the past as they are today. Yet we do not know, for instance, how native peoples may have understood blindness. We can assume that European colonists imported attitudes about blindness from their native countries. In some cases, they may have perceived blindness, like other impairments, as a sign of divine retribution for past sin. Harsh conditions of early colonial life would have made blind people who could not support themselves appear to impose additional hardship on FAMILY members and the COMMUNITY at large.

ESTABLISHING EDUCATION FOR THE BLIND

By the early 19th century American philanthropists, inspired by Enlightenment ideals about human rights and universal EDUCATION, began to investigate the possibility that blind people, with proper training, could become contributing members of society. SAMUEL GRIDLEY HOWE (1801–76) undertook to educate a few blind CHILDREN in his father's home in 1832. With funds from the state legislature and the financial support of other prominent Bostonians such as THOMAS HANDASYD PERKINS (1764–1854), Howe opened an institution in South Boston which later became known as the PERKINS SCHOOL FOR THE BLIND. Similar schools soon opened in other cities around the country. Howe modeled the school on the Royal Institute for the Young Blind in Paris, the first school for the blind, founded in 1785. Pupils were taught to read using texts with embossed print. They also received musical training, supporting the idea that blind people are gifted with musical talent. They were also taught gender specific skills: girls learned housekeeping, sewing, and other needlework, while boys learned carpentry, chair caning, broom making, and piano tuning. Like its Parisian counterpart, the Perkins School held regular exhibition events at which pupils demonstrated their skills to visitors, as a way to raise public awareness and monetary support. Renowned English author Charles Dickens (1812–70), visited Perkins in 1842 and was enthusiastic in his praise for the school's advanced methods.

In 1824 LOUIS BRAILLE (1809–52), a student at the Institute for the Young Blind in Paris, invented a reading and writing system that revolutionized the lives of blind people around the world. Braille's system featured patterns of raised dots rather than the embossed Roman alphabet that had been used previously. BRAILLE could be read more rapidly and efficiently than embossed letters, and texts were easier to produce. Braille's system also allowed blind people to write and to read their own writing without sighted assistance. Although it was several decades before braille was accepted as an approved reading and writing method in the Paris school, blind students were quick to adopt the system for their own use, and soon it found its way to blind schools in America. In 1892 the first Braille typewriter was invented at the Illinois School for the Blind. Later the design was perfected, and the machines came to be called Perkins Braillers. Different versions of the code were developed at different schools and by different individual practitioners, leading to the so-called WAR OF THE DOTS. It was not until 1932 that a uniform braille code for all English-speaking countries was established.

As schools for the blind proliferated across the country, many graduates found EMPLOYMENT as teachers and administrators. Others found work as music teachers, piano tuners, and in other fields. But educated blind people did not always fare well when seeking employment outside the blind institutions. Howe and other educators argued that factory assembly lines could be designed for blind workers, but manufacturers were unconvinced. Some schools established

> *"Three years ago I was struck by a car and I been blind two years. I can just 'zern' the light. When I was able to be about I used to vision what it would be like to be blind and now I know."*
>
> —Ben Hite, age 74, born into slavery in Tennessee; interviewed in Pine Bluff, Arkansas by Bernice Bowden in 1938, as part of the Federal Writers Project

SHELTERED WORKSHOPS where blind employees received a small stipend or room and board to produce handicrafts to be sold in school gift shops or in fund-raising appeals. There were few resources available to people who became blind as adults. Those without FAMILY support were often compelled to sustain themselves through begging (see BEGGARS AND BEGGING).

In 1880 HELEN KELLER (1880–1968) was born in Tuscumbia, Alabama. At the age of 19 months she became DEAF and blind following an illness assumed to be either scarlet fever or meningitis. In 1887 her parents hired ANNE SULLIVAN MACY (1866–1936), a recent graduate of the Perkins School, to be her teacher. Sullivan had been blind for much of her childhood but had recently had her sight partially restored. She used methods pioneered at Perkins to teach the DEAF-BLIND. Soon Keller learned to read and write, and went on to graduate from Radcliffe College, to publish articles and books, and to appear on the lecture circuit and the Vaudeville stage. She supported many reform movements, including women's suffrage and workers' rights, but was chiefly known for her inspirational message about overcoming adversity. Although both deaf and blind, Keller was primarily associated with blind issues. In the 1920s she helped to found the AMERICAN FOUNDATION FOR THE BLIND, and spent the rest of her long life as a national and international spokesperson for the organization, promoting educational and vocational programs.

ORGANIZATIONS OF AND FOR THE BLIND

The 20th century saw a rise in ORGANIZATIONS, opportunities, and innovations for the blind. In 1932 the National Library Service for the Blind was established. The library service distributed texts in Braille, and also phonograph recordings known as TALKING BOOKS. These materials as well as the special record players required for the talking books were mailed, free of charge, between regional libraries and eligible subscribers. In later decades, the recorded discs were replaced by cassette tapes. In the 21st century the NLS began to shift to digital delivery systems.

In 1954 the SOCIAL SECURITY ACT Amendments established a national standard of "legal blindness" to determine eligibility for rehabilitation and educational programs. To be considered legally blind, a person has a visual acuity of 20/200 or less, or a visual field of 20 degrees or less in the better eye with corrective lenses. Prior to this time, different state agencies employed a variety of methods to ascertain whether a person was blind enough to receive services or support. The national standard made it easier for people with a wide range of visual impairments to take advantage of a growing number of programs, such as the vendor system created by the RANDOLPH-SHEPPARD ACT of 1936, which gives priority to blind people to operate newsstands and other vending facilities on public property.

By the mid 20th century blind Americans had begun to organize to demand a say in the ways new programs were administered. The NATIONAL FEDERATION OF THE BLIND (NFB) was founded in 1940 and has since become one of the largest consumer and advocacy ORGANIZATIONS in the country. The NFB philosophy promotes the idea that the biggest problem blind people face is not the impairment itself but rather the prejudice of sighted people who assume they are inept and helpless. With the proper training, the NFB asserts, blindness can be reduced to the level of a minor nuisance. The NFB has fought the paternalistic attitudes of many administrators in the rehabilitation system, and lobbied Congress to insure the civil rights of blind people. The NFB also founded its own residential training centers, rivals to a growing number of state-sponsored programs, where blind people can acquire mobility training and learn Braille and other adaptive techniques. At the NFB Centers many of the instructors are also blind. As with many large organizations, inner conflicts developed. Another organization comprised of blind people, the AMERICAN COUNCIL OF THE BLIND, was founded in 1961. Though the two organizations were often in conflict, by the end of the century they had become allied around many issues.

Blind VETERANS of the 20th century's wars also founded new organizations and services. For example, THE SEEING EYE was founded in 1929 to train dogs as guides for blind people. Inspired by a program for blind veterans of WORLD WAR I in Germany, Dorothy Harrison Eustis (1886–1946) imported the training methods to America. Dogs wear special harnesses and receive special training to help guide blind users. After WORLD WAR II the BLINDED VETERANS ASSOCIATION was founded to provide rehabilitation training and job placement. Also, Recordings for the Blind (RFB) opened in Princeton, New Jersey, recording college textbooks for use by blind veterans who wanted to take advantage of the educational programs of the GI Bill. Later, RFB expanded its services to include all blind students of any age.

INCREASED CULTURAL INCLUSION

By the 1960s there was a movement away from RESIDEN-TIAL SCHOOLS, so that blind children could stay at home and go to neighborhood schools. Typically, blind children received textbooks in Braille or large print and attended tutoring sessions with itinerant teachers to help with braille and other specialized blindness skills. New technologies such as recorded books and new magnification lenses and devices were touted as superior to Braille for children with some usable sight. The unintended consequence of these trends was a sharp decline in Braille literacy during the second half of the century. Later research established that proficiency in Braille correlated to higher levels of education and employment.

The NFB and other blindness organizations conducted campaigns to ensure that Braille instruction would be available for any blind student who requested it. In 1976 RAY KURZWEIL (1948–   ), a computer scientist specializing in artificial intelligence, invented the first reading machine for the blind. The machine used a flat bed scanner and OPTI-CAL CHARACTER RECOGNITION technology to translate print material into synthesized speech. Early versions of the machine were cumbersome, inaccurate, and expensive. The first machine covered an entire tabletop and was purchased by the blind musician STEVIE WONDER (1950–   ). In the decades since that first machine, text-to-speech technology became more streamlined and accurate, making it possible for blind people to use computers, browse the worldwide Web, and download electronic books.

In the final decades of the 20th century other services and technologies became available to enhance blind Americans' independence and cultural inclusion. Audio descriptive services were developed to aid blind people's enjoyment of THEATER, movies, TELEVISION, and art museums. Global positioning technology has also been adapted for use by blind people to aid in independent MOBILITY.

By the early 21st century blind Americans found employment in many fields, including business, education, technology, and the ARTS. Despite the AMERICANS WITH DISABILITIES ACT (1990) and other legislation meant to fight discrimination, however, unemployment levels for blind people continue to hover around 70 percent. Public perceptions about the capabilities of blind people lag behind the many advances in education, training, and technology of the past two centuries.

See also ASSISTIVE TECHNOLOGY AND ADAPTIVE DEVICES; AUDIO DESCRIPTION; COMMUNITY; GUIDE DOGS; LONG CANES.

Georgina Kleege

Further Reading:

Koestler, Frances A. *The Unseen Minority: A Social History of Blindness in the United States.* New York: AFB Press, 2004.

Matson, Floyd. *Walking Alone, Marching Together: A History of the Organized Blind.* Baltimore: NFB Press, 1990.

Blind Boys of Alabama

The Blind Boys of Alabama is a male Gospel group, originating in the southern states. There are several contradictory accounts by MUSIC writers about the group's origins, ranging from the original numbers to how they met, but it is generally accepted that there were five early members: George Scott, Clarence Fountain, Jimmy Carter, Eric McKinnie, and Velma Bozman Traylor.

The original members met in 1937 at the Alabama School for the Negro Blind, during the years of institutional racial segregation in the Deep South. The history of their school was important to the direction of the group. It was founded in 1892 as the Alabama School for the Negro Blind on the original industrial asylum model, which meant that its students' main EDUCATION consisted of training in repetitive tasks, such as cane weaving. In these schools the only creative activity pursued was singing, mostly in the institution's traditional church services. This music little reflected the Blind Boys' musical interests or home background as it consisted of songs preferred by their white teachers. Their own group came about as a glee club, which reflected the more spiritual Gospel music they heard on the radio.

The Blind Boys did not become a fully formed group until 1939. The group started singing professionally in local army camps during WORLD WAR II, sneaking out of school to perform. After finishing their education, they became a touring and recording outfit called the Happy Land Jubilee Singers, signing for labels such as Savoy, House of Blues, and Speciality. It was not long afterward that members decided to change their name to compete directly with a group called the Blind Boys of Mississippi. Eventually, the Alabama group eclipsed the other in popularity and some members of the Mississippi group joined them.

In 1983 the group changed musical direction when members were recruited for *The Gospel at Colonus,* a musical performed both off and on Broadway. After this show they developed a more contemporary, commercial approach to Gospel, adapting to styles such as Funkadelic—an approach that mixed disco and funk. They then recorded songs written by such diverse artists as Tom Waits, Jimmy Cliff, Fat Boy Slim, Macy Gray, and Bob Dylan. They received many musical awards, including their first Grammy nomination in 1992 for Best Traditional Gospel Album, followed by a Grammy AE Award in 2001 in the same category.

Over the years the group has undergone many personnel changes, including the addition of sighted members. By 2008 it retained only two original members: Clarence Fountain and Jimmy Carter. Despite their title, the Blinds Boys of Alabama are not often linked with the disability movement or with their disability. In the media and in history accounts, the group's racial composition is more often the subject of interest than the blindness of their founding members, even though their disability experiences are shared with other popular musicians of color, such as RAY CHARLES and STEVIE WONDER.

See also BLIND; POPULAR CULTURE; RACE.

Simon Hayhoe

Further Reading:

D'Aponte, Mimi Gisolfi. "The Gospel at Colonus (and other Black Morality Plays)." *Black American Literature Forum* 25, no. 1 (Spring 1991): 101–111.

Green, Amy S. *The Revisionist Stage: American Directors Reinvent the Classics.* Cambridge: Cambridge University Press, 1994.

Rabkin, Gerald. "Lee Breuer: On 'The Gospel of Colonus.'" *Performing Arts Journal* 8, no. 1 (Winter 1984): 48–51.

Blinded Veterans Association

As a consequence of combat injuries, infectious diseases, and accidents, approximately 1,400 American servicemen emerged from WORLD WAR II with visual impairments. The majority were VETERANS of the army, which maintained a BLIND rehabilitation facility at Old Farms, a former boarding school in Avon, Connecticut. The Blinded Veterans Association (BVA) was founded at Old Farms in March 1945 by some 100 veterans, who were then undertaking MOBILITY and orientation training in preparation to reenter civilian life. Soon joined by blinded veterans from the navy and the marines, who were undergoing rehabilitation at the Philadelphia Naval Hospital, the organization grew rapidly to include, by 1948, 850 exclusively male veterans, 60 percent of visually impaired veterans of the WAR. In 1958 the BVA was officially incorporated under federal law, and thereafter became the organization the federal government recognized as the most important authority in blinded veterans affairs. One of the oldest single-disability veterans' ORGANIZATIONS, the BVA remains today a leading advocate on behalf of the rehabilitation, EMPLOYMENT, and the social needs of blinded veterans.

From its inception, the BVA has taken a comprehensive view of the needs of the visually IMPAIRED veteran. In forming its agenda, it has emphasized overcoming the practical challenges that impeded living an independent, normalized existence in the world of the sighted majority, characterized by both mobility and employment in the mainstream economy. But it has also placed an emphasis on confronting the psychological challenge of blindness incurred in adulthood after a lifetime of being sighted and the difficulties the visually impaired incur as a consequence of prejudice and discrimination.

The BVA has sought to mobilize resources from a variety of external and internal sources to meet these challenges. From the beginning, the BVA has sought to ensure that blinded veterans received the material and medical assistance from the federal government they need to make an effective, practical, and permanent transition into civilian life. One of its first campaigns was for the establishment of a permanent Veterans Administration blind rehabilitation institution to replace Old Farms and other military facilities, which were closed after the war. Opened in 1948, the Central Blind Rehabilitation Center was placed at Hines, Illinois, and put under the direction of Russell Williams, a blinded World War II veteran and one of the founders of the BVA. For years the BVA operated job-counseling and job-finding efforts on its own small budget through a field service program. Near the end of the VIETNAM WAR in 1974, however, it successfully negotiated a cooperative arrangement with the U.S. Department of Labor, which vastly expanded its resources for job placement of blinded veterans. Until the law embodying the arrangement expired in 1989, by which time the work of rehabilitating the Vietnam veterans was supposed to have been completed, with the assistance of the federal government the BVA placed thousands of blinded veterans in a great variety of professional, technical, and industrial jobs.

While aware that federal assistance is necessary both for it own work and for the rehabilitation of blinded veterans, the BVA has been wary of excessive dependence on the federal government, especially when it comes to the lives of individuals. The BVA has always had the goal of empowering blinded veterans by stimulating self-help and political ACTIVISM among its members through the organization of local campaigns against discrimination in employment and in public accommodations, such as restaurants, that impeded their reentry into civilian life. A common fear among the founders was that they would share the fate of the civilian blind, about whom these veterans actually knew little, and with whom they had little contact. Their rehabilitation took place exclusively in military facilities, and, like most other organizations for disabled veterans in the United States, there was little systematic outreach by the BVA to the civilian disabled. Nonetheless, the World War II blinded veterans assumed that the civilian blind were objects of pity and scorn, abandoned in the backrooms of their parents' houses and in SHELTERED WORKSHOPS. The early leadership of the BVA feared the temptation to use federal benefits to drop out of ordinary social existence, and hence end up as isolated as they believed the civilian blind to be. But the founders understood, too, the difficulties men who had always been sighted faced in adjusting to blindness, and they knew how strong that temptation might be.

Understanding this, the founders were influenced by Reverend Thomas Carroll (1909–71), a Catholic priest and blindness worker, who was one of the BVA's first chaplains. Carroll believed that the loss of sight required for adults a veritable rebirth. Out of these concerns and understandings came a strong commitment to solidarity among BVA members, who sought to empower one another, as individuals and by means of a formal field representative program, to meet the test of rehabilitation and to overcome the difficulties accompanying reemergence in civilian life. One result of this commitment to EMPOWERMENT through solidarity was an especially strong stand against racism and anti-Semitism, which the larger organizations for veterans usually accommodated out of deference to the social views of the majority of their members. Regional BVA chapters, which numbered around 40 at the beginning of the 21st century, have always been integrated by RACE, RELIGION, and ETHNICITY, and leadership positions are shared among members of all backgrounds. The early BVA was exclusively male, but, as the armed forces have become increasingly integrated by gender, women have entered its ranks in growing numbers. The organization has also established an auxiliary membership program to include veterans whose visual impairment was incurred not in the military but in civilian life, largely as the result of AGING.

In 2006 the BVA had a membership totaling 11,010 members, of whom 10,500 were visually impaired while serving in the armed forces, and 510 were auxiliary members. Its membership constituted approximately 9 percent of the 120,000 blinded veterans in the United States.

See also VOCATIONAL REHABILITATION.

David A. Gerber

Further Reading:

Blinded Veterans Association Web site. URL: http:// www.bva. org. http://www.1.va.gov/VS0/index.cfm?template=viewpo int&org_ ID+32-16K.

Brown, Robert. *The Fight Goes On: Perspectives on the Blinded Veterans Experience and the Work of the Blinded Veterans Association.* Washington, D.C.: Blinded Veterans Association, 1994.

Brown, Robert, and Hope Schutte. *Our Fight: A Battle against Darkness.* Washington, D.C.: Blinded Veterans Association, 1991.

Gerber, David A. "Blind and Enlightened: The Contested Origins of the Egalitarian Politics of the Blinded Veterans Association." In *The New Disability History: American Perspectives,* edited by Paul Longmore and Lauri Umansky, 313–334. New York: New York University Press, 2001.

Board of Education v. Rowley

In 1982 the Supreme Court was charged with interpreting Public Law 94-142, enacted in 1975 and now called the INDIVIDUALS WITH DISABILITIES EDUCATION ACT, which entitled all individuals with disabilities to a "free appropriate education." This occurred in the *Board of Education of the Hendrick Hudson Central School District v. Rowley* case, which involved a young DEAF girl in Peekskill, New York, named Amy Rowley, who fared better than the average child in her mainstream classroom without the assistance of a SIGN LANGUAGE INTERPRETER. Amy's deaf parents requested a sign language interpreter for their daughter. After the school denied their request because Amy appeared to be succeeding without assistance, they sought redress in federal court. In dispute was whether Congress had provided adequate guidance for the meaning of the term "free appropriate education."

Under Public Law 94-142 states are only required to provide ACCESS to public EDUCATION programs. This means that the state satisfies its burden when students benefit, even marginally. Amy was by all accounts a well-adjusted and intelligent child. And, although it was argued that she was being denied access to key information because of her deafness, the Supreme Court ruled that the school did not have to provide a sign language interpreter for her. In a 6 to 3 decision written by Justice William Rehnquist, the Court upheld the school's position that the law did not require the provision of services to maximize each child's potential, only that they be provided with an equal educational opportunity. The Court determined that Amy's ability to succeed was not being hindered and thus she was receiving equal access to an education. The decision also cautioned that courts should avoid substituting the state's judgment with its own since courts lacked expertise in educational policy. The act placed decision-making authority on how to educate children with disabilities with the state, leaving the person with a disability without input once the requirements of the act are met.

This decision is considered a milestone in the history of disability; it unequivocally locates people with disabilities as second-class citizens in the United States. That is, the decision allows the educational institutions to abdicate their responsibility to provide people with disabilities all of the tools to become competitive members of our society. Amy's ability to succeed without access was detrimental to her parents' case against the school district, and, according to Rehnquist's interpretation, Congress did not intend for students with disabilities to excel academically. Furthermore, the mode of instruction was intended to be unilaterally determined by the educational institution, not the person with a disability.

Three outcomes proceeded from this ruling: (1) Public Law 94-142 was interpreted to mean that Congress had only intended children with disabilities to have access to educational services but made no claim as to whether the child was guaranteed to benefit from the services; (2) Schools were not obligated to maximize a student's learning potential; and (3) The Court should not substitute the opinions of educational professionals with its own. All of these outcomes began a trend that is still enforced today. The Court has continuously opted to conservatively interpret legislation intended to benefit people with disabilities; it grants decision-making authority for accommodations to people other than the person with the disability.

Since this decision, people with disabilities have fought to demonstrate they are able to manage their own lives, both inside and outside the classroom. Although the wording may differ, laws pertaining to the provision of an accommodation, regardless of setting, have yet to provide the authority to determine when and what accommodation is needed to the person with a disability.

See also LAW AND POLICY.

Jeremy L. Brunson
Holly M. Manaseri
Steven J. Taylor

Further Reading:

Board of Education of the Hendrick Hudson Central School District v. Rowley, 458 U.S. 176, 102 S. CT. 3034 (1982).

National Center for Law and Deafness. *Legal Rights: The Guide for Deaf and Hard of Hearing People.* Washington, D.C.: Gallaudet University Press, 1992.

Rothstein, Laura. *Disability Law: Cases, Materials, Problems.* 3d ed. Newark, N.J.: Mathew Bender, 2002.

Smith, R. C. *A Case about Amy.* Philadelphia: Temple University Press, 1996.

Taylor, Steve J., and Stanford J. Searl. "The Disabled in America: History, Policy, and Trends." In *Understanding Exceptional Children and Youth,* edited by P. Knoblock, 16–63. Glenview, Ill.: Scott Foresman, 1987.

———. "Disability in America: Controversy, Debate, and Backlash." In *Understanding Exceptional Children and Youth,* edited by P. Knoblock, 64–96. Glenview, Ill.: Scott Foresman, 1987.

Board of Education v. Rowley (1982)

Amy Rowley was a deaf girl who was mainstreamed at Furnace Woods School, a public school in Peekskill, New York. Rowley had relied on lipreading and was considered a strong student, but her parents, in an effort to enhance her access to learning, requested that the school provide her with a sign language interpreter. When the school refused the request, the Rowleys sued, claiming that Furnace Woods had violated the "free appropriate education" clause of the Education for All Handicapped Children Act of 1975. When the case reached the Supreme Court in 1982, the justices upheld the school's decision with a 6–3 majority, asserting that the law only required an equal educational opportunity for Rowley, which she had received. This narrow interpretation of disability rights laws has continued into the 21st century.

Board of Education v. Rowley
458 U.S. 176 (1982)
BOARD OF EDUCATION OF THE HENDRICK HUDSON CENTRAL SCHOOL DISTRICT, WESTCHESTER COUNTY, et al., v. AMY ROWLEY, by her parents, ROWLEY et al.
U.S. Supreme Court

Justice [William] Rehnquist delivered the opinion of the Court.

This case presents a question of statutory interpretation. Petitioners contend that the Court of Appeals and the District Court misconstrued the requirements imposed by the Congress upon States which receive federal funds under the Education for All Handicapped Children Act. We agree and reverse the judgment of the Court of Appeals.

. . . This case arose in connection with the education of Amy Rowley, a deaf student at the Furnace Woods School in the Hendrick Hudson Central School District, Peekskill, New York. Amy has minimal residual hearing and is an excellent lip reader. During the year before she began attending Furnace Woods, a meeting between her parents and school administrators resulted in a decision to place her in a regular kindergarten class in order to determine what supplement services would be necessary to her education. Several members of the school administration prepared for Amy's arrival by attending a course in sign-language interpretation, and a teletype machine was installed in the principal's office to facilitate communication with her parents who are also deaf.

At the end of the trial period it was determined that Amy should remain in the kindergarten class, but that she should be provided with an FM hearing aid which would amplify words spoken into a wireless receiver by the teacher or fellow students during certain classroom activities. Amy successfully completed her kindergarten year.

As required by the Act, an IEP was prepared for Amy during the fall of her first-grade year. The IEP provided that Amy should be educated in a regular classroom at Furnace Woods, should continue to use the FM hearing aid, and should receive instruction from a tutor for the deaf for one hour each day and from a speech therapist for three hours each week. The Rowleys agreed with the IEP but insisted that Amy also be provided a qualified sign-language interpreter in all of her academic classes. Such an interpreter had been placed in Amy's kindergarten class for a two-week experimental period, but the interpreter had reported that Amy did not need his services at that time. The school administrators likewise concluded that Amy did not need such an interpreter in her first-grade classroom. They reached this conclusion after consulting the school district's Committee on the Handicapped, which had received expert evidence from Amy's parents on the importance of a sign-language interpreter, received testimony from Amy's teacher and other persons familiar with her academic and social progress, and visited a class for the deaf.

When their request for an interpreter was denied, the Rowleys demanded and received a hearing before an independent examiner. After receiving evidence from both sides, the examiner agreed with the administrators' determination that an interpreter was not necessary because "Amy was achieving educationally, academically, and socially" without such assistance. *App. to Pet. for Cert. F-22.* The examiner's decision was affirmed on appeal by the New York Commissioner of Education on the basis of substantial evidence in the record. *Id.,* at E-4. Pursuant to the Act's provision for judicial review, the Rowleys then brought an action in the United States District Court for the Southern District of New York, claiming that the administrators' denial of the sign-language interpreter constituted a denial of the "free appropriate public education" guaranteed by the Act.

The District Court found that Amy "is a remarkably well adjusted child" who interacts and communicates well with her classmates and has "developed an extraordinary rapport" with her teachers. 483 F. Supp, 528, 531. It also found that "she performs better than the average child in her class and is advancing easily from grade to grade," *id.,* at 534, but "that she understands considerably less of what goes on in class than she would if she were not deaf" and thus "is not learning as much, or performing as well academically, as she would without her handicap," *id.,* at 532. This disparity between Amy's achievement and her potential led the court to decide that she was not receiving a "free appropriate public education" which the court defined as "an opportunity to achieve [her] full potential commensurate with the opportunity provided to other children." *id.,*

at 534. According to the District Court, such a standard "requires that the potential of the handicapped child be measured and compared to his or her performance, and that the remaining differential or 'shortfall' be compared to the shortfall experienced by nonhandicapped children." *Ibid.* The District Court's definition arose from its assumption that the responsibility for "giving content to the requirement of an 'appropriate education'" had 'been left entirely to the federal courts and the hearing officers.' *Id.,* at 533.8

. . . This is the first case in which this Court has been called upon to interpreter any provision of the Act.

. . . When the language of the Act and its legislative history are considered together, the requirements imposed by Congress become tolerably clear. Insofar as a State is required to provide a handicapped child with a "free appropriate public education," we hold that it satisfies these requirements by providing personalized instruction with sufficient support services to permit the child to benefit educationally from that instruction. Such instruction and services must be provided at public expense, must meet the State's educational standards, must approximate the grade levels used in the State's regular education, and must comport with the child's IEP. In addition, the IEP, and therefore the personalized instruction, should be formulated in accordance with the requirements of the Act, and if the child is being educated in the regular classrooms of the public education system, should be reasonably calculated to enable the child to achieve passing marks and advance from grade to grade.

. . . Applying these principles to the facts of this case, we conclude that the court of Appeals erred in affirming the decision of the District Court. Neither the District Court nor the Court of Appeals found that petitioners had failed to comply with the procedures of the Act, and the findings of neither court would support a conclusion that Amy's educational program failed to comply with the substantive requirements of the Act. On the contrary, the District Court found that the "evidence firmly establishes that Amy is receiving an 'adequate' education, since she performs better than the average child in her class and is advancing easily from grade to grade." 483 F Supp., at 534.

In light of this finding, and of the fact that Amy was receiving personalized instruction and related services calculated by the Furnace Woods school administrators to meet her educational needs, the lower courts should not have concluded that the Act requires the provision of a sign-language interpreter. Accordingly, the decision of the Court of appeals is reversed and the case is remanded for further proceedings consistent with this opinion.

. . . Justice [Harry] Blackmun, concurring in the judgment.
Although I reach the same result as the Court of the Education for All Handicapped Children Act differently.

. . . [T]he question is whether Amy's program, viewed as a whole, offered her an opportunity to understand and participate in the classroom that was substantially equal to that given her nonhandicapped classmates. This is a standard predicated on equal educational opportunity and equal access to the educational process, rather than upon Amy's achievement of any particular educational outcome.

. . . By concentrating on whether Amy was "learning as much, or performing as well academically, as she would without her handicap," 483 F. Supp. 528, 532 (SDNY 1980), the District Court and the Court of Appeals paid too little attention to whether, on the entire record, respondent's individualized education program offered her an educational opportunity equal to that provided her nonhandicapped classmates. Because I believe that standard has been satisfied here, I agree that the judgment of the Court of Appeals should be reversed.

Source: Board of Education of the Hendrick Hudson Central School District v. Rowley. 458 U.S. 176 (1982).

Boggs, Elizabeth (Elizabeth Monroe) (1913–1996)
parent activist

Elizabeth Monroe Boggs was a leader in the mid 20th-century movement for the rights and services of people with developmental disabilities. She is also credited with coining and popularizing the concept and term "DEVELOPMENTAL DISABILITY" in policy contexts.

Elizabeth Monroe was born on April 5, 1913, in Cleveland, Ohio. She studied chemistry at Bryn Mawr College before earning a doctorate in chemistry at Cambridge University in 1941, the same year she married another scientist, Fitzhugh Boggs. During WORLD WAR II, she worked in the federal Explosives Research Laboratory in Bruceton, Pennsylvania. Her only child, Jonathan David Boggs, was born in 1945. Soon after birth, David developed a serious infection; he survived with brain injuries that resulted in developmental disabilities. Dr. Boggs turned her research skills to learning about developmental disability and advocating for children and families who were otherwise excluded from schools and other programs. In 1950 she joined the board of directors for the newly formed National Association of Retarded Children (today THE ARC), and served as a delegate to the White House Conference on Children and Youth.

Through the 1950s and into the 1970s, Boggs was active on the state and national levels in shaping policy concerning people with developmental disabilities. In 1961 she was appointed to President John F. Kennedy's President's Panel on Mental Retardation. She was the first woman president of the National Association of Retarded Children (1956–58), president of the New Jersey Association for Retarded Children (1966–67), chair of the National Advisory Council on Services and Facilities for the Developmentally Disabled (1971–74), and chair of the New Jersey State Developmental Disabilities Council (1971–79), among many other positions. At the international level, she chaired a United Nations task force on Implementation of the Declaration of Rights of Mentally Retarded Persons (1972–78). In her 70s, she was co-chair of the Congressional Task Force on the Rights and Empowerment of Americans with Disabilities, sharing duties with JUSTIN DART JR., toward crafting the legislation that became the AMERICANS WITH DISABILITIES ACT.

Boggs's husband died in 1971 and she died on January 27, 1996, at the age of 82, from injuries sustained when she lost control of her car on an icy road. She was survived by her son David Boggs, who lived at the Hunterdon Developmental Center from 1952 until his death in 2000. There are collections of Boggs's papers in the Kennedy Presidential Library and at the Samuel Gridley Howe Library in Waltham, Massachusetts. The Elizabeth M. Boggs Center on Developmental Disabilities at the University of Medicine and Dentistry of New Jersey (UMDNJ), created by the New Jersey legislature in 1983, is part of the network of University Centers for Excellence in Developmental Disabilities, funded through the U.S. Department of Health and Human Services. Since 1996 the Elizabeth Monroe Boggs Award for Young Leadership has been given annually by the President's Committee for People with Intellectual Disabilities.

See also DEVELOPMENTAL DISABILITY; INDIVIDUALS WITH DISABILITIES EDUCATION ACT; KENNEDY, JOHN F.; MENTAL RETARDATION; PARENT ADVOCACY GROUPS.

Penny L. Richards

Further Reading:

Groce, Nora. *The U.S. Role in the International Disability Activities: A History and a Look towards the Future.* Washington, D.C.: U.S. Department of Education, 1992.

Saxon, Wolfgang. "Dr. Elizabeth Monroe Boggs, 82, Founder of Group for Retarded," *New York Times,* 30 January 1996.

Bookshare

Ever since Johannes Gutenberg invented the printing press in the 15th century and literacy replaced oral tradition, BLIND people and others unable to read printed material have dreamed of being able to pick up a book and read it in real time. Bookshare.org, a project of Benetech, located in Palo Alto, California, was created in 2002 by Jim Fruchterman in an effort to provide access to printed works for blind users. Bookshare offers electronically scanned books to subscribers via the INTERNET. Various factors, including technology, advocacy, and the goal of full ACCESS, have shaped the history of ASSISTIVE TECHNOLOGY leading to Bookshare.

Although there is evidence of attempts at speech synthesis since the 18th century, it was not until the 1920s and 1930s that the development of electrical sound-producing devices came to fruition. During this era both industrial and advocacy interests produced innovations in speech synthesis. Following the pioneering research of ALEXANDER GRAHAM BELL, BELL LABORATORIES, founded in 1925, actively pursued research in telephonic equipment and in studying the properties and analysis of human speech. At the same time, the advocacy organization AMERICAN FOUNDATION FOR THE BLIND (AFB) gained financial support from the Carnegie Foundation in 1932 to research sound recording options for blind readers. By 1934 AFB, collaborating with companies such as RCA Victor, had produced several TALKING BOOKS. In 1936 Bell Laboratories employee H. W. Dudley, developed the voice coder or "voder," the world's first electronic speech synthesizer. It required an operator with a keyboard and foot pedals to supply "prosody"—the pitch, timing, and intensity of speech that gives it the intonation that makes it understandable. Many modern electronic synthesizers use the basic design pattern of the voder. Over the next few decades formats for Talking Books changed from LP records to more portable versions of magnetic and cassette tapes.

The technology upon which Bookshare is specifically based, synthetic speech and OPTICAL CHARACTER RECOGNITION (OCR), began to mature in the 1970s. For example, in 1975, in partnership with the advocacy group NATIONAL FEDERATION OF THE BLIND, RAYMOND KURZWEIL developed a synthetic speech reading machine. He drew on the knowledge of blind readers, his expertise in artificial intelligence, and a speech synthesizer operating on previously established principles to develop his device.

By 1985 synthetic speech had evolved to the point where it was produced by automatic text-speech conversion. Four years later, Jim Fruchterman, an engineer dedicated to using technology to solve social problems, founded Arkenstone, which produced the effective and popular OpenBook OCR product. Arkenstone's business model, a not-for-profit embedded in a for-profit company, enabled it to develop the first affordable OCR system, which allowed everyday users to scan printed material from a device connected to their personal computers and listen to this material through increasingly improving speech synthesizers installed in their computers. While Kurzweil's original reading machine cost more than $50,000, Arkenstone's product and a parallel version offered by Kurzweil cost one-tenth as much. Through the 1990s, scanning technology and OCR software improved so much that, by the 21st century, blind people were scanning books for private use at an exponentially increasing rate.

In 2000, after selling Arkenstone, Fruchterman formed Benetech ("good technology") to further his mission of developing technologies to solve social problems. Realizing that his Arkenstone OCR devices had created an as-yet uncollected library of scanned books stored in the computers of thousands of blind people, by modifying the model developed by file sharing service Napster for electronic storage and dissemination of music he created the innovative Bookshare project.

Since 2000 advancements in personal computer processors and software programs, coupled with the rise of Internet technology, have enabled the Bookshare concept to flourish. Bookshare asks blind people to send books they have scanned to its Palo Alto headquarters. Fruchterman's staff proofread the contributions to eliminate scanning errors and make them available via the Internet for download to other users who wish to "borrow" them from the Bookshare library. Bookshare staff also scan books to increase the library collection, enabling Bookshare to serve people more quickly, produce more works that are accessible and in a variety of electronic formats, and keep up with the rapidly changing world of printed books.

Bookshare.org currently has over 34,800 books and 150 periodicals in its library, ready for download by subscribers. Through the powerful combination of advocacy, technology, and literacy provided by Bookshare, blind and other print-disabled people have gained full access to tens of thousands of books and literary items.

Anthony C. Candela

Further Reading:

Charlson, Kim. "Visionary Ideas." *Kirkus Reviews* 75, no. 2 (January 2007): 12–13.

"History of Speech Synthesis." Helsinki University. Available online. URL: http://www.acoustics.hut.fi/~slemmett/dippa/chap2.html. Accessed November 11, 2007.

Kornblum, Janet. "*Bookshare*.org Opens Up Choices for Disabled Readers," *USA Today,* 21 February 2002.

Reid, Calvin. "*Bookshare*.org Offers Titles for Blind Readers," *Publishers Weekly,* 11 March 2002, p. 16.

Taylor, John M. "Serving Blind Readers in a Digital Age." *American Libraries* 35, no. 11 (December 2004): 49–51.

Boone, John William ("Blind Boone") (1864–1927) *musician*

Pianist and composer John "Blind" Boone performed thousands of concerts throughout the United States in the late 19th and early 20th centuries. His life story highlights important themes in disability history, including RACE, EMPLOYMENT, and artistic expression.

John William Boone was the son of Rachel Boone, who lived in SLAVERY until the CIVIL WAR. Rachel Boone was working as a cook for Union troops in 1864 when she gave birth to her son at Miami, Missouri. Surviving documents offer conflicting and vague details about his birth, but likely it was on May 17. The baby's father was said to be the camp's bugler. At six months, Boone fell seriously ill. As part of the treatment, his eyes were removed, possibly to relieve pressure on his brain, or because they were scarred or infected. Boone's mother worked as a domestic servant in Warrensburg, Missouri, and brought along "Willy" at times. In the homes of Rachel Boone's employers, young Boone first heard piano MUSIC. At age five, he was given a tin whistle, which he played for passersby in a group of boys on horns, harmonicas, and drums.

When he turned nine, Boone was sent to the Missouri Institution for the Education of the Blind in St. Louis, his expenses paid by the citizens of Warrensburg and Johnson County. Young Boone did not perform well in academic classes at the St. Louis school; instead, he was encouraged to learn the trade of broom-making. He was not admitted to music classes, despite his strong interest and previous experience with music. He found a fellow student to teach him the basics of piano anyway, and, in a year, he was playing well enough to be invited to entertain in homes and churches. At the Missouri institution, he played for visiting dignitaries, but he also left campus without permission to hear live music in a rougher part of town. For his repeated infractions, he was expelled. "They wouldn't let me play the piano all the time—they made me make brooms—so I ran off," he explained years later in a 1921 interview. After a short stint touring with exploitative promoters, the boy was returned to Warrensburg, where he worked for the town school. He headed out again, but this time as part of a trio that toured the Southwest successfully. At 14, he was solo again, playing at church services and teaching music.

In 1880 Boone was set to play a concert with the older African-American blind pianist, "BLIND TOM" BETHUNE, at the Garth Hall in Columbia, Missouri. Newspapers concocted a rivalry between the men, but the main result of the concert was to bring Boone to the attention of promoter John Lange Jr., who paid Boone's mother $10 a month for the opportunity to represent her son while he was still young. The Blind Boone Concert Company was formed, with the motto, "Merit, not Sympathy, Wins." This traveling company included several musical performers at any given time, and they appeared on a bill with Blind Boone starring. A young woman singer usually performed with them. The other musicians were always African-American, as was Boone's business partner, John Lange. As an all-black touring company, they often stayed in private homes, because few southern hotels would admit them. Through Lange's contacts, Boone got further training at various colleges, and his repertoire grew. Boone is said to have played over 10,000 concerts in his professional career, spanning 47 years, and covering all of North America. He played classical music by Beethoven, Liszt, and Chopin, church hymns, popular songs, and ragtime compositions. One famous original piece by Boone, "The Marshfield Tornado," re-created the sounds of a tornado hitting Marshfield, Missouri, in 1880, including fire bells, chimes, a church service, thunder, and dripping water.

In 1889 Boone married Lange's younger sister Eugenia. Boone made recordings in the form of piano rolls beginning in 1912, which have since been transcribed. His mother died in 1901, and his manager Lange died in 1916, both severe blows to Boone. He played his last concert in May 1927 and died a few months later, on October 4, from a heart attack. His burial in Columbia, Missouri, was a major public event, but the grave was left unmarked until 1971.

Today there is a Blind Boone Park in Warrensburg, complete with a life-sized statue of Boone playing a floating keyboard. There's a Blind Boone Ragtime and Early Jazz Festival celebrated in Columbia, Missouri, and an annual Blind Boone Music and Arts Festival in Warrensburg. His home in Columbia is on the National Register of Historic Places, and the John William Boone Heritage Foundation has been working to restore it. In addition, there is a Blind Boone Community Center in Columbia. A collection of memorabilia associated with Boone's career is in the Western Historical Manuscript Collection. Music written by Boone is available on CD.

Penny L. Richards

Further Reading:

Batterson, Jack A. *Blind Boone: Missouri's Ragtime Pioneer.* Columbia: University of Missouri Press, 1998.

Fuell-Cuther, Melissa. *Blind Boone: His Early Life and His Achievements.* Nappanee, Ind.: Evangel Publishing, 1918.

Sears, Ann. "John William 'Blind' Boone, Pianist-Composer: Merit, Not Sympathy, Wins." *Black Music Research Journal* 9, no. 2 (1989): 225–247.

Swindell, Warren C. "William 'Blind' Boone's Chicago Itinerary." *Black Music Research Journal* 12, no. 1 (Spring 1992): 113–125.

Booth, Edmund (1810–1905) *newspaper editor, Deaf community leader*

A writer, newspaper editor, and leader in the American DEAF COMMUNITY, Edmund Booth was a pioneer and Renaissance man.

Booth was born on a farm in Chicopee, Massachusetts, on August 24, 1810. In 1815 he contracted meningitis and became profoundly deaf in his left ear, partially deaf in his right ear, and totally BLIND in his left eye. His father died at this time of the same illness. Booth lost the remaining hearing in his right ear two years later. He attended the first permanent school for the deaf in the United States, the AMERICAN SCHOOL FOR THE DEAF in West Hartford, Connecticut, and studied under LAURENT CLERC, the first deaf teacher in the country. Graduating in 1830, Booth was soon appointed to a full-time teaching position at the school.

In 1839 Booth left Connecticut for Iowa, where one of his former students, Mary Ann Walworth, then lived with her FAMILY. There, he experienced a decade of frontier life, working at mills and building dams. After marrying Walworth, he was elected county recorder, and three years later he was made enrollment clerk to the Iowa House of Representatives. Booth's adventurous spirit and his dislike for farming led him to join the California gold rush in 1849. Leaving his wife and two children with relatives, he traveled with a deaf friend for six months in wagons to the West Coast. For five years Booth mined for gold near Sonora, sending home enough money for Mary Ann to purchase a five-acre tract of land for a home. Unfortunately for the family, his earnings from the gold ran out quickly after he returned to Iowa in 1854.

The next several decades mark a time of social commentary and political ACTIVISM for Edmund Booth. His career as a writer and newspaper editor for the *Anamosa Eureka* began in 1856. Within a few years he asked his son Thomas to jointly manage this prosperous weekly with him. In the late 1850s Booth participated in a significant debate then raging in the deaf cultural COMMUNITY. He opposed deaf activist JOHN J. FLOURNOY's proposal to establish a Deaf commonwealth, a colony in the West where hearing people could not take a leadership role. Booth challenged this deaf "utopia," arguing that it was unconstitutional as well as economically impossible. Booth took strong positions on national mainstream conflicts as well. When the CIVIL WAR began in 1861,

his abolitionist writings frequently angered readers who supported SLAVERY and state's rights.

After the war, Booth again turned to issues affecting deaf people in America. In 1880 he became a founding member of the NATIONAL ASSOCIATION OF THE DEAF (NAD), whose purpose was to represent the national deaf community in addressing economic, political, and social discrimination. Booth's son, Frank, a close associate of ALEXANDER GRAHAM BELL, became a strong advocate of ORALISM in the EDUCATION of deaf children, but Booth and his wife never substantially joined in that controversy.

All his life, Booth maintained connections with other deaf people, earning the Deaf cultural community's respect as a statesman. At the same time, he moved comfortably in, and made a lasting mark on, mainstream society in Iowa. Booth retired as editor of the *Anamosa Eureka* in 1895. He died on March 24, 1905, in Anamosa. All of the businesses and the district court there closed for his funeral.

Edmund Booth's life highlights how an educated deaf person can be a leader in the Deaf community as well as in hearing society. His story also reveals how deaf people participated fully in major historical events such as westward expansion, the Gold Rush, and the Civil War.

Harry G. Lang

Further Reading:

Lang, Harry G. *Edmund Booth, Deaf Pioneer.* Washington, D.C.: Gallaudet University Press, 2004.

Lang, Harry G., and Bonnie Meath-Lang, eds. "Edmund Booth (1810–1905) American Editor/Writer." In *Deaf Persons in the Arts and Sciences: A Biographical Dictionary.* Westport, Conn.: Greenwood Press, 1995.

Born on the Fourth of July

Based on the searing 1976 autobiography of disabled Vietnam VETERAN Ron Kovic, the movie *Born on the Fourth of July* (1989) might well be understood as a movie with two lives. Originally slated for production in 1978 with William Friedkin as director, *Born on the Fourth of July* was less than a week away from the start of filming when its funding collapsed. Its neophyte screenwriter, a Vietnam veteran named Oliver Stone, vowed to Kovic that he would revive the project if he ever achieved success as a Hollywood director. Though the process took several years, Stone made good on his promise after breaking through with *Platoon* in 1986 and *Wall Street* in 1987. Working closely with Kovic on a revised screenplay, Stone coproduced the FILM, directed it himself, and oversaw its release in 1989.

Born on the Fourth of July tells the story of Kovic (Tom Cruise), a young patriotic Long Islander who, steeped in the tradition of John Wayne and Audie Murphy WAR movies of the 1940s and 1950s, eagerly joins the marines and goes

Holding an upside-down flag in protest, disabled veteran Ron Kovic attends an antiwar march in 1972. Four years later, he wrote *Born on the Fourth of July*, a searing portrait of his wartime experiences. *(AP Images)*

off to fight in the VIETNAM WAR. A bullet shatters his spine at the T6 level, leaving him paralyzed from the mid-chest down. The film follows Kovic as he gradually undergoes a transformation from staunch WAR supporter to passionate antiwar activist. Along the way, *Born on the Fourth of July* explores such issues as the horrific conditions of Veterans Administration HOSPITALS and the psychological and sexual readjustments faced by newly disabled men.

The film suggests that Kovic's disability has left him symbolically disempowered, that he lost his manhood in Vietnam while ironically attempting to prove it. In keeping with earlier movies representing the disabled Vietnam veteran experience, most notably COMING HOME (1978) and *Cutter's Way* (1981), *Born on the Fourth of July* shows its central character reclaiming his manhood by engaging in a heroic activity. After he and other antiwar activists have been forcibly ejected from the 1972 Republican National Convention, for instance, Kovic takes charge by telling his fellow protestors that "we're gonna take the hall back" and he then leads them against the convention security guards and the police.

If Kovic as co-screenwriter was aware of such a symbolic dimension to his on-screen persona, he has given no indication of this in interviews. "I was able to see my story come out the way I wanted to see it and the way I felt it should come out," he said simply in an *American Film* article. Though some viewers may take issue with such touches and with the liberties the film takes with history (Abbie Hoffman did not speak at a Syracuse antiwar rally attended by Kovic, for example, nor did police brutally break it up), *Born on the Fourth of July* is noteworthy as a relatively rare Hollywood film co-created by a disabled person.

See also MEMOIR; POPULAR CULTURE.

Martin F. Norden

Further Reading:

Burgoyne, Robert. *Film Nation: Hollywood Looks at U.S. History.* Minneapolis: University of Minnesota Press, 1997.

Norden, Martin F. "Bitterness, Rage, and Redemption: Hollywood Constructs the Disabled Vietnam Veteran." In *Disabled Veterans in History,* edited by David Gerber, 96–116. Ann Arbor: University of Michigan Press, 2000.

———. *The Cinema of Isolation: A History of Physical Disability in the Movies.* New Brunswick, N.J.: Rutgers University Press, 1994.

Seidenberg, Robert. "To Hell and Back." *American Film* (January 1990): 28–31, 56.

Boswell, Connie (1907–1976) *popular singer*

One of the foremost stars of the 1930s and 1940s, Connee Boswell (she later changed her first name to Connie) was one of the first female popular singers, in the modern sense of the term. She was a major influence on other singers and musicians, including Ella Fitzgerald, Bing Crosby, the Dorsey brothers, and Glenn Miller.

Born in Kansas City, Missouri, on December 3, 1907, but raised from early childhood in New Orleans, Connie contracted poliomyelitis (POLIO) at the age of three and lost most of her MOBILITY in her legs. Her mother did not trust conventional treatments to bring about the best outcome for her daughter; instead, she devised her own regime of vigorous physical therapy, and insisted that Connie be treated no differently from her sisters Martha (1905–58) and Vet (1911–88). All three girls were musical; they sang and played together as a trio called the Boswell Sisters. In 1925 they cut their first record in New Orleans, and they enjoyed a brief spell on vaudeville circuits in the Midwest. Because they could not initially afford a WHEELCHAIR, Martha and Vet carried Connie everywhere in a "fireman's lift" grip. They moved to California in 1929, where they found work on radio and in the infant talking pictures industry.

In late 1930 they "broke" on national radio, and they moved to New York on a contract with NBC. Very soon afterward, both the Boswell Sisters as a trio, and Connie as a soloist, signed with Brunswick Records. For five years they were a compelling force in American entertainment, as stars of stage, screen, radio, and recordings. The sisters continued singing together until 1936, when Martha and Vet stopped performing in order to concentrate on marriage and family. Connie was also wed in 1936 to her manager, Harry Leedy, but when her sisters retired she opted to continue her singing career.

The years between 1936 and America's entry into WORLD WAR II in 1941 were probably her most successful, with No. 1 hits with both the Boswell Sisters ("The Object of My Affection") and Bing Crosby ("Alexander's Ragtime Band"), and almost continual exposure on the radio and in film. In 1938 she headlined with Crosby for the launch of the MARCH OF DIMES Appeal, and she continued to host the annual radio extravaganza for the next five years.

World War II had a significant impact on her career, as she was not allowed to take part in Veterans Service Organizations tours due to her need for a wheelchair; moreover, her recording schedule was curtailed by the 1942 ban on making records (shellac was needed for the WAR effort) and the subsequent Musicians' Union strike. She moved into cabaret, and, in the late 1940s and 1950s, she was one of the first artists to appear in new Las Vegas venues. Her last major engagement was on TELEVISION, in the 1959 NBC serialization of Jack Webb's *Pete Kelly's Blues,* starring as the club singer Savannah Brown. She died in New York on October 11, 1976, of CANCER.

Connie Boswell made no secret of her disability although, except for a brief period just after the Boswell Sisters split, she made an effort to conceal it on stage. Initially, this was because she wanted to be sure that her success was not founded on sympathy, but she came to believe her wheelchair presented too much of a challenge to her audience. Occasionally, her disability would form the basis of a headline, as in 1938, when *Down Beat* ran a story titled, "Boswell Would Refuse Cure for Paralyzed Legs to Help Economic Cripples!" and in 1951, she was heralded by the *Boston Sunday Post* as "The

Nation's Most Successful Cripple," in an article that described both her stage wardrobe and her wheelchairs in detail. By this time, she had perfected her live act, using a tall chair that was set on ball bearings and covered with a taffeta skirt, over which she would wear layers of ballgowns that could be stripped away easily in the wings for quick costume changes. Her piano was mounted on a platform so that she did not have to negotiate a piano stool; and, although she could not propel the chair across the stage herself, she would engage an emcee who would lead her by the hand with just enough pressure to set the chair in motion.

White, female, and disabled, Boswell was nonetheless a giant of jazz and pop MUSIC. Despite her contributions to the popular style, her work slipped into obscurity with the advent of rock and roll. However, on the 30th anniversary of her death in October 2006, she was honored in New Orleans with a full jazz "funeral" and second line procession.

Laurie Stras

Further Reading:

Friedwald, Will. *Jazz Singing: America's Great Voices from Bessie Smith to Bebop and Beyond.* 3d ed. New York: Da Capo Press, 1996.

Stras, Laurie. "White Face, Black Voice: Race, Gender and Region in the Music of the Boswell Sisters." *Journal of the Society for American Music* 1, no. 2 (2007): 207–255.

Sudhalter, Richard M. *Lost Chords: White Musicians and Their Contribution to Jazz, 1915–1945.* New York and Oxford: Oxford University Press, 1999.

Bourne, Randolph (1886–1918) *author and reformer*

During the 1910s Randolph Bourne was an influential spokesman for a younger generation of American intellectuals and reformers. His essays in leading journals of thought, politics, and culture such as the *Atlantic Monthly* and the *New Republic* tackled every contemporary concern. Rejecting the genteel tradition, he called for a literature grounded in American experience, psychologically and sociologically realistic. He advocated for progressive reform of public schools, favoring education geared to life. He supported feminism to free women from economic dependency on men but criticized separatist feminists. He fiercely and bravely condemned U.S. involvement in WORLD WAR I, seeing it as an outgrowth of the inevitable militaristic propensities of the modern industrial state. Predicting that wartime repression would kill social reform, he was one of the few Anglo-American intellectuals to dissent from the WAR. His essays on the assimilation of immigrants rejected the idea of the "melting pot," envisioning instead a "trans-national America" that would embrace ethnocultural diversity.

Progressive reformer and prolific author Randolph Bourne (1886–1918) discussed in various essays the discrimination he faced as a person with visible disabilities. This photo portrait of Bourne only hints at the facial disfigurement, curved spine, and short stature that were mocked by those challenged by his ideas and his presence. *(Randolph Bourne Papers, Rare Book and Manuscript Library, Columbia University)*

Bourne had a highly visible disability. His birth in Bloomfield, New Jersey, on May 30, 1886, was difficult, and forceps delivery left his face, mouth, and ear twisted. Spinal TUBERCULOSIS at age four stunted his growth and severely curved his spine. In adulthood, he was just under five feet tall. His labored breathing made it difficult for him to project his voice in large rooms. Still, "he talked with a slow relentless flow of words," said a friend, and he had boundless energy.

But the greatest impact on him of his "situation," as he called it, was the prejudice he frequently met. Poet Amy Lowell, who bitterly opposed his radicalism, scornfully said, "His writing shows he is a cripple. Deformed body, deformed mind." Novelist Theodore Dreiser, who admired Bourne's work, called him "as frightening a dwarf as I had ever seen." During the six years after he graduated high school in 1903, employers repeatedly turned him away because of his appearance. He finally secured low-wage work perforating player piano rolls and giving piano lessons. In 1909, at age 23, he won a scholarship to Columbia University but remained forever fearful that disability-based discrimination would again shut him out of productive paid work.

In his well-known essay "The Handicapped" (1911), revised as "A Philosophy of Handicap" in his collection *Youth and Life* (1913), Bourne explained the "handicapped man's" "situation": the endless demoralizing struggle to counter the prejudicial ideology of "handicap" and combat discrimination. Yet he also said that the experience of disability bias led him to inquire into the causes of other forms of social INJUSTICE by delving into the writings of radical social philosophers such as Henry George. From those readings and his own experience of disability-based prejudice and discrimination, he developed his radical perspective on society, culture, and politics. Historians have often misinterpreted the place of "handicap" in Bourne's thought, misreading this seminal essay as expressing his efforts to OVERCOME personal adversity. Part of the misunderstanding stems from contradictions in Bourne's own thinking. The first part of the essay analyzes the "handicapped man's" dilemma from a sociological and social psychological perspective and takes a radically militant stance toward the world. But the second part adopts an individualistic approach to resolving that situation. These contradictions reflected not only the incomplete nature of Bourne's analysis but also the difficulty of achieving a critical understanding of the ideology of "handicap" fashioned in that era. That framing, which rationalized the cultural devaluation of "HANDICAPPED" people and institutionalized discrimination against them, shaped not only Bourne's life but also the lives of people with disabilities for generations after.

On December 22, 1918, amidst the worldwide pandemic that was partly generated by the war he so forcefully opposed, Bourne died from Spanish influenza.

See also DEFORMITY; DISCRIMINATION; IDENTITY; STIGMA.

Paul K. Longmore

Further Reading:

Bender, Thomas. *New York Intellect: A History of Intellectual Life in New York City, from 1750 to the Beginnings of Our Own Time*. Baltimore: Johns Hopkins University Press, 1988.

Blake, Casey Nelson. *Beloved Community: The Cultural Criticism of Randolph Bourne, Van Wyck Brooks, Waldo Frank and Lewis Mumford*. Chapel Hill: University of North Carolina Press, 1990.

Lasch, Christopher. "Randolph Bourne and the Experimental Life." In *The New Radicalism in America, 1889–1963: The Intellectual as a Social Type*. New York: W.W. Norton, 1986.

Longmore, Paul. "The Life of Randolph Bourne and the Need for a History of Disabled People." In *Why I Burned My Book and Other Essays on Disability*. Philadelphia: Temple University Press, 2003.

Randolph Bourne's America. URL: http://www.randolphbourne.columbia.edu/.

Bove, Linda (1945–) *deaf actress*

Actress Linda Bove has been credited with widening career opportunities for DEAF people. She also has used her acting roles to expose others to AMERICAN SIGN LANGUAGE and served as a role model for deaf and disabled CHILDREN.

Bove was born on November 30, 1945, in Passaic, New Jersey, to Italian-American deaf parents. Several members of her extended FAMILY were also deaf. Raised among many other deaf people, Bove grew up using sign language as her primary means of communication. As a child, she attended two oral schools: St. Joseph's School for the Deaf in New York City and Marie Katzenbach School for the Deaf in West Trenton, New Jersey. After graduating high school in 1963, she entered Gallaudet College (later renamed GALLAUDET UNIVERSITY) as a preparatory student.

Bove performed in her first play as a Junior at Gallaudet College in 1967. The following summer she attended a summer DRAMA program offered by the NATIONAL THEATRE OF THE DEAF (NTD), a professional troupe that included deaf and hearing performers. After graduation Bove joined NTD, performing with them for nine years. In 1968 she founded the Little Theatre of the Deaf, along with other members of NTD. This theater troupe specialized in performances for deaf children. In the early 1970s she began working on TELEVISION shows. Her most famous role was Linda the Librarian on the children's show *Sesame Street*. For 32 years Bove was a guest and regular character on the series, modeling sign language. Her deafness and use of signs reflected the inclusive message projected in *Sesame Street* and generations of children learned rudimentary signs from the show. The popularity of her character also reflected and fueled the growing recognition of American Sign Language.

By meeting with producers and directors Bove expanded EMPLOYMENT opportunities for other deaf people and herself. By placing Bove in different performing roles, producers and directors came to recognize the capabilities of deaf performers, influencing them to cast other deaf performers in their productions. She also joined the Committee of Performers with Disabilities to encourage the casting of people with disabilities as disabled characters. In 1988 Bove worked with deaf art students at California State University at Northridge teaching them about the acting profession and the television industry. During this time of expanding opportunities and deaf pride in deaf culture, Bove served as a role model for aspiring performers.

In 1991 Bove and her husband of 30 years, deaf ACTOR ED WATERSTREET, established a deaf performance troupe in Los Angeles called Deaf West. This performance group created opportunities for deaf people to enjoy performances in their primary language, ASL. In recent years, Bove primarily has performed in live theater and created her own plays. Reflecting her earlier work on *Sesame Street,* Bove regularly performs shows for children.

Linda Bove, like AUDREY NORTON, PHYLLIS FRELICH, and MARLEE MATLIN, represents one among an important corps of deaf actresses who have shaped the ways Americans view deafness and sign language. Her successful work on television and stage highlights deaf peoples' abilities, as well as society's increasing awareness of deaf culture. Bove continues to live and work in Los Angeles, California.

Elizabeth Bush

Further Reading:

"Bove, Linda." Biographical File. Washington, D.C.: Gallaudet University Archives.

Phillips, Elizabeth. *Women and Girls with Disabilities: An Introductory Teaching Packet.* New York: Organization for Equal Education for the Sexes, 1986.

Sartwell, Maria, and Robert Ruffner, eds. *Profiles in the Arts.* Washington, D.C.: U.S. Government Printing Office, 1986.

Bowe, Frank (1947–2007) *disability rights advocate, author, and teacher*

A prolific author, scholar, and activist, Frank G. Bowe played a crucial role in the implementation of both SECTION 504 of the Rehabilitation Act of 1973 (see VOCATIONAL REHABILITATION ACT), the world's first civil-rights legislation for people with disabilities, and the AMERICANS WITH DISABILITIES ACT of 1990. He was also the main architect of the TELEVISION DECODER CIRCUITRY ACT of 1990, which was extended by the Telecommunications Act of 1996. A longtime professor at Hofstra University, he wrote more than 25 books, including *Handicapping America* (1978), the first comprehensive report on social policy and disability.

Born on March 29, 1947, in Milton, Pennsylvania, Bowe grew up in nearby Lewisburg, Pennsylvania. His father was a steel mill manager, and his mother worked as a reporter during WORLD WAR II. After three encounters with measles by the age of three, he was totally DEAF in his left ear and severely deaf in his right ear. Upon his parents' insistence, he attended public schools, struggling with vocabulary and enduring the prejudices of his classmates. After much perseverance, he made it into a college preparatory academic program, graduated 17th in a class of 188, and he became an accomplished writer.

At Western Maryland College (now McDaniel College), Bowe majored in English and philosophy and graduated summa cum laude the first deaf graduate to do so in 1969. He received a master's degree in special education from Gallaudet College (later renamed GALLAUDET UNIVERSITY) in 1971 and a doctorate in educational psychology from New York University in 1976.

In 1976 Bowe became the first executive director of the AMERICAN COALITION OF CITIZENS WITH DISABILITIES, the first national cross-disability advocacy ORGANIZATION. On April 5, 1977, he directed the largest PROTEST by disabled people in American history, a nationwide SIT-IN PROTEST AT THE HEALTH, EDUCATION, AND WELFARE DEPARTMENT in Washington, D.C., and its 10 regional offices. Although legislation had been passed in 1973 prohibiting discrimination, there had been little enforcement. The protest led to the landmark 1977 regulations for Section 504 of the Rehabilitation Act of 1973, PL 93-112, banning discrimination on the basis of handicap and requiring equal ACCESS for people with disabilities at federally funded facilities and programs.

In 1981 Bowe served as the U.S. representative to the United Nations Planning Committee for the Year of Disabled Persons, the first-ever representative with a disability. Subsequently, he was invited to Israel, Japan, and other countries to make recommendations regarding accommodations for people with disabilities. As president of his own company, FBA, Inc. from 1981 to 1984, he was a consultant on disability issues to Bell Atlantic, IBM, Xerox, NYNEX, and other large corporations.

At the U.S. Architectural and Transportation Barriers Compliance Board from 1984 to 1987, Bowe administered research contracts for the design of accessible telecommunications systems. From 1984 to 1986, he chaired the U.S. Congress Commission on Education of the Deaf whose final report containing 52 recommendations for education and rehabilitation appeared in 1988, just prior to and giving impetus to the DEAF PRESIDENT NOW! movement at Gallaudet University. Due to Bowe's input, the monumental Americans with Disabilities Act was drawn up and signed into law in 1990. In the same year, Bowe drafted the Television Decoder Circuitry Act of 1990, which mandated that most TELEVISIONS display closed captions (see CLOSED CAPTIONING), and also had a hand in the TELECOMMUNICATIONS ACT OF 1996, which required that broadcast and cable programs be captioned. In addition, for several years Bowe served as a regional commissioner in the Rehabilitation Services Administration, U.S. Department of Education, supervising six state VOCATIONAL REHABILITATION agencies, rehabilitation centers, training programs, and independent living centers.

Bowe was the author of more than 25 books on disability rights, SPECIAL EDUCATION, EMPLOYMENT issues, and technology, including *Rehabilitating America* (1980), *Personal Computers and Special Needs* (1984), and *Making Inclusion Work* (2005). In "Two-Way Technologies: A History of the Struggle to Communicate," a 2005 paper distributed by Representative Fred Upon (R.-Mich.), chair of the U.S. House of Representatives Subcommittee on Telecommunications and the Internet, Energy and Commerce Committee, Bowe discussed communications issues, especially how public policy has preceded and succeeded technology. In another policy paper, "Disability in America 2006," Bowe provided recommendations concerning HEALTH CARE, employment, and entitlements.

The recipient of many honors and awards, Bowe received an honorary doctor of laws (L.L.D) from Gallaudet University in 1981. In 1982 he was selected as one of the Ten Outstanding Young Americans by the U.S. Jaycees. In 1992 he was awarded the Distinguished Service Award by President George H. W. Bush for his life achievements. In 1994 he was inducted into the National Hall of Fame for People with Disabilities. At Hofstra University, where he was involved in training more than 2,000 special education teachers, Bowe was named "Distinguished Teacher of the Year" in 1996.

Frank G. Bowe died on August 21, 2007. Arguably the "Father of Section 504," Bowe was a champion of disability rights, fighting for equal access, educational accommodations, and employment opportunities.

See also ACTIVISM AND ADVOCACY; EMPOWERMENT; LAW AND POLICY.

Cynthia Pettie

Further Reading:
Bowe, Frank G. *Changing the Rules.* Silver Spring, Md.: T.J. Publishers, 1986.
"Dr. Frank Bowe." *Potomac Deaf Times,* 26 August 2007.
Moore, Matthew S., and Robert F. Panara. *Great Deaf Americans.* 2d ed. Rochester, N.Y.: Deaf Life Press, 1996.

Bowen, Eli (1842–1924) *performer*

Although Eli Bowen worked as an exhibit performer in museums, sideshows, and traveling circuses for more than five decades, relatively little is known about his life.

Bowen was born in Richland County, Ohio, on October 14, 1842. One of eight CHILDREN born to Robert and Sarah Bowen, Eli Bowen had phocomelia, a rare congenital condition in which his feet were attached to nearly absent legs, making him appear "legless." The young child learned to move about by walking on his hands, ultimately employing wooden blocks held in his hands to elevate his body. It is likely that Bowen helped out on the FAMILY farm and by early adulthood he had developed exceptional upper-body strength.

Although it is often reported that Bowen began working at Major Brown's Coliseum at the age of 13, census records show that he lived with his parents and attended school in 1860. It was most likely his father's death in 1865 that prompted his entry into the museum and carnival business. Beginning with the 1870 census, Bowen listed his profession as "showman." Bowen used his strength to develop an acrobatics and tumbling routine, enhancing his exhibit.

As with many "freaks" who worked the museum and carnival circuits in the 19th century, inflated titles, such as "Captain Eli Bowen" and "Master Eli Bowen," were used to market Bowen as a dignified yet amusing attraction. In his numerous *carte de visites,* or visiting cards that he handed out,

Bowen is dressed in suits, frequently with a sash to make him appear regal. Bowen was also known as "The Handsomest Man in Showbiz," "The Wondrous Man with Feet and No Legs," and "The Legless Acrobat." Bowen worked in most of the major museums and traveling shows of the day, including P. T. Barnum's circus. In the late 1890s Bowen allegedly teamed up with Charles Tripp (the "armless wonder") for a popular tandem bicycle act in which Tripp would pedal and Bowen would steer.

Bowen married Martha Haines (also known as Mattie Haight) in 1872 and the couple had four sons. His wife and children were frequently featured with him in visiting cards produced and sold for profit. In part, the curiosity of Bowen was the fact that he married a "NORMAL" wife and had four "normal" children. This fact was repeatedly used in printed

Known commonly as "The Legless Acrobat," Eli Bowen (1842–1924) was exhibited in sideshows, museums, and P. T. Barnum's shows during the 19th and early 20th centuries. He is shown in a family portrait with his wife and four sons. *(USU Merrill-Cazier Library, Special Collections & Archives)*

publicity materials as well, such as the pamphlet called "The Wonder of the Wide, Wide World: The True History of Mr. Eli Bowen" published in 1880. In the context of a society increasingly attracted to EUGENICS, a pseudoscience that categorized people by their genetic "worth," Americans expressed deep concerns about the intimate relationships and childbearing of people with disabilities. It appears that Bowen and his handlers were quick to capitalize on these anxieties but also potentially buffered direct intervention of the family by displaying them as freaks.

Bowen continued to work in the industry right up to his death. By most accounts Bowen was financially successful enough to retire and so it appears he voluntarily remained in his profession. Bowen died of pleurisy on May 4, 1924, while working for Dreamland Circus Sideshow in Coney Island, New York. He is buried in Lowell Lake County, Indiana.

See also FREAKERY; REPRESENTATION; SEXUALITY.

Sarah Smith

Further Reading:

Bogdan, Robert. *Freak Show: Presenting Human Oddities for Amusement and Profit.* Chicago: University of Chicago Press, 1988.

Mannix, Daniel P. *Freaks: We Who Are Not as Others.* New York: RE/Search Publications, 1976, 1999.

Boy in the Bubble   See VETTER, DAVID.

Brace, Julia (1807–1884) *deaf-blind woman*

Julia Brace was the first disabled American woman to be portrayed in popular juvenile LITERATURE and achieve celebrity status. New England educators and humanitarians in the 19th century used Brace's story to promote educational opportunities for people with disabilities. Her life experiences provided a seminal model for chronicling how individuals with disabilities adapted to new circumstances and learned new tasks.

Brace, the daughter of a poor cobbler living in Hartford County, Connecticut, was born on June 13, 1807. She was five years old when she contracted typhus fever, causing total sight and hearing loss. Prior to her illness, Brace contributed to the family economy by caring for younger siblings and helping in the family business. After her illness, Brace's inability to communicate verbally created problems within her FAMILY. With assistance from a local benevolent society, Brace was sent to a small school operated by Lydia H. Sigourney during her teen years. She was taught to sew and knit, but Sigourney was unable to teach Brace any sign language beyond simple home signs to communicate instructions, approval, and discipline. Away from fam-

ily, her frustration grew when she could not keep up with other students. In 1825, at the age of 18 years, she was admitted to the American Asylum at Hartford for the Education and Instruction of the Deaf and Dumb, the first RESIDENTIAL SCHOOL for the DEAF in America, now the AMERICAN SCHOOL FOR THE DEAF. Brace made limited progress at the school, in part because of her limited language skills. She learned how to manipulate wooden letters and pins on a cushion to form letters for object lessons, and mastered communicating with sign language used in the deaf community. Being the only DEAF-BLIND student in a COMMUNITY of deaf individuals, Brace drew attention to the institution and the need to fund such schools. Administrators at the institution allowed visitors to observe her practicing domestic skills such as needlework and sewing, an activity that would draw crowds to visit subsequent deaf-blind women like LAURA BRIDGMAN and HELEN KELLER at the PERKINS SCHOOL.

In 1828 Sigourney, Brace's former teacher, wrote an account of the deaf-blind woman's early life called, "The Deaf, Dumb and Blind Girl" for *Juvenile Miscellany* (May 1828), which was reprinted in *Religious Intelligencer* (August 2, 1828). This essay was freely copied in popular religious and juvenile periodicals and readers, including *Cobb's Juvenile Reader* (1834). In 1841 she met pioneering educator of the deaf-blind Dr. SAMUEL GRIDLEY HOWE of the Perkins Institute in Boston (see PERKINS SCHOOL FOR THE BLIND) and his star pupil Laura Bridgman. In 1842 Brace enrolled at the Perkins Institute for one year. Apparently she made little educational advancement there and thus returned to the American School for the Deaf as a boarder. She traveled to live with a married sister in Bloomfield, Connecticut, in 1860. She died at her sister's residence on August 12, 1884, and was buried in an unmarked grave at West Hill Cemetery.

Although less recognized today, Julia Brace was an important figure in 19th-century American LITERATURE and history. She appeared in popular juvenile literature as a model of pity and desolation, oversimplified perceptions that would follow people with disability throughout the next two centuries. At the same time, her story inspired parents to research and support institutional reforms that resulted in advances in educational opportunities for the deaf-blind. Brace created interest in mainstream society that would later enable Laura Bridgman and Helen Keller to become national and international role models for deaf-blind people and also challenge some of the STEREOTYPES of individuals with this dual disability.

Meredith Eliassen

Further Reading:

Klages, Mary. *Woeful Afflictions: Disability and Sentimentality in Victorian America.* Philadelphia: University of Pennsylvania Press, 1999.

Schwartz, Harold. *Samuel Gridley Howe: Social Reformer, 1801–1876.* Cambridge, Mass.: Harvard University Press, 1956.

Bragdon v. Abbott

Bragdon v. Abbott is a 1998 Supreme Court decision interpreting the AMERICANS WITH DISABILITIES ACT (ADA) of 1990 that addressed the issues of (1) whether asymptomatic human immunodeficiency virus (HIV) infection is a disability protected by the ADA, and (2) whether reproduction should be considered a "major life activity" under the ADA's definition. Since 1986 Sidney Abbott of Maine had been infected with HIV but was asymptomatic at the time of the following incident. In 1994 Abbott went to the office of Dr. Randon Bragdon for a routine dental appointment and disclosed that she had HIV. While completing the routine dental examination the dentist found a cavity. After discovery of the cavity, the dentist informed Abbott of the office policy against filling cavities of HIV patients in the dental office. The dentist offered to perform the dental services to repair the cavity in a hospital with no added fee. Since the services would be performed in a HOSPITAL, however, Abbott would have been responsible for the cost of using the hospital facilities. Abbott declined the dentist's offer and filed a lawsuit pursuant to the ADA and Maine state law. The lawsuit alleged discrimination on the basis of her disability.

In 1995 the U.S. District Court for Maine granted summary judgment in favor of Abbott (912 F. Supp. 580), and the U.S. Court of Appeals for the First Circuit affirmed the decision in 1997 (107 F.3d. 934). Bragdon filed a petition for certiorari, which is a request for review of the decision, to the U.S. Supreme Court. In delivering the opinion of the Supreme Court, Justice Anthony M. Kennedy determined that HIV, even when in the asymptomatic stage, is a disability that is covered by the definition of disability in the ADA (42 U.S.C. § 12102(A)) because HIV is a physical impairment that substantially limits the major life activity of reproduction in two ways. First, the Court stated that a woman with HIV who tries to conceive a child imposes a significant risk on the man. Second, the Court stated that a woman with HIV risks infecting the child during both gestation and childbirth because even with antiretroviral therapy the risk to the child is about 8 percent that they will contract HIV. The Court found that an 8 percent risk of transmitting a potentially fatal disease to a child is a substantial limitation on the woman's ability to reproduce. In addition, the Court stated that its finding that HIV in the asymptomatic phase is an impairment that substantially limits a major life activity is supported by the regulations issued by agencies with authority to interpret the ADA. The Court further

stated that whether a person with a disability poses a health risk to the treating physician must be determined based on objective medical evidence and not the physician's belief that a health risk exists. In reaching its decision, the Court stated that "the ADA does not ask whether a risk exists, but whether the risk is significant considering very few activities in life are completely free of any risk." The Court found that the dentist failed to present any objective, medical evidence showing that treating the respondent in a hospital would be safer or more efficient than a well-equipped dentist office. Therefore, the Court remanded the case to the U.S. Court of Appeals to determine whether the Supreme Court's analysis of some of the studies would alter the ruling that the dentist had neither presented objective medical evidence or a triable issue of fact.

The issue of whether HIV should be covered under the Americans with Disabilities Act provoked a great deal of controversy during the passage of the ADA, and *Bragdon v. Abbott* was considered a victory by both AIDS and disability rights activists. The decision affirmed that persons living with HIV or AIDS are protected from discrimination by the ADA, and stipulated the need for scientific evidence of actual risk rather than fear of potential risk to justify disparate treatment of people with disabilities.

See also BACKLASH; LAW AND POLICY; REPRODUCTIVE RIGHTS.

Cynthia Smith

Further Reading:

Americans with Disabilities Act of 1990, P.L. 101-336, 104 Stat. 327 (July 26, 1990), codified at 42 U.S.C. § 12101 et seq.

Bragdon v. Abbott, 524 U.S. 624 (1998). URL: http://www.ncd. gov/newsroom/publications/2002/supremecourt_ada. htm.

Bragdon v. Abbott (1998)

In 1986 Sidney Abbott was diagnosed as HIV-positive but showed no symptoms of her illness. In 1994 dentist Randon Bragdon refused to fill her cavity at his office after she had disclosed her medical condition, offering instead to perform the procedure at a hospital. Abbott refused, and initiated a lawsuit, invoking antidiscrimination protections outlined in the 1990 Americans with Disabilities Act (ADA). In 1998 Supreme Court justices hearing the case decided in favor of Abbott. They confirmed that HIV qualified as a significant impairment and concluded that the doctor offered no objective evidence that his own health would be better safeguarded if he performed the cavity filling in a hospital versus his own office. Both AIDS and disability activists consider Bragdon v. Abbott *an important victory because it upheld the view that persons with HIV and AIDS are protected against discrimination under the ADA.*

Bragdon v. Abbott
No. 97—156 (1998)
RANDON BRAGDON, PETITIONER v.
SIDNEY ABBOTT et al.
Justice [Anthony M.] Kennedy delivered the
opinion of the Court.

We address in this case the application of the Americans with Disabilities Act of 1990 (ADA), 104 Stat. 327, 42 U.S.C. § 12101 *et seq.*, to persons infected with the human immunodeficiency virus (HIV). We granted certiorari to review, first, whether HIV infection is a disability under the ADA when the infection has not yet progressed to the so-called symptomatic phase; and, second, whether the Court of Appeals, in affirming a grant of summary judgment, cited sufficient material in the record to determine, as a matter of law, that respondent's infection with HIV posed no direct threat to the health and safety of her treating dentist.

. . . In light of the immediacy with which the virus begins to damage the infected person's white blood cells and the severity of the disease, we hold it is an impairment from the moment of infection. As noted earlier, infection with HIV causes immediate abnormalities in a person's blood, and the infected person's white cell count continues to drop throughout the course of the disease, even when the attack is concentrated in the lymph nodes. In light of these facts, HIV infection must be regarded as a physiological disorder with a constant and detrimental effect on the infected person's hemic and lymphatic systems from the moment of infection. HIV infection satisfies the statutory and regulatory definition of a physical impairment during every stage of the disease.

. . . We ask, then, whether reproduction is a major life activity. We have little difficulty concluding that it is.

. . . The inclusion of activities such as caring for one's self and performing manual tasks belies the suggestion that a task must have a public or economic character in order to be a major life activity for purposes of the ADA. On the contrary, the Rehabilitation Act regulations support the inclusion of reproduction as a major life activity, since reproduction could not be regarded as any less important than working and learning. Petitioner advances no credible basis for confining major life activities to those with a public, economic, or daily aspect. In the absence of any reason to reach a contrary conclusion, we agree with the Court of Appeals' determination that reproduction is a major life activity for the purposes of the ADA.

. . . Our evaluation of the medical evidence leads us to conclude that respondent's infection substantially limited her ability to reproduce in two independent ways. First, a woman infected with HIV who tries to conceive a child imposes on the man a significant risk of becoming infected.

. . . Second, an infected woman risks infecting her child during gestation and childbirth, *i.e.*, perinatal transmission.

. . . In the end, the disability definition does not turn on personal choice. When significant limitations result from the impairment, the definition is met even if the difficulties are not insurmountable.

. . . The determination of the Court of Appeals that respondent's HIV infection was a disability under the ADA is affirmed.

Source: Randon Bragdon, Petitioner v. Sidney Abbott, et al. No. 97–156 (1998).

Bragg, Bernard (1928–) *actor, director, and playwright*

Bernard Bragg is an internationally acclaimed DEAF performer. His personal and professional experiences offer important insights into the meaning of deaf THEATER and deaf cultural IDENTITY.

Bragg was born on September 27, 1928, in Brooklyn, New York, to deaf parents. He grew up watching his father, Wolf, direct and act in a local deaf theater company. In 1933 young Bernard was enrolled at the Fanwood School for the Deaf in White Plains, New York, where his dream of becoming an actor was nurtured by Robert Panara, a deaf teacher. After graduating from Fanwood in 1947, Bragg attended Gallaudet College (later renamed GALLAUDET UNIVERSITY) in Washington, D.C. During his college years he twice won Best Actor of the Year awards. In addition to serving as editor of the *Buff and Blue*, the student newspaper, Bragg established in 1950 the first deaf Jewish student group at Gallaudet. In 1952 Bragg graduated from the college and accepted a teaching position at the California School for the Deaf in BERKELEY, where he remained for the next 15 years. Active in both the school's drama department as well as local deaf community theater, Bragg believed that mime might be a way for him to perform without voice.

In 1956 Bragg went to see French mime, Marcel Marceau, who was on his first American tour. Bragg went backstage to meet Marceau, who promptly invited him to Paris. Bragg consented and spent the summer in Europe; upon his return, he created a mime show, performing in San Francisco and Los Angeles nightclubs. Between 1959 and 1964 Bragg also appeared weekly on PBS's San Francisco affiliate, KQED as *The Quiet Man,* performing mime and DRAMA that viewers had requested by calling in to the show.

In 1967 David Hays, a Broadway set designer, sought Bragg's support in forming a professional sign language theater, NATIONAL THEATRE OF THE DEAF (NTD). Bragg recruited deaf actors for its first production, *Experiment in Television: An NBC Special.* The hour-long program introduced mainstream viewers to the concept of sign language as an art form. Bragg remained with NTD for 10 years and taught at its summer institute for 35 years.

The art of translating the written word for stage suited Bragg well because of his understanding of stage techniques, mime, acting, and AMERICAN SIGN LANGUAGE (ASL). Because of his belief that the basic nature of ASL is cinematic, he developed a technique called Visual Vernacular, which incorporated cinematic rules of film with mime and sign language. He has shared this technique in hundreds of workshops and productions around the world over the past four decades.

As a PLAYWRIGHT he collaborated with deaf colleague Eugene Bergman in 1981 to develop and produce *Tales from a Clubroom.* Set in a fictional deaf club, this play vividly expressed the universal experiences of the deaf COMMUNITY and the richness of Deaf culture.

Bragg has received numerous awards as well as an honorary degree in humane letters in 1988 from Gallaudet University for his work and service to the international deaf community. A long-time resident of Los Angeles, Bragg continues to teach playwriting and directing at California State University, Northridge. In the spring of 2006 Bragg began touring with his one-man show "Theatre in the Sky."

Bragg's diverse contributions highlight the importance of FAMILY and school life, signed communication, and the power of theater to express and promote deaf cultural identity.

Jane Norman

Further Reading:

Lang, Harry G., and Bonnie Meath-Lang. *Deaf Persons in the Arts and Sciences.* Westport, Conn.: Greenwood Press, 1995.

Padden, Carol, and Tom Humphries. *Inside Deaf Culture.* Cambridge, Mass.: Harvard University Press, 2005.

"Spotlight on Bernard Bragg," National Theatre of the Deaf. Available online. URL: http:/www.ntd.org/bernardbragg. html. Accessed April 2, 2007.

Braidwood, John (1784–1820) *deaf educator*

As one of the first persons to establish a school for the DEAF in America, John Braidwood is credited with bringing formalized deaf EDUCATION to the United States. His educational efforts exemplify the importance placed on oral deaf pedagogy (teaching speech and lipreading) in the early history of the United States.

Braidwood was born in 1784 (the exact date is unknown) into a prestigious family lineage rooted in deaf education. John was the grandson of Thomas Braidwood, the founder of the Braidwood Academy in Scotland. The FAMILY was famous for their profitable, yet highly protected pedagogy in deaf education, which was based on oral methods.

Braidwood followed his predecessors in the field of deaf education. In 1810 he assumed responsibility for the satellite Braidwood Academy in Edinburgh. His tenure there was short-lived; he left in 1812 without explanation. However, his drinking habits, flagrant spending of the institution's budget, and abrupt departure from his position consequently contributed to the demise of the satellite academy.

In an effort to escape his failed efforts in Britain, Braidwood came to the United States in 1812. Braidwood had ambitions to settle in Baltimore and to establish the first formal school for the deaf in America. Following the precedent in Scotland, Braidwood envisioned a private institution catering to affluent families. His family's name drew attention, helping him recruit students. Colonel William Bolling of Virginia, whose deaf siblings had attended the Scottish academy, knew of John Braidwood and immediately recruited him to teach his own deaf children.

Braidwood and Bolling met in the late spring of 1812 and initiated plans for establishing the American deaf institution. Braidwood traveled north to Baltimore and Philadelphia to recruit potential students. Problems resulting from Braidwood's alcoholism resulted in scrapes with the law, which distressed his benefactor and undermined the school's prospects. After discussions, Braidwood agreed to return to Bolling's estate.

During the fall of 1812 Braidwood began tutoring Bolling's five children, two of whom were deaf, at the Bolling "Cobbs Manor" in Virginia. This arrangement continued until March 1815, when the school was officially opened and enrolled five students. The original program at Bolling's estate marked the first attempt to establish an oral school for the deaf and is known today as the COBBS SCHOOL for the deaf. In the summer of 1816 Braidwood's alcoholism and trouble managing his various responsibilities apparently overwhelmed him, and he abandoned his position at Cobbs. The limited enrollment at the relatively new institution, high tuition costs, and lack of competent teachers led to the collapse of the Cobbs school after one year.

Bolling, still wanting an education for his deaf children, was willing to give Braidwood another chance. In 1817 he paired Braidwood with John Kirkpatrick, a minister from Manchester, Virginia. Bolling hoped that Braidwood would share his family's undisclosed pedagogical methods and that the partners would open another school for the deaf. But Braidwood's struggles continued, and he was removed from the position one year later. This was Braidwood's last attempt in the field of deaf education. He later became a bartender in Manchester, Virginia. He died at the age of 36 on October 25, 1820.

Braidwood's life has received only modest attention from scholars of deaf education. Still, his efforts reflected the close ties in deaf educational endeavors between America and Europe, the powerful role of families in educating disabled children, and the belief in oral values from an early period in American history. The challenges of ADDICTION and social expectations greatly influenced the outcome of his educational endeavors.

See also AMERICAN SCHOOL FOR THE DEAF; ORALISM.

Lindsey Patterson

Further Reading:

Bass, R. Aumon. *History of the Education of the Deaf in Virginia.* Staunton: Virginia School for the Deaf and Blind, 1949.

Braidwood, John. Biographical file. Gallaudet University Archives, 2007.

Crouch, Barry, and Brian Greenwald. *Hearing with the Eye: The Rise of Deaf Education in the United States.* Washington, D.C.: Gallaudet University Press, 2007.

Unterberger, Betty Miller. "The First Attempt to Establish an Oral School for the Deaf and Dumb in the United States." *Journal of Southern History* 13, no. 4 (November 1947): 1–18.

Van Cleve, John Vickrey, and Barry Crouch. *A Place of Their Own: Creating the Deaf Community in America.* Washington, D.C.: Gallaudet University Press, 1989.

Braille, Louis (1809–1852) *inventor of Braille code for blind and low-vision readers*

Louis Braille was a BLIND French educator and the inventor of BRAILLE, the tactile reading system named after this young inventor. While still in his teens, Braille refashioned a reading code designed for soldiers working in the dark into a versatile and multifunctional system that is now universally accepted as the premier reading system for blind persons around the world.

Born near Paris in Coupvray, France, on January 4, 1809, Braille lost his sight at the age of 10 following an accident in his father's saddling shop. While the injury initially affected only one of Braille's eyes, the other eye soon succumbed to the autoimmune disease of sympathetic ophthalmia. Not long after losing his sight, Braille earned a scholarship to the Institution Royale des Jeunes Aveugles (the Royal Institution for Blind Youth) in Paris in 1819. He would spend the rest of his life there, as a student and eventually as a teacher. Beyond his career as a talented educator and inventor, Braille was also a noted organist, a skill that allowed him to travel widely in France.

While still in his early teens at the Institution Royale des Jeunes Aveugles, Braille became interested in tactile writing systems that would enable his colleagues at the school to read independently. Prior to Braille's invention, the only form of writing accessible to blind students was a basic form of raised tactile letters that corresponded exactly to the Roman alphabet. Braille recognized that this system, developed by the school's founder, Valentin Haüy, was impractical due to its immense size, weight, and awkwardness.

An 1823 visit to the school by Charles Barbier, a captain in the French army who had developed a tactile writing system developed for use in darkness on the front lines, inspired the 14-year-old Braille. Known as "night writing," Barbier's system looked nothing like traditional Roman letters. Instead, Barbier's system consisted of 12 dots on a 3 x 3 grid that represented sounds rather than characters. Braille recognized that this system marked a considerable improvement over Haüy's simple raised letters on a page. To make it practical, however, it too would need to be revised.

While still in his teens, Braille radically modified "night writing" to be more usable for persons who were BLIND. He reduced the maximum numbers of dots to six on a 2 x 3 grid, so that each character would fit under the sensitive pad on the fingertip of the reader. He also made each character correspond to an actual letter rather than a sound, so that it mirrored Roman writing. Later, along with his friend Pierre Foucault, he developed Braille musical and mathematical notation, along with a frame for writing Braille by hand. In 1829 he published the key to his system in "System for writing words, music and plainchant for the use of the blind and arranged for them by M. Braille."

For the next 14 years, Braille taught at the Institution Royale des Jeunes Aveugles. By 1843 he became too ill to continue teaching full-time, though he remained in residence at the school until his death. He died at the age of 43 of TUBERCULOSIS on January 6, 1852.

Although popular among students at the Institution Royale des Jeunes Aveugles during Braille's life, the system would not be widely recognized in France until after his death. Schools for the blind in the United States gradually began to adopt Braille in the 1860s. This code strongly shaped blind education and the experiences of blind Americans through the late 19th and much of the 20th centuries. Educators especially debated the assets and limits of this system versus other reading codes for blind people. This "WAR OF THE DOTS" as it became known raised important issues about access, as well as about publishers who served the blind community.

To this day, many blind Americans consider Louis Braille an important figure in our national history even though he never spent time in the United States. His efforts to empower blind peers, as well as his techniques for promoting ACCESS, demonstrate the importance of ACTIVISM and EDUCATION. His life story illustrates the many global connections people with disabilities share.

Bradley Kadel

Further Reading:

Mellor, C. Michael. *Louis Braille: A Touch of Genius*. Louisville, Ky.: National Braille Press, 2006.

Braille code

Invented in 1824 by 15-year-old LOUIS BRAILLE (1809–52), then a student at the Parisian Royal Institution for Blind Youth, the Braille code was created to enable BLIND people to read and write more easily. Rather than emboss the shapes of print letters, which were inherently hard to distinguish by touch and impossible to write, Braille devised a cell of six raised dots arranged in two columns three dots high in which the presence or absence of specific dots coded for a letter of the print alphabet, a number or, later, musical notation. The Braille code's history in the United States embodies several important themes in disability history, including ACCESS, EDUCATION, and EMPOWERMENT.

The Braille code was introduced in the United States in 1854 by Simon Pollack, one of the founders of the Missouri School for the Blind, who had seen the raised dot system during a visit to Paris. Over the next few decades, several people attempted to develop various embossed codes to improve literacy skills among blind students. They included Joel West Smith, a blind teacher at the PERKINS SCHOOL FOR THE BLIND in Boston, who in 1878 invented "American Braille," which made writing Braille easier by having the most frequently used letters of the alphabet coded by Braille cells that used the least number of dots. Several factors complicated its use and status in the United States: For example, a specific dot configuration did not represent the same letter of the alphabet that it would in English Braille, which closely followed the original French version. The status of Braille in the United States was further complicated for blind people by the presence of New York Point (NYP), another highly competitive raised dot code. Invented in 1868 by William B. Wait, superintendent of the New York Institute for the Blind, NYP resembled a Braille cell on its side; it was just two dots high but up to four (or more) dots wide. This was the official type supported by the American Association of Instructors of the Blind, the leading professional educational ORGANIZATION. The Boston linetype also was used widely in America at the time. This embossed print remained dominant even at the Perkins school after Smith had devised American Braille. Braille also was resisted by organizations, such as the AMERICAN PRINTING HOUSE FOR THE BLIND, that had invested huge sums, some of it federal government subsidies, in producing books in New York Point and embossed print. To redo them in Braille was a costly proposition. Competition and controversy over codes for blind readers became known as the "WAR OF THE DOTS."

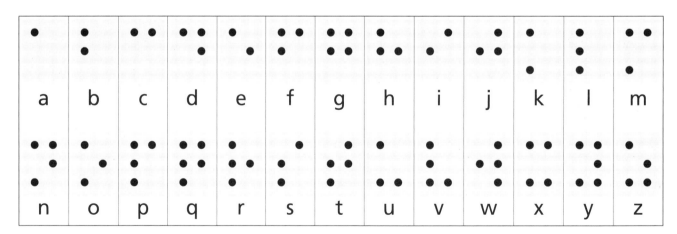

Invented by Louis Braille in 1824, the Braille code uses various combinations of raised dots to represent letters of the print alphabet, punctuation, and other signs, including musical notation. This chart offers the simplest representation, but advanced levels of Braille use other raised-dot combinations to create contractions that allow faster reading.

Although by 1907 NYP still was more widely used, the Braille code was gaining popularity, and it ultimately became the standard reading and writing code in the United States. Students also found that Braille was easier to read than were books with embossed print, and Braille music was far better than other tangible systems of musical notation. Writing Braille with a slate and stylus was (and still is) easy, but writing speeds became much faster with the invention of braille-writers, analogous to typewriters, in the 1890s. A cadre of instructors and administrators at blind schools also increasingly promoted the American Braille code; for example, a subcommittee of the American Association of Instructors of the Blind recommended this code in 1892. After objective tests, conducted under the auspices of the Uniform Type Committee (formed in 1905 by the American Association of Workers for the Blind and later also sponsored by the American Association of Instructors of the Blind), the superiority of Braille as a reading and writing code was finally ascertained. Still, decades of emotional debate among blind people themselves and among professionals in the field ensued before one standard Braille code for the English-speaking world was agreed upon in 1932 in a document often called the Treaty of London.

With the invention of the TALKING BOOK in the 1930s many experts in the field of blindness wrongly predicted that Braille would become obsolete. The Braille code's imminent death was again predicted in the 1970s, when talking computers were developed thanks to various researchers and organizations, including RAYMOND KURZWEIL. Portable audio players, which allowed blind people to read audio books whenever and wherever they wanted, did not eliminate the use of Braille either.

"Refreshable" Braille displays, which emerged in the late 1970s, further promoted Braille by presenting it without paper. Instead, a line of Braille cells is displayed by means of pins, controlled electronically, that move up above the surface or retract beneath it. A reader of such devices slides his or her fingers over a line of 20 or so cells, presses a button when the fingers reach the right side of the display, which is instantly "refreshed" to display the next line of Braille in the document.

Since the 1960s the national policy of MAINSTREAMING blind students into regular public schools rather than having them attend state RESIDENTIAL SCHOOLS has, unintentionally, adversely affected the teaching of Braille. With blind students widely dispersed, it became less practical to teach them Braille. Decades of experience have, however, made clear that Braille is important for literacy because reading Braille is analogous to reading print; reading by listening does not allow readers to learn how to spell and use correct punctuation. Since 1997 more than 30 states have passed laws stating that schools must teach Braille to all blind children capable

"It wasn't until after I had finished the course, some ten months after I began, that I started to see the benefits of learning Braille. . . . [One] benefit was that I could read to my wife, and the unexpected benefit was that we found something that we liked to do together. As I write this, I have been reading Braille for two years, and I'm on my fourth Braille novel. Not too many days go by that we don't sit down to read together."

—Mike Jolls, a student in the Nebraska Commission for the Blind's adult training center, on learning Braille code later in life, 2007

of learning it. While only 15 to 20 percent of blind people (mainly those who learned it as children) read Braille with ease, it has nevertheless been found that 90 percent of blind people who are employed full time can read Braille.

Technology in the late 20th and early 21st centuries has made Braille even more accessible. A print document can be scanned electronically, converted into Braille by software, and then embossed into paper. This means that a document required by just one or a few Braille readers can be quickly and economically produced. This is not to suggest that dedicated volunteer transcribers and proofreaders can be replaced by technology. Human intervention, whether by a blind or a sighted individual, is needed to correct aspects of translation and embossing that the computer does not do well.

By means of "web Braille" blind people can now download Braille books from a remote collection, such as that of the National Library Service for the Blind and Physically Handicapped. Instead of handling the bulky books, or relying on the mail to deliver Braille magazines, the blind reader can download them to a computer, store them, and read them at leisure on a refreshable display. Because it is flexible and amenable to digitization (it is, after all, a digital code) Braille still plays a vital role in the education, EMPLOYMENT, and recreation of blind people more than 180 years after its invention.

See also BRAILLE MUSIC.

C. Michael Mellor

Further Reading:

Irwin, Robert. "The War of the Dots." In *As I Saw It*. New York: American Foundation for the Blind, 1955.

Koestler, Frances A. *The Unseen Minority*. New York: McKay, 1976. Reprint, New York: American Foundation for the Blind, 2004.

Mellor, C. Michael. *Louis Braille: A Touch of Genius.* Boston: National Braille Press, 2006.

———. "Making a Point: The Crusade for a Universal Embossed Code in the United States." In Proceedings, Second International Conference on the Blind in History and the History of the Blind. Paris, Association Valentin Haüy, 1998 [French and English].

Braille music

Braille music is a system of tactile notation, widely used by visually impaired musicians, that employs an embossed six-dot cell to represent musical details. Louis Braille (1809–52) first set forth this alternative to print notation in 1829, and since then the code has been revised many times. Efforts are underway to develop one international standard, the most recent being the Braille Music Code in 1997. Many libraries house large collections of Braille music scores, including the Library of Congress in the United States, the National Library for the Blind in the United Kingdom, and the Canadian National Institute for the Blind.

Braille music does not directly translate printed notation. While both notational forms are quite useful, there remain conceptual and syntactical differences between them. For example, print music symbols share many properties with the musical features they represent, in essence plotting notes as points on a symbolic graph with axes designating pitch and time. Readers of print notation envision the rise and fall of melody, in which vertically aligned notes occur simultaneously and notes that are closer together horizontally move more quickly.

Braille music, on the other hand, is an alphabetic code that describes music using the 63 possible configurations of the Braille cell. The cell itself is arranged in two columns of three dots each numbered 1 through 6; the upper four dots represent pitch, while the lower two designate rhythmic values. Additional cells indicate register, intervals, articulations, and other expressive features. Unlike print music symbols, which have limited significations, each Braille cell has many meanings. For example, the cell containing only dot 1 has at least nine possible definitions in music code, and additional meanings if it appears in combination with other cells. This economy of signs results in some interesting quirks. The eighth notes C-D-E-F-G-A-B, for instance, use the same Braille symbols that stand for the alphabet letters d-e-f-g-h-i-j, respectively, creating an almost cipher-like substitution.

Despite its dissimilarity with print notation, Braille music has particular advantages. Since many musicians need their hands to play their instruments and therefore cannot scan Braille and play at the same time, Braille notation needs to be easily committed to memory. Due to its alphabetic nature, it can omit many of the elements present in print notation,

Braille symbols									
Alphabet letters	d	e	f	g	h	i	j
Note names	C	D	E	F	G	A	B

Providing blind musicians and singers access to musical scores, Braille music notation, shown here, represents musical information using an embossed six-dot cell that differs from standard Braille. Variations of this code have been used since the 19th century; all seek to create more inclusive ways of learning and performing music. *(Shersten R. Johnson)*

including staves, clefs, and beams. It also has a number of devices such as *doubling* and *grouping,* which cut down on repeated cells, aiding memorization.

In its earliest form, Braille music was transcribed by embossing each dot on heavy paper by hand with a stylus. Later on, machines allowed for faster production of Braille scores. Although many scores are still transcribed by certified Braille transcribers today, new possibilities are available using computer technology. Programs that read, edit, and publish music employ .niff (Notation Interchange File Format) or .midi (musical instrument digital interface) files to transcribe Braille into print and vice versa. Scanners, speech synthesizers, and other assistive technologies allow musicians of varying abilities to create scores in both notational formats. While these technologies are still being refined, they promise great advances in accessibility for visually impaired musicians.

See also ACCESS AND ACCESSIBILITY; MUSIC.

Shersten R. Johnson

Further Reading:

Braille Authority of North America. URL: http://www.Brailleauthority.org/.

Braille Music Subcommittee of the World Blind Union. *New International Manual of Braille Music Notation.* Compiled by Bettye Krolick. Zurich: Braille Press Zurich, 1997.

Krolick, Bettye. *How to Read Braille Music: An Introduction.* 2d ed. San Diego: Opus Technologies, 1998.

brain injury   See TRAUMATIC BRAIN INJURY.

Breslin, Mary Lou (1944–) *advocate*

As a legal and policy reform advocate, Mary Lou Breslin has played a significant role in the DISABILITY RIGHTS MOVEMENT.

Scholars know relatively little about Breslin's early years. Born in Louisville, Kentucky, in 1944, she contracted POLIO in 1955 and has primarily used a WHEELCHAIR for MOBILITY since. In 1957 she went to the Georgia Warm Springs Polio Foundation, a primary treatment center for polio. Her experiences at Warm Springs motivated Breslin's personal commitment to making accessibility a right, not a privilege, for all Americans. Childhood observations of racism directed against the African-Americans employed by her FAMILY further buttressed Breslin's commitment to social justice.

She completed high school in Louisville in 1962 and then enrolled at the University of Illinois, Champaign-Urbana, graduating four years later with a major in sociology and a minor in psychology. After taking her first job as a psychiatric social worker at Chicago State Hospital, she moved to Oklahoma, later to South Dakota, and then to New Mexico. In the fall of 1973 she settled in California.

During the 1970s Breslin became active in the California disability community as well as in social protest movements. In 1973 she began working at the University of California at Berkeley's Physically Disabled Students' Program; in the same year, she became involved in its Center for Independent Living and its Disability Law Resource Center. She participated in the historic 1976 sit-in protest that demanded implementation of SECTION 504 of the Rehabilitation Act of 1973. She also developed a training program for implementing Section 504.

In the late 1970s and early 1980s Breslin emerged as a leader focusing on issues of EMPOWERMENT and EDUCATION. In 1979 she cofounded the DISABLED RIGHTS AND EDUCATION AND DEFENSE FUND (DREDF). A grassroots ORGANIZATION, the DREDF is dedicated to policy reform and litigation by building alliances with civil rights leaders and government officials. In 1993 she founded the DREDF Development Partnership, a corporation that supports DREDF programs. Recognizing the need to document the lived experiences of American disability history, Breslin collaborated with Susan O'Hara in 1995 to design the Disability Rights and Independent Living Movement Oral History Project. The collection is housed in the Bancroft Library at the University of California, BERKELEY.

As the DREDF's Senior Policy Advisor in the early 21st century, Breslin has been working on internal LAW AND POLICY. Breslin also trains, lectures, and consults on disability and civil rights issues throughout Europe and Asia. She has taught at the McLaren School of Management at the University of San Francisco and currently is teaching at the University of California, Berkeley.

For her advocacy work, Breslin has received many awards, including a MARY E. SWITZER Merit Fellowship in 1995, the PAUL A. HEARNE Award from the Physical and Mental Disabilities Rights Committee of the American Bar Association in 2000, and the Henry B. Betts award in 2002.

ACCESS and EMPOWERMENT are two intertwined and fundamental issues in American disability history, and Mary Lou Breslin's advocacy to expand access through laws and policy and training reflect many dimensions of this civil rights goal, including HEALTH CARE, independent living, positive REPRESENTATION, education, and COMMUNITY ties. Breslin currently lives in Berkeley, California.

See also ROOSEVELT WARM SPRINGS INSTITUTE FOR REHABILITATION; SIT-IN PROTEST AT THE DEPARTMENT OF HEALTH, EDUCATION AND WELFARE.

Sara Newman

Further Reading:

Blackwell-Stratton, Marian, Mary Low Breslin, Arlene Byrnne Mayerson, and Susan Bailey. "Smashing Icons: Disabled Women and the Disability and Women's Rights Movements." In *Women Transforming Politics: An Alternative Reader,* edited by Cathy J. Cohen, Kathleen B. Jones, and Joan C. Tronto, 519–530. New York: New York University Press, 1997.

Breslin, Mary Lou, and Silvia Yee. *Disability Rights Law and Politics. International and National Perspectives.* Ardsley, N.Y.: Transnational Publishers, 2002.

O'Hara, Susan. "Mary Lou Breslin: Cofounder and Director of the Disability Rights Education and Defense Fund, Movement Strategist." Interview. Berkeley, Disability Rights and Independent Living Movement Oral History Series, 1996–1998. URL: http:// content.cdlib.org/ark:/13030/kt8r29n9sp/.

Potok, Andrew. *A Matter of Dignity: Changing the World of the Disabled.* New York: Bantam Books, 2003.

Bridgman, Laura (1829–1889) *celebrated deaf-blind woman*

Laura Bridgman won international fame in the 1840s as the first DEAF-BLIND person to be educated in verbal language. Instructed by SAMUEL GRIDLEY HOWE, director of the PERKINS SCHOOL FOR THE BLIND in Boston, she learned to read raised print, write, and converse with others, thus proving that the deaf-blind, who had previously been regarded as incapable of any understanding, could gain access to human culture. Fifty years older than HELEN KELLER, who would later eclipse her, Bridgman was celebrated in her day as the subject of important scientific and educational research and as the heroine of an inspiring tale of rescue and Christian redemption.

Born into a farm FAMILY in Hanover, New Hampshire, on December 21, 1829, Bridgman suffered an attack of scarlet fever that left her DEAF, BLIND, and with little sense of smell or taste. Before her illness, she had been a talkative two-year-old, just beginning to form sentences; afterward, as deafness caused language to fade from her conscious memory, she devised gestures to communicate her needs, but she could not always control her angry frustration. Although her parents had little time for her, her friendship with Asa Tenney, a mentally IMPAIRED farm hand who devoted himself to her care, saved her from the psychic disintegration that can overwhelm undereducated deaf-blind CHILDREN.

Bridgman's life changed in 1837, after Howe, who had been searching for a bright deaf-blind pupil, persuaded her parents to let him take eight-year-old Laura to Perkins, the nation's first school for the blind. Howe wanted to use her to prove that a deaf-blind child could be educated, a feat that had been considered impossible. He saw this not only as a philanthropic challenge but also as an opportunity for scientific research: Like others, he believed that because the deaf-blind received no auditory or visual information, their minds were mostly blank. Studying their behavior as their education progressed would show which mental qualities and ideas were innate and which were learned.

Howe, who disapproved of sign language without understanding it, based his approach on the system devised in 1800 for Victor, the famous Wild Boy of Aveyron, a languageless,

Considered the first successfully educated deaf-blind person in America, Laura Bridgman (1829–1889) was a cultural icon in the 19th century. Her dark glasses in this portrait highlight blindness, while her refined clothing and traditional pose represent her intellect and success.   *(Bettmann/CORBIS)*

unsocialized, apparently feral child who had been educated by Jean-Marc Gaspard Itard, resident physician at the Paris Institute for Deaf-Mutes. Using raised letters, Howe and his female assistants taught Bridgman to match objects with labels, but the real linguistic breakthrough came when she learned FINGERSPELLING, using the manual alphabet. Once she understood that language would empower her to converse with others, she made astonishing progress. Howe publicized her achievements in reports that circulated throughout the world, inducing Charles Dickens to come to see her when he traveled from England to Boston in 1842; his rhapsodic account of her in *American Notes* made her a celebrity and major tourist attraction, visited by thousands and widely discussed in sermons and scientific treatises.

By the 1850s Bridgman's fame was fading, for she was no longer the appealing little girl the public had adored and Howe had lost interest in her as a scientific project. She would have liked to marry or contribute to her own support, but neither he nor her family had ever considered how or where she might live as an adult. Lacking Helen Keller's beauty and winning ways, and with no teacher like ANNE SULLIVAN MACY of her own, Bridgman turned increasingly inward, devoting herself to religious meditation and prayer; in 1862, she defied Howe, a Unitarian rationalist, by embracing the fervent Baptist faith of her parents. Although she visited her family regularly, she felt isolated at home and preferred to pass most of her life at Perkins, teaching needlework. She died there on May 24, 1889, not long after meeting the young Helen Keller.

Elisabeth Gitter

Further Reading:

Freeberg, Ernest. *The Education of Laura Bridgman: First Deaf and Blind Person to Learn Language.* Cambridge, Mass.: Harvard University Press, 2001.

Gitter, Elisabeth. *The Imprisoned Guest: Samuel Howe and Laura Bridgman, the Original Deaf-Blind Girl.* New York: Farrar, Straus & Giroux, 2001.

Lamson, Mary Swift. *Life and Education of Laura D. Bridgman.* Boston: Houghton Mifflin, 1878.

"Miss Bridgeman's Anniversary" in *The Washington Post* (December 23, 1887)

Laura Bridgman (1829–89) was one of the most well known Americans in the 19th century. After becoming deaf-blind from scarlet fever when she was a child, Bridgman attended the Perkins School for the Blind in Boston in the late 1830s and 1840s. Visitors came from all over the world to view this "peculiar" child, and School administrator Samuel Gridley Howe gained fame for Bridgman's educational success. As this 1887 Washington Post *article notes, Bridgman (which the* Post *misspells "Bridgeman") became a symbol for the Perkins institution and for educational reforms. It also raises important questions about the representations of people with disabilities and mainstream society's understanding of those deemed different.*

"Miss Bridgeman's Anniversary"
The Washington Post, December 23, 1887

LAURY DEWEY BRIDGEMAN held a reception Wednesday at the Perkins Institution for the Blind in South Boston, to commemorate the fiftieth anniversary of her entrance into that home, an event which happened when she was eight years old.

No person in this country, so far as is known, has ever lived in it in so peculiar a condition, Born in New Hampshire fifty-eight years ago last Wednesday, with all the usual brightness, intelligence and vivacity of a New England child, she lost her sight and hearing when two years old through scarlet fever, and the loss of speech necessarily and soon followed.

Through all these years she has lived with but practically one sense, that of touch, and with it she has been able not only to cultivate her own mind beyond the degrees to which the majority attain, but to become at the institution in which she has so long been an inmate a teacher of those less afflicted than herself.

DR. SAMUEL G. HOWE, now dead, the husband of JULIA WARD HOWE, made Miss BRIDGEMAN's education the great work of his life, and he lived long enough to realize that however imperfect the clay image may be there is always a way of assertion for an immortal soul.

Source: "Miss Bridgeman's Anniversary," *The Washington Post,* 23 December 1887, p. 4.

Bristo, Marca (1953–) *disability rights activist and leader*

Marca Bristo is a leader within DISABILITY RIGHTS MOVEMENTS both in the United States and internationally. Her life has been committed to ensuring equal ACCESS to educational, vocational, and residential services for disabled people.

Marca Bristo was born in Albany, New York, in 1953 and lived on a farm in Castleton-on-Hudson until she was 10 years old. Later, Bristo attended Beloit College in Wisconsin, graduating in 1974. It was at Beloit that Bristo became involved in feminism, which she says has helped to formulate her future ACTIVISM. She then trained as a nurse a received a degree from Rush University. In 1977 Bristo became disabled due to a diving accident. It was after the accident that Bristo became aware of the discrimination that disabled women experience especially in relation to issues of reproduction and SEXUALITY. This knowledge led Bristo to attend a conference on sexuality and disability in 1978 in Berkeley. After attending this conference, Bristo became more active in the emerging disability rights movement.

In 1980 Bristo helped found Access Living, an independent living center in Chicago, one of the first 10 funded by the federal government. She was appointed director of Access Living in 1980. In 1982, under Bristo's leadership, Access Living, along with other independent living centers, helped to form the NATIONAL COUNCIL ON INDEPENDENT LIVING (NCIL), an ORGANIZATION whose mission is to advance independent living and the rights of people with disabilities through consumer-driven advocacy. Bristo served as president of NCIL from 1985 to 1989. Additionally, Bristo helped to formulate the early drafts of the AMERICANS WITH DISABILITIES ACT (ADA) during this period.

In 1994 Bristo was appointed chairperson by President Clinton to head the National Council on Disability (NCD), an independent federal agency that provides disability-related policy guidance to the president and Congress. Bristo was the first disabled person to hold this post. The NCD has legal authority to monitor the implementation of the ADA. During her time as chair of the NCD, Bristo petitioned the government to strongly enforce the legislative intent of the ADA. During Bristo's tenure at the NCD, town hall meetings were held to generate feedback on the effectiveness of the ADA. Under Bristo's leadership the NCD sought to reform government policies for individuals with psychiatric impairments. Specifically, the NCD released a report promoting an individual's right to resist psychiatric treatment and advocate for their own medical care. The report highlighted civil rights abuses against individuals with psychiatric impairments, including forced care and physical, sexual, and psychological ABUSE. Bristo also spearheaded NCD programs to promote leadership development for youth with disabilities and greater access to technology for disabled people throughout the United States. Both of these programs have been replicated in the larger disability COMMUNITY. While at the NCD, Bristo also became a vocal critic of Princeton University's decision to appoint PETER SINGER as a professor of bioethics because of Singer's position advocating infanticide of disabled infants.

Since leaving the NCD in 2002, Bristo returned as president and chief executive officer of Access Living. She is active in promoting disability activism and cultural activities in Chicago. Bristo has also provided leadership within the international disability rights communities in helping to create the United Nations Convention on the Rights of People with Disabilities, the first of its kind internationally, which was approved in 2006. Additionally Bristo has overseen the construction of Access Living's new headquarters in downtown Chicago, which received the 2007 PARALYZED VETERANS OF AMERICA's Barrier-Free America Award, for its universally accessible design and measures to create a green space in Chicago.

Bristo has received numerous awards for her work as a disability rights leader and activist, including the Henry B. Betts Award and the Americans with Disabilities Act Award.

See also ACTIVISM AND ADVOCACY; EMPOWERMENT; REPRODUCTIVE RIGHTS.

Michael Gill

Further Reading:
Bristo, Marca. "ADA at a Crossroads." In *Employment, Disability, and the Americans with Disabilities Act,* edited by Peter David Blanck, 463–468. Evanston, Ill.: Northwestern University Press.
Fleischer, Doris James, and Frieda Zames. *The Disability Rights Movement: From Charity to Confrontation.* Philadelphia: Temple University Press, 2000.
Yednak, Crystal. "Champion for the Rights of the Disabled: The President of a Chicago Advocacy Group Takes the Fight for Fair Treatment to an International Level," *Chicago Tribune,* 10 August 2005.

Brown, Mordecai ("Three Finger Brown")
(1876–1948) *baseball player*

Known to baseball fans as "Three Finger Brown," Mordecai Peter Centennial Brown was one of the greatest pitchers in baseball history. He compiled an excellent career won-lost record of 239 and 129. His career earned run average (ERA) of 2.06 is the third-lowest in Major League Baseball history. He pitched in the major leagues from 1903 to 1916 and was voted into the Baseball Hall of Fame in 1949.

Brown was born in the small farming community of Nyesville, Indiana, on October 19, 1876, the centennial year. As a young boy, Mordecai caught his hand in his uncle's corn shredder. The machine severed most of his right index finger and about half of his right pinkie. Shortly afterward he broke the two remaining fingers of his right hand.

If Brown had devoted his life to farming, he would likely have been lost to history. Many farming and industrial accidents of this era left countless Americans with physical impairments. However, Brown grew into a strong, athletic young man, and he nurtured a love of baseball. Brown's

With a career won-lost record of 239 and 129, Mordecai "Three Finger" Brown (1876–1948) was one of baseball's greatest pitchers. His impairment, caused by a farm accident when he was young, enabled him to throw a ball in unique ways that overpowered batters. He was elected to the Baseball Hall of Fame in 1949. *(Bettmann/CORBIS)*

unusual right hand permitted him to grip and to spin a baseball in ways that others could not. He was thus able to throw both a superb rapidly spinning curve ball and a superior knuckle ball that did not spin. Ty Cobb, one of baseball's greatest hitters, called Brown's curve ball "the most devastating pitch I ever faced."

Brown played semi-pro ball in his early 20s and reached the major leagues in 1903. After a lackluster rookie year with the St. Louis Cardinals, Brown moved to the Chicago Cubs, where he began to dominate his sport. He led the Cubs to National League pennants in 1906, 1907, 1908, and 1910 and World Series championships in 1907 and 1908. In the eight-year span from 1904 through 1911, Brown won 170 games while losing only 75, a remarkable winning percentage of .694. Over that same period, Brown pitched 2,192 innings and allowed only 418 earned runs, for an extraordinary eight-year ERA of 1.72. His league leading ERA in the 1906 season was 1.04, the second-lowest single-season mark in Major League Baseball history for a starting pitcher. In the modern era, only Bob Gibson approached this mark, posting an ERA of 1.12 in 1968.

A contemporary comparison would be to Brown's longtime friend and rival, New York Giants ace Christy Mathewson, known as "the big six" for his height and as "the Christian gentleman" for his character. Mathewson's career was longer than Brown's, and Mathewson was inducted into the Baseball Hall of Fame some years before Brown. But Brown won most of the games in which the two met head-to-head, including a streak of 10 consecutive victories from 1905 to 1908. The contests between these two stars were extensively advertised, avidly followed, and heavily attended.

The attitudes that Brown and his contemporaries displayed toward his pitching hand varied in tone and emphasis, but few if any were negative. One opposing pitcher spoke of Brown's condition during a 1908 vaudeville performance. A heckler suggested that the performer cut off one of his own fingers in order to improve his performance. Brown himself expressed no regrets about his condition, stating, "That old paw served me pretty well in its time. It gave me a firmer grip on the ball, so I could spin it over the hump. It gave me a greater dip." Newspaper articles detailed Brown's achievements and explained how he threw his beguiling pitches.

Brown earned the respect of his manager, Hall of Fame first baseman Frank Chance, as well as that of other great players of his era. Chance considered Brown the most reliable member of the Cubs's pitching staff and also ranked him "above Mathewson as a money pitcher." Chance also called Brown a great teacher of young ballplayers. Teammate and Cubs great Johnny Evers stressed Brown's "nerve, ability and willingness to work at all times under any conditions."

While there have been other celebrated athletes with physical impairments, such as one-armed pitcher JIM ABBOTT, few have been as successful as Brown. More common examples of disabled SPORTS figures have been men of short stature who have batted in the major leagues, but they have largely been perceived as novelties, which was how they were promoted.

Whether "Three Finger Brown" possessed a disability remains open to debate. In the context of professional baseball in the early 20th century, his impairment—the unusual condition of his throwing hand—was socially constructed as a distinct advantage. Due to his exceptional skills and great success, Brown escaped much of the discrimination and exclusion that disabled persons typically encounter.

Retiring as an active player at the age of 40, Brown returned to Indiana. While he appeared in a number of "old-timers" ball games, he wore his fame gently and lived a quiet life as a small businessman until his death on February 14, 1948, in Terre Haute, Indiana, at the age of 71.

See also POPULAR CULTURE; SOCIAL CONSTRUCTION OF DISABILITY.

Franklin K. Wyman

Further Reading:
The Official Mordecai "Three Finger" Brown Web site. URL: http://www.cmgww.com/baseball/brown/index.html.
Reichler, Joseph L., ed. *The Baseball Encyclopedia: The Complete and Official Record of Major League Baseball.* 7th ed. New York: Macmillan, 1988.
Thomson, Cindy, and Scott Brown. *Three Finger—The Mordecai Brown Story.* Lincoln: University of Nebraska Press, 2006.
"Three Finger Brown, History of His Career," *Portsmouth* (Ohio) *Evening Times,* 14 December 1909, p. 8.

Bubble Boy   See VETTER, DAVID.

Buck, Carrie (1906–1983) *plaintiff in Supreme Court case* Buck v. Bell

The young white woman who became the subject of a test case for INVOLUNTARY STERILIZATION was a victim of history and circumstance. Carrie Elizabeth Buck was born in Charlottesville, Virginia, in 1906, the daughter of Frank W. Buck and Emma A. Harlow Buck. Her father died when she was very young. In April 1920 her mother was committed to the VIRGINIA COLONY FOR EPILEPTICS AND FEEBLE-MINDED in Lynchburg, Virginia, with a diagnosis of "FEEBLEMINDEDNESS," the term then used for MENTAL RETARDATION, a description that was probably less of a psychological finding than a reflection of community distaste for her sexual behavior and alcohol consumption. Carrie had been removed from her mother's care when she was three and placed with a foster FAMILY, the Dobbs. She attended local schools, where her records indicate NORMAL progress each year, but before she completed sixth grade her foster family withdrew her from school to perform housework for them.

In 1923 Carrie Buck became pregnant, by her account as the result of rape committed by a nephew of the foster family with whom she had lived for almost 14 years. Believing that the pregnancy was evidence of promiscuity and thus of feeblemindedness, and not acknowledging the involvement of their nephew, the foster family sought to have her committed, like her mother, to the Virginia Colony for Epileptics and Feeble-Minded. Following the birth of her daughter, Vivian Alice Elaine Buck, in March 1924, Buck was committed to the Virginia State Colony in Lynchburg. Her foster parents took Buck's infant into their home, and they gave her their family name, Dobbs.

Shortly after Buck's commitment, Albert Sidney Priddy, superintendent and physician at the Virginia Colony, selected her to be the subject of the test case of the constitutionality of Virginia's recently enacted involuntary sterilization statue. This law provided that the commonwealth could forcibly sterilize anyone found to be incompetent because of alcoholism, EPILEPSY, feeblemindedness, INSANITY, or other factors. Underlying the law was the EUGENIC assumption that these traits were hereditary and that sterilization would thus prevent their transmission. Uncertain that the new law could withstand a constitutional challenge, however, its framers and supporters arranged to test it in court before performing the surgery. They chose Buck in the belief that she had inherited her feeblemindedness from her mother, and that her daughter showed signs of slow mental development as well.

The litigation went to circuit and appeals courts in Virginia, where the judges approved Buck's sterilization. Eventually styled *Buck v. Bell* (referring to John Hendren Bell, the superintendent of the Virginia Colony following Priddy's death in 1925), the case moved forward to the U.S. Supreme Court in April 1927. In May of that year the Court ruled that Virginia's law was constitutional, and that Buck should be sterilized. In the majority opinion, Justice Oliver Wendell Holmes declared that the "principle that sustains compulsory vaccination is broad enough to cover cutting the Fallopian tubes." In an oft-quoted phrase, he concluded that "three generations of imbeciles are enough." Consequently, Buck and approximately 8,300 other Virginians, including her younger half sister, were sterilized under the state law between 1927 and 1972. The Supreme Court decision encouraged the passage of similar laws in other states, and it has been linked to the development of sterilization laws in Nazi Germany in the 1930s.

After being sterilized in October 1927 and released from the Virginia Colony to work for a family in Bland County, Virginia, Buck married William Eagle, a widowed carpenter,

As the plaintiff of the landmark 1927 Supreme Court case *Buck v. Bell*, Carrie Buck (1906-1983) figures prominently in American disability history. Seated here with her mother, Emma (who was also institutionalized), Buck unsuccessfully fought to protect her right against forced sterilization. *(Arthur Estabrook Papers. M.E. Grenander Department of Special Collections & Archives, University at Albany Libraries)*

in May 1932. He died in 1941, and, 24 years later, she married Charles Detamore, of Front Royal, Virginia, in 1965. Friends, relatives, and professionals who knew her later in her life denied the accuracy of her diagnosis of mental retardation. She was independent and a helpful person to others for most of her life. Carrie Elizabeth Buck Eagle Detamore died on January 28, 1983, in a nursing home in Waynesboro, Virginia. She was buried in Oakwood Cemetery in Charlottesville. Vivian Dobbs, the daughter from whom Carrie was separated shortly after giving birth, is buried on an adjacent hillside. Belying Justice Holmes's famous opinion, Vivian was an honor student when she died of enterocolitis in 1932 at age eight. The practice of involuntary sterilization did not cease in Virginia institutions until 1972, and the enabling act remained in effect until April 1974.

In 2002 Governor Mark Warner issued a formal apology for Virginia's forcible sterilization of thousands of its citizens. His apology coincided with the 75th anniversary of the Supreme Court's decision in *Buck v. Bell*. He also noted that the EUGENICS movement propagated a shameful ideology, that Virginia should never have been involved in its promotion, and that this mistake needed to be remembered to prevent it from being repeated. The life of Carrie Buck stands as a testament to this mistake.

See also VIRGINIA COLONY FOR EPILEPTICS AND FEEBLEMINDED.

J. David Smith

Further Reading:
Lombardo, Paul A. "Eugenic Sterilization in Virginia: Aubrey Strode and the Case of *Buck v. Bell*." Ph.D. diss. University of Virginia, Charlottesville, 1982.
———. *Three Generations, No Imbeciles: Eugenics, the Supreme Court, and* Buck v. Bell. Baltimore: Johns Hopkins University Press, 2008.
Smith, J. David, and K. R. Nelson. *The Sterilization of Carrie Buck*. Far Hills, N.J.: New Horizon Press, 1989.
———. "Three Generations, No Imbeciles: New Light on *Buck v. Bell*." *New York University Law Review* 60 (1985): 30–62.

Buck, Pearl (1892–1973) *author and advocate*

Pearl Buck was a prominent American author and winner of the 1938 Nobel Prize in Literature. Her daughter Carol Buck (1920–92) was cognitively disabled, and was born during a period when public figures typically concealed the presence of COGNITIVE DISABILITY in their families. Buck's *The Child Who Never Grew* (1950) revealed Carol's disability and explored Buck's experience as her mother. Buck was the only nationally known figure at that time to publicly identify herself as the parent of a son or daughter with MENTAL RETARDATION, the term then preferred by activists and advocates.

Pearl Buck was born in Hillsboro, West Virginia, on June 26, 1892, and grew up in China as the child of Presbyterian missionaries. She attended Randolph-Macon Woman's College in Virginia, then married her first husband, John Lossing Buck, in 1917. Buck continued to live in China, where she taught English literature and began to write magazine articles. Buck's first novel *East Wind, West Wind* was published in 1930. Her best-selling second novel *The Good Earth* (1931) established her fame as an author. In 1934 she returned to the United States, and, in 1935, she was divorced and married her second husband, Richard Walsh.

Buck's daughter Carol was born in 1920, early in her career. Carol was later diagnosed with phenylketonuria (PKU), a genetic condition that leads to impaired brain development. However, the disorder was then unknown, and Carol's disability was identified only after Buck slowly recognized her delayed development and sought medical help. On the advice of doctors, Buck placed her daughter in a residential institution, the Training School at Vineland, New Jersey, in 1929. She believed that her daughter was better off in what she described as a homelike, loving, and protected environment. Carol Buck remained at VINELAND TRAINING SCHOOL until her death at age 72.

As Buck's fame grew in the 1930s, she was secretive about Carol's existence. Even longtime acquaintances were often unaware that Buck had an institutionalized daughter. Parents of cognitively disabled sons and daughters were subject to enormous STIGMA; cognitive disability was often seen as some vague moral and intellectual flaw, presumably hereditary, that might taint the entire family. Buck maintained her insistence on privacy until a parent-led advocacy movement began to grow in the late 1940s. The publication of *The Child Who Never Grew* served as both a response to and an inspiration for other parents who sought a new kind of publicity for mental retardation. Buck did not take a formal role in organized mental retardation advocacy. However, she corresponded regularly with individual parents and groups of parents, offering advice and support.

The Child Who Never Grew was primarily an account of Carol Buck's early childhood and INSTITUTIONALIZATION. It recounted Buck's painful recognition of her daughter's disability and her decision to place Carol at Vineland Training School. Buck also wrote more generally about mental retardation and the overwhelming problems faced by families. She stressed the innocence and vulnerability of individuals with mental retardation, portraying them as sweet-tempered children whose needs for protection and nurturing remained constant regardless of chronological age. The understanding of cognitive disability embodied in Buck's account has been strongly criticized for its failure to recognize the adult status of people with cognitive disabilities. However, this child-centered model was central to early mental retardation advocacy. *The Child Who Never Grew* provided an eloquent example of how to use this model to demand sympathy and attention from a hostile public. It was also one of the very few writings available at that time that could help families understand their own experience in positive terms. By publishing her narrative, Buck, who died on March 6, 1973, became a role model for how to move mental retardation from the status of private problem to the sphere of public advocacy.

See also ACTIVISM AND ADVOCACY; FAMILY; PARENT ADVOCACY GROUPS.

Katherine L. Castles

Further Reading:
Buck, Pearl S. *The Child Who Never Grew.* 1950. Reprinted with introduction and afterword by James A. Michener, Martha M. Jablow, and Janice C. Walsh. Bethesda, Md.: Woodbine House, 1992.

Castles, Katherine. "'Little 'Tardies': Mental Retardation, Race, and Class in American Society, 1945–1965." Ph.D. diss., Duke University, 2006.

Conn, Peter. *Pearl S. Buck: A Cultural Biography.* New York: Cambridge University Press, 1996.

Harris, Theodore F. *Pearl S. Buck: A Biography.* Vol. 2, *Her Philosophy as Expressed in Her Letters.* New York: John Day, 1971.

Buck v. Bell

The international EUGENICS movement, which sought to "improve" the human race through better breeding, fed widespread fear of and contempt for people with disabilities in the early 20th century, but few incidents generated by the eugenicists had the long-term practical and symbolic impact of the 1927 U.S. Supreme Court case of *Buck v. Bell.* The *Buck* case grew out of a 1924 law passed by the state of Virginia that allowed state-run institutions—mental HOSPITALS, ASYLUMS for the "FEEBLEMINDED," and the like—to surgically sterilize residents involuntarily in order to prevent them from having CHILDREN. The law focused on the "socially inadequate," a group that included those with "hereditary forms of insanity that are recurrent, IDIOCY, imbecility, feeble-mindedness or EPILEPSY."

The same year that the Virginia sterilization measure became law, CARRIE BUCK was declared "feebleminded" and "morally degenerate." Pregnant, but not married, Buck was committed to the VIRGINIA COLONY FOR EPILEPTICS AND FEEBLEMINDED, where her mother Emma Buck already resided. A cursory examination of Buck's six-month-old baby Vivian was used to suggest that she too was "not quite NORMAL," and she completed the trio of Bucks supposedly touched by hereditary defect. Doctors at the Virginia Colony solicited testimony to prove Buck family "defects" to the Colony Board of Directors, which then voted to sterilize Carrie Buck.

Through her state-appointed lawyer, Buck challenged the sterilization order. In a 1924 county court trial, a local Virginia judge determined that the sterilization law had been properly applied to Buck. Her lawyer filed an appeal in the Virginia Supreme Court, but it also endorsed the trial decision. The case was then appealed to the U.S. Supreme Court where Colony superintendent Dr. John Bell, defended the Virginia law in the case that became known as *Buck v. Bell.*

The *Buck* case, decided by the Supreme Court in 1927, generated one of the most notorious written opinions in Court history. With encouragement from former president and then Chief Justice William Howard Taft, Justice Oliver Wendell Holmes Jr. described Carrie Buck as a "feebleminded white woman . . . the daughter of a feeble-minded mother . . . and the mother of an illegitimate feeble-minded child." "It is better for all the world," Holmes wrote, for society to prohibit people like Buck—the "manifestly unfit"—from having similar children. Borrowing from the Court's public health precedent case authorizing mandatory vaccination to prevent smallpox, Holmes argued: "the principle that sustains compulsory vaccination is broad enough to cover cutting the Fallopian tubes." Then with a dramatic flourish that would become the rallying cry of sterilization advocates, he declared: "Three generations of imbeciles are enough." Seven other justices joined the Holmes decision. Only Justice Pierce Butler, who wrote no opinion, dissented.

The Supreme Court decision in *Buck v. Bell* provided legal justification for sterilization laws eventually passed in more than 30 states. Twenty years after the *Buck* decision, Nazi doctors on trial in Nuremberg for "experimental" sterilizations as part of death camp human "research" during WORLD WAR II relied on the *Buck* precedent in their own defense. By the late 1970s, when the last operations had been done under the aegis of those laws, eugenic sterilization totals in the United States exceeded 60,000.

Historical scholarship has since demonstrated that Carrie Buck's illegitimate child was the result of rape. Vivian Buck went on to perform adequately as a student, at one time earning a spot on her school's "honor roll." The dismal performance of Buck's lawyer Irving Whitehead—who failed to call a single witness on her behalf—has been explained by an unethical conflict of interest. He had been a long-standing supporter of sterilization, and had even served as a director on the board of the very facility where *Buck* was confined. In 2002 an historical marker commemorating the Buck case was erected in her home town of Charlottesville, Virginia, and the governor of Virginia issued a formal apology for past eugenic laws. The *Buck* case, however, has never been overturned; it remains as a Supreme Court precedent.

See also INSTITUTIONALIZATION; INVOLUNTARY STERILIZATION; LAW AND POLICY; REPRODUCTIVE RIGHTS; STIGMA.

Paul A. Lombardo

Further Reading:

Carlson, Elof Axel. *The Unfit: A History of a Bad Idea.* Cold Spring Harbor, N.Y.: Cold Spring Harbor Laboratory Press, 2001.

Lombardo, Paul A. *Three Generations, No Imbeciles: Eugenics, the Supreme Court, and* Buck v. Bell. Baltimore: Johns Hopkins University Press, 2008.

Buck v. Bell (1927)

Many scholars refer to the 1927 Supreme Court case of Buck v. Bell *as a watershed in the eugenics movement. The lawsuit concerned the constitutionality of Virginia's 1924 compulsory sterilization law and its application to Carrie Buck, a young mother who was incarcerated at the Virginia Colony for Epileptics and Feebleminded. Soon after the law's passage, Buck sued Dr. J. H. Bell, superintendent of the Virginia institution. Representing the majority (8–1) decision, Justice Oliver Wendell Holmes's harrowing assertion that "three generations of imbeciles are enough" reflected the common view that sterilizing people deemed "defective" served the common good. By the 1970s, roughly 60,000 Americans would be forcibly sterilized.* Buck v. Bell *has never been overturned.*

Buck v. Bell
274 U.S. 200 (1927)

Justice [Oliver Wendell] Holmes delivered the opinion of the Court.

This is a writ of error to review a judgment of the Supreme Court of Appeals of the State of Virginia affirming a judgment of the Circuit Court of Amherst County by which the defendant in error, the superintendent of the State Colony for Epileptics and Feeble Minded, was ordered to perform the operation of salpingectomy upon Carrie Buck, the plaintiff in error, for the purpose of making her sterile. 143 Va. 310. The case comes here upon the contention that the statute authorizing the judgment is void under the Fourteenth Amendment as denying to the plaintiff in error due process of law and the equal protection of the laws.

. . . An Act of Virginia, approved March 20, 1924, recites that the health of the patient and the welfare of society may be promoted in certain cases by the sterilization of mental defectives, under careful safeguard, &c.; that the sterilization may be effected in males by vasectomy and in females by salpingectomy, without serious pain or substantial danger to life; that the Commonwealth is supporting in various institutions many defective persons who, if now discharged, would become a menace, but, if incapable of procreating, might be discharged with safety and become self-supporting with benefit to themselves and to society, and that experience has shown that heredity plays an important part in the transmission of insanity, imbecility, &c.

. . . We have seen more than once that the public welfare may call upon the best citizens for their lives. It would be strange if it could not call upon those who already sap the strength of the State for these lesser sacrifices, often not felt to be such by those concerned, in order to prevent our being swamped with incompetence. It is better for all the world if, instead of waiting to execute degenerate offspring for crime or to let them starve for their imbecility, society can prevent those who are manifestly unfit from continuing their kind. The principle that sustains compulsory vaccination is broad enough to cover cutting the Fallopian tubes. *Jacobson v. Massachusetts,* 197 U.S. 11. Three generations of imbeciles are enough.

But, it is said, however it might be if this reasoning were applied generally, it fails when it is confined to the small number who are in the institutions named and is not applied to the multitudes outside. It is the usual last resort of constitutional arguments to point out shortcomings of this sort. But the answer is that the law does all that is needed when it does all that it can, indicates a policy, applies it to all within the lines, and seeks to bring within the lines all similarly situated so far and so fast as its means allow. Of course, so far as the operations enable those who otherwise must be kept confined to be returned to the world, and thus open the asylum to others, the equality aimed at will be more nearly reached.

Source: *Buck v. Bell, superintendent.* 274 U.S. 200 (1927).

Bunker, Chang and Eng (1811–1874)
internationally celebrated conjoined twins
Chang Bunker and Eng Bunker were twin brothers whose condition and birthplace became the basis for the term *Siamese twins.* They were born in Siam (now Thailand) on May 11, 1811, in the province of Samutsongkram, to a Chinese father and a half Chinese/half Siamese mother.

Chang and Eng mean "right" and "left" but whether these are their birth names is unknown. The twins took the name "Bunker" when they entered show business.

The Bunkers were joined at the chest by a small tunnel of connective tissue. Their livers were also joined in the tunnel but functioned independently. Although medicine and surgery could not do so at the time, modern advances would have made their separation a simple procedure. In 1829 they were "discovered" in Siam by a British merchant named Robert Hunter. He exhibited them as a curiosity during a world tour. After fulfilling their contract with Hunter, the twins went into business for themselves exhibiting themselves as curiosities, including work with the famed showman P. T. BARNUM. In 1839 they visited Wilkes County, North Carolina. They were treated very kindly there and eventually made their home in that area, becoming naturalized citizens of the United States.

The brothers finally settled on a farm in nearby Surry County and adopted the name Bunker. They prospered as farmers and were accepted as respected members of the community. On April 15, 1843, they married two sisters: Chang to Adelaide Yates and Eng to Sarah Yates. Chang and Adelaide had 10 children; Eng and Sarah had 12. After their weddings, the twins and their wives established two separate households on the farm and the twins would alternate spending three days at each home. While in the home of Eng, Chang apparently became passive and quiet. When they rotated to Chang's home and family, Eng became the passive twin. It appears that this was a way that they devised to create an alternating autonomy, enabling each of them to establish a relatively separate life. A friend of the twins for many years described this phenomenon as a "surrendering of the will" that allowed each twin to have a measure of freedom and individuality in his life, at least psychologically.

During the American CIVIL WAR (1861–65) Chang's son, Christopher, and Eng's son, Stephen, both fought for the Confederacy. Their fathers were slave owners before the war. Following the war the twins found that their Confederate currency was no longer negotiable. The market for the crops they raised was devastated. Therefore, like many of their North Carolina neighbors, they found themselves in difficult times. Unlike their neighbors, however, they had a special option they could exercise in an attempt to overcome their new financial challenges. As undesirable as it must have been for the aging men, they turned again to the business of displaying themselves as human curiosities, as "freaks." Chang and Eng made several tours around the United States, each usually accompanied by one of his children. They invested the money they made and were soon on a secure financial footing. They also toured Europe in a series of successful EXHIBITIONS in 1870.

Exhibited by P. T. Barnum and others, conjoined twins Chang and Eng Bunker (1811–1874) were successful performers and later farmers in North Carolina. Their class status is reflected in this traditional family photograph of the two brothers with their wives and two of their children. *(The Granger Collection, New York)*

At several times during their lives the twins had investigated the question of whether they could be separated and survive. They were most concerned about how the illness or death of one of them would affect the other if they remained conjoined. During their trip to Europe in 1870, they consulted with the most respected surgeons in several countries on this question. They found no surgeon who would give them any encouragement concerning the possibility of a successful separation. Part of their motivation for seeking separation was their concern for the welfare of their families should both of them die, which would be the case with a fatal illness of either of them. During this final visit to Europe Chang suffered a stroke. He was immediately paralyzed on his right side, leg, and arm. A series of medical consultations apparently resulted in no improvement in his health. They returned immediately to their homes in North Carolina.

On the night of January 17, 1874, Eng called out to his son that his Uncle Chang had died. Eng complained of agonizing pain and distress. He was comforted by his wife and children while a son went for a doctor. By the time the physician arrived both twins were dead.

The bodies of the twins were sent to Pennsylvania for autopsy. Afterward, they were buried in the cemetery near Mount Airy, North Carolina, behind the church where they had been faithful members. The fused liver of the Bunker brothers, a plaster cast of their bodies, and other material regarding the twins are on display at the Mütter Museum in Philadelphia.

The lives of Chang and Eng Bunker serve as a contradiction to a restricted view of humanity. The idea that heredity and environment are the only factors that can possibly influence human development and the character of human life is defied by their stories. They shared a common genetic

IDENTITY (CONJOINED TWINS are always identical twins) and they shared a common environmental experience (they were always together). And yet they were distinctly different individuals. Accounts of those who knew them best consistently point to their differences in temperament, personality, and interests. Their lives also serve as evidence of the potential for purpose, choice, and dignity even in complex human circumstances.

See also FAMILY; FREAK SHOWS; POPULAR CULTURE.

J. David Smith

Further Reading:

Smith, J. David. *Psychological Profiles of Conjoined Twins: Heredity, Environment, and Identity.* New York: Praeger, 1988.

Wallace, Irving, and Amy Wallace. *The Two: The Story of the Original Siamese Twins.* New York: Simon & Schuster, 1978.

Burke, Chris (1965–) *actor*

Chris Burke is an ACTOR, singer, and author with DOWN SYNDROME. Burke starred in ABC's television series LIFE GOES ON from 1989 to 1993. The show was the first television series that featured a central character with Down syndrome.

Burke was born on August 26, 1965. He attended schools in New York, Massachusetts, and Pennsylvania for people with mental disabilities and he always hoped to be an actor. His parents initially questioned the professional aspirations of someone with Down syndrome. Even though his siblings had brief but profitable stints as child models, his FAMILY tried to dissuade him from an acting career. But when Burke saw a younger adolescent with Down syndrome, Jason Kingsley, on TELEVISION, he wrote to Kingsley and his mother, a writer for the PBS series *Sesame Street.* This correspondence fostered a relationship, and when Kingsley's mother learned that an ABC movie, *Desperate,* would include a role for a young man with Down syndrome, she suggested Burke. Burke won the role, and although the movie did not become a series, his performance was impressive enough that network executives sought a show featuring the young actor.

Life Goes On featured Burke as Corky Thatcher, a high school student with Down syndrome. Patti Lupone and Bill Smitrovich played his parents, and Kellie Martin played his sister. The show was notable for its portrayal, in more or less realistic ways, of the life and concerns of an individual with Down syndrome. Not every episode centered on Corky. The last years of the show introduced Chad Lowe as Martin's love interest, Jesse McKenna, a character who was HIV-positive. The show was nevertheless recognized as challenging societal assumptions about what people with Down syndrome were capable of achieving. While *Life Goes On* was only modestly successful in terms of ratings, it won critical acclaim among television critics and among disability advocates. Burke was nominated for a Golden Globe award in 1989 for best supporting actor.

According to Burke's 1991 MEMOIR, *A Special Kind of Hero,* filming a series with an actor with an intellectual disability presented challenges. Key to success were appropriate supports such as a dialogue coach and good rapport among the cast and crew.

Burke appeared in several television and movie roles after the series ended, including a recurring role in *Touched by an Angel* and appearances in *The Commish, Heaven and Hell,* and the 2003 movie *Mona Lisa Smile.* Since 1993 he has recorded MUSIC albums with Joe and John DeMasi, including the 1998 release "Forever Friends," which won a Parents Choice Gold Award for Excellence. He also serves as a spokesperson for the National Down Syndrome Society, the National Down Syndrome Congress, and the McJobs program, a program designed to encourage the EMPLOYMENT of people with mental disabilities in McDonald's restaurants.

See also COGNITIVE AND INTELLECTUAL DISABILITY.

David Penna

Further Reading:

Burke, Chris, and Jo Beth McDaniel. *A Special Kind of Hero.* New York: Dell, 1991.

Uzoigwe, Chioma. "Life Goes On with Chris Burke." *The Scientific Aesthetic Quarterly* (December 7, 2008). Available online. URL: http://scientificaesthetic.com/2008/12/07/life-goes-on-with-chris-burke.html#more.

C

Callahan, John (1951–) *cartoonist*

John Callahan is the author of eight cartoon collections and two autobiographical books. He has published cartoons in more than 50 publications, and, as a writer and singer, he released a CD in 2006. Callahan is also a quadriplegic, whose spinal cord is severed between the fifth and sixth vertebrae. He draws his "stick-like" cartoon characters by holding the pad of paper on his lap, and placing the pen loosely in his right hand while stabilizing it with his left.

Callahan's cartoons explore the construction of disability in American culture, utilizing a sharp and somewhat shocking sense of HUMOR. In one of his signature cartoons, he depicts a man with hooks for his arms standing outside a building with a tin cup on the ground and a sign that states, "Will refrain from shaking hands with you. $5.00."

Callahan was born on February 5, 1951, in Portland, Oregon, to an unmarried mother who allowed David and Rosemary Callahan to adopt her son. The Callahans eventually had five biological children and John later reflected that he never felt a strong sense of belonging within his adopted FAMILY.

At age six Callahan created his first series of cartoons, which lampooned Aretha Franklin ("Urethra Franklin"), Frank Sinatra ("Frank Snotra"), and the nuns at his grade school ("nun with spear through head"). Through high school, Callahan excelled at art in its traditional forms, but the gag cartoon was his favorite and his drawings were influenced by Don Martin, the irreverent cartoonist of *Mad* and *Cracked* magazines.

As Callahan entered his early 20s, he struggled with emotional issues, alcohol abuse, and binge drinking. In 1972, while on a drinking binge with a friend, the friend accidentally drove into an electric pole at 90 miles an hour. While the friend sustained minor injuries, the crash severed Callahan's spine, making him a C5-6 quadriplegic. Callahan is able to move his triceps and half of his deltoids so he can extend his fingers, but he cannot close them around a fork or a pen. He is also able to move half of his diaphragm, but from the diaphragm down he has no sensation and no voluntary bodily control.

After the car accident, Callahan spent more than a year between inpatient physical rehabilitation, in an apartment with a personal aide and in a nursing home. Throughout it all he continued to abuse alcohol by enlisting the help of staff members. During this time, Callahan was able to earn credits toward a college degree and later graduated from Portland State University.

By 1978, six years after the car accident, Callahan was still drinking heavily. Then in June 1978 his aide left a bottle of alcohol within reach as was their practice. After spending an hour trying to remove the cork with his teeth, Callahan dropped the bottle. Staring at the bottle for hours Callahan at last realized that his problem was not quadriplegia but alcoholism and he decided then to change his life.

Although Callahan had studied art in high school, he had little formal training as a cartoonist, however, he found himself doodling cartoons to entertain others. After studying

Cartoonist John Callahan uses satire to critique common views of people with disabilities. In this 1990 depiction of a blind person spraying Braille graffiti on a wall, Callahan pushes his audience to reconsider their limited expectations of their blind peers, as well as other individuals with disabilities. (Reprinted by permission of John Callahan/Levin Represents)

a book by *National Lampoon* cartoonist Sam Gross, Callahan realized his desire to publish humorous cartoons. He contacted Gross and other successful cartoonists to learn more about the business and started submitting gag cartoons to local newspapers in 1980. Gross, who later became a friend and mentor, provided Callahan with his first big break by purchasing some of his cartoons to publish in an edited volume. Callahan then began to achieve success, publishing cartoons in national magazines such as *Hustler, Penthouse, National Lampoon,* and the *New Yorker.*

Because no American health insurance company sells medical policies to quadriplegics, Callahan relies on MEDICAID for health insurance. Although Callahan could manage his monthly bills, he could not manage without HEALTH CARE. Therefore despite his success in order to qualify for the level of medical aid needed, he could no longer sell his cartoons for profit.

Since the 1980s Callahan has used his artistic work to critique POPULAR CULTURE and mainstream society. As in childhood, his favorite style for challenging the stigmatized attitudes toward people with disabilities is the classic gag cartoon. While many of Callahan's cartoons exploit negative STEREOTYPES of disability in order to diminish their force, his works also are characterized by the ability to see humor in desperation. For instance, in one cartoon Callahan depicts a three-legged alien society where the alien with two legs is considered disabled. In another cartoon, he portrays a man bathing in a hotel lobby fountain with a WHEEL-CHAIR parked beside it. The manager of the hotel is shown desperately promising him, "I will personally find you a room with an accessible bathroom!!!" These cartoons provide a force of resistance by taking the stereotypes against people with disabilities to a ridiculous extreme and poking fun at the attitudes of persons who cling to their status of able-bodiedness.

John Callahan's humor poignantly highlights the complementary nature of comedy and tragedy. His popularity is evident in the diverse publications that have carried his work, including *Omni,* the *New Yorker, Penthouse, National Lampoon, Whole Earth Review, Lear's, Clinton Street Quarterly, Variations,* and *American Health.*

Some have viewed his cartoons as distasteful and inappropriate, while others have praised him for his efforts to counteract negative stereotypes of people with disabilities. Callahan has collected irate letters from disgruntled readers and various advocacy groups offended by his gag cartoons, who accuse him of being a sexist, ageist, fascist, Communist, and, ironically, of being harmful to persons with disabilities. Other letters have come from supporters such as former president Bill Clinton, comedian Robin Williams, and groups such as Media Access Office, Inc. To all of this Callahan simply responds, "I am merely a cartoonist."

Callahan's life story and artistic contributions highlight the importance of cultural REPRESENTATIONS of disability. The varied responses to his work, from deep connection and laughter to discomfort or disapproval, reflect the diverse meaning and understanding of disability in America today.

Kara Shultz
Darla Germeroth

Further Reading:

Callahan, John. *Don't Worry, He Won't Get Far on Foot.* New York: Vintage, 1989.

——. *Will the Real Callahan Please Stand Up?* New York: William Morrow, 1998.

Shultz, K., and Darla Germeroth. "Should We Laugh or Should We Cry? John Callahan's Humor as a Tool to Change Societal Attitudes toward Disability." *Howard Journal of Communication* 9, no. 3 (1998): 229–244.

Cameron, Thomas Amis (1806–1870) *Southern planters' son*

Thomas Amis Dudley Cameron was born in Hillsborough, North Carolina, on July 25, 1806, the second child of Duncan and Rebecca Bennehan Cameron. Duncan Cameron was a lawyer, and Rebecca Cameron inherited lands and resources enough for the family to be considered quite wealthy. By the time Thomas was eight years old, it was clear to his parents and teachers that he had difficulty learning. Tutors described him as inattentive and indolent; his older sister was disappointed that he couldn't read her letters from school. During this period, educators and medical experts had no standard definition for Cameron's condition. In this way, his life story demonstrates the fluid nature of disability categories.

In 1820 Thomas was enrolled in a boys' school in New Jersey run by a clergyman. Four years later, Thomas became a student at the American Literary, Scientific, and Military Academy in Vermont. The family's choice of a northern locale and a military education for Thomas reflected the common belief of the time that the southern climate caused some weakness of mind and body, and a hope that northern winters would brace the young man's constitution. Thomas Cameron's teachers at both schools sent frequent reports to his parents, explaining his activities and progress. Thomas also wrote a few letters home, most of them with clear evidence of adult assistance.

After his schooling, Thomas Cameron returned to his family homes in North Carolina. He served the family business by riding his horse between plantations, reporting back on conditions and carrying written messages. He also escorted his sisters and sister-in-law when other male relatives were unavailable. He held the job of postmaster at Stagville, a post office near his family's lands, for six years.

In 1837 Cameron was riding alone between Raleigh and Orange County when he was attacked by bandits and shot in the eye and shoulder. Treatments for his injuries included galvanism and opium, and a consultation with an oculist in Philadelphia. His recovery through the 1830s and 1840s was marked by constant bereavements—four of his sisters died from TUBERCULOSIS in these years, followed by the deaths of his mother, a beloved uncle, and, in 1853, his father. With his father's death, Thomas Cameron became a property holder, with his brother and sister as trustees.

Paul Cameron took charge of his older brother's affairs in the 1850s; he instructed Thomas Cameron's tailors and sat at his bedside during bouts of illness. During the CIVIL WAR (1861–65), Paul Cameron, brother-in-law George Mordecai, and other relatives held leadership roles in the Confederacy, but Thomas spent much of the WAR at the family's Fairntosh plantation, tending to the familiar routines of farmwork.

Thomas Cameron lived the last years of his life with his sisters Margaret and Mildred in Raleigh, North Carolina. He died after a short illness on January 21, 1870, at the age of 63. A handsome obelisk marks his grave in Raleigh's Oakwood Cemetery, with the inscription "blessed are the pure of heart, for they shall see God." Thomas Cameron was understood by FAMILY and friends as "pure of heart." While he would today meet the criteria for having a DEVELOPMENTAL DISABILITY, in his own time Cameron had no medical or educational label—his needs were addressed informally, within his family and COMMUNITY. The story of his experience with developmental disability, as read in the letters of his loved ones (in the extensive holdings of the Southern Historical Collection) is a story of affection, support, and participation in family, work, and social life.

The Camerons had access to extraordinary resources, but Thomas Cameron's circumstances were not otherwise unusual for his time: only later in the 19th century would many young people with abilities similar to his face exclusion from EDUCATION, EMPLOYMENT, and other settings.

Penny L. Richards

Further Reading:

Richards, Penny L. "Thomas Cameron's 'Pure and Guileless Life,' 1806–1870: Affection and Developmental Disability in a North Carolina Family." In *Disability in the South: An Historical Anthology,* edited by Hannah Joyner and Steven Noll. Athens, Ga.: University of Georgia. Forthcoming.

Richards, Penny L., and George H. S. Singer. "'To Draw Out the Effort of His Mind': Educating a Child with Mental Retardation in Early-Nineteenth-Century America." *Journal of Special Education* 31, no. 4 (1998): 443–466.

camps

Camping—the usually outdoors, usually summertime, retreat from everyday life, for recreational purposes of health,

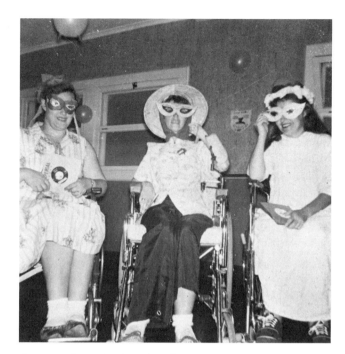

Camps and camping have long been mainstays of American culture. Dressed in costume, the female wheelchair users in this 20th-century photo are sharing in the revelry of camp life. *(Post-Polio Health International, St. Louis)*

education, or social bonding—is an American tradition. Scholarship on the history of camping and disabled people is rather slim. Documentation may be minimal, or just informal and dispersed, resisting coherent study. Nonetheless, the American "camping experience" has always been a diverse and complicated phenomenon, which may represent a rich vein of historical research covering changing conceptions of access, COMMUNITY, and inclusion.

The ingrained American cultural belief that outdoor communal living is wholesome, healthful, and invigorating for young people, a belief developed with growing fervor through the later 19th century, led to specialized, separate camps for CHILDREN with disabilities. Progressive reformers, including pioneering social worker Jane Addams, encouraged children with TUBERCULOSIS to enjoy "fresh air breathed in joy and freedom." During the 1920s, camps for children with diabetes were opened by physicians in Boston and Cleveland; other camps at the time served children with visual and hearing impairments, cardiac DISEASES, EPILEPSY, and asthma. By 1929 over 300 "SPECIAL" or disability camps had opened, with 35,000 children attending their programs. The 1930 White House Conference on Child Health and Protection addressed recreational services for the handicapped, based on President Hoover's interest in the Boys' Club as well as first lady Lou Henry Hoover's lifelong focus on the Girl Scouts. By the following year, 31 camps serving "crippled" children had been established, and, by 1945, over

50 such camps had opened, with approximately 5,000 children enrolled.

The Outing Association for Crippled Children in the late 1930s, with social workers' encouragement, began to view camps as a new option for treatment. Herrick House, built in Illinois and opened in 1940, operated as a year-round camp to serve children with DIABETES, blindness, EPILEPSY, and heart problems. Its guiding philosophy emphasized freedom under necessary limits. Others, including Eleanor Eell, worked during the Great Depression to adapt camps to include services for children with emotional and behavioral problems based on a belief in the "milieu therapy" that cultivated skills through a recreational repertoire. Eell asserted that camps needed supportive, not intrusive, supervision with challenges and teamwork. In 1943 Eell organized the Committee on Specialized Camping Services; working with the National Society for Crippled Children and Adults, committee members focused on standards and programs for children with physical disabilities, emphasizing what a child could do safely and competently rather than on cautious limitations.

Increasing recognition of diversity among disabled children motivated individualized approaches to camping over the next decades. After WORLD WAR II, the American Camping Association at their 1946 annual meeting in Boston placed more attention on serving "special populations" and "HANDICAPPED" children with priorities given to developing counselor qualifications and appreciating children as individuals. Dr. HOWARD RUSH wrote in a 1948 *New York Times* essay that summer camping as a rich group living experience was especially valuable to children with disabilities, who might be cut off from typical child development experiences. Author Cornelia Goldsmith argued in *Activities for Summer Camps* (1948) that, in camping for young children, consideration should always be given on how each child feels and how each child differs from another. Specialized camps serving disabled children flourished in this era, growing from 200 centers in 1920 to 3,200 by 1948. The National EASTER SEALS Society for Crippled Children began operating camps for children with CEREBRAL PALSY or POLIO. In the 1950s, despite fears of polio epidemics during summer months, camps increased for all children. Several million boys and girls attended over 15,000 camps. Day camps also increased during the postwar era.

Interest in civil rights issues shaped the camping movement in the 1960s and 1970s, influencing options for disabled campers. For example, camp analyst Dale Fink, whose sister had DOWN SYNDROME, recalled her story of drinking pine needle tea at an overnight YMCA camp run in Indianapolis, a sustaining memory for his sister's development. ORGANIZATIONS had no legal obligations in 1965 to enroll children with disabilities, but Fink's parents worked diligently to enroll their daughter. Disability rights victories, such as the 1970 Education of the Handicapped Act and the 1975 EDUCATION FOR ALL HANDICAPPED CHILDREN ACT, included most summer camps as educational centers with an integrated, rather than segregated, approach. This meant that young people with disabilities had legal support to attend most camps.

Over the next few decades, other disability civil rights laws expanded options for disabled campers. For example, greater application of the 1968 ARCHITECTURAL BARRIERS ACT and the 1990 AMERICANS WITH DISABILITIES ACT has resulted in increasing numbers of trails, park services, and park facilities that are accessible to disabled campers. Guidebooks on disability and camping, access passes for disabled campers, and research projects focused on access issues in national parks and federal recreation lands represent more recent efforts to promote greater inclusion of people with disabilities in camping.

POPULAR CULTURE representations of camp reflect both prejudicial attitudes toward people with disabilities as well as the impact of disability civil rights advocacy. For example, advertisements for scouting historically have emphasized able bodies and physical conditioning that complement social and moral conditioning. Young adult novels set in camps, such as the series *Camp Fire Girls*, which ran from the 1910s through the 1930s, reinforced ableist beliefs (discriminatory attitudes against people with disabilities) in idealized bodies as reflections of human worth. STEREOTYPES of disabled people pervade comedic FILMS set in camps since the 1970s; this popular subgenre commonly depicts cruel adolescent antics that reflect ableist beliefs (see ABLEISM): torturing kids who seem physically weak, who have speech impediments, vision impairments, or who are otherwise labeled as misfits. Camp films, such as Disney's *Camp Nowhere* (1994) and

---

"The campers—they were a sociable lot. They could see that we had no experience and were so willing to show us their maps, equipment, and all as well as to recommend certain ways and to avoid others. . . . All in all camping is unquestionably the best way to see our country. We became acquainted with the streams, hills, lakes of our neighboring states and we are thrilled with the prospect of visiting the rest of the country—and knowing it intimately."

—Alice Manning Williams, a 1907 graduate from the Clarke School for the Deaf, on her family's camping trip in 1934

Heavyweights (1995), also regularly poke fun at fat children. In contrast, works by people with disabilities about camp offer more empowering representations. For example, disability activist and scholar HARRIET MCBRYDE JOHNSON's 2006 coming of age novel, *Accidents of Nature,* details the experiences of teenagers with disabilities at "crip camp," the label given to "Camp Courage" by a main character in the story. Johnson sharply critiques general misperceptions of and condescension toward people with disabilities; the novel's vivid scenes of positive COMMUNITY and its theme of disability pride distinguish this work in the broad history of cultural REPRESENTATIONS both of camp and of disabled adolescents.

A quintessential American pastime, camping represents an important area for examining disability in our past. As scholars, activists, and campers continue to ponder the historical meaning of camping, questions concerning the ways camping has excluded, included, and shaped people with disabilities and their communities offer new directions for research and understanding.

Lisa L. Ossian

Further Reading:

Fink, Dale Borman. *Making a Place for Kids with Disabilities.* Westport, Conn.: Praeger, 2000.

Johnson, Harriet McBryde. *Accidents of Nature.* New York: Random House, 2006.

Zeller, Janet, Ruth Doyle, and Kathleen Snodgrass. *Accessibility Guidebook for Outdoor Recreation and Trails.* Missoula, Mont.: U.S. Department of Agriculture, Forest Service, Missoula Technology and Development Center, 2006.

cancer

Cancer is a diseased condition of the body characterized by cells that divide rapidly and abnormally. Such cells often spread, or metastasize, through the body. Masses of cancerous cells are called tumors, and most cancers result in tumor formation. Common sites of cancer in the body are the breasts, lungs, skin, prostate gland, and colon. If cancer is left untreated, it will typically spread through the body until death results. The history of cancer is important because it illustrates themes that are relevant to understanding disability history in the United States, such as treatment options, patient advocacy, and inequalities of ACCESS to HEALTH CARE.

In colonial America there were differing ideas about the nature and origin of cancer. Some scientists believed it was caused by injury or infection. Physicians knew that if they surgically removed tumors, they typically grew back, which led to varying theories about how cancer spread: from an imbalance of the body's "humors," through the lymphatic system, or as a diffusion as a liquid from a primary tumor site.

The 19th century brought many dramatic changes in the medical approach to cancer. German doctor Rudolf Virchow pioneered the field of cell pathology in the 1840s, allowing for precise cancer diagnoses through the examination of cells through a microscope. The growing use of anesthesia in surgery resulted in successful surgical treatments for cancer. Notably, in 1882 American physician William Stewart Halsted developed successful radical mastectomy surgery for breast cancer that entailed removal of the entire breast, the underlying muscles, and all adjacent lymph nodes.

During the late 19th and 20th centuries other significant developments in the treatments for cancer including hormone therapy, radiation therapy, and chemotherapy emerged; these treatments have caused both temporary and permanently disabling side effects for some people. Early experiments in hormone therapy came in 1896 when the Scottish scientist Thomas Beatson learned that removal of the ovaries could halt the development of advanced breast cancer in women. This led to an understanding of the role of estrogen in the development of breast cancer and also aided later connections between testicular hormones and prostate cancer. Radiation therapy for cancer was first used in the early 20th century. However, in the early days dosages were imprecise and side effects could outweigh the benefits of such treatment, given that radiation can both treat and cause cancer. In later decades, radiation equipment was refined; in the 21st century, targeted radiation therapy remains a major treatment modality for many cancers.

Chemotherapy was first developed in the 1940s by scientists working for the U.S. Department of Defense who found that nitrogen mustard, a chemical warfare agent, suppressed tumor formation. Further research led to additional discoveries of chemical agents that disrupted the growth and proliferation of cancer cells. In 1965 adjuvant therapy, or chemotherapy combined with the surgical excision of the primary tumors, was found to yield much higher success rates than chemotherapy alone. Treatments developed in this era aimed to maximize the ability to effectively eliminate cancer growth while moderating the physical side effects of undergoing dangerous and sometimes toxic therapies. Because of the potential risks of many cancer treatments, some patients may choose alternative therapies, which include acupuncture, meditation, or botanical medicines. Sometimes such alternative therapies may also be used along with conventional medical treatment.

In the 20th century researchers aimed to find the causes of cancer, and identified many cancer-inducing compounds such as tobacco smoke, radiation, and various chemicals. These compounds are called carcinogens and effect abnormalities in the genetic material of cells. POVERTY is often a confounding risk factor for cancer, given that levels of carcinogenic chemicals and pollutants tend to be higher in areas with low socioeconomic status. Additionally, many manual laborers are exposed to carcinogens in their workplace. "Cancer clusters," or high outbreaks of similar cancers, may result from occupational or neighborhood exposure to carcinogens.

Demographic information on cancer reveals other important social dimensions, including RACE, ETHNICITY, and sex. According to the American Cancer Society, in 2008 white women have a greater chance of getting breast cancer but black women are more likely to die from it. African-American men are 1.5 times more likely to get prostate cancer than other American males and are two to three times less likely to survive this condition. GENDERed pharmaceutical use, such as oral contraceptives and postmenopausal hormone therapy, may affect the likelihood of acquiring different forms of cancer. Certain forms, such as colorectal cancer, are more prevalent in people of Ashkenazi Jewish descent and specific American Indian groups, such as Alaska Native or Northern Plains. Researchers also have found that cancers tend to occur at different times in the life span differently, highlighting the important role of age (see AGING) in understanding the biological and social components of cancers.

In the late 20th and early 21st centuries, even with greater scientific understanding of the causes of cancer and increasingly effective treatment regimens, cancer has continued to be a leading cause of death in the United States. According to reports published in 2008, in the United States. one in four deaths occur from cancer and more than 1,500 people per day die of this disease. Sixty-six percent of cancer patients will live five years past diagnosis. Some researchers suggest that climbing cancer rates may be due to carcinogenic exposure and lifestyle choices, such as smoking, overeating, and sunbathing. Researchers also point out that increased longevity contributes to higher cancer incidence. Because of the high cost of cancer treatment and the likelihood that some cancers will return after several years of remission, it can be difficult for many cancer patients to obtain health insurance without an exclusion for a preexisting condition. Many cancer patients also face difficulty in obtaining life insurance. A study conducted on patients diagnosed with cancer in 1999 reveals that patients without health insurance are 1.6 times more likely to die within five years of diagnosis than patients with private HEALTH CARE coverage.

Although cancer is not specifically defined as a disabling condition in the 1990 AMERICANS WITH DISABILITIES ACT, patients who are disabled from cancer may seek accommodations and benefits for their condition. For example, many cancer patients may request disability leave from work for surgery or chemotherapy treatments, or patients who are disabled by cancer or who have advanced-stage cancers might apply for Social Security benefits, such as Social Security Disability Insurance or SUPPLEMENTARY SECURITY INCOME.

Several foundations offer aid for cancer patients or funds for cancer research. The American Cancer Society is a common source for cancer information and operates a wide variety of support programs for patients. They also promote cancer awareness and early detection. The Susan G. Komen Foundation is a well-known advocacy and fundraising group for breast cancer. Each year the foundation sponsors "Race for the Cure" events that draw thousands of participants. While the "pink ribbon" campaigns and breast cancer fund-raising efforts are hailed by many as important steps to fighting this common disease, critics point out that many businesses profit from "pinkwashing," namely, selling pink products while donating small portions of their proceeds to cancer research. Additionally, critics point out that other forms of cancer are neglected because of the popularity of breast cancer activism. In contrast to disability fund-raising, which tends to depict the helplessness of people with disabilities, cancer-related fund-raising events tend to emphasize the ubiquity of the disease and the strength of those who are "fighting" cancer.

Despite the large numbers of people diagnosed with cancer each year, there remains a social STIGMA surrounding the disease that may stem from a belief that the cancer is the fault of the patient, as many types of cancer may be linked to lifestyle choices. A cancer diagnosis may also carry the stigma of imminent death although survival rates for most cancers have increased markedly in recent decades. Because many cancer treatments involve surgical excision of tumors, removal of body parts or organs may result that may have long-term social and physical impact, similar to other disabling diseases or conditions.

Because many cancer patients now survive treatments, research is focusing on the long-term effects of undergoing cancer treatments. One 2006 study showed that former cancer patients have difficulties in the workplace and have a higher tendency for DEPRESSION. Survivors are also at risk for other chronic medical conditions. These study results suggest that cancer and cancer treatment may have more far-ranging health effects than are currently addressed by medical professionals and national legislation.

While cancer has been known in America since its earliest days, the social and scientific understandings of cancer have changed dramatically in the past 200 years. Therapeutic developments have increased survival rates from the disease, but the continued rise of cancer incidence and inequities in health care point to larger issues about cancer prevention and treatment that remain unresolved. While being a cancer patient may be socially distinguished from having a disability, cancer patients may find that identifying their condition as a short- or long-term disability may aid their applications for state and federal benefit programs. Like the broad history of disability in America, the history of cancer raises important questions about individual agency, medical research, and access to health care benefits.

See also DISEASE.

Jana Remy

Further Reading:

Coleman, Norman. *Understanding Cancer: A Patient's Guide to Diagnosis, Prognosis, and Treatment.* Baltimore: Johns Hopkins University Press, 2006.

Davis, Devra Lee. *The Secret History of the War on Cancer.* New York: Basic Books, 2007.

Leopold, Ellen. *A Darker Ribbon: Breast Cancer, Women, and Their Doctors in the Twentieth Century.* Boston: Beacon Press, 1999.

Wailoo, Keith. *How Cancer Crossed the Color Line: Race and Disease in 20th Century America.* Bethesda, Md.: National Library of Medicine, 2005.

Wishart, Adam. *One in Three: A Son's Journey into the History and Science of Cancer.* New York: Grove Press, 2007.

canes   See LONG CANES.

Cannon, Annie Jump (1863–1941) *astronomer*

Before the mid-20th century, computers were not machines: rather, they were human beings. A "computer" at the Harvard College Observatory in 1900 was a woman, one of a corps of science-minded women hired to make the tedious but crucial calculations required for precise astronomical measurement. Annie Jump Cannon began her career as one of these computers. This research work led Cannon into a pioneering career as an astronomer.

The daughter of a shipbuilder, Cannon was born in Dover, Delaware, on December 11, 1863. Her mother taught her to name the constellations in childhood. When Cannon went to Wellesley College, she studied astronomy with professors Maria Mitchell and Sarah Frances Whiting and earned a degree in physics in 1884. For the next 10 years, she lived at home, caring (see CAREGIVING) for her ailing mother. During her early adulthood, she became DEAF as an aftereffect of scarlet fever and used a HEARING AID thereafter.

In 1893 Cannon returned to Massachusetts to pursue graduate work at Wellesley. At that time Harvard had a fine observatory, and scientists were recruiting computers to assist them with their research. In 1896 she went to work as a computer under physicist Edward C. Pickering, who directed the college's observatory for 42 years. By 1911 Cannon was the curator of photographs at the observatory, and, from 1915 to 1924, she worked on the Draper Catalogue, a compilation of data on more than 200,000 stars. In this work, Cannon devised a classification system for stellar spectra commonly remembered by the mnemonic device "Oh Be a Fine Girl—Kiss Me" (O, B, A, F, G, K, M being star types). Cannon's classification system would become a standard for generations to come. To add to the Draper Catalogue's compedia, Harvard sent her to Peru to photograph stars visible only in the Southern Hemisphere.

Despite her contributions to the field, Cannon was not offered an official Harvard appointment until 1938. And, though she won the Henry Draper Medal from the National Academy of Sciences, she was refused membership in the same body on the basis of her gender and disability. Cannon used prize monies to fund several college scholarships for young women in the sciences; after her death on April 13, 1941, the American Association of University Women established the annual Annie J. Cannon Award in Astronomy.

Annie Jump Cannon was the first woman elected an officer of the American Astronomical Society and the first woman to be awarded an honorary doctorate at Oxford University, but she was not the only deaf woman astronomer at Harvard College Observatory. The head of stellar photometry, Henrietta Swan Leavitt (1868–1921), was also deaf from an illness in early adulthood, and she also started as a computer under Pickering. In an era when jobs for women in science were scarce, and jobs for deaf women in science scarcer still, the Harvard College Observatory offered an important niche for Cannon and Leavitt and their peers. Their work demanded concentration and precision, not strong hearing. Cannon wrote with obvious pride in her work, "Classifying the stars has helped materially in all studies of the structure of the universe. No greater problem is presented to the human mind." Both Cannon and Leavitt have lunar craters named in their honor.

Penny L. Richards

Further Reading:

Greenstein, George. "The Ladies of Observatory Hill." *American Scholar* 62 (1993): 437–446.

Lang, Harry G. *Silence of the Spheres: The Deaf Experience in the History of Science.* Westport, Conn.: Bergin & Garvey, 1994.

Mack, Pamela E. "Straying from Their Orbits: Women in Astronomy in America." In *Women of Science: Righting the Record,* edited by G. Kass-Simon, P. Farnes, and D. Nash, 72–116. Bloomington: Indiana University Press, 1990.

caregiving

Caregiving is the activity undertaken by individuals who look after the health, well-being, and safety of a mentally or physically disabled, chronically ill, or elderly person. The population of caregivers is as diverse as America, and it has historically included FAMILY and COMMUNITY members, paid and enslaved workers (see SLAVERY), and volunteers, as well as professionals and informal caregivers. A study of caregiving, therefore, reveals the complex ways work, relationships, gender, economics, and rights shape the lives of people with disabilities and those who know them.

The term *caregiving* is relatively modern, having been in use since the mid 1960s to describe persons who provide care to ill and disabled people. The term is not universally embraced, however; scholars and activists point out that the "giving" segment implies a one-way relationship, and it obscures the economic value of the activity. The preferred term in the United Kingdom is *carer,* a word that appears to have been in use since the late 17th century. An alternative term is *carework,* which is widely used in Europe, Africa, and Asia.

Since colonial times, primary caregiving responsibility for disabled, ill, or elderly people has typically been undertaken by a family member or an informal caregiver, most commonly a wife, mother, or daughter. Before the 19th century there were no formal medical or social facilities available so it was considered a family's responsibility to care for a loved one with a disability, illness, or who was elderly. Community support was also important, and often was provided by a system of mutual aid among women—help in the sickroom was returned with similar help as needed. Such informal care networks kept disabled people in the community physically, and they might have served to make communities more close-knit, but they also had the disadvantage of often unskilled care and lack of privacy.

To assist families and neighbors who were unable to meet the care needs of a household member, privately paid in-home caregivers have been an important source of community-based care during and since the colonial era. Until the end of the CIVIL WAR in 1865, another form of private home caregiving came from enslaved African-American women in the South. Some women were forced to forgo providing care for their own ill, disabled, or elderly family members until they returned to the slave quarters at night, and they often found themselves too exhausted to do so.

> "He's fragile, very fragile. It's not humanly possible to do this without help."
>
> —Amparo Denney, a California mother interviewed about at-home nursing care for her teenaged son, December 2007

A strong social support network often developed among enslaved women living in close proximity, meeting their family's mutual care needs.

This community-based care system began to change in the mid 19th century, as the fields of medicine, social service, and education were professionalized and as reliance on professional expertise grew. Formal services for people with developmental, mental, and physical disabilities were established, and care shifted to a public, custodial model, relying on INSTITUTIONALIZATION rather than home or community care. In the latter half of the 19th century and into the 20th, public policies and LAWS increasingly focused on creating state and local institutions to provide professional care for disabled people. The policy and institutional goals have varied widely; some seek CURES and EDUCATION while others focus on rehabilitation and protection measures. Ongoing critical debates highlight assets and limitations of segregated caregiving for people with disabilities, as well as the complexity and diversity of care. The care provided in many asylums and HOSPITALS was poor, either through misguided policies or the failings of individuals, and various reform movements over the past 150 years have sought to improve the harsh treatment and ABUSE found in such settings.

During WORLD WAR II, many conscientious objectors who refused to serve in the military were assigned to work in institutions, providing direct care to patients. After the WAR, the network of these carers joined others to build a movement for DEINSTITUTIONALIZATION. Proponents believed that those with MENTAL ILLNESS and physical disabilities could be returned into the community. Under laws that were passed to enforce this shift, community-based services were initiated in the form of schools, day activity programs, and residences in the community.

In the 1970s, other disability advocacy efforts focused on personal care assistants as part of the larger INDEPENDENT LIVING MOVEMENT. The professionalization of personal care assistants recognized both the many demands of this work and the rights and needs of disabled adults. Centers for Independent Living particularly advocated for personal care assistants; activist ORGANIZATIONS increasingly drew attention to personal assistance by the 1990s. The American Disabled for Accessible Public Transit (ADAPT) changed its name to AMERICAN DISABLED FOR ATTENDANT PROGRAMS TODAY in 1990, reflecting the association's commitment to attendant care issues.

According to the U.S. Department of Health and Human Services, in 2000 there were over 50 million informal or family caregivers in the United States providing care for a chronically ill, disabled, or aged family member or friend; at that time, family caregivers were providing 80 percent of long-term care in the nation. The emotional and physical well-being of caregivers has recently become a matter of some professional and media interest: "caregiver stress" is a phrase found throughout the literature on ALZHEIMER'S DISEASE, for example, and it is increasingly addressed by support groups and online communities. As a legislative response to the issue, the Family Medical Leave Act of 1993 (FMLA) requires employers to grant employees weeks of unpaid leave to handle home care responsibilities. (Some states have additional provisions for paid leave or other workplace accommodations for careers.)

Female family members still largely carry out caregiving with approximately 60 percent of family caregivers being women. Feminists have longed argued that in our society caregiving of any kind is seen as "women's work." As such, the nature of caregiving has always been an important topic of discussion for feminists who disagree with the view of caregiving as a "natural" instinct, not a skilled profession. They argue that because of this view, women are automatically given the "burden" of care because it is devalued in our society and poorly paid.

Caregiving is an important topic for understanding American and disability history because it provides a valuable historical and sociological tool that mirrors the changes in the roles, expectations, and treatment of the many minority groups in American society.

See also AGING; ASYLUMS AND INSTITUTIONS; GENDER; PATIENT RIGHTS.

Judith Gerber

Further Reading:

Abel, Emily. *Hearts of Wisdom: American Women Caring for Kin, 1850–1940.* Cambridge, Mass.: Harvard University Press, 2000.

Levine, Carol. *Always on Call: When Illness Turns Families into Caregivers.* New York: United Hospital Fund of New York, 2000.

Longmore, Paul, and Lauri Umansky, eds. *The New Disability History: American Perspectives.* New York: New York University Press, 2001.

Carlin, John (1813–1891) *deaf artist and writer*

Like many of his DEAF cultural peers, the 19th-century artist John Carlin believed that Deaf people should be viewed as equal to hearing people, but he distinguished himself by opposing the use of sign language.

John Carlin was born on June 15, 1813, in Philadelphia to a poor cobbler FAMILY. Historical documents suggest that he and his younger brother were born deaf or became deaf during infancy. Because Carlin's parents could not communicate clearly with John, they did not give him many responsibilities; this allowed the deaf boy to wander about Philadelphia and pursue his interest in drawing. While

roaming the city one day he met David Seixas, the director of a small school for the deaf. In 1820 Carlin joined Seixas's school as its youngest pupil. That same year the state took responsibility for overseeing Seixas's institution and renamed it Mt. Airy School, enabling more deaf students and teachers to join the institution.

Communication played a central role in Carlin's formative experiences at the school. Like other early state schools for the deaf in the United States, the Mt. Airy School primarily employed sign language and FINGERSPELLING for communication. As an emerging language system, however, this method appeared inconsistent and inelegant to Carlin. His frustration with signing likely contributed to his later opposition to its use in deaf schools. After four years at Mt. Airy, Carlin graduated in 1825. His family was financially unable to support additional education for him, so Carlin began to work as a sign and house painter for the next seven years.

As a house painter he used his spare time to study art, English, and other languages. Establishing his own painting business at the age of 19, he saved a modest profit that enabled him to study portrait painting from well-known artists such as John Neagle and J. R. Smith for one year. Over the next few years he saved up enough money to travel to London and Paris in 1838 to study under leading European artists such as Paul Delaroche. His finances depleted, Carlin returned to New York City in 1841 and established a studio where he painted miniatures, portraits, and landscapes for wealthy families. The rise of the daguerreotype at this time decreased the popularity of portraiture, leading him to search for a new artistic career.

While living in New York City, Carlin married a former student from the New York Institution for the Deaf, Miss Wayland, in December 1843. They later had five hearing children. Over the next 10 years, he became increasingly interested in writing as well as in advocacy on behalf of deaf people. He first studied POETRY under an English professor in New York and became a "local celebrity" with his most famous poem "The Mute's Lament," written in 1847. The deaf cultural COMMUNITY was impressed that he was able to master the rhythm, rhyme, and intricacies of the English language. Carlin also dabbled in writing articles for deaf publications (see LITTLE PAPER FAMILY), lectures, and works about architecture.

In many articles for deaf publications, such as the *AMERICAN ANNALS FOR THE DEAF,* Carlin took controversial positions on pressing issues of his day. For example, he challenged his peers to reconsider their support for sign language. Although he used sign language to communicate with other deaf people and in his lectures, Carlin maintained that sign language was an inferior language and a barrier to communicating with the broader hearing community. He believed that fingerspelling and ORALISM were better methods of communicating.

Carlin felt that deaf people would never equal hearing people in their learning or the elegance of their language, yet they could still be valuable and influential to the larger society. According to Carlin, deaf people would be useful citizens and leaders in their chosen careers of manual labor, but few would be considered successful compared with the greater population. Carlin also debated with JOHN FLOURNOY, who advocated the establishment of an exclusive community of deaf signers in the western United States. In his critical appraisal of Flournoy's proposal, Carlin asserted that English was superior to sign language.

On other issues, however, Carlin was considered an important advocate of the general deaf community. For example, he helped raise $6,000 for the building of St. Ann's Episcopal Church in New York City, the first church for the deaf. He proposed the erection of a monument to THOMAS HOPKINS GALLAUDET, the founder of the first school for the Deaf in the United States in Hartford, Connecticut, as a way to honor deaf heritage. In addition to chairing the finance committee for the Gallaudet monument, he headed the fund-raising committee for the Gallaudet Home for the Aged and Infirm Deaf. Widely recognized as a leader in the deaf world, Carlin was invited to give a speech at the first graduation ceremony for the Columbia Institution for the Deaf (later renamed GALLAUDET UNIVERSITY) in 1864. Administrators awarded him the first degree, an honorary master's degree. Many members and allies of the deaf community mourned his death on April 23, 1891.

While Carlin's views about the use of sign language were controversial in the deaf cultural community, he was admired to as an important and respected leader because of his many advocacy campaigns. His life story highlights the complexity of historic deaf IDENTITY, the meaning and use of sign language, and the tenacity of deaf activists.

See also AMERICAN SIGN LANGUAGE; COMMUNICATIONS DEBATE; PAINTERS.

Elizabeth Bush

Further Reading:

Ackerman, Gerald M. *American Orientalists: ACR Edition.* Paris: ACR Edition International, 1994.
Domich, Harold. *John Carlin: A Biographical Sketch.* Washington, D.C.: Gallaudet College Press, 1939.
Van Cleve, John Vickrey, and Barry A. Crouch. *A Place of Their Own: Creating the Deaf Community in America.* Washington, D.C.: Gallaudet University Press, 1989.
"A Very Detailed Account of the Life of John Carlin 1813–1891," *The Deaf Mute's Journal,* New York, 30 April 1891.

carpal tunnel syndrome

Carpal tunnel syndrome (CTS) is characterized by pain, numbness, and weakness of the fingers, hand, and wrist.

Swelling of tissue around the median nerve in the wrist slows or blocks the transmission of nerve signals, leading to the described symptoms. The history of CTS demonstrates the powerful impact of INDUSTRIALIZATION and technology, as well as of treatment.

The first cases of CTS were described in the 19th century. A median nerve compression at the wrist was first described by British surgeon Sir James Paget in 1854. In the United States, the public awareness for chronic wrist injuries increased after passage of the Workman's Compensation Act of 1911. The act made it possible for workers to file claims with their employers for reimbursement of medical expenses and coverage of some lost wages due to work-related injuries. In return, they waived the right to hold employers liable for pain and injuries incurred on the job. Even before the passage of this act, reports on occupational injuries, then called "writer's cramp," "seamstress cramp," "watchmaker's cramp," or "telegraphist cramp" could be found in the American press. These terms have largely disappeared from current views and discussions of occupational injuries. Scholars know very little about the particular living circumstances of people with these injuries since it traditionally affected workers, women, and immigrants, people who were generally not the focus of media or scientific interest.

The first surgery to relieve pressure from the carpal tunnel passage was performed in the 1930s by the surgeon James Learmonth. The term *carpal tunnel syndrome,* a compression of the nerves in a small passageway of the wrist, was introduced by neurosurgeon Frederick Moersch in 1938. After repeated observations in the Orthopaedic Surgery Department of the Cleveland clinic, in a first large-scale study, G. S. Phelan, a surgeon, concluded in the 1950s that CTS was likely made worse by repeated forceful hand movements.

During the 1960s reports about CTS became more frequent. However, the DISABILITY RIGHTS MOVEMENT that emerged in this period in the United States advocating equal civil rights for people with disabilities largely overlooked CTS as a disabling condition. In the 1980s strikes in the meatpacking industry that shifted in focus from winning higher wages and job security to work environment and occupational health and safety issues brought renewed attention to CTS in the workplace. The highest rates of CTS have since been found for occupations and jobs with intensive manual exertion, such as meatpacking and automobile assembly. These jobs are typically performed by a fairly unskilled and comparatively poorer labor force. Jobs that carry a higher risk for CTS development are often linked to minority or immigrant status, and low-paid, unskilled labor is carried out by people who often cannot afford health insurance. If CTS remains untreated because medical help is not sought, for example, because of a lack of insurance, symptoms may quickly become severe, risking permanent IMPAIRMENT of hand function. Ultimately, workers may be forced to give up their jobs and lack of alternative career skills may make it difficult to find new EMPLOYMENT.

While researchers have speculated about a genetic basis of CTS to this day there is no scientifically grounded or reliable test that would predict who is at risk. With increasing emphasis on genetic screening, new sources for stigmatization and discrimination of workers with CTS are likely. Employers may want to minimize the risk of hiring someone who may develop CTS on the job and use these screening tools—should they exist—without considering environmental factors.

While in the eyes of the public CTS is associated with office work, particularly keyboard use, studies have shown that CTS is up to three times more likely among assembly-line workers than data entry personnel. Research conducted by the Mayo Clinic in the United States showed that heavy computer use (up to seven hours per day) did not increase the risk of CTS.

Social as well as legal debates continue to influence the meaning and status of CTS. After the AMERICANS WITH DISABILITIES ACT (ADA) was passed in 1990, cases involving individuals with CTS quickly came to the fore in debates over the meaning of "disability." In the case of *Toyota Motor MFG., Ky., Inc. v. Williams* (2002), for example, the Supreme Court rejected the plaintiff's claim that her CTS, acquired through repetitive manual work, qualified as a disability. The same year, the U.S. Court of Appeals for the Ninth Circuit ruled that CTS is not a disability under federal law. However, people may still be covered by state legislation and in 1997 a former employee of a major coffee manufacturing company successfully sued her employer under the ADA and the Florida Civil Rights Act. In 2004 an army employee who lost his job because alternative job tasks and positions could not be identified that did not make his CTS worse, was not protected by the ADA. Under the ADA, employees have to prove that their disability prevents them from performing specific job duties while they are able to perform job responsibilities with appropriate assistance or modification or alternative work duties. Moreover, job applicants who may be prone to developing CTS are not protected under the ADA. The vast majority of lawsuits claiming that CTS is a disabling condition in the definition of the ADA have been rejected by the courts.

Carpal tunnel syndrome has been highlighted as a good example for the social construction of "disability." Depending on the circumstances, environments, and performance situations, individuals may be perceived or self-identify as "more or less" disabled. Employers supported by court rulings may not perceive CTS as functionally limiting and disabling in situations where employees may. Conversely, insurance companies and employers may view job applicants with a history of CTS as a liability and risk irrespective of job task requirements.

With growing public awareness of CTS, attention has been focused on its social dimensions. Questions about who is at increased risk of developing the condition as a result of his or her social position in society are being asked. Similarly, psychosocial characteristics, such as the perceived control over work processes and stress management, have been discussed. Scholars have yet to fully understand how social and demographic characteristics, such as EDUCATION, GENDER, RACE, ETHNICITY, workplace and task characteristics (duration, frequency), time on the job, and occupational ergonomics interact. Little is known about the long-term consequences of CTS. Specifically, it is unclear to what extent delayed or unsuccessfully treated CTS will lead to permanent disabling consequences and loss of employment.

A study conducted by the Mayo Clinic in Scottsdale, Arizona, and other sources have estimated that more than 3 percent of the U.S. population will experience at least one episode of CTS during their lifetime. The incidence rate in other developed countries seems to be similar to that found in the United States. Nearly 27,000 Americans working in the private sector missed at least one day of work due to CTS in 2001. In the 21st century, carpal tunnel syndrome has accounted for workers losing a median of 25 days of work per year, more than any other occupational injuries reported in the private sector.

The changing representations, treatments, and experiences of carpal tunnel syndrome are important for understanding American history. Tied closely to labor, medicine, and policy, CTS embodies more than a pathological condition. As scholars, activists, researchers, and lawmakers learn more about CTS, new insights into the meaning of disability are likely to emerge.

Thilo Kroll

Further Reading:

Erkulwater, J. L. *Disability Rights and the American Social Safety Net.* Ithaca, N.Y.: Cornell University Press, 2006.

Messing, K., and P. Östlin. *Gender Equality, Work and Health: A Review of the Evidence.* Geneva, Switzerland: World Health Organization, 2006.

National Institute for Occupational Safety and Health. U.S. Department of Health and Human Services. Centers for Disease Control and Prevention. *Worker Health Chart Book.* Atlanta, Ga.: National Institute for Occupational Safety and Health, 2004.

O'Brien, R. *Crippled Justice: The History of Modern Disability Policy in the Workplace.* Chicago: University of Chicago Press, 2001.

castration   See INVOLUNTARY STERILIZATION.

census   See UNITED STATES CENSUS.

Center for Independent Living   See INDEPENDENT LIVING MOVEMENT.

Center for Research on Women with Disabilities

Prior to 1992, research projects relating to women with disabilities received sporadic and minimal funding in the United States. Unlike Canada, which funded numerous investigations and publications, disabled women in the United States struggled to find basic research on SEXUALITY, EDUCATION, and VIOLENCE. In response to advocacy by disabled women, in 1992 the National Institutes of Health issued a major grant to a team led by Margaret A. Nosek, Ph.D., to conduct the first National Study on Women with Disabilities. The team discovered that disabled women faced numerous barriers to health, including ACCESS to HEALTH CARE, dismissal of health needs, and psychosocial barriers to personal romantic interactions. They also recognized the need for an ongoing research center on disabled women and health. In response to this need, in 1993 they created the Center for Research on Women with Disabilities (CROWD) at Baylor College of Medicine.

CROWD's approach challenged many community-based beliefs about the role of medicine and medical research for women with disabilities. Many disabled women suffered negative experiences during prior medical encounters causing them to delay health care appointments. Yet CROWD openly embraced medicine, believing that the tools of medical research can yield important information for women with disabilities.

Since its founding, CROWD has amassed a body of work demonstrating the value of their approach, publishing many journal articles and a book on women with disabilities. The topics are diverse and include the AMERICANS WITH DISABILITIES ACT, health care, health promotion, independent living, personal assistance services, psychological health, secondary conditions, sexuality and reproductive health, social issues, spirituality, and violence.

Finding a representative sample of women with disabilities is always difficult. To its credit, CROWD readily acknowledged the challenges in obtaining an appropriate research sample pool and worked hard to counter those challenges in its research methods. They found that educated Caucasian women respond to mail surveys while disabled women of color respond better to direct contact. Even with extensive outreach, it is still difficult to get a representative sample. For example, according to CROWD, only 9 percent of women with disabilities have a college education, yet their study *Violence Against Women with Physical Disabilities* (2002) reveals that 49 percent of the women studied had a postsecondary education. The same study included respondents who were African American (24 percent), Hispanic (21 percent), American Indian or Asian/Pacific Islander (8 percent), and Caucasian (49 percent). These women, regardless of education, had a median personal income of $7,000 and a median household income of $15,000.

Dr. Nosek continues to lead CROWD and its many research projects. With over 100 publications and a definitive book, *Women with Physical Disabilities: Achieving and Maintaining Health and Well Being* (1996), CROWD remains at the forefront of health research on women with disabilities.

See also ACTIVISM AND ADVOCACY; ORGANIZATIONS; REPRODUCTIVE RIGHTS.

Corbett Joan O'Toole

Further Reading:

Center for Research on Women with Disabilities. "Violence Against Women with Physical Disabilities." Available online. URL: http://www.bcm.edu/crowd/index.cfm?pmid=1347. Accessed December 30, 2006.
———. "Investigating Violence against Women with Disabilities." Available online. URL: http://www.bcm.edu/crowd/index.cfm?pmid=2081. Accessed December 30, 2006.
Center on Women Policy Studies. "The Barbara Waxman Fiduccia Papers on Women and Girls with Disabilities." Available online. URL: http://www.centerwomenpolicy.org/programs/waxmanfiduccia/default.asp. Accessed December 30, 2006.
Disabled Women's Network Ontario. Available online. URL: http://dawn.thot.net. Accessed December 30, 2006.
Krotoski, D., M. A. Nosek, and M. A. Turk, eds. *Women with Physical Disabilities: Achieving and Maintaining Health and Well Being.* Baltimore: Paul H. Brookes Publishers, 1996.

Center on Human Policy

The Center on Human Policy is a Syracuse University–based advocacy, policy, and research institute that was founded by Burton Blatt in 1971. Blatt had exposed conditions at institutions for people with intellectual disabilities in a 1966 book, CHRISTMAS IN PURGATORY, and in 1967 article in *Look* magazine. He had come to Syracuse University to chair its division of SPECIAL EDUCATION and rehabilitation in 1969. Although Blatt held his doctorate in special education and had spent his career as a public school teacher and then a special education professor, he recruited social scientists who had no experience in the area of disability to work at the Center on Human Policy because he believed that the field of special education needed fresh perspectives to confront the problems facing people with disabilities in society.

The late 1960s and the 1970s were a turbulent era in what was then known as the field of MENTAL RETARDATION. Civil rights attorneys, often working with parent groups, filed lawsuits challenging the school exclusion of children with intellectual and other disabilities and alleging abuse and neglect in institutions across the country. The Center on Human Policy used nonlegal strategies, including community organizing, exposing institutional conditions, and preparing educational materials, to advocate for educational rights, DEINSTITUTIONALIZATION, and later full inclusion in schools and communities. According to historians David J. Rothman and Sheila M. Rothman in their 1984 book, *The Willowbrook Wars: A Decade of Struggle for Social Justice,* the center's staff included "the most radical thinkers in the field." In 1979 the center issued *The Community Imperative,* a declaration supporting the rights of *all* people with disabilities to community living, which was endorsed by reform-minded disability, parent, and professional leaders. By the 1980s the center's staff included not only social scientists and professionals but also parents of children with disabilities and people with developmental disabilities. Although many of the center's efforts have focused on people with intellectual disabilities and their families, it has also advocated publicly for the right to a local education for DEAF children, accessible public TRANSPORTATION, the removal of architectural barriers, life-sustaining care and treatment for people with severe cognitive disabilities, and home and community-based services for people with physical disabilities and elderly persons.

As a university-based institute, the Center on Human Policy has always been involved in research and teaching. The research of faculty, staff, and students at the center has been based on qualitative methods, including participant observation, in-depth interviewing, and the analysis of historical sources and archival records. They have published books and articles on the life stories of people with disabilities, ethnographies of institutions, schools, and community settings, the experiences and perspectives of people with disabilities and their families, and the history of disability as well as on qualitative research methods themselves. Faculty associated with the center created the graduate DISABILITY STUDIES program at Syracuse University in 1995. In 2005 the center joined with other Syracuse University units involved in disability LAW AND POLICY to create the Center on Human Policy, Law, and Disability Studies.

See also ACTIVISM AND ADVOCACY; COGNITIVE AND INTELLECTUAL DISABILITY; DEVELOPMENTAL DISABILITY; FAMILY; PARENT ADVOCACY GROUPS.

Steven J. Taylor

Further Reading:
Center on Human Policy, Law, and Disability Studies. URL: http://disabilitystudies.syr.edu.

Rothman, David J., and Shiela M. Rothman. *The Willowbrook Wars: A Decade of Struggle for Social Justice.* New York: Harper & Row, 1984.

Taylor, S. J., and S. D. Blatt. *In Search of the Promised Land: The Collected Papers of Burton Blatt.* Washington, D.C.: American Association on Mental Retardation, 1999.

cerebral palsy

Cerebral palsy, or CP, is a nonprogressive disorder affecting muscle coordination and body movement in young CHILDREN and adults. Doctors use the term *cerebral palsy* to refer to any one of a number of neurological disorders that appear in infancy or early childhood and permanently affect body movement and muscle coordination. The disorders do not worsen over time. However, the development of secondary orthopedic difficulties such as ARTHRITIS and osteoporosis are fairly common. The term *cerebral* refers to the two hemispheres of the brain, in this case, to the cerebral cortex, which is the part of the brain that directs muscle movement. *Palsy* refers to the loss or IMPAIRMENT of motor function.

The existence of cerebral palsy prior to the 19th century has not been formally recorded, although it is fairly certain that cerebral palsy has existed as long as there have been human beings. Historically, those with CP and their families often experienced harassment and isolation due to the common public misperception that individuals with cerebral palsy were the products of incest or partial smothering. Parents also would keep their own children away from children with cerebral palsy based on another false belief that CP resulted from poor sanitary habits. Due to these misperceptions, a large majority of people with cerebral palsy were stigmatized and shunned by the rest of the population. Many were sent to ASYLUMS because they did not fit in with "NORMAL" society.

In 1861 cerebral palsy was first documented by English surgeon William Little, who observed young children who had stiff, spastic muscles in their legs and arms, which made it difficult for them to grasp objects and walk. He noted that most of these children were born prematurely or had highly complicated deliveries, and the doctor suggested their condition was the result of oxygen deprivation during birth. The lack of oxygen damaged sensitive brain tissues controlling movement, causing cerebral palsy. Over time and into adulthood, the conditions faced by these children in their youth did not better or worsen. Little named the condition "Little's Disease," which is now known as spastic diplegia, one of the several disorders affecting motor control classified as cerebral palsy.

In 1897, however, the noted psychiatrist SIGMUND FREUD disagreed. He observed that children with cerebral palsy often had other neurological problems such as MENTAL RETARDATION, visual disturbances, and seizures. Freud then suggested that the disorder might have roots earlier in life, where brain development faced complications in the womb. However, Freud's explanation was not highly regarded; doctors and families agreed that birth complications caused cerebral palsy.

It was not until the 1980s when scientists funded by the National Institute of Neurological Disorders and Stroke analyzed extensive data from more than 35,000 newborns and their mothers, and discovered that complications during birth and labor accounted for less than 10 percent of the infants born with cerebral palsy. In most cases, they could find no single, obvious cause. The studies prompted doctors and researchers to explore alternative causes for cerebral palsy, as well as the increasing incidence of the disorder, since technology has enabled more premature and low birth weight babies to survive past infancy.

Before the 1940s few children with cerebral palsy survived to adulthood. In the 21st century, because of the latest improvements in medical care and assistive technologies, 65 to 90 percent of children with cerebral palsy live into their adult years. There is, however, a downside to the increase in life expectancy for individuals with CP. Cerebral palsy is accompanied by a rise in medical and functional problems—some of them beginning at a relatively early age. The most prevalent medical problem is premature AGING. Individuals with cerebral palsy experience premature aging by age 40 because of the added stress and strain the disorder places on their bodies. Additionally, the developmental delays that often accompany cerebral palsy keep some organ systems from developing to their full capacity and level of performance, thus requiring extra strain on organs to perform at optimal level.

There have been many notable individuals with cerebral palsy: Stephen Hopkins, a signer of the Declaration of Independence in 1776, was believed to have cerebral palsy as he was quoted to say "My hand trembles, but my heart does not"; Christy Brown, an Irish painter and author of *My Left Foot* (1954), which was adapted into a FILM in 1989; HALE J. ZUKAS, a pioneer in DISABILITY RIGHTS MOVEMENTS; HARILYN ROUSSO, an author, psychotherapist, and social worker who founded the Association of Mental Health Practitioners with Disabilities; GERI JEWELL, ACTOR and comedian, best known for her role on *Diff'rent Strokes* in the early 1980s; Bill Porter, an American salesman whose inspirational story was made into the TNT TELEVISION movie *Door to Door* in 2002; Josh Blue, an American comedian and winner of the fourth season of NBC's *Last Comic Standing* in 2006; and Susie Maroney, a world record–holding marathon swimmer.

Cerebral palsy is the second-most expensive DEVELOPMENTAL DISABILITY to manage over the course of a person's lifetime, with an average lifetime cost per person of $921,000 (in 2003 dollars). The incidence in the United States is approx-

imately an average of 2 per 1,000 live births that develop CP per year; and there has been a slight increase in recent years. United Cerebral Palsy estimates that 800,000 children and adults in the United States are living with one or more of the symptoms of cerebral palsy. Although there have been significant improvements in neonatal nursing to help reduce the number of babies who develop cerebral palsy, these improvements also mean that the incidence of CP could increase due to the survival of low birth weight babies.

The population of adults with cerebral palsy continues to grow in the early 21st century. With this growth accompanies the need for greater independence and advocacy. Issues such as independent and multigroup homes, EMPLOYMENT opportunities, and VOTING rights are the focus for advancing the independence of people with disabilities.

The implementation of group home arrangements has greatly increased the independence of adults with cerebral palsy. These homes are specialized for easy accessibility and located in urban and suburban areas, fully integrated into the neighborhood. As the improvements in medicine and therapy are constantly advancing the independence of persons with cerebral palsy, the need for additional group homes and independent living situations greatly increases as well. The U.S. Department of Housing and Urban Development helps fund a number of such projects nationwide. Though many problems remain, a major victory for the disability COMMUNITY is the significant decrease in the number of children and adults with cerebral palsy in institutions since the 1950s and 1960s.

Other important issues for those with CP to consider are employment rights and opportunities. Since 1990, when Congress passed the AMERICANS WITH DISABILITIES ACT (ADA), the government has formally recognized the rights of persons with disabilities as related to employment, TRANSPORTATION, housing, and communication ACCESS, among others. Federal support has facilitated accommodations in job placement and rights in the workplace. In a 2000 survey, the Department of Labor estimated that 4.2 million people with disabilities are employed within the United States.

Outside of governmental organizations, disability advocacy groups and CP activists serve an important role in the CP community. ORGANIZATIONS such as UNITED CEREBRAL PALSY assist adults in job placement, housing, therapy, ASSISTIVE TECHNOLOGY training, early intervention programs, individual and FAMILY support, social and recreation programs, community living, state and local referrals, and advocacy.

Despite many achievements, the majority of people with cerebral palsy and other types of disabilities still do not enjoy complete rights. Increasingly, laws and court decisions have narrowed the protections granted by the ADA, and state and federal budgets have reduced money for services and programs that benefit people with disabilities. As a consequence, awareness and advocacy continues to be the key ingredients for helping people with cerebral palsy and other disabilities.

See also ACTIVISM AND ADVOCACY; CEREBRAL PALSY JOURNAL; LAW AND POLICY.

Aneri Mehta

Further Reading:
Centers for Disease Control and Prevention. Economic Costs Associated with Mental Retardation, Cerebral Palsy, Hearing Loss, and Vision Impairment, United States, 2003. MMWR 2004;53:57-9. Available online. URL: http://www.cdc.gov/mmwr/preview/mmwrhtml/mm5303a4.htm.
Department of Labor, Office of Disability Employment Policy. Available online. URL: http://www.dol.gov/odep/archives/ek01/stats.htm.
National Institute of Neurological Disorders and Stroke. Available online. URL: http://www.ninds.nih.gov/disorders/cerebral_palsy/detail_cerebral_palsy.htm#109883104.

Cerebral Palsy Journal

Cerebral Palsy Journal, a quarterly publication "of, for, and by" people with CEREBRAL PALSY, was published by the Institute of Logopedics (now known as "Heartspring") from 1940 to 1968 under three different names: *Spastic Review* (1940–49), *Cerebral Palsy Review* (1949–65), and *Cerebral Palsy Journal* (1965–68). The history of this journal demonstrates some of the pressing issues surrounding cerebral palsy and society's responses to people with cerebral palsy.

Dr. Martin Franklin Palmer, director of the Institute of Logopedics, served as the journal's technical consultant from 1940 until 1965. Although especially directed toward to scientists and workers who wanted to share the results of research and professional experiences, the publication also was intended for a diverse range of readers affected by cerebral palsy, including individuals with cerebral palsy, their families, and educators. Topics in the journal ranged widely, including book reviews of medical publications, issues in research, communication methods, COMMUNITY opinions, EDUCATION and treatment methods, and available grants for research into cerebral palsy. Editors actively sought international contributions to the publication and promoted original works in the field.

The *Cerebral Palsy Review* was renamed twice. From 1940 until 1949 the journal was known as *Spastic Review,* but greater sensitivity to the negative connotations associated with the term *spastic* motivated editors to retitle the journal the *Cerebral Palsy Review.* In 1965, shortly after Palmer's death, it acquired the name *Cerebral Palsy Journal.* When, in 1968, a new administration financially restructured the Institute of Logopedics, the *Cerebral Palsy Journal* ceased publication.

This journal, like many other medical publications about disabilities, demonstrates the powerful role scientists, doctors, and educators play in the understanding and REPRESENTATION of people with disabilities. As historical sources, publications such as the *Cerebral Palsy Review* reveal many of the pressing issues of its time.

See also MEDICAL MODEL OF DISABILITY; PRINT MEDIA.

Elizabeth A. Marotta

Further Reading:
"Child Behavior toward the Parent: A Factor Analysis of Mothers' Reports of Disabled Children." *Journal of Autism and Developmental Disorders* 14, no. 2 (1984).
Hallahan, Daniel P., et al. "Selective Attention in Cerebral Palsied and Normal Children." *Journal of Abnormal Child Psychology* 1, no. 3 (1973).
Hunt, Jacob T. "Children with Crippling Conditions and Special Health Problems." *Review of Educational Research* 33, no. 1 (1963): 99–108.
"Influencing Work and Social Attitudes of Cerebral Palsied Clients." *Cerebral Palsy Review* 24, no. 6 (1963): 9–11.
Love, Russel, J., et al. "Speech Performance, Dysphagia and Oral Reflexes in Cerebral Palsy." *Journal of Speech and Hearing Disorders* 45 (1980): 59–75.

Cerebral Palsy Review See CEREBRAL PALSY JOURNAL.

Chamberlin, Judi (ca. 1944–) *activist and advocate for mental health consumers/survivors/ex-patients*

Judi Chamberlin is widely regarded as one of the most effective PSYCHIATRIC SURVIVOR activists and ex-patient advocates. *Ex-patient's movement* is a term used to describe the collective interests of people who have experienced psychiatric treatment and hospitalization. For psychiatric survivors, consumers, and ex-patients, this movement represents compassion, choice, humanity, and self-EMPOWERMENT.

Beyond the fact of her birth about 1944, scholars know few details about Chamberlin's early years and life story until she adopted her role as an activist and advocate in 1971, years after repeated psychiatric hospitalizations left her feeling marginalized and abused. In that year Chamberlin joined other ex-patients to found the Mental Patients Liberation Front in Boston. In 1978 her most popular book, *On Our Own: Patient-Controlled Alternatives to the Mental Health System,* was published. This work, which has become a classic text in the psychiatric survivor movement, challenged the biomedical interpretation of MENTAL ILLNESS and called upon psychiatric survivors to engage actively in policy decisions over treatments. Since that time, Chamberlin has written extensively about the ABUSES of human rights that, in her view, characterize psychiatric practice.

A desire to bring awareness to these issues has shaped much of her ACTIVISM during and since the 1970s. For example, in 1986, Chamberlin cofounded the NATIONAL ASSOCIATION OF PSYCHIATRIC SURVIVORS (NAPS). Formerly known as the National Alliance of Mental Patients, NAPS rejected all forms of involuntary treatments and its members produced newsletters and gave public presentations that challenged traditional views of the mental health system. Chamberlin also supported the development of mutual help centers, such as the Ruby Rogers Advocacy and Drop-In Center, a mental health clinic founded in 1986 and run by and for persons with mental illness. The Mental Patients Liberation Front helped plan its creation and raised funds for this clinic. Since 1989 she has served as the director of education and training, senior consultant on survivor perspectives, and project director for the Center for Psychiatric Rehabilitation with Boston University. In 1992 she helped found the National Empowerment Center (NEC). The NEC's mission is to "carry a message of recovery, empowerment, hope and healing to people who have been labeled with mental illness" through education, media, referrals, networking, research, and policymaking.

In recognition of her work, Chamberlin was awarded the Distinguished Service Award by President George H. W. Bush in 1992. In 1995 she received the David J. Vail National Advocacy Award and the Pike Prize, an honor given to those demonstrating outstanding service to people with disabilities.

In the early 21st century, Chamberlin has remained an active board member with the National Association for Rights Protection and Advocacy, the Center for Public Representation, Mental Disability Rights International, and MindFreedom International; she also serves on several committees, including the Massachusetts Mental Health State Planning Council, the Disability Law Center Governing Board, the Coalition for the Legal Rights of People with Disabilities, and the Consumer/Survivor Mental Health Research and Policy Work Group.

Chamberlin's scholarship and activism directly challenge the fundamental assumption that inpatient psychiatric treatment is helpful and that psychiatric drugs are safe and effective. Her radical interpretations of mental illness represent a significant although often underexamined perspective in history, challenging both mainstream society and many disability rights activists to reconsider the social meaning of psychiatric differences and the status of people with—or perceived to have—mental illness.

See also SOCIAL CONSTRUCTION OF DISABILITY.

Kim A. Gorgens

Further Reading:
Chamberlin, Judi. "Human Rights, Not Patient Rights." Available online. URL: http://www.contac.org/j1.htm. Accessed March 15, 2008.

———. *On Our Own: Patient-Controlled Alternatives to the Mental Health System.* New York: McGraw-Hill, 1978.
———. "A Working Definition of Empowerment." *Psychiatric Rehabilitation Journal* 20 (2007): 43–46.

Chaney, Lon (1883–1930) *silent film actor*

Born in Colorado Springs, Colorado, on April 1, 1883, to DEAF parents Frank and Emma Chaney, Lon Chaney achieved fame as Hollywood's first character actor star. Featured in more than 150 silent FILMS and one talking motion picture, Chaney is best known today for his portrayals of the characters Quasimodo and Erik in the classic silent films *HUNCHBACK OF NOTRE DAME* (Universal, 1923) and *Phantom of the Opera* (Universal, 1925), respectively. Identified popularly as the "Man of a Thousand Faces," Columbia Studios produced a fictional film version of Chaney's life with that title in 1957, which featured actor James Cagney as Chaney. Previously honored with a star on the Hollywood Walk of Fame, the U.S. Postal Service issued a 32-cent stamp in 1994 with his image as the *Phantom* character Erik as part of a series of classic Hollywood monster actors.

One of four hearing children born to his deaf parents, Lon Chaney developed communication skills of sign, gesture, pantomime, and mimicry that he used to good advantage in vaudeville, THEATER, and movies. Withdrawing from school at an early age to care for his ill mother and younger siblings, he eventually found EMPLOYMENT as a stagehand and actor in local and touring theater companies. After an unhappy divorce from his first wife, singer Cleva Creighton, Chaney moved to Hollywood. By 1918 he had earned more than 100 film credits, and one year later Chaney received critical acclaim for his role as "the Frog" in *The Miracle Man* (Paramount/Artcraft, 1919). Pretending to be "a cripple," Chaney's con-artist character is repeatedly cured by a DEAF-BLIND faith healer in order to win contributions from amazed onlookers. When a disabled onlooker is actually cured, the gang of fakes mends their larcenous ways.

In order to play the "miraculous" scene in which the character Frog unravels his DEFECTIVE legs and walks upright, Chaney endured the physical pain of binding his legs and feet behind him into a harness. Through use of extensive makeup together with the leather harnesses, the actor contorted his body and face into numerous roles as disabled characters; so many of such roles that historian Martin Norden has referred to Chaney as the "Man of a Thousand Disabilities." Despite the grotesque appearance of his characters, contemporary audiences and critics commented that the actor always managed to reveal the humanity of the character beneath the makeup.

After the box office and critical successes of *Hunchback* and *Phantom,* Chaney became one of Metro-Goldwyn-Mayer's top stars. At MGM, Chaney worked with writer-director Todd Browning in several films that featured characters with a physical disability. However, Chaney's most popular MGM film was *Tell It to the Marines* (1927) in which, divested of any grotesque makeup he played a marine sergeant. In 1930 he made a successful talking picture debut in *The Unholy Three* (MGM, 1930). Chaney died shortly after the film's release.

After his death on August 26, 1930, contemporary newspapers reported many movie theaters held memorial services in his honor. Within the deaf COMMUNITY, Chaney continues to be cited as an early example of a successful hearing child of deaf parents.

See also CHILDREN OF DEAF ADULTS (CODAS); POPULAR CULTURE; REPRESENTATION.

John S. Schuchman

Further Reading:

Anderson, Robert G. *Faces, Forms, Films: The Artistry of Lon Chaney.* New York: Castle Books, 1971.

Blake, Michael F. *The Films of Lon Chaney.* Lanham, Md.: Madison Books, 2001.

Norden, Martin F. *The Cinema of Isolation, A History of Physical Disability in the Movies.* New Brunswick, N.J.: Rutgers University Press, 1994.

charity

From enduring cultural figures like the "crippled" child Tiny Tim in Charles Dickens's 19th-century novella, *A Christmas Carol,* to charitable organizations such as the MUSCULAR DYSTROPHY ASSOCIATION in the 20th century, charity has played a defining role in American disability history.

Notions of charity have strong religious roots that early Americans employed as part of their participation in organized, spiritual doctrine. Particularly since the early 19th century when religious revivals spread rapidly across the young nation, charity accrued specific social functions. For example, charity as a value expressed in organized action enabled women, especially white middle-class women, to lead "helping" programs; charitable work included a variety of services, including administering medical and health services, as well as literacy, job, and religious training. Through these efforts, charity activists helped define the meaning of disability in America by judging and labeling certain populations worthy of support.

The change in the late 19th and early 20th centuries of the idea of charity—a social relationship framed by one's desire to alleviate distress—had a strong impact on individuals with disabilities. Progressive reformers of the era implemented what they termed "scientific charity," a concept based on empirical evidence used to determine appropriate relief. Still, there were always those who believed that in a truly just society charity would be unnecessary. Thus some Progressives attempted to move away from a sentimentalizing, paternalizing approach to charity. These reformers sought to emphasize rehabilitation over handouts, lobbying state and national legislatures to pass new initiatives on urban reform measures, including WORKERS' COMPENSATION. It was the humiliating image of disability inextricably linked with charity that the LEAGUE OF THE PHYSICALLY HANDICAPPED, an early disability rights ORGANIZATION, sought to dispel. In the 1930s league members fought to remove the letters "PH" (for Physically Handicapped) that were stamped on their work records because many potential employers would thus deem them unemployable. The existence of the league effectively challenged earlier assumptions that disabled individuals were incapable or unwilling to find work, which, by extension, undermined the foundational premise of charity: the disadvantaged individual necessarily requires benevolent intervention rather than the league's call for social justice.

An important and contradictory figure in the history of charity and disability led the nation at this time. President FRANKLIN D. ROOSEVELT, who had contracted infantile paralysis (POLIO) over a decade before his inauguration in 1933, both challenged and reinforced notions of charity toward people with disabilities. Powerful, resourceful, and privileged, President Roosevelt rejected expressions of charity toward himself personally and actively hid his disability from public view. Yet he also played a central role in the proliferation of organized charities addressing disability conditions. For example, in 1938 Roosevelt helped create the NATIONAL FOUNDATION FOR INFANTILE PARALYSIS (NFIP) to provide resources and undertake research toward the treatment and eventual CURE of infantile paralysis. It was one of America's first highly mobilized, sophisticated charity ORGANIZATIONS.

The NFIP revolutionized organized charity by infusing benevolence with glamour and excitement. Emerging from

> "You are sorry for me!!!
> Eternal God! Am I then that thing
> As to excite pity!
> Give me deep scorn, without disguise,
> Most rancorous hate, abhorrence
> Any thing, but pity!"
>
> —Joseph Lyons, a deaf South Carolina man,
> in his diary, April 1833

the Warm Springs Foundation, the NFIP adopted its distinctive fund-raising campaigns: the annual Birthday Balls. These events were held each January from 1934 to 1945 in cities across the country to coincide with Roosevelt's birthday. The balls, gala events hosted at country clubs and hotels, featured entertainment and pageantry. These events enabled citizens to exercise their social and moral responsibility to improve the health of America's youth while simultaneously demonstrating their patriotic allegiance in supporting the president and the health of the civic body. Funds collected helped pay for individuals' care and rehabilitation as well as for medical research. The charitable giving to eradicate polio especially constituted a form of enlightened self-interest as those who donated understood that their generosity embodied a means by which they could protect themselves and those whom they loved.

The NFIP was also the first organization to realize the ideological, social, and political power of modern media. Using radio broadcasts, FILMS, and print ads (see ADVERTISING), the MARCH OF DIMES campaigns conveyed the image of the frightened, "pathetic" polio child across the country in order to galvanize support. The first POSTER CHILD, a product of the March of Dimes, established this practice as a charitable organization convention. Later, parent-initiated organizations, such as UNITED CEREBRAL PALSY and the MUSCULAR DYSTROPHY ASSOCIATION, employed techniques learned from the March of Dimes to raise money for the needs of CHILDREN with other disabilities. In addition to raising money to advance ongoing research, the March of Dimes also provided polio patients with a wide range of medical, financial, and personal support without means testing. Furthermore, it sponsored Jonas Salk's research that resulted in the 1955 discovery of the Salk polio vaccine, which ended five decades of polio epidemics in the United States.

As the charity industry evolved, methods to raise awareness and generate emotional interest in individuals with disabilities became more sophisticated. The rise of the charity TELETHON, pioneered by the Muscular Dystrophy Association in 1966 and hosted by comedian JERRY LEWIS, enhanced an accepted practice of exhibiting children with disabilities as DEPENDENT and pitiful subjects as a way of obtaining financial support. In a similar vein, the 1998 TELEVISION special, *Christopher Reeve: A Celebration of Hope,* represented disability as a pitiful condition. Reeve's TV program was presented as an informational/educational special designed to raise awareness about spinal cord injuries and to secure funds for his organization. These strategies, common to many charity fund-raising campaigns, position people with disabilities as sentimental figures as a means of raising money.

The cultural messages of the late-20th century charity movements pervaded other aspects of American life. As late as 1970, a postage stamp was issued titled, "Hope for the Crippled," picturing a person seated in a wheelchair, rising to stand up. As scholars like PAUL LONGMORE have shown, charities commonly foster expectations that the recipients must "OVERCOME" their impairments in order to be truly worthy. In this way, charities contribute to the STIGMA of disability as well as the disempowerment of people with disabilities who are unable or unwilling to achieve these expectations.

The DISABILITY RIGHTS MOVEMENT, which had gained considerable momentum by the 1970s, marked an effort to counter the firmly entrenched and continually reiterated connection between disability and charity. Through demonstrations, sit-ins, public court appearances, and other forms of social PROTEST to gain equal ACCESS to EDUCATION, EMPLOYMENT, and the built environment, disability rights activists distinguished themselves from the "Tiny Tim" STEREOTYPE that had implanted itself in the public consciousness. These activists specifically have challenged charitable models of disability by presenting individuals with disabilities who—as neighbors, community members, parents (as well as children), active citizens, students, and workers of all kinds—continue to enrich society as they demonstrate another way of being in the world. Other scholars have pointed out contradictions in organized charities, including the prevalence of nondisabled administrators leading associations and profiting personally from the business of charity. Continued and heated debates over the assets, limitations, and overall place of charity in the lives of people with disabilities reflect the diverse and changing meaning that charity embodies.

As a social value, interpretive model, as well as organized activity and policy, charity offers a rich and enduring field for study in American history. Its many intersections with disability raise new questions about REPRESENTATION, power, and IDENTITY—central themes in our nation's evolution.

See also ACTIVISM AND ADVOCACY; ORGANIZATIONS; RELIGION; ROOSEVELT WARM SPRINGS INSTITUTE FOR REHABILITATION; STIGMA.

Doris Zames Fleischer

Further Reading:

Drake, Robert F. "A Critique of the Role of the Traditional Charities." In *Disability and Society: Emerging Issue and Insights,* edited by Len Barton, 147–166. New York: Longman, 1996.

Fleischer, Doris Zames, and Frieda Zames. *The Disability Rights Movement: From Charity to Confrontation.* Philadelphia: Temple University Press, 2001.

Gallagher, Hugh Gregory. *FDR's Splendid Deception.* Rev. ed. Arlington, Va.: Vandamere Press, 1994.

Klages, Mary. *Woeful Affliction: Disability and Sentimentality in Victorian America.* Philadelphia: University of Pennsylvania Press, 1999.

Charles, Ray (Ray Charles Robinson) (1930–2004)
musician and singer

Ray Charles remains one of the most famous Americans with a disability. A gifted pianist, Charles performed in a variety of styles, including rhythm and blues, gospel, jazz, country, crossover popular MUSIC, and rock and roll.

Ray Charles Robinson was born on September 23, 1930, in Albany, Georgia, and grew up mostly in Greenville, Florida. When he was five years old, Ray witnessed his brother George drown in a tub. That same year he was diagnosed with glaucoma, which, over the following year, resulted in his complete BLINDNESS.

From 1937 to 1945 he attended the St. Augustine (Florida) School for the Deaf and Blind, an institution that practiced multiple types of segregation: teachers separated boys from girls and whites from blacks. Ray, who was black, learned to read BRAILLE quickly, including braille musical notation (see BRAILLE MUSIC). He also learned to play piano, clarinet, and saxophone. Much to his chagrin, his teachers encouraged students to study the music of classical composers Frederic Chopin and Johann Strauss and discouraged them from playing boogie woogie. Radio provided Ray with the music of Duke Ellington, Count Basie, Benny Goodman, Artie Shaw, and Glenn Miller.

His mother, Aretha Williams Robinson, died when Ray was 15. She had instilled in young Ray a commitment to self-reliance, and she encouraged him to "OVERCOME" blindness by using his mind and other senses. Consequently, throughout his life, Charles refused to use GUIDE DOGS or canes to assist him. Because there was already a famous Ray Robinson in the boxer Sugar Ray Robinson, the musician dropped his last name and became known as Ray Charles.

From the late 1940s through the 1970s Charles distinguished himself as a skilled musician in several genres, including rhythm and blues (R&B), gospel, jazz, and country. For example, by 1948 he had moved to Seattle and formed the Maxim Trio, an ensemble that played in a style reminiscent of Nat King Cole. "Confession Blues" (1949) was a major R&B hit. In 1952 Charles signed a recording contract with Atlantic Records of New York, and he released the gospel song "It Should Have Been Me." He performed jazz with Milt Jackson of the Modern Jazz Quartet at the 1958 Newport Jazz Festival. He then moved his contract to ABC-Paramount Records in 1959. That same year he performed in Carnegie Hall. His popular 1961 tune, "Georgia on My Mind," was named the official state song of Georgia in 1979. In 1962 he broadened his repertoire to include country music with songs such as "I Can't Stop Loving You."

In 1964, after being arrested at Logan Airport in Boston for possession of marijuana and heroin, Charles decided to end his 16-year drug habit abruptly, and he sought treatment during the winter of 1965 at St. Francis Hospital in Lynwood, California. While there, he substituted the urge for drugs by learning chess. As a beginner, he felt the pieces before and after each move, and eventually he memorized the board's layout. After he completed his rehabilitation, Charles generally did not discuss his experiences with ADDICTION.

Although never a major figure in either the African-American civil rights movement or the DISABILITY RIGHTS MOVEMENT, Charles had promoted both causes, providing financial contributions as well as occasional public support. For example, Charles worked with the National Association for Sickle Cell Disease, which advocates for greater research and treatment for a condition often found among African Americans. Treatment for an inner ear pain in 1983 caused by an opening in his Eustachian tube drew Charles to the Los Angeles nonprofit organization, Ear International. His donations and fund-raising supported research on various hearing and SPEECH DISORDERS. Several disability advocacy ORGANIZATIONS have honored Charles, including the AMERICAN FOUNDATION FOR THE BLIND, which awarded him the Helen Keller Personal Achievement Award in 1994. Shortly before his death, he was asked what effect blindness had had on his career. Charles replied, "Nothing, nothing, nothing." He died on June 10, 2004, in Beverly Hills, California, from acute liver disease.

Ray Charles remains one of the most recognized American pop icons with a disability. Like several other African-American blind musicians, Charles generally downplayed his disability, often casting himself as a stereotypical "overcomer" of disability. Yet his blindness and experiences with addiction shaped both his professional options as well as his reception by society.

See also POPULAR CULTURE; RACE; REPRESENTATION.

Ralph Hartsock

Further Reading:

Charles, Ray. *Brother Ray: Ray Charles' Own Story.* New York: Dial, 1978.

Lydon, Michael. *Ray Charles: Man and Music.* New York: Routledge, 2004.

Ritz, David. *Ray Charles: Voice of Soul.* New York: Chelsea House, 1994.

children

Historically, the subjects of childhood and disability have often been linked because of negative cultural STEREOTYPES portraying persons with disabilities as dependent or child-like. More positively, however, disability has for centuries presented an educational challenge, thus focusing attention on the young. With the emergence of the field of child psychology late in the 19th century, a new awareness of normative childhood and adolescent development led to greater awareness of physical, cognitive, or social-behavioral differences among children. It is more than coincidental that the first decades of the 20th century, which reformers hoped would be "the Century of the Child," saw the beginning of public school SPECIAL classes and ORGANIZATIONS such as the COUNCIL FOR EXCEPTIONAL CHILDREN.

In colonial New England, despite danger of exposure to infectious DISEASE, more children than elsewhere survived to assume essentially adult roles by adolescence. Since the young were important contributors to the FAMILY economy, a high premium was placed on familial responsibility, obedience, and self-control, values underscored by Puritan doctrine and enforced by the community. Conversely, the response to youthful expressions of anger, disobedience, and sloth could be harsh. Since literacy was far less critical than physical ability and moral behavior, most children with cognitive delays probably blended into the community. It is also likely that such children, as well as those with mild physical IMPAIRMENTS, were among those enrolled in the Massachusetts colony "dame schools" established through a 1647 statute. But more than two centuries passed before much schooling was available to more than a minority of American children.

When services for persons with disabilities were first instituted in the United States with the opening of the American Asylum for the Deaf and Dumb in 1817 and the New England Asylum for the Blind in 1832, their clientele were mainly adolescents and adults, rather than children. Recognizing the difficulty of attempting to reeducate older students, however, by midcentury the former had set age 10 as optimal for beginning an intended five-year course of study. With the spread of state RESIDENTIAL SCHOOLS, children with impaired vision or hearing virtually never began their schooling before age 10, if then. This seeming neglect of childhood can be attributed in part to the belief that, not early childhood, but rather adolescence was the "critical period" for learning. Also, sensory and other physical impairments were often incurred in middle childhood, resulting from diseases such as scarlet fever or accidents incurred in farm work. Another basis for deferring schooling for children with disabilities lay in awareness of childhood: residential school attendance required prolonged separation from family, something most parents of very young children were unwilling to countenance.

The later practicability of day classes due to motorized TRANSPORTATION coincided with growing awareness of the importance of early learning. Begun in Germany in the mid 19th century and readily adopted in the United States, Friedrich Froebel's kindergarten concept had enormous impact on schooling for children with disabilities. Kindergartens were established for children with visual impairment in the 1880s, when a network of kindergartens for DEAF children was also formed. As "ungraded" classes,

pioneered in New York in 1889 by Elizabeth Farrell, began to target pupils with MENTAL RETARDATION, "kindergartners" (women trained as kindergarten teachers) were considered ideal potential teachers of such classes.

However, only a minority of children with significant disabilities—and virtually no African-American or Native-American children, with or without disabilities—were provided schooling until the late 19th century. Segregated residential schools or school units began to serve BLIND African-American students in the 1860s, at which time nearly two-thirds of inmates languishing in the many ALMSHOUSES were children, many of whom had sensory or other impairments, including, according to reformer DOROTHEA DIX, "INSANITY." Young casualties of the CIVIL WAR were by no means limited to youth who had actually fought; loss or incapacity of parents vastly increased the number of children in orphanages or roaming city streets. The latter increased the perceived need for a succession of reformatories and "Houses of Refuge," while the former added to the 80 or more orphanages that had already been established.

The 1860s also saw the emergence of HOSPITALS for children and ORTHOPEDIC HOSPITALS, many of whose patients were children with such impairments as congenital club foot, joint inflammation, and paralysis resulting from SPINAL CORD INJURY. With the later emergence of "fresh air" or "open air" classes as part of the campaign to stop the spread of TUBERCULOSIS, hospital schools were established to serve "pupil-patients" with diverse medical needs.

From the 1880s to 1920, great waves of immigrants from southern and eastern Europe coincided with the increasing inclusiveness of the Common School. In coastal cities, increasingly diverse schools established "vestibule" or "steamer" classes to Americanize immigrant children as rapidly as possible, with special emphasis on English language competence, a model later extended to serve children who actually experienced speech impairments. Settlement houses, an important facet of the Progressive Movement and a central influence in the origin of services for children with disabilities, represented a significant exception to the nonwelcoming response to this massive immigration. Health problems keeping many out of school was a particular concern of settlement workers, shared by psychologists such as J. E. W. Wallin, who asserted that more than half the pupils in urban schools had POVERTY-related physical and learning problems.

By the 1930s, school policies excluding children for reasons of health or disability were a concern of parents, who would later successfully advocate for services, as did many physicians and other professionals. These concerns, which would lead ultimately to enactment of the EDUCATION OF ALL HANDICAPPED CHILDREN ACT (PL 94-142) in 1975, constituted important influences in the creation in 1965 of

Project HEAD START, which, in 1974, mandated a 10 percent rate of inclusion of children with disabilities. While subsequent social policy reforms, medical and behavioral science discoveries, and continuing advocacy have positively affected the lives of American children, including children with or at biological or environmental risk for developmental delays and disabilities, inequities in HEALTH CARE and educational opportunity continue.

Philip L. Safford

Further Reading:

Byrom, Brad. "A Pupil and a Patient: Hospital-Schools in Progressive America." In *The New Disability History,* edited by Paul K. Longmore and Lauri Umansky, 133–156. New York: New York University Press, 2001.

Ferguson, Philip M. "Mapping the Family: Disability Studies and the Exploration of Parental Response to Disability." In *Handbook of Disability Studies,* edited by Gary L. Albrecht, Katherine D. Seelman, and Michael Bury, 375–395. Thousand Oaks, Calif.: Sage Publications, 2001.

Safford, Philip L., and Elizabeth J. Safford. *A History of Childhood and Disability.* New York: Teachers College Press, 1996.

Safford, Philip L., and Elizabeth J. Safford, eds. *Children with Disabilities in America: A Historical Handbook and Guide.* Westport, Conn.: Greenwood Press, 2006.

"The Handicapped Child's Bill of Rights" by William J. Ellis (1930)

Children with disabilities historically have been viewed as inherently vulnerable and in need of protection and care. Since the 1960s, disability rights advocates have challenged such negative and narrowly medical interpretations, pressing for more empowering representations. This exceptional document from 1930 reflects an early example of a "rights-based model of disability." According to the Committee on the Physically and Mentally Handicapped Child (the terms then used to describe various disability conditions), children with disabilities should be entitled to expect appropriate educational options, social inclusion, and positive self-identity. Many of the values listed in this "Bill of Rights" still serve as guiding principles for advocates of children with disabilities in the 21st century.

"The Handicapped Child's Bill of Rights"
by William J. Ellis
1930

The Handicapped Child's Bill of Rights*
As an integral unit of our human society the handicapped child has a right:

1. To as vigorous a body as human skill can give him;

2. To an education so adapted to his handicap that he can be economically independent and have the chance for the fullest life of which he is capable;

3. To be brought up and educated by those who understand the nature of the burden he has to bear and who consider it a privilege to help him bear it;

4. To grow up in a world which does not set him apart, which looks at him, not with scorn or pity or ridicule—but which welcomes him, exactly as it welcomes every child, which offers him identical privileges and identical responsibilities;

5. To a life on which his handicap casts no shadow, but which is full day by day with those things which make it worth while, with comradeship, love, work, play, laughter, and tears—a life in which these things bring continually increasing growth, richness, release of energies, joy in achievement.

*Developed by the Committee on the Physically and Mentally Handicapped Child, 1930 White House Conference.

Source: "The Handicapped Child's Bill of Rights." Developed by the Committee on the Physically and Mentally Handicapped Child, 1930. White House Conference. Reprinted in William J. Ellis. "The Handicapped Child." *Annals of the American Academy of Political and Social Science* 212 (November 1940): 138–145.

Children Limited   See THE ARC.

Children of a Lesser God

Children of A Lesser God by Mark Medoff is an award-winning drama (World Premier, Mark Taper Forum, Los Angeles, 1979) and FILM (Paramount, 1986) that introduced mainstream (hearing) audiences to issues of DEAF culture and provided many DEAF and HARD OF HEARING ACTORS with professional theatrical EMPLOYMENT. Set in a residential deaf school, the play's plot revolves around a romance between a hearing (oralist) speech teacher, James Leeds, and a deaf graduate of the school now working there as a janitor/maid, Sarah Norman. The play, and to a lesser extent the film, touched on the need for an increase in deaf educators, deaf cultural pride, and the recognition of AMERICAN SIGN LANGUAGE as a communication system equal to spoken language. Though these issues were familiar to the deaf COMMUNITY of the late 1970s, it was new subject matter for mainstream American theater. For the first time deaf and hard of hearing characters were the protagonists of a DRAMA, and they were played by trained deaf and hard of hearing actors. The play's success also strengthened efforts in professional theaters to provide sign language interpreted performances for deaf and hard of hearing audience members.

Though the playwright Mark Medoff is hearing, the play was developed in a collaborative process with deaf actress PHYLLIS FRELICH over the span of several years, starting in 1978 in a five-month long residency at New Mexico State University, with Medoff, Frelich, and her hearing husband Bob Steinberg, a scenic/lighting designer and actor. They developed additional roles for deaf actors, the characters Orin Dennis and Lydia, both students. Based on this first draft, prominent theater producer and director Gordon Davidson offered Medoff and Frelich a production slot in the 1979 mainstage season at his Los Angeles theater, the Mark Taper Forum, with actor John Rubenstein replacing Bob Steinberg in the role of teacher James Leeds. The play underwent extensive rewriting during the rehearsal process, opened in late 1979 under the direction of Davidson, and was a critical and audience success. *Children* transferred to Broadway, where it won the 1980 Tony awards for Best Play, Best Performance by a Lead Actor, and Best Performance by a Lead Actress, as well as several Drama Desk Awards and nominations. A British production in 1981 garnered the Laurence Olivier awards for Best Play, Best Actor in a New Play, and Best Actress in a New Play.

A film version of the play was produced in 1986 starring deaf actress MARLEE MATLIN (who won an Oscar for Best Actress) and William Hurt. The film script, coauthored by Medoff and Hesper Anderson, departs significantly from the play, focusing more narrowly on the love story between Leeds and Norman. The play's secondary plot, a discrimination suit targeting the lack of deaf teachers brought against the school by the militant hard of hearing student Orin Dennis, or other suggestions of collective action on the part of the deaf community, was deleted. Leeds's attempts at oralist training methods are more successful in the film, and in general the deaf characters have less ability to move the plot forward; for example, they have no experience with popular dance until Leeds introduces them to disco. The film does add a deaf role model for Norman, a deaf economist Marian Loesser (played by deaf actress LINDA BOVE), and, as in the play, Norman resists Leeds's oralist teaching efforts as she fights for an autonomous (nonspeaking) voice.

Children established a theatrical convention for scenes using oral speech and sign in a play—the speaking character orally translates the signing and then responds in speech, while signing. This convention allows for real-time, bilingual communication between characters, but it serves audience members unequally. Hearing audiences experience a flowing conversation while deaf audiences have to rely on ASL interpreters usually placed on the side aprons of the stage for translation of all other speech in the play.

In both theatrical and film formats, *Children of a Lesser God* remains an important example and source in American disability history, marking changes in REPRESENTATION— symbolic and actual—of deafness and deaf people. At the same time, the work's different messages point to the contested expectation of what deaf people can and should be.

See also COMMUNICATION DEBATES; ORALISM; SIGN LANGUAGE INTERPRETERS AND INTERPRETING; THEATER.

Victoria Ann Lewis

Further Reading:
Brueggemann, Brenda Jo, and Susan Burch, eds. *Women and Deafness: Double Visions.* Washington, D.C.: Gallaudet University Press, 2006.

Fellemen, Susan. "Fluid Fantasies: *Splash* and *Children of a Lesser God.*" *Camera Obscura: A Journal of Feminist Cultural and Media Studies* 19 (January 1989): 109–133.

Lane, Harry G., and Bonnie Meath-Lang. *Deaf Persons in the Arts and Sciences.* Westport, Conn.: Greenwood Press, 1995.

Schuchman, John S. *Hollywood Speaks: Deafness and the Film Industry.* Urbana: University of Illinois Press, 1988.

children of deaf adults (codas)

It has been estimated that between 80 and 90 percent of children of DEAF parents have NORMAL hearing. These children, while hearing, grow up with the language and in the culture of the Deaf, thus occupying a unique social position. In 1983, recognizing this position and the need to articulate and represent it, Millie Brother, herself the adult hearing child of Deaf parents, thus coined the terms and *codas*—an acronym for *children of deaf adults*—and founded CODA, an international organization.

Within the deaf COMMUNITY, the AMERICAN SIGN LANGUAGE phrase "Mother-Father-Deaf" traditionally has been used to identify, accept, and explain the presence of coda individuals. Exposed to spoken language through other FAMILY members, neighbors, and school as well as exposure to the sign language of their Deaf parents and the Deaf community, many of these children identify themselves as belonging to both deaf and hearing cultures. But until the early 1980s, when Millie Brother founded CODA, these children had no way to formally identify themselves.

In 1983, in the introductory issue of the CODA *Newsletter,* Brother explained that the term derived from the

> "It is quite a treat to see the young faces of all those 'typical children of deaf parents,' and, especially when they happen to belong to old school-mates of youthful days."
>
> —deaf reader E.F.I., of Iowa, complimenting a newspaper series on hearing children of deaf parents, in 1904

musical term *coda,* which names the concluding segment of a musical piece. According to Brother, the coda is "dependent upon the preceding musical development; yet, it is an altered version of the original. In my eyes, I was the human analogy to this musical form." In other words, Brother saw herself as a part of the deaf community through her parents even though she was not deaf; like the musical coda, she was an "altered version."

Today, the term *coda* is used to describe the adult hearing offspring of one or more deaf parents and the term *koda* (kids of deaf adults) is used to apply to them as CHILDREN. The CODA group is now an international organization with regional chapters. Its membership is open to adult hearing children of both signing and nonsigning deaf parents. CODA provides annual conferences primarily in the United States but occasionally in other countries. The organization supports scholarships for young codas and sponsors an annual "Mother Father Deaf Day Celebration" on the last Sunday in April "to honor our deaf parents and recognize the gifts of culture and language we received from them."

The coda experience is myriad and complex. Many codas actively participate in the deaf community; others choose to leave it. Today there is much research about these experiences as well as biographical descriptions and fictional accounts of codas and their family lives. The CODA organization also continues its commitment to dispel myths about deaf parents and their hearing children.

See also IDENTITY.

John S. Schuchman

Further Reading:

Bull, Thomas. *On the Edge of Deaf Culture, Hearing Children/ Deaf Parents. Annotated Bibliography.* Alexandria, Va.: Deaf Family Research Press, 1998.

Davis, Lennard. *My Sense of Silence: Memoirs of a Childhood with Deafness.* Urbana: University of Illinois Press, 2000.

Preston, Paul. *Mother Father Deaf, Living between Sound and Silence.* Cambridge, Mass.: Harvard University Press, 1994.

Children's Bureau

The U.S. Children's Bureau is a division of the U.S. Department of Health and Human Services under the Administration on Children and Families (ACF). President William Howard Taft established the bureau in the Department of Commerce on April 9, 1912, as an investigatory and reporting agency on child welfare. Its current budget exceeds $7 billion; it is responsible for partnering with state and other federal programs to advance the welfare of all CHILDREN.

The idea for the agency came from Progressives Florence Kelley, representing the National Consumer's League, and Lillian Wald of the Henry Street Settlement House, who joined in 1903 to advance child welfare at the federal level. With significant grassroots campaigning and a boost from President Theodore Roosevelt's 1909 Conference on the Care of Dependent Children, they helped push through the founding legislation authorizing an agency of 16 employees and a budget of $25,640. Its first chief was Julia Lathrop, a veteran of Hull House in Chicago. Since then the bureau has had a nomadic existence within the government, reflecting the changing perception of the needs of American children, shifting from the Department of Commerce to the Department of Labor, the Social Security Administration, and the Department of Health, Education and Welfare (HEW) as well as to agencies within HEW, including the Social and Rehabilitation Service, the Public Health Service, and now the ACF.

The initial activities of the bureau related to child labor (hence its placement in the Department of Commerce), infant mortality, orphans, and delinquency, among others. These activities had an impact on disabilities and disability-related services, though not always directly. As many children working in unsafe settings at a very young age became disabled through work-related injuries, as children acquired TUBERCULOSIS and other chronic and acute disabling infections, and as malnutrition threatened children with conditions of deficiencies such as rickets, the Children's Bureau had an unfocused but significant impact on the incidence and experience of disability among children and their mothers. But in 1935, with the signing of the SOCIAL SECURITY ACT, and particularly Title V, the Children's Bureau was assigned the task of overseeing the $2.85 million distributed for the provision of services to children with disabilities.

In addition to allocating funds in collaboration with state governments, the bureau also generated a wealth of social research and guidance documents about topics relating to children with mental and physical disabilities, including surveys and position papers. In its allocative role, the bureau served as a leading sponsor of the multidisciplinary model in rehabilitative care.

Today, the bureau has a broad mandate, which includes a focus on preventing and mitigating child ABUSE, including aspects related to disabilities. The ACF also houses the Administration on Developmental Disabilities, which is in charge of implementing the Developmental Disabilities Assistance and the Bill of Rights Act of 2000.

See also FAMILY; LAW AND POLICY.

Walton O. Schalick, III

Further Reading:

Children's Bureau Web site. URL: http://www.acf.hhs. gov/programs/cb/.

Lindenmeyer, Kriste. *"A Right to Childhood": The U.S. Children's Bureau and Child Welfare, 1912–46.* Urbana: University of Illinois Press, 1997.

Markel, Howard, and Alexandra Stern, eds. *Formative Years: Children's Health in the United States, 1880–2000.* Ann Arbor: University of Michigan Press, 2002.

Chlorpromazine   See THORAZINE.

Christmas in Purgatory

Starting in the 1960s and 1970s, institutions for people with intellectual disabilities or MENTAL RETARDATION—commonly referred to as state schools, training schools, or state HOSPITALS—were challenged by exposés of abusive and dehumanizing conditions. One of the most influential of these was *Christmas in Purgatory,* a book written by Burton Blatt and with photographs by Fred Kaplan published in 1966.

"There is hell on earth," wrote Blatt, "and in America there is a special inferno. We were visitors there during Christmas, 1965." Blatt, then a professor at Boston University, had followed the controversy surrounding Senator Robert Kennedy's unannounced visits to New York's Willowbrook and Rome State schools in the fall of 1965. Kennedy publicly denounced conditions at the institutions. In response, public officials and supporters of Governor Nelson Rockefeller accused Kennedy of painting a misleading picture of conditions at the institutions based on superficial tours. Blatt believed that Kennedy had accurately portrayed the nature of conditions found at institutions.

With the aid of a friend, photographer Fred Kaplan, Blatt decided to expose institutional conditions on his own. He arranged for visits to four large state institutions in the Northeast at which Kaplan secretly took pictures of conditions on "back wards" with a camera secured to his belt. Blatt and Kaplan then visited Connecticut's Seaside Regional Center, a small, relatively new facility, where Kaplan openly took pictures of brightly lit wards, well-dressed residents, decorated dormitories, and educational programs.

Blatt and Kaplan's photographic exposé *Christmas in Purgatory* was published in 1966. The first part of the book depicted horribly overcrowded wards, naked and half-clothed residents, and barren rooms full of idle people. The second part showed the relatively positive scenes from Seaside. The back cover of *Christmas in Purgatory* included testimonials to its importance from Senator Edward Kennedy, Michigan governor George Romney, and Minnesota governor Karl Rolvaag.

One year later, Blatt, together with senior editor Charles Mangel, published a version of the exposé in *Look Magazine* titled "The Tragedy and Hope of Retarded Children." The article began: "These children do not have to be locked up in human warehouses. Yet, to our shame, this is where we put them—in back wards, without compassion, without even basic care."

In 1967 Blatt was invited to give a keynote address at a special session of the Massachusetts legislature convened at one of the state schools. He reviewed his findings in *Christmas in Purgatory* and urged the commonwealth to develop a "network of small, community-centered residential facilities."

When he first exposed the institutions, Blatt advocated for institutional reform. Before long, he had given up hope that institutions could be reformed. In a follow-up exposé published with two junior colleagues in 1979, Blatt concluded, "We must evacuate the institutions for the mentally retarded."

Blatt had moved to Syracuse University in 1969 to become director of the Division of Special Education and Rehabilitation. In 1971 he founded the Center on Human Policy, which continues to distribute *Christmas in Purgatory.* This work remains an important historical source, reflecting a long history of disability ACTIVISM as well as comprising a vivid commentary on institutional life.

See also ASYLUMS AND INSTITUTIONS; BAZELON CENTER FOR MENTAL HEALTH LAW; COGNITIVE AND INTELLECTUAL DISABILITY; DEINSTITUTIONALIZATION.

Steven J. Taylor

Further Reading:

Blatt, Burton. *Exodus from Pandemonium: Human Abuse and a Reformation of Public Policy.* Boston: Allyn & Bacon, 1970.

Blatt, Burton, and Fred Kaplan. *Christmas in Purgatory: A Photographic Essay on Mental Retardation.* Boston: Allyn & Bacon, 1966.

Blatt, Burton, and C. Mangel. "The Tragedy and Hope of Retarded Children." *Look Magazine,* 31 October 1967, pp. 96–99.

Blatt, Burton, A. Ozolins, and J. McNally. *The Family Papers: A Return to Purgatory.* New York: Longman, 1979.

Chronic Fatigue Syndrome

Chronic Fatigue Syndrome (CFS) is a CHRONIC ILLNESS that may manifest itself in severe neurological problems, flu-like symptoms, brain dysfunction, pain, sleep disorders, heart problems, and dozens of other symptoms. Many individuals with CFS are occupationally disabled and others are indefinitely bedridden. Its history reveals much about society's skepticism of and assumptions about disabilities.

American awareness of CFS emerged in 1984 when doctors Paul Cheney and Dan Peterson treated a cluster outbreak of an undetermined illness in Incline Village, Nevada. The doctors summoned researchers for the Centers for Disease Control (CDC), today the Centers for Disease Control and Prevention, to survey this new pathology. In *Osler's Web: Inside the Labyrinth of the Chronic Fatigue Syndrome Epidemic* (1996), journalist Hilary Johnson alleged that these officials arrived with a tautological reasoning: if the patients didn't look that sick (only a limited number of live patients or lab results were examined), there must not be a serious epidemic. Activists later asserted that subsequent use of the term "fatigue" trivialized the condition. After originally terming the DISEASE "Chronic Epstein-Barr Virus (CEBV)," CDC researchers named the illness "chronic fatigue syndrome" in 1988. A nearly identical illness named myalgic encephalomyelitis (ME) had existed in the medical literature since 1938. Although debate continues over whether ME and CFS are synonymous terms, they are frequently used interchangeably. Both ME and CFS occur in epidemic and sporadic forms.

Many in POPULAR CULTURE, academia, and the medical profession treated CFS as a metaphor for a stressed-out society. Since Incline Village was affluent, *Time* nicknamed the illness "yuppie disease," with a cartoon portraying a well-dressed man sleeping in an opulent dinner setting. Many then batted around the derogatory term "yuppie flu." This biased depiction affected CFS politics much as "Gay-Related Immune Deficiency" had haunted AIDS in the early 1980s. CFS cuts across racial lines and is most common among the working class, but early myths were hard to dispel. CFS jokes infiltrated popular culture, and Princeton professor Elaine Showalter made a highly publicized attempt to define CFS as a hysterical epidemic in her 1997 book, *Hystories: Hysterical Epidemics and Modern Media.*

The term CFS remains controversial. The largest patient advocacy ORGANIZATION, the CFIDS Association, took on the patient-coined name "chronic fatigue immune dysfunction syndrome" (CFIDS). The ME Society of America adopted the historical name of the illness, believing ME to be more medically accurate. Doctors and journalists often shorten the illness name to the misnomer "chronic fatigue." Nonspecific chronic fatigue is a condition that afflicts 10 to 25 percent of those seeking medical care, and bears no resemblance to the incurable chronic fatigue *syndrome*. As terminological debates raged in the 1990s, the CDC spent much of its CFS funds on other research accounts. CDC researcher William Reeves came forward under the whistleblowers' act to reveal these improprieties. In 2006 the CDC recognized the valid-

ity of the illness. While releasing new genomic studies, it launched a public awareness campaign to spread information about the illness and its severity. Current research has also studied CFS deaths, which were largely ignored in earlier decades. A 2006 study found CFS patients to be more susceptible to deaths from heart failure, CANCER, and suicide. Pathologists studying the case of 32-year-old Sophia Mirza, a bedridden woman in the United Kingdom who died of CFS in 2005 after being forcibly "sectioned" to a locked psychiatric ward, noted damage to her brainstem, liver, and kidneys.

Over a million Americans of all ages have CFS. Despite the publication of 3,000 research studies on CFS, its etiology remains unclear. In recent years activists have managed to overturn some misconceptions about CFS, but the low diagnostic rate indicates that STIGMA toward this condition lingers.

Peggy Munson

Further Reading:

Centers for Disease Control CFS Web site. URL: http://www.cdc.gov/cfs.

Jason, Leonard, Karina Corradi, Sara Gress, Sarah Williams, and Susan Torres-Harding. "Causes of Death among Patients with Chronic Fatigue Syndrome." *Health Care for Women International* 27 (2006): 615–626.

Munson, Peggy. *Stricken: Voices from the Hidden Epidemic of Chronic Fatigue Syndrome.* Philadelphia: Haworth Press, 2000.

Verrillo, Erica F., and Lauren M. Gellman. *Chronic Fatigue Syndrome: A Treatment Guide.* New York: St. Martin's Griffin, 1998.

chronic illness

Chronic illness, a set of conditions that progress slowly and over long periods of time, are relevant to American disability in various ways. Some chronic illnesses result in disabilities (and vice versa), but the historical social, political, economic, medical, and embodied features of chronic illness also relate to and occasionally complicate notions of disability.

Modern medicine usually separates illness into one of two categories, either *acute illness* (which typically begins abruptly and lasts a short period) or *chronic illness*. Chronic illnesses are sometimes characterized by insidious onset, with subtle or hard-to-diagnose symptoms. Chronic illnesses are also often characterized by a course in which periods of active DISEASE are succeeded by periods of remission. These remissions, in turn, are followed by periods of active disease, the entire process occurring repeatedly over an individual's lifetime. Thus, one of the key differences between acute and chronic illnesses is that acute diseases are resolved after a relatively short time, while the course of a chronic disease can

> *"I look upon the period of a long confinement by rheumatism just at the period of manhood not hardly as a fortunate accident of life, but as one of the most providential incidents that could have been allotted to me. Under it, I first learned to reflect and became sensible of moral responsibility. . . . Dear Elizabeth need not therefore look upon the period of her confinement as time wasted. She may improve it to much advantage, and I hope she will do so."*
>
> —Thomas Ruffin (1787–1870), a North Carolina judge, in a letter advising his eldest daughter Catherine about her sister Elizabeth and on the benefits of the sickbed, January 22, 1835

wax and wane over a lifetime. Both types of illness can have lasting effects on an individual in the form of IMPAIRMENT or disability, and some chronic illnesses such as multiple sclerosis can also be classified as a disability. In addition, acute and chronic diseases differ in the ways they unfold over time, in the type of health care relationship they require, in the type of psychosocial adjustments the individual may have to make, and in the type of social strategies the individual may adopt. Both acute and chronic illnesses can be understood as primarily "physical" or primarily "psychological" in nature; or, as is often the case, contain some element of each. Both acute and chronic illnesses may be infectious; TUBERCULOSIS is an example of a disease both infectious and chronic. Both may also be stigmatized, leading to the social isolation of those thought to have the disease. Persons with EPILEPSY, for example, were confined in separate institutions well into the 20th century, and persons with Hansen's disease (LEPROSY) or MENTAL ILLNESSES are still often confined today.

Although references to chronic illnesses appear in a wide array of American historical documents, little scholarship has focused on the experiences of these conditions or on their implications for understanding broader society. Evidence suggests the important role, for example, that economics has played in the history of chronic illness. Two of the great shifts occurred in the 19th and 20th centuries. Americans' life expectancy increased at the same time the principal causes of death shifted from acute illnesses (short-lived illnesses) to chronic ones. For instance, in 1900, the overall life expectancy for whites in the United States was approximately 48 years, and the average life expectancy for nonwhites was approximately 33 years. In 1900, 60 percent of all U.S. deaths were due to acute illnesses such as pneu-

monia and intestinal diseases, and approximately 20 percent of all deaths were caused by three chronic conditions: heart disease, cancer, and stroke. One hundred years later, the life expectancy for whites rose to approximately 80 years, and the life expectancy for nonwhites was approximately 74 years. By the year 2002, seven out of the 10 most important causes of death were chronic illnesses, including cardiovascular disease, CANCER, respiratory diseases, and DIABETES. These demographic changes were due both to medical advances as well as to increases in the standard of living.

Because life spans have been increasing since the turn of the 20th century, more people lived long enough to develop chronic illnesses, many of which first appear during adulthood and middle age (see AGING). Advances in medical knowledge during this time led to changes in our knowledge and classification of diseases as either acute or chronic. For example, in the early 20th century diabetes was an acute disease with no effective treatment. Virtually all patients died within a few years of onset. The discovery of insulin therapy in the 1920s transformed diabetes from an acute fatal disease to a chronic disease that could be managed over a long life span. However, as people with diabetes lived longer, new health problems emerged, including blindness, kidney failure, and cardiovascular disease that were a consequence of the management of this now chronic disease.

In the 21st century people with some chronic illnesses live a "NORMAL" lifespan, and adaptations now enable many people with chronic illnesses to enjoy new forms of social support. This has made it possible for people with even relatively rare chronic illnesses to interact with others with the same chronic illness through support groups. The rise of the INTERNET has enabled some to have virtual contact that can be directed to very specific populations, such as young women with chronically fatiguing conditions or with the families of people who are elderly and have a specific chronic disease. These increased exchanges and interactions have emerged because of a number of developments.

In the past five decades, many people with chronic illnesses have lived longer, and efforts to deinstitutionalize men and women since the 1960s have resulted in additional FAMILY responsibilities and support networks for CAREGIVING. Because chronic illnesses often have varying degrees of intensity, individuals, their families, and the social support system need to be constantly aware of changes in the disease. Those supplying care to persons with a chronic mental illness, for instance, report being constantly "on alert," because symptoms of some chronic mental illnesses can manifest at any time.

Chronic illnesses present a unique challenge in DISABILITY STUDIES since they do not entirely fit either the social or MEDICAL MODELS OF DISABILITY. Because chronic illnesses often vary in intensity, there can be times when an individual can appear to be "cured." However, during intense episodes, the individual may be quite disabled. Because of the remissions and relapses of chronic illnesses, many of these disorders can never be "cured," while acute illnesses often can. We speak of cancer as in remission, but we say that the patient was cured of her or his pneumonia. As scholars Anselm Strauss, Juliet Corbin, and Kathy Charmaz have shown, chronic illness has a significant impact on social relationships in addition to physical conditions. Episodes of remission and relapse may occur repeatedly in an individual's life, as is true with some cases of LUPUS, MULTIPLE SCLEROSIS, and HIV/AIDS.

The example of infection with HIV highlights the possible change of an illness from acute to chronic, in large part because of medical interventions and advances. When the virus was first isolated, infection with HIV seemed an inevitable death sentence, as this acute illness went through its stages rapidly and the individual died, often in a matter of months or at best a few years after infection. With discoveries of newer medications, applicable procedures, and prompt detection, HIV infection can be a chronic illness to be managed over years, and the person who finds they have the virus may be able to participate in a demanding career or to be the biological parent of a child—goals that were unthinkable during the early days of the AIDS epidemic in the 1980s.

Another point to stress is the social construction of chronic disease, which may change over time with effects on our understanding of and attitudes toward the chronic illness. For instance, the mental change produced in combatants during war was termed shell shock during WORLD WAR I, battle fatigue during WORLD WAR II, and posttraumatic stress disorder following the VIETNAM WAR in the 1970s and early 1980s. Shifts in terminology and treatment and different ideas about environmental factors and attitudes toward war and military expectations, as well as changing attitudes about expectations of care and the meaning of disability represent some of the prominent social dimensions in the history of chronic illness.

The decisive shifts in the 20th century from acute illnesses to chronic illness as the primary causes of death have had profound implications for the character of society as well as for the life of an individual. Chronic illnesses require a different model of treatment and care than acute illnesses. Chronic illnesses require a level of cooperation among health care providers, support groups, and individuals with the chronic disease that is qualitatively and quantitatively different from the needs of the person with an acute illness: the care that the health care system provides must be long-lasting, if needed; thorough and deep in character and dedication; ethically complex, sometimes involving painful moral positions and decision making and the excruciating choices of life and death involved in weighing of benefits and disadvantages—all this in general contrast to the medical care involved in acute illness. Importantly, the treatment of chronic illness requires conscious cooperation and negotiation between the health care team and the patient, and among the various health care providers who make up the team. The treatment of chronic illness, then, is much more dependent on social interaction and social relationships than is the case for acute illness.

See also CURES; DAILY LIFE; LANGUAGE AND TERMINOLOGY; SOCIAL CONSTRUCTION OF DISABILITY; STIGMA.

Carol Brooks Gardner
William P. Gronfein

Further Reading:
Dormandy, Thomas. *The White Death: A History of Tuberculosis.* New York: New York University Press, 2000.

Feudtner, Chris. *Bittersweet: Diabetes, Insulin, and the Transformation of an Illness.* Chapel Hill: University of North Carolina Press, 2003.

Friedlander, Walter J. *The History of Modern Epilepsy.* Westport, Conn.: Greenwood Press, 2001.

Kirk, Stuart, Herb Kutchins, and Dorothy Rowe. *Making Us Crazy: DSM—The Psychiatric Bible and the Creation of Mental Disorders.* London: Constable, 1999.

Swiderski, Richard M. *Multiple Sclerosis through History and Human Life.* Jefferson, N.C.: McFarland and Company, 1998.

circus

The display of the extraordinary body has been an integral part of the circus since its inception in the 18th century. Within the space of a circular arena surrounded by an audience, human beings fly from a trapeze, dance atop animals, lift prodigious weights, and juggle fire, while horses walk on their hind legs, elephants form pyramids, and tigers fly through hoops. Historically, people with disabilities performing unusual bodily feats (like an armless person sewing with her feet or a legless man walking with his arms) constituted an important part of the circus's constellation of extraordinary bodies.

The EXHIBITION of disabled human performers had a long history at medieval fairs, royal courts, and among itinerant entertainment troupes. But the organized display of disabled people in a commercial space dedicated to the exhibition of so-called human oddities occurred only with the advent of the sideshow (also known as the FREAK SHOW) in the mid-19th century. In 1841 the amusement proprietor P. T. BARNUM laid the foundation for the modern circus sideshow with his purchase of Scudder's American Museum on Broadway in New York City. This looming five-story structure was filled with fossils, bones, shells, and stuffed birds. Barnum painted fanciful images of wild animals from around the world on the building's exterior to lure the crowds, and he supplemented the taxidermy features with highly profitable live human and animal exhibitions. The display of disabled performers was a central part of the show. Other enterprising showmen copied Barnum's formula and a new entertainment genre was born. After the American Museum burned to the ground a second time, Barnum swore off the museum business for good and launched his own traveling circus in 1871.

Sideshow audiences paid to watch "freaks" who were both "born" and "made." Born freaks included performers with congenital deformities, disabilities, or unusual features such as abundant bodily hair. In line with the racist norms of the era, born freaks included people of color who played so-called savages or missing links. By contrast, made freaks were comprised of physically able performers who cultivated bizarre bodily skills such as glass eating, sword swallowing, fire eating, or live goldfish regurgitation. The distinction between the born and the made, however, was often hazy, because acts often enhanced their extraordinary bodies with specific tricks of the growing sideshow trade: giants, for instance, often wore lifts or towering hats, while DWARFS sat in oversized furniture. To heighten public interest in their sideshow performers, Barnum and other showmen such as Adam Forepaugh and the Ringling brothers crafted elaborate marketing campaigns such as a faux marriage between the Fat Lady and the Skeleton Man. Many disabled freaks such as the armless woman Mrs. Anne E. Leak Thompson, or the three-legged man Lentini became celebrities—facilitated by the sophisticated national marketing campaigns that showmen used to sell their circuses.

Sideshow performers themselves actively participated in the making of their occupational identities. An armless 17-year-old named Charles Tripp, for example, joined Barnum's sideshow in 1872, where he painted portraits, performed carpentry, and wrote flawlessly with his feet for the next 50 years. Like other sideshow performers, Tripp supplemented his income with postcard sales of himself. During the 19th-century craze for *cartes de visite,* middle-class consumers enthusiastically purchased postcard images of their favorite stage and sideshow performers and placed them in treasured photograph albums in their parlors, alongside family portraits and pictures of presidents and generals.

The circus offered disabled people the opportunity for a decent income in a society in which there were few other EMPLOYMENT opportunities for them. However, greedy and unscrupulous managers exploited several performers. The English CONJOINED TWINS, Daisy and Violet Hilton, lived in virtual bondage in the early 20th century. Cruel managers beat the young twins and kept them locked in a room between show dates in circuses, vaudeville, and carnivals, lest the paying public get a free look. In 1931 the twins legally won their freedom at the age of 23.

The circus sideshow was a highly profitable institution from the 1840s until approximately 1970. However, the display of disabled performers declined rapidly thereafter. In an age when medical authorities—not showmen—now explained the physiological basis for disability, the circus gradually lost its explanatory power. Moreover, as an integral part of the social movements of the 1960s and 1970s, disabled rights activists charged that the display of disabled people for profit at the sideshow was a unilaterally exploitative enterprise. Consequently, they demanded the dissolution of the circus sideshow. Although sideshow displays of made freaks—glass eaters, fire eaters, elastic skin men, and others—have enjoyed a resurgence at concerts and carnivals today, the display of disabled circus sideshow performers has wholly vanished.

See also COMMUNITY; EXPLOITATION.

Janet M. Davis

Further Reading:
Adams, Rachel. *Sideshow U.S.A.: Freaks and the American Cultural Imagination.* Chicago: University of Chicago Press, 2001.

Bogdan, Robert. *Freak Show: Presenting Human Oddities for Amusement and Profit.* Chicago: University of Chicago Press, 1988.

Cook, James. *The Arts of Deception: Playing with Fraud in the Age of Barnum.* Cambridge, Mass.: Harvard University Press, 2001.

Davis, Janet M. *The Circus Age: Culture and Society under the American Big Top.* Chapel Hill: University of North Carolina Press, 2002.

Jensen, Dean. *The Lives and Loves of Daisy and Violet Hilton: A True Story of Conjoined Twins.* Berkeley, Calif.: Ten Speed Press, 2006.

Kunhardt, Philip B., Philip B. Kunhardt III, and Peter W. Kunhardt. *P. T. Barnum: America's Greatest Showman.* New York: Alfred A. Knopf, 1995.

City Lights

When Charlie Chaplin released the movie *City Lights* in 1931, many of his Hollywood colleagues thought him out of step with the times. Not only did he refuse to convert the film into a "talking picture" at a time when audiences were flocking to such FILMS, but he also imbued it with highly sentimental views that seemed hopelessly dated by the 1930s. Nevertheless, *City Lights* fared well with audiences and critics alike, and it is considered by many today to be Chaplin's masterpiece. Produced, directed, cowritten, and coedited by Chaplin, who also starred in it and composed much of its musical score, *City Lights* was one of the first synchronous sound-era films to feature a disabled character in a prominent role.

In this film, Chaplin's world-beloved "Little Tramp" character—a hard-luck vagabond outfitted in a too tight jacket, too loose pants, and jaunty bowler—encounters a young BLIND woman (Virginia Cherrill) who peddles flowers on a busy street corner. In a bit of wishful thinking, the young woman mistakes the Tramp for a wealthy man. The Tramp is so charmed by her that he maintains the charade while secretly raising money for a sight-restoring operation. This decision leads him into a series of misguided fund-raising efforts, including comic turns at street sweeping and boxing, before a besotted millionaire offers him the necessary cash. The Tramp turns the money over to the young woman shortly before the police, believing he has robbed the millionaire, arrest him. After his eventual release from prison, the Tramp meets the young woman again but under very different circumstances; her vision restored, she now works professionally as a florist. Dressed in clothes more tattered than usual, the Tramp is a strange and pitiable figure to her; she assumes he is merely a bum looking for a bit of kindness. The film ends on a note of high pathos when she finally recognizes her benefactor.

City Lights is perhaps the most famous illustration of Hollywood's interest in turning young disabled women into figures of childlike perfection. Like many other disabled female characters before her, Virginia Cherrill's flower seller is sweet, pure, docile, sexless, and, importantly for Chaplin, attractive. As he wrote in his autobiography in 1964, one of his biggest hurdles as the film's producer "was to find a girl who could look blind without detracting from her beauty. So many applicants looked upward, showing the whites of their eyes, which was too distressing."

In addition, *City Lights* follows the pattern established by many movies of the 1910s and 1920s by subscribing to the view that "good" disabled people, especially those who are pleasant to look at, should be rewarded with miracle CURES. Indeed, the Tramp's quest that drives the movie is to raise money for a corrective operation. Tapping into the all-too-common belief that disabled people are sexless, the film also implies that the young woman's SEXUALITY has been restored along with her eyesight; initially portrayed by Cherrill as a demure and childlike ingénue, the flower seller turns into a rather spunky soubrette after her operation.

In addition to its antiquated views on disability, *City Lights* is noteworthy for a less apparent reason; it was the final film for a DEAF ACTOR named GRANVILLE REDMOND. One of California's most famous impressionist painters, Redmond had become close friends with Chaplin during the 1910s and appeared in a half-dozen of the latter's films. With pantomimic cinema quickly giving way to the Talkies during the early 1930s, Redmond's brief, unbilled appearance in *City Lights* marked the end of his film acting career.

See also GENDER; POPULAR CULTURE; STEREOTYPES.

Martin F. Norden

Further Reading:

Chaplin, Charles. *My Autobiography.* New York: Simon & Schuster, 1964.

Norden, Martin F. *The Cinema of Isolation: A History of Physical Disability in the Movies.* New Brunswick, N.J.: Rutgers University Press, 1994.

Schuchman, John S. *Hollywood Speaks: Deafness and the Film Entertainment Industry.* Urbana: University of Illinois Press, 1988.

civil rights   See DISABILITY RIGHTS MOVEMENT.

Civil Service Reform Act

Methods to improve the efficacy of civil service have been a subject of contention throughout American history. The Civil Service Reform Act of 1978 (CSRA) embodied the culmination of President Jimmy Carter's effort to enhance the performance of federal agencies through revision of personnel selection, authority, and pay mechanisms. The directive established important rights for disabled VETERANS working in civil service.

The Civil Service Reform Act of 1978 replaced the Civil Service Commission, an organization first established by the Pendleton Act in 1883 to abolish the "spoils system"—corruption through political patronage—with three new agencies to oversee civil service personnel. The bill met with contention from conservatives who were opposed to the idea of expanding government, but it was eventually passed after some concessions. The Office of Personnel Management was established to research, examine, and direct personnel selection. The Merit Systems Protection Board was created to process the appeals of civil servants and civil service applicants, and the Federal Labor Relations Authority was created to deal with employee collective bargaining through unions.

These agencies sought to ensure that "fair and equitable" treatment be given to personnel and applicants at all levels of civil service regardless of race, gender, political or cultural association, marital status, AGE, or disabling condition; they also provided safeguards for those who reported such discrimination. At the same time, the programs specifically created opportunities for certain people with disabilities. For example, preferential policies for disabled veterans were greatly expanded.

The Pendleton Act of 1883 provided disabled veterans the foundation for more expansive policies nearly a century later. The Veterans' Readjustment Assistance Act of 1974 and additional legislation in 1976 provided preference for wartime veterans—both disabled and NONDISABLED—as well as for disabled peacetime veterans. The CSRA provided veterans with 30 percent or greater disability special appointing authority as well as a lifetime preference in hiring and retention. The Civil Service Reform Act that President Carter originally presented to Congress included these benefits to all veterans, but lawmakers scaled back the measure to apply only to disabled veterans. The CSRA also ensured specific accommodations, such as "interpreting assistants for DEAF employees."

The 1978 CSRA was not intended to directly modify the operations of civil service but to regulate the positions and incentives provided to civil servants with the aim of ultimately improving those operations. Through the agencies the CSRA established, President Carter hoped that a more efficient, better-managed executive branch would emerge. However, the enactment met heavy opposition immediately after its passing, and the measure had much less of an impact than expected. In the 1980s the Reagan administration reoriented the agencies established by the CSRA to focus on administrative efficiency rather than on creating an environment for operational efficiency. In the 21st century the act lacks much of the influence that Carter intended, but, by creating an explicitly protected space in the federal EMPLOYMENT system for disabled veterans, it has left a lasting legacy.

See also SIGN LANGUAGE INTERPRETERS AND INTERPRETING.

Arthur Holst

Further Reading:

Garson, D. *The Civil Service Reform Act of 1978*. Available online. URL: http://cwx.prenhall.com/bookbind/pubbooks/dye4/medialib/docs/civilser.htm. Accessed January 24, 2006.

Jaeger, Paul T., and Cynthia Ann Bowman. *Understanding Disability: Inclusion, Access, Diversity and Civil Rights*. Westport, Conn.: Praeger, 2005.

Longmore, Paul K., and Lauri Umansky, eds. *The New Disability History: American Perspectives*. New York: New York University Press, 2001.

Vaughn, Robert G. *Civil Service Reform Act (1978)*. Available online. URL: http://www.novelguide.com/a/discover/mac_01/mac_01_00046.html. Accessed January 23, 2006.

Civil Service Reform Act (1978)

Signed into law by President Jimmy Carter on October 13, 1978, the Civil Service Reform Act was intended to improve the assessment of employees, payment systems, and administration. Embedded within this act are protections for disabled veterans, including special appointing authority and hiring and retention measures. It also provided accommodations such as interpreters for deaf employees. It was considered an important victory for disability advocates. These selections from the act highlight the focused policies that applied to disabled veterans.

Civil Service Reform Act of 1978
Public Law 95-454 (S 2640)

An act to reform the civil service laws. October 13, 1978

... INTERPRETING ASSISTANTS FOR DEAF EMPLOYEES

... "(d) The head of each agency may also employ or assign, subject to section 209 of title 18 and to the provisions of this title governing appointment and chapter 51 and subchapter III of chapter 53 of this title governing classification and pay, such reading assistants for blind employees and such interpreting assistants for deaf employees as may be necessary to enable such employees to perform their work."

... VETERANS AND PREFERENCE ELIGIBLES
Sec. 307. (a) Effective beginning October 1, 1980, section 2108 of title 5, United States Code, is amended—,

... 'preference eligible' does not include a retired member of the armed forces unless—,

"(A) the individual is a disabled veteran; or

... "Section 3112. Disabled veterans; noncompetitive appointment

"Under such regulations as the Office of Personnel Management shall prescribe, an agency may make a noncompetitive appointment leading to conversion to career or career-conditional employment of a disabled veteran who has a compensable service-connected disability of 30 percent or more."

Source: Excerpted from the U.S. Equal Employment Opportunity Commission Web site at http://www.eeoc.gov/abouteeoc/35th/thelaw/civil_service_reform-1978.html.

Civil War (1861–1865)

The nation's bloodiest WAR, the Civil War (1861–65) altered the meaning of disability in American life. Antebellum DISEASE and accidents had been more debilitating than they are today, but the WAR inflicted unprecedented damage on minds and bodies. Hundreds of thousands of VETERANS returned to civilian life with physical and mental scars, including an estimated 45,000 amputees, stimulating a tripling of patents for PROSTHETIC devices.

The federal government had provided pensions and soldiers' homes for survivors of earlier wars, but the Civil War's enormous toll forced an extraordinary expansion of individual entitlements to aid. In 1862 the government began compensating veterans for inability to do manual labor, as long as the cause was traceable to military service; specific injuries were soon added at higher rates, from a maximum of $25 per month in 1864 to $72 in 1878 and $100 in 1889.

The number of pensioned Union veterans approached 400,000 in 1890, but more than two-thirds of Civil War survivors had not yet received a pension. Seeking advantage in an era of close competition and prodded by the Grand Army of the Republic, the Union veterans' largest organization, Republican Party politicians in Congress engineered a major expansion that provided pensions for all soldiers with disabilities regardless of their origin. In 1907 eligibility was further enlarged when old AGE (defined as 62) became the legal basis for a pension. Pensions following other wars had likewise been gradually liberalized, but they never carried social impact: in 1910, 28 percent of all American men over age 65 received a Civil War pension.

But many veterans, with an exceptionally severe disability or without a FAMILY, needed more than cash payments. In 1866 Congress authorized creation of an "asylum" (soon renamed a "home") for Union veterans. With branches eventually reaching from to coast to coast, the system provided bed and board, medical care, and military routine for residents. By 1908, when these homes (plus ones established by a number of states) reached a peak of nearly 47,000 residents, they had evolved into assisted-living institutions for elderly veterans.

Some ex-soldiers, suffering from the anxiety, antisocial behavior, and flashbacks that are associated today with post-traumatic stress disorder, could not stay in soldiers' homes. Shuttled among family, jail, and insane ASYLUMS, psychologically disturbed veterans fell through the cracks of 19th-century therapeutic philosophies: authorities could not decide whether to treat ex-soldiers' psychological problems as mental or physical in origin. An unknown number of disabled veterans ended their suffering with suicide.

Governments of the former Confederate states had fewer resources and faced greater public opposition to individual aid, so they were slower in assisting their veterans. States initially did little more than subsidize artificial limbs, but, as the scale of deprivation and disability became widely known after 1880, southern governments began to grant modest pensions and establish soldiers' homes. A survey in 1915 found half of all surviving Confederate veterans receiving pensions of about $60 per year, and nearly 2,400 veterans residing in state-operated soldiers' homes.

The plight of the Civil War veteran brought unprecedented attention to the reality of disability: evidence can

Private Benjamin Franklin from Minnesota, shown in this 1886 photograph, had parts of all four limbs amputated during the Civil War.   *(The Otis Historical Archives, The National Museum of Health & Medicine)*

be seen in the images and preserved body parts of wounded soldiers at the Army Medical Museum, founded in 1862, and in the massive *Medical and Surgical History of the War of the Rebellion,* filled with hundreds of lithographs of Civil War participants and their wounds. The new awareness also led to a complex national conversation about disability. A senator from Massachusetts declared that "a man who has lost both his arms is totally or nearly totally helpless; his life is a constant burden, and there is not a minute of the day that he does not feel that he is a captive to some other person"; other Americans, convinced that fraud and abuse were the inevitable result of legislated compassion, were infuriated by reports of undeserving pensioners.

Yet there were also assertions of pride by and on behalf of disabled veterans. Photographers, for example, could have retouched their clinical images to render wounded veterans anonymous, but they seldom did so—AMPUTEES and other severely wounded ex-soldiers are fully identified and typically gaze directly into the camera. Many amputees also rejected the notion that their lives were "a constant burden." Relying on the importance of self-control in the 19th-century conception of masculinity, veteran George Warren, who had lost his right arm in the war, wrote that he "gave [my arm] up willingly for I had the assurance that it could not be given for a nobler or better cause."

Since most disabilities were less obvious than a missing limb, a public-assistance model, based on the long-standing distinction between worthy and unworthy recipients, governed aid to veterans. The key gatekeepers in this system were the medical examiners, one of whom testified that his job was to "form an opinion of [an applicant's] character." Such opinions contributed to biases in access to pensions: African-Americans, immigrants, and veterans with stigmatized mental disabilities were reluctant to apply and denied pensions more frequently than native-born, white soldiers.

Some of the changes inspired by the Civil War reveal that governmental aid for people with disabilities and their assertions of dignity are not recent developments. It is equally important to remember, however, that the weight of numbers behind official policies and the primacy of individual responsibility in expressed attitudes firmly rooted the policies and attitudes in their own time.

Larry M. Logue
Peter Blanck

Further Reading:

Blanck, Peter, et al. *Disability Civil Rights Law and Policy: Treatise, Cases and Materials.* St. Paul, Minn.: Thomson West Publishing, 2004–2006.

Connor, J. T. H., and Michael G. Rhode. "Shooting Soldiers: Civil War Medical Images, Memory, and Identity in America." *Invisible Culture: An Electronic Journal for Visual Culture* 5 (2003). URL: http://www.rochester.edu/in_visible_culture/Issue5.

Dean, Eric T., Jr. *Shook Over Hell: Post-Traumatic Stress, Vietnam, and the Civil War.* Cambridge, Mass.: Harvard University Press, 1997.

Figg, Laurann, and Jane Farrell-Beck. "Amputation in the Civil War: Physical and Social Dimensions." *Journal of the History of Medicine and Allied Sciences* 48 (1993): 454–475.

Logue, Larry M., and Peter Blanck. "'There Is Nothing That Promotes Longevity Like a Pension'": Public Policy and Mortality of Civil War Union Army Veterans." *Wake Forest Law Review* 39 (2004): 49–67.

"When Johnny Comes Marching Home" and "Paddy's Lamentation" (1860s)

The Civil War (1861–65) was one of the most profound events in American history. For disability historians, the war is significant not only for producing thousands of disabled veterans but also for influencing attitudes, policies, and technology related to disability. In these two popular songs from that era disability plays a central role. "When Johnny Comes Marching Home" suggests an expectation of social acceptance for wounded soldiers upon their return;

"Paddy's Lamentation," in contrast, points to the lack of real support and the challenges faced by those disabled in the carnage. Such popular cultural representations reveal the pervasive but often overlooked presence of disability in America.

"When Johnny Comes Marching Home"

When Johnny comes home the girls will say,
Hurrah! Hurrah!
We'll have sweethearts now to cheer our way,
Hurrah! Hurrah!
And if they lost a leg, the girls won't run,
For half a man is better than none,
And we'll all feel gay
When Johnny comes marching home.

Source: From Irwin Silber and Jerry Silverman, *Songs of the Civil War.* Courier Dover Publications, 1995, p. 175. This verse of "When Johnny Comes Marching Home" is credited to "California minstrel, Ben Cotton." Available online. URL: http://hauntedfieldmusic.com/Lyrics.html#Irish%20Vol. Accessed June 26, 2008.

"Paddy's Lamentation"

General Meagher to us said
'If you get shot or you lose your leg
Every mother's son of you will get a pension.'
But in the war I lost my leg
And all I got's a wooden peg
Oh me boys, it's the truth to you I mention.

Source: From "Paddy's Lamentation," Anonymous, as found in David Kincaid's CD *The Irish Volunteer: Songs of the Irish Union Soldier, 1861–65.* This verse is believed to be a postwar addition, 1860s. Available online. URL: http://hauntedfieldmusic.com/Lyrics.html#Irish%20Vol. Accessed June 26, 2008.

Clarke School for the Deaf

The foremost institution in oral EDUCATION for the DEAF for the past 150 years is the Clarke School for the Deaf in Northampton, Massachusetts. Often viewed as an antagonist within the cultural deaf community, the Clarke School has been a driving force behind the American oral movement and the teaching of speech and lipreading.

After the CIVIL WAR, when oral education in the United States began to take firm root, Northampton merchant and philanthropist John Clarke endowed the establishment of an institution for deaf CHILDREN dedicated to teaching speech. The school later was named in his honor. The Clarke School opened on October 1, 1867, with 20 pupils; Harriet Rogers was the school's first principal. Rogers upheld the oral school's mission to assimilate deaf children into hearing society. CAROLINE YALE succeeded Rogers and remained principal of the Clarke School for over 47 years. The two women were successful in promoting the growth of their institution, enhancing both social and financial networks.

During her tenure at the Clarke School, Yale fostered close friendships with leaders in the oral movement. ALEXANDER GRAHAM BELL and his father-in-law Gardiner Hubbard Green proved to be important allies to the institution, as they both devoted personal, educational, and financial support to the school. Both men also served as chairmen of the board of directors for numerous years.

The astute leaders of the Clarke School capitalized on the importance of FAMILY in the lives of deaf children. Aiming to reach the parents of deaf children, the school implemented educational programs, instructing mothers and fathers in the values of ORALISM. The success of this campaign has been a contributing factor to the continued presence of oralism in the United States.

The Clarke School was a prominent leader in the rise of female teachers entering the field of education in the late 19th and early 20th centuries. Reinforcing the mainstream ideology of how deaf children should behave in public, such as proper breathing, eating, and speaking, the Clarke School relied on a strong base of young female teachers who embodied such values. Principal Yale recruited female teachers heavily from the "Seven Sister Schools" (elite female colleges in the North), especially Smith College, since it was located across the street from the Clarke School. Yale established a teacher training program at the school in 1892, graduating generations of female teachers during her tenure. The influx of hearing females in deaf education under the Clarke program and those at other institutions resulted in the displacement of deaf male and female teachers before WORLD WAR II.

Much of the Clarke School's prominence can be attributed to its strong networking among influential leaders during the Progressive Era of the early 19th century. For example, Grace Goodhue, a former teacher and alumna of the teaching program at Clarke, married the politician and future U.S. president Calvin Coolidge in 1905. Although Goodhue taught at the Clarke School only for three years, she maintained close ties with the institution. During her husband's presidency in the 1920s, Goodhue raised over $2 million for the endowment of her previous employer.

Since World War II, Clarke has maintained close connections to the medical establishment, promoting assistive devices such as COCHLEAR IMPLANTS and aural work (using residual hearing to enhance speech training). In the late 20th and early 21st centuries, the Clarke School has continued to grow, developing early intervention programs for children and establishing satellite locations in Boston, Philadelphia, New York City, and Jacksonville, Florida.

Embodying ideals of assimilation and Americanization, the Clarke School has sought to "restore" deaf children to mainstream society. As a driving force in the oral movement, the institution holds a significant place in deaf and disability history. Exemplifying the importance of social networking with prominent leaders and the effects of feminization in the field of education, the Clarke School symbolizes mainstream society's historical push to assimilate deaf people into the hearing world, an issue that remains hotly contested by deaf cultural advocates.

See also GENDER; RESIDENTIAL SCHOOLS.

Lindsey Patterson

Further Reading:
Burch, Susan. *Signs of Resistance: American Deaf Cultural History, 1900 to World War II.* New York and London: New York University Press, 2002.

Clarke School Web site. URL: www.clarkeschool.org.

Florentine Films. *Through Deaf Eyes.* Documentary film. PBS, Washington, D.C.: March 2007.

Gannon, Jack R. *Deaf Heritage: A Narrative History of Deaf America.* Silver Spring, Md.: National Association of the Deaf, 1980.

Van Cleve, John Vickrey, and Barry Crouch. *A Place of their Own: Creating the Deaf Community in America.* Washington, D.C.: Gallaudet University Press, 1989.

Cleland, Max (1942–) *disabled veteran and U.S. senator*

Joseph Maxwell Cleland has served as secretary of the Veterans Administration, Georgia secretary of state, and U.S. senator from Georgia. Born in Atlanta, Georgia, on August 24, 1942, he grew up in nearby Lithonia, the only child of Hugh, a salesman and WORLD WAR II VETERAN, and Juanita, a secretary. At 6′2″ and 215 pounds, Cleland was a robust athlete and straight-A student at Lithonia High School.

Cleland became interested in politics while majoring in history at Florida's Stetson University. After graduating in 1964, he campaigned for U.S. congressional candidate Jim Mackay, a progressive Democrat. He joined the army in 1966 after a year of graduate school at Emory University, where he received a master's degree in history in 1968.

From 1967 to 1968 Cleland was a Signal Corps officer in Vietnam, setting up communications equipment. On April 8, 1968, with a month left in his tour, he picked up a grenade that he thought he had dropped. It exploded, taking off both his legs and his right arm. He spent 18 months rehabilitating in army HOSPITALS. The army awarded him a Silver Star for Gallantry in Action and the Bronze Star for Meritorious Service.

In 1970 Cleland ran for the Georgia state senate and won, becoming at age 28 the youngest Georgia state senator ever elected. In 1977 President Jimmy Carter appointed Cleland secretary of the Veterans Administration. The first Vietnam veteran and severely disabled person to hold the position, as well as the youngest, Cleland established psychological counseling centers for veterans in the first initiative ever to deal specifically with the emotional trauma of WAR.

In 1980 Ronald Reagan's defeat of Jimmy Carter ended Cleland's tenure as secretary of the Veterans Administration. Cleland returned to Georgia, serving as secretary of state for 13 years, from 1983 to 1996. His implementation of the National Voter Registration Act increased the number of disabled registered voters in Georgia.

In 1996 Cleland was elected to the U.S. Senate, where he supported improved health services for veterans and enacted fair access VOTING reforms. Cleland lost his Senate seat in 2002 to Republican Saxby Chambliss in a controversial campaign in which Chambliss accused Cleland of being unpatriotic and weak on national security in the wake of the SEPTEMBER 11, 2001, terrorist attacks.

Following his senatorial defeat, Cleland taught political science at American University until 2003, when he joined the Export-Import Bank of the United States. In August 2007 he joined the Pennsylvania Association of Individuals with Disabilities (PAID), an ORGANIZATION dedicated to promoting EMPLOYMENT of disabled persons.

Cleland's career has been fraught with challenge. In the Georgia state senate, inaccessible buildings inspired his legislation requiring public facilities to be accessible, legislation that would later served as a model for the AMERICANS WITH DISABILITIES ACT of 1990. As a U.S. senator, he had to use the women's restroom because the men's room was not WHEELCHAIR accessible. He credits these and other challenges for much of his success because they provided a clear and meaningful direction for his life as an activist and political leader. Many disability activists claim Cleland as a true ally to the DISABILITY RIGHTS MOVEMENT, acknowledging his public advocacy. While many aspects of his life story are exceptional, Cleland's example highlights common factors in disability history, including the quest for equality, ACCESS, and REPRESENTATION.

Former Georgia senator Max Cleland has had a long and illustrious political career, including a 14-year appointment as the head of the United States Department of Veterans Affairs. *(George Loper)*

See also ACTIVISM AND ADVOCACY; AMPUTEES AND AMPUTATION; VIETNAM WAR.

Robin Feltman

Further Reading:
Barabak, Mark Z. "Poster Boy," *Los Angeles Times,* 18 July 2004. Available online. URL: http://www.sun-sentinel.com/business/la-tm-cleland29jul18,0,4458836.story?page=3. Accessed August 5, 2007.
Cleland, Max. *Strong at the Broken Places.* Atlanta: Long Street Press, 2000.
Williams, Rudi. "Amputee Ware Hero U.S. Senator Still Fights for Survival," American Forces Press Service. Available online. URL: http://www.defenselink.mil/news/newsarticle.aspx?id=44298. Accessed August 3, 2007.

Clerc, Laurent (Louis-Laurent-Marie Clerc) (1785–1869) *deaf teacher, advocate, and community leader*

Louis-Laurent-Marie Clerc is one of the most important figures in American DEAF cultural history. As both a teacher and advocate who helped spread sign language in the United States in the 19th century, his life story highlights various central themes in the development of the deaf COMMUNITY, including EDUCATION, LANGUAGE, EMPOWERMENT, and cultural IDENTITY.

Clerc was born on December 26, 1785, in the village of La Balme les Grottes, near Lyon, France. His father served as the town's notary, tax collector, and mayor. Clerc became deaf while a small child. He attributed his deafness to a fall into the fire at his family's home that also destroyed his sense of smell. A stroke of fingers against cheek, representing the scar that remained from that long ago fall, became his name in sign language.

At the age of 12, Clerc entered the national school for deaf students in Paris. His teacher was Jean Massieu, a deaf man and former student of the school's director Abbé Roch-Ambroise Sicard. Clerc quickly learned sign language and became recognized as one of the school's outstanding students. In 1805 he became a tutor at the school, and a year later he was appointed teacher. In 1815 Sicard traveled to England to demonstrate French methods for teaching deaf CHILDREN, in which emphasis was placed on signing, reading, and writing, and Clerc was among those selected to accompany him.

When Clerc was in London the Rev. THOMAS HOPKINS GALLAUDET, a minister from the United States who had been engaged by MASON FITCH COGSWELL, a prominent Connecticut doctor and father of a deaf daughter, attended one of Sicard's demonstrations. Gallaudet, in Europe to study methods of teaching deaf students and bring these methods back to the United States, was impressed by the eloquence and sagacity of Clerc's written and signed responses at the demonstration. He traveled to the Paris school in spring 1816, and Clerc became Gallaudet's teacher.

The two men communicated through gestures, written French, and perhaps a smattering of English that Clerc had studied in preparation for his trip to England. They agreed that Clerc would come to the United States to help Gallaudet set up a school for deaf students. A contract dated June 13, 1816, specified that Clerc would teach grammar, language, arithmetic, geography, history, and religion, and that, in Protestant New England, he would be able to practice his Catholic faith and not be forced to teach anything that conflicted with it.

Within days of signing the contract, the two men boarded the *Mary Augusta* and sailed for the United States. After a voyage of 52 days—during which Gallaudet continued to teach Clerc English and Clerc continued to teach Gallaudet signs—they arrived in New York in August 1816. The Connecticut legislature had passed legislation to establish the AMERICAN SCHOOL FOR THE DEAF, in Hartford, and Clerc and Gallaudet embarked on fund-raising for the new school, which opened on April 15, 1817. Clerc taught at the school for the next 41 years until he retired in 1858.

In 1819 Clerc married Eliza Boardman, one of his former students, and the couple had six children. With the rise of residential schools, it became increasingly common for deaf people to marry each other. In addition to his teaching duties, Clerc traveled to Washington, D.C., to garner support for deaf education. In January 1818 he addressed the U.S. Congress and met President James Monroe. In 1821, when the Pennsylvania School for the Deaf, the third oldest in the country, was in danger of closing, Clerc served as acting administrator and helped stabilize the school. Clerc returned to his native France to visit, writing extensively of his visits with friends and French schools for deaf students and contributing to links between the French and American deaf communities that would endure for generations.

The New England Gallaudet Association, a social, civic ORGANIZATION of deaf people, held its first general convention in 1857, and Clerc delivered the major address. In 1858 Clerc addressed the assembly again, and he used the opportunity to support the integration of the deaf and hearing communities. Early in his career, Clerc had suggested that land given by the federal government to Alabama for a state school be used as a national headquarters for deaf people, and JOHN FLOURNOY, one of his students, had advocated the establishment of a state comprised of exclusively deaf people. At this point, however, Clerc spoke against "exclusivity," noting that the involvement of hearing individuals in educational and advocacy organizations was helpful for a variety of practical reasons. This sophisticated understanding of cultural identity and empowerment has yet to be fully examined by scholars.

In 1864, when an act of Congress gave the school for deaf students in Washington, D.C., the right to award college degrees (thus establishing what would later become GALLAUDET UNIVERSITY), Clerc was invited to address those assembled for the college's official opening. He died four years later, on July 18, 1869, in Hartford, Connecticut.

Clerc's influence on the early education of deaf students in the United States was profound. The students he taught and the teachers he trained fanned out across the country using the sign language and the pedagogy he brought from France. When linguists analyzed AMERICAN SIGN LANGUAGE, they found that most American signs derived their origin from the French signs that had arrived in Clerc's hands. Equally important, as the first schools for deaf students sought funding from a dubious public, Clerc provided a living example of potential success, irrefutable proof of the sophistication and aptitude of deaf people. Deaf people have honored Clerc in various ways, including naming educational programs after him, placing historic plaques at places of significance during his life, and requesting or devising the production of busts, paintings, and plays.

Cathryn Carroll

Further Reading:

Canlas, Loida. "Laurent Clerc: Apostle to the Deaf People in the New World." Gallaudet University, 2007. URL: http://clerc-center.gallaudet.edu/Literacy/MSSDLRC/clerc/.

Gannon, Jack. *Deaf Heritage: A Narrative History of Deaf America.* Silver Spring, Md.: National Association of the Deaf, 1981.

Lane, Harlan. *When the Mind Hears.* New York: Random House, 1989.

Van Cleve, John Vickrey, and Barry Crouch. *A Place of Their Own: Creating the Deaf Community in America.* Washington, D.C.: Gallaudet University Press, 1989.

Excerpts from *The Diary of Laurent Clerc's Voyage from France to America in 1816*

On June 18, 1816, French deaf educator Laurent Clerc joined American Reverend Thomas Hopkins Gallaudet on the ship Mary Augusta, *which sailed from Le Havre, France, to New York. In April 1817 the two would become "founding fathers" of the American School for the Deaf, the first permanent school for the deaf in the United States, located in Hartford, Connecticut. As part of his effort to learn English, Clerc kept a diary during his 52-day voyage to America. These selections from that journal demonstrate his exceptional linguistic skills, his interactions with many hearing people on the ship, and his evolving relationship with Gallaudet.*

The Diary of Laurent Clerc's Voyage from France to America in 1816
by Laurent Clerc
1816

A Recital of all that I have done and seen, since my departure from Havre till my arrival at New York. I warn the Reader who may read this relation, that I have not written it for him, but for myself, and particularly to exercise and perfect myself in the English Language.

—Laurent Clerc

The ship named Mary-Augusta the provisions all being ready in the morning of Tuesday the 18th of June 1816, we waited for nothing but the high water to take our departure. In fine, at three o'clock in the afternoon, the tide having risen, we left Havre, a pretty little City of France, surrounded by a crowd of spectators. The persons who knew us wished us a happy voyage and good health. We were in number six passengers without counting the Captain, whose name was Mr. Hall, and twelve strong and skillful sailors.

. . . We soon lost sight of Havre. We descended into our cabin where we supped; after supper, we prayed to God, and after prayer, we wished each other a good evening and went to bed. For my own part, I slept very profoundly.

. . . Thursday, June the 20th. The hour of our breakfast being fixed at eight o'clock, that of our dinner at two o'clock and that of our supper at eight o'clock, I take care to rise every morning half an hour before breakfast, which consists usually of the same things which I have before related. I employed all the morning in studying English, and in making some exercises on some verbs which I judge convenient to record here:

to let down . . . . . . They let down, during the night, the lanterns of the streets to light them.

to abridge . . . . . . Your letter is too long, you must abridge it.

to shorten . . . . . . My pantaloons are too long, I must get them shortened.

to buy . . . . M. Gallaudet has bought all that we want for our voyage.

. . . I did nothing extraordinary the rest of the day, except, that having perceived one of our companions had mounted the shrouds, I thought that it was necessary that I should advise the Captain of it. I took then a sheet of paper and wrote this to the Captain with my pencil: "Sir, it is forbidden to the passengers to mount, the shrouds, under pain of being condemned to pay an honorable forfeit, but that gentleman has ascended in spite of that prohibition. I advise you to condemn him to pay to the sailors six bottles of wine." Before showing this advertisment to the Captain, I presented it to Mr. Gallaudet, begging him to correct it. He cast a glance of the eye upon it, with the goodness which characterizes him, and when he had corrected it, I wrote it fair. The Captain in reading it, laughed, and agreed that I had reason in what I had said, but he did not follow my advice. He asked me where I had learned that prohibition. I answered him that it was when I went from France to England.

. . . Friday, June the 21st. . . . After breakfast, M. Gallaudet desiring to encourage me to learn good English, suggested to me the thought of writing this journal, and it is in consequence of his advice that I do it. I began it therefore on the spot and I wrote my diary of the 18th of June, which busied me all the day. It was a long time for so small a matter, but if you deign to consider that I was obliged, every moment, to seek in my dictionary the words which I did not understand, you would say of it, I am sure, that I could not do it more quickly. When I had finished my first day, I presented it to Mr. Gallaudet, praying him to correct it. He did it with his ordinary kindness. Afterwards I wrote my work fair in my stitched book.

. . . Thursday, July the 18th. It continued to rain at intervals and to blow with violence, but much more violently than the preceding day, and so violently that the gallant sail of our ship was rent. Nobody perceived it except the Captain who saw it after dinner. He at once called all the sailors and ordered them to mount above. They did it, and when they were there, they busied themselves in uniting and letting down the top gallant sail, in order to substitute another in its place. This was soon done, and our ship continued her way as she had been doing.

Almost at the same time we discovered before us another ship which we soon overtook and passed by, but without having approached it, for it was at the north and we at the west, and we always have it in sight, but at a great distance. In the evening, the sea was extremely agitated. It cast water here and there upon deck, and also a certain kind of I do not know what fish, which the sailors gathered and showed us. After supper, being seated on deck near M. Gallaudet who held my slates, I took it from him and wrote upon it that the East was very avaricious, for since thirty days we have been on the sea and it has not granted us a single morsel of wind. He laughed upon reading it. The Captain having come up to sit at my side, I told him that, seeing the bad wind, we should yet be on the sea during a month and a half, and that I was rather uneasy lest we should begin to fail of water; but he removed my fears by saying that if we used our provisions with economy we might remain at sea three or four months longer and yet fail of nothing.

. . . Thursday, August the 8th. Oh, great joy among us all! We are told that we are approaching America, that if the wind continues, we shall be in sight of New York in two days at latest. May God grant that this hope may be realized! But whatsoever He may please to command, we are all disposed to resign ourselves to His orders, and whatsoever may happen.

Source: Laurent Clerc. *The Diary of Laurent Clerc's Voyage from France to America in 1816.* West Hartford, Conn.: American School for the Deaf, 1952. Available online. URL: http://www. disabilitymuseum.org/lib/docs/687.htm?page=print. Accessed June 20, 2008.

Cloak of Competence, The

In 1967 anthropologist Robert Edgerton published *The Cloak of Competence: Stigma in the Lives of the Mentally Retarded*, a highly influential study in the field of COGNITIVE DISABILITY. Edgerton examined the experiences of 48 "mildly mentally retarded" former patients of Pacific State Hospital in California. Together with a team of researchers, Edgerton conducted interviews and participant observation with the former patients as they went about their lives in the community. Whenever possible, the research team also interviewed or observed FAMILY members, friends, and acquaintances of the 48 former patients.

The Cloak of Competence reports on the findings and conclusions of Edgerton's study. Edgerton used the concept of STIGMA developed by ERVING GOFFMAN in his 1963 book to understand the people in his study. Goffman had argued that a stigma was a deeply discrediting physical, personal, racial, national, or religious attribute that threatened to damage people's identities in their relations with others. Edgerton applied the concept directly to the experiences of former patients. Having MENTAL RETARDATION, he concluded, was a deeply discrediting and stigmatizing attribute that could harm people's self-esteem. The former patients went to great lengths to deny their mental retardation, to hide their past INSTITUTIONALIZATION, and to "pass" as "NORMAL" people. Edgerton also reported that the former patients relied on NONDISABLED "benefactors" for assistance in managing daily problems, in denial, and in passing in the community.

Edgerton and colleagues published follow-up studies of some of the former patients in the original study in 1976, 1984, and 1991. Of those who could be located, most were faring far better in the community than Edgerton would have predicted in 1967. They had become more independent, less reliant on benefactors, and less consumed with denial and passing than when they had been studied initially.

The Cloak of Competence transformed treatment and understanding of cognitively disabled people in the late 1960s and 1970s. It helped to popularize sociological and anthropological methods and concepts in a field that had been dominated by medicine and psychology. Edgerton's work also sensitized professionals in the field to the stigmatizing nature of the concept of mental retardation and the potentially harmful effects of diagnosing someone as mentally retarded. *The Cloak of Competence* was later criticized by sociologists Robert Bogdan and Steven Taylor and historian

David Gerber. In a 1982 book containing the life histories of two former residents of a state institution for people with mental retardation, Bogdan and Taylor argued that Edgerton did not question the concept of mental retardation itself and that mental retardation was a label imposed on people by others according to arbitrary standards. The title of Edgerton's book, claimed Bogdan and Taylor, suggested that people labeled mentally retarded tried to hide their incompetence. They maintained that people so labeled had a cloak of incompetence put over them. Gerber questioned whether the former patients included in Edgerton's study had an objective disability condition and suggested that social and economic factors had played a major role in their institutionalization. In a revised and updated version of *The Cloak of Competence* published in 1993, Edgerton defended his original study and expressed disagreement with what he referred to as "extreme social constructionist views" of mental retardation or intellectual disability held by some of his critics.

Steven J. Taylor

Further Reading:

Bogdan, Robert, and Steven J. Taylor. *Inside Out: The Social Meaning of Mental Retardation.* Toronto: University of Toronto Press, 1982.

Edgerton, Robert B. *The Cloak of Competence: Stigma in the Lives of the Mentally Retarded.* Rev. ed. Berkeley: University of California Press, 1993.

Gerber, D. A. "Listening to Disabled People: The Problem of Voice and Authority in Robert B. Edgerton's *The Cloak of Competence*." *Disability, Handicap & Society* 5 (1990): 3–23.

Goffman, Erving. *Stigma: Notes on the Management of Spoiled Identity.* Englewood Cliffs, N.J.: Prentice Hall, 1963.

Close, Chuck (1940–) *artist*

Chuck Close is an artist best known for the large portrait work he has done since the 1970s. Known for his massive realistic "heads," usually painted on seven-by-nine-foot canvases, Close described himself in a 1995 issue of the eminent art journal, *ARTNews*, as a "poor white-trash kid from a mill-town in Washington state," but the same issue listed him among the "50 Most Influential People" in the art world. Close's work encompasses a range of media, including painting, prints, paper sculptures, photographs, holograms, daguerreotypes, and film. Many critics identify Close with the photorealists of the 1970s. These New Realists see the world as an image, take parts from that world and incorporate them into their own work, with the goal of bringing life and art closer together. They are often linked to the Pop Art movement in New York because of their use of mass-produced commercial objects. Rather than aligning himself with this group, Close says he

would label his work as "New Artificialist" (his own term), feeling that he does not have much in common with the New Realists because he does not try to create something "real."

Close was born on July 5, 1940, in Monroe, Washington. His love for creating art began at age four, and, by age five, his parents had bought him his own set of oil paints. His first art teacher, a woman his father hired at a local diner and who Close identifies as a prostitute, helped him to establish the foundations of his future work and provided a bevy of nude bodies to paint.

As a child, Close struggled in school, having difficulty reading and remembering factual information, difficulties that might today be identified by educators and psychologists as dyslexia. Close's learning disability influenced the way he worked after graduating from Yale University in 1964 with a master's degree in fine art. His consistent use of a grid placed over the subject of study stems from the process he used to learn information as a child—break it into small manageable pieces and then bring it all together to make a whole. Close works on one grid of the canvas at a time, and he does not move on to the others until he has finished.

Critics say he replicates the veracity of a photograph while simultaneously undermining the objectivity of PHOTOGRAPHY. Close states that he wants to present the information in his "heads" in the most neutral, straightforward way, without editorial comment.

Close explains the large size of his paintings in three ways: First, that is how tall his ceiling was when he first began to paint the "heads." Second, a seven-by-nine-foot canvas is directionally proportional to a five-by-seven- or eight-by-ten-inch photograph. Lastly, the larger something is, the longer it takes to walk by it in the gallery.

Chuck Close's first solo show was in 1970 at the Bykert Gallery in New York City. By 1988 Close's work had appeared in 60 solo shows and had been seen in hundreds of group shows around the world.

In 1988, as a result of a spinal blood clot, Close developed incomplete tetraplegia, also known as quadriparesis or incomplete quadriplegia. While Close does use a WHEELCHAIR, his upper arms have movement and he has feeling and some movement in his legs. Following his changed circumstances, Close found that continuing to paint was the best thing he could do to rehabilitate his mind and body. With the help of his wife, Leslie, and his rehabilitation team, Close devised a way to strap a paint brush to his hands and work in miniature form, having just enough strength to make two-inch paintings. Eventually, Close moved into a fully accessible studio, with a moving easel to lift his signature-sized canvases up and down.

In November 1991 Chuck Close opened a new show at Pace Gallery in SoHo. Continuing the tradition of his earlier work in terms of size and content, the new paintings were somehow different. Close says the difference comes in his palette—he returned to the colors of his earlier work, which was greatly influenced by renowned 20th-century PAINTER Willem de Kooning.

Close does not like being described as a disability hero, and he does not like to talk about "overcoming adversity" (see OVERCOME AND OVERCOMING). He states that he was lucky because he was already "somebody" before his tetraplegia. He was self-employed and did not have to worry about an employer refusing to allow him to return to his job. Financially, he could afford to get back to work and to restructure his life to accommodate his work.

Chuck Close's work continues to be shown worldwide in traveling exhibits that focus on his self-portraiture, prints, process, and collaboration. One of his most recent shows was at the Pace Gallery, "Recent Paintings (2002–2005)," in 2005.

Heidi A. Temple

Further Reading:

Guare, John. *Chuck Close—Life and Work 1988–1995.* New York: Thames & Hudson, 1995.

Tully, Judd. Personal Interview with Chuck Close. Archives of American Art, Smithsonian Institution, 14 May 1987.

closed caption decoders

CLOSED CAPTIONS are captions that can be turned on and off by the viewer. The closed caption (CC) decoder is part of a system for providing access to TELEVISION. This equipment or circuitry makes it possible to display television captions or to turn them off.

The system was developed in the 1970s with leadership and funding from the U.S. Department of Health, Education and Welfare (HEW). Dr. Malcolm Norwood, a DEAF leader who is widely credited as the "father" of closed captioning, played a pivotal role as chief of the Media Services and Captioned Films for the Deaf Branch of HEW. The federal department sponsored market research to determine whether television viewers who could hear would accept "open" captions—captions that you cannot turn off—on televisions. The research found that many people would accept captions, but too large a projected number would not accept them; the number of hearing people who would not accept them was larger than the projected audience of DEAF and hard of hearing people who would be added to the audience. HEW continued to explore open captioning by funding production of captions for a number of series captioned by Public Broadcasting Service (PBS) affiliate WGBH in Boston. At the same time, as a result of industry resistance to open captioning, HEW funded work on development and testing of a closed caption system, which would display captions only on televisions equipped with a special decoder.

Other federal agencies and groups of advocates joined the effort. For example, in 1970, the National Bureau of Standards proposed a method of transmitting hidden caption information in the television signal and PBS developed and carried out tests on the decoder with funding from HEW. The First National Conference on Television for the Hearing Impaired, which was held in Knoxville, Tennessee, on December 14–16, 1971, brought together deaf and hard of hearing adults, parents of deaf and hard of hearing CHILDREN, producers, and representatives of television networks. This conference helped build momentum for organized and supported captioned television development. Five years later, in 1976, the Federal Communications Commission approved the use of part of the broadcast signal (Line 21) for closed captions. On March 16, 1980, the first closed captioned television shows appeared on NBC, ABC, and PBS stations.

The first decoders were set-top boxes. In the 1980s there was only one television model with a built-in decoder. Later the circuitry for closed caption decoders was built into television sets in the United States as a result of the TELEVISION DECODER CIRCUITRY ACT OF 1990.

The market for digital television and home theater technology has led to changes in the nature of the equipment itself. Systems are sold as a collection of components. Screens do not always include television-receiver components. Although it is illegal to sell a television without a decoder, the definition of television has become more difficult to pin down. It is possible to buy a home theater system that has no television, but not be able to buy a CC decoder for it—built-in or separate.

Closed captioning currently is available in digital video media other than television, across many but not all video formats. Closed captions for many video formats can be stored in a separate media file, and many media players integrate the caption file with the video file so that the captions appear, synchronized with the audio, under the video image. In this case, no CC decoder equipment is required.

The history of the closed caption decoder is important for many reasons. Many civil rights movements emphasize ACCESS and inclusion, and the development of decoders represents an important victory for many groups that were excluded by early television and other media technology. It also shows that it is possible for government, industry, and consumer advocates to work together to provide accessibility. In addition, this assistive technology—and the EMPOWERMENT movement that helped shape it—contributed to new laws, industries, and social attitudes toward deaf, HARD OF HEARING, and other marginalized peoples.

See also ASSISTIVE TECHNOLOGY AND ADAPTIVE DEVICES.

Judy Harkins

Further Reading:
Strauss, Karen P. *A New Civil Right: Telecommunications Equality for Deaf and Hard of Hearing Americans.* Washington, D.C.: Gallaudet University Press, 2006.

closed captioning

The advent and proliferation of closed captioning marks an important advancement in American DEAF and disability history. Closed captions provide text accompaniment to video media (such as TELEVISION programs or movies) but they are only seen when a special decoder is used. The captions are either superimposed on the video or displayed just below the video image and are synchronized with the speech of the soundtrack. Captions also contain text information about the audio programming, including descriptions of the sound effects or the type of background music used.

Particularly since the 1930s when moving pictures first incorporated sound, deaf and HARD OF HEARING people have sought alternative ways to access fully mainstream video entertainment. From WORLD WAR II through the 1960s, some progress was made using open captions (text, such as subtitles, that are visible to all viewers), but this applied only to certain types of FILMS. Television, the most popular and powerful media form since the 1950s, however, remained inaccessible to many deaf and hard of hearing consumers. In the 1960s the movement to make films accessible began to shift, focusing increasingly on television as a vital area for access improvement. Captioning became the primary means to achieve this.

Television captioning was developed in the 1970s under the leadership of the U.S. Department of Health, Education and Welfare (HEW) and the Public Broadcasting System (PBS). The first television captioning used "open" captions visible to all viewers. With HEW funding, WGBH, a PBS affiliate in Boston that remains active in captioning services and accessibility research today, open captioned its 1972 broadcasts of *The French Chef* with Julia Child; later it provided open captions of a children's series called *Zoom* and, on commercial television *The ABC Evening News.* For many deaf and hard of hearing viewers, these shows provided the first opportunity to ACCESS mainstream video media on a par with their hearing peers.

Feedback to these broadcasts and related market research later revealed that while some people heralded captions, many hearing viewers found the new format invasive and unappealing. The relatively small numbers of people who relied on captioning, coupled with the outcry against open captions, motivated the U.S. Department of Education, PBS, and other government agencies to develop a system to display captions only on command—to "close" them. The result was the creation of closed captioning and of decoders to read them.

In 1979 the National Captioning Institute was established as a nonprofit company to manufacture and sell decoders that could receive and display closed captions. The first decoders were sold in the early 1980s and were set-top boxes; only one model of TV had a built-in decoder. Increasing deaf and disability rights ACTIVISM helped fuel the passage of the 1990 TELEVISION DECODER CIRCUITRY ACT, which mandated that all manufacturers since the 1990s build the CLOSED CAPTION DECODER into their televisions.

For more than 25 years, the U.S. Department of Education helped to pay for captioning of broadcast television programs. Through the TELECOMMUNICATIONS ACT OF 1996, Congress finally began to shift the responsibility for captioning of television, including cable television, to the television program providers. The Federal Communications Commission established an eight-year phase-in period for this purpose, directing the television industry to increase captioning of television incrementally, to its current level of nearly 100 percent, or approximately 20 hours per day, beginning in 2006. Although the Department of Education still subsidizes some television captioning, these subsidies are now nominal, and reserved only for programming that is appropriate for use in the classroom setting, and which is not otherwise funded by television producers or programming distributors. Thirty years after closed-captioning was first developed, a very large proportion of television is finally accessible.

Access, however, remains a concern. Because legal mandates for video accessibility apply only to television, other forms of captioning access are beginning to lose ground; movies shown in movie theaters and on Internet video, DVDs, MP3, and videotapes, for example, still are not required by law to be captioned. Voluntary captioning of numerous DVDs and videotapes has occurred, but many others are still not captioned, nor is most video on the INTERNET.

The rise of closed captioning embodies many common features in deaf and disability history. The desire for full and equal access as an outgrowth of civil rights ideology strongly defines advocacy for captions. As with other examples of UNIVERSAL DESIGN, an approach that seeks to make things accessible to and inclusive of all people, captions ultimately serve more than the originally intended consumers. Individuals learning English, for example, have benefited from captioned programs. And changing technologies, such as the Internet, present both new communication possibilities for deaf and disabled people as well as new challenges as access remains a pressing issue.

See also ACCESS AND ACCESSIBILITY.

Judy Harkins
Karen Peltz Strauss

Further Reading:
National Captioning Institute. "A Brief History of Captioned Television." URL: http://www.ncicap.org/Docs/history.htm. Accessed January 19, 2007.

Strauss, Karen P. *A New Civil Right: Telecommunications Equality for Deaf and Hard of Hearing Americans.* Washington, D.C.: Gallaudet University Press, 2006.

Cobbs school

One of the first attempts to establish a school for the DEAF in the United States was the Cobbs school in Chesterfield, Virginia, in the early 19th century. The brief life of this institution demonstrates the disparate approaches to American education for the Deaf. Its demise would leave a void in Deaf EDUCATION that the AMERICAN SCHOOL FOR THE DEAF, the birthplace of deaf cultural history, would fill a year later.

Inspired by his two deaf CHILDREN, colonel and prominent planter William Bolling sought to establish a deaf school in the United States. Prior to 1815, only affluent families enjoyed formal options for deaf education; some sent their children to Scotland to study at the Braidwood Academy, a private oral institution established by Thomas Braidwood. While William Bolling could hear, he knew firsthand of the FAMILY disruptions and the expenses involved in sending children to Europe for an education, since his deaf siblings, Thomas John and Mary, had attended the Braidwood Academy.

In 1812, contemporaneously with Bolling's efforts to establish deaf EDUCATION in America, JOHN BRAIDWOOD, the grandson of the founder of the Braidwood Academy, came to the United States to start a school based on his family's teaching methods. Bolling contacted Braidwood and asked him to come to Virginia to meet with his deaf children at his estate, Cobbs Manor.

After a series of dramatic events during Braidwood's travels from New York to Virginia, including a carriage accident that left him with minor injuries and an arrest for accumulated debts, he finally arrived at Cobbs Manor. However, the War of 1812 between the United States and Great Britain proved to be another obstacle to the establishment of Bolling's and Braidwood's school. Bolling vouched for Braidwood's presence in the United States and promised to keep him under close watch, allowing for his continued residence in America. Then, while Bolling went off to WAR, Braidwood tutored his benefactor's deaf and hearing children for one year before opening his instruction to more children.

The Cobbs school for the deaf officially opened in March 1815, enrolling five students. The school catered to affluent families and taught speech and lipreading. However, Braidwood's alcoholism and reckless lifestyle precluded his ability to effectively head the school, and, after only one year, he left in 1816. With few students and no instructor, the first attempt to establish an oral deaf school in America collapsed after Braidwood's departure.

Although the Cobbs school proved short-lived, its role in American deaf history remains vital. It reflected growing efforts to gain educational opportunities for deaf children, advocacy that would succeed with the American School for the Deaf and other state-sponsored institutions later in the 19th century. The emphasis on oral training presented at the Cobbs school likewise embodies the long-standing belief in training deaf people to adapt to hearing society and values. Its failure, as some historians note, likely enabled alternative models for deaf education to take root more fully at that time. The Cobbs school further contributes to our understanding of American history, as it exemplifies the state of education in the United State prior to broad governmental support.

The Cobbs school is memorialized with a bronze plaque that hangs in the main hall of Virginia's state school for the deaf in Staunton.

See also ORALISM.

Lindsey Patterson

Further Reading:
Bass, R. Aumon. *History of the Education of the Deaf in Virginia.* Staunton: Virginia School for the Deaf and Blind, 1949.
Crouch, Barry, and Brian Greenwald. "Hearing with the Eye: The Rise of Deaf Education in the United States." In *The Deaf History Reader,* edited by John Van Cleve. Washington, D.C., Gallaudet University Press, 2008.
Van Cleve, John Vickrey, and Barry Crouch. *A Place of Their Own: Creating the Deaf Community in America.* Washington, D.C.: Gallaudet University Press, 1989.

cochlear implants

Cochlear implants represent a recent attempt in a long history of efforts by researchers, educators, and others to mitigate the effects of hearing loss through technological means. Advances in cochlear implant technology, increased awareness of bioethical issues, and disability civil rights ACTIVISM have fueled some of the ongoing controversies over this device.

The cochlea, located in the inner ear, is a very small, fluid-filled, snail-shaped tube about one-third of an inch in diameter that contains thousands of microscopic hair cells. When these hair cells are unable to stimulate the adjacent auditory nerve fibers, the auditory nerve, which connects the cochlea to the cortex of the brain, is unable to transmit sounds to the brain. This results in a sensorineural hearing loss. A cochlear implant is designed to do the job of the hair cells and stimulate the auditory nerve fibers.

A cochlear implant consists of external and surgically implanted internal parts. The external components consist of a battery, a small microphone, a microcomputer, and a headpiece that magnetically connects to an internal receiver. The internal components consist of the receiver and a wirelike electrode array that runs from the receiver into the cochlea. Sounds received by the microphone are converted into digital information by the microcomputer and transmitted via radio waves to the internal receiver and along the electrode array. This process differentiates a cochlear implant from a conventional HEARING AID, which simply amplifies sound.

Cochlear implants are designed for those who receive minimal or no benefit from a hearing aid. Like hearing aids, implants can be turned off, if desired. The external parts of the device are usually removed during vigorous physical activity, bathing, and before sleeping; the internal components are never removed, except when medically necessary.

The first experimental cochlear implant surgeries on DEAF adults were performed in France in 1957 and in the United States in 1961. At that time, the devices were bulky, cumbersome, and minimally effective. Research continued in the 1960s and 1970s, primarily in the United States, Europe, and Australia, and the first deaf child received an implant in 1977, also in France. Research to make cochlear implants both more technologically sophisticated and much smaller than earlier models continues; almost all implants are now behind-the-ear devices.

At the present time more than 100,000 people have had cochlear implant surgery; in the United States, approximately 22,000 adults and 15,000 children have received the device. It is not known, however, how many recipients have discontinued using their implant for one reason or another. Cochlear implant surgery is very expensive, costing upwards of $50,000, and is typically covered by health insurance. Implantation is rare in the less affluent nations of the world, however, and, in the United States, relatively prosperous, white cochlear implant recipients continue to be overrepresented in the implanted population.

Since the late 1970s controversies and unresolved issues regarding cochlear implants have arisen. A number of deaf people have repeatedly questioned the need for an implant because they do not see themselves as impaired or disabled and in need of a "CURE." They resist the narrow medical interpretation of disability that views deafness in strictly pathological terms. Moreover, historical examples abound that demonstrate how deaf people are living full, satisfying, and rewarding lives without being able to hear. This is particularly true for those who use AMERICAN SIGN LANGUAGE (or some other sign language) and participate in Deaf COMMUNITY activities.

Most of the opposition to cochlear implants has been directed toward implantation in CHILDREN. Since the late 1990s at least half of the implant surgeries performed internationally have been done on deaf children. Changes in U.S. Food and Drug Administration (FDA) guidelines, which now permit implantation in children as young as 12 months

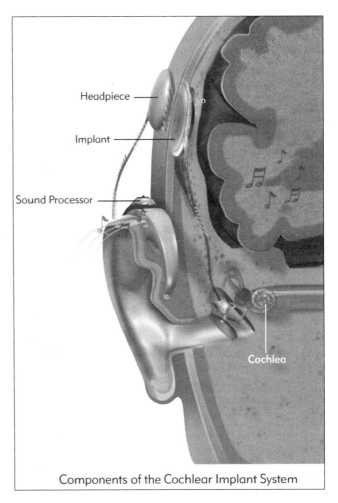

Components of the Cochlear Implant System

This diagram shows the various parts of a cochlear implant and where they are placed on people who undergo this procedure.   *(Advanced Bionics)*

of age, as well as a large body of research findings that show considerably improved language and speech development for children implanted by age three, have contributed to the increase in the number of children receiving implants. Today, it is routine to implant children as young as one year, or even younger if it is deemed medically necessary, FDA guidelines notwithstanding. Such early implantation might occur in cases of spinal meningitis when cochlear ossification could make later implantation problematic.

One reason for the opposition to pediatric implantation is the presumption that implant surgery should be seen as elective surgery and, as such, ought to be postponed until children are old enough to decide whether or not they want the device. This is based on the bioethical principle of self-determination and the right of the individual to make informed decisions. One example of this opposition was a 1991 position paper on cochlear implants issued by the NATIONAL ASSOCIATION OF THE DEAF (NAD) that criticized both the FDA for approving pediatric implantation and parents for following through with the surgery when insufficiently informed about the Deaf community.

In recent years, as the number of pediatric implantations has increased, the opposition to these implants has subsided. The NAD issued a revised position paper in 2000 that recognized the right of parents to make informed choices for their child, including the right to get a cochlear implant and other assistive devices, while at the same time actively supporting an interactive visual environment that incorporates sign language and English. Other associations dealing with deaf and HARD OF HEARING individuals have indicated even stronger support for pediatric cochlear implantation, thereby reflecting the diversity of opinion in the broader deaf and hard of hearing community. It is also important to note that current disability studies do recognize that disability is a natural part of human diversity and have at times questioned the need for cochlear implants for deaf persons who are part of a vibrant culture. At the same time, many disability advocates typically embrace technology in order to improve quality of life.

While research has demonstrated the benefits of implanting the child at a relatively early age in order to facilitate spoken language development, implanted children almost invariably require intensive post-implant speech and auditory therapy in order to benefit from the equipment since it does not restore "NORMAL" hearing. In educational settings, children with cochlear implants frequently require a variety of support services, including classroom amplification systems, media captioning, and SIGN LANGUAGE INTERPRETERS. With appropriate services, many deaf children have clearly benefited from cochlear implants. At the same time, many other deaf children have performed very well academically and socially without implants.

As many scholars have noted, cochlear implantation raises important historical and social questions, including the meaning and view of deafness, SCIENCE AND TECHNOLOGY, and authority.

See also ASSISTIVE TECHNOLOGY AND ADAPTIVE DEVICES; IMPAIRMENT/IMPAIRED; MEDICAL MODEL OF DISABILITY.

John B. Christiansen
Irene W. Leigh

Further Reading:

Chorost, Michael. *Rebuilt: How Becoming Part Computer Made Me More Human.* New York: Houghton Mifflin, 2005.

Christiansen, John B., and Irene W. Leigh. *Cochlear Implants in Children: Ethics and Choices.* Washington, D.C.: Gallaudet University Press, 2002, 2005.

Komesaroff, Linda, ed. *Surgical Consent: Bioethics and Cochlear Implantation.* Washington, D.C.: Gallaudet University Press, 2007.

Coelho, Tony (Anthony Lee) (1942–   ) *politician and disability advocate*

Anthony (Tony) Coelho is best known in the disability COMMUNITY for his advocacy of disability issues, including his support for the AMERICANS WITH DISABILITIES ACT (ADA) while serving in the U.S. House of Representatives as majority whip in 1988. Coelho's personal experience with EPILEPSY helped lead to this advocacy role while representing California's 15th congressional district from 1978 to 1989 and subsequently while chairing the PRESIDENT'S COMMITTEE ON EMPLOYMENT OF PEOPLE WITH DISABILITIES.

Born on June 15, 1942, Coelho grew up in the farming community of Los Banos, California. Coelho's life changed suddenly at age 15 when a truck accident flipped his pickup truck and left him with headaches that developed into grand mal seizures within a year. However, it was not until his senior year at Loyola University in Chicago, while serving as student body president, that Coelho was diagnosed with epilepsy. The diagnosis meant that Coelho's health insurance was canceled, his driver's license was revoked, and he became unable to pursue his goal of becoming a Catholic priest.

After graduating from Loyola University in Los Angeles in 1964, Coelho worked for Bob Hope, the celebrated actor and comedian. Hope was instrumental in turning Coelho toward politics and helped Coelho find a staff position with Congressman Bernie Sisk. Coelho worked first as Sisk's legislative assistant, rising to become his chief of staff from 1971 to 1977. Following Sisk's retirement, Coelho won his congressional seat in 1978, despite criticism that his epilepsy would preclude his ability to serve as a member of Congress.

Coelho rose quickly in the Democratic leadership. From 1981 to 1987 he chaired the Democratic Congressional Campaign Committee, and, in 1988, he attained the powerful position of House majority whip. His public reputation was shaped by his prominent success at raising funds for Democratic candidates from corporate sources typically unsympathetic to the Democratic Party.

Coelho was forced to resign from Congress in 1989, due to controversial allegations of his involvement with junk bonds. However, he continued to work on behalf of people with disabilities, particularly "hidden disabilities" such as epilepsy. In 1994 President Bill Clinton appointed Coelho as chair of the President's Committee on Employment of People with Disabilities (where he served until 2001) and, in 1998, as vice chair of the National Task Force on Employment of Adults with Disabilities and as co-chair of the U.S. Census Monitoring Board. In 1999–2000 Coelho was general chairman of the presidential campaign of Democratic candidate Al Gore. For many years, Tony Coelho has raised funds on behalf of the EPILEPSY FOUNDATION of America, and, in 2007, he served as chair of the Foundation's National Board of Directors.

Edmund Vu

Further Reading:

Epilepsy Foundation of America Web site. URL: http://www. epilepsyfoundation.org/aboutus/coelho.cfm. Accessed February 13, 2007.

McMahon, Brian, and Linda Shaw. *Enabling Lives: Biographies of Six Prominent Americans with Disabilities.* Boca Raton, Fla.: CRC Press, 2000.

cognitive and intellectual disability

As is often the case with the social history of oppressed groups, we are more familiar with the people who intervened in the lives of intellectually disabled individuals at various points in time than with those individuals themselves. We know much more about the superintendents of the so-called "idiot asylums" that arose in 19th century America than we do about the "idiots" upon whom they built their reputations. We know more of the ideas and opinions of American psychiatrist HENRY GODDARD than we do of Deborah Kallikak—the alias for the woman whose FAMILY heritage was used by Goddard in the early 20th century as the prototypical justification for eugenic sterilization and segregation of the intellectually disabled population. We know much more of Joseph Kennedy and all of his other CHILDREN (including John, Robert, Eunice, and Edward), than we do of his daughter ROSEMARY KENNEDY, upon whom Joseph had a LOBOTOMY done followed by a lifetime of INSTITUTIONALIZATION. For most of our country's history, people with intellectual disabilities have been collectively anonymous and invisible, though individually familiar and present throughout our society.

Until the middle of the 19th century, many adults with milder levels of intellectual disability were left to make their own way in a largely rural and agrarian society. Such "simpletons" (as they were often called) would sometimes wander from town to town, perhaps working for food or living on handouts from relatives and friends. For many of these Americans in the colonial and early national periods, their daily lives were characterized by what might be called a "benign neglect": neither targets of abuse nor recipients of support; occasionally ridiculed and often ignored; but accepted as an inevitable part of the social landscape. Those with more severe intellectual disabilities probably fared less well, subjected to the harsh and ineffective treatments of the largely uninformed medical profession, or hidden away by embarrassed families who feared the accusations of those who saw signs of divine retribution in the birth of severely disabled children.

With the spread of ALMSHOUSES in the late 18th and early 19th centuries, the social response to disability became more economically guided. Those with intellectual disabilities who were unable to support themselves were increasingly placed with other groups of poor people (widows, orphans, the mentally "insane" and physically "decrepit") within the confines of the local poor farm or almshouse. As the reformer DOROTHEA DIX would document in her numerous reports to state legislatures in the mid-19th century, the conditions in many of these facilities were shamefully neglectful at best and shockingly abusive at worst. Yet for most leaders in EDUCATION and HEALTH CARE, there was little beyond improved custody that could be envisioned for this segment of the dependent population. Most commonly referred to as "idiots" or "imbeciles," these individuals were seen as largely beyond help. However, that was to change in the middle of the century.

ESTABLISHING INSTITUTIONS FOR EDUCATION

In December 1844 SAMUEL GRIDLEY HOWE, the superintendent of the Perkins Institution and Massachusetts Asylum for the Blind (later known as the PERKINS SCHOOL FOR THE BLIND) in Boston, wrote Samuel B. Woodward, his fellow superintendent at the Massachusetts State Lunatic Hospital at Worcester, in response to Woodward's inquiry about "IDIOCY." Earlier that year Woodward had called the directors of the nation's 23 insane asylums to meet in Philadelphia to form a national association of medical superintendents. Among these physicians, there were complaints that patients whose "idiocy" appeared more prominent than their INSANITY had become a part of the several asylums' incurable populations. Woodward had shared the superintendents' concern with Howe, who acknowledged that on several occasions he too had received pupils at his BLIND school whose blindness, he later discovered, was complicated by "idiocy."

With his interest peaked by his exchange of letters with Woodward, Howe read shortly thereafter an article by John Conolly in the January 1845 edition of the *British & Foreign Medical Review.* In the article, Conolly, chief physician of the county lunatic asylum at Hanwell, England, described his visits to Parisian institutions. At the Bicêtre Hospital, he observed an idiot school that had opened in 1842. Under the direction of the lead teacher, EDOUARD SÉGUIN, this school had shown that pupils of even the most limited cognitive abilities could learn. Encouraged by his correspondence with Woodward and by Conolly's article, Howe persuaded the Massachusetts legislature to fund a three-year experimental school for people with cognitive disabilities. In October 1848 the first pupils were admitted to the newly founded "experimental school" (a new wing of the already existing Perkins Institution and Massachusetts Asylum for the Blind). As the "school" designation suggests—as well as following the pattern of his work with blind (and DEAF-BLIND) children— Howe's intent with this new educational experiment was to demonstrate the educability of CHILDREN, even when outwardly "damaged" and "DEFECTIVE." The optimistic goal was one of improvement—if not CURE—to the point of returning the newly able children to lives in the community as productive members of society. At the same time, it is important to note that Howe (and others), even at their most optimistic, would acknowledge that at least some children and adults with the most severe disabilities might be beyond the help of any intervention, and should be confined to purely custodial facilities.

In 1847 HERVEY WILBUR, a young Massachusetts physician without an established practice, also read reports about Séguin's work with idiots. The next year he opened a private school for cognitively disabled children at Barre in western Massachusetts. Three years later, in 1851, he moved to New York to become the superintendent of the recently opened New York State Asylum for Idiots. Adding to the excitement of the time, Séguin immigrated to the United States in 1850. During the 1850s, Howe, Wilbur, and Séguin published reports and articles about their successes in educating people with cognitive disabilities. Interest in this EDUCATION spread around the nation, and, by 1865, Pennsylvania, Ohio, Connecticut, Kentucky, and Illinois had opened residential schools.

SHIFTING ATTITUDES TOWARD INSTITUTIONALIZATION

If the two decades after the opening of the first "idiot" schools was a period of educational optimism, the seeds of a shift to pessimism after the CIVIL WAR lay just below the surface. Less than two years after his school opened, Howe had privately written Massachusetts town officials to take back a pupil who, despite Howe's best efforts, did not improve. Howe and others in the early 1850s also noted the presence of so-called moral idiots, young people whose minds, he claimed, were devoid of moral faculties. In 1858 Isaac Kerlin, the superintendent of the Pennsylvania Training School for Feeble-Minded Children, published *The Mind Unveiled; or, A Brief History of Twenty-two Imbecile Children*. In it he recounted the stories of several "moral idiots" or "moral imbeciles." Born with the absence of moral judgment but usually fairly intelligent, these particular kinds of weak minds threatened the good order of the COMMUNITY. As such, it was in the community's best interest to protect itself from the vices of moral imbeciles by keeping them safely guarded in the institution. By the 1870s the theme of feeblemindedness had become intertwined with moral deficiency.

Pessimism after the Civil War was fed by both the concept of degenerative heredity and the economic depression of the 1870s. Census counts in 1870 and 1880 suggested that there were more "FEEBLEMINDED" citizens than in prewar estimates. (Throughout the last half of the century, the term "feebleminded" came to replace "idiocy" as the generic term of reference for all levels of intellectual disability. "Idiocy" and "imbecility" became part of the evolving professional taxon-

omies referring to more severe levels of feeblemindedness.) The economic downturn also led to widespread unemployment, which seemed to call greater attention to rural vagabonds and "tramps," the roaming poor who moved from town to town, and urban "deadbeats," or the able-bodied BEGGARS increasingly visible on the streets of large cities. For the aging Kerlin and younger superintendents such as Connecticut's George Knight, Illinois's William Fish, and New York's J. C. Carson, the best way to stop the hereditary transmission of feeblemindedness was to ensure lifelong custodial care for the weak-minded. At the same time, economic problems made it difficult for superintendents to find employment outside the institution for their educated inmates. In this context, by the mid-1880s superintendents increasingly spoke of the "burden of the feebleminded" on society. Old distinctions made between educational pupils and custodial cases gave way to custodialism for most institutional inmates.

Between 1880 and 1910 the "burden of the feebleminded" became a rationale for institutional growth and expansion. With the focus of services so completely on the institution, superintendents found new ways to organize their enlarging facilities. In their professional association, the American Association of Medical Officers of American Institutions for Idiotic and Feeble-Minded Persons, superintendents shared the newest ways to classify inmates—with high-grade imbeciles in the highest range of ability and low-grade idiots at the lowest. Besides classification, superintendents worried about the costs of operating large institutions. To meet these costs, superintendents turned to the inmates themselves. Now likely never to leave the facility—in contrast to the previous generation of cognitively disabled students—inmates could best pass their time working on the institution's farm or in CAREGIVING for less-capable fellow inmates. Along with keeping inmates busy, the work reduced the costs that institutional officials would otherwise have had to pay to hired workers.

If the image of social burdens justified custodialism in the last decades of the 19th century, two events in the first decades of the 20th century reframed the image of intellectually disabled people from social burdens to social menaces. The first event was the introduction of Mendelian genetics into what superintendents had long claimed was an association between feeblemindedness and heredity. As the work of the Austrian botanist and geneticist Gregor Mendel became known after 1900, superintendents and social welfare authorities came to believe that the proper application of the new genetic information would demonstrate this connection. Accompanying Mendelian genetics in the first years of the new century was the development of so-called higher order mental testing. In 1908 Henry H. Goddard, a psychologist at the VINELAND TRAINING SCHOOL in New Jersey, introduced a translation of a new test of intelligence developed by the French psychologist, ALFRED BINET. By the beginning of the next decade the IQ (intelligence quotient) test, although going through several refinements, became the principal academically sanctioned tool for measuring, first, the intelligence of feebleminds and, eventually, of all school children. Combining the interest of authorities in heredity with the new tool for measuring intelligence, Goddard in 1912—less than four years after he introduced Binet's test—published *The Kallikak Family: A Study in the Heredity of Feeble-Mindedness.*

According to Goddard, the pseudonymously named KALLIKAK FAMILY with its double lineage—one with a line of respectable, law-abiding citizens and another line with law-breaking, sexually promiscuous "low lifers"—showed inevitable transmission of inferior stock through multiple generations. Besides the predictable transmission of bad genes, the new linkage of GENETICS and IQ testing showed, Goddard claimed, the "fecundity of the inferiors." Yet unlike easily identified idiots and imbeciles, families such as the Kallikaks were numerous, but neither their inferiority nor their promiscuous tendencies were readily recognized. To classify this newly identified group of feeble minds, Goddard constructed a new label, "MORONS." Unlike idiots and imbeciles, morons usually remained outside the confinement of the institution. Goddard and most of his colleagues warned that these morons were perhaps the greatest social menace of all: moving unnoticed and uncontrolled among the public, inferior in intelligence, breeding frequently, prone to vice and law-breaking, and spreading the consequences of their immoral behavior throughout society.

INSTITUTIONAL INCARCERATION AND THE EUGENICS MOVEMENT

What had been "the burden of the feebleminded" in the last decades of the 19th century had by 1915 become "the menace of the feebleminded." The new menace rhetoric became linked with the emergence of the eugenics movement in the second and third decades of the 20th century. The proponents of eugenics, which included institutional superintendents but also politicians, academics, business leaders, and other prominent Americans, called for controlling the reproduction of inferior people. Intellectually disabled people, already associated with inferior intelligence, fecundity, and vice, were prominent among those people who, eugenicists argued, needed to be controlled. To carry out this control, superintendents and their eugenic supporters turned to a familiar solution, institutional incarceration. They also set their sights on a new means of control, sterilization. Two new surgical operations—the tubal ligation for women and the vasectomy for men—both developed at the turn of the century, provided simple procedures whose purpose was the prevention of procreation. Even into the 1970s some states continued the practice of INVOLUNTARY STERILIZATION for eugenic purposes.

By 1920 the invention of the "moron" in the midst of rhetoric on the "menace of the feebleminded" had ironically produced a growing perception that, despite institutionalization and sterilization, there were in the general population too many feebleminded people to control. Not all feeble minds, especially feebleminded children, could be institutionalized. Given this perception, public schools, especially in the nation's urban communities, developed special classrooms and schools for so-called mentally DEFECTIVE children. Although these classes failed to educate most disabled children, they reflected the growing concern among social welfare authorities that public resources had to provide care for working families burdened by disability. Intellectually disabled children, these authorities claimed, could learn basic work skills for their future low-level employment or they could learn social skills for their eventual placement in a public residential institution.

The expansion of residential institutions, on the one hand, and public school classes for "SPECIAL children," on the other, continued through the 1920s. This expansion occurred just as the EUGENICS movement began losing its scientific legitimacy while, ironically, gaining greater public support. The years of the Great Depression and WORLD WAR II saw little institutional construction. Although states lacked funds to build new institutions, the demand to take more residents from economically distressed families and communities had never appeared so great. To accommodate the demand, institutions took in ever larger numbers. Even before the nation entered World War II in 1941, residential institutions for the intellectually disabled were crowded. Superintendents during the 1930s and 1940s complained about bedrooms and hallways filled with beds. In some facilities residents were sleeping two to a bed. Community demands for institutions to take more residents exacerbated this situation, and the reduction in available staff, many of whom had been drafted into the armed services, made overcrowding even more acute.

By the end of the war in 1945, public institutions had become "snake pits," a vivid new term popularized by both a bestselling novel and an award-winning movie of the same name to refer to these dangerous and overcrowded facilities. The 1950s saw efforts by the states to alleviate the overcrowding of the previous decades. Also in the 1950s the first national organization of parents, the National Association of Retarded Children (NARC, now known as THE ARC), was incorporated. Despite the association's advocacy for special education services, it was not until 1961, when JOHN F. KENNEDY became president, that "MENTAL RETARDATION" gained national attention. Led by the new president's sister, Eunice Kennedy Shriver, the President's Panel on Mental Retardation influenced congressional legislation during both the Kennedy and the Johnson administrations in the 1960s.

An important early goal of NARC and other groups was the construction of new public institutions, and the federal government funded such construction during the decade.

DEINSTITUTIONALIZATION AND COMMUNITY-BASED SERVICES

As these new facilities appeared, the seeds of their destruction also emerged. The late 1960s and early 1970s saw two sources of pressure develop that would change from support for improving public institutions to support for their closure. The first source was economic. The states had used federal funds to construct and upgrade their institutions. Federal construction funding, however, did not include support for HOSPITAL maintenance and staffing costs. By the mid 1970s officials in many states had concluded that the day-to-day costs of their residential facilities were stressing their state's budget. Accompanying this economic stress was a second source of pressure. The decades of the 1960s and 1970s were a period when many Americans questioned long-held suppositions about all sorts of social arrangements. Assumptions about the care and control of mentally retarded citizens were no exception. Parents, service providers, academics, and media representatives began to argue that residential institutions were inhumane places that served neither the best interests of the retarded consumer nor the public interest. In place of the institution, critics such as former executive director of the NARC GUNNAR DYBWAD and psychologist Wolf Wolfensberger argued for the "NORMALIZATION" of services in local communities. Several federal and state judicial rulings of the period supported this new perspective. By the mid 1970s state financial pressures became linked with growing efforts of activists to move growing numbers of institutionalized individuals back to their home communities.

Federal legislation in the form of Title 19 of the SOCIAL SECURITY ACT, or MEDICAID, made this linkage possible. Medicaid was passed in 1965 as a part of the Johnson administration's Great Society program. A decade later state officials discovered that Medicaid provided a way to shift service costs from the states to the federal government and at the same time shift state services from institutions to local communities. Beginning in the mid-1970s and continuing into the 21st century, states reduced the population of their residential facilities and, in many cases, completely closed several of their institutions. Around the nation, residents of public institutions moved to community apartments, GROUP HOMES, and other residential homes. In public schools, too, students with intellectual and other disabilities were increasingly "mainstreamed" into ordinary classroom activities. In 1975 the Education of All Handicapped Children Act (now the INDIVIDUALS WITH DISABILITIES EDUCATION ACT or IDEA) established for the first time at the national level the explicit right of every child, regardless of type or level of disability, to a "free, appropriate public education" in the "least restrictive environment." Like DEINSTITUTIONALIZATION, this new emphasis on integration shifted education in special classes to regular classrooms where these "least restrictive" alternatives provided for the individual educational needs of each student. By the 1980s and for the first time in American history, intellectual disabilities had become the concern of local communities rather than of state-operated institutions.

In the early 21st century the community has remained the locus of services. Building the capacity of both schools and adult services to provide inclusive programs has become the official policy and the increasingly common practice. By 2008 nine states had closed all of their large, congregate facilities for people with intellectual disabilities. Another nine had fewer than 150 of its citizens remaining in such facilities. There are now growing numbers of intellectually disabled citizens who never have—and in all likelihood, never will—live in an institution. For this new generation, the community has been the only location of their education, job training, and DAILY LIFE. For them opportunities for normal social integration have opened new educational, social, and occupational options that would have been impossible a generation earlier. For other people who moved from residential institutions to communities, life has often improved. Some have acquired regular jobs, gotten married, and become part of the social fabric of ordinary American communities. Similarly, in neighborhood schools throughout the country, examples of successful approaches to inclusive education can be found. In just a little over three decades of changed policy (i.e., the passage of the original Individuals with Disabilities Education Act in 1975), students with even the most severe intellectual disabilities are not only guaranteed a free, appropriate, public education, but also are often seen obtaining that education side by side with their nondisabled peers in general education classrooms, with the supports needed to help them succeed.

Others, it must be added, have fared less well. Progressive federal mandates of the 1970s were followed by reduction of federal funds during the Reagan administration in the 1980s, and federal funding has remained inadequate to support community-based residential and educational programs at the level of demonstrated need, leaving thousands of individuals across the country on so-called wait lists for services that remain in scarce supply. Although medicaid funding has allowed for community-based living arrangements, in many states the principal benefactors of this funding have been for-profit operators of nursing facilities. In these "homes," intellectually disabled adults live with a dozen or more residents. Their days are "institutional" in their sterile routines and impersonal support. They rarely choose who their friends will be or in what activities they will participate. In short, their lives have become a privatized version of the large congregate care of earlier public facilities.

In many public schools, inclusion has become an empty policy for many students. Pupils with intellectual disabilities are rarely integrated into regular classrooms in either elementary or secondary schools. Instead they spend most of their days in "special classes" even if the classes are not called SPECIAL. If school officials attempt to integrate intellectually disabled students into regular classes, they often limit the integration to so-called nonacademic classes such as physical education, music, and art.

With this mixed history of partial success and frustrating failures, the future for people with intellectual disabilities seems anything but settled. Certainly, the visibility of this segment of the disability COMMUNITY and their families seems unlikely to allow a permanent acquiescence to the unfulfilled promises of past reforms. At the same time, the narrative of failed reforms and unintended consequences that marks the history of this group suggests that their struggles will continue. The "islands of excellence" that can now be found with individuals flourishing in classrooms and communities are still fairly small in number. If the social "experiment" of the large public institution seems to be drawing slowly to an end then the "experiment" of the truly inclusive community has yet to be fully begun.

See also INCLUSION EDUCATION; INTELLIGENCE TESTS; MAINSTREAMING; SELF-ADVOCATES AND SELF-ADVOCACY; *SNAKE PIT, THE*.

Philip M. Ferguson

Further Reading:
Castellani, Paul J. *From Snake Pits to Cash Cows: Politics and Public Institutions in New York*. Albany: State University of New York Press, 2005.

Ferguson, Philip M. *Abandoned to Their Fate: Social Policy and Practice toward Severely Retarded People in America, 1820–1920*. Philadelphia: Temple University Press, 1994.

Noll, Steven. *Feeble-Minded in Our Midst: Institutions for the Mentally Retarded in the South, 1900–1940*. Chapel Hill: University of North Carolina Press, 1995.

Shattuck, Roger. *The Forbidden Experiment: The Story of the Wild Boy of Aveyron*. New York: Farrar, Straus & Giroux, 1980.

Trent, James W., Jr. *Inventing the Feeble Mind: A History of Mental Retardation in the United States*. Berkeley: University of California Press, 1994.

Cogswell, Alice (1805–1830) *deaf cultural icon*

As with many other DEAF cultures around the world, the origins story of America's minority linguistic-cultural group involved a child. Alice Cogswell is credited as the inspiration for what became the first cultural "place" for deaf people in the United States: a permanent RESIDENTIAL SCHOOL.

The third daughter of prominent New England surgeon MASON FITCH COGSWELL and Mary Austin Cogswell, Alice was born on August 21, 1805. In 1807 as a toddler, she developed "spotted fever" (cerebra-spinal meningitis) and consequently lost her hearing. Her FAMILY sought ways of educating their daughter. At this time, however, few options existed for deaf Americans. Affluent families occasionally sent their children to Europe, especially to the Braidwood Academy in Great Britain. Some historical sources now credit Connecticut poet Lydia Huntly Sigourney as Alice's first teacher, and they suggest that the young deaf girl attended classes from 1813 to 1817 with her hearing sisters in an early bilingual environment.

Geographic location and timing played a critical role in the direction of young Cogswell's life. Next door to the Connecticut family lived the Gallaudets, a family whose younger CHILDREN played with Alice. In 1814 THOMAS HOPKINS GALLAUDET, an aspiring missionary at Andover Seminary, returned home for a visit and met Alice. According to the iconic tale, Gallaudet attempted to teach Alice how to communicate by writing the word "hat" in the sand and then pointing to his hat.

In 1814 Thomas Hopkins Gallaudet, with help from Mason Cogswell and others, embarked on a European expedition to learn advanced methods for educating deaf people. Ultimately he returned to America with French teacher of the deaf LAURENT CLERC (1785–1869), who helped found the first permanent residential school for the deaf in Hartford, Connecticut. The American Asylum for the Deaf and Dumb (later renamed the AMERICAN SCHOOL FOR THE DEAF, or ASD) opened in April 1817 and Alice Cogswell was the first of seven students enrolled.

Alice Cogswell apparently was a diligent student who tended to write about religious topics. Her teachers complimented her for her humility, affection, and piousness, traits that were particularly admired in females from the wealthy classes in America at this time.

She completed her schooling at ASD in 1823. Available sources offer little information about her activities over the next seven years. In December 1830 her father succumbed to pneumonia. Soon after, Alice also became ill. Reports describe her delirium, noting that she was calmed when her former teacher Thomas Hopkins Gallaudet came to sit and sign with her. Alice Cogswell died on December 30, 1830.

As a cultural icon in the deaf world, Alice Cogswell embodies inspiration and potential. Sculptures of Cogswell at the American School for the Deaf and at GALLAUDET UNIVERSITY, America's premier university for the deaf and HARD OF HEARING, depict her as a young girl, holding a book in one arm and looking either forward to the future or upward at her benefactor, Thomas Hopkins Gallaudet. Short stories and plays such as "Sign Me Alice" (1973) commonly present her in sentimentalized ways that echo early 19th-century

LITERATURE: She is seen as sweet, affectionate, devoted to her father, compliant, and physically beautiful.

In reality, scholars know relatively little about the young woman who helped spark the beginnings of American deaf culture. Her GENDER makes it difficult for others to see and understand her experience since, as with many females from this era, the life she led was largely concealed or veiled. Instead, leaders in the early 19th century—and historians since—have generally pointed to the more visible figures, men like Gallaudet and Clerc, as the true heroes of early deaf EDUCATION and COMMUNITY development.

Susan Burch

Further Reading:

Eastman, Gilbert. *Sign Me Alice.* Videorecording. Washington, D.C.: Gallaudet College TV Studio, 1973.

Gannon, Jack R. *Deaf Heritage: A Narrative History of Deaf America.* Silver Spring, Md.: National Association of the Deaf, 1981.

Root, Grace Cogswell, ed. *Father and Daughter: A Collection of Cogswell Family Letters and Diaries, 1772–1830.* West Hartford, Conn.: American School for the Deaf, 1924.

Van Cleve, John Vickrey, and Barry Crouch. *A Place of Their Own: Creating the Deaf Community in America.* Washington, D.C.: Gallaudet University Press, 1989.

Letter from Alice Cogswell to Emily Phillips (May 30, 1821)

For many deaf Americans, Alice Cogswell (1805–30) is a cultural icon. The deaf daughter of Mason Fitch Cogswell (1761–1830), a prominent Connecticut physician, Alice Cogswell sparked a movement that led to the founding of the American School for the Deaf (ASD), the first permanent school for deaf children in the United States. In this letter written on May 30, 1821, the 15-year-old Cogswell describes meeting French deaf educator and ASD cofounder Laurent Clerc (1785–1869) and details the school's early development. Because language is a key feature in deaf history and because many deaf people communicated primarily in sign language, Cogswell's written English (which may have been assisted by her teachers) is particularly valuable to scholars.

From Alice Cogswell to Emily Phillips
May 30, 1821

Mrs. Emily Phillips,
Philadelphia, Pa.
Hartford, May 30th, 1821.
My dear Mrs. Phillips,-

. . . You cannot imagine how I was glad at the arrival of Mr. Clerc. Every Hartford body is extremely happy to see him. He is fleshy, happy and healthy. He has made a great deals of travels in the part of Europe. When you come here you will undoubtedly feel glad to see him again. I suppose you have not heard of this, that the new Asylum is completely finished, and the deaf and dumb persons live already there now. I used to go to school nowadays, sometimes in a chaise when it rains. But I dine with the D. and D. every noon. It is a most delightful and cool place and has as fine a prospect as I ever saw or felt. When you are in this town I will show you the apartments of the new Asylum. In the highest story it is a very large garret called the hall and has four arched windows. You will be delighted to view the prospect.

The new Asylum has been dedicated about a few weeks ago. A great number of people assembled to hear Mr. Gallaudet's sermon, and a dedicatory hymn written by Mrs. Sigourney was sung. I will tell you about circumstances of this when I see you for it is too long an account.

Source: Alice Cogswell to Emily Phillips, May 30, 1821. *Father and Daughter: A Collection of Cogswell Family Letters and Diaries (1772–1830)*. Hartford, Conn.: American School for the Deaf, 1924. Available online. URL: http://www.disabilitymuseum.org/lib/docs/698.htm. Accessed June 5, 2008.

Cogswell, Mason Fitch (1761–1830) *physician and Deaf education advocate*

One of the most influential Americans of the DEAF community was Mason Fitch Cogswell, a prominent physician and surgeon in Hartford, Connecticut, and father of ALICE COGSWELL (1805–30). Their story is centrally involved with the 1817 founding of North America's first permanent and publicly supported school for deaf CHILDREN.

Mason Fitch Cogswell was born in Canterbury, Connecticut, on September 28, 1761, to a family of five children. After the death of his mother in 1772 and his father's relocation later that same year, Mason Cogswell was left in the care of Samuel Huntington, a prominent Connecticut citizen who later served in the Continental Congress and signed the Declaration of Independence in 1776. During the AMERICAN REVOLUTION (1775–83), Cogswell attended Yale College, where he graduated as valedictorian in 1780. He soon started studying medicine under his brother James, a surgeon in the Continental Army, and later at a soldier's hospital in New York City. In 1789 Cogswell returned to Connecticut to practice medicine, settling permanently in Hartford. He eventually became well known in the field of surgery across the country and was the first to perform the removal of eye cataracts and the tying of the carotid artery.

Cogswell married Mary Austin Ledyard on April 13, 1800. The couple had five children, the third of whom was Alice, born in 1805. At the age of two Alice contracted "spotted fever" and became deaf. Because of her deafness and his reluctance to send her overseas for an EDUCATION, Cogswell recruited a neighbor and friend, Reverend THOMAS HOPKINS GALLAUDET, to help teach Alice.

Having a deaf daughter impelled Cogswell to take practical measures for the general education and welfare of deaf children. He solicited wealthy New Englanders, parents, and friends to support a school. As part of their plans, Gallaudet traveled to Europe in 1815 to study the best methods of teaching deaf children; he returned a year later with LAURENT CLERC, a deaf Frenchman and an experienced teacher.

The combined efforts of Cogswell, Gallaudet, and Clerc culminated in the opening in Hartford on April 15, 1817, of the Connecticut Asylum for the Education and Instruction of the Deaf and Dumb Persons (later renamed the AMERICAN SCHOOL FOR THE DEAF), the first permanent institution for deaf children on the North American continent. Cogswell remained closely affiliated with the institution, serving as a member of the Board of Trustees as well as on several school committees. In addition to his private practice, Cogswell treated members of the school as the institution's physician. He died of pneumonia on December 17, 1830.

Scholars have yet to examine Cogswell's general attitude toward people with other disabilities. His primary advocacy work focused on deaf people, stemming from his affection for his daughter. This ACTIVISM, however, contributed to growing reform movements on behalf of other disabled Americans, including educational options for BLIND and cognitively disabled children. It is likely that Cogswell's insistence on deaf people's capabilities and demands for governmental support encouraged others to reconsider some of the limited views people held toward their disabled peers. His work also serves as an early example of an advocacy movement by parents, an organized effort that gained momentum roughly a century later.

To this day, America's Deaf cultural community commonly views Cogswell as an ally, on a par with pioneers Gallaudet and Clerc, and credit him with helping lay the foundations of deaf education in America. As a hearing parent of a deaf child, Mason Fitch Cogswell presents an important example of the positive collaborations between deaf and hearing people as well as the powerful role FAMILY plays in shaping history.

See also PARENT ADVOCACY GROUPS.

Clifton F. Carbin

Further Readings:
Braddock, Guilbert C. *Notable Deaf Persons.* Washington, D.C.: Gallaudet College Alumni Association, 1975.
Gannon, Jack R. *Deaf Heritage: A Narrative History of Deaf America.* Silver Spring, Md.: National Association of the Deaf, 1980.
Van Cleve, John Vickrey, and Barry A. Crouch. *A Place of Their Own: Creating the Deaf Community in America.* Washington, D.C.: Gallaudet University Press, 1989.

comedy   See HUMOR.

comic books

Comic books originated in the 1930s as an influential form of popular literature and had a significant cultural impact that has only recently been understood outside of comic fandom. Superhero comics in particular constitute one of the most enduring genres of comics, and disability has emerged as a subtheme in many of these works.

Blindness is one of the chief disabilities experienced by superheroes. Notably all of the BLIND heroes embody or express the powerful cliché about justice being blind. The first blind hero was featured in *The Black Bat* (1934). In this comic, the reader is introduced to Tony Quinn, a district attorney who is blinded when criminals attempt to destroy evidence by dousing it in acid. Quinn finds a surgeon to perform an eye transplant and his new eyes give him the superpower to see in "the inkiest blackness." As the Black Bat, Quinn operates as a vigilante to bring to justice those criminals whom the law proved unable to apprehend. As Quinn, the district attorney, he uses a white cane and feigns blindness.

The next blind superhero appeared in 1941 in *Dr. Mid-Nite.* In this series, Dr. Charles McNider is badly injured by criminals as he tries to save the life of an assaulted government witness. While healing, he discovers that although he cannot see in the light he has gained the ability to see in the dark. He becomes a vigilante pursuing the mobsters and criminals that initially attacked him. Dr. Mid-Nite, unlike the Black Bat, does not fully recover his eyesight, and he is considered to be the first disabled superhero.

The last, and most important, blind superhero to appear was Marvel's 1964 launching of *Daredevil* (this is the second Daredevil, the first originating in 1940 was temporarily a mute). The young hero, Matt Murdock, is hit by a truck and blinded by radioactive material. Murdock discovers that this loss of sight heightens his other four senses. After adolescence, Murdock attends college and becomes a well-respected lawyer. Like the Black Bat, Murdock continues practicing law by day while also seeking justice as a vigilante who pursues those whom the law cannot reach by night. In addition to its significant commercial success, Daredevil has been one of the longest continuing superhero comics to emerge in the "Silver Age" of this genre (1956–68).

One of the most important features in superhero comics is the use of disability to disguise the superpowered nature of the hero. For example, in a 2003 story, "Out," Matt Murdock relies on his blindness to persuade the public that he is not Daredevil after a newspaper revealed his secret identity. Similarly, in the short-run comic *The Fighting Armenian* (1980), Soviet super soldier Sergei Baginski poses as a deaf mute to maintain his secret identity. In the initial run of *Thor* (1962), Thor's secret identity is initially embedded in Donald Blake, a disabled physician. Disability figured as an important disguise for superpowers because, in mainstream thinking, disability represents the exact opposite of superpowers—to be superpowered is to have *more* abilities, whereas to be disabled it to have *less* abilities. As a result, the use of disability as disguise at once reinforces beliefs that people with disabilities are not capable of the types of physical heroism necessary for superheroes while also subverting this paradigm by showing that some disabled individuals (particularly Daredevil) are indeed capable heroes.

One superhero comic book to directly deal with issues of disability was the 1977 *The Human Fly*, written by Bill Mantlo, illustrated by Lee Elias, and published by Marvel Comics. In this series, the Human Fly is disabled in a car accident that also takes the lives of his wife and children. According to the comic, the car accident leaves every bone in the Human Fly's body broken, and he is told that he will never walk again. After numerous reconstructive surgeries from which he gains a steel skeleton, he dedicates himself to proving his doctors wrong, and eventually, after four years, he teaches himself to walk and becomes especially physically fit. While in the hospital he meets several people disabled from the Vietnam War and industrial accidents who have given up their will to live. He decides to dedicate his life to helping these people and others like them overcome their "handicaps." In the first issue (September 1977), he thought to himself: "*He* had fought against separation [from mainstream society] and won. *They* had lost, because the motivation was not there and was not being supplied by the world without." He often surrounded himself with characters who, although disabled, saw themselves more as differently abled. In addition to helping people through his interpersonal relationships, the Human Fly, a stuntman, raised money for charities that would benefit people with disabilities. This comic ran for 19 issues and was regarded by comic scholars as one of the most positive portrayals of the disability COMMUNITY, although the "overcomer" image advocated by the comic was often simplistic and the writing was poor. Also, the inherent didactic quality of the comic probably undercut its appeal to disabled readers. One of the most remarkable aspects of the comic was the Human Fly's insistence on equal opportunity for disabled people.

Most frequently in comic books, super villains, more than superheroes, appear as disabled. INSANITY and DISFIGUREMENT figure prominently among motivations for two of Batman's enemies, the super villains Joker and Two-Face. Psychologists Nancy Weinberg and Rosina Santana argue that people with disabilities are more likely to be seen as "especially moral or especially corrupt" in comic books and they found negative portrayals of disability to be more common than positive portrayals. However, Weinberg and Santana fail to take into account the visual nature of comic books, which often use graphic cues (such as disfigurement) to indicate a character's warped moral nature. Certainly negative portrayals of disability continue, but the recent celebration of superheroes such as the blind Daredevil, the paraplegic Oracle, and the DEAF Echo offer positive images to counter the negative. Each of these characters is uniquely and better developed than super villains tend to be.

Other disabled superheroes include: The Mask (1940, temporarily blind), Captain Marvel Jr. (1942, disabled), Rackman (1947, dwarf), Professor X (1963, paraplegic), Captain Storm (1964, amputee), NoMan (1965, paraplegic), Son of Vulcan (1965, lame), Tom Thumb (1971, dwarf), Badger (1983, schizophrenic), Oracle (1988, paraplegic), and Echo (1999, deaf). The comic *X-MEN* continually grapples with physical otherness through its mutant, sometimes disabled, characters.

Disability has also been featured prominently in comics produced by independent presses, particularly in *Omaha the Cat Dancer, Stray Bullets,* and *The Spiral Cage.* Because alternative comics tend to focus on the day-to-day experiences of life, disability, both physical and mental, has been an important theme. Many of the writers of alternative comics are themselves disabled or have had extensive interaction with the medical establishment. Web comics also emerged in the 1990s as an important venue for discussing disability issues. INTERNET publishing has provided a forum for artists and writers who are disabled or have worked intimately with people with disabilities to develop comics that address various aspects of disability. Two noteworthy examples are Jon and Claire Lytle's *DizAbled* and Rob McCarthy's *Hell on Wheels.* Both alternative comics and Web comics reflect the changing perceptions of disability emphasizing the constructed nature of ability. Also, both formats tend to express a sense of HUMOR about ability and disability that is lacking in superhero comics.

See also OVERCOME AND OVERCOMING; POPULAR CULTURE; REPRESENTATION; STEREOTYPES.

Jessica Pliley

Further Reading:

Benton, Mike. *The Comic Book in America: An Illustrated History.* Dallas, Tex.: Taylor Publishing, 1993.

Bongco, Mila. *Reading Comics: Language, Culture, and the Concept of the Superhero in Comic Books.* New York: Garland Publishing, 2000.

Goulart, Ron, ed. *The Encyclopedia of American Comics.* New York: Facts On File, 1990.

Reynolds, Richard. *Super Heroes: A Modern Mythology.* Jackson: University of Mississippi Press, 1994.

Rovin, Jeff. *The Encyclopedia of Superheroes.* New York: Facts On File, 1985.

———. *The Encyclopedia of Super Villains.* New York: Facts On File, 1987.

Coming Home

One of the first mainstream American FILMS to critique the VIETNAM WAR openly, *Coming Home* (1978) presents a severely injured VETERAN as its central figure: Luke Martin (Jon Voight), a one-time marine who uses a wheelchair due to a wartime SPINAL CORD INJURY. Initially bitter and angry, Martin evolves into a wise and saintly figure with the help of Sally Hyde (Jane Fonda), a politically naive "military wife" with whom he has an affair. After the drug-overdose death of a fellow veteran at a Veterans Administration HOSPITAL, Luke takes his transformation one step further, becoming an impassioned antiwar protestor.

Written by Waldo Salt and Robert C. Jones and directed by Hal Ashby, *Coming Home* is noteworthy for, among other things, its frank treatment of SEXUALITY. With its unusually graphic lovemaking scene between Martin and Hyde, *Coming Home* did more than any other film up to that point to shatter the widespread myth that disabled people are nonsexual beings.

The film is also notable for the simplest of reasons; unlike the vast majority of disability-themed movies that preceded it, *Coming Home* addresses issues of ACCESS AND ACCESSIBILITY as well as the indifference faced by disabled people on a daily basis. After Martin arrives at Hyde's home for dinner and discovers that her abode is not equipped with a ramp, he is forced to get out of his chair and scoot backward up her front steps. In another scene, Martin is accidentally blocked in a grocery store by a NONDISABLED woman; when he asks to get past her, she acts as if he does not exist.

In addition to these small but compelling touches, *Coming Home* benefits from the presence of actual disabled Vietnam veterans who played themselves in several improvised scenes. Cinematographer Haskell Wexler, who found working with the vets "the most interesting and exciting part of the whole film," created a special camera dolly that allowed him to avoid high angles—and the sense of weakness and insignificance they often connote—while photographing the veterans in their WHEELCHAIRS.

In many ways, *Coming Home* is a transitional film. It is indebted to some extent to such movies of the post–WORLD WAR II period as *THE BEST YEARS OF OUR LIVES* (1946) and *THE MEN* (1950) in its showing the rehabilitative process of severely wounded veterans. By showing Martin engaged in a wide variety of day-to-day post-rehabilitative activities, however, it moves well beyond these earlier films and their typical "overcoming" perspective. *Coming Home* is not without its flaws; indeed, it was widely criticized for conflating romantic and political issues and for showing Martin engaged in solitary political acts at a time when group protests were far more common. Nevertheless, it remains one of Hollywood's most honest and forthright representations of the disabled experience.

See also ACTORS; *BORN ON THE FOURTH OF JULY;* OVERCOME AND OVERCOMING; REPRESENTATION.

Martin F. Norden

Further Reading:

Keller, David. "Making *Coming Home:* An Interview with Haskell Wexler." *Filmmakers Newsletter,* March 1978.

Norden, Martin F. "Bitterness, Rage, and Redemption: Hollywood Constructs the Disabled Vietnam Veteran." In *Disabled Veterans in History,* edited by David Gerber, 96–114. Ann Arbor: University of Michigan Press, 2000.

———. *The Cinema of Isolation: A History of Physical Disability in the Movies.* New Brunswick, N.J.: Rutgers University Press, 1994.

communication debates

Communication methods have been the most controversial aspect of American DEAF EDUCATION since schools for the deaf were established in the early 19th century. Communication debates about them have taken various forms. They have included both technical arguments concerning the effectiveness of different methods in achieving particular educational goals and value-laden arguments about the overarching purpose of deaf education itself. The latter controversies have focused especially on whether the primary purpose of education is to make deaf people figuratively less deaf or whether it is to develop their full potential as individuals. These matters continue to lie at the heart of most discussions about deaf people in America today.

LAURENT CLERC and THOMAS HOPKINS GALLAUDET, the founders in 1817 of the first permanent school for deaf CHILDREN in the United States, the AMERICAN SCHOOL FOR THE DEAF (ASD), believed that deaf people communicated most successfully and most easily with "the natural language of signs," that is, grammatical movements of the hand, fingers, face, and body that were standardized through usage by deaf people and that bore little or no relation to spoken language. They argued that this sign language, similar to today's American Sign Language (ASL), was effective in accomplishing the school's goals, which included teaching religious studies, socializing deaf children, and helping them acquire a vocation. They also believed, however, that using signs in English word order, sometimes with invented grammatical markers, and including more spelling out of English words with specific finger shapes, a system called "methodical signs," would be useful for the specific task of teaching deaf students to read and write English.

Within two decades of ASD's founding, American educators disagreed sharply about the value of each of these methods. Some argued that natural sign language was more effective in conveying any knowledge base because it was easier to learn visually and more appropriate to the physiology of body movements than methodical signs. Others countered that teaching students one language, natural sign language, when the target language, English, bore no resemblance to it was illogical. Despite these disagreements over the efficacy of different kinds of signed communication, most teachers, schools, and parents continued to accept ASD's emphasis on deaf education as a primarily moral and practical endeavor and ASD's belief that signing was essential to reaching the minds of deaf children.

The late 19th century brought challenges to sign communication in any form and to previously accepted ideas about the purpose of deaf education. Individuals called "oralists," led by Alexander Graham Bell, argued that deaf Americans could and should be trained to use their voices to convey their thoughts and to comprehend spoken language by interpreting movements of the lips, tongue, and mouth. Oralists argued that deaf people who learned to speak and read lips would be figuratively less deaf, more "normal." They would not become an ASL-using class apart. They would not need special educational facilities, at least not after a few years of training in speech and lipreading, and they would likely marry hearing people, therefore reducing the number of deaf children in future generations.

Oralism quickly became popular. Americans worried about the social pressures created by different cultures and languages, and, concerned about the genetic health of society, welcomed the oralists' views. Parents of deaf children, the vast majority of whom were hearing themselves, were drawn to oralism by the promise that their children would become more like them, able to speak and to comprehend English. An increasingly urban, diverse, and secular society rejected the old belief that education should emphasize religious objectives. Governing boards, parents, and educational leaders encouraged schools for the deaf to stress social and linguistic conformity and the acquisition and development of skills that would force deaf people into the dominant oral culture.

Many deaf Americans resisted these efforts and fought to keep sign language, ASL, alive and in the schools. From the late 19th century until well into the middle of the 20th century, they wrote ASL dictionaries, filmed master users of ASL, created stories and plays in ASL, and lobbied in various states to attempt to convince educators to keep signing as the primary learning tool in schools. Local and state organizations and the National Association of the Deaf argued for the importance of sign language to deaf children, and they decried the emphasis on speech and lipreading, arguing that many deaf people could never learn these skills well enough to use them in their adult lives. Even as deaf Americans preserved ASL for themselves, however, the schools increasingly reduced its pedagogical role. Deaf students spent countless hours attempting to learn to speak and lipread. Those who could not do so, generally students who were born profoundly deaf, were labeled "oral failures" and consigned to vocational classes.

The late 20th century saw the gradual rehabilitation of sign language, now termed ASL, as academic studies demonstrated that it was a full, rich, and complex human language, and as American society became more welcoming to cultural diversity. Yet ASL's use in education remained contested. Most schools moved slowly from oralism toward signing that reflected English word order and that was usually accompanied by speech. Later, some schools tried a different approach termed "bi-cultural and bilingual." Supporters claimed that ASL was the only effective form of signing, that simultaneous signing and speaking was unintelligible to deaf people, that ASL could be used to teach written English, and that deaf children could and should grow up to accept both hearing culture, based solidly in English, and deaf culture, rooted equally in ASL.

Research has not settled the communication debates. If the primary goal of deaf education is for deaf children to learn to use written English as accurately and idiomatically as their hearing counterparts, no method has yet proven successful. The widespread acceptance of cochlear implants as a means to improve access to spoken English, and the many efforts to modify the genes responsible for some forms of deafness, suggest that American society remains committed to a pathological model of deafness, one that cannot be addressed through alternative communication methods but requires a technological or medical alteration in deaf people themselves.

See also activism and advocacy; identity; language and terminology; National Association of the Deaf sign language film preservation campaign.

John Vickrey Van Cleve

Further Reading:

Baynton, Douglas C. *Forbidden Signs: American Culture and the Campaign against Sign Language.* Chicago: University of Chicago Press, 1966.

Burch, Susan. *Signs of Resistance: American Deaf Cultural History, 1900 to World War II.* New York: New York University Press, 2002.

Stedt, Joseph D., and Donald F. Moores. "Manual Codes on English and American Sign Language: Historical Perspectives and Current Realities." In *Manual Communication: Implications for Educators,* edited by Harry Bornstein, 1–20. Washington, D.C.: Gallaudet University Press, 1990.

community

Examining disability history through the lens of community illuminates much of what it has meant to be a person with a disability in the United States. Community implies a sense of human connectedness and a shared IDENTITY, and many Americans with various disabilities have seen themselves since the 1960s as forming a self-directed community. Explaining how and why this came about is an important goal of disability history.

The growth of disability communities has been uneven. Some groups of people with disabilities formed communities long before others. Asking why it took so long for the development of a cross-disability community to form opens up larger questions about the entire relationship between disability and community in the American past. The very concept of a cross-disability community faced difficult intellectual, political, and social obstacles. Most nondisabled Americans viewed disability as a "problem" to be solved within communities rather than the basis of community itself. There may have been disability *in* communities, but relatively few Americans built communities *of* disability. Ironically, the solutions proffered, including segregation in large institutions, fostered shared identities and interests and ultimately the growth of disability communities.

The classic formulation of what community means was published by the German sociologist Ferdinand Tönnies in 1887. Tönnies contrasted *Gemeinschaft,* or community, and *Gesellschaft,* or society. *Gemeinschaft* implied an almost familial sense of belonging, a heartfelt cohesiveness, and personal commitment to the unified interests of the group. *Gesellschaft,* a consequence of modernity, was an impersonal sense of association directed by rational calculations of self-interest. Community, which largely emanated from feelings, and society, which largely relied on common beliefs, were not exclusive terms. In the real world, groups could be, and most likely were, combinations of the two. Sociologists focus on structures and settings of community, but community also has profound psychological implications. For individuals, an organic sense of community can be the most important factor in shaping a person's identity.

In early America, different communities defined disability in very different ways. For Native American groups that valued the vision quest, for example, an individual with what today would be considered a psychiatric disability could be a shaman with high status and a community leader. Colonial Europeans in America sometimes accused people who exhibited possible MENTAL ILLNESSES of demonic possession. Such contrasts highlight the fluidity of disability. The historical meanings of disability vary depending on context, and community can be one of the most important locations of historical context.

For the European colonists of eastern North America, strong communities were necessary for survival, especially in the early years of settlement. Individualism could be fatal in the face of DISEASE, food shortages, and warfare. Where communal ties were weak, as in 17th-century Virginia, death rates were high. Where communities were tightly knit, as in early New England, death rates were considerably lower. The level of cohesion especially affected the survivability of people with disabilities.

New England's strong sense of community was not just practical. It was also ideological, based on Puritan religious beliefs. Puritanism, with its attendant mission to build "a city upon a hill," inculcated a strong communal ethos that had both positive and negative consequences for people with disabilities. While a physically disabled indentured servant in early Virginia could expect little assistance from a planter whose life revolved around extracting tobacco from land and labor, a New Englander who became physically disabled would likely be cared for by the family, the "little commonwealth," as well as by the town and local church.

Disability in New England could also act as the impetus for communal catharsis, a violent purging of "otherness" from the sanctified community. Even minor physical abnormalities could render a person vulnerable. To have SCHIZOPHRENIA in Salem, Massachusetts, in 1692 could invite execution for witchcraft. Such practices, if not sensational witchcraft trials, lasted well into the 19th century. Josiah Spaulding, Jr., for example, the son of the Congregationalist minister in Buckland, Massachusetts, argued incessantly, refused to follow his father's career, and was a bit of a practical joker. The minister, fearing INSANITY, had his son placed in a cage in 1810. Josiah Spaulding remained there until his death 57 years later. The local community paid the bill for his upkeep.

A more positive communal response to disability developed on the island of MARTHA'S VINEYARD, Massachusetts, where many inhabitants shared a genetic predisposition for deafness. An inclusive community grew there before 1800 because of the widespread use of sign language among both

This poster by Alberta Pepin reflects specific disability communities as well as the place of people with disabilities in mainstream society. *(The Center on Human Policy at Syracuse University)*

DEAF and hearing people. The sign language system used on Martha's Vineyard was so common that hearing people sometimes used it to communicate with other hearing people. The shared language allowed for a community that integrated people with a sensory difference into all areas of life. Deaf Vineyarders faced neither the STIGMA nor the isolation so commonly endured by other people with disabilities in early America.

Communities composed of people with disabilities became possible during the 19th century. Probably the first such community was created by deaf people at the AMERICAN SCHOOL FOR THE DEAF in Hartford, Connecticut. Its founder, THOMAS HOPKINS GALLAUDET (1787–1851), was a Congregationalist minister with his own sense of mission. Gallaudet sought to bring deaf people, individuals he called "the heathen among us," into a Christian community of believers. Explicitly linking his efforts to the worldwide missionary efforts ignited by the Second Great Awakening, Gallaudet viewed deafness as a tragic affliction that isolated individuals from a religious community. His alliance with France's LAURENT CLERC (1785–1869) brought sign language, ultimately AMERICAN SIGN LANGUAGE, to the United States, and with it came the basis for a deaf cultural community, reinforced through shared experiences in RESIDENTIAL SCHOOLS.

By the 1840s, HORACE MANN (1796–1859), the prominent EDUCATION reformer who before the CIVIL WAR advocated a common elementary schooling for all Americans, rejected deaf education as practiced by Gallaudet. As historian Douglas C. Baynton shows, the deaf community, which included, among other things, sign language, intermarriage, and clubs for and by deaf people, drew more sustained negative attention during the latter half of the 19th century. Many oralists (supporters of teaching speech and lipreading) as well as eugenicists (believers in the system that evaluated humans by notions of biological worth) considered the "clannishness" of deaf Americans to be detrimental to themselves and to society in general. Efforts to eliminate or at least undermine deaf community ties gained momentum in the early 20th century, particularly through educational policies and technological advances in HEARING AIDS. Many scholars and activists assert that the efforts to mainstream deaf people and to promote COCHLEAR IMPLANTS in the late 20th and early 21st centuries built on these earlier campaigns. Still, deaf people's own accounts of their affinity for a distinctive deaf community reveal an important if underrecognized part of American history.

In addition to deaf schools, antebellum institutions, whatever the intentions of their founders, fostered a sense of community among people with disabilities, if only by gathering them in one place. With the reforms advocated by DOROTHEA DIX beginning in the 1840s, people with psychiatric disabilities were removed from local jails and ALMS-HOUSES and placed in larger specialized institutions, usually under the aegis of state government. MORAL TREATMENT, the proposition that people could be nurtured back to psychic health in homelike environments, made possible opportunities for forming communities that would have been unthinkable earlier and for a long time afterward. One of the more interesting and little-known examples of this occurred at New York State Insane Asylum in Utica during the 1850s. Evidence of an ASYLUM community emerges from the pages of THE OPAL, a highbrow literary journal published by the inmates of the asylum between 1851 and 1860, apparently as part of their treatment. Fellow inmates are referred to as citizens of "Asylumia," and articles written by the "Opalians" raised questions about treatment, freedom, and restraints at the institution. In general, articles emphasized a commonality of interests and sought a mutually supportive atmosphere for those confined in the asylum. After the CIVIL WAR, as institutions became larger and more impersonal, the amenities described in The Opal disappeared.

Antebellum reformers of various sorts made possible the first disability communities, but they never truly supported their growth and stability. Antebellum sentimentality should not be confused with support for diversity. For both sentimental reformers and medical authorities, people with disabilities remained a negative reference group that somehow impeded perfectionist aspirations. For them, disability remained a problem to be solved, through either pity or SCIENCE, not a source of communal identity.

A very different kind of disability community became possible because of the business ventures of entrepreneur and showman P. T. BARNUM. Beginning in the 1840s, Barnum's American Museum in New York City was a place where a paying public could gaze upon people with disabilities. Though this sort of entertainment, later enshrined as the CIRCUS sideshow, would ultimately be rejected as disreputable, Barnum's patrons were exemplars of middle-class respectability. Historians continue to debate whether the FREAK SHOW should be interpreted as positive or negative in its effects on people with disabilities. The variety of freak shows hints at a continuum between EXPLOITATION and self-determination. In terms of community, freak shows created among the people with disabilities involved with them a sense of "insider" and "outsider." This suggests the growth of a community based on the common experiences of performing, traveling, and living together. Members of the audience, disdainfully called "rubes," could never be, as chanted in the climactic scene from the film FREAKS (1932), "one of us." Freaks portrayed a powerful, if disconcerting, communal ethos when the performers join forces to punish the adulterous wife of a little person, killing her strong-man lover and then surrounding her en masse before violently turning her into a deformed freak.

If POPULAR CULTURE brought people with disabilities together, so did WAR. One of the outcomes of the Civil War was to make disability much more common. Lacking a germ theory and antibiotics, surgeons often fought infection by amputating damaged limbs. With rising casualties and pressing manpower shortages, the Union War Department created the Invalid Corps in April 1863. The Invalid Corps served garrison duties and worked in HOSPITALS. As the war progressed, the sheer scale of casualties overwhelmed the abilities of traditional communities to deal with disability, and new ORGANIZATIONS such as the U.S. Sanitary Commission sought national remedies to help disabled VETERANS. Though advocating the quick return of disabled veterans to their local communities, the U.S. government authorized in 1865 the construction of a National Asylum for Disabled Volunteer Soldiers. By gathering disabled soldiers together, the Invalid Corps and the National Asylum may have fostered some sense of community based on disability. That the community of disabled veterans never formed its own organization in the aftermath of the war may suggest the difficulties in reconciling 19th-century notions of manliness with disability (see GENDER).

In late 19th-century America, dominant ideas of manliness and disability also made it difficult for men to form viable communities based on working-class status. By equating "independence" with manliness, 19th-century able-bodied workers contrasted themselves with their disabled fellows. Railroad workers, for example, pushed disabled workers out of the workforce rather than accept them as equals. During the 1880s, the railroad brotherhoods, working in an industry in which disabling accidents were a common occurrence, even allied with their employers to castigate disabled workers as "cripples" unworthy of services or inclusion in their labor communities. Bodily status thus trumped class status in determining community membership.

With SOCIAL DARWINISM and EUGENICS in ascendance, the turn of the 20th century was a particularly difficult time for communities based on disability. Institutions for people with disabilities were crowded and underfunded. Involuntary sterilizations were increasingly performed on those with mental disabilities. Disability as the basis of a shared identity was discounted by mainstream social norms.

In an isolated town in rural Georgia in the 1920s and the 1930s a community based on physical disability flourished. Made famous because one of its members went on to become president of the United States, the Georgia Warm Springs Foundation gathered POLIO survivors from across the country for rehabilitation services. The sunny and optimistic setting, a reflection of FRANKLIN D. ROOSEVELT's direct involvement, contrasted markedly from the typical hospital of the period. No longer adjusting to life with a disability in isolation, people who came to Warm Springs found a community of "polios." Though Roosevelt's public persona obscured his own physical disability, the disability community of which he was a part in Warm Springs was privately very important to him.

Feelings of community permeated the pages of *The Polio Chronicle,* a monthly magazine published by the Patients' Committee of the Warm Springs Foundation in the early 1930s. Socializing, HUMOR, and romance were at the center of life at Warm Springs. In an article called "Playing Polio at Warm Springs," the rehabilitation center seemed much like a vacation resort, though one in which most people danced in WHEELCHAIRS and "physios," or physical therapists, and attendants replaced hotel workers. What made the atmosphere especially appealing was the accessibility of the buildings at Warm Springs. At a time when ramps were unheard of in public buildings, Warms Springs was, in the words of "Playing Polio," a "stairless Eden."

No matter how socially active, the community at Warm Springs did not foster a sustained political identity around disability. Ultimately, much of the energy that could have molded such a political consciousness was expended in a rehabilitation ideology and in fund-raising efforts that ultimately led to the creation of the MARCH OF DIMES. Though residents at Warm Springs shared ideas about accessible design and assistive technologies, they never fomented a drive for disability rights. During the Great Depression of the 1930s, however, one group did promote such an agenda, decades before the appearance of the DISABILITY RIGHTS MOVEMENT. THE LEAGUE OF THE PHYSICALLY HANDICAPPED represented a political community of people with disabilities, a group of individuals whose shared experiences led to a commitment to societal change. Stressing political identity over medical diagnosis, the league rejected the prevailing NEW DEAL disability policies of CHARITY and SHELTERED WORKSHOPS. Instead, they used tactics such as the sit-down strike in 1935 to fight against bias in the workplace and in government hiring. Such a consciousness and similar tactics would become a hallmark of the disability rights movement.

Though WORLD WAR II, like all wars, made disability more common, the cultural atmosphere in its immediate aftermath was not conducive to the spread of communities of people with disabilities. *THE BEST YEARS OF OUR LIVES* (1946), winner of the Academy Award for Best Picture in 1947, emotionally illustrates the dominant approach to disability among returning veterans. The film follows three veterans, all with psychiatric or physical disabilities, as they reintegrate into civilian society. *The Best Years of Our Lives* clearly implies that a successful transition could take place only within the nuclear FAMILY and with the guidance and support, not of other disabled veterans, but of a caring and loving woman. The crucial community for these returning

Group identity is a fundamental part of American disability history. This 1959 photograph of people picnicking is but one example of the way community is experienced.   *(Post-Polio Health International, St. Louis)*

veterans was the suburban neighborhood, not an association of other people with disabilities.

The prominence of the nuclear family in the postwar United States fostered a new ACTIVISM on the part of parents of CHILDREN with developmental disabilities. Probably historically the most stigmatized disability group, people with cognitive disabilities lived in the shadow of EUGENICS, often institutionalized and ignored or feared. In the immediate aftermath of World War II, exposés of deplorable conditions existing in public institutions were published by both journalists and the conscientious objectors who had worked as attendants during the war. A community of parent activists (see PARENT ADVOCACY GROUPS) arose out of those expo-

sés. The spate of confessional autobiographies by parents of mentally disabled children, such as PEARL BUCK (1892–1973), and DALE EVANS ROGERS (1912–2001), made it easier to speak in public about what had hitherto been an unmentionable shame. Middle-class parents of the 1950s, for whom successful parenting was an imprimatur of successful personhood, joined together to form the National Association for Retarded Children, today THE ARC of the United States. Sharing their experiences, the parent community lobbied local, state, and federal authorities to provide better services to their children.

One of the most important communities in American disability history formed at the University of California at

Berkeley. When ED ROBERTS enrolled at Berkeley in 1962, the campus was on the verge of tumultuous upheavals over students' rights, civil rights for African-Americans, and women's rights. A similar movement for disability rights would grow out of a disability community on campus. The "ROLLING QUADS" fought for accessibility and attendant services. Their ultimate goal was independent living. The movement could not have achieved the successes it did were if not for the shared feelings of community among the students with disabilities.

Examining disability within the context of community continues to be an important task for disability historians. The varied responses of American communities to disability significantly shaped the lived experiences of people with disabilities. Since community relies on feelings of attachment, these responses were emotional rather than rational or bureaucratic and frequently had negative consequences for people with disabilities. The most common emotional responses of able-bodied communities were fear and pity, and how and why fear and pity have acted in differing circumstances raises all sorts of new areas of study for historians. Understanding the crucial role of past communities in the lives of people with disabilities also illustrates quite vividly the relational nature of disability. Disability is an evolving, multidimensional social construct, not a medical diagnosis. Finally, and on a more positive note, there remains much work to be done on the self-directed communities created by people with disabilities. Through newly uncovered primary sources or the reexamination of old ones, those communities can be brought back to life. Such prospects are what make disability history such an exciting, innovative, and emerging field.

See also DAILY LIFE; DISABILITY ART AND ARTISTIC EXPRESSION; DISABILITY CULTURE; GROUP HOMES; INVOLUNTARY STERILIZATION; RESIDENTIAL SCHOOLS; ROOSEVELT WARM SPRINGS INSTITUTE FOR REHABILITATION; SOCIAL CONSTRUCTION OF DISABILITY.

Graham Warder

Further Reading:
Baynton, Douglas C. *Forbidden Signs: American Culture and the Campaign against Sign Language.* Chicago: University of Chicago Press, 1996.

Bogdan, Robert. "The Social Construction of Freaks." In *Freakery: Cultural Spectacles of the Extraordinary Body,* edited by Rosemarie Garland Thomson, 23–37. New York: New York University Press, 1996.

Gerber, David A. "The 'Careers' of People Exhibited in Freak Shows: The Problem of Volition and Valorization." In *Freakery: Cultural Spectacles of the Extraordinary Body,* edited by Rosemarie Garland Thomson, 38–55. New York: New York University Press, 1996.

———. "Heroes and Misfits: The Troubled Social Reintegration of Disabled Veterans in *The Best Years of Our Lives.*" *American Quarterly* 46, no. 4 (December 1994): 545–574.

Longmore, Paul, and David Golderger. "The League of the Physically Handicapped and the Great Depression: A Case Study in the New Disability History." *Journal of American History* 83, no. 3 (December 2000): 888–932.

Pelka, Fred, ed. *The Civil War Letters of Colonel Charles F. Johnson, Invalid Corps.* Amherst: University of Massachusetts Press, 2004.

Shapiro, Joseph P. *No Pity: People with Disabilities Forging a New Civil Rights Movement.* New York: Three Rivers Press, 1993.

Trent, James W., Jr. *Inventing the Feeble Mind: A History of Mental Retardation in the United States.* Berkeley: University of California Press, 1994.

Williams-Searle, John. "Cold Charity: Manhood, Brotherhood, and the Transformation of Disability, 1870–1900." In *The New Disability History: American Perspectives,* edited by Paul K. Longmore and Lauri Umansky, 157–186. New York: New York University Press, 2001.

Cone, Kitty (Curtis) (1944–   ) *activist*

Curtis "Kitty" Cone played a vital role in the DISABILITY RIGHTS MOVEMENT in the San Francisco Bay Area during the 1970s, 1980s, and 1990s. She was a key political strategist and organizer in several important actions and is widely recognized for her leadership during the 1977 SIT-IN PROTEST AT THE DEPARTMENT OF HEALTH, EDUCATION AND WELFARE offices in San Francisco, a 25-day demonstration in support of SECTION 504 of the Rehabilitation Act of 1973 (see VOCATIONAL REHABILITATION ACT), Title V, which guaranteed the rights of disabled people to access federally funded services. She became a national and international activist for the rights of disabled people, particularly their rights to become parents and to have access to housing, attendants, and TRANSPORTATION.

Kitty Cone was born on April 7, 1944, in Champaign, Illinois. She was misdiagnosed several times in her first 15 years, and finally correctly diagnosed with MUSCULAR DYSTROPHY in the late 1950s, at age 15. In her early years she attended schools in Tokyo, Japan, Washington, D.C., Kentucky, and Georgia. During her time in Richmond, Kentucky, and Augusta, Georgia, Cone was struck by the racism she witnessed and was drawn to the emerging civil rights movement. She began protesting racial discrimination in the early 1960s.

In 1963 she enrolled at the University of Illinois at Urbana-Champaign as part of a program sponsored by the Rehabilitation Center at the university. She quickly became a political leader in the civil rights and antiwar movements but like many other disabled people did not make the connections to the discrimination and attitudinal barriers faced by people with disabilities. After leaving the university without graduating in 1967, Cone worked with activist ORGANIZATIONS in Chicago, Atlanta, and Washington, D.C., before coming out as a lesbian and moving to BERKELEY, California, in the summer of 1972. Unable to find accessible housing in Berkeley, she purchased a home and installed a ramp. The following year she was asked to go on the JERRY LEWIS Telethon to talk about the WHEELCHAIR she was given by the MUSCULAR DYSTROPHY ASSOCIATION. On the TELETHON she explained that while she loved her wheelchair, it was not useful for getting her from home to work because there were no curb ramps in Oakland. This represented the impromptu beginning of her involvement with disability politics.

In 1974 Cone learned of the Center for Independent Living (CIL) in Berkeley, and she became deeply involved in the INDEPENDENT LIVING MOVEMENT. Impressed by the effectiveness of this fledgling movement in empowering people with disabilities, she began volunteering at CIL, eventually applying her experience with political organizing. Soon after, as chair of the Committee for an Accessible Oakland, Cone was elected to the board of the Chinatown Community Development Committee and was able to secure money for curb ramps in downtown Oakland. In 1975 she worked on the BART (Bay Area Rapid Transit) Handicapped Task Force and with the AC (Alameda–Contra Costa) Transit system addressing public transit accessibility policies. After a short hiatus from activism in Mexico in the fall of 1975, Cone returned to the East Bay area and to her work with CIL. In 1977 she met disability rights activist JUDY HEUMANN, learned about Section 504 of the Rehabilitation Act, and was offered a job organizing sit-ins at the Department of Health, Education and Welfare offices in San Francisco. That demonstration, for which she is most well known, began April 5, 1977, and lasted 25 days. As a result of the sit-in, Section 504 was implemented, but it was not fully enforced for several years following its passage. During that time, Cone doggedly pursued its implementation by state and local agencies, protesting at the San Francisco Transbay Terminal in 1978, organizing Disabled People's Civil Rights Day in October 1979 in San Francisco, and lobbying in Washington against the Cleveland Amendment, which would have allowed local agencies to provide meager and inconvenient paratransit services rather than creating truly accessible public transportation systems.

Through her involvement in the disability rights movement Kitty Cone encountered many disabled women who were raising CHILDREN. Wanting to become a parent herself, Cone moved to Tijuana, Mexico, in 1981 where she adopted a child named Jorge. They returned to California in March 1984. Cone notes that raising Jorge has been the single most important part of her life, and she strongly supports the rights of disabled people who want to be parents (see FAMILY).

A keen interest in international issues drew her into global ACTIVISM in the 1980s. For example, in December 1980 she traveled to Nicaragua with the Disabled International Support Effort to meet and work with members of the disability community there. After returning from Mexico in 1984, Cone began work at the WORLD INSTITUTE ON DISABILITY where she researched international personal care assistance programs.

In the late 1980s she returned to local activism, organizing demonstrations and advocating policies for accessible transportation in the Bay Area. In 1990 Cone began working for the DISABILITY RIGHTS EDUCATION AND DEFENSE FUND (DREDF) lawyer referral service, and she became the development director there in 1993. Since 1998 she has served on the Board of Directors at DREDF.

Cone currently lives in Albany, California.

See also ACCESS AND ACCESSIBILITY; EMPOWERMENT; PROTEST; REPRODUCTIVE RIGHTS.

Laurel A. Clark

Further Reading:
Cone, Kitty. "On Parenting and the Disability Rights Movement." Video clip from an interview on March 9, 1998, the Disability Rights and Independent Living Movement collection, Regional Oral History Office, University of California, Berkeley. Available online. URL: http://bancroft.berkeley.edu/collections/drilm/collection/items/cone1.smil. Accessed December 15, 2007.
———. "Political Organizer for Disability Rights, 1970s–1990s, and Strategist for Section 504 Demonstrations, 1977." An oral history conducted in 1996–1998 by David Landes, Regional Oral History Office, the Bancroft Library, University of California, Berkeley, 2000. URL: http://content.cdlib.org/ark:/13030/kt1w1001mt/. Accessed December 15, 2007.
"Handicapped End Demonstration," *New York Times*, 1 May 1977.
O'Brien, Ruth. *Crippled Justice: The History of Modern Disability Policy in the Workplace.* Chicago: University of Chicago Press, 2001.

conjoined twins

Conjoined twins, often referred to as *Siamese twins,* are identical twins born with a physical connection, which may be as simple as a band of tissue, or as complex as an extensively shared body with joint organs and limbs. Conjoinment, which has been observed in many animal species, occurs when a fertilized egg begins to split into twin embryos, but, for unknown reasons, does not complete the process. Estimates of human conjoined twins' frequency vary from 1 in 50,000 to 1 in 200,000 births. About 50 percent of conjoined twins are stillborn, while another 30 percent do not survive more than a day. Currently, in the United States, there are about 40 live births of conjoined twins each year.

Conjoined twinning has occurred throughout human history, appearing in ancient carvings and the earliest written records. In the premodern period, such twins were generally viewed as wondrous monsters or portents. In the 19th and early 20th centuries, conjoined twins were among the most popular attractions at American "FREAK SHOWS." CHANG AND ENG BUNKER (1811–74), the original Siamese twins, exhibited themselves on the freak show stage for a number of years before settling in North Carolina, where many of their descendants still reside. Other notable conjoined twins exhibited during this period include Millie and Christine McKoy (1851–1909), Giacomo and Giovanni Tocci (ca. 1875–unknown), and Daisy and Violet Hilton (1908–69).

American cultural fascination with conjoined twins is apparent in the many references to Chang and Eng in 19th-century America, of which the best known is Mark Twain's 1869 sketch, "Personal Habits of the Siamese Twins." Twain was also inspired by viewing the Tocci brothers to compose his 1892 short story, "Those Extraordinary Twins." In the 20th and 21st centuries, this fascination has continued with a number of FILMS, such as *Freaks* (1932), *Twin Falls, Idaho* (1999), and *Stuck on You* (2003); and novels, such as *Geek Love* (1989), *Chang and Eng* (2000), and *Half-Life* (2006). These cultural REPRESENTATIONS generally present conjoined characters existing in opposition and struggle with one another, while most accounts by real conjoined twins tell a very different story of cooperation, mutual nurturing, and companionship—a perspective more accurately reflected in Lori Lansens's 2005 novel *The Girls*.

While conjoined twins have been successfully separated as early as 1690, the advent of modern medicine meant that separation became increasingly viewed as the only acceptable response to conjoinment. In the 20th century, doctors have attempted hundreds of risky separation surgeries that have often resulted in the death of one or both twins. In 1996 it was estimated that about 200 attempted separations had been reported, although it is likely actual numbers were higher, due to surgeons not wishing to advertise "failures." A 1994 study found that only 5 percent of separated conjoined twins were ever discharged from the HOSPITAL. In the first decade of the 21st century, more twins are surviving separation, which almost always takes place in early childhood.

Nearly all conjoined twins who survive to adulthood, however, strongly reject the idea of separation. For example, while Chang and Eng did seek medical advice, largely at the urging of their wives, for most of their lives they rejected the idea of separation, including at the end of life. There are also many historical cases of twins refusing separation when one had died, with the surviving twin stating that he or she would rather die than live separated. In 2003, 29-year-old Iranian citizens Laden and Laleh Bijani became the first conjoined twins to consent to separation; neither survived the procedure. Their story was widely publicized and influential in the American media. In contrast, the much publicized story of Abby and Brittany Hensel, born in the American Midwest in 1990, has brought greater attention to the ability of some extensively conjoined twins to grow into healthy and functional adulthood. In the Hensels' case, it is clear that surgical separation would have produced significant IMPAIRMENT and possible death. Sharing a single body with two arms and legs, the Hensels have defied doctors' predictions by learning to walk, run, ride a bicycle, and play softball, and by their development of distinct and intelligent personalities.

Disability historians have analyzed conjoined twins in relation to issues of visibility and enfreakment, debating in particular how the public exhibition of conjoined twins can be seen as both exploitative and empowering—Millie and Christine McKoy, for example, used their public careers to achieve wealth and independence rarely available to African-American women in the 19th century. Although live exhibition of conjoined twins is no longer a common practice in the United States, media and medical representations of conjoined twins continue to fuel discussions regarding the nature of individuality, privacy, and bodily self-determination, which are central to the concerns of disability scholars and activists.

Ellen Samuels

Further Reading:
Clark, David L., and Catherine Myser. "Being Humaned: Medical Documentaries and the Hyperrealization of Conjoined Twins." In *Freakery: Cultural Spectacles of the Extraordinary Body,* edited by Rosemarie Garland Thomson, 338–355. New York: New York University Press, 1996.
Dreger, Alice Domurat. *One of Us: Conjoined Twins and the Future of Normal.* Cambridge, Mass.: Harvard University Press, 2004.
Face to Face: The Story of the Schappell Twins. Directed by Ellen Weissbrod. A & E Television, 2000. Documentary film.
Twain, Mark. "Personal Habits of the Siamese Twins." In *Collected Tales, Sketches, Speeches, & Essays, 1852–1890.* New York: Library of America, 1992.

Council for Exceptional Children

EDUCATION is an important issue in American disability history, and the history of the Council for Exceptional Children (CEC) highlights the changing approach to teaching and advocating for CHILDREN with disabilities.

The CEC was founded in 1922 as the International Council for the Education of Exceptional Children at a time when the demand for SPECIAL EDUCATION teachers was growing and members of the profession were isolated owing to their placement outside mainstream education. (The organization changed its name to the Council for Exceptional Children in 1958.) The council filled a void created by the 1918 dissolution of the National Education Association's (NEA's) Department of Special Education and the 1922 collapse of the National Association for the Study and Education of Exceptional Children, groups formed to address the isolation felt by people in special education and their need for professional affiliation and greater knowledge of exceptionality.

The International Council for the Education of Exceptional Children was formed by a group of students and faculty at Columbia University Teachers College in New York. Faculty member Elizabeth E. Farrell, a prominent innovator in SPECIAL education who had held leadership positions in NEA's Department of Special Education, was elected as the council's first president. Three aims were set forth at the inaugural meeting: "To unite those interested in the educational problems of the 'special child.' To emphasize the education of the 'special child'—rather than his identification or classification. To establish professional standards for teachers in the field of special education."

These aims formalized into a constitution, resolutions, and goals during CEC's early years. CEC called for suitable educational opportunities for exceptional children, highly qualified educators, professional guidance, research, involvement of members in their state's education work, and a role for the council in providing legislative information and suggestions. CEC was strengthened as a professional association by these documents and the communication offered to members by the publication of *Council Review* in 1934, which evolved into the *Journal of Exceptional Children* in 1942 (renamed *Exceptional Children* in 1951).

In the 1940s and 1950s CEC's membership increased, as did member participation in association governance. Additionally, CEC established a national headquarters in Washington, D.C., in 1950, preparing a foundation from which greater programs and action could be taken. In the 1960s CEC issued its first professional standards statement, incorporated as an independent organization, and took on a greater role as a publisher of special education literature. CEC received a U.S. Office of Education grant to develop and operate an Education Resource Information Center (ERIC) Clearinghouse on Exceptional Children and began the practitioner journal *TEACHING Exceptional Children*.

CEC's legislative voice gained influence as state legislatures looked to the council's Model State Law for the Education of the Handicapped in the 1970s. This state-level movement served as the principal force behind the Education For All Handicapped Children Act and its passage in 1975, the statute that is now known as the INDIVIDUALS WITH DISABILITIES EDUCATION ACT (IDEA). In the 1990s CEC issued a new publication, *CEC Today*, and focused its efforts on improving special education teaching conditions. In the 21st century CEC has adopted a new governance structure, held its first memberwide election for officers, and helped guide Congress in the reauthorization of IDEA in 2004.

Since its inception, CEC has supported the work of special education professionals and others working on behalf of individuals with exceptionalities through advocacy, education, and professional standards. While great advances have resulted from CEC's work and laws such as IDEA, professionals serving individuals with exceptionalities and the individuals themselves continue to have a need for collaboration, research, professional development, and organizational voice in legislation.

See also ACTIVISM AND ADVOCACY; LAW AND POLICY.

Kate Zoellner

Further Reading:

Council for Exceptional Children. *The Council for Exceptional Children.* URL: http://www.ideapractices.org/.

Kode, Kimberly. *Elizabeth Farrell and the History of Special Education.* Arlington, Va.: Council for Exceptional Children, 2002.

Crippled Children's Services

Crippled Children Services (CCS), Part 2 of Title V of the 1935 SOCIAL SECURITY ACT (SSA), allocated federal grants to states for services "and facilities for crippled children or for children suffering from conditions which lead to crippling." The Children's Bureau, founded in 1912 to protect the rights of children, found that many states provided services to disabled CHILDREN, but efforts were uncoordinated and often substandard, particularly in rural areas. The CCS was intended to facilitate and compel states to coordinate their services.

The Children's Bureau played the central role in ensuring that the Social Security Act addressed child welfare and health issues, and included disabled children's services within its initial proposals for maternal and child health. Advocacy groups, such as the National Society for Crippled Children, however, fought to make CCS a separate section within the SSA, arguing that access to medical, educational, and rehabilitative services for disabled children would allow fuller participation in society.

States were required to match grants from the CCS and establish administrative procedures, including plans to handle funding. Thirty-eight states received funding, and the remaining states soon added services to their health and welfare departments. Until 1959 states were allowed to define the term "crippled," but the federal guidelines excluded mentally retarded children and children with congenital heart disease from services. The scope of CCS eventually widened to include children with any disability or CHRONIC ILLNESS, and to serve urban areas.

Since its inception Title V, including Services to Crippled Children, has been amended a number of times and undergone several bureaucratic shifts, including a transfer in 1969 from the U.S. Labor Department to the U.S. Public Health Service. In 1981 Title V became part of the Omnibus Budget Reconciliation Act, which extended block grants to states. In 1985, reflecting the broadening definition of disabled, CCS was renamed Children With Special Health Care Needs. The agency currently monitors and evaluates the status of children with SPECIAL needs under the auspices of the Maternal and Child Health Bureau, Health Resources and Services Administration, and the U.S. Department of Health and Human Services.

While the inclusion of children in the Social Security Act signaled recognition of childhood as a unique category, the Crippled Children's Services program recognized the distinct medical and educational needs of disabled children, as well as the role of federal and state government in the lives of disabled children. As the status of people with disabilities continues to be considered among the lowest of all minority groups in the United States, however, it is unclear if the Crippled Children's Services made as much of a difference in the lives of people with disabilities as originally intended.

See also HEALTH CARE.

Lee S. Polansky

Further Reading:

Bremner, Robert, ed. *Children and Youth in America: A Documentary History.* Vol. 3, 1933–73, pts. 5–7. Cambridge, Mass.: Harvard University Press, 1974.

Breslow, Lester, ed. *Encyclopedia of Public Health.* New York: MacMillan Reference USA, 2002.

Lindenmeyer, Kriste. *"A Right to Childhood": The U.S. Children's Bureau and Child Welfare, 1912–1946.* Urbana: University of Illinois Press, 1997.

Crosby, Fanny (Frances Jane) (1820–1915) *hymnist, poet, social worker, and educator*

BLIND from infancy, Frances Jane "Fanny" Crosby, wrote texts to 9,000 hymns and numerous CIVIL WAR ballads. She also wrote eulogies to two presidents: William Henry Harrison (published in the *New York Herald* in 1841), and Zachary Taylor (published in Edward Marshall's *The Book of Oratory* in 1856). "Dixie for the Union," her abolitionist ballad set to music by Daniel Emmett, was distributed throughout the country on broadsides, its chorus stating: "Go meet those Southern traitors with iron will." She later set a temperance song, "The Banner of Temperance" to the tune used for the "Star Spangled Banner." Her creative and reform contributions to American society highlight unique connections between RELIGION, GENDER, MUSIC, and disability.

Fanny Crosby was born on March 24, 1820, in the town of Southeast, New York, about 60 miles from New York City. Before she was two months old, Fanny developed an eye infection. Some accounts suggest a stranger claiming medical knowledge placed hot poultices on the infant's eyes as a supposed CURE, which caused Fanny's blindness. Recent studies, however, suggest that Crosby had a congenital eye DISEASE, and the application of poultices merely served to accelerate her blindness.

During Fanny's preadolescent years, the Crosbys lived in Ridgefield, Connecticut, and boarded with a devout church member named Mrs. Hawley. As Hawley cared for Fanny, she noticed the child's interest in the Bible and encouraged this further, reading several passages repeatedly, along with POETRY, and helping young Fanny to memorize them.

In 1835, at age 15, Crosby entered the New York Institution for the Blind. Here she studied writing and geography under future president Grover Cleveland; she also learned how to play piano, organ, harp, and guitar with Anthony Reiff of the New York Philharmonic. Crosby excelled in history, science, philosophy, and grammar but had difficulty learning BRAILLE.

In 1845 Crosby completed her coursework, and in 1847 she became an instructor of rhetoric, grammar, and American history at the New York Institution for the Blind. While serving as a teacher, she continued her musical work. During the 1850s she collaborated with composer George F. Root (1820–95), widely respected in gospel music circles and previously a teacher at the Institution, and wrote prolifically. During the 1860s Crosby drafted numerous hymn texts for composer William Bradbury (1816–68). Due to her extremely high volume of poems, the Bradbury Company, which had hired Crosby to write hymn texts for his music, assigned her pseudonyms. Crosby's first hymn, "We Are Going," also titled "Our Bright Home Above," was published in Bradbury's *The Golden Censer* (1864). Crosby later wrote for revivalists Dwight L. Moody and Ira D. Sankey, who credited their evangelical success in part to Crosby's hymns. Some of her most popular hymns that endure today are "Blessed Assurance," "Safe in the Arms of Jesus," and "Pass Me Not, O Gentle Savior."

In 1858 she married Alexander Van Alstyne, another white blind teacher at the institution. Crosby then left the institution, kept her maiden name, and embarked on a poetic career. In 1859 Crosby bore a child, who died during infancy. She never spoke publicly or wrote about her motherhood. Different outlooks on finances, among other issues, caused strains in the marriage. The couple separated amicably in 1885.

Faith inspired Crosby in her sixties to do rescue mission work in New York, at the Bowery Mission and the Door of Hope, a mission for women. At age 80 Crosby moved to Bridgeport, Connecticut, continued her mission work, and lived with her sister, Carolyn Ryder. When Ryder died in 1906, Crosby remained in Bridgeport with her niece, Florence Booth. Fanny Crosby died on February 12, 1915, in Bridgeport, Connecticut, as the result of a massive stroke.

Crosby's life story reveals important perspectives about gender, religion, RESIDENTIAL SCHOOLS, and disability in the late 19th century. Like many other gifted people with sensory disabilities, Crosby benefited from the rise of residential schools for blind and DEAF Americans. The institution offered her an academic education as well as musical training that expanded her EMPLOYMENT options at a time when able-bodied women were rapidly entering the workforce and disability became particularly stigmatized. Crosby's affiliation with the blind school also opened her to a social COMMUNITY that was important to her throughout her life. At a time when disabled women commonly were discouraged from marrying, Crosby married a blind man. Her reference to her blindness as a blessing reflects both a personal interpretation of disability and common, gendered social frameworks.

See also REPRODUCTIVE RIGHTS; SOCIAL WORK; VOCATIONAL TRAINING.

Ralph Hartsock

Further Reading:

Blumhofer, Edith L. "Fanny Crosby and Protestant Hymnody." *Music in American Religious Experience,* edited by Philip V. Bohlman, Edith L. Blumhofer, and Maria M. Chow, 215–231. New York: Oxford University Press, 2006.

———. *Her Heart Can See: The Life and Hymns of Fanny J. Crosby.* Grand Rapids, Mich.: William B. Eerdman's, 2005.

Burger, Delores. "Home Missionary: Fanny J. Crosby." In *Women Who Changed the Heart of the City.* Grand Rapids, Mich.: Kregel, 1997.

Ruffin, Bernard. *Fanny Crosby.* Philadelphia: United Church Press, 1976.

"The Blind Girl's Lament" by Fanny Crosby (1842)

Born in Southeast, New York, Frances "Fanny" Crosby (1820–1915) was a prolific writer, poet, and hymnist. While a student at the New York Institution for the Blind in the 1830s, Crosby gained advanced training in music, and over subsequent decades, she worked with leading composers and musicians. This poem, titled "The Blind Girl's Lament," represents her traditional, sentimental, and deeply personal writing style. Crosby often downplayed her blindness, and, as this piece shows, her strong religious convictions and representations of common suffering draw the greatest attention.

"The Blind Girl's Lament" by Fanny Crosby February 1842

Again the well remembered spot I thread,
The spot of all in earth most dear to me;
Ye scenes of childhood, now forever fled,
Fond memory brings you back, with all your glee.

When morn's fair goddess wide her gates did ope,
I've wandered here to greet her early dawn;
When tuneful birds their melodies awoke,
I've heard thy murmurs, lonely Horicon.

But on thy placid bosom now to gaze
These sightless orbs, alas! do strive in vain,
The golden sun sheds not for me it's rays,
To light o'er once familiar scenes again.

Oh! what is sight; a gift I ne'er can know,–
But let me never murmur or repine–
Why should these eyes with tears of grief o'erflow
For that which never, can be mine.

Here have I roamed at twilight's pensive hour,
When stars illum'd the blue ethereal sky;
Here breathed the fragrance of each sleeping flower
And heard the balmy zephyrs gently sigh.

But where are those my bosom held so dear,
Who in my joys and sorrows shared a part,
Whose accents fell like music on my ear?
How sacred is their memory to my heart!

Alas their dwelling is the stranger's home,
I call, but echo's voice alone replies;
And as I wander o'er the spot, alone,
Unbidden tears of grief suffuse mine eyes.

When sorrow blights some fondly cherished flower
We've nourished long and tenderly caressed,
Is there a balm that in that cheerless hour
Can sooth the anguish of the troubled breast?

Oh, yes! Hope fondly whispers in mine ear,
That with those loved ones I shall meet again;

She from my cheek doth wipe the gushing tear,
And bids my anxious heart no more complain.

Source: Fanny Crosby. "The Blind Girl's Lament." *Sixth Annual Report of the New York Institution for the Blind* (February 1842): 35–36 Available online. URL: http://www.nyise.org/fanny/words.html. Accessed April 1, 2009.

crutches

Crutches, along with splints, are among the oldest assistive devices known to humans. They are a type of orthotic device and have been used since antiquity as MOBILITY aids for those with injured or impaired legs. One of the earliest representations of a crutch is a carving on the entrance to an Egyptian tomb dated to 2830 B.C.E. In the United States, increased use of orthotics (assistive devices such as crutches and splints) and limb PROSTHETICS (replacements) accompanied every WAR, particular epidemics, and injury-provoking transitions such as INDUSTRIALIZATION.

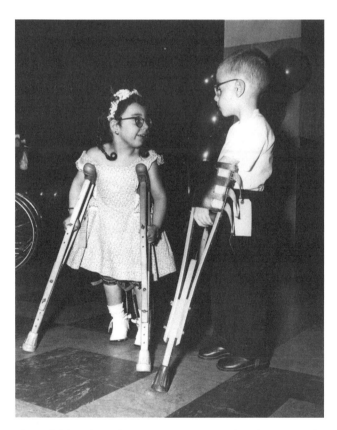

These children from the 1960s are using crutches that adjusted for various heights. The leg braces they wear made walking impossible without crutches. *(Smithsonian National Museum of American History, Division of Medicine and Science)*

> "You have no idea how I rejoiced that you had been able to leave your room, even with the aid of crutches. What a relief it must have been to you after so long & painful a confinement. . . . I hope ere this that you can even walk a little without your crutches, and are able to attend to some of the domestic duties of which you were so fond."
>
> —Virginia teacher Thomas Bailey in a letter to his mother, Priscilla Brownrigg Bailey (1800–1874) of Swannanoa, North Carolina, who had fallen from a mule in spring 1859 and was just starting to use crutches months later on December 16, 1859

For example, crutches were especially important for the AMPUTEES who survived the CIVIL WAR, and they were further developed to assist those who survived POLIO in the 20th century. The wide use of crutches to bridge temporary impairments such as broken legs and sprained ankles has made them a familiar cross-over experience for people who might not otherwise be aware of barriers that people with a disability encounter.

Crutches have undergone design changes over time to make them lighter, more comfortable, and less likely to slip. The basic crutch is a long slender pole with some kind of pad or grip to enable the user to transfer his or her weight onto the crutch and move forward. Underarm crutches reach from the ground to the armpit, have a pad under the arm and a handgrip. Forearm crutches, also known as Canadian crutches, were popularized by polio patients and developed in the 1940s and 1950s. They are used by slipping the forearm through a cuff and holding onto a hand grip. Variations on these designs include crutches that have broader soles, multiple or pivoting tips to distribute weight more evenly and allow for smoother walking gaits, knee support crutches for the lower leg, and platform crutches for those with disabilities that affect hand grip. Since the 1960s crutches made from wood have mostly been replaced by lighter materials such as aluminum and titanium. Rubber and gel tips and pads have made them more comfortable to lean on and grip and less likely to slip or cause joint pain with long-term use.

One of the 20th-century controversies related to crutch use is the result of the growth of a disability consciousness among users. Some people question whether it is better to use crutches and risk further injury from falls and strains but gain the prestige of "walking" or use a WHEELCHAIR or scooter, which are safer but might increase social STIGMA.

This image from the 1950s captures one of the pleasures of daily life. The man's crutch is a typical, somewhat awkward, wooden design of the era.   *(Smithsonian National Museum of American History, Division of Medicine and Science)*

Since the 1990s crutch designs have become more expressive. Crutches have become fashion accessories in addition to their usefulness as assistive technologies. Crutches in the 21st century come in a range of colors and some have "skins" that can be substituted, to match the user's mood. This playfulness around formerly stigmatized objects reflects the success of the DISABILITY RIGHTS MOVEMENT in redefining the beauty of the human body and acceptance of difference.

Crutches illustrate the ingenuity, simplicity, and antiquity of both mobility devices and the important role assistive devices play in the lives of many people with disabilities and impairments.

See also ASSISTIVE TECHNOLOGY AND ADAPTIVE DEVICES; IMPAIRMENT/IMPAIRED.

Laurel A. Clark

Further Reading:

Epstein, Sigmund. "Art, History and the Crutch," in *Classics of Orthopaedics,* edited by Marshall R. Urist, Philadelphia: Lippincott, 1976.

Fetterman, Thomas. "Crutches Anyone?" *Post-Polio Health* 14, no. 3 (Summer 1998).

Cued Speech

Developed in 1966 by Dr. Orin Cornett at GALLAUDET UNIVERSITY, Cued Speech is a visual-manual system of communication of handshapes and placements (cues) that represent the phonemes of spoken languages. Phonemes are the basic building blocks of any language; with spoken languages, we typically think of them as the sound parts that make up syllables and words. For example, the word *cat* has three phonemes: /k/, /a/, /t/. The cues must coincide with the normal mouth movements of traditionally spoken languages for complete phonemic access.

The term "cued language" refers to any language expressed via cues. As of 2006, Cued Speech has been adapted to 60 languages and dialects around the world (e.g., cued French, cued Spanish, cued Hebrew, etc.).

In cued American English, eight handshapes represent consonants and four placements around the lower face area represent vowels. As many words have similar mouth shapes and patterns, speech-reading alone can lead to misunderstandings. For this reason, Dr. Cornett systematically assigned similar-looking consonants to different handshape groups to help distinguish between visually ambiguous phonemes. For example, the phonemes /m/, /b/, and /p/ are assigned to different handshapes. He followed the same process for assigning specific vowels (e.g., /e/ as in *bet* and /i/ as in *bit*). Therefore, each handshape and placement represents groups of consonants and vowels that are visually different on the mouth.

A handshape plus a placement equals one cue or syllable. The use of cues and mouth movements together visually represent the phonemes of spoken languages without ambiguity. For example, the following three phrases all look similar from the perspective of a DEAF speech-reader: (1) *I love you*, (2) *all of you*, and (3) *olive juice*. Also, the following words look virtually identical: *ban, man, pan, pen, Ben,* and *men*. When cues are added, the phrases and words become distinct.

Cues follow the phonemic representation of words, not their written spelling. *Here, gear, cheer,* and *tier* all have the same vowel representation and /r/ as an ending. While the beginnings of those words have different handshapes, the endings follow the same movement pattern. Also, similarly spelled words with different vowel phonemes, such as *tough, though, cough, through,* and *bough,* have different placements and handshapes.

Research indicates that native deaf cuers typically develop reading skills comparable to those of hearing peers because they have developed internal phonological awareness and language-processing skills. They are able to identify and spontaneously generate rhyming pairs—an indicator of spoken language awareness and ability.

In the 1960s many people equated speech ability with language development. We now know that speech and language are not interrelated. However, many who see the term "Cued

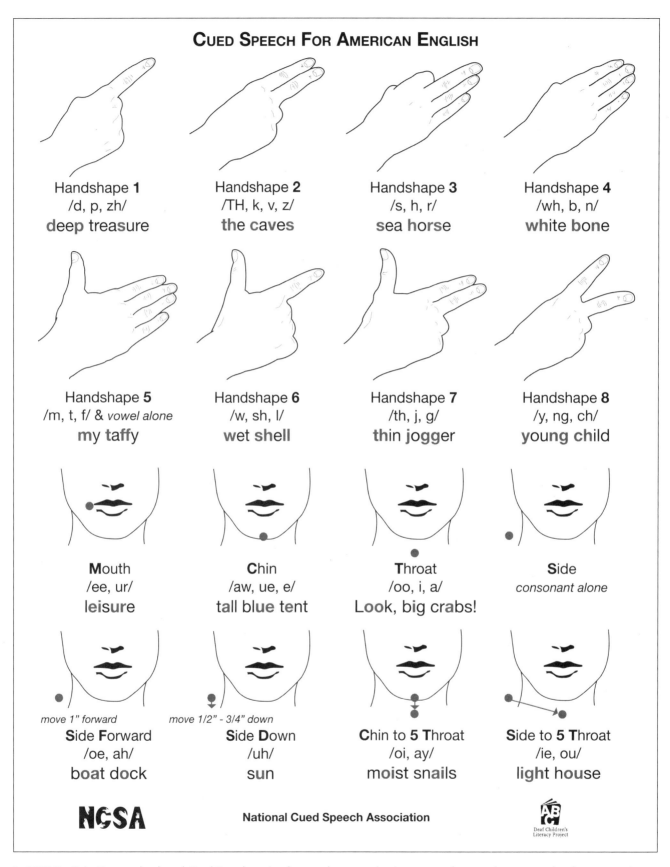

CUED SPEECH FOR AMERICAN ENGLISH

Handshape 1
/d, p, zh/
deep treasure

Handshape 2
/TH, k, v, z/
the caves

Handshape 3
/s, h, r/
sea horse

Handshape 4
/wh, b, n/
white bone

Handshape 5
/m, t, f/ & *vowel alone*
my taffy

Handshape 6
/w, sh, l/
wet shell

Handshape 7
/th, j, g/
thin jogger

Handshape 8
/y, ng, ch/
young child

Mouth
/ee, ur/
leisure

Chin
/aw, ue, e/
tall blue tent

Throat
/oo, i, a/
Look, big crabs!

Side
consonant alone

move 1" forward
Side **F**orward
/oe, ah/
boat dock

move 1/2" - 3/4" down
Side **D**own
/uh/
sun

Chin to **5** **T**hroat
/oi, ay/
moist snails

Side to **5** **T**hroat
/ie, ou/
light house

NCSA

National Cued Speech Association

AB C
Deaf Children's
Literacy Project

In 1966 Dr. Orin Cornett developed Cued Speech, a visual-manual communication system that supplements spoken language using handshapes and placements (cues). Charts such as the one shown here demonstrate common techniques used.   *(National Cued Speech Association)*

Speech" still believe that either speech is a required component or the purpose of the system is to improve speech skills. Cued Speech, which makes visual biofeedback possible, can be used in speech therapy situations. However, Cued Speech is primarily used as a communication tool for providing ACCESS to the language foundation needed for attaining literacy.

Recent trends in deaf EDUCATION have led to the idea of bilingual fluency in AMERICAN SIGN LANGUAGE and written English. The National Cued Speech Association endorses using cueing as part of this bilingual approach as a means to achieving proficiency in reading and writing English.

Gene Mirus
Hilary Franklin

Further Reading:

Cornett, R. O., and M. E. Daisey. *Cued Speech Resource Book for Parents of Deaf Children.* Raleigh, N.C.: National Cued Speech Association, 1992.

Fleetwood, E., and M. Metzger. *Cued Language Structure: An Analysis of Cued American English Based on Linguistic Principles.* New York: Calliope Press, 1998.

LaSasso, C., K. Crain, and J. Leybaert. "Rhyme Generation in Deaf Students: The Effect of Exposure to Cued Speech." *Journal of Deaf Studies and Deaf Education* 8, no. 3 (2003): 250–270.

National Cued Speech Association Web site. URL: http://www.cuedspeech.org.

cultural deprivation theory

Developed by sociologists and educators in the United States and Great Britain after WORLD WAR II and especially influential during the 1960s, cultural deprivation theory attempts to explain the differences between the educational achievements of poor and middle-class children by reference to the social structure of their families. From this perspective, certain kinds of families, specifically black and low income, often do not raise CHILDREN who are successful in school because they do not instill in their offspring an interest in and aptitude for EDUCATION. As a result, children with disabilities (of learning, cognition, speech, and hearing, for example) are considered disadvantaged and different compared to their "NORMAL" classmates. The perspective has also been applied to the sociology of health and illness. Thus, lifestyle choices such as smoking, alcohol consumption, and eating habits determine ill-health, and middle-class families make better choices in these areas. On the one hand, elements of this perspective remain in current social consciousness, particularly those about lifestyle choices. On the other hand, the idea that disabilities are caused by deficits in a child's socioeconomic background has been largely abandoned.

To resolve the many problems perceived as arising from deprived families, advocates of cultural deprivation theory promote "compensatory education," that is, schools supply families or communities with the basic cultural competences which they are said to lack, competencies involving reading and math skills. Compensatory education began in the United States in the early 1960s during the presidency of JOHN F. KENNEDY, which President Lyndon Johnson continued under "Operation Head Start" as part of his "War on Poverty." Although these and other programs invested additional resources in preschool educational facilities for the poor, working-class students' academic performances showed no significant improvement.

Since multicultural, diversity, and disability approaches to education first appeared in the 1970s, cultural deprivation theory has been debated and largely refuted not only because of its statistical failures but also because of the assumptions about culture and families on which it rests. By suggesting that the average middle-class family is the norm against which the average low-income family must be judged, the theory characterizes the poor as deficient rather than different with respect to that norm. The theory also assumes that only low-income families, not middle-class families and schools, must change. From a pedagogical viewpoint, the theory stereotypes students in ways that negatively influence how they are taught. By definition, teachers perceive students understood as culturally deprived as unable or slow to improve. Accordingly, students with disabilities are often separated from other students and asked to work toward lower educational goals.

But not all families, even middle-class white ones, behave in similar ways nor does any evidence suggest that middle-income homes have a monopoly on raising children who become educated and successful adults. Recent research also indicates that changes in teaching style or curricula and MAINSTREAMING rather than separating students improve all students' learning, not only the so-called culturally deprived or those with disabilities. Thus, more recent approaches to education, which focus on cultural diversity and on ability rather than deprivation and disability, consider differences to be strengths as well as sources of potential in all children, regardless of socioeconomic background. In so doing, approaches to disability no longer link learning deficits directly with POVERTY or RACE.

See also HEAD START.

Sara Newman

Further Reading:

Bilton, Tony, et al. *Introductory Sociology.* 3d edition. London: Macmillan, 1996. "Cultural Deprivation." URL: http://www.sociology.org.uk/tece1eg.htm.

Deutsch, Martin. *Disadvantaged Child: Selected Papers of Martin Deutsch and Associates.* New York: Basic Books, 1967.

"Education Reforms and Students at Risk: A Review of the Current State of the Art." January 1994. Available online. URL: http://www.ed.gov/pubs/EdReformStudies/EdReforms/chap5a.html. Accessed February 5, 2008.

curb cuts

Curb cuts represent a key victory in disability rights history because they mark the start of increased awareness of the importance of ACCESS for individuals with physical disabilities. The curb cut is a small ramp, or lowered indentation, built into the curb of a sidewalk to ease passage to the street, particularly for persons whose MOBILITY needs benefit from this design, such as wheelchair users, bicyclists, and pedestrians with baby carriages. These safety ramps facilitate movement from one level to another.

Student ACTIVISM at the University of California, BERKELEY campus in the late 1960s and early 1970s first drew attention to curb cuts and ultimately helped make them a national priority. Disability rights leader and UC Berkeley student ED ROBERTS, along with other activists, fought for curb cut inclusion in both the campus and the city ARCHITECTURE. Frustrated by city-and campuswide challenges posed to WHEELCHAIRS, disabled Berkeley students began urging the city of Berkeley's public works department to construct cement curb ramps, primarily at intersections near campus. It is believed that these curb cuts in Berkeley were the first installed by a city government to promote independent living for wheelchair users. Within a year, students with disabilities on the Berkeley campus were demanding curb cuts be implemented throughout the city itself. In 1970 the city of Berkeley began installing curb cuts throughout the city.

As grassroots disability activism grew throughout the country, the architectural shifts in Berkeley prompted more widespread changes throughout major American cities. SECTION 504 of the 1973 Rehabilitation Act, which prohibited discrimination on the basis of disability, contributed to an increase in curb cut construction. Under this law, organizations receiving federal funds were required to make programs accessible. This included making sidewalks and entryways accessible to the extent that they enabled wheelchair access to programs and events. Centers for independent living also played a role in promoting accessible design. As individuals with disabilities began building up activist bases around the nation, they collectively placed pressure on state legislators, themselves bound by Section 504 requirements, to make their cities more accessible.

Although curb cuts continued to be installed around the country, they were by no means a priority of cities. It was not until the landmark AMERICANS WITH DISABILITIES ACT of 1990 (ADA) that more widespread national inclusion of curb cuts began. Modeled in part after Section 504

> "The bureaucrats could have avoided the problem entirely if they had consulted someone who will be using the ramps, instead of deciding they know what is best for the handicapped."
>
> —Noel Rudd, a wheelchair user in Burbank, California, on the city's badly designed curb cuts, quoted July 4, 1976

of the Rehabilitation Act, the ADA required that state and local governments make their programs and services accessible to citizens with disabilities. Title II of the ADA required city governments to ensure that all programs, services, and activities were accessible to people with disabilities. Once the ADA passed, more cities began installing curb cuts as part of compliance to Title II.

Despite the ADA mandate, not all municipalities currently provide curb cuts where necessary. Many factors affect reluctance or delay in curb cut installation. Typical challenges include local governments' failure to ensure that a city's services, municipal buildings, and programs meet ADA requirements. Another challenge is that city governments are not required to construct curb ramps on existing roads and sidewalks. When streets and roads are newly built or altered, however, they must have ramps wherever they intersect with streets or where there were previously uncut curbs. The ADA required all city governments to complete a self-evaluation of their facilities, programs, policies, and practices by January 26, 1993. Continual self-evaluation can work to allow a city to budget for necessary changes and can help avoid lack of compliance, whether intentional or not.

Disability activists continue to place pressure on urban areas to improve curb cut availability. Thus, as curb cuts have become more prevalent in most major U.S. cities, the need to refine the curb cut design has emerged. In particular, visually impaired individuals have argued for a more universal curb ramp design that would include a safe way to alert the pedestrian when the crosswalk ended and the street began. Beginning in 2001 the ADA was revised to require Tactile Detectable Warnings on all curb cuts built after 2001. Tactile warnings are designed to facilitate street crossing, particularly for individuals who are visually IMPAIRED or BLIND. Tactile ramps are constructed with raised bumps that offer a color contrast (often yellow or red), are detectable under foot, and in some cases elicit a sound on contact.

Although there is work to be done with respect to installation of curb cuts, those cities that do offer improvements tend to enforce their purpose. For example, many cities impose fines against blocking a curb cut, much in the same way that a disabled parking space reserved solely for patrons displaying proper signage is protected. Curb cuts have improved access and ease of mobility for both the disabled and the able-bodied and will undoubtedly become more prevalent in the 21st century.

Dawn Reynolds

Further Reading:

Charlton, James I. *Nothing About Us Without Us: Disability Oppression and Empowerment.* Berkeley: University of California Press, 2000.

Preiser, Wolfgang, and Elaine Ostroff. *Universal Design Handbook.* New York: McGraw-Hill, 2001.

Russell, Marta. *Beyond Ramps: Disability at the End of the Social Contract.* Monroe, Me.: Common Courage Press, 1998.

"University of California at Berkeley News." Available online. URL: http://www.berkeley.edu/news/media/releases/2005/01/12_disability_history.shtml. Accessed August 9, 2007.

cures

Cures—or the prospect of cures—have been a prominent and critical aspect of the disability experience throughout American history. Often celebrated in mainstream society, efforts to seek cures for illnesses and disabilities reveal deeply held beliefs about the meaning and place of disability and people with disabilities in American society.

Cures are a central feature in what disability studies scholars call the MEDICAL MODEL OF DISABILITY, which is based on an assumption of normalcy and emphasizes the individual's "abnormal" condition. The SOCIAL CONSTRUCTION OF DISABILITY also holds cures as a central feature of the disability experience, but the interpretation is far different: according to the social model of disability, cures—especially cures for conditions that are not life threatening or painful—are part of a broader effort to control and eliminate specific types of difference. This trend, as well as its scholarly interpretation, offers important insights into American history.

While cures have been part of disability throughout American history, until relatively recently, the possibility of curing or effectively treating many illnesses was remote. Mass production of antibiotics, effective psychiatric drugs, chemotherapies for CANCER, and joint and organ replacement are mid to late 20th-century modalities. Even antiseptic surgery and scientifically tested drugs were uncommon until the 20th century. With such a sea change in medicine, cures prescribed for disability before the 20th century might not be recognizable as such today.

In colonial America, many of today's disabilities or impairments were not identified as such. Disability and impairment were often unremarkable because they were widely experienced. For example, before refraction of lenses, fine gradations in eyesight were not very apparent, let alone in need of correction or cure. During this time as well as long into the 20th century, self-dosage was the rule. People generally decided for themselves about treatments including when further treatment was not desired. Those without the same legally recognized rights as others, such as CHILDREN and institutionalized people, often had treatment or "cure" thrust upon them. In colonial America, institutions were rare, scientific knowledge was limited, and the medical profession did not enjoy the respect it received in the 20th century. Drastic medical intervention was often dangerous and therefore uncommon: for example, before antiseptic techniques were developed, surgery was likely to cause infection, which could be fatal. During the colonial period, serious medical cures and advice included prayer or theological instruction, reflecting moral dimensions attached to the acquisition or persistence of many disabilities. People with disabilities were liable to be subjected to proselytizing and moral condemnation. Just as proselytizing and moral condemnation of certain disabilities have continued to a limited extent to the present day, people with disabilities living in colonial times were also subject to chemical and physical interventions of the sort most commonly recognized as cures today.

During the 19th century, scientific knowledge expanded and medicine became an influential profession practiced by respectable men. Popular acceptance of the medical profession by communities was reflected in the rapid growth of HOSPITALS at the end of the century. Effective cures for major illnesses and disabilities remained limited. This did not prevent the enthusiastic marketing or medical acceptance of new "scientific" cures, even when they were dangerous, ineffective, or not needed. Doctors prescribed toxic mercury pills throughout the 19th century for conditions ranging from parasites to DEPRESSION and VENEREAL DISEASE. During this time, INSTITUTIONALIZATION of people with disabilities expanded, leaving more individuals vulnerable to new and experimental cures.

This shift in the role and respect accorded medicine and SCIENCE paralleled other shifts in thinking. The same decades that saw the explosive growth and popular acceptance of science and medicine were also witness to the beginning of the EUGENICS movement. Traits and conditions that had been seen before as part of God's will, part of an individual, or unfixable were recast by eugenicists as defects to be fixed by cures or prevented from being passed down through sterilizations (see INVOLUNTARY STERILIZATION).

The turn of the 20th century saw science and medicine expand with new cures for new disabilities or defects.

Surgeries were more widely used by orthopedic surgeons in rehabilitation. The new cures were sometimes inspired by other fields: AIRPLANE pilots commonly took paying DEAF customers for rides intended to cure their condition through rapid changes in air pressure. Radiation and radioactive substances were prescribed as cures for patients. At the same time that scientists and doctors were inventing new cures, they also discovered new defects to cure. Part of the redefinition of certain traits as defects arose from the widespread popular acceptance of the MEDICAL MODEL OF DISABILITY, which emphasized disabilities as abnormalities or bodily problems instead of constituting a natural part of human variation or social phenomena. Psychologists used INTELLIGENCE TESTS to create new definitions of intelligence based on arbitrary measurements. Scientific ideas of evolution combined with eugenics to create SOCIAL DARWINISM, which turned certain behaviors previously labeled immoral into hereditary defects of the brain or constitution.

The trend toward normalization through medical intervention gained momentum in the middle of the 20th century. Scientific advances in biology and chemistry fueled the discovery and production of some of the first effective cures. By the end of WORLD WAR II penicillin was mass-produced, allowing numerous diseases, including syphilis, to be completely cured. Antiseptic techniques allowed surgery to expand from absolute necessities to more complicated procedures such as hysterectomies, spinal fusions, and lobotomies (see LOBOTOMY).

These cures came at a price. Human experimentation constituted an inherent part of the scientific development and testing of cures. Officially, scientists asked for volunteers or experimented upon themselves. However, vulnerable populations were repeatedly exploited and subjected to experimentation. Famous accounts of such experimentation were recorded after World War II in the Nuremberg trials and officially banned, but involuntary participation in human experimentation did not end with the NUREMBURG PRINCIPLES adopted in 1947. People with disabilities were repeatedly used as test subjects for possible cures, as in the case of the Willowbrook school, where cognitively disabled students may have been infected with hepatitis B to test the effectiveness of gamma globulin in combating the DISEASE. In some cases, such as the TUSKEGEE SYPHILIS STUDY, human experimentation led to the coerced acquisition of disabilities.

The middle of the 20th century brought not only the development of drugs and procedures that effectively treated root causes of disabilities, it also saw a narrowing definition of normality. New sedatives administered to people in psychological institutions reduced the range of acceptable behaviors as it drastically curtailed violent behavior. Physicians also prescribed sedatives for numerous housewives as cures for unhappiness in their lives, and lobotomies were applauded as procedures that made compliant patients out of violent individuals with psychological disabilities. People with psychological disabilities were targeted most noticeably by these cures, but abnormality associated with other disabilities was targeted as well. Notably, ORALISM, the behavioralist method that cured the outward appearance of Deafness by teaching Deaf people to lipread and speak, peaked in popularity during this time.

The 1970s and 1980s brought two contradictory developments. First, a backlash against science and medicine called into question both cures and conditions identified as defects. In the 1970s national anxiety over cures was apparent in support of increased federal power to regulate and remove problematic cures from the market. Cures that altered behavior were especially called into question. The PATIENT RIGHTS movement advocated for the right of disabled people to refuse treatments and critiqued the use of lobotomies and tranquilizers as coercive control instead of a cure. Strict oralism lost popularity with the linguistic defense of AMERICAN SIGN LANGUAGE as a legitimate language. Elsewhere, numerous new advocacy organizations pushed for increased research and funding for cures for cancer and HIV/AIDS, and later for ALZHEIMER'S and PARKINSON'S DISEASE.

New cures that modified behavior toward an arbitrary and coercive normative state reemerged at the very end of the 20th century, often marketed as cures that changed individual defects. Advances in science and technology fueled the development of COCHLEAR IMPLANTS for deaf individuals, behavioral treatments for AUTISM, and new psychopharmaceuticals. While scientific cures and their theoretical basis may be accepted widely by the majority of the American public, reception of these new cures has been mixed in the com-

> "'One day [the Rev. Henry Duncan, who was deaf] was sitting by a window, when lightning struck a tree nearby. He was knocked senseless by the shock, and when he recovered could hear perfectly.' We clip the above from an exchange and give it for what it is worth, which, we judge is very little. But if any of our deaf friends think that Mr. Duncan has found a sure cure for deafness, we advise them to call our second baseman a liar. The effect will not be distinguishable from a stroke of lightning, and there will be no tree spoiled."
>
> —an anonymous contributor to a deaf newspaper, mocking various proclaimed "cures" for deafness, September 1890

munities of those they were designed to cure. Some disabled individuals and communities have welcomed new cures as beneficial and helpful, while others have found them stigmatizing, unnecessary, misleading in the statements of their effectiveness, and, in the case of cochlear implants, threatening to their culture and way of life.

See also ABLEISM; ACTIVISM AND ADVOCACY; DEFECTIVE; IMPAIRMENT/IMPAIRED; LOBOTOMY; NORMAL AND NORMALCY; STIGMA.

Katherine Randle

Further Reading:

Byrom, Brad. "A Pupil and a Patient: Hospital-Schools in Progressive America." In *The New Disability History: American Perspectives,* edited by Paul Longmore and Lauri Umanski, 133–157. New York: New York University Press, 2001.

Pappworth, M. H. *Human Guinea Pigs: Experimentation on Man.* Boston: Beacon Press, 1968.

Through Deaf Eyes. Directed by Larry Hott. Florentine Films/PBS, 2007.

Valenstein, Elliot S. *Great and Desperate Cures: The Rise and Decline of Psychosurgery and Other Radical Treatments for Mental Illness.* New York: Basic Books, 1986.

cyborg

The term *cyborg,* short for *cybernetic organism,* typically refers to biological organisms enhanced by, and blended with, technology. Scientists Manfred Clynes and Nathan Kline coined the term in the 1960s to refer to a rat that had been fitted with an osmotic pump to control the injection of chemicals under its skin; both men worked for the U.S. space program and were exploring the possibilities of biochemically, electronically, and physiologically modifying human beings so that they could function more efficiently in space. Their project parallels science fiction stories, FILMS, and novels in which writers explore the boundaries between humans, other organisms, and machines; from STAR TREK's Borg to the *Terminator* series, American POPULAR CULTURE is richly populated with boundary-crossing creatures—cyborgs—that do not fit nicely into distinct categories of human, animal, or machine. Eventually the term began to refer to more mundane, and medical, blendings, with bionic limbs, pacemakers, dialysis machines, and COCHLEAR IMPLANTS all seen as establishing cyborgian relationships between human beings and machines. Some cyber-theorists, such as the editors of *The Cyborg Handbook,* expand the definition even further, arguing that the proliferation of wireless and handheld technologies, the expansion of the INTERNET, and the increasing use of computers in schools, homes, and workplaces has led to widespread "cyborgization;" in the words of theorist Donna J. Haraway in her groundbreaking 1985 "A Manifesto for Cyborgs": "we are all cyborgs."

According to Haraway, the cyborg figure serves not only as an apt description of humans' literal interface with machines and other species but also as a metaphor for progressive politics. She argues that the cyborg, in its position on the margins between human and machine, allows for a revisioning of the relationships among culture, technology, and nature, insisting that any boundaries between these entities are contingent and permeable. As hybrid boundary-crossers, cyborgs pose a challenge to the "naturalness" of nature, suggesting that nature and technology are not diametrically opposed. There is no idyllic, pure nature untouched by technology, and any appeal to such is misguided; our understandings of nature are always mediated through language and culture.

Haraway uses the boundary-blurring of the cyborg as a resource for feminist theory and politics. She reads the work of women of color through the figure of the cyborg, articulating a model of feminism that does not assume all women are equally positioned within society or that all women share the same experiences. The cyborg figure, which cannot be contained in a single category, models an ironic feminism, one that does not recognize "woman" as a discrete, coherent category, and one that favors lobbying around shared goals instead of shared identities. For Haraway, the cyborg is a useful figure for thinking about difference differently, and other theorists have taken up the cyborg in their own work, speculating on its continued usefulness to feminism and other social justice projects. DISABILITY STUDIES scholars joined this exploration in the mid 1990s, debating whether the figure serves as a useful tool for disability IDENTITY or whether it glorifies a MEDICAL MODEL OF DISABILITY.

For some disability theorists, the boundary-blurring cyborg is a helpful guide in conceptualizing disabled bodies, identities, and politics. Rosemarie Garland Thomson argues, for example, that the cyborg's hybrid nature provides a productive model of embodiment for people with disabilities, many of whom have incorporated adaptive technologies (e.g., WHEELCHAIRS and ventilators), other human beings (personal attendants), and animals (GUIDE DOGS) into their lives, embodying the human/animal/machine couplings figured by the cyborg. Cyborg theory, with its focus on permeability, fluidity, and blurred boundaries, rejects the notion that "wholeness" is possible or desirable, a position that resonates for disability theorists challenging the marginalization of those with bodies and minds deemed broken, incomplete, or dysfunctional. Moreover, because of its refusal to adhere to fixed boundaries, the cyborg can be a useful metaphor for theorists interested in disrupting the able-bodied/disabled binary. As many disability theorists have noted, there is no fixed, permanent, or stable boundary between disabled and nondisabled people; the boundary-crossing cyborg embodies this lack well. Finally, Haraway's desire for a politics based on political affinity rather than biological identity is a useful resource for disability studies scholars and activists crafting a movement among people with different impairments. A cyborg politics does not require an amputee, a BLIND person, and a PSYCHIATRIC SURVIVOR to present their identities and experiences as the same, or all amputees' experiences as the same; rather, it encourages the formation of flexible coalitions to achieve shared goals.

Other disability theorists are less convinced, arguing that cyborg theory too often erases or ignores the material realities of disabled people's lives. With its focus on human/machine couplings, cyborg theory celebrates the boundary-crossing potential of adaptive technology, such as high-tech prosthetic limbs, but ignores the fact that such boundary-crossing is often painful. Tobin Siebers writes, for example, about how the same leg brace that facilitates his movement and renders him cyborgian also leads to sores on his calf; he argues that cyborg theory wrongly presents the human/technology interface as wholly positive. Moreover, argue Nirmala Erevelles, David Mitchell, and Sharon Snyder, many people with disabilities cannot afford, and therefore have no ACCESS to, the advanced technologies heralded in cyborg theory; prosthetic limbs, lightweight wheelchairs, and other adaptive equipment are simply beyond the reach of most people with disabilities. Casting the cyborg figure as a role model for disabled people's (alleged) interface with technology both obscures and leaves intact this economic reality. Critics of cyborg theory also note that disability often appears in cyborg theory as an individual problem that can and should be solved through technological intervention. Although Haraway presents the cyborg as a challenge to ideologies of wholeness, they argue that cyborg theory's celebration of technological intervention and human/machine couplings perpetuates the ableist assumption that disabled bodies are broken and require "fixing." As a result, urges Rosemarie Garland Thomson, cyborg theorists must begin paying attention to the political effects of theoretical discourse.

See also ABLEISM; AMPUTEES AND AMPUTATION; PROSTHETICS; SCIENCE AND TECHNOLOGY.

Alison Kafer

Further Reading:
Erevelles, Nirmala. "In Search of the Disabled Subject." In *Embodied Rhetorics: Disability in Language and Culture,* edited by James C. Wilson and Cynthia Lewiecki-Wilson, 92–114. Carbondale: Southern Illinois University Press, 2001.

Garland Thomson, Rosemarie. "Integrating Disability, Transforming Feminist Theory." In *Gendering Disability,* edited by Bonnie G. Smith and Beth Hutchison, 73–106. New Brunswick, N.J.: Rutgers University Press, 2004.

Kirkup, Gill, Linda Janes, Kath Woodward, and Fiona Hovenden, eds. *The Gendered Cyborg: A Reader.* London: Routledge, 2000.

cystic fibrosis

Cystic fibrosis (CF) is a chronic DISEASE, which from a medical perspective means that it is lifelong, progressively disabling, and often fatal. Understanding the relation between cystic fibrosis and disability involves recognizing how medical views interact with other cultural interpretations of disease and disability to shape how people throughout society experience the bodily impairment of the person with CF. It also means understanding how persons with CF and their families have negotiated such interpretations of this chronic disease in the course of everyday life.

The needs and experiences of people with CF are bound to the way modern medicine conceptualizes CF. Physicians first recognized CF as a distinct clinical entity in the late 1930s while treating small children who demonstrated a severe inability to absorb nutrients. American physician Dorothy Andersen gave the disorder the name "cystic fibrosis of the pancreas" in 1938. However, by the 1950s, physicians were beginning to notice that this childhood disease was not localized to any one organ. They redefined CF as a systemic disorder that stemmed from viscous secretions produced by the mucous glands throughout the body. Diagnosis of the condition became easier in the mid 1950s as it became clear that electrolytes in the sweat of CF patients were elevated. With each new discovery came the growing realization that CF was a complex clinical puzzle and a multifaceted disorder. By the mid 1960s a medical portrait of CF emerged that envisioned the disease as, at once, a hereditary condition, a lung disorder, a digestive problem, a form of pancreatic insufficiency, and a cause of liver cirrhosis and infertility (in males) as well as a systemic malady defined by mucous overproduction.

Because CF is a multifaceted disorder, the experience of having this disease can vary considerably from person to person and, therefore, significantly affect the ways in which people experience it as a disability. In the 1960s and 1970s the lung manifestations of the disease began to dominate medical and popular portrayals of CF largely because it was the disease's impact on the lungs that was causing most of the suffering and deaths among people with CF. Mucous would collect in the lungs, become an ideal host for bacterial infections, and lead to irreparable tissue scarring that over time would slowly but surely destroy the lungs. Death by CF frequently meant drowning in your own mucous. This grim reality motivated people with CF, their families, and physicians to emphasize this dimension of the disease over others. Not surprisingly, personal writings about the CF experience often emphasize this dimension of the disease over others.

Prominent examples include Laura Rothenberg's posthumous MEMOIR, *Breathing for a Living,* and Frank DeFord's 1983 best-seller, *Alex: A Life of a Child,* which movingly narrates the death of his daughter from CF.

The life experiences of people with CF have also varied considerably owing to their individual and social circumstances and the character and quality of the care they receive over the course of their lives. In recognition of such diverse challenges, parents of CF patients began collaborating with medical specialists in the 1950s and formed a national advocacy ORGANIZATION in 1955 known as the Cystic Fibrosis Foundation. Over the past five decades the CF Foundation has generated tremendous awareness of the disease, raised considerable monies for research and treatment, and successfully lobbied the federal government for added resources.

Medical management of CF has dramatically transformed the life prospects of people with CF over the past several decades. By the early 21st century, CF was no longer the child killer it used to be. More than 40 percent of registered CF patients in the United States were adults; and, on average, the person with CF could expect to live to the age of 33. This reflects tremendous medical progress, but it is also stands as an accomplishment earned by people with CF, their families, and advocates.

Stephen Pemberton

Further Reading:

Deford, Frank. *Alex: Life of a Child.* New York: Viking, 1983.

Doershuck, Carl, ed. *Cystic Fibrosis in the 20th Century: People, Events, and Progress.* Cleveland, Ohio: AM Publishing, 2001.

Gawande, Atul. "The Bell Curve: What Happens When Patients Find Out How Good Their Doctors Really Are?" *New Yorker,* 6 December 2004, pp. 82–91.

Rothenberg, Laura. *Breathing for a Living: A Memoir.* New York: Hyperion, 2003.

Wailoo, Keith, and Stephen Pemberton. *The Troubled Dream of Genetic Medicine: Ethnicity and Innovation in Tay-Sachs, Cystic Fibrosis, and Sickle Cell Disease.* Baltimore: Johns Hopkins University Press, 2006.

D

daily life

A central feature of social history, studies of daily life are important for understanding the meaning of being an American as well as of being in America. To date, however, virtually no historical scholarship directly examines the daily lives of people with disabilities or of the ways disability is experienced by those who live and work with these individuals. While scholars examine, for instance, early 20th-century immigrants' daily life in major cities, almost no attention has been paid to disabled immigrants and their families. This absence of study in part reflects the strong impact of the MEDICAL MODEL OF DISABILITY that historically has marginalized people with impairments of all varieties into strictly medical frameworks that stigmatize disability as a hardship that marks individual bodies, and that occurs primarily in medical context, such as HOSPITALS or within a HEALTH CARE system.

Although daily life is inherently complicated to document and fully understand, aspects of disability further com-

Everyday experiences vary widely and represent a significant aspect of American disability history. Marianne McHugh (1930–1978), born with Down syndrome, appears in personal snapshots such as this one *(front right)*, fully participating in the daily life of her family.   *(Colleen E. McHugh)*

plicate interpretations and information gathering: restricted access to EDUCATION limited literacy in some disabled populations in the past, which in turn limited the possibility of written documents, such as diaries and letters; for other people with disabilities, restriction on marriage and FAMILY formation meant that there was no one who cared to preserve their written record or to remember their daily lives in oral histories. Where scholars can find evidence of disabled people's daily lives in the past, they are shaped, like all other lives are, by folk or vernacular knowledge, adaptation and improvisation, and the creation of personal connections. Such factors by themselves may comprise the smallest of adjustments, but they compound to produce a distinctive DISABILITY CULTURE of daily living. For this reason, the historical study of daily life holds rich possibilities for disability history.

It is commonly assumed in the 21st century that individuals and families living with disabilities will naturally consult and follow expert advice from doctors, therapists, and educators (in fact, there are times when such advice must be followed, to remain within the LAW). However, until fairly recently such advice was either nonexistent or of minimal impact on everyday life. Instead, culturally transmitted "common knowledge" was more often the source of guidance for everyday decisions and arrangements. Such folk or vernacular knowledge includes beliefs, not only about disability itself but also about health and contagion, about childhood and adulthood, about GENDER and RACE, and about inheritance, blame, and fate. This fund of information is encoded in common language, which may describe and explain disability in ways that differ sharply from expert jargon.

For example, the everyday comments that greet the birth of a child with apparent differences, or the diagnosis of a young child, reveal much about ordinary beliefs and priorities, and they preview the way that child will be treated in the FAMILY and in the COMMUNITY. Long before medical explanations were available, people explained disability in religious or philosophical terms, with far-ranging consequences both good and ill. For example, when Fanny Maury's son George was born in 1818 in Norfolk, Virginia, "the poor little fellow['s]" apparent deformities of hands and feet were much discussed by friends: "I am pleased to tell you they bear their misfortune with the reflection that it will be able to write as the forefinger and thumb are at liberty, and that it is not a daughter." Indeed, George Maury grew up to become a bookseller in Virginia and the community's earliest expectations for his education and EMPLOYMENT were fulfilled. Other CHILDREN in other times and places found far different reception. When Ruth Austin (1892–1918) began to show clear signs of developmental delays, her grandmother in rural California dashed off a note to the girl's mother, the writer Mary Austin, saying: "I don't know what you've done, daughter, to have such a judgment upon you." As such a harsh judgment suggests, this child's mere existence would be hidden from many, a subject of shame and guilt for her parents and other relations. In the crowded tenements of the Lower East Side of New York City during the great wave of immigration from eastern Europe in the late 19th and early 20th centuries, young Herschey Lang's scarred face and sickly appearance were enough to draw stares and exclamations; "pregnant women . . . would stick their thumbs in their belts and immediately look away," recalled his sister, describing the superstitious gesture she saw far too often in the short life of her brother, who died at age five in 1917.

Everyday attitudes, beliefs, and superstitions shaped the activities, objects, and settings of disabled people's lives. Without expert input on such matters, many families and individuals improvised: handmade and personally tailored adaptations to ordinary tools and rituals are found across disability history, and they reveal much about the conditions of everyday life. A well-known example of this improvisation is "home sign," or the idiosyncratic gestural language developed in families without or before access to a more standard and elaborate form of sign language.

Other common domestic accommodations—handcrafted tableware, bell systems for calling help, tactile tags in clothing, beds equipped with wedges and rails—point to the creativity with which many managed impairment in the past. Impromptu adaptations sometimes extended beyond the home into the community: When circus performers ANNA SWAN and her husband Martin Bates settled in Seville, Ohio, in 1874, their home and furniture were specially constructed for their height (both were over seven feet tall), but the nearby Baptist church also built a custom pew for the couple. This pattern of improvisation continues into recent decades. In 1948 Candido Jacuzzi of San Francisco fabricated a submersible bathtub pump for his young son Kenneth, who had rheumatoid arthritis. He later patented and marketed a version of the device, and the Jacuzzi whirlpool bath is now so widely used that its disability roots are seldom recalled.

Activist ED ROBERTS's motorized WHEELCHAIR is an icon of disability history, now held at the Smithsonian National Museum of American History; it is also an improvisation, customized in the mid 1970s from a Porsche seat, headlights,

> "I don't think that my disability really changed anything as far as my relationship with my wife and children. . . . [When] our daughter Louisie was in school (she must've been really little), the teacher said to her, 'Your dad is Bob Gurney. He's the one who is handicapped.' Well, Louisie told her, 'No he's not. He's my daddy!'"
>
> —Robert Gurney, a polio survivor, in a 1996 oral history interview

duct tape, and bumper stickers, to match Roberts's needs and personality. Today's homemade adaptations range from the low-tech, such as clothing and toys, to software and electronic devices. The everyday material culture of disability history is a subject that surely will reward much further study as museum collections and archives grow to meet the interests of researchers.

Beyond customized objects, everyday practices and decisions have been adapted to better serve disabled people within the family. Parents barred from enrolling their children with disabilities in school devised their own methods of educating, through trial-and-error and close attention to the child's particular needs. Couples have long worked out improvised means of courtship and intimacy (a social history that may be particularly challenging to reconstruct, but a record of long, loving partnerships and children born to disabled parents tells us that creativity has, indeed, often triumphed). Even the basic question of where to live has been solved around impairment considerations: writer Celia Thaxter retreated to an island with her son Karl in the 1870s in hopes that the isolation would be more calming to his temper, and that he would keep from harm in such a remote location. A whole wave of migration to the American Southwest in the late 19th and early 20th centuries was sparked by a search "for the healthful air," and its anticipated benefits to people with lung ailments such as TUBERCULOSIS. In recent decades, despite federal laws such as the INDIVIDUALS WITH DISABILITIES EDUCATION ACT (1974) and the AMERICANS WITH DISABILITIES ACT (1990), differences in state and local laws and programs have prompted families and individuals to make similar hopeful relocations.

To gain knowledge, to learn about material and practical innovations, and simply to share the experience of disability, people seek the connections and alliances that are integral to the living of everyday lives. Some of these connections began with shared culture: A common language among culturally DEAF people has created a natural basis for fellowship through most of American history, spinning in the more developed communities into churches, sports leagues, literary and arts clubs, and charitable ORGANIZATIONS. Other connections began with common exclusions—the SPECIAL EDUCATION class or state school, for example, or no school at all. Marcella Nelson of Seattle remembered what she was told when her son was born with CEREBRAL PALSY in 1936: "One doctor said, 'There's nothing out there for your kids. If you want something to happen, you're going to have to do it for yourself.'" And that is what many families of disabled children did, especially beginning in the early 20th century. They started programs themselves, sometimes hatched by friends over coffee at the kitchen table. Mothers Dixie Henrikson and Mary Schallert of North Hollywood, California, founded Activities for Retarded Children in 1969. "A lot of people think Easter and Christmas parties are enough," Henrikson explained later, "but these kids have the same needs as any teenagers, and other teenagers don't say, 'Oh I've been out this month, so I think I'll stay home now.'" Recognizing the need to work together for social opportunities and systemic change, families and individuals across the United States started local, regional, state, and national networks of support and common interests.

While much disability history can be read in the annual reports of asylum superintendents or the text of laws and court decisions, the history of everyday life for people with disabilities is found elsewhere: in personal correspondence, diaries and mimeographed newsletters, oral histories and photo albums, handmade and well-worn tools, and domestic architecture, recipe boxes, and clothes trunks. The retrieval of this history in coming years will depend on the survival of such ephemeral materials, always a tenuous prospect. It will also require historians to access and interpret these texts resourcefully, taking an eclectic approach to assembling a picture of how disabled lives have been lived beyond asylums, courtrooms, schoolgrounds, and legislative chambers. The reward for such careful gathering and reading will be a deeper historical understanding of the rich diversity of disability cultures and experiences.

See also ASYLUMS AND INSTITUTIONS; ASSISTIVE TECHNOLOGY AND ADAPTIVE DEVICES; REPRODUCTIVE RIGHTS; SEXUALITY.

Penny L. Richards

Further Reading:

Berube, Michael. *Life as We Know It: A Father, a Family, and an Exceptional Child.* New York: Vintage, 1998.

Griffin, John Howard. *Scattered Shadows: A Memoir of Blindness and Vision.* Maryknoll, N.Y.: Orbis Books, 2004.

Groce, Nora. *Everyone Here Spoke Sign Language.* Cambridge, Mass.: Harvard University Press, 1985.

Linton, Simi. *My Body Politic.* Ann Arbor: University of Michigan Press, 2007.

Schwartzenberg, Susan. *Becoming Citizens: Family Life and the Politics of Disability.* Seattle: University of Washington Press, 2005.

Shreve, Susan Richards. *Warm Springs: Traces of a Childhood at FDR's Polio Haven.* Boston: Mariner, 2008.

dance

Throughout the last century of American history, the categories of dance and disability have moved through an interesting and complex tango of connection and disconnection. Since the 1930s when choreographer George Ballanchine created a new American icon of a dancer with his form of ballet, many Americans primarily envisage dancers as thin, long-limbed, swanlike creatures who leap gracefully through the air, landing softly in a classically beautiful pose. Twentieth-century choreography, costumes, and lighting have helped to create the illusion of a perfectly able body—one completely unhampered by sweat, pain, or the evidence of any physical negotiation with gravity. Despite this illusion, the history of dance has many intersections with disability, including the emergence of inclusive dance troupes.

People with disabilities have been dancers for all of American history, but the types of dance options and social responses to their dancing has varied. For example, since the mid-19th century schools for DEAF and BLIND CHILDREN, as well as psychiatric institutions, regularly included dance as both therapy and entertainment. Some scholars believe that the racist, stereotypical character "Jim Crow" evolved in the 1830s from a minstrel song and dance that involved a "crippled" African-American. Anecdotal evidence suggests that white stage performer T. D. Rice met "Jim Crow," an African-American with a deformed body and perhaps other disabling conditions and adopted Crow's distinct movement and poses as he developed his minstrel art.

In the 20th century, the modern dance tradition, led by such visionary women as Isadora Duncan, Ruth St. Denis, and Martha Graham, promoted values that resonated with disability performers and activists. Modern dance is committed to the idea that anyone and everyone can (and should) express their inner selves through a range of movement possibilities. Throughout the 20th century, modern dance educators believed expressive, improvisational dancing constituted an important therapy for all children, introducing the practice to CAMPS and schools for deaf and blind children, as well as those with emotional problems. Despite this legacy of egalitarianism in modern dance, it was not until the late 20th century that disabled dancers began to share the professional stage with NONDISABLED dancers.

The roots of this aesthetic shift of priority from visual line of the body in space to lived experience, including a focus on the particularities of the disabled figure, lay in the cultural rev-

People with disabilities have expressed themselves through dance throughout American history. As this image of Axis Dance company performers shows, it can be used to celebrate and empower everybody.   *(Matt Haber/www.matthaber.com)*

olutions sparked by the civil rights ACTIVISM of the 1960s and the women's movement of the 1970s. At this time, youth culture reflected the growing interest in African-American MUSIC and the mixture of styles that evolved into early rock and roll. The resultant dance styles privileged individualistic, improvisational movement in the midst of a supportive COMMUNITY of peers. No longer was it necessary or desirable to execute specific moves; what was really important was the freedom to express one's self in an open, nonjudgmental manner.

One of the most exciting areas of mixed ability dancing is embedded in the global practice of Contact Improvisation, a dance form developed in the early 1970s by a group of people interested in exploring the dancing produced by the exchange of weight between two (or more) people. The movement in Contact Improvisation is structured by the specific physics of this exchange, which explores the changing dynamics of weight, space, momentum, and force, and can include such movement as shifting balance or one person lifting or carrying another. The focus in contact training on the flow of movement through the spine (and not just the spatial placement of the limbs) as well as the commitment to experienc-

ing awkward moments within the improvisation allows this dance form to include many differently-abled bodies. Two of the most active participants in teaching and performing this dance are Emery Blackwell and Alito Alessi who both live in Eugene, Oregon, a city in the forefront of design for WHEEL-CHAIR accessibility. Blackwell served as the president of OIL (Oregonians for Independent Living) until he resigned to devote himself to dance. Alessi, a veteran "contacter" who has had various experiences with physical disabilities (including an accident that severed the tendons on one ankle), has been coordinating the DanceAbility workshops in Eugene. In addition to their participation in this kind of forum, Blackwell and Alessi have been dancing together for over a decade, creating both choreographic works such as their duet "Wheels of Fortune" and improvisational duets performed throughout the world.

The rise of the DISABILITY RIGHTS MOVEMENT and the emergence of the AIDS epidemic in the early 1980s have also directly influenced dance and dancers. Spurred by a renewed emphasis on making individual bodily identities visible and a political awareness generated by the disability rights movement, an increasing number of contemporary dance companies are working to integrate visibly disabled and visibly nondisabled dancers. This is evidenced by the creation of troupes such as Dancing Wheels (Cleveland, 1980) and AXIS DANCE (San Francisco, 1987).

While these radical artistic endeavors point to the evolving meaning of disability and its REPRESENTATION, various factors hinder full progress. For example, mainstream print and television news, as well as the dance press, commonly tokenize disability dance, casting it in terms of "SPECIAL" human interest profiles rather than reviews of choreographic rigor. Financial issues present other complications. It can still be prohibitively expensive to travel as a disabled person, especially if one needs to bring an aide along. Consequently, nondisabled dancers in grassroots ORGANIZATIONS with limited resources often receive much more touring and teaching work than even the most highly renowned disabled dancers.

Because every dancer knows someone who has been seriously injured or permanently disabled, this work in mixed ability dance has created a continuum of possibilities for dancers. This new openness replaces the previous either/or mentality, which forced many dancers to abandon the art form they loved because they could not (or would not) fit into the traditional image of the classical ballet dancer leaping gracefully across the stage. Whether disabled or nondisabled, contemporary dancers are more apt to perform later in life and with more physical limitations than ever before. As a result, audiences are increasingly trained to look for an individual expressivity that is not limited by traditional notions of virtuosity. Finally, American dance is beginning to look truly democratic.

Ann Cooper Albright

Further Reading:

Albright, Ann Cooper. *Choreographing Difference: The Body and Identity in Contemporary Dance.* Middletown, Conn.: Wesleyan University Press, 1997.

Garland Thomson, Rosemarie. *Extraordinary Bodies: Figuring Disability in American Culture and Literature.* New York: Columbia University Press, 1997.

Kuppers, Petra. *Disability and Contemporary Performance: Bodies on Edge.* New York: Routledge, 2003.

Sandahl, Carrie, and Philip Auslander, eds. *Bodies in Commotion: Disability and Performance.* Ann Arbor: University of Michigan Press, 2005.

Waters, Hazel. *Racism on the Victorian Stage: Representation of Slavery and the Black Character.* Cambridge: Cambridge University Press, 2007.

Dark Victory

The 1939 "women's" melodrama *Dark Victory* presents Bette Davis playing Judith Traherne, a young, wealthy socialite dying from a brain tumor. Her ultimately stoic acceptance of her terminal condition makes Traherne a combination of several of Hollywood's stereotypical REPRESENTATIONS of a person with disabilities.

Based on a short-run Broadway play in 1934 by George Brewer, Jr., and Bertram Bloch, *Dark Victory* solidified the star appeal of actress Bette Davis, who received an Academy Award nomination for Best Actress. Davis plays Judith Traherne, the playgirl who starts to experience headaches, accidentally burns herself with cigarettes, and, most spectacularly, has an accident while horseback riding, her vision blurring into a rotating triplicate version of the hurdle into which she rides her horse. In trying to show the audience what Traherne was experiencing with the blurred, rotating, triplicate vision, the film at times puts the viewer into the subjective role of Traherne. For most of the film, however, the camera assumes a more distant perspective. Traherne consults a doctor, Frederick Steele (played by George Brent), who quickly diagnoses her neurological symptoms and does surgery on her glioma, the brain tumor causing her problems. The surgery only temporarily resolves the condition, and Steele, who has fallen in love with his patient, decides not to tell her that she has only a few months left to live. Judith, who has fallen in love with her doctor, accidentally discovers her prognosis and enters into a raging self-destructive drinking spree, until she finally resolves to live her final months to their fullest. The two wed and enjoy a brief idyllic marriage until Traherne suddenly begins to lose her vision—the sign, Steele had told Traherne's friend, that she had only a few hours until a painless death—at just the same time as Steele is called into the city to present his medical research. Traherne hides her BLINDNESS and lets her husband leave without telling him of her imminent death, choosing instead to die by herself. Max Steiner's melodramatic musical score exerts its greatest manipulative power in the closing scenes, as the music accompanying her solitary death employs wordless choirs and harps, traditional musical codes for things associated with heaven.

The FILM offers several fictions about Traherne's medical condition as it supports a number of stereotypical representations of a person with disabilities. After her operation, all of her symptoms instantly disappear, and only a tiny patch of her hair appears to have been shaved for her brain surgery; in reality, neither of these things would have happened. The precision with which Steele predicted both the amount of time left for Traherne as well as the painless way she would be affected in her final hours were also beyond his ability to know.

Traherne's angelic resignation to her fate combines elements of the tragic victim and the sweet innocent, two frequently recurring disability stereotypes common to Hollywood cinema. The film could be categorized as a "woman's film" or "weepie," designed especially for a female audience expecting drama and emotional catharsis. As it often does in other FILMS, disability in *Dark Victory* serves as a vehicle to heighten vulnerability, tragedy, and drama. Scholars of disability commonly point to Hollywood's important role in shaping images and representations toward disability. *Dark Victory* thus offers an example of not only cinematic successes but also the widespread and historical stereotypes of disabled people.

See also GENDER; POPULAR CULTURE; REPRESENTATION.

Neil Lerner

Further Reading:

"Bette Davis, Interviewed by Rex Reed." In *The Norton Book of Interviews: An Anthology from 1859 to the Present Day,* edited by Christopher Silvester. New York: W.W. Norton, 1996.

Doane, Mary Ann. "The 'Woman's Film': Possession and Address." In *Home Is Where the Heart Is: Studies in Melodrama and the Woman's Film,* edited by Christine Gledhill, 283–298. London: British Film Institute, 1987.

Leaming, Barbara. *Bette Davis: A Biography.* New York: Simon & Schuster, 1992.

Norden, Martin F. *The Cinema of Isolation: A History of Physical Disability in the Movies.* New Brunswick, N.J.: Rutgers University Press, 1994.

Dart, Justin, Jr. (1930–2002) *entrepreneur, activist*

Justin Dart Jr. was the rebellious son of wealthy parents, a successful business entrepreneur in Japan, and a tireless advocate for the rights of individuals with disabilities. He was influential in securing the passage of the AMERICANS WITH DISABILITIES ACT (ADA) in 1990.

Dart was born in Chicago, Illinois, on August 29, 1930. His father was an affluent businessman and his mother a patron of the arts. A young rebel, he attended seven different high schools without graduating. In 1948 he contracted POLIO, which left him reliant on a WHEELCHAIR for life. Dart's experience in the HOSPITAL and his introduction to the philosophy of Indian leader Mohandas Gandhi redirected his life. He attended the University of Houston and earned bachelor's and master's degrees in history and political science. He hoped to teach, but the university refused to grant his teaching certificate because he used a wheelchair. Dart then went into business in Mexico and Japan, starting several successful companies, including Japan Tupperware. He always made it a practice to hire people with disabilities for his companies. While in Japan he married his partner, Yoshiko Saji.

A visit to a polio rehabilitation center in Vietnam in 1966 motivated Dart to sell his businesses and reconfigure his life path. He and Yoshiko spent six years at an isolated farmhouse in Japan studying and meditating. They decided to commit their lives to disability rights. They moved to Texas in 1974 and became involved in local disability ACTIVISM.

Beginning in 1980 Dart accepted appointments to a number of governmental agencies and boards concerned with people with disabilities. He served on the Texas Governor's Committee for Persons with Disabilities from 1980 to 1985, including a term as its chair. President Ronald Reagan appointed Dart as vice chair of the National Council on Disability in 1981, a platform from which Dart would campaign for the passage of the ADA. In 1983 he became the head of the Rehabilitation Services Administration. He was later asked to resign for having pointed out the agency's failures in serving people with disabilities. In 1989 Dart chaired the PRESIDENT'S COMMITTEE ON EMPLOYMENT OF PEOPLE WITH DISABILITIES.

During this time Dart campaigned nationally for passage of the ADA. He and his wife toured every state, building support for the act. He and his allies also lobbied Congress. Their efforts were rewarded when the act passed and President George H. W. Bush signed the legislation on July 26, 1990.

When the ADA came under attack by conservatives, Dart established Justice For All in 1995 to bring together disability activists to protect the rights guaranteed by the ADA and to lobby for additional legislation. President Bill Clinton awarded Dart the Presidential Medal of Freedom in 1998. Heart attacks in 1997 limited Dart's ability to travel, but he worked for the rights of individuals with disabilities until his death on June 21, 2002.

Justin Dart demonstrates how an individual can make a difference both by serving in official government positions and by taking up the role of advocate when change proceeds too slowly. Dart always acknowledged the assistance of his colleagues, but he was a crucial catalyst in the campaign for disability rights.

See also DISABILITY RIGHTS MOVEMENT.

Daniel J. Wilson

Further Reading:

Fleischer, Doris Zames, and Frieda Zames. *The Disability Rights Movement: From Charity to Confrontation.* Philadelphia: Temple University Press, 2001.

Shapiro, Joseph P. *No Pity: People with Disabilities Forging a New Civil Rights Movement.* New York: Times Books, 1993.

Davenport, Charles (1866–1944) *eugenics movement leader*

Charles Davenport was one of the most influential figures in the history of the American EUGENICS movement. His stature as a respected biologist in the early 20th century enabled him to play a leading role both in shaping American attitudes toward human differences and in passing public policies restricting the rights and behavior of those considered a threat to the eugenic health of the nation.

Davenport was born on June 1, 1866, in Stamford, Connecticut. He attended Harvard University, earning a doctoral degree in biology in 1892. Davenport's early work focused on zoology, and he became a prominent professor of the field at the University of Chicago before accepting a position as the director of the Eugenics Record Office (ERO) at Cold Spring Harbor, New York, in 1911. Eugenics purported to be a civic biology that claimed human beings differed according to superior and inferior hereditary traits passed down as dominant or recessive genes from one generation to another. As director of the ERO, Davenport sponsored research attempting to validate these ideas and influence public policy. While eugenics was based upon a flawed and rigidly deterministic conception of human heredity and many of Davenport's research studies lacked scientific rigor, he nonetheless was able to attract considerable philanthropic and political support, making the ERO the foremost center for American eugenic research in the 1910s and 1920s.

At the ERO, Davenport sponsored summer institutes for teachers, SOCIAL WORKERS, and officials from prisons and mental hospitals. Institute participants were taught how to detect "inferior traits," the definition of which included DEAFness, BLINDness, and a range of other mental and physical disabilities. Many of the institute graduates became ERO field workers who collected data on inmates in state custodial facilities and on poor rural and urban families who were considered eugenically "unfit." Based on these biased studies, Davenport wrote numerous articles and books calling for the elimination of "DEFECTIVE" germ plasm from the American population.

Davenport played a role in translating his hopes for eugenic public policies into actual federal and state legislation. This included his support for the 1924 Immigration and Restriction Act, which placed stringent national quotas on people entering the United States. Davenport and other eugenics advocates convinced many in Congress that southern and eastern European immigrants reflected disproportionate numbers of defective hereditary traits and therefore risked lowering the intellectual, moral, and physical health of the American population. On the state level, many of the studies made by Davenport's ERO field workers were used as evidence to support legislation aimed at sterilizing and segregating those considered mentally and physically unfit to reproduce. Tens of thousands of people deemed mentally or physically impaired were sterilized in the United States in the name of eugenic public health in the first half of the 20th century.

Davenport soon became a major figure in the international eugenics movement. He presided over conferences that brought together eugenic researchers from around the world, initiating collaboration with German eugenicists in the 1920s and supporting the 1930s Nazi laws that imposed sterilization on mentally and physically disabled persons. At the time of his death on February 18, 1944, Davenport remained steadfast in his eugenic views, despite increasing criticism from the scientific community and mounting evidence of the horrors perpetrated by the Nazis in the name of eugenics.

See also BELL, ALEXANDER GRAHAM; IMMIGRATION POLICY; INVOLUNTARY STERILIZATION; LAW AND POLICY.

Alan Stoskopf

Further Reading:
Kevles, Daniel J. *In the Name of Eugenics.* Cambridge, Mass.: Harvard University Press, 1995.

deaf (Deaf)

The term *deaf* implies that an individual cannot process auditory signals. Such an extreme physical condition, however, has been and remains rare. Most people who are labeled deaf hear sounds within some frequencies at particular decibel levels. In American history, "deaf" most often has signified a person who cannot understand speech by means of audition alone. The term therefore overlaps with HARD OF HEARING, a signification that came into common use in the early 20th century, replacing the term *semi-deaf,* which was often used by deaf people themselves to suggest a person who could understand some speech in some circumstances. Terms such as DEAF-BLIND, identifying individuals having more than one disability, came into use in the late 20th century, by which time application of the term *deaf,* particularly the self-application of the term, had taken on political and cultural meanings that were constrained, but not defined, by particular audiologic conditions.

CHANGING INTERPRETATIONS OF DEAFNESS

Indeed, the importance and cultural meaning of "deaf" have been contested throughout much of American history. Interpretations of hearing limitations and intertwined beliefs about human language—what forms it might take and what its use reveals about individuals' humanity—have changed through time, reflecting dominant social concerns at particular periods in history. Technological developments and new biological understandings also have influenced the interpretation of "deaf." Deaf people themselves, as individuals and as a collectivity, have approached their particular physical characteristic in a variety of ways, some of them directly contradictory, demonstrating the overarching influence of social norms in defining disability and the complicated mixture of attitudes deaf people hold, and have held, about deafness.

The colonial period shows no unanimity of what it meant to be deaf. Deafness was a low incidence condition, most frequently caused by illness or accident, giving it a random nature in most instances. The colonists' responses were locally determined rather than driven by a common view of deafness or disability. Many deaf people married, raised families, contributed to their local communities, and were seemingly accepted without significant STIGMA. Some accounts remark on deaf people's use of gestures as an adequate substitute for speech and hearing. In other instances, though, deaf individuals were excluded from social and religious activities and were assumed to be ineducable. General public discussion of what it meant to be deaf only began near the end of the 18th century when a few deaf CHILDREN were born to wealthy colonists.

Deaf voices themselves are almost completely absent before the 19th century, but one exception was that of Jonathan Lambert, who moved to the island of MARTHA'S VINEYARD in 1694 and lived most of his adult life there. Lambert was deaf because of a recessive gene that became widely shared among the Vineyard's early settlers. He had a successful life by contemporary measures, acquiring land and goods and participating in the activities of his community. Nevertheless, in his will, probated in 1738, Lambert singled out his two deaf children (he and his wife also had five hearing children) for special consideration because, he wrote, they could not speak for themselves, suggesting that Lambert saw deafness as a particular hindrance within his milieu.

Martha's Vineyard was an exception to the randomness of the meaning of deaf in early American history. Some scholars believe that the widespread incidence of recessive deafness in certain areas of the island in the late 18th and early 19th centuries created a situation in which deaf and hearing persons alike knew sign language and consistently used it when deaf individuals were present. Deafness itself was therefore not seen as a disability. The evidence for this interpretation is suggestive but not conclusive.

SCHOOLS AND ORGANIZATIONS FOR THE DEAF

The early national period in American history saw the formation of shared public attitudes about the meaning of deafness and sign language, as schools for deaf children were established, beginning with the AMERICAN SCHOOL FOR THE DEAF in 1817. Deaf people concentrated around these institutions and developed a common sign language (AMERICAN SIGN LANGUAGE, ASL). Public discourse at this time most often referred to uneducated deaf people as "unfortunates," largely because of their exclusion from religious understanding. EDUCATION, though, was believed to be capable of overcoming this shortcoming. Sign language in the early 1800s aroused little controversy. Some observers argued that it was superior to spoken language. An article in the *American Annals of Education* in 1834, for example, claimed

that the "signs and gestures" deaf people used were "far more expressive than words." Sign language was the primary communication method in all American schools for deaf children from 1817 until 1867, when the first permanent oral (speech and lipreading) schools, the New York Institution for the Improved Instruction of Deaf Mutes and the CLARKE SCHOOL FOR THE DEAF, opened, commencing a struggle between ORALISM and signing in the United States.

Deaf people's own ambivalent and sometimes contradictory attitudes toward their condition and their language became apparent in the early and middle 19th century. Deaf poet and artist JOHN CARLIN exemplified these conflicts. He argued that deaf people could assume nearly any profession if provided with educational opportunity, and yet he both lamented his deafness and believed that ASL was inferior to English. JOHN FLOURNOY, by contrast, insisted that deaf people should live apart in their own state. That way they would free themselves from hearing people's prejudice and gain complete self-determination, he argued. Writing in the *AMERICAN ANNALS OF THE DEAF* in 1856, Flournoy sounded like a modern disability rights activist, "The old cry about the incapacity of men's minds from physical disabilities, I think it were time, now in this intelligent age, to *explode*!" [Italics in original.] Yet Carlin and others ridiculed Flournoy and the idea that deaf people could govern their own state.

Whatever their ambivalence about deafness, many deaf Americans began to see themselves as an identifiable collectivity, a class apart, by the mid-19th century, and this perception grew stronger as the century progressed. Alumni from the American School for the Deaf in 1854 created the first organization of deaf Americans, the New England Gallaudet Association. Local and state ORGANIZATIONS followed. A convention of deaf people created the NATIONAL ASSOCIATION OF THE DEAF (NAD) in 1880. A founder stated in the convention proceedings that "deaf-mutes" were a "class by themselves."

DEFINING DEAFNESS

The term *deaf* was not yet in common usage. Indeed, the terminology employed to describe people who could not hear well enough to understand spoken language was contested in the 19th century, and it has undergone numerous modifications since. Hearing people tended to use the term DEAF AND DUMB to describe those who were deaf until the late 19th century, but deaf people more often labeled themselves "mutes" or sometimes "deaf-mutes." At that time in American history, the inability to speak articulately was not unequivocally associated with ignorance, mental incapacity, or inferiority, and deaf people were not ashamed of their lack of speech. The most venerated deaf leader in American history, LAURENT CLERC, cofounder of the American School for the Deaf, apparently never spoke vocally.

Mid-19th-century deaf leaders were acutely aware of the importance of defining their condition and their "class" in terms that were carefully drawn to unite deaf people, not to divide them. The constitution of the New England Gallaudet Association in 1854, for example, stated that "mutes" were welcome to join, as were people who were "only deaf." The latter sometimes referred to deaf people who did not know ASL, but more frequently it denoted people who could not understand speech themselves but who could use their voices to be understood by hearing people. These were most often people who became deaf after learning to speak or those who were able to hear enough to gain auditory cues to guide their own speech. The distinction between those deaf people who could speak and those who could not was important to hearing people, and it became more important in the late 19th century and beyond, but early deaf leaders showed that it was not important to them. The shared condition of deafness was all that mattered. Thus, the New England Gallaudet Association only excluded hearing people, not speaking deaf people, from membership.

STIGMATIZING DEAFNESS

Hearing people began to change radically the meaning of *deaf* in the late 19th century, adding greater stigmatization than was common before. Broad cultural movements were in part responsible for this. Educated Americans started to embrace Darwinian interpretations of cultural change and argue that sign language was primitive and had failed in competition with spoken language. To countenance its use by deaf people, therefore, would hold them back from realizing their full potential, according to this argument. Furthermore, nationalists worried that a country with multiple languages in common usage would be inherently weak, and nativists

> "Our needs are unique, and our goal is not to repair our physical system or 'restore' senses and skills we never had, but to impress on the world that we must be accepted as we are; that what is normal for the world may be abnormal for us . . . that through no fault of our own we may not read or write well, but we are capable of skills and strategies easily equal to the skills and strategies of others. . . . To be an integral part of the national deaf culture is a rich, rewarding experience, fulfilling in itself."
>
> —Bill White, in an essay to his deaf peers, in a community journal, in 1989

insisted that English was more evolved and therefore inherently superior to other languages, particularly those that were accompanied by gesture when spoken.

ALEXANDER GRAHAM BELL further stigmatized the meaning of "deaf" in 1883 when he argued in a paper to the American Academy of Sciences, later reprinted as *Memoir upon the Formation of Deaf Variety of the Human Race,* that deaf people's behavior represented a threat to America's well-being. Bell reasoned that as deaf people married each other in increasing numbers, they would be likely to pass on to their children genetic deafness. Through generations of intermarriage, Bell continued, the United States would produce a subclass of genetically deaf people. Bell was unequivocal in arguing that this would be a tragedy for the wider society. He claimed that deaf people contributed less to the common good and used more social resources than those who could hear. Bell's proposed solutions included forcing deaf children to use spoken English, banishing ASL from education, mixing hearing and deaf children in common schools, and taking strong efforts to discourage deaf people from marrying each other.

By 1900, the term *deaf* had therefore taken on new meaning in the United States. It no longer simply suggested "unfortunates," that is, people who did not have easy access to religious truth or education, as it had when the first school for deaf children had opened almost a century earlier. Neither did it mean, as deaf persons themselves increasingly saw it, a group of people who constituted a class apart because of their shared circumstances. Now it suggested people whose preferred language, ASL, was primitive and un-American; whose marriages were propagating a DEPENDENT class; and whose tendency to form their own cultural institutions—clubs, newspapers, advocacy organizations—was socially destructive and posed a threat to American cultural unity. *Deaf* now unambiguously denoted a pathology.

Deaf people generally reacted to this new interpretation by drawing together and resisting attempts to change the meaning of *deaf*. Local and national ORGANIZATIONS fought to maintain ASL as the primary language of instruction in deaf schools. They usually conceded that deaf people who could use spoken English and read it from the lips had advantages in hearing society, but they insisted that most deaf people could not do so and that using school time to teach speech and speech-reading interfered with deaf students' intellectual development and their acquisition of useful trade skills. The NAD filmed ASL masters to preserve the language for future generations, and deaf leaders reacted strongly to eugenicists' occasional suggestions that deaf people's right to marry might be curtailed or regulated in the interest of reducing the condition's incidence.

By the third decade of the 20th century, though, after years of cultural attack by nationalists and by language bigots, and after eugenicists had raised the specter of a dependent deaf class, deaf Americans themselves revealed new ambivalence and internal conflicts about their own interpretation of *deaf*. The NAD, for instance, in 1920 passed a resolution formally discouraging congenitally deaf people, that is, those who were born deaf and thus believed (erroneously) to be necessarily genetically deaf, from marrying each other. While deaf organizations, from deaf-only insurance companies such as the NATIONAL FRATERNAL SOCIETY OF THE DEAF to deaf-only sporting clubs became ever more popular, articles in deaf publications stressed how "NORMAL" deaf people were. Social news items in the deaf press celebrated marriages of deaf people to each other, whether the individuals were congenitally deaf or not, but similar notices also celebrated the birth of hearing children to deaf parents and emphasized the normality of deaf families and the success of the hearing progeny of deaf couples.

DEAFNESS AS A DISABILITY

The onset of the Great Depression in the 1930s brought forward another simmering conflict within the American deaf COMMUNITY. Since the late 19th century, deaf community leaders had insisted that deaf people should not be classified with Americans who were considered disabled or HANDICAPPED and therefore dependent on CHARITY. Deaf leaders were most often deafened later in life themselves and fluent in both written (and sometimes spoken) English and ASL. They usually held middle-class jobs, and they reasoned that deaf people would be most successful in American society if they were thought to be capable of competing with hearing people without being granted special favors. They had lobbied against rules that would exempt deaf people, along with disabled individuals, from vagrancy prosecution, for instance. Despite high deaf unemployment rates in the 1930s, reaching 40 to 50 percent, and despite overt discrimination against deaf workers by NEW DEAL federal relief programs, most deaf leadership opposed sections of the SOCIAL SECURITY ACT of 1935 that singled out disabled workers for special consideration. A few deaf leaders, especially Marcus Kenner of New York, argued that the federal government should create "mandated" EMPLOYMENT of deaf people, but most of Kenner's deaf cohorts refuted this position.

WORLD WAR II exasperated the tensions within the American deaf community over the meaning of *deaf*, even as it rapidly expanded job opportunities. Some deaf people argued that defining themselves as disabled would allow a valuable alliance with a larger social and political group to maintain wartime employment levels. Others clung to the traditional leadership view, which insisted that equating deafness with disability would lessen deaf people's independence and advance the perspective that deaf people were inferior to hearing people. Kenner and a few others believed

that the NAD should broaden its focus to include people who were hard of hearing, meaning those who could understand most speech with audition alone, and they argued that the NAD should align with disabled groups that were pushing for a federal commitment to preserve employment gains for disabled workers during the WAR. In the end, traditional deaf leaders were successful in maintaining the position that deaf Americans should de-emphasize their deafness, not seek any special consideration from the government, and not align themselves with disabled groups or accept the label "handicapped."

Numerous developments in the late 20th century further complicated the meaning of "deaf." Academic studies begun by Gallaudet College (later renamed GALLAUDET UNIVERSITY) researcher WILLIAM STOKOE and his colleagues concluded that ASL constituted a full-fledged human language. They argued that ASL was not poor English or a collection of gestures, as most hearing and many educated deaf people had believed, but a grammatical language separate from English and capable of expressing even the most complex thoughts clearly and unambiguously. Many advocates, deaf and hearing, interpreted this discovery to mean that deaf people should be seen primarily as an oppressed linguistic minority, like Spanish speakers, or an ethnic minority, like African-Americans, that had been discriminated against historically.

SOCIAL INCLUSION

The broader civil rights movements contributed to other changes within the community. Deaf community members confronted the impact of Jim Crow racism as RESIDENTIAL SCHOOLS and Gallaudet College desegregated. In 1964 the NAD officially admitted black members after several decades of white-only members; in the same year, female members were granted the right to vote. Greater attention to diversity within the community helped foster new organizations, such as DEAF WOMEN UNITED and NATIONAL BLACK DEAF ADVOCATES.

Theoretical models and advocacy strategies of the civil rights era also led some American deaf activists to frame their arguments for deaf rights within this context, and, in 1975, deaf college professor Tom Humphries coined a new word, *AUDISM*, indicating that the oppression of deaf people was similar to the racism that oppressed ethnic minorities. Other scholarly studies that presented a social interpretation of deafness contributed to the emergence of DEAF STUDIES as an interdisciplinary field.

Newly energized deaf leaders began pushing for communication accessibility of various kinds, even while disagreeing among themselves about the cultural meaning of deaf. In the 1960s a core group of oral deaf people, that is, individuals outside of the signing deaf community, developed teletypewriters, called TTYs, that could be used by deaf people to communicate over phone lines by means of written English. Members of the signing deaf community, on the other hand, took advantage of ASL's new linguistic status to argue that it should be used in mainstream media, particularly television, to better integrate deaf people into American culture. Various signed news programs began as a result, and a popular children's TELEVISION program regularly included a signing deaf character.

LEGISLATION

Changes in American law that most affected deaf people during this period ironically, however, were specifically targeted at persons who carried the label "disabled," not those considered linguistic or ethnic minorities. The VOCATIONAL REHABILITATION ACT of 1954, for example, expanded deaf Americans' opportunities and their access to federal and state resources in a number of significant ways, improving job training, paying for higher education, and extending "handicapped" social services to deaf people. The Education for All Handicapped Children Act of 1975, which was intended primarily to assure that disabled children received an appropriate education, also had the effect of decreasing the concentration of deaf children in SPECIAL schools and increasing their participation in regular public schools, where SIGN LANGUAGE INTERPRETERS were supposed to provide them equal ACCESS to education. Just as many deaf Americans were beginning to define themselves as an ASL-using linguistic minority, therefore, social and legal changes in the United States were weakening the institutions—the deaf residential schools—that were the prime agents for transmitting ASL from one generation to the next.

The rapidly fluctuating, unstable, and indeterminate meaning of *deaf* became even more obvious in the 1980s when the NAD, traditionally opposed to linkages between deafness and disability, supported passage of what became the AMERICANS WITH DISABILITIES ACT of 1990. Throughout most of the 20th century, deaf leaders had resisted overt cooperation with disability rights organizations or identification with supposedly dependent groups, fearing loss of their independence and challenges to their equality with hearing Americans. Now, though, they were ready to embrace the idea that deaf people were entitled to certain government programs or rights that were intended to assist disabled persons. They recognized that the ADA would extend deaf rights in employment, TRANSPORTATION, accommodations, and communication access, as it did. After the ADA's passage, federal support facilitated the creation of new technical devices and services to enhance deaf people's ability to communicate with each other and with hearing people. As if these changes were not sufficiently disruptive of any consistent understanding of deaf, new technologies challenged the core meaning of the term as the 20th century closed.

MEDICAL INTERVENTION

COCHLEAR IMPLANTS, devices that use microcomputers surgically placed in the head to bypass deaf individuals' dysfunctional cochlea, have raised completely new questions about the word *deaf*. On the one hand, the surgery required to implant these devices destroys any natural hearing an individual may have had. On the other hand, with the device implanted and functioning, some people who were previously audiologically deaf by any measure are able to function as though they were "hearing." That is, they can understand speech by audition alone, without visual cues. While not all individuals gain the same degree of auditory acuity from cochlear implants, as the devices improve, it is reasonable to expect that functional "deafness" will cease in persons with these devices. Perhaps, then, the term *deaf* will undergo yet another redefinition.

See also ACCESS AND ACCESSIBILITY; ACTIVISM AND ADVOCACY; ASSISTIVE TECHNOLOGY AND ADAPTIVE DEVICES; DEAF-BLIND; CHILDREN OF DEAF ADULTS; COMMUNICATION DEBATES; DEAF PRESIDENT NOW!; LANGUAGE AND TERMINOLOGY; LITTLE PAPER FAMILY; NATIONAL ASSOCIATION OF THE DEAF SIGN LANGUAGE FILM PRESERVATION CAMPAIGN.

John Vickrey Van Cleve

Further Reading:

Buchanan, Robert M. *Illusions of Equality: Deaf Americans in School and Factory, 1850–1950.* Washington, D.C.: Gallaudet University Press, 1999.

Burch, Susan. *Signs of Resistance: American Deaf Cultural History, 1900 to World War II.* New York: New York University Press, 2002.

Krentz, Christopher, ed. *A Mighty Change: An Anthology of Deaf American Writing, 1816–1864.* Washington, D.C.: Gallaudet University Press, 2000.

Lang, Harry G. "Genesis of a Community: The American Deaf Experience in the Seventeenth and Eighteenth Centuries." In *The Deaf History Reader,* edited by John Vickrey Van Cleve. Washington, D.C.: Gallaudet University Press, 2007.

Van Cleve, John Vickrey, and Barry A. Crouch. *A Place of Their Own: Creating the Deaf Community in America.* Washington, D.C.: Gallaudet University Press, 1989.

Deaf Abused Women's Network

The Deaf Abused Women's Network (DAWN) is a nonprofit ORGANIZATION serving the DEAF COMMUNITY to aid in the EDUCATION and the prevention of domestic VIOLENCE and sexual assault.

In 1995 Sandy McLennon, an assistant professor at GALLAUDET UNIVERSITY, envisioned building an advocacy group for abused women for the Washington, D.C., Deaf community. In 1998 McLennon and a group of five women received training in Seattle provided by the Abused Deaf Women's Advocacy Services (ADWAS), the first organization in the United States specifically established to address deafness and ABUSE. In 1999 DAWN was incorporated. It remains the only organization in the Washington, D.C., region that directly serves the Deaf community in the area of domestic violence.

Ralena McDevitt served as the first chair of the all-Deaf board of directors, the majority of whom are women. The organization promotes linguistic ACCESS through the use of AMERICAN SIGN LANGUAGE, as well as other cultural aspects of the Deaf community. DAWN has established networks throughout Washington, D.C., including HOSPITALS, police departments, and courts to ensure accessibility for their clients.

Location and demographics are integral to DAWN's successful outreach. Washington, D.C., represents one of the largest Deaf communities in America, and studies estimate that between 5,000 and 12,000 Deaf and HARD OF HEARING women in the Washington, D.C., metropolitan area will be abused during their lifetime. For various reasons, including social STIGMA, it is difficult to track actual incidents of violence against women in America. This issue is even more compounded with deaf women due to linguistic challenges and the insular nature of deaf communities. The desire to break down this language barrier as a way to empower more deaf women to report incidents of ABUSE especially motivated DAWN's creation.

The organization offers community workshops, outreach programs, and survivor support groups for Deaf women. Through these resources, DAWN's mission is to raise awareness within the Deaf community about domestic violence and sexual assault. Attempting to reach women of all ages, DAWN recruits college students for internships and advocacy work.

Through education, advocacy, and volunteer services, this emerging organization promotes the EMPOWERMENT of Deaf women. DAWN is a part of a larger movement of organizations that seek to address a pervasive but often overlooked aspect of the lives of women who are deaf and/or disabled. These initiatives not only provide resources for women who have been abused but also bolster the communities of Deaf and disabled women through EMPLOYMENT, volunteer opportunities, and leadership roles within the organization.

See also ACTIVISM AND ADVOCACY; AMERICAN SIGN LANGUAGE.

Lindsey Patterson

Further Reading:
DAWN Subject File. Washington, D.C., Gallaudet University Archives. Deaf Abused Women's Network Web site. URL: www.deafdawn.org.

deaf and dumb

Since ancient times, people have employed variations of the term *deaf and dumb* to refer to profoundly DEAF individuals. Its changing meaning over time demonstrates the power of language as well as contested notions of IDENTITY.

Before the 1600s most people assumed that human vocal chords and auditory organs were linked in ways that resulted in deaf people being incapable of producing articulate speech. Consequently, the terms *mute* and *dumb* were used interchangeably to describe the inability to speak. In 1591 German physician Salomon Alberti published *Discourse on Deafness and Speechlessness,* in which he proved that hearing and speech were separate functions. Over the next century, European deaf educators such as Samuel Heineke applied this knowledge as they began to train deaf people in ORALISM (lipreading and speech). Despite these scientific and educational changes, the term *deaf and dumb* continued to be the primary label used in Europe and America for roughly 200 years.

Early American schools for the deaf commonly incorporated the term *deaf and dumb* in their titles, such as the New York Institution for Instruction of the Deaf and Dumb (1817), the Ohio Institution for the Deaf and Dumb (1829), and the Nebraska Institute for the Deaf and Dumb (1869). The premier professional journal of the deaf educators was called the *American Annals of the Deaf and Dumb* from its origin in 1847 until 1886, when it assumed the title *AMERICAN ANNALS OF THE DEAF.* Throughout the 19th century, many American deaf people referred to themselves by these terms, interchanging "deaf and dumb" with "deaf-mute." Some deaf publications and ORGANIZATIONS also embraced the term *mute,* including the *DEAF MUTES' JOURNAL* and the *Deaf Mute's Companion.* Throughout this period, the label referred especially to deaf and HARD OF HEARING people who primarily used sign language communication, but sometimes, as with the New York–based oral club the *Deaf-Mutes Union League,* it marked members' deafness rather than language use.

The meaning of *dumb* began to change significantly in the late 19th and early 20th centuries. A primary factor was the rise of EUGENICS (the pseudoscience that evaluated humans, plants, and animals based on notions of superior and inferior "stock"). As scholars such as Lennard Davis and Douglas Baynton have shown, eugenic ideas emphasized deafness as a "defect" and viewed deaf people as inherently inferior; casting all "deviant" populations together, eugenicists, through classifications and policies, increasingly linked deaf people with others who had—or appeared to have—cognitive disabilities (see COGNITIVE AND INTELLECTUAL DISABILITY). By the 1920s this "menace of the FEEBLEMINDED," eugenicists explained, posed the greatest threat to America, sparking widespread concern over the intellectual caliber of all citizens. At the same time, attacks on deaf culture and specifically on sign language both reflected and reinforced the notion that spoken English was a superior form of language and that sign language was base and animalistic. These factors in part contributed to the new meaning of *dumb* as synonymous with "stupid" or "of low intelligence." Deaf people clearly distinguished the two meanings of "dumb" through the signs they used. The sign for dumb/mute is represented with a closed fist over the mouth; the sign for dumb/stupid shares the hand shape of a closed fist but is placed on the forehead, implying limited intellectual capacities. For most hearing people, however, the distinctions have been less obvious.

Responding to the negative connotations of the label, deaf culture advocates by the early 20th century aligned with oral advocates to challenge the stigmatized label. For example, in 1916 the leading oralist publication, *The Volta Review,* actively denounced the use of "deaf and dumb," claiming that it perpetuated a misconception that deaf people were unable to vocalize and erroneously demeaned them to the status of "brutes" or "animals." Likewise, the NATIONAL ASSOCIATION OF THE DEAF created committees on nomenclature that publicly rejected the terms, advocating "deaf" and "hard of hearing" as more appropriate labels. In the decades before WORLD WAR II, leaders at the Conference of Executives of American Schools for the Deaf also passed resolutions urging institutions and professionals, as well as mainstream society to cease using either deaf-mute or deaf and dumb.

With the rise of activist movements, including deaf and disability civil rights, the term *deaf and dumb* shifted meaning again, and it is commonly recognized today as a derogatory and outdated term. Still, the informal and continued references to deaf and dumb in media and elsewhere perpetuates a degrading STEREOTYPE of deaf people and highlights the power that LANGUAGE AND TERMINOLOGY play in our understanding of communities and individuals.

Sylvie Soulier

Further Reading:

Baynton, Douglas. *Forbidden Signs: American Culture and the Campaign against Sign Language.* Chicago: University of Chicago Press, 1998.

Burch, Susan. *Signs of Resistance: American Deaf Cultural History, 1900 to World War II.* New York: New York University Press, 2002.

Davis, Leonard. *Enforcing Normalcy: Disability, Deafness and the Body.* New York: Verso, 1995.

Gannon, Jack R. *Deaf Heritage: A Narrative History of Deaf America.* Silver Spring, Md.: National Association of the Deaf, 1981.

Van Cleve, John Vickrey. *Genetics, Disability and Deafness.* Washington, D.C.: Gallaudet University Press, 2004.

deaf-blind

The word *deaf-blind* describes people who have all types and degrees of both vision and hearing loss. One person may be born with a vision and hearing loss, or lose these senses early in life. Another person may be born DEAF or HARD OF HEARING, and lose his vision later. Yet another may be born BLIND or visually IMPAIRED, and experience a hearing loss in later years. Major issues, including access to information, community ACCESS, EDUCATION, citizenship, and advocacy, define the history of this group of Americans.

Although people born deaf-blind certainly lived in the United States prior to the 19th century we know little about them, primarily due to the widespread belief that they lacked both intellect and soul and thus were ineducable in any way, and because of the resulting exclusion of them from FAMILY, social, and public life. Institutional histories also tend to exclude deaf-blind people. In the early 19th century, reformers helped establish schools for deaf students and blind students, but for various reasons no formal programs were established for those who experienced both conditions. Consequently, deaf-blind individuals followed adapted courses at deaf or blind schools.

The first known example of a deaf-blind person to receive instruction in the United States was JULIA BRACE (1807–84), who entered the American Asylum for the Deaf in Hartford, Connecticut (see AMERICAN SCHOOL FOR THE DEAF), in 1825 and remained at the institution for over 30 years. Instructed using sign language, Brace, by most accounts, made limited progress in her education. Her ability to communicate facilely with others through signs demonstrated the capacity for deaf-blind people to learn, but neither the school nor members of the broader society drew much attention to her example.

In contrast, LAURA BRIDGMAN (1829–89) became an iconic figure in the 19th century, and her international fame reflects important themes in American society at that time. Bridgman had lost her hearing and vision at age two from scarlet fever. She began attending PERKINS SCHOOL FOR THE BLIND in Boston, Massachusetts, when she was eight. There, she learned to read by using raised letters, and she communicated through FINGERSPELLING. By age 12 she was writing letters and correspondence to family and friends. However, people often had mixed reactions upon meeting or hearing about Bridgman. Some saw her as an angel, unaffected by what was going on around her because of her limited knowledge of her environment. Others saw her as strange because of her odd behavior and mannerisms, which included "excessive" facial expressions and an exceptional ability to glean information through touch. Her teachers trained her to be well-behaved, obedient, and pleasant, but they regarded her as very different from most people, and she was not encouraged to be like others. Scholars such as Elizabeth Gitter and

Ernest Freeburg have argued that larger contests over religious beliefs, GENDER expectations, attitudes toward people with disabilities, and pedagogical experiments shaped Bridgman's education and her public REPRESENTATION.

In similar ways, Bridgman's "successor" as a noted individual who was deaf and blind in the 20th century, HELEN KELLER, represented emerging trends in American society. She, like Bridgman, lost her hearing and vision at an early age, 19 months. However, at age six she acquired a full-time teacher, ANNE SULLIVAN MACY, who taught her for many years. Like other "modern women" of the time, Keller attended college, graduating from Radcliffe College in 1904; she was the first deaf-blind person to obtain a bachelor's degree. An active reformer in the Progressive Era, she traveled around the world and advocated on the behalf of blind, visually impaired, and deaf-blind people. Keller achieved a degree of independence that Laura Bridgman never had. She accomplished her many activities because Sullivan and other teachers were with her almost all the time. Yet gender and disability discrimination still constrained her choices; for example, her friends and family discouraged her from marrying and having children.

The legal, social, and technological advances advocated by the DISABILITY RIGHTS MOVEMENT also gave people with combined vision and hearing loss greater access to education and EMPLOYMENT. In 1967 Congress funded the Helen Keller National Center for Deaf-Blind Youth and Adults (HKNC), a national rehabilitation center for people with both vision and hearing loss. The establishment of HKNC afforded deaf-blind people the opportunity to receive training in communication, independent living, and employment-related skills that they could use in their home communities. The establishment of laws such as PL 94-142 (later named the INDIVIDUALS WITH DISABILITIES EDUCATION ACT), the

Rehabilitation Act of 1973 (see VOCATIONAL REHABILITATION ACT), and the 1990 AMERICANS WITH DISABILITIES ACT (ADA) gave people with disabilities greater opportunities for access to education and employment. CHILDREN with dual vision and hearing loss also could be educated with their peers in a mainstream setting with supports such as interpreters, individual instruction, specially trained resource teachers, and assistive devices, in addition to being taught at schools for the deaf or the blind. The Rehabilitation Act and the ADA also gave deaf-blind people greater access to postsecondary education and employment.

Reflecting these changes, people in the deaf-blind COMMUNITY advocated for themselves. In 1979 deaf-blind activists renamed the American League for the Deaf-Blind, originally founded in 1937, the AMERICAN ASSOCIATION OF THE DEAF-BLIND (AADB) after several prior name changes. The ORGANIZATION shifted from service-oriented support to a community-based EMPOWERMENT model. Its new initiatives included efforts to promote independence and full inclusions of all deaf-blind people. At first, the AADB was primarily run by a volunteer board of directors, but, as part of an effort to professionalize the organization, the board of directors in 1984 hired a paid part-time bookkeeper, who later became a full-time program manager. In 2002 Jamie Pope, who is hard of hearing and has low vision, was hired as the first executive director. Pope remains as executive director today.

Similar to other disability organizations, AADB increasingly has become a national advocacy organization rather than mainly a social and recreational organization. To note one example, AADB is collaborating with organizations such as the REGISTRY OF INTERPRETERS FOR THE DEAF and the National Consortium of Interpreter Education Centers to foster specialized training and to standardize professional guidelines for interpreters who may work with this community. Such efforts arose in response to the deaf-blind community's need for greater access to interpreting and other services.

In recent decades, deaf-blind people have taken increasingly active public roles in their communities, starting from at least the late 1950s, when they began establishing their own deaf-blind associations and clubs. They continue to run local and state deaf-blind associations. They also serve on boards and commissions, and they advocate for their needs; for example, most state commissions for the deaf and hard of hearing, or telecommunications relay services, have at least one deaf-blind person on their advisory councils to give advice and input on the needs of the deaf-blind population.

More and more deaf-blind people have access to the INTERNET and e-mail, which gives them an opportunity to connect with each other and receive information from around the world. They are also able to use this information and their

> *"To survive in this world deaf-blind people have had to depend heavily on hearing and sighted people. . . . We no longer need to say that we are dependent on other people to live independently. Instead we can decide what we need and then look for the services to meet those needs. We are no longer 'clients.' We are 'consumers' and we need to shop around for the best services. By being smart 'consumers' we can live as independently as anyone else in the world."*
>
> —Lynette Boyer, describing in 1992 the deaf-blind community in her home state of Minnesota

connections to become more involved in their communities, and to advocate for needed and improved services.

One example of the politicization of the community is evidenced by a 2006 sit-in by a group of deaf and deaf-blind people at a doctor's office in northeast Ohio because the doctor did not provide SIGN LANGUAGE INTERPRETERS. This sit-in was successful as the office eventually provided sign language interpreters on a regular basis to consumers who needed them. In addition, the group provided training to other medical professionals and gave them information about sign language interpreting agencies the professionals could use to procure interpreters.

Examples from mainstream media reflect the changing status of deaf-blind Americans. For example, the film THE MIRACLE WORKER (1962) reinforced the image of deaf-blind people such as Helen Keller as eternally childlike; few media examples before the 1970s depicted adults who were deaf-blind or who were independent and happy. The rise of disability rights ACTIVISM, however, has contributed to new REPRESENTATIONS of deaf-blind people. In 1989, for example, Barbara Walters interviewed a deaf-blind couple, Michelle and Robert Smithdas, on the TELEVISION program 20/20. The episode focused on their daily lives: how they communicated with each other and other people; how they cooked, shopped, and cleaned; and how they traveled and accomplished everyday activities. It acknowledged their educational and career successes as well.

Exact statistics of deaf-blind people are unknown at present. However, the National Child Count of the National Consortium on Deaf-Blindness (a federally funded program providing information and training on children and youth who are deaf-blind) maintains a national Deaf-Blind Child Count. The National Deaf-Blind Child Count estimates that there are around 10,000 children in the United States with dual vision and hearing loss. Based on this prevalence data, we can estimate that around 40,000 to 70,000 deaf-blind people live in the United States today. Thousands more experience a vision and hearing loss, but they may not identify themselves as "deaf-blind."

Despite the advances in education and employment for people who are deaf-blind, challenges still remain today. In one example, people in the deaf-blind community are advocating for a national network of specially trained people known as support service providers (SSPs), who can provide environmental information to deaf-blind people and assist with such things as transportation and shopping so that deaf-blind people can receive more access to their communities. Currently, 13 SSP programs exist in the United States; however, they are not available in every state, and more trained support service providers are needed.

As scholars are only recently beginning to document, the changing representations of deaf-blind people over the course of American history reinforces the social interpretation of disability. Religious, political, economic, cultural, and social features have shaped this minority community and the way others have perceived them. Particularly in the latter 20th century, disability advocacy efforts in general and deaf-blind activism in particular have resulted in legal, educational, and employment reforms to promote fuller integration of marginalized people. Although considerable progress is evidenced by these changes, social barriers remain as many Americans have yet to realize the capabilities of people with combined vision and hearing loss. However, people with dual vision and hearing loss are becoming more and more involved in their mainstream communities. Thus, they are demonstrating to the world at large that they have the same skills, interests, and capabilities as everyone else.

See also ACCESS AND ACCESSIBILITY; MAINSTREAMING; PROTEST; RESIDENTIAL SCHOOLS; SELF-ADVOCATES AND SELF-ADVOCACY.

Elizabeth T. Spiers

Further Reading:

American Association of the Deaf-Blind Web site. URL: www.aadb.org.

Freeberg, Ernest. *Laura Bridgman: First Deaf and Blind Person to Learn Language.* Boston: Harvard University Press, 2001.

Gitter, Elisabeth. *An Imprisoned Guest.* New York: Farrar, Strauss & Giroux, 2001.

Keller, Helen. *The Story of My Life.* Mineola, N.Y.: Dover Press, 1903.

Smith, Theresa B. *Guidelines for Working and Socializing with Deaf-Blind People.* Burtonsville, Md.: Sign Media Press, 2002.

The Story of My Life by Helen Keller (1903)

In 1902 22-year-old Radcliffe College student Helen Keller began writing her autobiography. In it, the famous deaf-blind woman describes how her "whole body is alive to the conditions about [her]." This memoir is important for understanding Keller's sense of self as well as the ways she carefully crafted her public persona. For example, in these passages Keller details her "normal" interests in nature and museums, the domestic arts, and her affection for friends and her bull terrier, Phiz; at the same time her writings also clearly showcase her exceptional intelligence and literary skills, challenging those who questioned her capacities.

The Story of My Life by Helen Keller
1903

People who think that all sensations reach us through the eye and the ear have expressed surprise that I should notice any difference, except possibly the absence of pavements, between walking in city streets and in country roads. They forget that my whole body is alive to the conditions about me. The rumble and roar of the city smite the nerves of my face, and I feel the ceaseless tramp of an unseen multitude, and the dissonant tumult frets my spirit. The grinding of heavy wagons on hard pavements and the monotonous clangour of machinery are all the more torturing to the nerves if one's attention is not diverted by the panorama that is always present in the noisy streets to people who can see.

In the country one sees only Nature's fair works, and one's soul is not saddened by the cruel struggle for mere existence that goes on in the crowded city. Several times I have visited the narrow, dirty streets where the poor live, and I grow hot and indignant to think that good people should be content to live in fine houses and become strong and beautiful, while others are condemned to live in hideous, sunless tenements and grow ugly, withered and cringing. The children who crowd these grimy alleys, half-clad and underfed, shrink away from your outstretched hand as if from a blow. Dear little creatures, they crouch in my heart and haunt me with a constant sense of pain. There are men and women, too, all gnarled and bent out of shape. I have felt their hard, rough hands and realized what an endless struggle their existence must be—no more than a series of scrimmages, thwarted attempts to do something. Their life seems an immense disparity between effort and opportunity. The sun and the air are God's free gifts to all we say; but are they so? In yonder city's dingy alleys the sun shines not, and the air is foul. Oh, man, how dost thou forget and obstruct thy brother man, and say, "Give us this day our daily bread," when he has none! Oh, would that men would leave the city, its splendour and its tumult and its gold, and return to wood and field and simple, honest living! Then would their children grow stately as noble trees, and their thoughts sweet and pure as wayside flowers. It is impossible not to think of all this when I return to the country after a year of work in town.

What a joy it is to feel the soft, springy earth under my feet once more, to follow grassy roads that lead to ferny brooks where I can bathe my fingers in a cataract of rippling notes, or to clamber over a stone wall into green fields that tumble and roll and climb in riotous gladness!

Next to a leisurely walk I enjoy a "spin" on my tandem bicycle. It is splendid to feel the wind blowing in my face and the springy motion of my iron steed. The rapid rush through the air gives me a delicious sense of strength and buoyancy, and the exercise makes my pulses dance and my heart sing.

Whenever it is possible, my dog accompanies me on a walk or ride or sail. I have had many dog friends—huge mastiffs, soft-eyed spaniels, wood-wise setters and honest, homely bull terriers. At present the lord of my affections is one of these bull terriers. He has a long pedigree, a crooked tail and the drollest "phiz" in dogdom. My dog friends seem to understand my limitations, and always keep close beside me when I am alone. I love their affectionate ways and the eloquent wag of their tails.

When a rainy day keeps me indoors, I amuse myself after the manner of other girls. I like to knit and crochet; I read in the happy-go-lucky way I love, here and there a line; or perhaps I play a game or two of checkers or chess with a friend. I have a special board on which I play these games. The squares are cut out, so that the men stand in them firmly. The black checkers are flat and the white ones curved on top. Each checker has a hole in the middle in which a brass knob can be placed to distinguish the king from the commons. The chessmen are of two sizes, the white larger than the black, so that I have no trouble in following my opponent's maneuvers by moving my hands lightly over the board after a play. The jar made by shifting the men from one hole to another tells me when it is my turn.

If I happen to be all alone and in an idle mood, I play a game of solitaire, of which I am very fond. I use playing cards marked in the upper right-hand corner with braille symbols which indicate the value of the card.

If there are children around, nothing pleases me so much as to frolic with them. I find even the smallest child excellent company, and I am glad to say that children usually like me. They lead me about and show me the things they are interested in. Of course the little ones cannot spell on their fingers; but I manage to read their lips. If I do not succeed they resort to dumb show. Sometimes I make a mistake and do the wrong thing. A burst of childish laughter greets my blunder, and the pantomime begins all over again. I often tell them stories or teach them a game, and the wingéd hours depart and leave us good and happy.

Museums and art stores are also sources of pleasure and inspiration. Doubtless it will seem strange to many that the hand unaided by sight can feel action, sentiment, beauty in the cold marble; and yet it is true that I derive genuine pleasure from touching great works of art. As my finger tips trace line and curve, they discover the thought and emotion which the artist has portrayed. I can feel in the faces of gods and heroes hate, courage and love, just as I can detect them in living faces I am permitted to touch. I feel in Diana's posture the grace and freedom of the forest and the spirit that tames the mountain lion and subdues the fiercest passions. My soul delights in the repose and gracious curves of the Venus; and in Barré's bronzes the secrets of the jungle are revealed to me.

Source: Helen Keller. *The Story of My Life*. New York: Doubleday & Co., 1903. Available online. URL: http://www.afb.org/MyLife/book.asp?ch=HK-intro. Accessed June 20, 2008.

Deaflympics

Sport historically has been a vital feature in America's DEAF cultural world, and the development of international deaf games highlights important networks and sense of COMMUNITY. The Deaflympics, founded in 1924 by two notable Deaf SPORTS leaders, Eugène Rubens-Alcais of France and Antoine Dresse of Belgium, helped establish a new governing body called the Comité International des Sports Silencieux (known in English as the International Committee of Sports for the Deaf, or ICSD). At that time the ICSD sought to establish mutual cooperation among deaf sports federations and to govern the newly established International Silent Games, which would be held every four years. The name of these international games changed in 2001 to Deaflympics.

From its origin, the ICSD allowed only deaf people to administer the ORGANIZATION and participate in its sporting events, demonstrating a commitment to self-determination and autonomy. Robey Burns spearheaded the U.S. membership campaign to the ICSD in 1935. Since that time, the American deaf COMMUNITY has hosted two summer Deaflympics (in Washington, D.C., in 1965 and in Los Angeles in 1985) and two winter games (in Lake Placid, N.Y., in 1975 and in Salt Lake City in 2007). The first American president of Deaflympics was Jerald Jordan, who was elected in 1971.

The summer games include 20 different SPORTS, ranging from badminton to wrestling, and they feature more than 2,500 athletes from over 75 countries. The winter games are significantly smaller, with four sports: alpine skiing, cross-country skiing, snowboarding, and ice hockey (and curling soon to be added). Some 300 athletes participate from more than 20 countries. The only sport that is on the Deaflympics program that the Olympics do not have is the sport of orienteering.

The International Olympic Committee (IOC) has recognized ICSD since 1951, acknowledging its high standard of administration and sports activities. In May 1955 the IOC announced its unanimous recognition of the ICSD as an "International Federation with Olympic standing." However, the ICSD was not granted permission to use the term "Olympic" or the IOC's five-ring emblems. The ICSD logo, designed in 2003 by Ralph Fernandez, embodies fundamental elements: sign language, deaf and international cultures, unity, and continuity. The hand shapes for "ok," "good," and "great" overlap each other in a circle, echoing the original sign deaf people used for "Deaflympics." Together, these hand shapes also represent the sign for "united." The center of the logo symbolizes the iris of the eye, which reflects deaf peoples' use of signed communication, a visual language.

Currently, there are six voting members of the Executive Committee, and four nonvoting representatives from the regions within the ICSD structure: Africa, the Americas, Asia-Pacific, and Europe. There are approximately 95 full members, which consist of national deaf sports federations from all over the world. Associate membership is limited to deaf international single-sport governing bodies. As of 2009 there are approximately 7 million deaf athletes participating in different levels of sport competitions in over 35 different sports.

Many Deaf Americans historically have not identified with other disability groups or with able-bodied competitors. The desire to be among other deaf people and to celebrate their cultural connections and athletic abilities strongly influences how community members define themselves. The commitment to Deaflympics also shows that deaf Americans share a sense of kinship that transcends national boundaries.

Donalda Ammons

Further Reading:

Ammons, Donalda. "Unique Identity of the World Games for the Deaf." *Palaestra* 6, no. 2 (Winter/Spring 1990): 40–43.

Fosshaug, Siv. "Deaf Sports: An Empowerment Perspective." *WFD News* 17, No. 2 (December 2004): 5–6.

Lovett, John M., Jordan Eickman, and Terry Giansanti. *CISS 2001: A Review*. West Yorkshire, England: Red Lizard Limited, 2004.

Stewart, David. *Deaf Sport: The Impact of Sports within the Deaf Community*. Washington, D.C.: Gallaudet University Press, 1991.

Deaf Mosaic

Deaf Mosaic was an Emmy Award–winning nationally broadcast TELEVISION series in the 1980s and 1990s that portrayed DEAF people from various walks of life as individuals with interesting stories to tell, rather than as people with a disability that prevented them from living fulfilling, successful lives.

The series, produced by the television department at GALLAUDET UNIVERSITY in Washington, D.C., followed the increasing prominence of deaf people in creative public venues such as LINDA BOVE, who had a recurring role on PBS's *Sesame Street* from 1971 to 2003, and PHYLLIS FRELICH, who won the 1980 Tony Award for her role in the Broadway play *CHILDREN OF A LESSER GOD*.

Deaf Mosaic premiered on WETA, the Washington, D.C., public television station in 1985. The program featured Gilbert C. Eastman, a deaf professor from Gallaudet University's THEATER department and one of the founding members of the NATIONAL THEATRE OF THE DEAF as its genial host. In 1988 Mary Lou Novitsky, a deaf production specialist in the university's television department, joined the program as co-host. Novitsky eventually became one of the producers of the series.

Although not the first, *Deaf Mosaic* remains the longest running national series hosted by deaf individuals. The program, showcasing deaf people who were successful, contributing members of society, received considerable attention from both the Deaf community and mainstream society. During its 10-year run, the half-hour magazine format series, at various times, was shown on as many as 100 PBS stations across the United States. The Discovery Channel provided additional distribution beginning in the summer of 1985.

Deaf Mosaic's novel approach took advantage of technology and used AMERICAN SIGN LANGUAGE (ASL), voice-overs, and open captioning to produce a series covering a wide range of stories, which attracted deaf as well as hearing viewers. Many deaf people shared their video copies of the programs with their hearing families, friends, and coworkers, knowing that *Deaf Mosaic* was a positive way for hearing people to learn about signing deaf people, their culture, and way of life.

The episodes featured deaf people engaged in traditional and nontraditional professions, as well as their hobbies, national and international deaf events, politics, and RELIGION. Timely topics, such as the International DEAFLYMPICS, deaf people with HIV, the World Federation of the Deaf Conference, and the 1988 DEAF PRESIDENT NOW! protest at Gallaudet University were covered.

Deaf Mosaic, which received 18 regional Emmy Awards and numerous CINE Golden Eagles and Telly awards, ceased production in 1995 due to a lack of funding. There have been no similar programs in the United States since then.

See also COMMUNITY; EMPOWERMENT; REPRESENTATION.

Jane Norman

Further Reading:

Berke, Jamie. "Deaf Culture—Television Programming for the Deaf." URL: http://deafness.about.com/cs/culturefeatures3/a/tvfordeaf.htm?p=1.

Deaf Mosaic. Available online. URL: http://videolibrary.gallaudet.edu.

deaf-mute   See DEAF; DEAF AND DUMB; LANGUAGE AND TERMINOLOGY.

Deaf Mute's Journal *(New York Journal of the Deaf)*

The *Deaf Mute's Journal* played a vital role in the history of the American DEAF community. Used as a means to celebrate Deaf IDENTITY and promote cultural unity, it was the first Deaf newspaper with statewide subscriptions.

Deaf author Henry C. Rider created the original "Deaf Mute's Journal" in 1872 as a column in Henry Humphries's mainstream New York newspaper, the *Mexico Independent*. Due to the popularity of the column, editors allowed Rider to expand the piece to a full page. In 1874 Rider began his own printing business, enabling him to produce the *Deaf Mute's Journal* as an independent newspaper. This publication became the first and only weekly distributed newspaper by and for the Deaf at the time.

The New York School for the Deaf acquired publication of the *Deaf Mute's Journal* in 1878. Edwin A. Hodgson, the printing instructor at the New York School for the Deaf, became the new editor. Hodgson oversaw the *Deaf Mute's Journal* for 53 years, until his retirement in 1931.

For several reasons, newspapers such as the *Deaf Mute's Journal* were especially popular in the 19th and early 20th centuries. Vocational teachers used these publications to train students in printing, a secure and popular trade for many graduates. Deaf students and alumni in turn supported these newspapers as a means of communication across the nation in the decades before telecommunication devices and other accessible technologies were developed. Many of the columns provided detailed accounts of social events, from formal occasions such as balls to individual visits between deaf friends. Other essays summarized educational lectures delivered at various deaf schools or moral tales and brief history lessons. These regular features sought to enhance deaf people's general academic and civic knowledge. The *Deaf Mute's Journal* also focused on pressing educational and EMPLOYMENT issues while battling negative STEREOTYPES associated with the Deaf COMMUNITY. Impressed by the positive depiction of deaf people in the *Deaf Mute's Journal*, the NATIONAL ASSOCIATION OF THE DEAF, for example, voted in 1910 to name the *Deaf Mute's Journal* as its official publication.

In 1931 Dr. Thomas Francis Fox took over the responsibility of editing the *Deaf Mute's Journal*. When the New York School for the Deaf moved to White Plains in 1939 the *Deaf Mute's Journal* was renamed the *New York Journal of the Deaf*. It is likely that the growing stigma of the term "mute" in this period helped motivate the new name. The *New York Journal of the Deaf* was published until 1951.

In addition to fostering networks among Deaf Americans, the *Deaf Mute's Journal* and its successor promoted a sense of unity and pride among deaf people at a time when they had limited means to receive news and information. It had a significant impact on the American Deaf community, preserving the legacy of Deaf Americans and providing scholars and subsequent generations of community members with a window into the thoughts and aspirations of deaf people in the first part of the 20th century.

See also LITTLE PAPER FAMILY; PRINT MEDIA; VOCATIONAL TRAINING.

Sylvie Soulier

Further Reading:

Burch, Susan. *Signs of Resistance: American Deaf Cultural History, 1900 to World War II*. New York: New York University Press, 2002.

Van Cleve, John Vickrey, and Barry A. Crouch. *A Place of Their Own: Creating the Deaf Community in America*. Washington, D.C.: Gallaudet University Press, 1989.

Deaf President Now!

Deaf President Now! (DPN) is one of the most important civil rights PROTESTS in Deaf and disability history. DPN started with the selection of a new president at GALLAUDET UNIVERSITY, the world's only liberal arts university created specifically to serve DEAF and HARD OF HEARING students. By 1988 Gallaudet had been in existence for 124 years, and, of the six presidents who had served since 1864, none were deaf. In March of that year protesters at the Washington, D.C., institution successfully challenged a decision by the university's board of trustees to appoint a hearing person to lead the school. After a week of activities that garnered unprecedented media attention, Elisabeth A. Zinser, a hearing woman who had been selected as the university's seventh president resigned, and a deaf man, I. KING JORDAN, was selected as Gallaudet's eighth president.

DPN was not completely unexpected or spontaneous. A deaf administrator at the university had applied unsuccessfully for the presidency after Edward C. Merrill retired in 1982, and, by the mid-1980s, large numbers of deaf people, including many with advanced graduate degrees, had entered positions of leadership in schools, colleges, and businesses. Within Gallaudet University, the expectations of COMMU-NITY members had risen, and broad disability rights activism, which focused on empowering people with disabilities, had emerged as an important social movement during the quarter century preceding DPN.

Soon after Gallaudet's president Jerry C. Lee announced his resignation in August 1987, a variety of activities in support of a deaf president began. Advocacy campaigns on and off campus, led by established deaf leaders such as Alan B. Crammatte, Gary Olsen, and Astrid Goodstein, drew on tactics employed by pioneers of the civil rights movement as they developed their own goals and strategies. These activities included meetings, lobbying, letter writing, and media campaigns. Other advocacy efforts took place during the last few months of 1987 and well into 1988, and many of them were initiated by a group of six young deaf alumni who called themselves the "Ducks": Steve Hlibok, Mike O'Donnell, Jeff Rosen, Paul Singleton, James Tucker, and Fred Weiner. These emerging leaders would play a central role in the protest activities on Gallaudet's campus.

While various groups of activists organized, the university's board of trustees established a formal 11-member search committee in September 1987. Five of the members of this committee, including the chair and the vice chair, were deaf. By the end of the search, 67 people had applied for the position; nine of the candidates were deaf.

On March 1, 1988, a few days before the board selected a new president, some of those who had been working for months to promote a deaf president held an on-campus rally to encourage more people, including students, to become involved. A flyer prepared for this rally compared the effort at Gallaudet with struggles of other minority groups, including women and African Americans, and thus linked what was happening at the university to the wider civil rights movement.

A few days after the rally, three finalists were interviewed by the board of trustees. Two candidates were deaf administrators: the superintendent of the Louisiana School for the Deaf, Harvey Corson, and the dean of Gallaudet's College of Arts and Sciences, I. King Jordan; the third candidate was the hearing vice chancellor of the University of North Carolina, Greensboro, Elisabeth Zinser. After these interviews were completed, the board announced on Sunday, March 6, that they had selected Zinser as the new president of the university.

Many people arrived on campus in anticipation of the board's decision, and most of them expected the decision to be announced by a representative from the board or the administration. Instead, people learned that Zinser had been selected by reading flyers announcing her selection, and many were outraged. After discussing the implications of this news, people stormed out of the main entrance and congregated on a busy street in front of the campus. Hundreds

Holding a banner that reads "we still have a dream," these protesters in the 1988 Deaf President Now! Movement visibly linked their efforts to gain a deaf leader for Gallaudet University with earlier civil rights movements.   *(Gallaudet University Archives)*

of angry protesters subsequently flocked to the hotel where the board was staying to demand an explanation from the board's chairperson. The confrontation at the hotel was not productive, and agitated protesters returned to campus for the beginning of a week-long series of meetings, rallies, and marches.

During the week of the protest, classes were not held, other normal university business was suspended, and an ad hoc DPN Council was formed in order to bring some structure to the protest. As the week went on, Gallaudet's faculty and staff voted overwhelmingly to support the goals of the protest, thousands of dollars in donations were collected, and many people began to realize that DPN was more than just a local protest. It had clearly become an important civil rights movement that would have ramifications far beyond Washington, D.C.

On Friday, March 11, Elisabeth Zinser came to accept this interpretation as well and announced her resignation. The board soon met again and selected I. King Jordan as Gallaudet's president. Philip W. Bravin was selected as the first deaf chairperson of the university's board of trustees after Jane Bassett Spilman, the previous chairperson, resigned.

There were a number of reasons why DPN was successful. The association of DPN with previous civil rights struggles played an important role, as did the strong support of many faculty, staff, students, alumni, others in the deaf community (including SIGN LANGUAGE INTERPRETERS), local community groups, legislators, and representatives of the mass media. The goals of the protest were timely, persuasive, and clearly defined; in addition, articulate, charismatic student leaders, particularly Bridgetta Bourne, Jerry Covell, Greg Hlibok, and Tim Rarus, emerged to communicate these goals to the nation.

DPN represents a historic example of self-advocacy as people from within the Deaf world led the challenge to the board's decision. In addition, DPN both reflected some of the goals of the broader DISABILITY RIGHTS MOVEMENT and encouraged other disability rights activists to seek similar goals. Many activists for the disabled supported DPN, thus linking issues of EMPOWERMENT, EDUCATION, and other concerns from their own movements to the issues that emerged at Gallaudet.

Events subsequent to DPN are also noteworthy. In particular, the most important legislation in the history of disability rights in the United States, the AMERICANS WITH DISABILITIES ACT, was signed into law only two years after DPN, and many observers credit the protest for changing the political climate that made this historic legislation possible.

See also ACTIVISM AND ADVOCACY; PRINT MEDIA; REP-
RESENTATION; SELF-ADVOCATES AND SELF-ADVOCACY.

John B. Christiansen

Further Reading:

Christiansen, John B., and Sharon N. Barnartt. *Deaf President
Now!: The 1988 Revolution at Gallaudet.* Washington, D.C.:
Gallaudet University Press, 1995.
Gannon, Jack R. *The Week the World Heard Gallaudet.* Washing-
ton, D.C.: Gallaudet University Press, 1989.
Shapiro, Joseph P. *No Pity: People with Disabilities Forging a New
Civil Rights Movement.* New York: Random House, Three
Rivers Press, 1994.

Deaf studies

Like other interdisciplinary fields that examine minority communities and issues of IDENTITY, Deaf studies reflects and promotes the critical examination of DEAF peoples and notions of
what it means to be deaf. Deaf studies commonly draws on
the fields of history, sociology, communication, EDUCATION,
anthropology, LITERATURE, and linguistics, as well as other
interdisciplinary approaches, such as FILM studies and GEN-
DER studies. Its emergence and evolution has both shaped and
been shaped by broad trends in American society.

Very little scholarly study has addressed the historical
evolution of this field, but various factors likely motivated
its creation and early development. Since the late 1950s and
1960s, the linguistic studies of various researchers, including WILLIAM STOKOE, provided compelling evidence that
AMERICAN SIGN LANGUAGE (ASL) was an authentic language and not a simplified form of English expressed in
gestural form. Although such revelations initially drew critical responses from some hearing and deaf people, this recognition fostered positive and empowering approaches to
understanding the deaf COMMUNITY and its culture. Civil
rights ACTIVISM of the 1960s and 1970s also contributed
to reassessments of marginalized people, drawing attention
to systems of oppression and strategies for EMPOWERMENT.
Efforts to enhance communication and access during this
era, such as telecommunication devices for the deaf (TTYs)
and CLOSED CAPTIONING, demonstrated deaf peoples' ability
to marshal resources and their increasing adoption of rights-
based campaigns.

By the early 1980s scholar-advocates such as JACK
GANNON began documenting COMMUNITY histories in the
hope of educating deaf people about their cultural roots.
Published by the NATIONAL ASSOCIATION OF THE DEAF in
1981, Gannon's *Deaf Heritage: A Narrative History of Deaf
America* remains an important reference tool in the field.
Later in the decade, other prominent scholars, including
Carol Padden and Tom Humphries, examined the boundaries of deaf identity, outlining cultural features that especially
distinguish this minority community, including residential
school experiences, use of sign language, shared folklore,
participation in deaf ORGANIZATIONS, and other social connections. This emerging scholarship challenged traditional
scholarly REPRESENTATIONS of deaf people emanating from a
MEDICAL MODEL OF DISABILITY. Such works, usually written
by nondeaf educators and "experts" in the field of deafness,
focused especially on auditory conditions and deaf people as
objects of study rather than as active agents in their lives and
communities.

In 1981 Boston University established the first formal
Deaf studies program. Since its inception, the university commonly has offered its courses in ASL, an approach adopted
by many other Deaf studies programs elsewhere. However,
different emphases, outlooks, and goals shape Deaf studies
programs across America. For example, Boston University
historically has emphasized educational issues and teacher
training as part of its curriculum and is housed in the university's School of Education, while Towson University in
Maryland offers among its options a concentration in human
services and deaf culture; this program draws connections
between Deaf Studies, Audiology, and Speech-Pathology
and is part of the College of Health Professions. GALLAUDET
UNIVERSITY in Washington, D.C., has one of the largest
programs with undergraduate major and minor degree programs, as well as a master's degree. Affiliated with the College
of Arts and Sciences and linked with the ASL program, it
especially emphasizes deaf history, American Sign Language,
and cultural studies. Since the 1990s increasing numbers
of universities and colleges offer courses, certificates, and
workshops in Deaf studies. Scholars in the field continue to
discuss and assess the scholarly and cultural implications of
program placement and faculty training, as well as the goals
of individual programs. A deep interest in global and trans-
national issues has motivated Deaf studies experts to sponsor
international events, such as the Deaf Way conferences, the
first of which was held in Washington, D.C., in 1989.

In more recent years, scholars have expanded their study
of the meaning of "deaf" to consider its relationship to notions
of "hearing-ness." One development is the concept of AUDISM,
which critically examines ways that society has constructed
systems of oppression based on the belief that hearing and
being a hearing person is superior to deafness and being
deaf. The contested relationship between some culturally
deaf people and people with disabilities, as well as between
Deaf studies and DISABILITY STUDIES has drawn attention as
well. At the 2006 SOCIETY FOR DISABILITY STUDIES conference, for example, experts in both fields joined in a plenary
session to discuss the commonalities and distinct differences
between the groups and fields. Other researchers have begun
to reexamine the boundaries of deaf culture by considering

the experiences and identities of codas (CHILDREN OF DEAF ADULTS), HARD OF HEARING people, and multiply disabled deaf people. Responding to broader studies in multiculturalism, educators have added classes in Deaf studies that extend beyond the traditional scope of white, male, privileged deaf Americans. In addition, bioethical concerns over innovations in technology, including genetic testing and COCHLEAR IMPLANTS, has prompted new areas of study.

As an energetic and expanding field, Deaf studies demonstrates the fusion of civil rights activism and scholarly pursuit. Building from other interdisciplinary approaches to minority experiences, Deaf studies has made distinct contributions to the broader understanding of American society.

See also GENETICS; RESIDENTIAL SCHOOLS; SCIENCE AND TECHNOLOGY.

Yerker Andersson
Susan Burch

Further Reading:

Baynton, Douglas C. *Forbidden Signs: American Culture and the Campaign against Sign Language.* Chicago: University of Chicago Press, 1998.

Burch, Susan. *Signs of Resistance: American Deaf Cultural History, 1900 to World War II.* New York: New York University Press, 2002.

Gannon, Jack R. *Deaf Heritage: A Narrative History of Deaf America.* Silver Spring, Md.: National Association of the Deaf, 1981.

Lane, Harlan, Robert Hoffmeister, and Ben Bahan. *A Journey into the Deaf-World.* San Diego: DawnSignPress, 1996.

Padden, Carol, and Tom Humphries. *Deaf in America: Voices from a Culture.* Cambridge, Mass.: Harvard University Press, 1990.

Deaf Women United

Deaf Women United (DWU) is a leading grassroots organization for DEAF and HARD OF HEARING women in North America. A nonprofit ORGANIZATION that came into being in 1985, DWU's mission is to recognize and empower deaf and hard of hearing women of diverse socioeconomic status, RACE, ETHNICITY, and sexual orientation.

In the early 1980s Marcella Meyer, then the executive director of the Greater Los Angeles Council on Deafness, joined with peers to form a committee that began planning the first national conference for deaf women. The resulting 1985 "Deaf Women United" conference in Santa Monica, California, drew attention to the double "handicap" of ACCESS and GENDER that deaf women commonly faced.

The positive response to this event motivated the creation of an organization that also took the name Deaf Women United. The first DWU Board of Officers, composed of "CB" Buchholz, Allie Joiner, Marsha Kessler-Nowak, Sheila Conlon-Mentkowski, Betty G. Miller, Sandra Ammons-Rasmus, and Gwen Speakes, drafted a mission statement and obtained funding and assistance from the Women's Technical Assistance Project. After bylaws were drafted and passed, DWU became incorporated in the state of Maryland on November 23, 1987, and received a not-for-profit tax-exempt status a year later. A second national conference, at which both the board and the bylaws were expanded, followed in 1987 at George Mason University in Fairfax, Virginia. Since that time the group has sponsored a biannual conference.

In succeeding years DWU worked to put out a quarterly newsletter, conducted a national membership drive, established chapters, designed a new brochure for national distribution, and adopted a logo. By 1999 DWU had created a Web site and began to sponsor two awards: the Deaf Women of Achievement, which recognizes the accomplishments of a deaf woman, and the Wall of Honor, which pays tribute to a deaf woman who has markedly assisted her local COMMUNITY. In 2000 member Tina Jo Breindel published *Know That: Quotes from Deaf Women for a Positive Life* to celebrate the achievements of deaf women.

In the 21st century DWU has maintained its mission to promote and instruct deaf women in EDUCATION, EMPLOYMENT, politics, and culture by way of a network of individuals and organizations that represent and serve deaf women. A Speakers Bureau, mentoring system, on-site training at its chapters, and scholarship programs represent various initiatives the organization sponsors. In recent years DWU has affiliated with other national organizations, such as the NATIONAL ASSOCIATION OF THE DEAF and the National Organization for Women, to address ways of empowering deaf women. As of 2008 it boasted 15 chapters across the country.

The creation of Deaf Women United marks an important moment in deaf history. The desire for EMPOWERMENT has defined American history generally and deaf history specifically, and DWU's growth reflects this tradition. Since the 1980s, increasing awareness of diverse experiences, including those shaped by sex and gender, has altered what it means to be deaf and how members of the broad deaf COMMUNITY have responded to advocacy issues.

See also ACTIVISM AND ADVOCACY.

Cynthia Pettie

Further Reading:

Breindel, Tina Jo. *Know That: Quotes from Deaf Women for a Positive Life.* San Diego: DawnSign Press, 2000.

Deaf Women United, Inc. *Enlighten Yourself!* URL: www.dwu.org.

Holcomb, Mabs, and Sharon Wood. *Deaf Women: A Parade through the Decades.* San Diego: DawnSignPress, 1989.

defective

Defective is an adjective that emerged by the 15th century in Europe that means faulty, deficient, or incomplete. Historically, this term was used to describe a disabling physical or mental defect, and it was more generally applied to people with a disability. The changing meaning and use of this word is important for understanding the history of disability in the United States.

Scholars have yet to chart the evolution of this specific term in American disability history, but many have shown that in the late 19th century the rise of EUGENICS (the pseudoscience that judged and categorized people based on notions of genetic superiority and inferiority) enhanced the meaning of this term. Specifically, eugenicists applied this label to a wide array of people, including criminals, poor people, and members of racial minority groups, but it was most commonly targeted at people with cognitive disabilities (see COGNITIVE AND INTELLECTUAL DISABILITY). For example, in an 1898 article in the *American Journal of Sociology,* eugenic advocate Alexander Johnson described "FEEBLEMINDED" individuals (a general term that included cognitive disabilities) as "defective" in his warning that this group of people must be controlled so as not to undermine American society. The ramifications of this label were considerable. For example, eugenic efforts to limit the spread of genetically "defective" people included INSTITUTIONALIZATION and prohibitions against marriage. Various scholars have noted that people with—or perceived as having—cognitive disabilities were particularly vulnerable to eugenic programs aimed at defectives. Between 1907 and 1964 over 60,000 such individuals were victims of INVOLUNTARY STERILIZATION. The common use of the term as a noun ("defectives" rather than "defective people") that emerged by the early 1900s both reflected and reinforced stigmatizing notions of disability that have lasted to varying degrees since.

After the 1940s, however, the term *defective* was used less frequently to describe the broad category of people with disabilities. It is likely that the Nazi atrocities of WORLD WAR II contributed to Americans' increasing rejection of the label. Individuals with disabilities also had a direct impact on the evolving meaning and use of the term. Disabled VETERANS, for example, frequently viewed themselves and were viewed as heroes rather than defectives. The rise of the DISABILITY RIGHTS MOVEMENT, which gained momentum in the 1960s, also influenced the meaning of defective as activists directly rejected the use of defective as demeaning. Disability studies scholars, particularly since the 1980s and 1990s have demonstrated the historical and changing social values of the term. By so doing, they have challenged common assumptions that scientific terms, such as defective, are static and objective. This has further changed the meaning of the label and its relation to people who were cast as defective or having defects.

Still, many medical experts and others in the early 21st century continue to use the term *defect* to describe a variety of disability conditions. "Birth defects," for example, are often used to refer to congenital disabilities. Most dictionaries use "speech defects" as an appropriate example of defect. The application of the term *defective* to describe specific conditions rather than the full person suggests important progress in the understanding of people with disabilities. The continued debates over whether any application of the term in relation to human traits is appropriate demonstrates the powerful impact of language on IDENTITY in American history.

See also LANGUAGE AND TERMINOLOGY; MEDICAL MODEL OF DISABILITY; REPRODUCTIVE RIGHTS.

William J. Peace

Further Reading:

Deutsch, Helen Elizabeth, and Felicity Nussbaum, eds. *"Defects": Engendering the Modern Body.* Ann Arbor: University of Michigan Press, 2000.
Pernick, Martin. "Defining the Defective: Eugenics, Aesthetics, and Mass Culture in Early-Twentieth-Century America." In *The Body and Physical Difference: Discourses of Disability,* edited by David T. Mitchell and Sharon L. Snyder, 89–110. Ann Arbor: University of Michigan Press, 1997.

deformity

Deformity is understood in aesthetic terms as the opposite of beauty, or more generally as a deviation from NORMAL appearance. It may be accidental, the product of illness, or occur naturally through congenital aberration. Deformity is influenced by standards of taste and might vary historically and between different countries of the world. How a society defines a particular body as "deformed" tells us much about its ideals of bodily perfection and the perception of those whose bodies deviate from these norms.

Since ancient times, physical deformity has carried STIGMA. In the Platonic tradition, beauty was equated with good and deformity with sinfulness and evil. In early modern Europe, "monstrous births"—the birth of congenitally deformed children—were sometimes regarded as signs of divine punishment. By the 18th century the stigma of deformity was also associated with certain "inferior" racial types in European and American thought. In his oration given before the Philosophical Society in Philadelphia in 1787, Samuel Stanhope Smith argued that "fair" skin denoted superior qualities of the mind and exalted feelings, whereas blackness was both a physical deformity and a sign of "idiotism."

Both racially exotic and congenitally deformed people were exhibited as "freaks" in the 19th and 20th centuries. Between 1840 and 1940 the EXHIBITION for profit of "LIT-

TLE PEOPLE," "giants," "human skeletons," "armless and leg-less wonders," "half men/half women," "fat people," "Siamese twins" (see CONJOINED TWINS), and other extraordinary humans was a popular feature of fairs, circuses, dime museums, and carnivals across the United States. At the same time as "FREAK SHOWS" encouraged the ogling of deformed people for entertainment, under the influence of EUGENICS there were renewed attempts from the late 19th century to regulate bodies that failed to fit an aesthetic ideal based on health and productivity. Coinciding with attempts to institutionalize people with disabilities, from the 1880s until WORLD WAR I American cities passed so-called UGLY LAWS that sought to prevent the maimed and physically "unsightly" from appearing in public areas. Some of these remained on the statute books until the 1970s.

In contrast to the association of deformity with sin, some religious writers from the 18th century have instead emphasized that living with the "affliction" of deformity might encourage the virtue of forbearance. However, the idea that deformity acts as a bar to social acceptance has remained a constant. The correction of deformity through aesthetic surgery became popular in the 20th century, beginning with attempts to reconstruct the faces of WAR VETERANS after World War I.

Historians have sometimes viewed early modern discussions and REPRESENTATIONS of "deformity," which covered both physical IMPAIRMENT and more general aberration from prescribed bodily ideals, as a precursor to modern notions of disability. In modern usage, the terms *disability* and *deformity* overlap, but they have different connotations. While the one relates to the body's functional competence and the other to appearance, they share a history of social devaluation.

See also ABLEISM; CIRCUS; EXHIBITIONS; RELIGION; SOCIAL CONSTRUCTION OF DISABILITY.

David M. Turner

Further Reading:

Garland Thomson, Rosemarie, ed. *Freakery: Cultural Spectacles of the Extraordinary Body.* New York: New York University Press, 1996.
Gilman, Sander L. *Making the Body Beautiful: A Cultural History of Aesthetic Surgery.* Princeton, N.J.: Princeton University Press, 1999.
Leroi, Armand Marie. *Mutants: On Genetic Variety and the Human Body.* New York: Viking, 2003.
Nussbaum, Felicity A. *The Limits of the Human: Fictions of Anomaly, Race and Gender in the Long Eighteenth Century.* Cambridge: Cambridge University Press, 2003.
Snyder, Sharon L., and David T. Mitchell. *Cultural Locations of Disability.* Chicago: University of Chicago Press, 2006.
Turner, David M., and Kevin Stagg, eds. *Social Histories of Disability and Deformity.* New York: Routledge, 2006.

degeneration

From the middle of the 19th century into the middle of the 20th century, many intellectuals used the term *degeneration* to describe what they perceived as the decline both of the human animal and of human culture. These writers included physical and social scientists, physicians and cultural critics, both in Europe and in America. While many were openly racist, nearly all believed that some groups of human beings had degenerated more quickly than others. In addition to believing that African-Americans were "degenerate," they also attached the degenerate label to persons with disabilities, immigrants, and the poor. The impact of these beliefs was significant and wide-ranging.

Charles Darwin's publication of the *On the Origin of Species* in 1859 heightened interest in degeneration, but the idea had preceded Darwin's seminal work on evolution. The idea that humankind had been developing over time had enjoyed increasing popularity for about half a century before the *Origin,* and, after that publication, the notion of SOCIAL DARWINISM allowed many to argue that some persons, or groups of persons, were fit to survive, while others represented a step backward, and were considered degenerates.

Thinkers in the United States readily adapted the views of European scientists and philosophers to American conditions. Yale sociology professor William Graham Sumner was a fervent follower of Herbert Spenser's Social Darwinist evolutionary theory. In 1883 he published a collection of essays titled *What Social Classes Owe to Each Other,* in which he argued that the upper classes owe the lower classes nothing. Sumner believed that the poor were poor because of their own laziness or other bad habits or because of their inferior heredity. Thus, for Sumner, no amount of social change or governmental intervention could help the degenerate poor, some of whom would be considered disabled today.

In the new century, many American academics cast disabled persons as degenerate. For example, in 1901, American anthropologist Amos W. Butler addressed his colleagues on the subject of degeneration at a meeting of the American Association for the Advancement of Science. Butler focused on the threat of the "FEEBLEMINDED," individuals thought to have intellectual impairments. He feared the SEXUALITY of these "degenerates," and their potential for breeding to excess and overwhelming the society at large. This was particularly true, he felt, because most needed custodial care but might be hard to control. He also stressed hereditary risk, since "NORMAL" parents could sometimes produce feebleminded CHILDREN. Thus, Butler believed that mental disability was expensive, threatening, and insidious.

During the early 20th century a complex system developed in the United States to study, categorize, and control those persons whom scientists deemed to be degenerate. Scientist CHARLES DAVENPORT founded the Eugenics Record

Office in Cold Spring Harbor, Long Island, in 1910 and worked to compile family histories on as many Americans as possible in order to trace and classify the "fit" and the "unfit." Unfit and degenerate often meant virtually the same thing. EUGENICS, then treated as a serious science, sought to improve the human race by selective breeding.

Another example of this trend was psychologist HENRY H. GODDARD, head of the VINELAND TRAINING SCHOOL in New Jersey. In his 1912 study of the KALLIKAK FAMILY, Goddard traced the history of a "feebleminded" Vineland resident and argued that a brief affair between a Revolutionary War soldier and a degenerate woman produced, over the generations, over 100 feebleminded or otherwise socially undesirable persons, while this same soldier's later marriage to a woman of good heredity resulted in generations of upstanding and productive citizens. Goddard believed that most such "DEFECTIVES," particularly those diagnosed as idiots and imbeciles, should be institutionalized.

Early 20th-century fears of new immigration patterns led some to describe three races of Europeans, two of which were, in effect, degenerate. Socially prominent New York attorney Madison Grant published THE PASSING OF THE GREAT RACE (1916), which sought to arouse fear of the loss of Nordic (that is, English, German, and Scandinavian) dominance in the United States due to immigration from southern and eastern Europe, whose inhabitants he called Alpines and Mediterraneans. In 1933, in his The Conquest of a Continent, Grant took his argument further, claiming that the presence of African-Americans in the United States posed a threat to the stability of the nation. The significance of these early theories for disability history is that they set an intellectual tone that differences between individuals and groups of people were only innate, that is, within the person himself or herself, that therefore no amount of social or educational uplift (or even what today might be called "accommodations") would help those who began as degenerates, and that therefore no resources should be expended on such persons.

The developing notion of "degeneration" led to schemes and policies of classification and exclusion that had significant impact on disabled persons for several generations in both Europe and the United States.

Franklin K. Wyman

Further Reading:

Cotkin, George. *Reluctant Modernism: American Thought and Culture, 1880–1900.* New York: Twayne Publishers, 1992.

Higham, John. *Strangers in the Land: Patterns of American Nativism, 1860–1925.* New York: Atheneum, 1973.

Hofstadter, Richard. *Social Darwinism in American Thought.* 1944. Reprint, Boston: Beacon Press, 1983.

Menand, Louis. *The Metaphysical Club.* New York: Farrar, Straus & Giroux, 2001.

Trent, James W., Jr. *Inventing the Feeble Mind: A History of Mental Retardation in the United States.* Berkeley: University of California Press, 1994.

deinstitutionalization

Deinstitutionalization refers generally to the movement of people with psychiatric and intellectual and developmental disabilities out of public institutions (mental HOSPITALS or psychiatric centers; training schools or developmental centers). It is a complex issue, simply because deinstitutionalization has been pursued for different reasons and has been carried out in various ways.

The concept of deinstitutionalization can be traced at least as far back as the 1930s, but it did not become popular in mental health and developmental disabilities until decades later. The population of people in state and county mental hospitals reached its peak at 558,922 in 1955. Following that year, the population started a steady decline. By 1971 slightly more than 300,000 people remained at public mental hospitals. The population declined as a result of shorter stays at the institutions (admissions to mental hospitals actually increased over this period). The initial decline in mental hospital populations has been attributed generally to advances in psychiatric treatment and the development of psychoactive medications. In the 1960s and 1970s some critics of deinstitutionalization charged that it was motivated by the desire of government officials to reduce state budgets for mental health services.

The idea that people with psychiatric or intellectual disabilities should be treated in the community whenever possible became popular in the 1960s. In 1963 President JOHN F. KENNEDY proposed a national program in mental health and MENTAL RETARDATION to improve care in public institutions and to expand community services. Congress subsequently passed legislation to fund community mental health centers and mental retardation facilities. Around the same time, scholars such as ERVING GOFFMAN and psychiatrist THOMAS SZASZ began to examine the negative effects of INSTITUTIONALIZATION and to oppose the involuntary commitment of people to mental hospitals.

State institutions for people with intellectual and developmental disabilities reached their maximum population of 194,650 in 1967 and have declined steadily ever since. The deinstitutionalization of people in state schools or training schools, as they were called in the 1960s and 1970s in most states, was spurred by the public exposure of institutional conditions in Burton Blatt's CHRISTMAS IN PURGATORY and elsewhere and the growing acceptance of the principle of NORMALIZATION. Many proponents of deinstitutionalization also argued that people with intellectual disabilities could learn daily living skills better in community settings than in segregated institutions. An increasing number of states no longer operate state institutions for people with intellectual or developmental disabilities.

In the 1970s public interest and civil liberties attorneys challenged institutionalization and a wide range of institutional practices. The U.S. Supreme Court and lower federal courts ruled that it was unconstitutional to confine people involuntarily in custodial institutions who were nondangerous and capable of living safely on their own in the community or to unnecessarily restrict the civil liberties and rights of people by segregating them in institutions. Legal challenges to institutions fueled the depopulation and eventual closure of many large public facilities.

Deinstitutionalization became extremely controversial in the fields of mental health and mental retardation in the 1970s. Critics charged that deinstitutionalization had resulted in the transfer of people from public institutions to substandard private institutions, including nursing homes, and the creation of large, homeless urban populations of former institutional residents. Some unions representing public employees at institutions waged aggressive public relations campaigns against deinstitutionalization. Public officials and community members in some locales fought the opening of GROUP HOMES designed to house people with psychiatric or developmental disabilities. A number of mental health and mental retardation experts argued that there was not sufficient research evidence on the benefits of institutions versus community living to justify large-scale deinstitutionalization, especially for people with severe disabilities.

Disability rights groups, including "PSYCHIATRIC SURVIVOR" and self-advocacy or "people first" ORGANIZATIONS, have strongly supported deinstitutionalization as a human rights issue. AMERICAN DISABLED FOR ATTENDANT PROGRAMS TODAY and other organizations representing people with disabilities have advocated for the passage of federal legislation mandating a shift of funds from nursing homes and other institutions to community services and supports. In the field of intellectual and developmental disabilities, major professional and family organizations have expressed support for deinstitutionalization and community living.

As a concept, deinstitutionalization has been, at best, incomplete. It focused attention on the release of people with disabilities from public institutions. For people who need personal assistance, medical services, and other supports, simply being released from an institution or never being admitted to one is insufficient. There must be services and adequate housing to enable them to live successfully in the community. People with even the most severe disabilities can live in the community if adequate supports are available. States have varied in the degree to which they have provided adequate funding and resources for community services.

See also ACTIVISM AND ADVOCACY; ASYLUMS AND INSTITUTIONS; COGNITIVE AND INTELLECTUAL DISABILITY; COMMUNITY; DEVELOPMENTAL DISABILITY; LAW AND POLICY; MAD PEOPLE AND MADNESS; MENTAL ILLNESS; *ONE FLEW OVER THE CUCKOO'S NEST*; SELF-ADVOCATES AND SELF-ADVOCACY; *SNAKE-PIT, THE*.

Steven J. Taylor

Further Reading:
Grob, Gerald N. *From Asylum to Community: Mental Health Policy in America.* Princeton, N.J.: Princeton University Press, 1991.
Rothman, David J., and Sheila M. Rothman. *The Willowbrook Wars: Bringing the Mentally Disabled into the Community.* New Brunswick, N.J.: Aldine Transaction, 2005.
Taylor, Steven J., and Stanford J. Searl. "Disability in America: A History of Policies and Trends." In *Significant Disability: Issues Affecting People with Significant Disabilities from a Historical, Policy, Leadership, and Systems Perspective,* edited by E. D. Martin, 16–33. Springfield, Ill.: Charles C. Thomas, 2001.
———. "Disability in America: Controversy, Debate, and Backlash." In *Significant Disability: Issues Affecting People with Significant Disabilities from a Historical, Policy, Leadership, and Systems Perspective,* edited by E. D. Martin, 64–96. Springfield, Ill.: Charles C. Thomas, 2001.

De Kroyft, Helen (Sarah Helen Aldrich) (1818–1915) *blind memoirist, essayist*

Sarah Helen Aldrich De Kroyft was a woman who, after going BLIND in her 20s, became a prominent author.

Born on October 29, 1818, near Rochester, New York, Sarah Helen Aldrich attended the Genesee Wesleyan Seminary in Lima, a coeducational institution that had opened in 1822. Her studies included French, Italian, and mathematics, and she taught in her local public school during the winters of the seven years she attended Lima Seminary. In 1845 she married Dr. William De Kroyft of Rochester, who had developed a "hemorrhage of the lungs;" later, on their wedding day, he died. According to her own account, De Kroyft cried so much after her husband's death that she developed an inflammation of the eyes, and she found herself "in one short month a bride, a widow, and blind."

Shortly afterward she began attending the New York Institution for the Blind and soon began to write essays for New York City newspapers and magazines about her experiences, becoming one of the first blind women to write for a public audience. In 1849 she published *A Place in Thy Memory*, a volume of some 40 of the letters she had written to friends and FAMILY during her years at the New York Institution, describing the changes blindness had created in her philosophic and spiritual beliefs. The preface to the book apologetically confesses that only the necessity of supporting herself could prompt the proper middle-class woman to present her private thoughts to the reading public; the preface also describes the process by which De Kroyft shared her prospectus with a wide range of wealthy New Yorkers to gather subscriptions to pay her publishing expenses. The volume proved highly successful, selling over 200,000 copies in 67 editions during De Kroyft's lifetime, and was endorsed for its idealism and philanthropic inspiration by political figures including President Zachary Taylor and First Lady Abigail Fillmore, who reportedly invited "the Blind Authoress" to a ceremony at the White House library in 1852.

De Kroyft published a children's book, *Little Jakey,* in 1871, which she claimed was the true story of the blind child of German immigrants, whom the author had met at the New York Institution for the Blind. Awash in popular sentimental STEREOTYPES, including an abusive alcoholic father and a dying mother, and narrated in Jakey's heavily stilted German-accented English, the tale depicts how the blind boy's innate purity and goodness, and his angelic death, serve as a moral lesson to all around him. This book was reprinted in raised type for blind students, and it was one of the first books HELEN KELLER read for herself at the PERKINS SCHOOL FOR THE BLIND in Boston in the 1880s. In 1876 De Kroyft published *The Soul of Eve,* a rewriting of the Edenic myth that grants to Eve, as the prototype of True Womanhood, a redemptive and prescient form of perception not limited to her physical senses; as in her writings about her own blindness, she attributes to the blind and to women a special mode of consciousness not linked to bodily configuration. *Mortara,* published in 1888, followed in De Kroyft's particular sentimental and romantic vein to present a series of letters written to an imaginary mythic hero who is both a saviour and a suitor to the blind author. Another book of personal essays on her spiritual beliefs and the true meaning of her blindness, *The Foreshadowed Way,* appeared in 1908. As the first and most famous blind woman writer of the 19th century, De Kroyft's work affirmed the sentimental and spiritual portrayal of blindness common in Victorian writings, while her efforts to sell her own works as her means of economic support helped contradict the STEREOTYPE of the blind woman as helpless DEPENDENT. She died in 1915; the exact date and place are unknown.

See also GENDER; LITERATURE; POPULAR CULTURE; REPRESENTATION.

Mary Klages

Further Reading:

Klages, Mary. *Woeful Afflictions: Disability and Sentimentality in Victorian America.* Philadelphia: University of Pennsylvania Press, 1999.

Ryan, James Emmett. "The Blind Authoress of New York: Helen De Kroyft and the Uses of Disability in Antebellum America." *American Quarterly* 51, no. 2 (1999): 385–418.
"Sarah Helen DeKroyft." Available online. URL: http://www. nyise.org/text/dekroft.html. Accessed December 4, 2006.

Deliverance

A feature-length silent FILM from 1919, *Deliverance* is a semi-fictionalized story of HELEN KELLER's life. The real Helen Keller (1880–1968), 38 years old when the movie was made, and her teacher ANNE SULLIVAN MACY (1866–1936) act as themselves in part of the film. Depicting Keller's EDUCATION and her adaptations to DEAF-BLINDNESS as an epic battle to OVERCOME "ignorance" through education, "patience," and "love," the film is an example of how Keller's life has been shaped in the popular media to embody ideals that the real Helen Keller, who was a socialist, did not necessarily hold.

The film has three acts. Act I, Childhood, depicts Keller's birth and disabling illness, her family's appeals to ALEXANDER GRAHAM BELL for help, and her early interactions with Macy, including the famous scene at the well in which Keller discovers language. Later, Keller learns to speak at the Horace Mann School for the Deaf in Boston. This process is depicted as a battle for independence parallel to "America's struggle for Independence," which is presented in dreamlike historical reenactment scenes evoked by Keller and Macy's tour of Boston's historical sites. The film presents ORALISM, the use of speech and lipreading rather than signing, as a valuable avenue toward deaf independence.

Act II, Maidenhood, chronicles Keller's secondary and postsecondary education, her growing fame, and her typically adolescent daydreams of love. In Act III, Womanhood, Keller, her mother, brother, and Macy appear as themselves. Having graduated from Radcliffe, Keller is labeled the "Eighth Wonder of the World." She alternately studies and works, or enjoys such leisure activities as dancing and an airplane ride. In a fictional sequence, Keller parades on horseback as a messenger of freedom. This heroic image is accompanied by a quote from Keller, in which blindness and deafness are metaphors for moral deficits: "Only those are blind who do not see the truth. Only those are deaf who do not hear the oracle of their better selves."

Deliverance treats Keller's life as a moral lesson of how commitment to EDUCATION and hard work is rewarded with fame, security, and happiness. The film stresses this by contrasting Keller's story with that of another, fictional girl, Nadja. A first-generation American, Nadja rejected schooling when Keller embraced it. Forced to work a factory job, and to cope with the tragic death of her husband and the war-blinding of her son, the metaphorically BLIND and DEAF

Nadja ironically ends up more spiritually and socially impoverished than the physically blind and deaf Keller.

Keller and Macy signed on to this film project with economic goals that went unrealized due to the film's brief, though well-received, run. Having quarreled with synopsist Francis Trevelyan Miller, the women were not very invested in the final film. Keller wanted it to endorse the socialist cause of the International Workers of the World, while Miller maintained its focus on less politically divisive values. True to her principles, Keller refused to attend the premiere in New York City because it would have meant breaking an Actor's Equity strike.

Susan Crutchfield

Further Reading:

Cohen, Paula M. "Helen Keller and the American Myth." *Yale Review* 85 (January 1997): 1–20.

Deliverance. 1919. Directed by George Foster Platt. Helen Keller Film Corp. Filmstrip. Library of Congress.

Herrmann, Dorothy. *Helen Keller: A Life.* Chicago: University of Chicago Press, 1999.

Keller, Helen. *The Story of My Life.* New York: Bantam Books, 1990.

Lash, Joseph P. *Helen and Teacher: The Story of Helen Keller and Anne Sullivan Macy.* Reading, Mass.: Addison-Wesley Publishing, 1997.

Nielsen, Kim E. *The Radical Lives of Helen Keller.* New York: New York University Press, 2004.

dementia

The term *dementia* was first used by Philippe Pinel, the French psychiatrist widely regarded as the founder of modern PSYCHIATRY, in 1797 at the Bicêtre Hospital in Paris, but the modern concept of dementia coalesced only in the late 19th century. Prior to the rise of modern medicine, dementia was a diffuse category that included a broad range of symptoms and conditions implying social incompetence. By the mid-19th century new understandings of neuropathology narrowed dementia to include only intellectual IMPAIRMENT. Noncognitive symptoms were moved into separate disease categories or regarded as secondary to the primary diagnosis of dementia.

New ideas about dementia coincided with the growth of modern America. In modern society, the crucial importance of cognitive ability in achieving selfhood fed a fear of dementia. During the same time period that the medical concept of dementia took shape, America was being transformed by the market revolution and the erosion of traditional social hierarchies. By the end of the 19th century selfhood was no longer an ascribed status bestowed at birth but the product of individual choice and lifelong effort. In modern society,

dementia's destruction of the cognitive abilities essential to the project of self-creation came to be seen as the most dreadful of all losses.

By the early 20th century physicians regarded dementia as a neuropsychiatric syndrome whose causes might be found in a number of distinct brain pathologies, the most common being the senile plaques and neurofibrillary tangles associated with ALZHEIMER'S DISEASE, and the cerebrovascular lesions characteristic of what is today called multi-infarct dementia. Despite these new views on the pathology of dementia, the relationship between dementia and AGING remained unclear. Since all people of advanced ages exhibit at least some of the supposed biological markers of dementia, doctors could regard dementia either as a DISEASE or as an extreme point on a continuum of brain aging. While the issue remained controversial, it was clear by 1900 that aging was the greatest single risk factor for dementia and that the prevalence of dementia increased steadily with age, hence the continued use in the medical literature of "SENILITY" and related terms through the 1980s. According to the Alzheimer's Association, about 10 percent in the population over 65 years of age and nearly 50 percent in the population 85 and older have Alzheimer's disease.

Dementia is also connected in important ways to the history of institutional care in the United States. Until the late 19th century, when elderly people with dementia could not be cared for at home, they were regarded as "merely senile" and typically cared for in poor houses (see ALMSHOUSES). When states assumed the cost of caring for people with mental illness around the turn of the 20th century, elderly patients with dementia were increasingly likely to be classified as insane and admitted to state mental HOSPITALS. Psychiatry viewed the proliferation of aged dementia patients in the state hospital system with alarm, but could do little to stop the trend. DEINSTITUTIONALIZATION and passage of MEDICARE and MEDICAID in 1965 led to the emergence of the modern nursing home industry, and older patients with dementia were shifted out of public psychiatric hospitals and into these new institutions.

Dementia emerged as a major public issue in the second half of the 20th century as it became clear that the United States was an aging society. In 1900 just over 4 percent of the U.S. population was 65 and older; in 2000, more than 12 percent of the population was 65 or older, and with the aging of the baby boom generation, this is projected to grow to more than 20 percent by 2050, with fully 5 percent of the population 85 and older. By the 1980s public debates on dementia were framed in terms of an "apocalyptic demography" in which the economic and social burdens of dementia were seen as an impending tidal wave threatening to overwhelm society. Such concerns resulted in a dramatic increase in federal spending on biomedical research but also increased the

STIGMA and anxiety associated with dementia in particular and aging in general.

See also AGE AND AGEISM; ASYLUMS AND INSTITUTIONS.

Jesse F. Ballenger

Further Reading:

Ballenger, Jesse F. *Self, Senility and Alzheimer's Disease in Modern America: A History.* Baltimore: Johns Hopkins University Press, 2006.

Berrios, G. E. "Dementia and Aging since the Nineteenth Century." In *Dementia and Normal Aging,* edited by F. A. Huppert, C. Brayne and D. W. O'Connor. Cambridge: Cambridge University Press, 1994.

Whitehouse, Peter J., Konrad Maurer, and Jesse F. Ballenger, eds. *Concepts of Alzheimer Disease: Biological, Clinical and Cultural Perspectives.* Baltimore: Johns Hopkins University Press, 2000.

Department of Veterans Affairs

The Department of Veterans Affairs (VA) is the agency of the federal government with responsibility for serving VETERANS of the U.S. Armed Forces and their families through programs of HEALTH CARE, financial assistance, and burial benefits. The VA also conducts extensive research on chronic DISEASES, including neurotrauma, SPINAL CORD INJURIES, PROSTHETICS, hearing and vision loss, alcoholism, and mental health. While the department was originally named the Veterans Administration, which was referred to by the abbreviation VA, the acronym VA is commonly used to refer to both the agency's historical and current names.

Prior to WORLD WAR I, disabled veterans had received health care from the U.S. Public Health Service and disability pensions through the U.S. Pension Bureau. With the tremendous demand for services from disabled World War I veterans returning from Europe, in 1921 Congress created an independent agency, the Veterans Bureau, with responsibility for veterans health facilities. However, the bureau faced numerous charges of fraud and corruption in its hospital program during the 1920s, and, in 1930, President Herbert Hoover signed Executive Order 5398, renaming and organizing it as the Veterans Administration, an independent federal agency. At its founding, the VA operated 54 veterans hospitals, and it was also assigned responsibility for administration of military pensions.

As the end of WORLD WAR II approached, Congress unanimously passed the Servicemen's Readjustment Act (P.L. 78-346), which President FRANKLIN D. ROOSEVELT signed on June 22, 1944. This law became known as the G.I. Bill of Rights, and it offered subsidized home loans and extensive education benefits to veterans, which were administered by the VA. In addition to operating HOSPITAL and benefit systems, the VA became responsible in 1973 for a system of national cemeteries previously operated by the U.S. Army, although the Army maintained control of Arlington National Cemetery and the U.S. Soldiers' and Airmen's Home National Cemetery. In 1989 the VA was raised to cabinet status in legislation signed by President Ronald Reagan, and its name was changed to the Department of Veterans Affairs.

In fiscal year 2006, the VA operated 155 medical centers in every state in the country, as well as 872 outpatient clinics, 135 nursing homes, 45 residential rehabilitation treatment programs, 209 Veterans (counseling) Centers, and 108 home-care programs. In that year, the VA also provided $34.4 billion dollars to 3.6 million recipients in disability compensation, death compensation, and pensions to veterans disabled by injuries or diseases that were incurred or aggravated during active military service.

For much of the VA's history, it has been subject to criticism by veterans ORGANIZATIONS over the amount paid in disability benefits as well as over what conditions should make veterans eligible for VA benefits and services. Prominent veterans groups have included the American Legion and the DISABLED AMERICAN VETERANS, founded after WORLD WAR I, the Veterans of Foreign Wars, founded in 1899 by Spanish-American War veterans, and the PARALYZED VETERANS OF AMERICA, established after WORLD WAR II. These groups typically have advocated for veteran-specific programs and services, and they have frequently opposed any proposed merger of veteran programs into more generic government health and disability programs. Veterans organizations have also objected to the narrow definition of combat-related conditions used to qualify veterans for VA services, contending that many disabled veterans were not receiving needed assistance. Other critics, including two commissions chaired by former president Herbert Hoover in the late 1940s and the early 1950s, have charged that the VA unnecessarily duplicates other government programs, and that the VA HEALTH CARE system should be scaled back on grounds of efficiency.

In addition to their provision of services, VA facilities have served as locations that have been instrumental in the formation of formal organizations and informal networks of disabled veterans, who have sought enhanced services and benefits from the federal government, as well as promoting mutual assistance and support. Thus, by bringing veterans with disabilities together to receive services, and by serving as a target for PROTESTS and collective action, the Department of Veterans Affairs has indirectly helped to foster disability rights ACTIVISM and collective action. Debates over the mission and future of the VA, and over the claims of veterans to public assistance and support, have also been important examples of how we socially construct disability in the United States, distinguishing between the deserving and undeserving disabled, and the segregation or integration of people with disabilities into the societal mainstream.

See also ACTIVISM AND ADVOCACY; LAW AND POLICY; SOCIAL CONSTRUCTION OF DISABILITY; SPINAL CORD INJURY; WAR.

Richard K. Scotch

Further Reading:

Baker, Rodney R., and Wade E. Pickren. *Psychology and the Department of Veterans Affairs: A Historical Analysis of Training, Research, Practice, and Advocacy.* Washington D.C.: APA, 2006.

Department of Veterans Affairs. *Fact Sheet.* Washington, D.C., 2007.

Hamowy, Ronald. *Government and Public Health in America.* Cheltenham, England: E. Elgar, 2007.

dependent and dependence

Dependence is the condition of needing help from others to live and it is a fundamental fact of all human existence. Within the history of disability, however, this idea of dependence assumes a greater scope: It is often thought that people with disabilities are helpless, that disabled people require the constant assistance and intervention of NONDISABLED persons, and that disabled people as a group are dependent on the abilities and resources of the larger community in a way that many find pitiable or excessive. In stark contrast to this widely held view, disability scholars, activists, and others argue that people with disabilities have been held back, oppressed, and exploited by these attitudes, since conventional relationships between nondisabled and disabled often take the form of CHARITY or patronage on one side and passive dependence on the other. Within the limits of this model, people with disabilities have been forced into the position of children or even objects. Many thus argue that all relationships that reinforce dependent existence deny individuals, disabled or nondisabled, fundamental human freedoms: The opportunity to live and act independently, to take an active role in self-management, and to take part in the larger life of the community, including VOTING and participating in other aspects of civic life.

The idea that people with disabilities are dependent on the nondisabled is a long-standing tradition of Western history and is evident in ancient Greek texts as well as those of the Jewish and Christian Bibles. Likewise, this notion was present for centuries in European culture before the Westernization of the Americas beginning in the late 15th century.

In American history and culture, the idea of disabled dependence becomes most visible during the 19th century when specialized ASYLUMS AND INSTITUTIONS began to administer to the perceived needs of BLIND people, DEAF people, and those with cognitive disabilities (see COGNI-TIVE AND INTELLECTUAL DISABILITY) and MENTAL ILLNESS. In many respects, these institutions performed a useful and beneficial function, educating people excluded from mainstream venues, sheltering many from terrible POVERTY, and enabling the beginnings of what has become a rich and vibrant American DISABILITY CULTURE. At the same time, the movement toward INSTITUTIONALIZATION, which was particularly powerful in the United States, also strengthened the sense that people with disabilities could not and should not act for themselves. Since these institutions were, almost without exception, administered by nondisabled persons, they also institutionalized a hierarchy of nondisabled superiority and disabled inferiority, reinforcing not only the actual dependence of people with disabilities but also the cultural conception of disabled people as dependent.

American history offers many examples of people with disabilities locked into harmful relationships of dependence. Housed at the PERKINS SCHOOL FOR THE BLIND, well-known DEAF-BLIND woman LAURA BRIDGMAN (1829–89) was regularly displayed to tourists by director SAMUEL GRIDLEY HOWE, who used Bridgman's fame to help raise money for the school. The worst aspects of this structure of institutionalized dependency were symbolized in the late 20th century by the scandalous ABUSES that took place at the Willowbrook State School in New York, where cognitively disabled inmates were neglected, starved, and sexually assaulted.

It is not only in formal institutional settings, however, that disabled Americans have suffered EXPLOITATION from relationships of dependence. In the 20th century the idea of disabled dependence was enshrined by fund-raising campaigns for charitable ORGANIZATIONS founded to help people with disabilities. Employing strategies that relied on the use of a POSTER CHILD or a TELETHON, many of these organizations created manipulative images of disabled people as wholly dependent with the immediate result that many disabled individuals, especially disabled youths, were misrepresented and exploited. The enduring effect of these images, however, has been even more egregious: By confirming the popular notion that disabled people were mostly CHILDREN dependent on help from nondisabled adults, the telethon and poster-child approach to disability has done untold harm. By promoting an idea of disability that most disabled people find humiliating, these campaigns fostered the notion that disabled people cannot be independent mature adults with jobs, partners, and children of their own. By portraying disability as permanently dependent, the fund-raising that was intended to help people with disabilities actually strengthened attitudes of cultural contempt for disabled people, creating further bias in EDUCATION, the job market, politics, and general social intercourse.

Most prominent among the charitable groups criticized for this approach has been the MUSCULAR DYSTROPHY

ASSOCIATION (MDA). Headed by chairman JERRY LEWIS, the fund-raising techniques of the MDA have been the subject of bitter debate for a generation. Although Lewis continues to identify the subjects of his charity as "Jerry's Kids," a group of former telethon children identify themselves ironically as "Jerry's Orphans," marking disapproval of what they see as Lewis's damaging paternalism. A 1981 *New York Times* op-ed article by EVAN KEMP, later an architect of the AMERICANS WITH DISABILITIES ACT of 1990, gave voice to the views of many in the disability community when he criticized Lewis and the MDA, calling for a "no pity" approach to disability.

Kemp's essay was in keeping with the rising momentum of the DISABILITY RIGHTS MOVEMENT, which presented an ever greater challenge to the conventional role of disabled people as institutionalized dependents. Indeed, the movement in education toward MAINSTREAMING children with disabilities in general education classrooms showed that disabled children could very often perform independently, while the growing INDEPENDENT LIVING MOVEMENT proved that even severely disabled adults need not be restricted to the institutions that often encouraged dependent attitudes.

Despite tremendous gains in challenging the conventions that have often kept disabled people dependent, however, the issue of disabled dependency is still very much alive. Strong debate arose in the winter of 2007, for instance, over the treatment of a severely mentally disabled six-year-old girl known as "Ashley X," who received controversial medical treatment to stunt her growth and prevent her sexual development. Although doctors and her parents felt that the "Ashley treatment" was justified because it would enable the girl's parents to continue to provide long-term care for her at home, many in the disability COMMUNITY were outraged by the procedure, arguing that the convenience of her caregivers (see CAREGIVING), or the fact of Ashley's dependency, should not have entered into any decision to permanently alter her body.

Scholars of disability continue to debate the issues raised by dependency. Sociologist Tom Shakespeare, for instance, observes that "in the performance of help, we take on different and changing roles" but that "the ways in which we experience help can be profoundly different." He argues for change "so that these differences do not embody dependency and STIGMA." In a similar vein, writer Nancy Mairs invites readers to rethink attitudes toward help, pointing out that all human beings need both to be cared for and to take care of others in different ways. Being dependent, she suggests, is not an experience to be resisted, but one in which all humanity participates.

See also STEREOTYPES.

Julia Miele Rodas

Further Reading:

Gibbs, Nancy. "Pillow Angel Ethics" (in two parts), *Time,* 7 January 2007 and 9 January 2007. Available online. URL: http://www.time.com/time/nation/article/0,8599,1574851,00.html and http://www.time.com/time/nation/article/0,8599,1575325,00.html. Accessed September 28, 2007.

Kemp, Evan, Jr. "Aiding the Disabled: No Pity Please," *New York Times,* 3 September 1981.

Lane, Harlan L. *The Mask of Benevolence: Disabling the Deaf Community.* New York: Knopf, 1992.

Mairs, Nancy. "Taking Care." In *Waist-high in the World: A Life among the Nondisabled.* Boston: Beacon Press, 1996.

Shakespeare, Tom. *Help: Imagining Welfare.* Birmingham, England: Venture Press, 2000.

University of California, Berkeley. "The Disability Rights and Independent Living Movement." Available online. URL: http://bancroft.berkeley.edu/collections/drilm/index.html. Accessed September 28, 2007.

depression

The experience, definition, diagnosis, and treatments of depression have played an important but underexamined role in American history. Depression is often linked to the earlier concepts of MELANCHOLY and melancholia, which have appeared regularly in LITERATURE for at least 2,500 years. However, the path by which these concepts evolved toward the term *depression,* or our contemporary notion of clinical depression, is the subject of ongoing debate. The links between melancholy and depression are complex, but it is generally agreed that they share many features, including inertia, a feeling of pointlessness, and a tendency to turn negative feelings inward against oneself.

The term *depression* emerged in the later decades of the 19th century, during roughly the same historical period as the rise of PSYCHIATRY as a medical specialization. The image of depressed people (and all "MAD" PEOPLE, a term then used for MENTAL ILLNESS) shifted during this time from one of unfeeling animals to one of sick persons in need of pity and treatment. Still, for persons with depression—or those perceived as such—the STIGMA attached to "mad" states remained and even increased as medical experts categorized depression as an affliction.

The understanding and treatment of depression has changed over the past century. SIGMUND FREUD's classic essay "Mourning and Melancholia" (1917) often is cited as an early and key text in the historical study of depression. Its theory suggests a cause rooted in the unconscious, namely, the perceived loss of a parent's love. During the 1950s and 1960s, however, depression was believed to be either endogenous (inherent in the body) or neurotic (arising from an external event). In addition to psychoanalysis, forms of treatment have included electroshock therapy, which was especially prominent in the 1940s and 1950s, and again in the last several decades.

Concepts of depression since the civil rights era reflect an increased interest in the chemical and physical causes underlying the condition. For example, in 1980, the DIAGNOSTIC AND STATISTICAL MANUAL OF MENTAL DISORDERS *(DSM)* began classifying depression into more diverse types, and the focus of treatment shifted toward psychopharmacology, as American medical care entered what is popularly known as "the Prozac era," so named for the antidepressant drug PROZAC®, which became widely prescribed. While most researchers and clinicians working on depression argue for a mix of methods, an emphasis on chemical treatments of symptoms has increased steadily in the last 30 years.

Since 2000 the *DSM* (fourth edition, Text Revision) has categorized depression as a mood disorder, distinguished it from bipolar disorders, and identified the subcategories *major depressive disorder, dysthymic disorder,* and *depressive disorder not otherwise specified.* Although the *DSM IV-TR* is considered the standard tool for diagnosis and treatment of depression in the United States, it has been criticized for numerous reasons, including its adherence to a deficit model of description and treatment (one that posits that disability is a problem that inheres in an individual's body rather than a problem that is socially constructed), as well as its failure to address adequately the sociocultural contexts that accompany diagnoses of depression.

Feminist scholarship has called into question many previously accepted features of depression, including its disproportionate diagnosis in women, and its tendency to be associated with sexist terms such as "HYSTERIA." Testimonials and studies involving VETERANS of World Wars I and II, and particularly the Vietnam and Persian Gulf wars, have brought attention to the role of trauma and post-traumatic stress disorder, in depression. Today, although the causes of depression are not known, it is acknowledged that depression affects about 19 million people in the United States—approximately one in 16. Recent research suggests that there may be both genetic and socioeconomic factors involved.

Popular REPRESENTATIONS of depression highlight broader social understandings of depression. For example, a common STEREOTYPE of artists and writers who experience depression is a romanticized notion of the condition that casts these individuals as a suffering artist or genius. Issues of depression influence and pervade many artistic works, such as Edgar Allan Poe's "The Fall of the House of Usher" (1840), Sylvia Plath's poem "Lady Lazarus" (1962) and her autobiographical novel, *The Bell Jar* (1962), as well as CHARLOTTE PERKINS GILMAN's "THE YELLOW WALLPAPER" (1892) and various works by WILLIAM FAULKNER and TONI MORRISON. Other forms of POPULAR CULTURE frequently include issues of depression, from plays such as Eugene O'Neil's *Anna Christie* (1922) to FILMS such as *Sunset Boulevard* (1950) and *Girl, Interrupted* (1999).

Particularly in recent decades, numerous prominent Americans, including novelist William Styron, actor Jim Carrey, journalist Mike Wallace, and Kitty Dukakis (wife of 1988 presidential candidate Michael Dukakis), have chosen to share their experiences with depression through MEMOIRS or in other public forums. Stigmatizing reactions to such disclosures continue, as when actor Tom Cruise publicly attacked Brooke Shields in 2007 for using therapy and ANTIDEPRESSANTS to treat her postpartum depression. The mixed public response to Cruise's attack indicates that popular opinion of depression may be shifting, although slowly.

Depression continues to be a pervasive issue in American culture. Understanding the changing interpretations and approaches to depression can help reveal the changing nature of American attitudes on diverse topics, including GENDER, HEALTH CARE, and art.

See also PERSIAN GULF WAR; SOCIAL CONSTRUCTION OF DISABILITY; VIETNAM WAR; WORLD WAR I; WORLD WAR II.

Margaret Price

Further Reading:
Blazer, Dan G. *The Age of Melancholy: "Major Depression" and Its Social Origins.* New York: Routledge, 2005.
Danquah, Meri Nana-Ama. *Willow Weep for Me: A Black Woman's Journey through Depression.* New York: One World, 1999.
Russell, Denise. "Shifting Trends in Diagnosis." In *Women, Madness, and Medicine,* 51–71. Cambridge, Mass.: Polity Press, 1995.
Stoppard, Janet M., and Linda M. McMullen, eds. *Situating Sadness: Women and Depression in Social Context.* New York: New York University Press, 2003.
Styron, William. *Darkness Visible: A Memoir of Madness.* New York: Vintage, 1992.

Developmental Disabilities Assistance and Bill of Rights Act

The Developmental Disabilities Assistance and Bill of Rights Act (DDABRA) of 1975 is an important guarantee of the rights of people with developmental disabilities that also created a system of state public advocacy agencies to monitor those rights. Developmental disabilities (DD) were defined in the Act as MENTAL RETARDATION, CEREBRAL PALSY, EPILEPSY, AUTISM, and dyslexia and other neurological conditions that originated before the age of 18 and constituted "substantial handicaps." In 1978 this categorical definition was replaced by a definition based on functional limitations.

The DDABRA built on an earlier federal statute, the Mental Retardation Facilities and Community Health Centers

Construction Act of 1963 that had helped to create a system of community-based agencies to serve people with mental retardation and MENTAL ILLNESS as they were leaving state facilities as part of the movement for DEINSTITUTIONALIZATION. The 1963 act was reauthorized and expanded in 1970 with the Developmental Disabilities Services and Facilities Construction Amendments of 1970, which first used the term developmental disabilities and provided federal grants to states to provide services and construct facilities for people with developmental disabilities, and to establish state planning agencies to assess those services.

The DDABRA went further, establishing Protection and Advocacy (P & A) systems in each state to ensure the safety and well being of individuals with developmental disabilities. The P & A systems were designed to advocate for the rights of people with DD, and they were empowered to pursue legal, administrative, and other remedies to ensure those rights, including the right to appropriate treatment and services designed to maximize individual potential. The law specifically required that individuals residing in institutions receive appropriate services, and it prohibited the use of physical or chemical restraints except when "absolutely necessary," and mandated that visits from close relatives be permitted "at reasonable hours without prior notice." The act also funded new programs at universities to conduct DD services research and to provide education and training to DD service providers. Following the 1975 act, Congress passed subsequent reauthorizations and amendments in 1984, 1987, 1990, 1994, and 2000.

The DDABRA of 1975 constituted a significant step in bringing resources and attention to issues of support services for people with developmental disabilities. The act also proved instrumental in the promotion of disability rights, by providing public funding for legal advocacy efforts on behalf of people with disabilities, individuals who are often marginalized and lack the resources or expertise to pursue legal advocacy on their own. However, because the P & A systems are located within state governments, disability advocates have charged that P & A advocates often encounter bureaucratic and political barriers in their work on behalf of people with developmental disabilities.

See also COGNITIVE AND INTELLECTUAL DISABILITY; DEVELOPMENTAL DISABILITY; KENNEDY, JOHN F.; LAW AND POLICY.

Richard K. Scotch

Further Reading:

"Legislative History and Evolution of the DD Act." URL: http://www.md-council.org/Resources/DD_Act/History/history.html.

Pelka, Fred. *The ABC-CLIO Companion to the Disability Rights Movement.* Santa Barbara, Calif.: ABC-CLIO, 1997.

Developmental Disabilities Assistance and Bill of Rights Act

The Developmental Disabilities Assistance and Bill of Rights Act of 1975 guarantees the rights of people with developmental disabilities; as one measure to support these rights, the act established protection and advocacy programs to serve people with developmental disabilities. The act built on the 1963 Mental Retardation Facilities and Community Health Centers Construction Act and the 1970 Developmental Disabilities Services and Facilities Construction Amendments; the addition of "Bill of Rights" marks an important shift in approach to citizens with developmental disabilities and specifically addressed their rights to treatment and services intended to maximize their potential and provided public funding for legal advocacy work. Congress reauthorized the act and passed new amendments to it in 1984, 1987, 1990, 1994, and 2000.

Developmental Disabilities Assistance and Bill of Rights Act of 2000 Public Law 106-402

An Act to improve service systems for individuals with developmental disabilities, and for other purposes. October 30, 2000

. . . Purpose.—The purpose of this title is to assure that individuals with developmental disabilities and their families participate in the design of and have access to needed community services, individualized supports, and other forms of assistance that promote self-determination, independence, productivity, and integration and inclusion in all facets of community life, through culturally competent programs authorized under this title, including specifically—

(1) State Councils on Developmental Disabilities in each State to engage in advocacy, capacity building, and systemic change activities that—

(A) are consistent with the purpose described in this subsection and the policy described in subsection (c); and

(B) contribute to a coordinated, consumer- and family-centered, consumer- and family-directed, comprehensive system that includes needed community services, individualized supports, and other forms of assistance that promote self-determination for individuals with developmental disabilities and their families;

(2) protection and advocacy systems in each State to protect the legal and human rights of individuals with developmental disabilities;

(3) University Centers for Excellence in Developmental Disabilities Education, Research, and Service—

(A) to provide interdisciplinary pre-service preparation and continuing education of students and fellows, which may include the preparation and continuing education of leadership, direct service, clinical, or other personnel to strengthen and increase the capacity of States and communities to achieve the purpose of this title;

(B) to provide community services—

(i) that provide training and technical assistance for individuals with developmental disabilities, their families, professionals, para-professionals, policymakers, students, and other members of the community; and

(ii) that may provide services, supports, and assistance for the persons described in clause (i) through demonstration and model activities;

(C) to conduct research, which may include basic or applied research, evaluation, and the analysis of public policy in areas that affect or could affect, either positively or negatively, individuals with developmental disabilities and their families; and

(D) to disseminate information related to activities undertaken to address the purpose of this title, especially dissemination of information that demonstrates that the network authorized under this subtitle is a national and international resource that includes specific substantive areas of expertise that may be accessed and applied in diverse settings and circumstances; and

(4) funding for—

(A) national initiatives to collect necessary data on issues that are directly or indirectly relevant to the lives of individuals with developmental disabilities;

(B) technical assistance to entities who engage in or intend to engage in activities consistent with the purpose described in this subsection or the policy described in subsection (c); and other nationally significant activities.

(C) Policy.—It is the policy of the United States that all programs, projects, and activities receiving assistance under this title shall be carried out in a manner consistent with the principles that—

(1) individuals with developmental disabilities, including those with the most severe developmental disabilities, are capable of self-determination, independence, productivity, and integration and inclusion in all facets of community life, but often require the provision of community services, individualized supports, and other forms of assistance;

(2) individuals with developmental disabilities and their families have competencies, capabilities, and personal goals that should be recognized, supported, and encouraged, and any assistance to such individuals should be provided in an individualized manner, consistent with the unique strengths, resources, priorities, concerns, abilities, and capabilities of such individuals;

(3) individuals with developmental disabilities and their families are the primary decision-makers regarding the services and supports such individuals and their families receive, including regarding choosing where the individuals live from available options, and play decisionmaking roles in policies and programs that affect the lives of such individuals and their families;

(4) services, supports, and other assistance should be provided in a manner that demonstrates respect for individual dignity, personal preferences, and cultural differences;

(5) specific efforts must be made to ensure that individuals with developmental disabilities from racial and ethnic minority backgrounds and their families enjoy increased and meaningful opportunities to access and use community services, individualized supports, and other forms of assistance available to other individuals with developmental disabilities and their families;

(6) recruitment efforts in disciplines related to developmental disabilities relating to preservice training, community training, practice, administration, and policymaking must focus on bringing larger numbers of racial and ethnic minorities into the disciplines in order to provide appropriate skills, knowledge, role models, and sufficient personnel to address the growing needs of an increasingly diverse population;

(7) with education and support, communities can be accessible to and responsive to the needs of individuals with developmental disabilities and their families and are enriched by full and active participation in community activities, and contributions, by individuals with developmental disabilities and their families;

(8) individuals with developmental disabilities have access to opportunities and the necessary support to be included in community life,

have interdependent relationships, live in homes and communities, and make contributions to their families, communities, and States, and the Nation;

(9) efforts undertaken to maintain or expand community-based living options for individuals with disabilities should be monitored in order to determine and report to appropriate individuals and entities the extent of access by individuals with developmental disabilities to those options and the extent of compliance by entities providing those options with quality assurance standards;

(10) families of children with developmental disabilities need to have access to and use of safe and appropriate child care and before-school and after-school programs, in the most integrated settings, in order to enrich the participation of the children in community life;

(11) individuals with developmental disabilities need to have access to and use of public transportation, in order to be independent and directly contribute to and participate in all facets of community life; and

(12) individuals with developmental disabilities need to have access to and use of recreational, leisure, and social opportunities in the most integrated settings, in order to enrich their participation in community life.

... Sec. 109. Rights of Individuals With Developmental Disabilities.

(a) In General.—Congress makes the following findings respecting the rights of individuals with developmental disabilities:

(1) Individuals with developmental disabilities have a right to appropriate treatment, services, and habilitation for such disabilities, consistent with section 101(c).

(2) The treatment, services, and habitation for an individual with developmental disabilities should be designed to maximize the potential of the individual and should be provided in the setting that is least restrictive of the individual's personal liberty.

(3) The Federal Government and the States both have an obligation to ensure that public funds are provided only to institutional programs, residential programs, and other community programs, including educational programs in which individuals with developmental disabilities participate, that—

(A) provide treatment, services, and habilitation that are appropriate to the needs of such individuals; and

(B) meet minimum standards relating to—

(i) provision of care that is free of abuse, neglect, sexual and financial exploitation, and violations of legal and human rights and that subjects individuals with developmental disabilities to no greater risk of harm than others in the general population;

(ii) provision to such individuals of appropriate and sufficient medical and dental services;

(iii) prohibition of the use of physical restraint and seclusion for such an individual unless absolutely necessary to ensure the immediate physical safety of the individual or others, and prohibition of the use of such restraint and seclusion as a punishment or as a substitute for a habilitation program;

(iv) prohibition of the excessive use of chemical restraints on such individuals and the use of such restraints as punishment or as a substitute for a habilitation program or in quantities that interfere with services, treatment, or habilitation for such individuals; and

(v) provision for close relatives or guardians of such individuals to visit the individuals without prior notice.

(4) All programs for individuals with developmental disabilities should meet standards—

(A) that are designed to assure the most favorable possible outcome for those served; and

(B)(i) in the case of residential programs serving individuals in need of comprehensive health-related, habilitative, assistive technology or rehabilitative services, that are at least equivalent to those standards applicable to intermediate care facilities for the mentally retarded, promulgated in regulations of the Secretary on June 3, 1988, as appropriate, taking into account the size of the institutions and the service delivery arrangements of the facilities of the programs;

(ii) in the case of other residential programs for individuals with developmental disabilities, that assure that—

(I) care is appropriate to the needs of the individuals being served by such programs;

(II) the individuals admitted to facilities of such programs are individuals whose needs can be met through services provided by such facilities; and

  (III) the facilities of such programs provide for the humane care of the residents of the facilities, are sanitary, and protect their rights; and

  (iii) in the case of nonresidential programs, that assure that the care provided by such programs is appropriate to the individuals served by the programs.

  (b) Clarification.—The rights of individuals with developmental disabilities described in findings made in this section shall be considered to be in addition to any constitutional or other rights otherwise afforded to all individuals.

⬥

Source: Excerpted from the Web site of the U.S. Government Printing Office. URL: http://frwebgate.access.gpo.gov/cgi-bin/getdoc.cgi?dbname=106_cong_public_laws&docid=f:publ402.106.

developmental disability

Developmental disability is a catch-all term that only relatively recently has come to prominence in the United States. In many areas of the world the equivalent term is intellectual disability. *Developmentally disabled* is often used as a replacement for terms such as mentally disabled or mentally retarded, which are viewed as pejorative by many in the disability COMMUNITY; however, the term DEVELOPMENTAL DISABILITY refers to a wide range of significant life-long disorders. These conditions are due to mental or physical IMPAIRMENTS and include AUTISM spectrum disorders, CEREBRAL PALSY, DOWN SYNDROME, and many other conditions formerly called "MENTAL RETARDATION" as well as FETAL ALCOHOL SYNDROME and acquired cognitive impairments. The Centers for Disease Control and Prevention also includes hearing loss and vision impairment as developmental disabilities. According to the U.S. Administration on Developmental Disabilities, in 2007 there were approximately 4.5 million Americans with developmental disabilities, which it defines as a disability that substantially limits at least three of the following life functions: (1) capacity for independent living; (2) economic self-sufficiency; (3) learning; (4) mobility; (5) receptive/expressive language; (6) self-care; and (7) self-direction. Under this definition, the disability must be manifested before age 22 and must be a life-long condition.

Prior to the 19th century, most people with developmental disabilities lived with their extended families. They were largely viewed as a part of society and while sometimes subject to ridicule, according to scholar James Trent, they were "protected by the generosity and familiarity of the locals." With the rise of scientific research in the 19th century, reformers such as DOROTHEA DIX encouraged the creation of specialized ASYLUMS AND INSTITUTIONS for various disability populations, including developmentally disabled citizens.

While there exist accounts of these institutions as semi-utopian facilities, exposés and MEMOIRS in the early to mid 20th century depict many institutions as oppressive, dangerous, and inhumane. Unfortunately, ABUSE of people with developmental disabilities is a significant theme in the history of this group. Various factors, including communication barriers, isolation, and perceived or actual dependency have contributed to the vulnerability that people with developmental disabilities often experience. Indeed, concerns over GENETIC conditions and resentment of their dependency on others partially motivated eugenicists to demand that many people with developmental disabilities remain permanently institutionalized or forcibly sterilized in order to "protect" society from their "tainted" presence. In the late 19th and early 20th centuries, tens of thousands of people, mostly those with or perceived as having developmental disabilities, were sterilized in the United States.

At various times, FAMILY members, reformers, and journalists have brought the issue of abuse from the margins of society into public focus. For example, in a 1972 undercover TELEVISION report, journalist Geraldo Rivera documented deplorable conditions and abuse at the Willowbrook State School in Staten Island, New York. The television exposé sparked a lawsuit and the school eventually closed.

Motivated by concerns over abuse and oppression, disability advocates in the 1970s urged policymakers and medical experts to deinstitutionalize people with developmental disabilities. Activists proposed various community living options, including GROUP HOMES, as a means to promote autonomy and community integration. These options have benefited some individuals, but others have struggled due to inadequate community supports and difficulties assessing appropriate options.

EMPOWERMENT and self-advocacy have become prominent features in the history of people with developmental disabilities. For example, prior to the 1970s ORGANIZATIONS such as THE ARC and SPECIAL OLYMPICS originally served people with developmental disabilities but did not encourage members of this community to join its leadership. In 1974 People First, an activist organization comprised of people with cognitive disabilities, held its first convention. Since the 1970s organizations historically serving developmentally disabled people and associations of and for individuals with development disabilities have emphasized the important role of self-advocacy and empowerment training.

The many campaigns to improve educational, vocational, and social options for disabled Americans have provided tangible results. Visibility of people with developmental disabilities has grown in the last several decades in the United States, and media and POPULAR CULTURE depictions reflect this change. For instance, the television series *Facts of Life* (1980–84) included comedian GERI JEWELL and *Life Goes On* (1989–93) spotlighted actor CHRIS BURKE, both of whom have developmental disabilities.

In the general disability rights movement, people with developmental disabilities have been only partially involved. Although they share many of the limiting STEREOTYPES as other people with disabilities, people with developmental disabilities often have fewer options for sharing their personal viewpoints or for building a strong economic network to support their cause. Contested topics such as SEXUALITY and competency further complicate their status and choices. America's treatment of developmental disabilities reveals previously unquestioned assumptions about citizenship, worth, community, and competence. Disability studies of this topic will likely offer new insights into this feature of our common heritage.

See also COGNITIVE AND INTELLECTUAL DISABILITY; DEPENDENT AND DEPENDENCE; EUGENICS; INVOLUNTARY STERILIZATION; SELF-ADVOCATES AND SELF-ADVOCACY; SELF ADVOCATES BECOMING EMPOWERED.

David Penna
Vickie D'Andrea-Penna

Further Reading:

American Association on Mental Retardation. "World's Oldest Organization on Intellectual Disability Has a Progressive New Name." Press release, 2 November 2006. Washington, D.C.: American Association on Mental Retardation.

Blatt, Burton. *Exodus from Pandemonium.* Boston: Allyn & Bacon, 1970.

Trent, James W., Jr. *Inventing the Feeble Mind: A History of Mental Retardation in the United States.* Berkeley: University of California Press. 1994.

Williams, Paul, and Bonnie Shoultz. *We Can Speak for Ourselves.* Bloomington: Indiana University Press, 1984.

diabetes

Type 1 diabetes (or more properly diabetes mellitus) is a chronic autoimmune DISEASE in which the body does not produce insulin, a hormone that the pancreas creates that controls blood glucose levels. Currently there is no cure for Type 1 diabetes, although it can be controlled by insulin intake (either by injection or by a pump), blood glucose monitoring, diet control, and exercise. Type 1 diabetes, formerly known as Juvenile-Onset or Insulin Dependent Diabetes, is

characterized by the destruction of the insulin-producing beta cells of the pancreas and, without regular injections of insulin, the patient will die. In addition, if the patient does not check blood sugars and give appropriate insulin doses he or she will develop complications, including heart disease, blindness, kidney failure, nerve damage, and damage to the blood vessels that may lead to lower limb amputation. Its cause is unknown although genetic and environmental factors play a part in its onset. There are approximately 500,000 people worldwide with Type 1 diabetes and about 65,000 more are diagnosed each year.

Type 2 diabetes mellitus, formerly known as Adult-Onset Diabetes, results from the body's resistance to insulin and the inability of the body to produce enough insulin to overcome the insulin resistance. It is much more of a lifestyle disorder than Type 1 diabetes, as high blood pressure, poor diet, obesity, and lack of exercise are major causes of the disease. There are significantly larger numbers of Type 2 cases, with approximately 18 million people worldwide diagnosed with the disease. Numbers of individuals with Type 2 diabetes mellitus are increasing rapidly, reaching epidemic proportions, especially in the United States and western Europe. This is a result of increasing obesity among large segments of the population, even children, a population in which Type 2 diabetes was quite rare until approximately 1990.

Diabetes has been identified as a specific disease since about 1200 B.C.E. in Egypt. Ancient Greek physicians, including Hippocrates and Galen, also identified the disease as one in which the patient exhibits frequent urination and is often thirsty, although Galen wrongly viewed its origin in the kidneys. In approximately 150 C.E., Aretaeus, another Greek physician and contemporary of Galen, named the disorder "Diabetes," from the Greek word for siphon. He described the disease as "a melting down of the flesh and limbs into urine." He called this melting "rapid" and death "speedy." For the next thousand years, little more was known of the disease except that there was no CURE. As the Renaissance opened Europe to new ideas and thoughts, physicians and scientists began to look again at patients who exhibited the symptoms of diabetes. The Swiss physician Paracelsus hypothesized in the early 16th century that the disease was caused by an accumulation of salts in the body. In 1675 the English natural philosopher Thomas Willis determined that diabetes was a disorder of the blood and called the disease the "pissing evil" for the sweetness of the patient's urine. By the end of the 18th century, English and French doctors had developed dietary regimens that called for a decrease in the intake of sugars, which prolonged the lives of patients diagnosed with diabetes.

By the beginning of the 20th century, researchers had conclusively determined that the pancreas was somehow related to the onset of diabetes. German physician Paul

Langerhans discovered small cells within the pancreas, which would be named "Islets of Langerhans." In 1901 American pathologist Eugene Opie determined that there was a connection between these cells and the origins of diabetes. By 1920 the secretion of these islet cells was named insulin (Latin for island). In 1921–22 two Canadian scientists, Frederick Banting and Charles Best, isolated this secretion and developed a technique for injecting it into patients with diabetes. This provided the first real opportunity for patients to live with the disease. Their experimental patient, a 14-year-old boy identified as L.T., lived for 13 more years with the continued injections of insulin. Banting, but not Best, received the Nobel Prize for medicine in 1923.

The development of insulin changed the lives of patients with diabetes forever. Continued scientific developments, including new and better methods of blood glucose monitoring, have improved the life chances of patients with Type 1 diabetes. Since the mid 1990s, the development of an insulin pump delivery system offers freedom from injections for an increasing number of patients. Research is currently focused on improving both blood glucose monitoring and insulin delivery as well as on determining a cure for the disease.

Diabetes is currently considered a disability covered under the Americans with Disabilities Act (ADA) of 1990. However, as a result of three 1999 Supreme Court decisions (referred to as the Sutton trilogy), a person with diabetes will have to show that they still meet the definition of disability after taking any mitigating measures—such as insulin or oral medications. If after these measures, the individual is determined to be "stable," they cannot be covered under the provisions of ADA. Courts are required to undertake an individual assessment of each person, looking at how diabetes affects them. This includes such things as the impact of insulin and oral medication on the person and any diabetes-related complications.

People with diabetes have rarely been involved in the broader disabilities movement since the disease is not contagious and not linked to social class or obvious physical disability. Without those overt signs of disability, stigma has been less of a problem for those with diabetes. Insulin has "normalized" the lives of people with diabetes, making their relationship to disability rather tenuous. With the increasing numbers of persons with Type II diabetes and its association with lifestyle choices, however, the relationship between the disease and disability as a social construct may be increasing.

See also social construction of disability.

Steven Noll

Further Reading:
Bliss, Michael. *The Discovery of Insulin.* Chicago: University of Chicago Press, 1982.

Feudtner, John Christopher. *Bittersweet: Diabetes, Insulin, and the Transformation of Illness.* Chapel Hill: University of North Carolina Press, 2003.

Diagnostic and Statistical Manual of Mental Disorders

Published by the American Psychiatric Association, the *Diagnostic and Statistical Manual of Mental Disorders (DSM)* is the most widely used source of diagnostic criteria on mental illness and mental disorders in the United States. It is applied in a range of therapeutic contexts by mental health clinicians and researchers as well as by insurance companies, pharmaceutical companies, and policymakers. Now in its sixth version (that is, four classificatory editions with textual revisions of the last two), published in 2000, each successive version of the *DSM* refines the classification and diagnosis of mental disorders in light of current clinical perspectives. In so doing, each new edition attempts to be more inclusive of individuals with mental health disabilities in social programs, protected groups, and for insurance policies. Inevitably, however, each version leads to new ways to exclude these individuals from such programs and from society at large.

The first version of the *DSM* (1952) described 106 categories of mental disorder. The revised *DSM-II* (1968) presented 182 disorders responding to claims that the earlier edition did not establish clear boundaries erected between normal and abnormal. In its seventh printing in 1974, this edition included its best-known change: removing "homosexuality" as a category of disorder, replacing it with the category of "sexual orientation disturbance." The current *DSM-IV-TR* does not classify homosexuality as a disorder, and "sexual orientation disturbance" is no longer a diagnosis. Renaming and reorganizing of conditions have continued in the next two editions. The *DSM-III* (1980) and its text revision *DSM-III-R* (1987) list 292 disorders, while the *DSM-IV* (1994) and its text revision, *DSM-IV-TR* (2000), contain 297. The publication of the *DSM-V* is anticipated in 2011 or later.

The current version, the *DSM-IV*, is comprised of three major components: the diagnostic classification, the diagnostic criteria, and the descriptive text. The diagnostic classification lists the mental disorders that belong within the system of analytic criteria. Its major categories include disorders usually first diagnosed in infancy, childhood, or adolescence; delirium, dementia, amnesic and other cognitive disorders; mental disorder due to a general medical condition not elsewhere classified; mood disorders; anxiety disorders; somatoform disorders; factitious disorders; dissociative disorders; sexual and gender identity disorders; eating disorders; sleeping disorders; impulse-control disorders not elsewhere classified; adjustment disorders; and personality disorders. The diagnostic criteria assess each disorder based on five "axes": symptoms; patient's past history; relevant physical symptoms; associated psychosocial stressors; and patient's highest level of adaptive functioning within the past year. In establishing diagnosis, the descriptive text considers psychological, social, and cross-cultural variables.

The *DSM* has attracted criticism as well as praise. Critics contend that the manual not only invents illnesses and behaviors but also uses them to label individuals unfairly. These critics question whether many of the *DSM*'s categories— "disorder of written expression" is one example—are valid, demonstrable disorders. Others criticize the *DSM* because its categories, particularly in earlier editions, were neither properly field-tested nor informed by professional experience and expert opinion. Some professionals, however, commend the manual's carefully constructed categories and find its diagnostic criteria useful if applied with clinical knowledge, judgment, and experience.

See also LANGUAGE AND TERMINOLOGY; LGBT; MEDICAL MODEL OF DISABILITY.

Sara Newman

Further Reading:

American Psychiatric Association. *Diagnostic and Statistical Manual of Mental Disorders.* 4th ed. *(DSM-IV).* Washington, D.C.: American Psychiatric Association, 1994.
———. "DSM-IV Official Site." URL: http://dsmivtr.org/.
———. "DSM V Research Planning Activities." URL: http://www.dsm5.org/planning.cfm.
Cockerham, William C. *Sociology of Mental Disorder.* 4th ed. Upper Saddle River, N.J.: Prentice Hall, 1996.

disability art and artistic expression

Throughout American history, artistic expression has been a powerful vehicle for communicating ideas about disability. Artistic expression includes any form of creative REPRESENTATION intended for an audience, including the performing, literary, visual, and musical arts. From what is considered the high arts, such as THEATER and SCULPTURE, to what is considered the low arts, such as CIRCUS sideshows and stand-up comedy, the arts across media both reflect and contribute to the understanding of disability in American culture. Historically, artists have used representations of disability in ways that have contradicted the lived experience, feelings, and concerns of disabled people themselves. Primarily, artists have used disability to symbolize the grotesque and evil, or paradoxically, the inspirational and innocent. These representations have generally failed to capture the complexity of life lived with a disability.

DEVELOPMENT OF DISABILITY ART

Of course, artists themselves have always experienced disability both directly (through AGE, ILLNESS, accident, or birth) and indirectly (through relationships with friends and FAMILY). The term *disability art* tends to describe the work of artists with disabilities that overtly and intentionally references a disability experience. It is almost impossible to assess, however, the relationship between artists' experiences with disability and the representations they create in their work prior to the disability art movement that emerged alongside the DISABILITY RIGHTS MOVEMENT in the 1970s. Circus sideshow performers, such as little people CHARLES SHERWOOD STRATTON (1838–83) and LAVINIA WARREN STRATTON (1841–1919) or CONJOINED TWINS such as CHANG AND ENG BUNKER (1811–74) and Daisy and Violet Hilton (1908–69), were artists with disabilities whose work focused on their IMPAIRMENTS, but the extent to which these artists exercised creative control over their own representations is not fully understood. Other artists are known to have had impairments, including watercolorist Charles Demuth (1883–1935), who was a POLIO survivor; painter Horace Pippin (1888–1946), who had an arm damaged by WAR; writer CARSON MCCULLERS (1917–67), who had rheumatic fever and paralysis; and painter James Castle (1900–77) who was DEAF. It is difficult to determine, however, how these artists' work relates to their experiences of disability because they either did not self-identify as disabled, likely to avoid stigmatization (see STIGMA), or because their references to disability were covert or rare. Additionally, critics and art historians minimized the role of disability in these artists' lives or work, either ignoring it altogether or identifying it only in terms of a tragedy to OVERCOME on the way to success.

Significant changes in the 1970s, including the rise and spread of the disability rights movement, provided a rich context for artists with disabilities to begin generating work that self-consciously responded to mainstream society's narrow representations of disability. In the process they have redefined the meaning of disability for themselves, the disability rights movement, and the public at large. The explosion of the contemporary disability art movement is partly a result of civil rights legislation that has removed some of the barriers to the EDUCATION and training of disabled artists. Many of these artists have demonstrated an increased willingness to examine, and an interest in exploring, the lived experience of disability overtly in their work; a significant number have directly participated in or supported the disability rights movement. Others have had direct associations with Centers for Independent Living as employees, board members, or consumers. This work has had the powerful effect of redefining disability as a social or group identity made up of people who have different impairments but nonetheless consider themselves allies with shared cultural values.

ORGANIZATIONS FOR DISABLED ARTISTS

The coalescence of a group IDENTITY is reflected in the emergence of a number of theater and dance companies that include artists with a variety of impairments. Most support the development of original work on the subject of disability and deafness. National Theatre Workshop of the Handicapped, for example, was founded in 1977 in Belfast, Maine. This company provides professional theatrical training for artists with a variety of physical impairments. The NATIONAL THEATRE OF THE DEAF was founded in 1967 in Waterford, Connecticut, and Theater by the Blind was founded in 1979 in New York City. In 2008 Theater by the Blind changed its name to THEATER BREAKING THROUGH BARRIERS to reflect its efforts to include theater artists with various types of impairments in addition to those who are BLIND and low vision. Dancing Wheels (founded in 1980) in Cleveland, Ohio, AXIS DANCE COMPANY (founded in 1987), and in Oakland, California, Joint Forces Dance Company (founded in 1987) in Eugene, Oregon, were among the first physically integrated dance companies. Congruent with the disability rights movement's goal to integrate disabled and NONDISABLED people in society, all of these theater and DANCE companies include artists with and without disabilities.

ORGANIZATIONS have emerged to support and promote the work of artists with disabilities as well as provide technical assistance in providing accommodations to artists and audiences with disabilities. A sampling includes VSA ARTS of Washington, D.C. (founded in 1974 and formerly known as Very Special Arts), which has affiliates across the United States and internationally; the Alliance for Inclusion in the Arts in New York City (founded in and formerly known as the Non-Traditional Casting Project (founded in 1986); the National Arts and Disability Center at the University of California-Los Angeles (founded in 1994); and the International Archive of Deaf Artists (founded in 1998) at the NATIONAL TECHNICAL INSTITUTE FOR THE DEAF at Rochester Institute of Technology. The National Endowment for the Arts, along with VSA Arts, has been funding studies and focus groups nationwide to uncover the barriers and facilitators to careers in the arts for people with disabilities in an effort to improve conditions for disabled people attempting to make their livings as artists. Disability art festivals are held across the United States. A sampling includes the annual Superfest Film Festival (founded in 1980) in BERKELEY, CALIFORNIA; This/Ability at the University of Michigan–Ann Arbor (1995); Bodies of Work: the Chicago Festival of Disability Arts and Culture (2006); the annual Disability Pride Art and Culture Festival (founded in 2006) in Portland, Oregon, and the Independence Starts Here: Festival of Disability Pride Arts and Culture (2007) in Philadelphia. These festivals not only feature artists with disabilities but also have become models for providing audience accessibility to programming, such as accessible seating, BRAILLE programs, SIGN LANGUAGE INTERPRETERS, assistive listening devices, and AUDIO DESCRIPTION.

SELF-REPRESENTATION AND IDENTITY

As part of the process of redefining disability, many artists, across impairment type and artistic media, have explicitly addressed the STEREOTYPES of disability found in mainstream cultures. PLAYWRIGHTS Mike Ervin and Susan Nussbaum, for example, mocked stereotypes in their 1990 comedy revue *The Plucky and Spunky Show,* which premiered at the Remains Theatre in Chicago and was performed with disabled and nondisabled cast members. Poet, playwright, and performer LYNN MANNING's (1955–) widely published poem "The Magic Wand" (1997) angrily confronted audiences about stereotypes of African-American men and blind men. Manning wrote about how passersby who do not know he is blind see him only as a "black man" and assume he is a gang member, basketball player, or rapist. However, unfolding his traveling cane transforms him, like a magic wand, in others' eyes into a "blind man," a figure that historically has been cast as a saint or musical savant. Manning performs this poem as part of his one-man show, *Weights,* which premiered in 2001 at the Center Theatre Group in Los Angeles.

Although many do not identify with the disability arts movement, deaf cultural artists have created a community and artistic forms of representation that share with disabled artists the goal of EMPOWERMENT and recognition of distinct lived experiences. The De'Via Manifesto (Deaf View/Image Art), for example, was created in 1989 by deaf cultural artists Betty G. Miller and Paul Johnston to reflect defining characteristics of deaf cultural art. This includes metaphors and representations that embody deaf cultural values.

Deaf and disabled artists have replaced STEREOTYPES with stories from their own lives, often taking the form of autobiography, whether in the performing, literary, or visual arts. At the Mark Taper Forum Theatre in Los Angeles, Victoria Ann Lewis (1946–) founded THE OTHER VOICES PROJECT in 1981 to develop the talents of disabled theater artists. Early performance workshops focused on disabled actors' autobiographical material and culminated in two TELEVISION specials: *Tell Them I'm a Mermaid* (1983) and *Who Parks in Those Spaces* (1985). Nancy Mairs's *Plain Text* (1986) is an influential collection of essays that explored her feminist views on motherhood and work, complicated by her experiences of DEPRESSION, agoraphobia, and MULTIPLE SCLEROSIS. JOHN HOCKENBERRY's (1956–) *Moving Violations: War Zones, Wheelchairs and Declarations of Independence* (1996) chronicled his career as a journalist and tackled issues from war in the Middle East to fighting for accessible public TRANSPORTATION to the mechanics of sex as a PARAPLEGIC.

In 1996 Hockenberry performed excerpts from his MEMOIR in a one-man show called *Spoke Man* at American Place Theater in New York. Simi Linton's (1947–　) *My Body Politic* (2006) explored the emergence and growth of her disability identity through community with disabled scholars, activists, and artists. Independent filmmaker Laurel Chiten has made documentary FILMS in which people with disabilities dispel myths by telling stories about their own lives. Her 1994 film *TWITCH AND SHOUT* (1994) features people with TOURETTE SYNDROME, and her 2007 film *Twisted* features people with dystonia. Chiten, who also shares the diagnoses of dystonia and Tourette syndrome, is known for creating multifaceted portraits of her interview subjects, that are poignant, funny, irreverent, and fully human.

PAINTERS have been creating portraits of themselves and others to create complex images of people with disabilities that defy stereotypes. Jonathan Wos (1981–　) has created self-portraits across media—sculpture, painting, and drawing—that depict many different aspects of living with osteogenesis imperfecta. He uses a variety of representational strategies, ranging from parody to realism to abstraction, giving his body of work rich dimensions. Like Wos, painter Sunaura Taylor (1982–　) paints exquisitely realistic full-body portraits of herself and others. In her portraits, the subjects display expressions on their faces that are ambivalent. The viewer has permission to look unabashedly at the subjects' distinctive bodies; it is clear that the subjects are aware they are being looked at

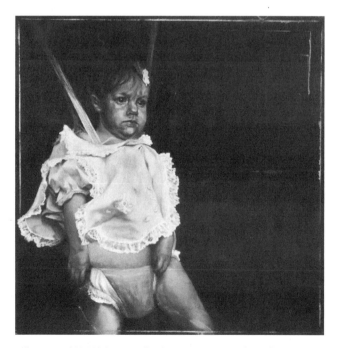

Jolly Jumper (2003) is one of painter Sunaura Taylor's first explorations of her childhood experiences with disability. The jumper apparatus holding her suggests both confinement to a space as well as an opportunity to explore movement. *(Sunaura Taylor)*

but unclear how they respond to such scrutiny. Thus, viewers are prompted to think about their interest in disabled bodies and the complicated emotions such an encounter provokes. These subjects cannot be neatly stereotyped.

In exploring the lived experience of disability in their work, numerous artists have addressed how their disability identity is informed by other aspects of their identity, such as RACE, class, GENDER, and SEXUALITY. Anne Finger's (1951–　) memoir *Past Due: A Story of Disability, Pregnancy and Birth* (1990) chronicles the tensions in the feminist community around issues of motherhood and REPRODUCTIVE RIGHTS. Johnson Cheu's POETRY and essays often take on experiences of disability within a Chinese-American FAMILY, as in his 1997 poems "Little Girl Gone" and "Banana Stealing." Poet and performer Leroy Moore (1967–　) has explored issues of African-American masculinity, disability, and sexuality in his work. With Todd Herman, he created a video called *Forbidden Acts: And Other Poems by Leroy Moore* (2003), which features three of his spoken word poems combined with Moore's dancelike movement sequences. Poet, essayist, and playwright Kenny Fries writes about his experiences as a gay, Jewish disabled man in his collection of poems *Anesthesia* (1996) and his memoir *Body Remember* (1997). These multifaceted expressions of identity enhance the understanding of disability.

STARING

Artists with visible impairments have also illuminated the daily experience of being the object of the curious public's intrusive stares. In the performing arts, especially, the experience of being stared at is overtly addressed, most likely because live performance offers an immediate opportunity to comment upon the dynamics of STARING. In his one-man show *Church of 80% Sincerity*, David Roche, who has a facial DISFIGUREMENT, begins the performance by asking the audience to chant in unison "What happened to your face?" He answers, satisfying his audience's curiosity so he can move on to other issues. Dancer and playwright Catherine Cole begins *Five Foot Feat* (2001) by crossing to center stage, facing the audience, and removing her PROSTHETIC left leg, letting the audience take in her unique physicality before continuing the performance with the other dancers.

Interdisciplinary and new media artist BILL SHANNON (1970–　), blurs the boundary between art on stage and art on the streets as a means of highlighting how he is expected to "perform" certain ideas about disability in DAILY LIFE. For example, his performance art piece "After the Fall" was performed and videotaped on the streets of Chicago in 1994 and Novogrod, Russia, in 1998. In this piece, Shannon performed everyday tasks or danced using his CRUTCHES. He videotaped passersby as they stared at him, offered to help him, or intruded into his personal space. In 2000 he incorporated the video documentation from "After the Fall" into a performance called "Spatial Theory," which premiered at Restless Gravity International Festival in Aberystwyth, Wales. In a lecture-type format, Shannon showed excerpts from the video to define for the audience different types of "looks" and offers of help he receives from the public. Like Shannon, stand-up comic Josh Blue (1978–   ) reflects back to audiences how they look at him, employing a technique he calls "reverse teasing." Blue became well known in 2006 for winning the NBC reality television series *Last Comic Standing.* In his act, Blue verbalized what he thinks people must be thinking about when they look at him. The result disarmed the audience through biting, but good-natured teasing.

Staring has the effect of isolating the person being looked at, effectively casting him or her as an anomalous individual. To counteract this trend in representation and in actual life, artists with disabilities have been creating collaborative projects that explore relationships between disabled people. In her highly acclaimed series of portraits, *Circle Stories* (begun in 1997), painter Riva Lehrer (1958–   ) creates intimate portraits of disabled artists and academics that invite viewers to linger over the images of her subjects, rather than coldly stare. In the process of staring, viewers usually attempt to categorize a disabled person, often drawing on their own stereotypical understanding of disability. Viewers encountering one of Lehrer's portraits, though, cannot easily categorize what they see. Lehrer creates her portraits through an extensive process of collaboration between the artist and her subjects. Lehrer has many conversations with her subjects and incorporates imagery from their lives into the work. Her subjects have a say in how they are depicted, whereas both in daily life and in artistic representations most disabled people have little control over how they are seen. The subjects in the final portraits directly meet the gaze of the viewer; they are not passive objects to be looked at. Viewers, in a sense, create a relationship with the subject and puzzle over the iconic images representative of the subjects' lives. Instead of overtly explaining the subjects' lives, the portraits compel viewers to create their own meanings pieced together from the clues that Lehrer and the subjects supply.

INNOVATION IN ART

German-born interdisciplinary artist Petra Kuppers (1968–   ) also collaborates closely with other disabled people to create new representations of people with disabilities. Kuppers is the artistic director of the Olympias Project (founded in 1998), which includes a series of community art projects including dance, poetry, installation, sound art, performance art, and video. These projects often involve professional artists with disabilities working side by side with disabled people new to art-making practices. This work provides opportunities for artistic expression and community building among people with disabilities, generating fresh perspectives, aesthetics, and material for their local communities and the international art world. Artists with disabilities also communicate to audiences their unique bodily, mental, and sensory experiences of the world. These artists are harnessing their bodies' particularities to provide new insights into their surroundings. Their work often challenges accepted aesthetic qualities of established artistic disciplines. Frank Moore (1946–   ) became infamous in the 1970s in the underground art community for his subversive, ritualistic performances that incorporate elements of theater or dance, but are neither. As a person with CEREBRAL PALSY who uses a laser pointer and a board with the alphabet, words, and numbers to communicate, he sought out means of connecting with others nonverbally. He coined the term "eroplay" in the 1980s to describe his nude performance events in which participants explored each others' bodies in nonsexual, but sensual and joyful ways. While Moore typically avoids being labeled as a disability artist, he is considered an influential pioneer and an ongoing contributor through his writing, INTERNET, and performance projects to the alternative art scene in general and Disability Art movement in particular. Charles Mee (1938–   ), who contracted polio in 1953, writes plays that are strongly influenced by his experiences of disability but are not explicitly about the topic of disability. Instead, he explains how his collagelike plays are not structurally "intact," but filled with brokenness and jagged edges, like his life.

Georgina Kleege's (1956–   ) book *Sight Unseen* (1999) includes a creative essay "The Mind's Eye," which is about how she experiences visual art as a BLIND person. She explains how she looks at a painting, using her peripheral vision, working her way around her blind spot, moving very close to paintings, scanning them, leaning to see from different angles, and then moving away. Her essay, which is a work of art in itself, expands the understanding of what constitutes a painting. The paintings of DAN KEPLINGER (1973–   ), who was featured in the 1999 Oscar-winning documentary *KING GIMP,* reflect his unique personal movement vocabulary as a man with cerebral palsy. Bold, bright, expansive brush strokes seem to leap from the canvas. Multimedia artist Stephen Lapthisophon, who is blind, has created installations that disorient his audiences by asking them to encounter out-of-kilter disability accommodations. In his installation *With Reasonable Accommodations* (2003), audiences encounter a ramp that leads into the wall, nonsensical signage, a walker dangling from the ceiling, and paintings that lean facing against the wall. Lapthisophon's installation encourages audiences to experience the confusion of navigating the world filled with inadequate and often absurd accommodations.

ADDRESSING THE MEDICAL MODEL
OF DISABILITY

Many artists with disabilities experience their bodies in relation to the MEDICAL MODEL OF DISABILITY. The mainstream public tends to think of people with disabilities solely in terms of their status as "patients," considering them as individuals in need of care or CURE rather than seeing them as fully rounded human beings. In contrast, through disability art, a much more complex and ambivalent relationship to medicine emerges. Some artists have incorporated medical imaging of their own bodies, such as X-rays, angiograms, or even written medical records, into their work. Medical imagery tends to make the body into an object for assessing pathology and devising a treatment or cure. Artists have turned this medical information into raw material for exploring their bodies and worldviews. Since having a stroke in 1997, Katherine Sherwood (1952–   ) has created abstract paintings that combine her post-stroke brain angiograms with medieval spiritual symbols. Paintings from the series "Golgi's Door" (2007) allude to the 19th-century Italian scientist Camillo Golgi (1843–1926), who developed a method of staining the brain's tissues to make their intricate structures visible. The angiograms of the blood vessels of her brain are transformed into beautiful abstract images that interweave with ancient magic symbols. Conceptual artist Harriet Sanderson transforms MOBILITY devices, such as WHEELCHAIRS and canes, into complex sculptures in her 1998–99 exhibit "RE-Vamp," which was shown in Seattle, Washington. This exhibit included sculptures made from cast-off wheelchairs, creating aesthetically pleasing "hybrid" objects of utility using materials such as natural fibers, walking canes, and vinyl. The exhibit included performances in which she interacted physically with the materials. Poet Jim Ferris makes use of language from his actual childhood medical records in his poem "From the Surgeons: Drs. Sofield, Louis, Hark, Alfini, Millar, Baehr, Bevan-Thomas, Tsatsos, Ericson, and Bennan," published in his 2004 collection titled *Hospital Poems.* Ferris wrangles language used to describe and analyze—language that was literally used to make decisions about the shape his body would take—into a poetic body of his own choosing.

A common practice among artists with disabilities is to focus explicitly on the body itself—its fleshiness, fluids, and feelings—to humanize medical imagery. Since the late 1980s painter Laura Ferguson has been creating self-portraits as part of the "Visible Skeleton Series." Ferguson's ethereal nudes are translucent, exposing the bones underneath her skin. To create her paintings, Ferguson references high-tech images of her body, such as X-rays and MRIs, and medical anatomy drawing. The figures twist and turn; backs, limbs, and torsos are presented from a variety of unexpected angles.

These angles accentuate the beauty of her spinal scoliosis as well as her emotional responses to and physical sensations of her body. Bob Flanagan (1952–96) created a series of performance installations, along with his life partner Sheree Rose, in which they eroticized medical equipment used to treat and manage his CYSTIC FIBROSIS. *Visiting Hours,* a 1994 installation at the New Museum of Contemporary Art in New York City, included sexually explicit photographs, SCULPTURE, and poetry, and even Flanagan himself in a hospital bed. In this installation, Flanagan explores how sexual experimentation, influenced by his medical experiences, empowered him to take control of, and even prolong, his life.

Taken together, the disability art movement has played a significant role in the creating of DISABILITY CULTURE and community (sometimes known as crip culture). Its rich examples reflect and embody the diverse range of disability experiences and offer important sources of study, empowerment, and cultural discovery.

See also PERFORMANCE ARTISTS.

Carrie Sandahl

Further Reading:

Crutchfield, Susan, and Nancy Epstein, eds. *Points of Contact: Disability, Art, and Culture.* Ann Arbor: University of Michigan Press, 2000.

Fries, Kenny. *Staring Back: The Disability Experience from the Inside Out.* New York: Plume, 1997.

Kuppers, Petra. *The Scar of Visibility: Medical Performances and Contemporary Art.* Minneapolis: University of Minnesota Press, 2007.

———. *Disability and Contemporary Performance: Bodies on Edge.* London and New York: Routledge, 2003.

Lehrer, Riva, and Sofia Zutautas, eds. *Humans Being: Disability in Contemporary Art.* Chicago: City of Chicago Department of Cultural Affairs, 2006.

Lewis, Victoria Ann. *Beyond Victims and Villains: Contemporary Plays by Disabled Playwrights.* New York: Theatre Communications Group, 2006.

Millett, Ann. "Disarming Venus: Disability and the Re-vision of Art History." *FemTAP: A Journal of Feminist Theory as Feminist Praxis* (Summer 2006). URL: http://femtap.com/id13.html.

Mitchell, David, and Sharon Snyder, directors. *Disability Takes on the Arts.* Brace Yourself Productions, 2004.

———. *Vital Signs: Crip Culture Talks Back.* Brace Yourself Productions, 2001.

Sandahl, Carrie, and Philip Auslander, eds. *Bodies in Commotion: Disability and Performance.* Ann Arbor: University of Michigan Press, 2005.

Sonnenstrahl, Deborah M. *Deaf Artists in America: Colonial to Contemporary.* San Diego: DawnSignPress, 2003.

disability culture

It is difficult to define or even discuss a disability culture without first defining a framework for the term *culture*. British cultural historian Raymond Williams calls culture "a way of life." People debate if disabled people have a shared or negotiated way of living, or whether there is an American disability culture history that can be traced. There are definitely cultural ways of dealing with disability: A wider culture might marginalize disabled people by institutionalizing them, shutting them from public view, or by assigning them specific public functions, such as fool or jester or wise person. Indeed, the study of disability and culture comprises a rich field for anthropologists and sociologists who compare the different treatments of disability and its diverse structural positioning in historical and contemporary cultures. But *disability culture* can also mean the willed coming together of people who begin to understand themselves as a cultural minority, as a band that needs to create together rituals, codes, languages, art, and behaviors in order to strengthen their position.

THE HISTORY OF DISABILITY CULTURE

The term *disability culture* emerged as part of the civil rights movement of disabled people in the 1960s and 1970s. Historically, people with disabilities have been defined through their disabilities as objects of pity, humiliation, or ridicule. As such, they have been marginalized and ostracized, kept out of public schools and the workplace, and often incarcerated for life in state institutions and nursing homes. They have been barred from marriage, parenthood, and, in the case of UGLY LAWS, from appearing in public. Many of these places of marginalization are now being rethought and reinvestigated as cultural communities. DEAF cultural communities, for example, flourished in America with the rise of RESIDENTIAL SCHOOLS. With the exception of deaf cultural historians, scholars have yet to fully examine the extent to which various cultures of disability formed in these and other institutions.

Still, anecdotal evidence suggests that small-scale independent groups expressed community and cultural affiliations in the United States during the 19th century. For example, SANITARIUMS for people with TUBERCULOSIS since the 1880s provided spaces for communal experiences and expression of shared values. As cultural scholars have demonstrated, romance and SEXUALITY represent important by-products of culture, and many relationships developed at these facilities thus reflect a possible example of early disability culture.

Organized SPORTS, such as DEAFLYMPICS, begun in the 1920s, wheelchair basketball, which has grown in popularity since the 1950s, and PARALYMPICS, which began in 1960, also may provide rich evidence of disability culture. Through disability sports, rituals, folklore, and HUMOR, relationships have flourished, drawing groups of Americans together over generations.

The broader civil rights movements of the 1960s contributed to disabled people gaining substantial national force and national attention, which also fortified and expanded disability culture. The INDEPENDENT LIVING MOVEMENT has been the backbone of the DISABILITY RIGHTS MOVEMENT, based on the premise that even the most severely disabled people have the fundamental right to live in the community. As such, in 1972 the first Center for Independent Living opened in BERKELEY, CALIFORNIA, not only to facilitate both the burgeoning disability rights movement and the continued goal of disability ACTIVISM, but also to serve as the focal point for the disability COMMUNITY. As Centers for Independent Living opened up around the country, they became, and often continue to be, gathering places for disability culture.

Scholars have debated the defining features of disability culture. Psychologist Carol Gill's highly influential *Disability Rag* article, "A Psychological View of Disability Culture" (published in extended form in *DISABILITY STUDIES QUARTERLY* [1995]), identifies disability culture as a strategy for survival, not only an outcome of a shared experience. She enumerates a range of core elements of disability culture: a cultural expression of long-standing social oppression, a reclamation in disabled people's art and humor, disabled people's work on creating a disability history, and work on LANGUAGE and symbols that are shared, all in the face of silencing, refusal of education, refusal of ACCESS to social spaces, and the inculcation of self-hate.

Social oppression allows people to find a core together, to create culture in order to survive. And so, although not formally identified as such, disability culture finds early forms of expression in the various segregated locales where disabled people live or work together. Institutions such as ASYLUMS, mental health wards, and long-term care HOSPITALS can provide not only places to rally against, to find emotional unity against an oppressor, but also potential places of assembly, places in which forms of culture can crystallize. Sitting together in a common room, disabled people find language and behavior for themselves, often language different from the overtly medicalized labels used by medical staff and wardens.

Few documents survive of the everyday practices employed in the 19th and early 20th centuries, or else their relevance for disability histories has not yet been explored. Glimpses open up at odd moments: In Tod Browning's *FREAKS* (1932), FREAK SHOW performers act out a demonic and yet strangely appealing community of crips as they celebrate the wedding of a fellow performer. Jack Cardiff's 1974 film *The Mutations* cites this iconic moment when "real-life" disabled people from the United Kingdom and the United States act as the background to another horror movie. In the film, the freaks have birthday parties, feel strongly about people being "one of us," and exhibit a code of living (and killing: it is the sensationalist aspects of freak show life that make it a rich vein for POPULAR CULTURE). Today, disability culture activists can use these films as (tenuous) evidence of freak show culture, and they can explore them together with other traces of a vanished COMMUNITY. They can access the oral histories of retired Sideshow performers, historical postcards from early 20th-century New York sideshows that show disabled people as stars manipulating their different bodies to attract audiences, or the institutional history of CIRCUS and side-show managers such as P. T. BARNUM. The American TELEVISION series *The X-Files* (1993–2002) used the behavioral roles of these precursors to create its own contemporary version of freak show camaraderie among disabled people. Many of these documents do not come directly from disabled people, are often created for a NONDISABLED market, and show more about the attitudes toward difference than the nature of disabled lives. But in the absence of so much in disability history, disability scholars are creative in their search for documents—and in the examples cited, disabled performers do appear, not just nondisabled people acting disabled. This alone makes these FILMS landmarks of disability history.

Sometimes, we have to look beyond national borders to find evidence for disability history. In *The Epidemic* (2006), a Danish movie shown at Superfest, a disability culture festival in Berkeley, California, the audience draws in its breath when they see historical footage of people with POLIO, living together, a community of crips. The film is astonishing because viewers can see community images of polio survivors, not just isolated people. In any context, European or American, this footage is rare, and it delights the cinema audience. In a documentary about performance artist Bob Flanagan, old Super-8 footage shows the performer singing at a CAMP for youth with CYSTIC FIBROSIS. These brief moments can speak to contemporary researchers about places where disability culture might have happened, and wait for researchers to come and explore further.

To find historical evidence for disability culture is hard. Painstaking historical research into late 19th century- and early 20th-century sources can find evidence for the congregation of mendicant PEDDLERS and BEGGARS, many disabled, with codes and modes of behavior that might fall under the category of "disability culture." The Oral History Archive at the University of California, Berkeley, has a section on the disability rights movement and the Independent Living Movement, as well as a special project dedicated to disabled artists. The archive holds many entries that help us shape knowledge of the early days of the movement, what it felt like to be part of it and to be in it. These oral histories constitute

important documents and recordings: They afford glimpses into the lives of disabled people as told by themselves, with much detailed and private information. Part of a movement of oral history and "history-from-below" activism, these archives try to find ways of preserving new forms of heritage: They work on the form of historiography, the writing of history, not just on the content. Thus, video recordings and innovative communication formats allow people whose voices were excluded from mainstream archiving to speak. Instant messaging can become part of interviewing techniques, as in the case of poet NEIL MARCUS, who communicates with significant speech differences, and the physical and interpretive challenges of historical labor become visible in the effort to establish communication. This focus on the specific communication patterns of different people shows disability culture as a culture of attention, improvisation, and (serious) play.

SITES OF DISABILITY CULTURE

Disability culture speaks about the specific cultural utterances, behaviors, and practices that occur when disabled people are together—practices that differ from nondisabled people's living. Many behaviors deemed unseemly in mainstream society are acceptable and encouraged in disability culture settings such as crip cabarets. Cabarets are a form of performance display often utilized by political movements that value individual life experiences: queer culture, radical feminists, and African-American pride movements all know forms of display that allow multiple solo performers or short community skits to share an evening stage. Oftentimes, these cabarets emerge in institutions—mental health asylums, nursing homes, hospitals—in which their (mythologized) roots lie in instantaneous improvised forms of self-expression away from the disciplining presence of wardens or hospital personnel. Furthermore, crip cabarets comprise an important development tool in the political education of disabled people: Many disability events feature these open-mike events as a way for people to find a voice, to experience the thrill of the stage and of self-display, and to find pride.

Other sites of disability culture include disability equality political meetings, meetings at Centers for Independent Living, and other sites and ORGANIZATIONS run by disabled people for disabled people. Such behaviors might include feeding one another; making noises and being tolerant of them, responding to them rather than trying to suppress or ignore them; sitting, standing, and lying down in ways that might be unexpected in mainstream settings; attending to each other's sensory needs; an awareness that things might take a while to get going as everybody's access is getting assured; foregrounding physical needs and bodily behavior with pride and enjoyment, rather than with embarrassment. As is probably already apparent from this list, disability culture is always emerging, never quite yet there, for certainly hierarchies and normative ways-of-being characterize many congregations of disabled people. Oppression and shame are deeply embedded qualities, and it takes more than just a call for disability culture to undo the rigorous regime of denying disabled people's right to be in the world. It is not just cultural pain that can alienate disabled people from themselves: physical PAIN and mental anguish also strand many in isolation. To call a culture into being allows disabled people to see their life experiences as important, exciting, and beautiful in their painfulness, exclusion, and difference. It is hard. But disability culture tries. It moves forward. It respects. It enjoys. It values people's differences in the world. And it mourns for the pain that discrimination and hate have caused both disabled and nondisabled people.

There are many different groups within disability culture that come together at different times, in different arenas of public and private life, and in different relation to the contemporary term *disability culture*. Freak shows, asylums, hospitals, and VETERANS meetings are all sites at which disabled people have congregated, willingly and unwillingly, and many disability artists use these sites as imaginary places to tell stories about disability histories. What is common to many examples of disability culture are exemplified in the specific cases of polio culture and BLIND culture.

While other subdivisions within disability culture solidify within institutional frameworks such as schools or asylums, polio culture has different roots. Of course, many polio survivors have historically been institutionalized; certainly, polio survivors have been marginalized. But polio is different because of the sheer number of people who have been afflicted with the disease beginning with the first major outbreak reported in the United States in Vermont in 1894, the very public nature of the DISEASE, and in the ability to advocate politically afforded by both numbers and publicity. Indeed, it is in disability civil rights that polio culture crystallized historically.

POLIO CULTURE

While polio had been present in the United States for decades, in 1916 the number of cases skyrocketed. In the 1916 pandemic, more than 9,000 cases were reported in New York City alone. In 1952, more than 58,000 cases of polio were reported in the United States at large. The sheer number of infections created a "polio hysteria" that made it more difficult to avoid the issue of polio than it had been to stifle earlier reform efforts to help other disabled groups. Consequently, when groups such as the Warm Springs Institute and the NATIONAL FOUNDATION FOR INFANTILE PARALYSIS, later the MARCH OF DIMES—both created by President FRANKLIN D. ROOSEVELT—and the Sister Kenny Foundation began to spring up around the country in the early 20th century

there was little resistance. Places such as Warm Springs, as well as many state and locally run rehabilitation hospitals, served not only as sources of medical treatment and relief but also as locales where polio survivors could congregate and discuss their current situations—much like the Centers of Independent Living provide in the 21st century. Polio survivors differed in that just as many of them continued to live in their homes, encountered the everyday difficulties of daily living, and faced marginalization and ostracism. While it is true that many polio survivors attempted to merge into the mainstream—and as such they did not form specific survivor groups or other epicenters for polio culture—it is nonetheless also true that the sheer number of polio survivors and the impact of the disease contributed to a larger national discussion on disability. The beginnings of the modern polio culture—one that solidified in a strictly formal sense only with the rise of post-polio syndrome in the 1980s in the formation of post-polio support groups—are nonetheless there in the early survivors. People argue that polio survivors spearheaded the disability civil rights movement of the 1960s.

The DISABILITY RIGHTS MOVEMENT pulled the disparate pockets of polio culture together, where formerly they had been separate, as polio treatments had varied so broadly. As one of the largest disabled groups in the world, and one with representatives in all social classes, the polio community was harder to silence; ironically, the disease had given them the numbers to make a political difference—there were 254,000 people paralyzed by polio living in the United States in 1977—and Warm Springs and the March of Dimes had given them the means and political voice to create some change. While the expansion of modern rehabilitation arguably began in the era of World War I, polio epidemics nonetheless created an exponential increase in the field—significant in that rehabilitation thus attained a more public and national focus. Key polio culture figures such as JUDY HEUMANN and ED ROBERTS were pioneers in the Independent Living Movement that built the first Center for Independent Living in Berkeley, California, and spearheaded the disability civil rights movement nationally. Roberts also formed the ROLLING QUADS, a grassroots group that not only built the CIL but also created the Physically Disabled Students Program (PDSP), which has since been extrapolated and applied to community residents at large. The goal of the polio culture has always been one of advocacy—not only for people with polio but also for the broader disabled community. That is not to say that disability advocacy through polio culture has been an easy, or even unproblematic goal; many polio patients in the post–WORLD WAR II era preferred mainstreaming to advocacy.

Polio culture is not confined to political spaces. It has the same rich artistic, scientific, and literary history as the larger disability culture of which it is a part. It continues to use art as advocacy and exploration, as in the work of Harriet

Sanderson, which deals primarily with self-image, intimate relationships, and the body's influence on physical and psychological existence.

Polio culture knows about STIGMA. The 1998 film *A Paralyzing Fear: The Story of Polio in America*, traces the history of the polio pandemic in the United States and sums up prevalent attitudes both on the disease and on survivors in a historical film from the March of Dimes titled *The Crippler*:

> "My name is virus poliomyelitis," growls the deep male voiceover as the camera pans over pastoral clouds from which emerges a shadow carrying the silhouette of a crutch. "I consider myself quite an artist, a sort of sculptor. I specialize in grotesques, twisting and deforming human bodies. That's why I'm called The Crippler."

Having demonized and personified the disease, medicine and the Salk vaccine descend to rescue the world from dehumanization. The implication in the scene is that a man with polio is the crutch, the grotesque, the deformed, the cripple. He is fashioned of his polio, and medicine and isolation are the only solution. This is the image against which polio culture still seeks to work, as the larger disability culture seeks to work against a reductive medical model, namely, through its art, through its advocacy, through the uniqueness of its voice. Works such as Anne Finger's *Elegy for a Disease: A Personal and Cultural History of Polio* (2006) use MEMOIR to speak about the complexity of experiences of polio, their intersections with gender roles, upward mobility, and popular culture, and the way that social attitudes toward disability shape life with polio. In addition, scholars Daniel Wilson and Marc Shell have provided social histories of polio that include revealing oral interviews from individuals with polio and post-polio. Similarly, in works by disabled artists, disability emerges as a cultural experience, a nexus of bodies, histories, personal stories, and cultural narratives.

BLIND CULTURE

The history of BLIND culture is as hard to chart as the history of the blind is difficult to trace. Scholars are left with accounts of "special persons" rather than generalized accounts of the blind acting in concert to achieve collective goals. Several theories serve to explain why narratives of blindness center around the individual rather than the collective: that blind people were kept in isolation, that there were no schools or institutions for the blind until the 1830s, that the prevailing 18th-century thought was that because sight was required to understand the essence of a thing, there was no point in educating the blind.

The first chartered school for the blind, the PERKINS SCHOOL FOR THE BLIND, opened in Boston in 1832 under the supposition that the blind could and should be educated and trained to become independent members of society, earning their own way in the world. Until the 1920s blind children were still segregated in classrooms. Blind culture advocates achieved their first major public victory with integration of blind students into public schooling. Blind culture continues to be deeply interested in public ACTIVISM, principally concerned with maintaining the goals of independent living. Such groups as the AMERICAN COUNCIL OF THE BLIND and the AMERICAN FOUNDATION FOR THE BLIND, the NATIONAL FEDERATION OF THE BLIND, and the NATIONAL LIBRARY SERVICE FOR THE BLIND AND PHYSICALLY HANDICAPPED work to provide access services. Such services include state-subsidized training with canes and seeing eye dogs; free access to tape recorders and mail-in lending services for books on tape (and discussions about which books are put on tape and which are not); access to home and work technologies such as speaking watches, devices that signal when a coffee mug is full, computer programs that read script; job and social services, and so forth.

School usually becomes the first communal gathering place for the blind in the United States and EDUCATION the means through which blind culture is inculcated. The latter point is more compelling than it may initially seem. Education is a cultural access point that denies blind people access to nondisabled culture in ways that the material fact of blindness does not. In the strata of a sighted family, for instance, education is the principal means of moving from one step to another. When a blind person is denied access to education, he or she cannot adequately understand her or his situation either physically or politically. Blind people in the United States were historically denied physical, mental, emotional, and cultural access to the mainstream world, which rendered them doubly isolated. Thus, the inception of schools for the blind gave physical access to other blind people, means of navigating the physical world via LONG CANE, GUIDE DOGS, and other technologies, and points of interface with the nondisabled culture that allowed blind people a means of entry and a means of establishing their own cultural norms and practices.

The ongoing fascination of mainstream culture for blindness and "second sight" can be fertile grounds for writers, who can explore their experiences across these realms of public and private thoughts. Poet Steven Kuusisto discusses both his personal experience of sensory difference and his encounter with (and his internalization of) ableist STEREOTYPES of blindness and with "for-the-blind" institutions in his memoirs, lyrical essays, and poems. In his work, the history of BRAILLE merges with his sense of words under his fingers, smells guide him through the city, and he takes care of his guide dog. The work opens up perspectives on blindness as a cultural complex of meanings and as a lived experience.

The social element of blind culture is frequently overlooked when the media profiles one of the blind advocacy groups. Independent living is one of the goals of blind culture, often gained through social groups. Blind culture concerns itself with the richest living experience, which includes practical, "how-to" questions of the body and spatial navigation but is more centrally concerned with the world it finds once it is given access to it. This interface between sensorial difference and image-based culture can lead to conundrums in access provision. For example, in 21st century debates in blind culture, the etiquette of audio description is a point of contention. Questions arise concerning what is to be described and what is not—how, for instance, RACE or body size in films should be described even if it is not directly thematized in the film or television program and whether or not access technologies such as AUDIO DESCRIPTION become part of the aesthetic vocabulary of art practices. These questions concern quality of life, and the fashioning of a sustainable, culturally rich lifestyle, and they make up parts of what blind culture is today.

EXPANDING DISABILITY CULTURE

In addition to these histories of impairment-focused groups, disability culture is consolidating itself through large-scale events organized by disabled people for disabled people. Examples include the 10-day, large scale Bodies at Work festival organized in Chicago in 2006, and many other smaller festivals in many places in the United States. Organizations such as VSA ARTS organize festivals that showcase disabled artists. Film, performance, and lecture series offer rich fare for people who are interested in how the movement portrays itself and in how many strands and different perspectives make up its agenda. Companies such as AXIS DANCE, the Mickee Faust Theatre, That Uppity Theatre Company, and the Olimpias offer opportunities for disabled people to become art creators and try out new aesthetics, building on earlier work in disability-focused workshops at the Mark Taper Forum in Los Angeles, integrated dance work in Contact Improvisation circles from the 1970s onward, and other art forms that value nonconformity, difference, and community outreach. With this, the development of disability culture is noticeably different from deaf culture. Deaf culture has its own language—AMERICAN SIGN LANGUAGE—and the long struggle to protect and preserve this language has strongly shaped the cultural identity and values of deaf Americans. Educational practices, historically including residential schools for the deaf, deaf publications, folklore, HUMOR, and intermarriage, reflect some of the wide-ranging cultural practices that have defined this distinctive culture.

Disability culture emerges at many different sites and develops on a continuum that ranges from integrative practices in which disabled and nondisabled people forge aesthetic alliances to radical crip work in which disabled people self-segregate. Disability culture intersects with other identity movements, as evidenced by Leroy Moore's Krip Hop black poetry performance work, and it has to find ways of responding creatively to the ways that different cultural groups address disability in their political understandings.

There is a utopian agenda in disability culture, a move outward from description of the status quo toward a world in which difference is valued, and where cultural and social forms respond to all of the contributions people make to their world.

To call for crip culture or disability culture is to call for a different political act than to ask to enter the mainstream, to have all difference vanish in a postmodern "melting pot." This tension presents itself to disability artists: Should they try to "make it" in the wider, so-called mainstream world, or should they embrace, work within, and explore the aesthetics that are particular to disabled people, or both, painfully, at the same time? Is to call something "disability culture" a restriction, or an avant-garde opening, a political intervention?

In the 21st century this dual pull on DISABILITY ART defines many art events that try to break out of older modes, such as the crip cabaret, and bring nondisabled audiences to the radical, complex, and searching work of disability culture artists. But it requires cultural capital, that is, access to knowledge, to read these art practices as part of a cultural movement rather than merely as individual expressions of witnessing or overcoming. That capital is not easily accessible to nondisabled audiences and to disabled audience members who are not aware of or in tune with the specific political ideas of social model disability or minority identity politics. There are tensions around access and inclusion, around whose voices are heard, and whose silenced, but to push for crip culture means to value the ability to find ways of living richly as disabled people, even and especially in the face of ongoing and internalized oppression.

Disability culture speaks for itself, claims ground, reinvents art practice, and changes the way people tell stories. Disability culture remembers its histories and creates its futures out of the agency of disabled people. Disability culture is important for the wider American culture: The history of disability culture, as sketchy and in need of further investigation as it is, speaks to the survival of people, to the resilience of spirit and flesh, to the existence of difference in multiple forms, and to the value of that difference. Cultural expressions of disabled people add dimension and depth to the common ways people perceive disability and those who have them. When we investigate, reveal, and debate the defining features of disability culture, we encourage those interested in understanding the past to pay attention to lived experiences, not just to STEREOTYPES of disability. Disabled artists can show what it means to experience the world in complex and shifting ways, and the cultures that shape themselves around these artistic expressions can provide a home for people to live in. When we look at disability culture we can find out how these homes withstand the storms of discrimination, so that we can build a more solid future for all of us, living together.

See also ACCESS AND ACCESSIBILITY; DISABILITY HISTORY ARCHIVES; LANGUAGE AND TERMINOLOGY; ROOSEVELT WARM SPRINGS INSTITUTE FOR REHABILITATION; SCULPTURE AND INSTALLATION ART.

Petra Kuppers
Melanie Wakefield

Further Reading:

The Epidemic. Niels Frandsen, producer and director. Denmark, 2007.

Finger, Anne. *Elegy for a Disease. A Personal and Cultural History of a Disease.* New York: St. Martin's, 2006.

Garland Thomson, Rosemarie, ed. *Freakery: Cultural Spectacles of the Extraordinary Body.* New York: New York University Press, 1996.

Gill, Carol. "A Psychological View of Disability Culture." *Disability Studies Quarterly* (Fall 1995). URL: http://www.independentliving.org/docs3/gill1995.html.

Kuppers, Petra. "Performing Determinism: Disability Culture Poetry." *Text and Performance Quarterly* 27, no. 2 (2007): 89–106.

Lewis, Victoria, ed. *Beyond Victims and Villains. Contemporary Plays by Disabled Playwrights.* New York: Theatre Communication Group, 2006.

Schweik, Susan. *The Ugly Laws: Disability in Public.* New York: New York University Press, 2008.

Shell, Marc. *Polio and Its Aftermath: The Paralysis of Culture.* Cambridge, Mass.: Harvard University Press, 2005.

Sick: The Life and Times of Bob Flanagan. Dick Kirby, producer and director, 1997.

Wilson, Daniel. *Living with Polio: The Epidemic and Its Survivors.* Chicago: University of Chicago Press, 2005.

"Disabled Country" by Neil Marcus

Neil Marcus (1954–) entered what he called "Disabled Country" when he was diagnosed with a rare neurological disorder called dystonia muculoram deformas, which produces involuntary spasms. A major poet and performance artist in the disability arts movement, Marcus self-identifies as an empowered and creative person with a disability. His work "Disabled Country" embodies many distinctive experiences common in disability history, includ-

ing oppressive medical views of disability, the struggle to embrace a positive identity as disabled, and the liberation of claiming this sense of self and community. As such, it offers a rich example of disability culture, art, and lived experience.

"Disabled Country"
by Neil Marcus

If there was a country called disabled,
I would be from there.
I live disabled culture, eat disabled food,
make disabled love, cry disabled tears,
climb disabled mountains and tell disabled
stories.
If there was a country called disabled,
I would say she has immigrants that come to
her
From as far back as time remembers.
If there was a country called disabled,
Then I am one of its citizens.
I came there at age 8. I tried to leave.
Was encouraged by doctors to leave.
I tried to surgically remove myself from disabled country
but found myself, in the end, staying and living there.
If there was a country called disabled,
I would always have to remind myself that I
came from there.
I often want to forget.
I would have to remember . . . to remember.
In my life's journey
I am making myself
At home in my country.

Source: Neil Marcus. "Disabled Country." Available online. URL: http://www.disabledandproud.com/prideart.htm#Neil. Accessed June 20, 2008.

"You Get Proud by Practicing"
by Laura Hershey (1991)

Formerly the 1973 poster child for the Muscular Dystrophy Association telethon, Laura Hershey (1962–) eventually became an activist in the disability rights movement, combining poetry and journalism in her efforts to empower people with disabilities. In this poem, "You Get Proud by Practicing," Hershey rejects the many forces of oppression and stigma that people with disabilities commonly face, offering self-pride and communal empowerment as answers to social fears and expectations. "You Get Proud by Practicing," thus reflects her personal mantra as well as her hopes for all members of the disability community.

"You Get Proud by Practicing"
by Laura Hershey
1991

If you are not proud
for who you are, for what you say, for how
you look;
if every time you stop
to think of yourself, you do not see yourself
glowing
with golden light; do not, therefore, give up
on yourself.
You can
get proud.
You do not need
a better body, a purer spirit, or a Ph.D.
to be proud.
You do not need
a lot of money, a handsome boyfriend, or a
nice car.
You do not need
to be able to walk, or see, or hear,
or use big, complicated words,
or do any of the things that you just can't do
to be proud. A caseworker
cannot make you proud,
or a doctor.
You only need
more practice.
You get proud
by practicing.

There are many many ways to get proud.
You can try riding a horse, or skiing on one
leg,
or playing guitar,
and do well or not so well,
and be glad you tried
either way.
You can show
something you've made
to someone you respect
and be happy with it no matter
what they say.
You can say
what you think, though you know
other people do not think the same way, and

you can
keep saying it, even if they tell you
you are crazy.
You can add your voice
all night to the voices
of a hundred and fifty others
in a circle
around a jailhouse
where your brothers and sisters are being held
for blocking buses with no lift,
or you can be one of the ones
inside the jailhouse,
knowing of the circle outside.
You can speak your love
to a friend
without fear.
You can find someone
who will listen to you
without judging you or doubting you or being
afraid of you
and let you hear yourself perhaps
for the first time.
These are all ways
of getting proud.
None of them
are easy, but all of them
are possible. You can do all of these things,
or just one of them again and again.
You get proud
by practicing.
Power makes you proud, and power
comes in many fine forms
supple and rich as butterfly wings.
It is music
when you practice opening your mouth
and liking what you hear
because it is the sound of your own
true voice.
It is sunlight
when you practice seeing
strength and beauty in everyone
including yourself.
It is dance
when you practice knowing
that what you do
and the way you do it
is the right way for you
and can't be called wrong.
All these hold
more power than weapons or money
or lies.
All these practices bring power, and power

makes you proud.
You get proud
by practicing.
Remember, you weren't the one
who made you ashamed,
but you are the one
who can make you proud.
Just practice,
practice until you get proud, and once you are
proud,
keep practicing so you won't forget.
You get proud
by practicing.

⊰◈⊱

Source: Laura Hershey. "You Get Proud By Practicing." 1991.
Available online. URL: http://www.cripcommentary.com/poetry.
html. Accessed April 1, 2008.

disability history archives

Disability history archives are collections of historically significant documents and photographs relating to disability. These are
often small collections, sometimes in paper form, but, increasingly, scholars and collectors are developing and maintaining
these archival resources electronically, often with the intention of supporting disability rights ACTIVISM and the academic
field of DISABILITY STUDIES. Disability history archives should
not be confused with collections on the history of medicine,
which cover texts and documents tracing a record of DISEASE
and impairment. Instead, disability history archives provide the
underpinnings of the study of disability as a social construction (see SOCIAL CONSTRUCTION OF DISABILITY), much in the
same way that GENDER, class, RACE, and nationality are used as
categories of analysis in other academic arenas.

Disability history archives vary widely in their content.
The Regional Disability Archives at the University of Toledo
Ward M. Canaday Center for Special Collections preserves
80 years of records of the Ability Center of Greater Toledo
from its incarnation as the Society for Crippled Children
in 1920 to the Center for Independent Living it is today.
The Toledo Sight Center collection includes documents in
BRAILLE. Assistance Dogs of America records contain news
clippings with photographs of service dogs partnered with
people with disabilities. Personal papers of individuals with
disabilities and their allies are also in the collection.

Disability history archives are also found online and
include such Web-based archives as the Beyond Affliction:
the 1988 Disability History Project, the Image Archive on the
American EUGENICS Movement, and the Disability Rights and
Independent Living Movement Archive. Some collections are
private, such as the more than 10,000 photographs and nega-
tives held by the disability rights photographer, TOM OLIN.

The Disability Rights and Independent Living Movement
Archive at the Bancroft Library at the University of California,
Berkeley, provides captioned videotaped oral histories of
the pioneers of the 1970s and 1980s INDEPENDENT LIVING
MOVEMENT in the United States. By contrast, the Image
Archive on the American Eugenics Movement reaches back
into the 19th century and utilizes newspaper articles and
photographs and scholarly papers and diagrams to document the efforts made by American eugenicists to eradicate
disabled people from the human genetic pool through laws,
medical procedures, and social control of reproduction (see
REPRODUCTIVE RIGHTS).

Sometimes archives not officially identified as sources of
disability history can provide excellent resources for scholars
of disability and activists for the disabled, such as the collection of organizational records of the Rotary Club of Toledo,
Ohio—founders of the Toledo Society for Crippled Children—
located in the Canaday Center archives at the University of
Toledo. Similarly, the ALEXANDER GRAHAM BELL family
papers (1862–1939) provide an excellent online disability
history archive, despite Bell's controversial place in disability
history, which includes the controversies around COCHLEAR
IMPLANTS, AMERICAN SIGN LANGUAGE, and ORALISM.

Disability history archives provide a much needed historical record of this unique aspect of American society and
culture.

See also DISABILITY HISTORY ASSOCIATION; DISABILITY
HISTORY MUSEUM.

Patricia A. Murphy

Further Reading:
Britton, Diane F., Barbara Floyd, and Patricia A. Murphy. "Over-
    coming Another Obstacle: Documenting the History of a
    Community's Disabled." *Radical History Review* 94 (Winter
    2006): 213–227.
Longmore, Paul K., and Lauri Umansky. "Introduction: Dis-
    ability History: From the Margins to the Mainstream." In
    The New Disability History: American Perspectives, edited
    by Paul K. Longmore and Lauri Umansky, 1–32. New York:
    New York University Press, 2001.

Disability History Association

The idea to form a scholarly ORGANIZATION devoted to
disability history grew out of informal conversations at a
six-week long Summer Institute on DISABILITY STUDIES in
the Humanities at San Francisco State University in 2000.
Excited by the lively discussions in critical disability studies,
yet concerned by the cavalier use of history by some non-
historians, a small group talked of forming an electronic

discussion list, H-DISABILITY. Participants hoped that such a forum would help draw out scholars both nationally and internationally who studied topics related to disability in past times and places, but who had not yet come to think of themselves as historians of disability. At the same time, they hoped that such a list would lead to greater recognition of the topic for the history profession as a whole. Thanks in part to the list that soon numbered several hundred subscribers, faculty and graduate students met informally at various national conferences, where they began laying the groundwork for the Disability History Association (DHA). The organization held its first board meeting in December 2004 and formally incorporated in 2007. Historian Kim Nielsen served as DHA's first president; Catherine Kudlick became president in 2006. Board members have included graduate students, independent historians, and senior scholars.

The organization claims as its mission to "promote the study of the history of individuals or groups with disabilities, perspectives on disability, representations/constructions of disability, policy and practice history, teaching, theory, and Disability and related social and civil rights movements." Like those working in critical DISABILITY STUDIES, the founders of the DHA sought to understand disability beyond a tragedy befalling isolated individuals. Instead, they have encouraged teachers and researchers to explore social, economic, and political forces that have shaped attitudes and policies. Using a minority group model that sees disability as a characteristic that forms a person much like RACE, ETHNICITY, GENDER, and sexual orientation, the leaders of the field have raised productive questions about STIGMA, normality, hierarchies, and what role difference plays in establishing and maintaining power relations. Welcoming "scholars, institutions and organizations, and others working in all geographic regions and all time periods," the association seeks to "define both history and disability widely," explaining that it is "both inclusive and international, reflected in our diverse topics and approaches."

The DHA currently works with the flagship American Historical Association (AHA) to make both the discipline and the profession of history more welcoming and inclusive. In summer 2006 the DHA achieved the important goal of getting the AHA to list "disability" as an interest category. It has also helped increase the number of presentations on disability topics at the AHA's annual meeting and is helping to foster a climate more conducive to recruiting, hiring, and promoting historians with disabilities. In summer 2008, it cosponsored an international disability history conference with the British Disability History Group and San Francisco State University. Since that time, the DHA has become an affiliated organization with the American Historical Association. While the Disability History Association works to create a more diverse, inclusive profession, its main goal remains the promotion of rigorous scholarly research and analysis on an important area of human experience. Future plans include scholarships and prizes to reward outstanding work in the field, conferences, and launching a scholarly journal.

See also DISABILITY HISTORY ARCHIVES; SOCIAL CONSTRUCTION OF DISABILITY.

Catherine Kudlick

Further Reading:
Disability History Association Web site. "About the DHA." URL: dha.osu.edu.
Kerber, Linda. "Enabling History." *Perspectives* 44, no. 8 (November 2006). URL: http://www.historians.org/perspectives/issues/2006/0611/0611pre1.cfm.
Kudlick, Catherine, and Paul Longmore. "Disability and the Transformation of Historians' Public Sphere." *Perspectives* 44, no. 8 (November 2006). URL: http://www.historians.org/perspectives/issues/2006/0611/0611for2.cfm.

Disability History Museum

Open to the public since 2001, the Disability History Museum (DHM) is an online resource for the study of the cultural history of disability in the United States. Created by Laurie Block, a media producer and independent scholar based in Conway, Massachusetts, the DHM seeks to promote historical understanding by preserving and interpreting the stories of people with disabilities.

The DHM grew out of Block's production of a four-hour National Public Radio documentary series, *Beyond Affliction: The Disability History Project,* first broadcast in 1998. An accompanying Web site included some primary and secondary sources. The DHM was designed to expand upon this effort with a custom-made, scaleable, and searchable database.

The DHM is sponsored by a nonprofit media company called Straight Ahead Pictures, Inc. The museum's Web site is divided into three sectors—Library, Education, and Museum. As of 2009, only the library is available publicly, though efforts to open the other sectors are continuing.

Images and texts, from single photographs to entire books from about 1800 through the 1990s, are currently included on the site. The collections are digitized from original materials kept at archival repositories and libraries around the country. The library is designed to be used both as an independent research tool and as a basis for building educational curriculum materials for high schools and colleges and for online museum exhibits.

The DHM Library crosses disability categories. At the macro level, materials are keyworded as physical, sensory, psychiatric, or COGNITIVE DISABILITY. The collections include thousands of historical documents such as cabinet cards and *cartes de visite,* institutional reports, exposés of ABUSE in institutions, pamphlets, and government documents. Among the

DHM's strengths are primary sources in disability history prior to the CIVIL WAR. There are images and texts about P. T. BARNUM's human exhibits, DOROTHEA DIX's efforts in ASYLUM reform, and the reform efforts that led to the creation of the AMERICAN SCHOOL FOR THE DEAF. For the 20th century, the strongest area collected thus far relates to FRANKLIN D. ROOSEVELT and POLIO. Funding has been secured to add considerable primary and secondary materials about HELEN KELLER and the people around her. The establishment and evolution of collections such as the Disability History Museum reflect the growing interest in and advocacy for disability rights and history. As the fields of DISABILITY STUDIES and disability history flourish, museums such as this will play a vital role.

See also ACTIVISM AND ADVOCACY; DISABILITY HISTORY ARCHIVES; PUBLIC HISTORY.

Graham Warder

Further Reading:

Disability History Museum Web site. URL: www.disabilitymuseum.org.

Umansky, Lauri. "Web Site Review." *Journal of American History* (June 2005). URL: http://www.indiana.edu/~jah/issues/reviews/921_wr03.shtml. Accessed July 8, 2007.

Disability History Week

In the early 21st century disability advocates began to campaign to create a state-supported Disability History Week during the third week in October, which coincides with National Disability Employment Awareness Month. This approach is similar to other awareness initiatives, such as Black History Month and Women's History Month, that have gained state and national support.

Advocates for Disability History Week seek to increase awareness nationwide and educate school-age CHILDREN about people with disabilities in American history. In efforts already begun, students are encouraged during the week to learn about people with disabilities that emphasize the changing ways society has responded to such individuals. Supplementary educational materials showcase broad reforms and other changes in America that have influenced the lives of disabled people; representing these citizens as self-advocates in their communities is a guiding theme in Disability History Week activities. The campaign to implement this program and its goals nationally exemplifies broader issues in history, including disability rights ACTIVISM, the rise of DISABILITY STUDIES, and expanding notions of citizenship.

Disability History Week is a project of the Museum of Disability History and People Inc., located in Williamsville, New York. The museum was started in 1998 by James M. Bolesto to increase understanding and acceptance of people

with disabilities and promote their independence. Disability History Week contributes to that mission and, along with staff members and the B. Thomas Golisano Foundation, the museum began meeting with state legislators, such as New York State Assembly Member Mark Schroeder, to gain official state sanction. The project has expanded to include local disability advocacy agencies such as statewide independent living councils. Momentum has increased nationally due to these efforts and ongoing communication between states as they share ideas and strategies. The museum is also helping states by disseminating universal lesson plans that provide an additional tool and resource for schools.

In March 2006 West Virginia became the first state to enact legislation authorizing a Disability History Week. Signed on April 3, 2006, the law mandates that during the third week in October public schools educate students about disability and disability rights. Several other states, including Idaho, Illinois, Iowa, Kentucky, Michigan, Pennsylvania, New York, North Carolina, and Washington, are considering similar legislation, as are Connecticut and Florida, where the Connecticut Youth Leadership Project and the Florida Youth Council are active. Some of the proposed LAWS vary slightly. Connecticut, for example, has considered declaring the first week in October as Disability History Week while Florida is considering legislating the first two weeks in October.

The grassroots drive to create a Disability History Week demonstrates the power of collective advocacy efforts to raise awareness about people with disabilities. It ties into the larger DISABILITY RIGHTS MOVEMENT, which focuses on expanding ACCESS, opportunity, and justice for disabled citizens. The evolution of Disability History Week provides a rich example of communication, networking, and teamwork between and among disability ORGANIZATIONS, the public educational system, and governmental officials.

See also ACTIVISM AND ADVOCACY.

Empish J. Thomas

Further Reading:

Fleischer, Doris Zames, and Frieda Zames. *The Disability Rights Movement.* Philadelphia: Temple University Press, 2001.

Malhotra, Ravi. "The Politics of the Disability Rights Movements." *New Politics* 8, no. 3 (Summer 2001).

Disability History Week Act (2006)

Passed by the West Virginia legislature on March 8, 2006, Disability History Week represents a successful effort by disability advocates to promote positive awareness of people with disabilities and their place in American history. The week is recognized annually during the third week of October, which is recognized as Disability History Month across the nation. The act outlines various options for acknowledging disability history, including additions to school curricula and recognition of young leaders in the disability rights movement by legislators. This selection from the bill offers a rationale for the week and ways of actively supporting it.

Disability History Week
H. B. 4491

AN ACT to amend the Code of West Virginia, 1931, as amended, by adding thereto a new article, designated §18-10O-1, §18-10O-2, §18-10O-3, §18-10O-4 and §18-10O-5, all relating to increasing the awareness and understanding of the history and contributions of people with disabilities in the state, nation and world; designating the third week of October as Disability History Week for the state of West Virginia; requiring integration of instruction on disability history, people with disabilities and the disability rights movement into the existing public school curriculum; legislative findings; and defined terms.

Be it enacted by the Legislature of West Virginia:
That the Code of West Virginia, 1931, as amended, be amended by adding thereto a new article, designated §18-10O-1, §18-10O-2, §18-10O-3, §18-10O-4 and §18-10O-5, all to read as follows:

Article 10O. Disability History Week.
§18-10O-1. Short title.
This article is known and may be cited as the "Disability History Week Act."

§18-10O-2. Legislative findings.
The Legislature finds that:

(1) According to the two thousand United States Census over four hundred thousand West Virginians have disabilities, which is nearly twenty-four percent of the state's general population;

(2) In order to ensure the full inclusion of people with disabilities into society, it is necessary to expand the public's knowledge, awareness and understanding of the history of disabilities and the disability rights movement;

(3) The disability rights movement is a civil rights movement that is an important part of the history of this state and this country;

(4) October is recognized nationally as Disability Awareness Month; and

(5) By designating the third week of October as Disability History Week, students and the public will have the opportunity to learn about the history and contributions of people with disabilities.

§18-10O-3. Purpose.
The purpose of this article is to increase the awareness and understanding of the history and contributions of people with disabilities in the state, nation and world by designating the annual observance of the third week of October as Disability History Week.

§18-10O-4. Definitions.
As used in this article the following words and phrases have the following meanings:

(a) "Disability history" means the people, events and timelines of the development and evolution of services to, and the civil rights of, people with disabilities. Disability history includes the contributions of specific people with disabilities; and

(b) "Existing school curriculum" means all the courses and curricula currently in place at a public school.

§18-10O-5. Disability History Week designated.

(a) The third week of October annually is designated as Disability History Week for the state of West Virginia.

(b) In recognition of and to further the purposes of Disability History Week, each public school shall provide instruction on disability history, people with disabilities and the disability rights movement. The instruction shall be integrated into the existing school curriculum in a manner such as, but not limited to, supplementing existing lesson plans, holding school assemblies or providing other school activities. The instruction may be delivered by school personnel or by guest speakers.

(c) State institutions of higher education are encouraged to conduct and promote activities that provide education, awareness and understanding of disability history, people with disabilities and the disability rights movement.

(d) The Legislature is encouraged to annually recognize Disability History Week by introducing a concurrent resolution to:

(1) Recognize youth leaders in the disability rights movement;

(2) Reaffirm a commitment to the full inclusion of people with disabilities in society; and

(3) Recognize the disability rights movement as an important part of the history of this state and nation.

(e) Recognized resources for information, materials and speakers regarding disability history, people with disabilities and the disability rights movement include, but are not limited to:

(1) Centers for Independent Living;

(2) The Statewide Independent Living Council;

(3) The Developmental Disabilities Council; and

(4) The State Americans with Disabilities Act Coordinator.

(f) The provisions of this article are not intended to create a burden, financial or otherwise, for public schools, teachers or state institutions of higher education.

Source: Excerpted from the Web site of the West Virginia Legislature at http://www.legis.state.wv.us/Bill_Text_HTML/2006_SESSIONS/RS/BILLS/hb4491%20enr. htm.

disability identity   See IDENTITY.

disability rights   See DISABILITY RIGHTS MOVEMENT; EMPOWERMENT; LAW AND POLICY.

Disability Rights and Education Defense Fund

The Disability Rights and Education Defense Fund (DREDF) was created in 1979 to advance and protect the rights of individuals with disabilities through legal, educational, and public policy efforts. Since its start it has been an integral part of the DISABILITY RIGHTS MOVEMENT. The grassroots organization, cofounded by MARY LOU BRESLIN, Robert Funk, and PATRISHA WRIGHT, serves as a national legal defense fund, providing support for disability advocates at the local, state, and federal levels. DREDF is managed by persons with disabilities and the parents of CHILDREN who are disabled. The organization maintains offices in BERKELEY, CALIFORNIA, and Washington, D.C.

DREDF's work is organized around the following areas of emphasis: (1) Legal Advocacy; (2) Public Policy and Legislation; (3) Children and Family Advocacy; (4) Training and Education; (5) International Programs; and (6) Research. In addition to representing clients in discrimination and compliance lawsuits, the organization files *amicus curiae*

briefs (legal memos reviewed by the court even though the persons or ORGANIZATIONS filing them are not litigants in the case) in cases of particular importance to disability law. Further, DREDF seeks to educate people about the rights of people with disabilities and provides training to law students, lawyers, business, and government officials. DREDF has had a significant impact on federal disability policy since the organization's start as a result of its advocacy efforts directed at Congress and several presidential administrations. For example, Patrisha Wright, DREDF's long-time director of governmental affairs, was instrumental in generating support for the AMERICAN WITH DISABILITIES ACT of 1990 (ADA). Prior to the ADA's passage, Wright also defended SECTION 504 of the 1973 Rehabilitation Act (see VOCATIONAL REHABILITATION ACT) against deregulation in the Reagan era in the 1980s. In the wake of a series of cases in which the U.S. Supreme Court has consistently narrowed the definition of what can be construed as a disability DREDF has been active in lobbying for the proposed Americans with Disabilities Act Restoration Act, which would expand the ADA's scope.

See also ACTIVISM AND ADVOCACY; BACKLASH; LAW AND POLICY.

Aaron Cooley

Further Reading:

"Let Us on the Bus!" *Mainstream* 22 no. 6 (March 1998): 9–12.

Oakes, Wayne Thomas. *Perspectives on Disability, Discrimination, Accommodations, and Law.* New York: LFB Scholarly Publishing, 2005.

Shapiro, Joseph. "Disability Policy and the Media: A Stealth Civil Rights Movement Bypasses the Press and Defies Conventional Wisdom." *Policy Studies Journal* 22, no. 1 (Spring 1994): 12–22.

———. "The New Civil Rights." URL: http://www.disabilityculture.org/course/article3.htm.

disability rights movement

Beginning in the late 19th century, disability-based political movements emerged that represented a range of constituencies. Although their agendas remained distinct, their perspectives became similar. From the 1970s on, these movements formed cross-disability political alliances to address issues of general concern. At various times, they cooperated or competed. They also operated in a growing number of countries and internationally. By the 21st century the disability rights movements had become diverse and complex, embracing people with a wide variety of disabilities.

RIGHTS FOR THE DEAF

The first of these movements began among DEAF people. Beginning in the mid 18th century schools to educate the deaf were founded in Europe and the Americas. In France, the United States, and some other countries, instruction and communication were carried out in various sign languages, while in Britain, Germany, and elsewhere in northern Europe ORALISM (speech and lipreading) dominated. These schools' graduates formed local and national deaf communities. For example, deaf Swedes founded the Stockholm Deaf Club in 1868. In the mid 19th century school alumni in the United States, who communicated in the AMERICAN SIGN LANGUAGE (ASL) they had developed, established newspapers, churches, and social clubs. During the late 19th and early 20th centuries an aggressive oralist movement challenged sign languages everywhere. Resisting oralism, the American deaf COMMUNITY formed state political associations and, in 1880, founded the NATIONAL ASSOCIATION OF THE DEAF. Deaf advocates fought the revamping of EDUCATION and defended ASL. In the early 20th century the American deaf community also battled various forms of discrimination: in the 1910s federal civil service hiring practices, in the 1920s state restrictions on driver's licenses (see AUTOMOBILES), and in the 1930s federal work relief policies barring their EMPLOYMENT. In the late 20th century activists campaigned for recognition of ASL as a true language and sought to reshape deaf education at all levels. The effort climaxed in the 1988 "DEAF PRESIDENT NOW!" demonstrations opposing appointment of a hearing person to head GALLAUDET UNIVERSITY, an institution of higher learning established in 1864 (as the Columbia Institution for the Instruction of the Deaf and Dumb and Blind) to educate deaf people. As a result, Gallaudet obtained its first deaf president.

RIGHTS FOR THE BLIND

From the 1890s through the early 1960s BLIND people also formed their own social and political associations. In 1896 graduates of several state schools in the Midwest established the American Blind People's Higher Education and General Improvement Association, which for several years published *THE PROBLEM,* a magazine aimed at improving public understanding of the situation and capabilities of blind people. During the 1930s several state ORGANIZATIONS were founded. In 1940 state leaders launched the NATIONAL FEDERATION OF THE BLIND, with JACOBUS TENBROEK as its first president. In 1961 other blind activists established the competing AMERICAN COUNCIL OF THE BLIND. The "organized blind" movement in the United States opposed domination by sighted professionals and called for empowering blind people regarding policies and programs affecting them. For example, in the 1920s Colorado advocates campaigned to have a strong say in that state's rehabilitation programs. Blind activists also criticized restrictive social welfare policies, segregation in SHELTERED WORKSHOPS, and discrimination in society at large. From the 1930s on they lobbied for local GUIDE DOG and "white cane" laws to guarantee blind people's right of ACCESS to and freedom of movement in public places; these were the first access and accommodations statutes. Meanwhile, blind people in Europe were also forming advocacy groups, for example, the Louis Braille Association in Portugal (1927) and the Panhellenic Association of the Blind in Greece (1932). Some of these organizations fought social prejudice. For example, the British National League of the Blind held a march in London in 1933 to PROTEST job discrimination.

INSTITUTIONS AND INSTITUTIONALIZATION

Although conditions in insane ASYLUMS had drawn criticism in the 1800s, self-advocacy by people with mental disabilities did not emerge forcefully until the 20th century. In 1908 CLIFFORD BEERS published *A Mind That Found Itself* to expose abusive conditions in mental hospitals in the United States. That same year the Society for Mental Hygiene, a self-advocacy group, began to campaign for improved treatment. In 1909, in New York City, Beers founded the NATIONAL COMMITTEE FOR MENTAL HYGIENE. In 1946 conscientious objectors, who during WORLD WAR II had done alternative service in mental HOSPITALS, established the National Mental Health Foundation to publicize oppressive conditions in institutions. Their effort helped launch the DEINSTITUTIONALIZATION movement. The following year, patients at Rockland State Hospital in New York City organized a self-help group, We Are Not Alone (WANA). A generation later in the early 1970s a more activist movement emerged, with the founding of local grassroots organizations, including the Insane Liberation Front in Portland, Oregon; the Mental Patients' Liberation Front in Boston; the Mental Patients' Liberation Project in New York; and the Network against Psychiatric Assault in San Francisco. *Madness Network News* began publishing in 1971. Parents of mental patients founded the NATIONAL ALLIANCE ON MENTALLY ILLNESS in 1979, and the NATIONAL ASSOCIATION OF PSYCHIATRIC SURVIVORS was established that same year. In 1973 a Conference on Human Rights and Psychiatric Oppression met at the University of Detroit, the first gathering of its kind. JUDI CHAMBERLIN's 1978 book *On Our Own: Patient Controlled Alternatives to the Mental Health System* served as a manifesto for the movement's more militant contingent. These many advocacy groups battled social prejudice, employment discrimination, compulsory INSTITUTIONALIZATION, and forced treatment. They filed lawsuits and lobbied for legislation to protect the rights of people with mental disabilities. Their legal victories included the U.S. Supreme Court's landmark ruling in *O'Connor v. Donaldson* (1975) that prohibited involuntary commitment unless it was determined that individuals were a threat to themselves or others. Their political accomplishments included the Mental Illness Bill of Rights Act (1985), which required states to provide protection and advocacy services for people with mental disabilities.

Compulsory institutionalization was also a key issue in the movement on behalf of and by people with intellectual disabilities. From the late 19th century and into the latter decades of the 20th many were confined in huge, harsh, state-run facilities. Outside institutions, CHILDREN with those disabilities were excluded from public schools. A movement of parents and some professionals emerged after World War II to address this situation. At first it aimed to ameliorate institutional conditions; by the 1960s it was promoting community-based living and mainstream schooling (see MAINSTREAMING). In 1950 delegates from several state associations of parents founded the Association for Retarded Children of the United States (later the Association for Retarded Citizens and finally THE ARC). Due to his family's personal experience, President JOHN F. KENNEDY in the early 1960s supported community alternatives to institutionalization, but Congress never adequately funded that initiative.

EDUCATION AND EMPLOYMENT

By the early 1970s advocates had directed their efforts increasingly toward political and civil rights action. SPECIAL EDUCATION teachers formed THE ASSOCIATION OF PERSONS WITH SEVERE HANDICAPS (TASH) in 1975 to promote educational rights. These educators and parent advocates were strongly influenced by the Scandinavian "NORMALIZATION" movement that emerged in 1960 to promote deinstitutionalization and integrated socialization of people with intellectual and developmental disabilities (see DEVELOPMENTAL DISABILITY). A self-advocacy movement emerged from Sweden, where the first such meeting of people with those disabilities was held in 1959. Following that precedent an American self-advocacy organization, People First, was founded in 1974. In the 1970s the movement of and for people with intellectual disabilities (see COGNITIVE AND INTELLECTUAL DISABILITY) made important advances through lawsuits and legislation. A U.S. federal district court barred institutionalization without rehabilitation or education in WYATT V. STICKNEY (1971). A state court in Halderman v. Pennhurst (1977) not only ordered improved conditions at a Pennsylvania facility but also provided an important precedent in establishing a right to community-based living. Perhaps the greatest impetus to deinstitutionalization came in 1972 with a media exposé of abusive conditions at Willowbrook State School in New York. A subsequent lawsuit enabled large numbers of people to move into the community. Congress expanded the protections granted in some of these lawsuits with passage of the DEVELOPMENTALLY DISABLED ASSISTANCE AND BILL OF RIGHTS ACT (1975), which established the rights of people with intellectual disabilities in institutions and authorized federal funding of programs serving them. However, parts of the law proved largely ineffective because Congress failed to include an enforcement mechanism.

The movement of parents of children with intellectual disabilities was also central to establishing the right to a free appropriate public education. Beginning in various states in the 1950s and 1960s, the parents advocacy movement moved to the national level, achieving its goals through both lawsuits and legislation. Two important federal district court decisions, MILLS V. BOARD OF EDUCATION and Pennsylvania Association of Retarded Children (PARC) v. Commonwealth of Pennsylvania (both 1972), affirmed the educational rights of children with disabilities and ordered that school districts no longer exclude them. Encouraged by those rulings, advocates in various states filed similar suits. This movement's most important achievement was the federal Education for All Handicapped Children Act (1975, later renamed the INDIVIDUALS WITH DISABILITIES EDUCATION ACT). This law guaranteed the right of children with disabilities to public schooling in the most integrated environments appropriate for each child according to an "individualized educational program." In the decades following its passage advocates lobbied for adequate federal funding and compliance by local school districts. Some also promoted "inclusive education," integration of all students with disabilities in mainstream classrooms.

Various movements of people with physical disabilities emerged in the United States. In 1935 the LEAGUE OF THE PHYSICALLY HANDICAPPED was founded in New York City to oppose job discrimination in a NEW DEAL federal work-relief program. Its militant protests resulted in the hiring of 1,500 physically disabled workers. In 1940 the AMERICAN FEDERATION OF THE PHYSICALLY HANDICAPPED was founded under the leadership of PAUL STRACHAN. The first cross-disability, national political organization in the United States, it worked to end employment discrimination.

Following World War II, physically disabled activists and their supporters worked to integrate higher education. Disabled VETERANS enrolled in schools that provided access and accommodations. By 1961 the student body at the University of Illinois at Champaign-Urbana included 163 students with disabilities, 101 of them WHEELCHAIR users. In 1962 ED ROBERTS, a quadriplegic ventilator user as the result of POLIO, fought University of California at BERKELEY administrators to gain admission. Other students with significant physical disabilities soon followed him. Disabled graduates of such schools as Illinois, Berkeley, and Boston University emerged as prominent disability rights leaders in the 1970s.

INDEPENDENT LIVING MOVEMENT

Young adults with significant physical disabilities spearheaded the INDEPENDENT LIVING MOVEMENT (ILM) that emerged in the 1970s to promote self-directed community-based living. Between 1972 and 1976 they established independent living centers (ILCs) in Berkeley, Boston, Houston, Denver, St. Louis, Los Angeles, and Chicago. These agencies offered peer counseling, facilitated personal assistance services, and lobbied for civil rights, accessibility, and government resources to support independent living. In the late 1970s the federal government started funding ILCs. By then 52 were operating in the United States; by the 1990s there were several hundred. In the latter era ILCs expanded their clientele beyond the original core of physically disabled people to include people with sensory, developmental, and mental disabilities of all ages and various ethnic minorities. In significant ways, the ILM complemented the deinstitutionalization movements for people with mental and intellectual disabilities and, over time, established connections with them. From the 1990s on, through the leadership of ADAPT (AMERICAN DISABLED FOR ATTENDANT PROGRAMS TODAY), the NATIONAL COUNCIL ON INDEPENDENT LIVING, and activist ILC leaders, the ILM lobbied for reallocation of federal funds from institutional placements to independent living. Beginning in 1977, British self-advocates conducted a similar national campaign to free people with disabilities from institutions. From 1980 on, independent living movements emerged in Canada, Europe, Asia, and Latin America.

ACCESSIBILITY AND TRANSPORTATION

Physical access and access to programs and services has been a goal of many disability rights movements. Returning disabled World War II veterans played prominent roles in the campaign to remove architectural barriers in the United States. A 1947 gathering of delegates from Veterans Administration HOSPITALS met at Birmingham Hospital in Van Nuys, California, to found PARALYZED VETERANS OF AMERICA (PVA). Together with such organizations as the National Easter Seals Society, PVA campaigned for national access standards and state and federal laws to enforce them. The barrier-free movement's first major legislative achievement was the ARCHITECTURAL BARRIERS ACT (1968), a federal law requiring that most facilities designed, built, altered, or leased with federal monies be accessible. Its enforcement provisions, however, were weak. Further lobbying prompted creation of the Architectural and Transportation Barriers Compliance Board (1973) to ensure compliance with the 1968 law. Additional legislation in 1976 mandated that facilities built with federal funds incorporate access features in their original design.

By means of both laws and lawsuits, activists also campaigned for accessible public transit (see TRANSPORTATION). The Urban Mass Transportation Act (1970) and the Federal-Aid Highway Act (1973) assured a right of equal access to public mass transit, but neither had adequate enforcement

mechanisms. Activists responded by filing lawsuits and engaging in direct action protests. For example, in a landmark 1972 ruling, PVA and other advocacy groups persuaded a court to order that the design of the new Washington, D.C., Metro transit system include access features. In 1978 activists organized a year-long civil disobedience campaign in Denver. Blocking buses they compelled the Regional Transit Authority to buy wheelchair lift-equipped vehicles. In the 1980s these and other advocates established ADAPT as a militant national group. From 1983 to 1990 the group employed civil disobedience at the semiannual meetings of the American Public Transit Association to PROTEST officials' resistance to making public transit accessible to people with disabilities. The AMERICANS WITH DISABILITIES ACT (ADA) of 1990 mandated such access but allowed long time lines for compliance. In the 1990s and on into the 21st century activists continued to campaign for accessible public transit in New York, Philadelphia, and other major U.S. cities. ADAPT also successfully used militant tactics to compel Greyhound and other interstate bus companies to comply with the ADA. Meanwhile, in Britain militant activism emerged in the early 1990s in the Campaign for Accessible Transport.

Accessibility involved more than wheelchair lifts. It also included Braille markings and auditory signals. Some organized blind advocacy groups supported the latter but the NATIONAL FEDERATION OF THE BLIND opposed them, declaring that those signals made blind people dependent on technology that would rarely be adopted. Meanwhile, the deaf community lobbied for captioned TV programming. In 1976 the Federal Communications Commission designated Line 21 on television sets for CLOSED CAPTIONING.

LEGISLATION

The two most noted U.S. civil rights laws relating to people with disabilities were the 1973 Rehabilitation Act's SECTION 504 and the 1990 Americans with Disabilities Act. Section 504 prohibited discrimination against "otherwise qualified handicapped" individuals in federally funded programs. For four years the Nixon, Ford, and Carter administrations avoided issuing the regulations that would implement it. Though activists had no part in drafting 504, their efforts for its promulgation became an effective means to mobilize disability rights advocacy. That campaign led to the first national cross-disability political organizing in the United States with the establishment of the AMERICAN COALITION OF CITIZENS WITH DISABILITIES in 1974. It climaxed in April 1977 with one-day sit-ins in 10 cities and the three-and-a-half-week occupation of a federal building in San Francisco that pressured the Carter administration to declare 504 as an enforceable civil rights statute. The political education produced by the 504 campaign resulted in more sophisticated and extensive alliance building during the 1980s that led to passage of the Americans with Disabilities Act. The ADA applied the principles of accessibility, reasonable accommodations, and protection against discrimination to the broader society.

The disability rights movements in the United States have remained largely white and middle class. There are notable exceptions, however, such as the NATIONAL BLACK DEAF ADVOCATES, organized in 1981 to address the double discrimination against deaf African-Americans. In addition, in some movements, such as the organized blind and the deaf community, men dominated in leadership roles, while in others, such as the Independent Living Movement, women played a prominent role. Beginning in the 1970s physically disabled feminists called on both disability rights advocates and nondisabled feminists to take up disabled women's issues. The DISABLED WOMEN'S NETWORK (DAWN) was founded in Winnipeg, Canada, in 1987 to combat another form of double discrimination: disability bias combined with sexism.

Because litigation constituted a major strategy of all disability rights movements, many supported legal centers. The first in the United States was the National Center for Law and the Handicapped at the University of Notre Dame (1971). Some centers, such as the Judge David L. BAZELON CENTER FOR MENTAL HEALTH LAW in Washington, D.C. (1972), have served particular disability constituencies. Others, such as the Western Center on Law and the Handicapped (1975, later the Western Center on Law and Disability Rights) in Los Angeles and the DISABILITY RIGHTS EDUCATION AND DEFENSE FUND in Berkeley (1979), have represented both specific disability constituencies and cross-disability issues.

CROSS-DISABILITY MOVEMENTS

Cross-disability political activism appeared even before formation of the American Coalition of Citizens with Disabilities. In 1970 DISABLED IN ACTION was founded in New York City with chapters later organized in other northeastern cities. It employed direct action protest tactics and lawsuits to advance disability rights. Its members represented a militant younger generation that identified with disabled people in general rather than particular disability constituencies. The annual meetings of the President's Committee on Employment of the Handicapped (later the PRESIDENT'S COMMITTEE ON EMPLOYMENT OF PEOPLE WITH DISABILITIES), first held in 1947, became another arena in which members of various disability communities came to recognize their similar perspectives and agendas. Cross-disability consciousness was also reflected in the Bill of Rights for the Handicapped adopted at the UNITED CEREBRAL PALSY ASSOCIATION's 1973 annual meeting in Washington, D.C., and in the celebration of Disabled People's Civil Rights Day, on October 20, 1979, which included rallies in major cities to declare solidarity

among Americans with disabilities. From the 1970s on, disability rights movements pursued both disability-specific and cross-disability concerns. These developments indicated the emergence of not only cross-disability political alliances but even of a common identity. A 1986 Harris poll documented that a younger generation of American adults with disabilities now viewed themselves as part of a minority group that faced discrimination.

Meanwhile, cross-disability political movements appeared in many other countries. While Norwegians founded a cross-disability association as early as 1950, most emerged in the 1970s and 1980s, including the Threshold in Finland (1973); the Union of Physically Impaired Against Segregation in Great Britain (1975); the Coalition of Provincial Organizations of the Handicapped in Canada (1976, later renamed the Council of Canadians with Disabilities); a national cross-disability association of 30 organizations in the Netherlands (1977); the United Front of the Handicapped in Sri Lanka (1977); the first National Forum for Disabled People in Scotland (1978); the British Council of Organizations of Disabled People (1981); the first national gathering in Brazil to organize a cross-disability association (1981); the Combined Disabilities Association in Jamaica (1981); the Congress on the Rights of People with Disabilities in Costa Rica (1982); the Disabled Persons Assembly in New Zealand (1982); and associations of physically disabled, blind, and deaf people meeting in Zambia to create a common secretariat (1983). At the same time, various disability movements formed international advocacy organizations, including the World Federation of the Deaf (1950) and the World Blind Union (1984). The first international conference on the civil rights of people with psychiatric disabilities met in 1984. In 1981 a global cross-disability advocacy organization, Disabled People's International (DPI), was founded in Singapore.

These movements often pursued civil rights or human rights objectives and used militant tactics. In Sweden in 1977 advocates successfully incorporated into building codes the requirement that multifamily housing include access features. Canada's Human Rights Act was amended to cover people with disabilities (1983) as was Australia's Bill of Rights (1985). Disabled People of South Africa was founded in 1986 as a national, interracial, and democratic association linked to the struggle against apartheid. In Japan a radical self-advocacy movement was launched in 1978, while in Germany a coalition of disability activist groups conducted a mock tribunal in 1981 that tried the nation for its segregation and ABUSE of people with disabilities. Six years later, over 500 Korean disability rights activists protested inaccessibility (1987), and in France 23,000 people joined a disability rights demonstration to demand greater government funding for personal assistance services and technical equipment (1999).

In Britain beginning in the early 1990s a broad coalition, the Direct Action Network, militantly campaigned on a range of issues that included accessible public transport, deinstitutionalization and community-based living, the rights of deaf people, and an end to psychiatric oppression. In 2006, after five years of negotiation, international advocates completed a United Nations' INTERNATIONAL CONVENTION ON THE RIGHTS OF PERSONS WITH DISABILITIES and then launched a campaign to get member states to adopt it.

Each of the disability-specific movements has focused its advocacy on issues and agendas of particular concern to their constituencies, but they historically operated from similar principles and often pursued comparable goals. Over time their developing ideologies of disability and disability rights not only challenged dominant perspectives but also moved toward a similar outlook. The ideological and political parallels support a historical explanation of them as components of a larger disability rights movement. By the end of the 20th century, virtually all disability movements operated from a common set of ideas. All substituted a Minority-Group or Social or Social-Political Model of disability for a MEDICAL MODEL OF DISABILITY. That is, they reframed "disability" as a social, cultural, and political status and identity, rather than simply a series of medical conditions requiring treatment. That basic shift in definition of the problems of people with disabilities led to a corresponding redirection of practical priorities and agendas. Although these movements demanded access to appropriate HEALTH CARE as a social right, they de-emphasized medical, educational, and vocational "treatments" to correct individuals and called instead for reform of society. They explained the social marginalization, vocational limitations, and economic disadvantages of many people with disabilities as not the inevitable outcome of physiological conditions but largely the result of social prejudice, institutionalized discrimination, inaccessibility, restrictive public policies, and bureaucratic and professional domination. They lobbied for legal protection from discrimination and due process in all professional or governmental decision making affecting people with disabilities. They also asserted the right of people with disabilities to the means to achieve social participation and integration. Those means included physical access, reasonable accommodations in programs and services, technological devices, and various educational and social services. They called for legal guarantees of these means as enforceable rights rather than dispensations of CHARITY.

These movements also challenged the power of medical, educational, and social service professionals and vendors of services and products over the lives of people with disabilities. They accused service providers and professionals of frequently advancing their own material and status interests at the price of the best interests of people with disabilities. Because activists saw relationships between professionals and people with disabilities as often adversarial, with disproportionate power on the professionals' side, they campaigned for EMPOWERMENT of individuals. But contrary to a common mistaken assumption, these movements supported more than personal autonomy. They called for not only personal self-advocacy and individual self-determination but also collective empowerment and COMMUNITY self-determination.

Late 20th-century political activism promoted a sense of identification across disability constituencies and a growing sense of universalistic disability IDENTITY. Even so, disability-specific interests and identities persisted. The continuing need to address the tension between particular constituencies, interests, and identities and a perception of common community and shared interests indicated the emergence of a historically significant transformation in consciousness among people with disabilities. At the beginning of the 21st century, all disability movements and a more general disability rights movement were moving toward a complex shared ideology of disability and disability rights and a complicated cross-disability agenda.

See also ABLEISM; ACCESS AND ACCESSIBILITY; ASSISTIVE TECHNOLOGY AND ADAPTIVE DEVICES; DISABILITY ART AND ARTISTIC EXPRESSION; DISABILITY CULTURE; DISABILITY STUDIES; INCLUSION EDUCATION; LANGUAGE AND TERMINOLOGY; LAW AND POLICY; PARENT ADVOCACY GROUPS; REPRESENTATION; SELF-ADVOCATES AND SELF-ADVOCACY; SIT-IN PROTEST AT THE DEPARTMENT OF HEALTH, EDUCATION AND WELFARE.

Paul K. Longmore

Further Reading:
Charlton, James. *Nothing About Us Without Us: Disability Oppression and Empowerment.* Berkeley: University of California Press, 2000.

Fleischer, Doris Zames, and Frieda Zames. *The Disability Rights Movement: From Charity to Confrontation.* Philadelphia: Temple University Press, 2001.

Longmore, Paul K. *Why I Burned My Book and Other Essays on Disability.* Philadelphia: Temple University Press, 2003.

Shapiro, Joseph P. *No Pity: People with Disabilities Forging a New Civil Rights Movement.* New York: Three Rivers Press, 1994.

Interview with Charles Carr (2001)

One of the early founders of Centers for Independent Living in Massachusetts in the 1970s and 1980s, Charles Carr has remained a staunch advocate in the disability rights movement. Reflecting in this 2001 interview on the history and outcomes of the movement, Carr recognizes the powerful impact of self-advocacy for people with disabilities. At the same time he points to important areas where work remains, including employment and transportation. Like many established leaders, Carr calls for a new generation of disability activists to continue fighting for full inclusion and full citizenship.

Charles Carr
Interview conducted by Fred Pelka
2001

So I feel that in terms of the disability rights movement, we got the ADA, but we didn't get full employment. We didn't even get partial employment. We don't have adequate housing. We don't have adequate transportation. So we didn't get all we wanted, but what we did get was our voices heard. We did get some political status. We are making gains that are measured gains. If you look back ten years, even, since the ADA was passed, and you look at the number of people with all types of disabilities that have assumed mantles of power on local, statewide, national levels, to me, as someone who's been around as long as I have, I'm very happy and I'm very pleased.

What I worry about, though, is this trend that I see now of apathy and stagnation. Some of the younger folks are feeling pretty apolitical and almost feeling like what Tip O'Neil [Speaker of the House Thomas P. O'Neil] said so eloquently, and that is that people that have made it in any movement have a tendency to say to hell with them, I have mine. And they settle for that. As a leader, I absolutely believe what he's saying is true. So if the younger folks are feeling like I've got my piece, I don't really need to fight any longer, they're really wrong. All they've got to do is look around in their community and look at any institution—state hospital, state schools, nursing home, whatever. They're filled to capacity. Look at the unemployment rate hovering around seventy percent and realize that we've just begun.

What we've done is we've made gains in integrating people into the community. Gains. But where's the rest of the dream? How many home owners are there with disabilities? How many people are gainfully employed? How many people have families and have reached their full potential? Not very many. So we have a lot of work to do.

Source: Charles Carr, interviewed by Fred Pelka, June 30, 2001. Available online. URL: http://bancroft.berkeley.edu/collections/drilm/collection/items/carr1_transcript.html. Accessed June 26, 2008.

disability studies

Disability studies refers to the examination of disability as a social, cultural, and political phenomenon. In contrast to clinical, medical, or therapeutic perspectives on disability, disability studies focuses on how disability is defined and represented in society. From this perspective, disability is not a characteristic that exists in the person so defined, but a construct that finds its meaning in a social and cultural context.

Although scholarship on the social and cultural meaning of disability can be traced at least as far back as the 1950s and 1960s, the phrase *disability studies* did not emerge until the 1980s. The Section for the Study of Chronic Illness, Impairment, and Disability of the Western Social Science Association, which had been established in 1982, was renamed the SOCIETY FOR DISABILITY STUDIES (SDS) in 1986. That same year, IRVING ZOLA, the first president of SDS, changed the name of the *Disability and Chronic Disease Newsletter*, which he published, to the *DISABILITY STUDIES QUARTERLY*.

Disability studies is a vibrant and diverse field of inquiry. First, it is multidisciplinary. Early disability studies scholarship was based on the social sciences, history, and political science. In the 1990s the humanities began to exert a strong influence on disability studies scholarship, with the publication of many books and articles and the increased presence of critical work on disability in academic organizations such as the Modern Language Association. Today, the field is informed by scholarship from history, sociology, LITERATURE, political science, LAW, policy studies, economics, cultural studies, anthropology, geography, philosophy, theology, gender studies, communications and media studies, the arts, and other disciplines.

Second, disability studies covers an extremely diverse group of people. People who are BLIND, DEAF, have HIV/AIDS, use WHEELCHAIRS, have chronic PAIN, learn at a slower pace or differently than most people, have psychiatric histories, and so on have vastly different experiences and perspectives. Even people within a single disability category can differ greatly from one another. This begs the question: does it make sense to lump such different human beings under a simple category such as disability? It does—not because they are the same in any biological or philosophical sense, but because society has placed them in this category, with consequences for how they are viewed and treated by the majority presumed to be NONDISABLED.

Although a disability studies perspective can be and has been applied to any group of people defined as having a disability, most scholarship identified with the phrase has focused on the "body" and people with physical or sensory IMPAIRMENTS. This is slowly changing with the recognition that people with intellectual, psychiatric, or nonapparent disabilities—or labeled as such—have been subjected to the same prejudice, stereotyping, and discrimination as other disabled people.

Finally, it is usually easier to define what disability studies is *not*—not medicine, rehabilitation, SPECIAL EDUCATION, physical or OCCUPATIONAL THERAPY, and other professions oriented toward the CURE, prevention, and treatment of disabilities—than to specify what it *is*. Disability studies scholars generally subscribe to the "minority model of disability" or the view that the status of disabled people as a minority shapes their experiences in society, but they disagree on other things. For example, some scholars view disability in terms of culture and IDENTITY, while others perceive disability as a social construct or label. Many British disability studies scholars, in particular, approach disability from a materialist perspective focusing on the political economy. Other scholars are interested in the social and cultural REPRESENTATION of disability.

Scholars even use different LANGUAGE to refer to the people at the center on inquiry in disability studies. "Disabled person" is used to draw attention to the centrality of disability in individual identity; "person with a disability" or "people first language" conveys the idea that having a disability is secondary to people's identities as human beings; "person labeled disabled" ("mentally retarded," "mentally ill," etc.) focuses on how disability is a socially constructed definition imposed upon people. Within subgroups, minor variations in language, spelling, or capitalization can carry tremendous significance. Thus, "deaf person" and "Deaf person" mean very different things, with the former simply indicating a person who is deaf and the latter emphasizing membership in a culture defined linguistically. Some scholars also believe that Deaf people represent a linguistic minority and not a disability group.

The Society for Disability Studies remains the major American scholarly association concerned with disability studies. SDS continues to publish *Disability Studies Quarterly*. The British journal *Disability & Society* is another major source of disability studies scholarship. By the early 21st century, more than 20 universities in North America offered formal undergraduate or graduate programs in Disability Studies, a number that is likely to grow. Disability studies courses are taught in academic departments at universities throughout the United States.

See also DEAF STUDIES; FEMINIST DISABILITY STUDIES; QUEER DISABILITY STUDIES; SOCIAL CONSTRUCTION OF DISABILITY.

Steven J. Taylor

Further Reading:

Davis, Lenny J. *Bending Over Backwards: Disability, Dismodernism & Other Difficult Positions.* New York: New York University Press, 2002.

Haller, Beth. "A Brief History of *DSQ*." *Disability Studies Quarterly.* Available online. URL: http://www.dsq-sds.org/history_of_dsq.html. Accessed December 19, 2006.

Linton, Simi. *Claiming Disability: Knowledge and Identity.* New York: New York University Press, 1998.

Longmore, Paul K. *Why I Burned My Book and Other Essays on Disability.* Philadelphia: Temple University Press, 2003.

Society for Disability Studies. "Society for Disability Studies General Information." Available online. URL: http://www.uic.edu/orgs/sds/generalinfo.html. Accessed December 19, 2006.

Taylor, Steven, B. Shoultz, and P. Walker. "Disability Studies: Information and Resources." Center on Human Policy, Syracuse University. Available online. URL: http://thechp.syr.edu/Disability_Studies_2003_current.html. Accessed December 19, 2006.

Disability Studies Quarterly

Disability Studies Quarterly (*DSQ*) is the oldest academic journal in North America focused on DISABILITY STUDIES. Published by the SOCIETY FOR DISABILITY STUDIES (SDS), *DSQ* is a peer-reviewed journal whose recent editors have included Brenda Jo Brueggemann, Scot Danforth and Stephen Kuusisto. *DSQ* is composed of a number of sections, one usually dedicated to a specific disability theme. Other sections include commentaries, peer-reviewed articles and reviews. Historically, the journal also has showcased an international section, creative works, and a section on pedagogy. It is published online at www.dsq-sds.org, and since autumn 2008, is available without a subscription.

DSQ grew out of an earlier publication edited by one of the SDS founders, IRVING K. ZOLA (1935–94), a professor of sociology at Brandeis University and a founding member of SDS, who had taken over a publication called the *Disability Newsletter* in 1982. This newsletter was started by sociologist Natalie Allon (1941–2001) in 1980 as part of the disability subsection of the Medical Sociology Section of the American Sociological Association. Zola began as editor with the publication of the second volume, at the same time renaming it the *Disability and Chronic Disease Newsletter*. In 1986 Zola changed the name again to *Disability Studies Quarterly* and officially established the connection between the publication and the society.

The early *DSQ* issues were in a photocopied and stapled format. They contained reviews and bibliographies of disability-related materials from numerous disciplines, an extensive calendar of disability-oriented events, and calls for papers. Early in the history of *DSQ,* Zola worked with guest editors to assign themes to three of each year's issues. (Winter issues were typically left as general issues.) Themes ranged widely, including topics such as public policy, media, the body, technology, and AGING. Each thematic issue had a guest editor with expertise on the focus topic. Articles were generally short, more often "think pieces" than research reports, and they were not peer reviewed beyond the guest editor and Zola. The journal was published from Brandeis University until Zola's death in 1994. David Pfeiffer (1934–2003), a political scientist at Suffolk University, took over as *DSQ* editor in the summer of 1995. The content continued to expand and began to include much more original research in the growing field of disability studies. Beth Haller of Towson University and Corinne Kirchner of the American Foundation for the Blind served as *DSQ* editors from 2004 until spring 2007.

In part to enhance ACCESS to the journal, *DSQ* moved exclusively to an online format in 2000, and, in 2002, the SDS board decided to rotate the editorship every three years. It also codified a statement of principles for *DSQ,* which helped define the emerging field of disability studies. This includes placing disability in a broader context of social, political, medical, and economic factors. Multidisciplinary and interdisciplinary approaches are common features of the field, as is the recognition that personal lived experiences have much to show us about disability and its meaning.

DSQ holds a unique place in the history of disability studies because from its beginning it has provided a unique space for scholars and writers across the disciplines to publish essays and start a "conversation" about the disabled in society. Although a number of other academic journals now include disability content, *DSQ* has continued to give authors an accessible and high-quality venue for publication.

Beth Haller

Further Reading:

Disability Newsletter 1 (1980). Publication of the disability subsection of the Medical Sociology Section of the American Sociological Association.

Garland Thomson, Rosemarie, and Paul Longmore. "*DSQ* Statement of Principles." Available online. URL: http://www.dsq-sds.org/principles.html. Accessed August 19, 2001.

Haller, Beth, and Corinne Kirchner. "Editor's Preface." *Disability Studies Quarterly* (Spring 2006): 26. Available online. URL: http://www.dsq-sds.org/_articles_html/2006/spring/editorspreface.asp. Accessed August 19, 2006.

Pfeiffer, David. "Editor's Preface." *Disability Studies Quarterly* 16 (Fall 1996): 1.

Zola, Irving K. "The Editors' Letter." *Disability Studies Quarterly* 10 (Fall 1990): 1.

Disabled American Veterans

Headquartered in Cold Spring, Kentucky, the Disabled American Veterans (DAV) is a federally chartered veterans' ORGANIZATION comprised exclusively of men and women disabled as a result of military service. Since its formation in 1920, the DAV has led an active campaign to improve the treatment of the nation's disabled VETERANS. As the largest association of disabled veterans in the United States, the DAV has also played a central role in mediating the social experience of WAR disability in modern America.

The DAV emerged in response to the dire conditions facing disabled veterans at the end of WORLD WAR I (1914–18). Despite the late entry of the United States into the conflict in 1917, Americans were ill prepared to meet the needs of the latest generation of war-disabled veterans. The rapid rate of sick and wounded combatants returning home from Europe—23,000 per month in early 1919—overwhelmed the government agencies responsible for their care. Disabled veterans seeking medical treatment, rehabilitation, and monetary compensation faced long delays and endless red tape. Making matters worse, economic recession and lingering public prejudices made it difficult for many disabled veterans to reintegrate smoothly into postwar society.

The DAV's roots can be traced to Cincinnati, Ohio, home to two loosely organized self-help groups for disabled veterans: the Ohio Mechanics Institute for Disabled Soldiers and a smaller faction of disabled veterans from the University of Cincinnati. The two groups eventually coalesced under the leadership of Robert S. Marx (1889–1960), a charismatic attorney who had been severely wounded mere hours before the war's end. Like many of the DAV's early leaders, Marx worried that the unique challenges faced by disabled veterans would be ignored by more inclusive groups of veterans. On September 25, 1920, delegates from across the country assembled in Cincinnati, and the Disabled Veterans of the World War was born (the name would be shortened in January 1941). The following summer, some 1,400 DAV members elected Marx the group's first national commander.

Over the next two decades, the DAV attracted tens of thousands of members and founded more than 1,200 local chapters and state offices across the country. Working closely with other groups of veterans, the DAV lobbied politicians to liberalize federal disability benefits and eliminate corruption within the Veterans Bureau. In its publicity campaigns, the DAV exalted the veteran with disabilities as a civic ideal, deserving of material comfort and public assistance. The group also functioned as a social safety net for disabled veterans and their families. Throughout the 1920s and 1930s, the DAV sponsored countless CHARITY entertainments, "Forget-Me-Not" Day celebrations, and disability-themed sporting events. In times of hardship, the group's Women's

Auxiliary distributed food, money, and cigarettes to needy disabled veterans.

Following WORLD WAR II, DAV membership swelled to more than 100,000. It continued to climb throughout much of the 20th century, as fresh cohorts of service-disabled veterans joined the DAV's ranks. In 1976, after the end of the Vietnam War, DAV members played a critical role in raising public awareness of post-traumatic stress disorder. In the 1990s and the early years of the 21st century, the DAV developed a wide array of social services and outreach programs to help disabled veterans recently returned from the PERSIAN GULF WAR (1990–91), Afghanistan, and Iraq. Now nearly 1.4 million members strong, the DAV remains the most forceful advocate for the fair treatment of disabled veterans in the United States.

See also ACTIVISM AND ADVOCACY; IRAQ WAR.

John M. Kinder

Further Reading:

"Annual Report of the Anthony L. Baskerville National Membership Director to the Disabled American Veterans," 85th National Convention, Chicago, Illinois, August 12–15, 2006. Disabled American Veterans. Available online. URL: http://www.dav.org/membership/documents/2006_annual_report.pdf. Accessed May 20, 2007.

Minott, Rodney G. *Peerless Patriots: Organized Veterans and the Spirit of Americanism.* Washington, D.C.: Public Affairs Press, 1962.

Ross, Davis R. B. *Preparing for Ulysses: Politics and Veterans during World War II.* New York: Columbia University Press, 1969.

Wars & Scars: A Diamond Anniversary History of the Disabled American Veterans. Cold Spring, Ky.: Disabled American Veterans, 1995.

Disabled in Action

Disabled in Action (DIA) has been an important cross-disability PROTEST ORGANIZATION since its founding by JUDY HEUMANN and other disabled students at Long Island University's Brooklyn campus in 1970. Heumann, a POLIO survivor, had filed an antidiscrimination lawsuit against the New York City Board of Education, which had refused to issue her a teaching certificate because she used a WHEELCHAIR and could not walk. The publicity surrounding this successful legal action attracted a number of individuals with disabilities, who joined with Heumann to establish DIA.

DIA is a grassroots organization with no office or paid staff. In addition to its first chapter in New York City, a Philadelphia chapter was established in 1973, and other chapters have existed in Baltimore, Maryland, and Syracuse, New York. DIA relies primarily on volunteer efforts by its members, but it has also raised money through a variety of foundation and government grants, and through performances by its musical group, the Disabled In Action Singers.

In its early years, DIA organized street protests in New York and Washington, D.C., following the vetoes by President Richard Nixon of two initial versions of what was to become the Rehabilitation Act of 1973 (see VOCATIONAL REHABILITATION ACT). These protests included a takeover of the Nixon presidential campaign office in New York City (in partnership with a group of disabled Vietnam VETERANS), blocking rush-hour traffic in the Wall Street financial district, and a demonstration at the Lincoln Memorial in Washington.

Another target for DIA protests has been fund-raising TELETHONS, which many disability rights activists criticize as promoting images of disabled people as tragically flawed and incapable of living NORMAL lives. DIA protested UNITED CEREBRAL PALSY telethons in 1976 and 1977 and the MUSCULAR DYSTROPHY ASSOCIATION in 1993 and 1994. DIA also has worked for accessible public TRANSPORTATION, enactment of the AMERICANS WITH DISABILITIES ACT, accessible public facilities such as the Empire State Building's observation tower, and removal of barriers in residences and local businesses through its One-Step Campaign.

DIA has sought change through legal actions as well, including *Hill v. New York City Board of Elections,* which, in 1994, successfully mandated wheelchair accessible local VOTING sites. DIA argued for accessible transportation in the 1976 case *Disabled in Action of Pennsylvania, Inc. v. Coleman* and the 1982 case *Dopico v. Goldschmidt.*

DIA has often worked in partnership with other disability groups, such as ADAPT and its WHEELS OF JUSTICE protests, the Eastern Paralyzed Veterans of America, and the AMERICAN COUNCIL OF THE BLIND. Since the passage of the Americans with Disabilities Act of 1990, DIA has focused its activities on health care reform and redirecting MEDICAID funding to promote independence and community-based services.

Richard K. Scotch

Further Reading:

Disabled in Action of Pennsylvania, Inc. Web site. URL: http://www.disabledinactionpa.org/.

Disabled in Action Web site. URL: http://www.disabledinaction.org/.

Fleischer, Doris Zames, and Frieda Zames. *The Disability Rights Movement: From Charity to Confrontation.* Philadelphia: Temple University Press, 2001.

Disabled Peoples Liberation Front

The Disabled Peoples Liberation Front (DPLF) represents a radical, local response to discrimination as well as a rich example of disability EMPOWERMENT.

In 1977 Jean Wassell, a teacher from western Massachusetts, James Brooks, from the Chicago housing projects, and former MARCH OF DIMES POSTER CHILD Richard Candelmo joined together in Boston to discuss civil rights for persons with disabilities. They also examined the connection between discrimination against people with disabilities and the ongoing discrimination against women, people of color, and those of different social classes. This informal discussion evolved into an ORGANIZATION called the Disabled Peoples Liberation Front, modeled on other radical social movements. The group stressed the specific inequities people with disabilities faced in areas such as housing, HEALTH CARE, EDUCATION, and EMPLOYMENT. Membership was free and open to all interested parties.

The same year, the three activists composed a manifesto that exposed the connections between RACE, class, and disability. They asserted that poor people "became" so unhealthy at a young AGE because of social conditions that kept them from access to good health care. Financial costs and a bureaucracy that devalued them, the activists added, contributed to their marginalized place. Similarly, people with disabilities were mostly poor; even when their specific health needs were addressed through surgery or drugs, their overall health generally was ignored.

DPLF members chose not to seek government subsidies for their organization, asserting that governments or government-funded agencies placed certain restraints on behavior and speech. Accepting government funds, they reasoned, would have forced them to be more circumspect in criticizing the social system. DPLF chose to use civil disobedience and to speak out against capitalism, two tactics that were familiar to other civil rights efforts but had remained outside the mainstream disability movement.

Focused on local action, the DPLF approached issues familiar to all disabled people. Members chained themselves to buses to draw attention to inaccessible public TRANSPORTATION. When Alan Friedberg, an executive of the Sack Theater chain, which owned many movie houses in the Boston area, refused to provide disability accommodations and dismissed the validity of protestors' civil rights arguments in 1978, DPLF members blocked Sack movie theaters throughout the region. The movie theater boycott lasted seven years, until 1985, when the company agreed to install ramps and elevators and to build accessible theaters in the future.

As other mainstream disability groups gained prominence locally and nationally in the 1980s, the DPLF sought to collaborate on issues upon which they agreed. One example was TELETHONS. The DPLF had distinguished itself as an early critic of telethons that presented disabled people as pitiful and objects of CHARITY. Various DPLF members were arrested many times for picketing the JERRY LEWIS Telethon. Other advocacy groups, such as Jerry's Orphans, also

actively challenged Lewis and the MUSCULAR DYSTROPHY ASSOCIATION telethon.

Throughout the 1980s and 1990s, the group also worked with unions, including bus drivers who worked with SPECIAL needs kids; partnering with antiracism organizations, the DPLF marched in Boston and Washington, D.C., to express opposition to the death penalty and its disproportionate impact on minority communities.

Other disabled people often publicly criticized the DPLF's stances and tactics as inappropriate. They strongly disagreed with the group's opinion that the 1990 AMERICANS WITH DISABILITIES ACT was merely another mainstream way to keep people with disabilities in line, in court, and stuck within the structure of the capitalist system. Differences in strategic planning and economic and political views often have continued to separate the DPLF from the mainstream DISABILITY RIGHTS MOVEMENT.

Beginning in the 1990s, the DPLF has worked almost exclusively with housing advocates to demand more affordable and accessible housing, and most recently to prevent foreclosures. It continues to collaborate selectively with other disability organizations and to work with unions and the poor. Its ultimate goals remain those first articulated in 1977.

As a radical local advocacy group, the DPLF offers an important example of the diversity within the disability rights movement. Its attention to the links between race, economic class, and disability reflect major challenges and common experiences of oppression in American history.

See also ACCESS AND ACCESSIBILITY; ACTIVISM AND ADVOCACY; POVERTY; PROTEST.

Karen Schneiderman

Further Reading:
Charlton, James I. *Nothing About Us Without Us: Disability Oppression and Empowerment.* Berkeley: University of California Press, 2000.
Russell, Marta. *Beyond Ramps: Disability at the End of the Social Contract.* Monroe, Me.: Common Courage Press, 1998.

DisAbled Women's Network Canada

The DisAbled Women's Network (DAWN) Canada holds a critical place in the history of disabled women in the United States. Founded in 1985, DAWN Canada provided early leadership on issues of women with disabilities. More importantly DAWN focused its efforts on creating publications to assist women with a variety of disabilities. Although DAWN Canada is not currently working on a national level, provincial chapters continue to produce publications and online resources.

Women with disabilities in the United States never succeeded in creating a national organization of disabled women, yet they created many important events that spurred the efforts of women with disabilities around the globe. DAWN Canada's early research publications enabled disabled women in the United States to document barriers facing women with disabilities.

Founded by a group of women with disabilities, DAWN Canada addressed the diversity of disabled women from the outset. The initial group included women with physical, mental, and sensory disabilities with varied sexual orientations, RACES, RELIGIONS, and classes. DAWN's founders focused their feminist work on issues critical to all women with disabilities: EMPLOYMENT, POVERTY, self-image, SEXUALITY, ACCESS to HEALTH CARE and other services, and VIOLENCE against women with disabilities.

In 1988 DAWN Canada surveyed women with disabilities across the country. In combination with interviews, these surveys formed the basis of four important publications: *Beating the Odds: Violence and Women with Disabilities* (1989); *The Only Parent in the Neighbourhood: Mothering and Women with Disabilities* (1989); *Who Do We Think We Are?: Self Image and Women with Disabilities* (1989); and *Different Therefore Unequal: Employment and Women with Disabilities* (1989).

While DAWN Canada developed national campaigns, local chapters blossomed and created additional material. Many of DAWN's publications became available in English and French and on audiotape and computer disk. In 1993 DAWN Ontario published brochures on motherhood: *I Want to be a Mother; Je veux être Mère*; health care: *You and Your Doctor: Partners in Care; Votre Medecin et Vous*; and sexuality: *Une Collaboration essentielle; Women with Disabilities Talk about Sexuality; Les Femmes handicapées parlent de leur Sexualité.*

Over the next decade DAWN and its chapters continued to create materials on health care, violence, substance abuse, smoking, and poverty. They wrote the first analysis of women with mental disabilities in the federal PRISON system, *Federally Sentenced Women with Mental Disabilities: A Dark Corner in Canadian Human Rights*. DAWN worked with Action des femmes handicapées de Montréal to highlight the issue of cancer in *Access to Breast Cancer Screening Programs for Women with Disabilities*. This work built on the CANCER experiences of Judith Rogers, a U.S. disabled cancer survivor, who initiated the project Breast Health Access for Women with Disabilities in BERKELEY, CALIFORNIA.

DAWN Canada also addressed legislative and policy barriers that thwarted their goal to countering poverty, isolation, discrimination, and violence for women with disabilities. With a specific focus on working in coalitions, DAWN Canada brought disabled women's issues to numerous peace and poverty-focused groups. DAWN Canada's ability to pursue national work has depended heavily on project-specific funding, while provincial chapters provide a regional presence with networks of volunteers.

See also ACTIVISM AND ADVOCACY; ORGANIZATIONS.

Corbett Joan O'Toole

Further Reading:
"Access to Breast Cancer Screening Programs for Women with Disabilities." Available online. URL: http://dawn.thot.net/afhm.html. Accessed December 30, 2006.

"Beating the Odds: Violence and Women with Disabilities." Breast Health Access for Women with Disabilities. Available online. URL: www.bhawd.org. Last updated February 19, 2006.

"Different Therefore Unequal: Employment and Women with Disabilities." 1989. Available online. URL: http://www.dawncanada.net/ENG/ENGdifferent.htm. Accessed November 10, 2008.

DisAbled Women's Network (DAWN) Canada Web site. URL: www.dawncanada.net Last updated February 22, 2005.

Disabled Women's Network (DAWN) Ontario. Available online. URL: www.dawn.thot.net. Updated daily.

"Federally Sentenced Women with Mental Disabilities: A Dark Corner in Canadian Human Rights." Available online. URL: http://www.elizabethfry.ca/submissn/dawn/1.htm. Accessed December 30, 2006.

The Only Parent in the Neighbourhood: Mothering and Women with Disabilities. 1989. Available online. URL: http://www.dawncanada.net/ENG/ENGmother.htm. Accessed November 1, 2008.

Ridington, Jillian. "Who Do We Think We Are?: Self Image and Women with Disabilities." Position Paper 1. Prepared for DAWN Canada: Disabled Women's Network Canada, 1989.

disasters and disaster recovery

Throughout the 20th century in the United States, emergency planning for people with disabilities relied primarily upon informal partnerships, personal relationships, and flexibility. In the event of natural hazards or technological emergencies, responders historically relied upon community networks to locate individuals with special needs and to improvise solutions to their requirements for emergency services, including the evacuation of individuals with MOBILITY impairments, medical care for the severely ill, and communication with members of the DEAF and BLIND populations. The second half of the 20th century also brought early efforts on behalf of entities such as the Administration on Aging to develop meaningful dialogues with emergency management organizations. Despite this history, the question of institutionalizing disaster response assistance for people with disabilities did not rise to the forefront of public discourse until the early 21st century.

The issue of formalizing structures for assisting people with disabilities in the event of an emergency emerged as a prominent political issue following the SEPTEMBER 11, 2001, attacks on the World Trade Center and the Pentagon; the dialogue then intensified following HURRICANE KATRINA's flooding of New Orleans, Louisiana, and other communities along the U.S. Gulf Coast in 2005. Reports surfaced from both incidents indicating that large numbers of individuals with mobility IMPAIRMENTS died while awaiting rescue and that emergency response and recovery personnel were unprepared to respond to the SPECIAL needs of large segments of the populations in question.

After the attacks on the World Trade Center and particularly after the devastation of Hurricane Katrina, disability advocacy groups and emergency response organizations began issuing reports focusing specifically on the needs of people with disabilities and examining after-action reports and analyses of earlier incidents (including the 1993 World Trade Center attack, the 1994 Northridge, California, earthquake, and the 1999 Hurricane Floyd) for lessons learned and smart practices pertaining to disaster and disability. Scholars also increased efforts toward studying the experiences of disabled populations during disaster, resulting in a burst of scholarly literature offering empirical evidence for the need to integrate strategy and tactics for assisting individuals with disabilities explicitly into formal and official standing emergency operations plans.

As a result of the increase in scholarly analysis and attention to the issue, many emergency response organizations subsequently initiated major efforts at integrating strategy and tactics to assist people with disabilities into disaster recovery plans and operations. Many of these efforts include programs designed to provide warnings and instructions in a variety of visual, tactile, and auditory formats. A number of entities also began working to modify shelter sites and disaster assistance centers to make them accessible to people with mobility impairments and to staff shelters with American SIGN LANGUAGE INTERPRETERS and individuals prepared to respond to severe medical conditions, including ALZHEIMER'S DISEASE, SPINA BIFIDA, and a variety of psychiatric disorders and cognitive impairments. Longer-term planning has focused on developing registries of individuals with special needs in order to reach them quickly in the event of an emergency and on developing effective outreach programs to people with disabilities. These outreach programs include communication about preparedness measures and efforts to create meaningful partnerships between emergency management organizations and disability advocacy ORGANIZATIONS, with the hope of allowing representatives of the disability COMMUNITY to assist in the developing disaster response plans tailored to the special needs groups residing in communities throughout the United States.

See also ACCESS AND ACCESSIBILITY; ACTIVISM AND ADVOCACY.

Katherine J. Worboys

Further Reading:

Barile, Maria, Catherine Fitchten, Vittoria Ferraro, and Darlene Judd. "Ice Storm Experiences of People with Disabilities: Knowledge Is Safety." Special Issue: Parting the Waters, Disability and Deliverance in the Wake of Disaster. *Review of Disability Studies* 2, no. 3 (2006): 35–48.

Congressional Briefing. "Emergency Management and People with Disabilities: Before, During, and After." November 10, 2005.

Hemingway, Laura, and Mark Priestley. "Natural Hazards, Human Vulnerability, and Disabling Societies: A Disaster for Disabled People?" Special Issue: Parting the Waters, Disability and Deliverance in the Wake of Disaster. *Review of Disability Studies* 2, no. 3 (2006): 57–67.

Wisner, Ben. "Disability and Disaster: Victimhood and Agency in Earthquake Reduction." In *Earthquakes,* edited by C. Rodrigue and E. Rovai. London: Routledge, 2002.

> *"I was told by a FEMA agent that looked at my record. He said that your disability is above the shoulder and I feel like you're being discriminated against. The state does not take those type [of] disabilities as serious disabilities. Even with your doctor's note, they're not taking you serious."*
>
> —Wayne English of Duplin County, N.C., on flood relief after Hurricane Floyd, interviewed on December 8, 1999

disease

Disease needs to be distinguished from illness, on the one hand, and disability, on the other. The terms *disease* and *illness* are often used interchangeably but are actually distinct. Both refer to what is commonly called sickness, but they describe different aspects of it. *Disease* refers to the pathological condition itself, as investigated by scientific research and as diagnosed and treated by clinicians; it refers to a sickness in the abstract and as manifested in medical patients. In contrast, *illness* refers to the individual's personal, often idiosyncratic, experience of the disease. Illness is thus always particular and concrete. Additionally, there is a sense in which, while illness has always existed, disease came into existence only with the founding of professional medicine. The disjunction between the physician's tendency to focus on disease and the patient's concern with illness has been a subject of much work in the medical humanities.

The distinction between disease and disability is less subtle; the terms are not typically used interchangeably. Nevertheless, the two entities are closely related and are occasionally confused, or falsely associated, with each other. One difficulty lies in the fact that, though distinct conceptually, disease and disability can include the other; for example, various diseases can cause BLINDNESS and DEAFNESS, and a short-term infection with the POLIO virus may lead to life-long impairment. Conversely, severe MOBILITY impairments may render individuals vulnerable to infectious diseases, especially in the lungs and bladder. Thus, disease and disability often overlap: The same individual may be both disabled and diseased. Another difficulty lies in the fact that some conditions, such as alcoholism or drug ADDICTION, may be seen as moral failings, diseases, or disabilities, depending on the time, cultural context, and individual perspective. Finally, disease, as well as disability, may qualify an individual for protection from discrimination under the AMERICANS WITH DISABILITIES ACT, which has been construed as applying to individuals with TUBERCULOSIS, HIV/AIDS, MENTAL ILL-NESS, and CANCER, among other diseases.

The significance of the difference between disease and disability goes beyond the conceptual to the matter of the consequences for the population in question. People with disabilities are not (by definition, at least) ill or diseased; typically, their impairments cannot be cured—and often not even alleviated—by medical intervention. Nevertheless, like the diseased, people with disabilities have often suffered from STIGMA and social ostracism. Societies have at times segregated, persecuted, even euthanized (see EUTHANASIA) those with physical or intellectual disabilities. Whereas QUARAN-TINE may be justifiable in the case of contagious, readily communicable, disease, quarantine makes no sense as a public health measure with disability. And EUGENICS, whether old (applied by governments and the power of the state) or new (applied by individuals on medical advice, as in the case of abortion of fetuses diagnosed with certain disabilities) tends to view disability as a pathology to be prevented, minimized, or eliminated from the body politic.

An additional consideration is the steady expanse of the reach of modern biomedicine, which tends to pathologize more and more human traits or behaviors. The discovery of a drug that can alleviate a condition once viewed as within the acceptable range of human variation—say, shyness—can create a new disorder—in this case, social anxiety disorder. Such disorders are ambiguous by their nature, but the fact of their moderation by medical intervention tends to characterize them as diseases. Thus, "disease" expands in scope and attracts more and more medical and economic resources.

Health insurance seems all the more necessary, universal HEALTH CARE all the more unaffordable.

The conflation of disability with disease depends on the insidious fantasy of transcending human frailty by eliminating disability as well as conquering disease. Even if all diseases could be cured and all hereditary and congenital disabilities prevented, accidents, environmental dangers, and intentional injury will always disable people. People with disabilities rightly resent the assumption that they are diseased and can be or should be cured, altered, or eliminated. For people with many disabilities the medical paradigm and the progress of medical science hold limited promise. Instead of looking to modern biomedicine for relief, they look to the social paradigm to address their condition; they seek rights, ACCESS, equality, not CURE.

See also COGNITIVE AND INTELLECTUAL DISABILI-TIES; IMPAIRMENT/IMPAIRED; SOCIAL CONSTRUCTION OF DISABILITY.

G. Thomas Couser

Further Reading:
Boorse Christopher. "On the Distinction between Disease and Illness." *Philosophy and Public Affairs* 5 (1975): 49–68.
Grob, Gerald. *The Deadly Truth: A History of Disease in America.* Cambridge, Mass.: Harvard University Press, 2002.

disfigurement

Disfigurement is commonly used to describe a pronounced deviation from so-called NORMAL appearance. Typically used to identify scarring, birthmarks, amputation, or other apparent "defects," especially on the face, the word disfigurement suggests that human appearance is supposed to display an underlying wholeness, integrity, balance, or uniformity and that any departure from this basic human "figure" is a deficit, or a negative feature.

From the standpoint of American disability history, the most significant issue surrounding disfigurement is whether it should be considered a form of disability. Mainstream American culture has often opposed understanding disfigured people as disabled and has been resistant to offering legal protections for otherwise NONDISABLED persons with disfigurements. Those who believe that disfigurement and disability belong to different categories argue that disfigurement affects appearance only and that since an unusual appearance does not cause physical impairment, disability and disfigurement must be considered separately.

From a disability perspective, this is understood as a false separation. Since many disability scholars and activists approach disability as a social construction—understanding that people with disabilities are "disabled" by social factors like prejudice and discrimination more than by any physical impairment—this group contends that similar social factors

"When I was ten I was hit by an automobile. This was 1912. I was four weeks unconscious. I had a fractured skull. They never figured I'd live. I was out of school for a year. It was a rich man who hit me so we got a shyster lawyer and went to court. The jury awarded me $250, but we lost on appeal. I was disfigured for life, and got nothing. I went back to selling papers. If stuck with papers at the end of the day I'd say, 'Extra! Extra! Big shipwreck in the subway! Two dead men found alive!'"

—Henry Dockter, in a 1989 oral history interview with his granddaughter, Gayle Goodman

Further Reading:

Bogdan, Robert. *Freak Show: Presenting Human Oddities for Amusement and Profit.* Chicago: University of Chicago Press, 1988.

Garland Thomson, Rosemarie. *Freakery: Cultural Spectacles of the Extraordinary Body.* New York: New York University Press, 1996.

Grealy, Lucy. *Autobiography of a Face.* Boston: Houghton Mifflin, 1994.

Partridge, J. *Changing Faces: The Challenge of Facial Disfigurement.* London: Penguin Books, 1990.

Schweik, Susan. "Disability Politics and American Literary History: Some Suggestions." *American Literary History* (February 16, 2008) 20, nos. 1–2 (2008): 217–237. Available online. URL: http://alh.oxfordjournals.org/cgi/content/citation/ajn001v1. Accessed October 4, 2008.

———. *The Ugly Laws: Disability in Public.* New York: New York University Press, 2009.

are at work against disfigured persons. For this reason, many DISABILITY STUDIES theorists argue for the inclusion of disfigured persons within the fold of disability IDENTITY.

The historical inclusion of unimpaired persons with significant disfigurements (for example, "bearded ladies") in American sideshows and FREAK SHOWS is a clear indication of the relationship between disfigurement and disability. Disability scholar Susan Schweik also demonstrates the connection between these two through her studies of the so-called American UGLY LAWS, local rulings that forbade persons with an "unsightly" or "disgusting" physical appearance from appearing in public. Within the realm of DISABILITY CULTURE, among the most important American texts lending support to the sense that disfigurement is a form of disability is *Autobiography of a Face* (1994) by LUCY GREALY (1963–2002). Describing the author's experience of childhood CANCER, through diagnosis, treatment, and full recovery, *Autobiography of a Face* ultimately focuses on the writer's realization that the experience of surviving cancer paled beside that of living with a facial disfigurement. "It was the pain," she writes, "from feeling ugly, that I always viewed as the great tragedy of my life. The fact that I had cancer seemed minor in comparison." Through Grealy's narrative, the reader is brought into a real and immediate understanding of the connection between disability and disfigurement.

Recently some disability theorists, most notably Rosemarie Garland Thomson, have raised objections to the term "disfigurement," pointing out that it continues to encourage prejudicial attitudes regarding human appearance. Thomson advocates instead for "unusual enfacement," or alternate terminology that challenges the dominant discriminatory LANGUAGE.

See also SOCIAL CONSTRUCTION OF DISABILITY.

Julia Miele Rodas

Dix, Dorothea (1802–1887) *social reformer*

Dorothea Dix's crusade against the harsh treatment of people with MENTAL ILLNESS and MENTAL RETARDATION, as well as the squalid conditions maintained in the jails and poorhouses where they were housed, captured national attention and made her one of the leading reformers in antebellum America. Her efforts led to better, more humane treatment of people with mental illness and the establishment of numerous institutions for their care.

Born in Hampden, Maine, on April 4, 1802, Dorothea Dix was the first of three children born to Joseph and Mary Dix. Because of her father's ADDICTION to alcohol and her mother's struggles with mental illness, Dix assumed the responsibility of caring for her siblings at a very young age. As a teenager, she became a schoolteacher in Massachusetts and later wrote several books.

Dix's career as a reformer began in 1841, when a young theological student assigned to provide Sunday school instruction to women at the East Cambridge jail in Massachusetts asked for Dix's advice. Dix immediately volunteered to take over the task. When she visited the jail the next Sunday, she was shocked by the filth, lack of heat, neglect, and signs of brutality. Especially troubling to Dix was that noncriminals with mental illness had been incarcerated in the jail as well, locked in cells and chained to walls.

Over the next two years, Dix toured ALMSHOUSES and jails throughout Massachusetts, documenting conditions that paralleled those at East Cambridge. Although local governments, which almost exclusively bore the responsibility for caring for the poor and for people with mental illness, sometimes offered "outdoor relief" (direct assistance to people in need), forced incarceration to the poorhouse, jail, or almshouse was the most common form of public assistance.

During this time, Dix met state legislator and doctor Samuel Gridley Howe, a social reformer and pioneer in the development of institutions for the BLIND and mentally retarded. Howe encouraged her to collect her observations and present them to the Massachusetts legislature.

Dix's speech to state lawmakers in 1843 sparked an uproar, and local officials and newspapers accused her of inaccuracies, distortion, and slander. Dix's supporters, however, included such nationally prominent figures as HORACE MANN, a champion for public education, and Charles Sumner, an abolitionist who later became a U.S. senator. When the controversy subsided, the legislature approved the enlargement of Worcester State Hospital in 1843 to accommodate people with mental illness.

Dix then took her crusade to other states, traveling tirelessly, touring poorhouses and reporting her findings to anyone who would listen. Between 1844 and 1852, Dix addressed the legislatures of New York, New Jersey, Pennsylvania, Kentucky, Tennessee, North Carolina, Mississippi, and Maryland, advocating the creation of separate mental HOSPITALS or asylums. She did not believe the poorhouses could be reformed, and she staunchly opposed outdoor relief and family care because they degraded those in need.

Dix also proposed that the federal government assist the states in their efforts by granting them public land that could be sold to fund mental hospitals or ASYLUMS. After six years of advocating for the land-grant bill, Dix persuaded Congress to pass what became known as the "12,225,000-Acre Bill" (10,000,000 acres for the "insane" and 2,225,000 acres for "deaf mutes"). President Franklin Pierce vetoed the bill in 1854, dismissing it as an unwarranted federal intrusion on state affairs.

During the CIVIL WAR, Dix served as the head of women nurses for the Union Army. After the WAR ended in 1865, she resumed her efforts on behalf of people with mental illness. Although Dix failed to convince the federal government to fund care of people with mental illness and mental retardation, her efforts, together with those of the emerging professional class, ultimately led states to take over responsibility for caring for people by establishing specialized hospitals and asylums. By 1860, 28 of the 33 states had established public insane asylums. According to historian Albert Deutsch, Dix was personally responsible for the founding or enlargement of 32 mental hospitals in the United States and abroad. The first state institution for the "FEEBLEMINDED" was opened in Massachusetts in 1848, and by 1890, 20 such asylums had been established. In 1881 Dix moved into an apartment at the first hospital she helped establish, the New Jersey State Hospital; she died there six years later on July 17, 1887.

See also CAREGIVING; INSTITUTIONALIZATION; PRISON.

Steven J. Taylor

Further Reading:

Brown, Thomas. *Dorothea Dix: New England Reformer.* Cambridge, Mass.: Harvard University Press, 1998.

Ferguson, Phillip. *Abandoned to Their Fate: Social Policy and Practice Toward Severely Retarded People in America, 1820–1920.* Philadelphia: Temple University Press, 1994.

Grob, Gerald. N. *The Mad Among Us: A History of the Care of America's Mentally Ill.* New York: Free Press, 1994.

Taylor, Steven J., and Stanford. J. Searl. "Disability in America: A History of Policies and Trends." In *Significant Disability: Issues Affecting People with Significant Disabilities from a Historical, Policy, Leadership, and Systems Perspective,* edited by E. Davis Martin, 16–63. Springfield, Ill.: Charles C. Thomas, 2001.

"Memorial Soliciting a State Hospital for the Protection and Cure of the Insane, Submitted to the General Assembly of North Carolina" by Dorothea Dix (1848)

Born in Hampden, Maine, in 1802, Dorothea Dix became a leading reformer, advocating for asylums to care for people with mental illnesses. As part of her crusade, Dix personally petitioned legislatures across the nation, drawing attention to the inhumane conditions in hospitals, almshouses, and prisons. In this 1848 letter to the North Carolina General Assembly, she draws on anecdotes of personal suffering, statistical evidence, and Christian benevolence to motivate change. Although institutionalization increasingly became a contested issue in the 20th century, many of Dix's ideas about protecting and respecting marginalized people remain relevant to critiques of disability in America.

"Memorial Soliciting a State Hospital for the Protection and Cure of the Insane, Submitted to the General Assembly of North Carolina" by Dorothea Dix November 1848

To the General Assembly of the State of North Carolina:
GENTLEMEN:—

I respectfully ask your attention to the subject herein presented and discussed; and solicit your prompt and favorable action upon the same.

I come not to urge personal claims, nor to seek individual benefits; I appear as the advocate of those who cannot plead their own cause; I come as the friend of those who are deserted, oppressed, and desolate. In the Providence of God, I am the voice of the maniac whose piercing cries from the dreary dungeons of your jails penetrate not your

Halls of Legislation. I am the Hope of the poor crazed beings who pine in the cells, and stalls, and cages, and waste rooms of your poor-houses. I am the Revelation of hundreds of wailing, suffering creatures, hidden in your private dwellings, and in pens and cabins—shut out, cut off from all healing influences, from all mind-restoring cares.

Could the sighs and moans, and shrieks of the insane throughout your wide-extending land reach you here and now, how would your sensibilities to the miseries of these unfortunates be quickened: how eager would you be to devise schemes for their relief—plans for their restoration to the blessing of a right exercise of the reasoning faculties. Could their melancholy histories be spread before you as revealed to my grieved spirit during the last three months, how promptly, how earnestly would you search out the most approved means of relief; how trifling, how insignificant, by comparison, would appear the sacrifices you are asked to make; how would a few dimes and dollars, gathered from each citizen, diminish in value as a possession, compared with the certain benefits and vast good to be secured for the suffering insane, and for their afflicted kindred, by the consecration and application of a sufficient fund to the construction of a suitable hospital in which the restoring cares of skilfully applied physical and moral treatment should be received and in which humane and healing influences should take the place of abuse and neglect and of galling chains and loathsome dungeons.

. . . But it is not to the State pride of the intelligent citizens of North Carolina that my appeal comes; it is to the liberal and humane hearts of this portion of my fellow citizens, its plea reaches; it *cannot* be rejected, it dares not consent to be put off, it claims with earnest importunity that its merits may be discussed, it would merge in oblivion the multiplied miseries resulting from past neglects and procrastination, by wakening to action the efficient energies of humanity and justice.

At present there are practiced in the State of North Carolina, four methods of disposing of her *more than one thousand* insane, epileptic, and idiot citizens, viz: In the cells and dungeons of the County jails, in comfortless rooms and cages in the county poor-houses, in the dwellings of private families, and by sending the patients to distant hospitals, more seasonably established in sister States. I ask to represent some of the very serious evils and disadvantages of each and all these methods of disposing of the insane, whether belonging to the poor or to the opulent classes of citizens.

It may be here stated that by far the larger portion of the insane epileptics, and idiots, are detained in or near private families, few by comparison, being sent to Northern or Southern State hospitals, and yet fewer detained in prisons and poor-houses, yet so many in these last, and so melancholy their condition, that were the survey taken of these cases alone, no stronger arguments would be needed to incite energetic measures for establishing an institution in North. Carolina adapted to their necessities, and to the wants of the continually recurring cases, which each year swell the record of unalleviated unmitigated miseries.

. . . [M]any persons adopt the idea that the insane are not sensible to external circumstances that to their perceptions the dungeon, chains, cold, nakedness, and harsh epithets are as acceptable as a comfortable apartment, freedom from shackles a pleasantly tempered atmosphere, decent clothing, kindly speech, and a courteous address. They assert that coarse, ill-prepared food is as palatable as that which is wholesome and well cooked, that cold and heat, sunshine and cloud, pure air and that loaded with noisome exhalations, liberty and confinement; are all one and the same to the insane, producing like impressions and results on the deranged intellect. Greater error of belief was never adopted; more serious mistakes, and conducting to more fatal results could not be propagated. The insane in most cases feel as acutely and distinguish as readily as the sane.

. . . As benefactors of the distressed whose mental darkness may, through your agency, be dispersed, how many blessings and prayers from grateful hearts will enrich you! As your last hours shall be slowly numbered, and the review of life becomes more and more searching, amidst the shades of uncompromising memories, how beautiful will be the remembrance that of the many of this life's transactions, oftenest controlling transient and outward affairs frequently conducting to disquieting results, and sometimes to those of doubtful good, you have aided to accomplish a work whose results of wide diffused benefits are as sanctifying as they are permanent: blessing through all Time—consecrating through all Eternity!

Gentlemen, the sum of the plea of your Memoralist is embodied in the solicitation for an adequate appropriation for the construction of a Hospital for the remedial treatment of the Insane in the State of North Carolina.

Respectfully submitted,

D. L. DIX.

Raleigh, November 1848.

Source: Dorothea Dix. "Memorial Soliciting a State Hospital for the Protection and Cure of the Insane, Submitted to the General Assembly of North Carolina" (November 1848). Raleigh, N.C.: Seaton Gales, 1848. Available online. URL: http://Docsouth. Unc.Edu/Nc/Dixdl/Dixdl.html. Accessed June 26, 2008.

Dole, Bob (Robert Joseph) (1923–) *politician*

Robert "Bob" Dole is a prominent political leader and three-time presidential candidate who served in the U.S. Congress for 36 years, both as a representative and as a senator from Kansas. His near-fatal injuries sustained during World War II led him to become a powerful and visible advocate for people with disabilities, particularly veterans, as well as an example of the changing role and status of disabled persons. Bob Dole is married to Elizabeth Hanford Dole, former U.S. senator from North Carolina, and he has a daughter, Robin, from a previous marriage.

Dole was born on July 22, 1923, in Russell, Kansas, the second of four children of Doran and Bina Dole. Midway through his sophomore year at the University of Kansas in 1942, Dole enlisted in the U.S. Army and was later assigned as a platoon leader for the 10th Mountain Division in Italy. During a battle in northern Italy on April 14, 1945, he was nearly killed and left temporarily paralyzed after being hit in the back by enemy machine-gun fire and shrapnel.

For the next seven months Dole remained encased in a full-body cast with extensive spinal cord injuries (see SPINAL CORD INJURY) as well as an irreparably damaged right arm and shattered right shoulder. While in the body cast, he developed a severe kidney infection that mandated the removal of the kidney, and later he nearly died from infections resulting from blood clots. He spent the next three years convalescing in army HOSPITALS, enduring nine surgeries and relearning to dress, eat, and walk. Although in time he regained his MOBILITY and the use of his left arm, he could never again fully use his right shoulder and arm.

Following his rehabilitation, Dole moved to Arizona, where he enrolled at the University of Arizona. He later transferred back to Kansas, graduating from Washburn University in Topeka in 1952 with combined bachelor's and law degrees. During his time in Topeka, he decided to enter politics, winning a seat in the Kansas Legislature, followed by four terms as the Russell County attorney. In 1960 he won election as U.S. representative from the 6th Congressional District, and eight years later he was elected to the Senate, where he served as both Majority and Minority Leader from 1984 through 1996. Dole was the Republican vice presidential nominee during President Gerald Ford's unsuccessful campaign for a full term in 1976, and he himself ran in the Republican presidential primaries in 1980 and 1988. In 1996 he was nominated as the Republican candidate for president, but ultimately was defeated by incumbent Bill Clinton.

During his years in the Senate, Dole was a powerful advocate for people with disabilities, likening their situation to that of other minority groups and calling for civil rights and equal access to EDUCATION, HEALTH CARE, and TRANSPORTATION. He was a key figure in the passage of the AMERICANS WITH DISABILITIES ACT of 1990 as well as the AIR CARRIER ACCESS ACT of 1986. Since leaving the Senate in 1996, Dole has served as chairman of the National World War II Memorial (2004) and cochair (with former secretary of health and human services Donna Shalala) of the President's Commission on Care for America's Returning Wounded Warriors (2007).

Malinda Hicks

Further Reading:

Bob Dole Web site. URL: http://www.bobdole.org.

Dole, Bob. *One Soldier's Story.* New York: HarperCollins, 2005.

Hilton, Stanley G. *Bob Dole: American Political Phoenix.* Chicago: Contemporary Books, 1988.

Doonesbury

Since its inception in 1970, Garry Trudeau's comic strip *Doonesbury* has been noted for its political and social satire. The strip has taken on subjects ranging from the behavior of college students to America's WARS from Vietnam to Iraq, and the politics of every president since Richard Nixon. Although Trudeau opposed both the Vietnam and Iraq wars, he portrayed some of his characters in battle, most notably his helmet-wearing, ex-quarterback B.D. In the tradition of WORLD WAR II cartoonist Bill Mauldin, Trudeau demonstrated considerable understanding of the challenges ordinary soldiers faced in confronting the enemy and in dealing with army command and bureaucracy. B.D. escaped largely unscathed from the earlier conflicts, but in Iraq in 2005 he loses a leg in a roadside bombing.

In a series of daily strips and then in two collections, *The Long Road Home: One Step at a Time* (2005) and *The War Within: One More Step at a Time* (2006), Trudeau follows B.D.'s experience from the time of the bombing through the arrival of the medics, his transfers to the field HOSPITAL, the evacuation hospital in Germany, Walter Reed Hospital in Washington, D.C., and finally home. Along the way Trudeau sensitively explores B.D's loss of his leg and his recognition that he is disabled. Trudeau treats the physical pain as well as the psychological PAIN associated with a war wound and amputation. After Trudeau began the series, the Pentagon invited him to meet with wounded soldiers and their physicians at Walter Reed Hospital. The strips reflect Trudeau's many conversations with soldiers wounded in Iraq and with the men and women who treat them.

Trudeau's portrayal of B.D's experience acknowledges that recovery from such a wound is as much psychological as physical and involves not only the wounded soldier but the FAMILY and friends. Trudeau explores the challenges of physical rehabilitation and of adjusting to a high-tech prosthesis. Equally important, he addresses the psychological challenge of adjusting to a disability and of dealing with post-traumatic stress disorder. Much of the second collection of strips deals with B.D's struggle to come to terms psychologically with what he saw and did in Iraq. Trudeau also examines the impact on B.D's wife and child and on his friends. B.D., like many individuals with disabilities, has good days and bad days, makes progress and slips backward. Trudeau also follows B.D's efforts to tackle both his memories and his growing reliance on alcohol by working with a sympathetic counselor at his local Veterans Center.

These *Doonesbury* cartoons about B.D's efforts to learn to live with his physical and psychological wounds are an important cultural statement about disability. Trudeau demonstrates that having a disability is an evolving experience. By portraying B.D's continuing struggles so vividly, Trudeau strips away some of the shame and STIGMA so often associated with having a disability. Although he is addressing a serious topic, Trudeau also finds HUMOR in unlikely places and gently satirizes the behavior of individuals including B.D. In bringing disability to the comic pages of 600 newspapers, Trudeau acknowledges that disability is part of the human condition and that an important part of disability is how we deal with it as individuals with disabilities and as a society.

See also AMPUTEES AND AMPUTATION; HUMOR; IRAQ WAR; POPULAR CULTURE; PROSTHETICS; REPRESENTATION; VETERANS; VIETNAM WAR.

Daniel J. Wilson

Further Reading:
Newton, Julianne H. "Trudeau Draws Truth." *Critical Studies in Media Communication* 24 (March 2007): 81–85.
Trudeau, Garry. "Death and Politics on the Funny Pages: Gary Trudeau Addresses American Newspaper Editors." *Critical Studies in Media Communication* 24 (March 2007): 86–92.

———. *The Long Road Home: One Step at a Time.* Kansas City, Mo.: Andrews McMeel, 2005.
———. *The War Within: One More Step at a Time.* Kansas City, Mo.: Andrews McMeel, 2006.

dopamine

Dopamine is a neurotransmitter (a chemical that stimulates or transmits nerve impulses) that has been instrumental in destigmatizing certain disabilities. Swedish researchers Arvid Carlsson and Nils-Åke Hillarp at the Laboratory for Chemical Pharmacology of the National Heart Institute are credited with first discovering the neurotransmitter in 1952. Studies of dopamine and certain dopamine receptors in the brain have provided evidence that both SCHIZOPHRENIA and ADDICTION are brain disorders. The discovery of dopamine's role in these diseases and further evidence of changes in certain types of dopamine receptors have led to an understanding in medicine and parts of society that schizophrenia and addiction are disorders, not moral failings.

Schizophrenia was seen for centuries as a personal failing, with a variety of possible causes. In the 1950s schizophrenic symptoms became more treatable with the introduction of Chlorpromazine, a drug that blocked dopamine receptors. Research into the mechanisms of Chlorpromazine and other drugs like Haldol helped lead to the formation and widespread acceptance of the Dopamine Hypothesis of schizophrenia. In its most basic form, the hypothesis states that altered dopamine activity is associated with schizophrenia. Though simple, this hypothesis has been one of the strongest supports for the understanding of schizophrenia as a DISEASE and not a personal failing. However, acceptance of the dopamine hypothesis has been attacked repeatedly by a variety of critics. Many scientists believe that attributing all of schizophrenia to dopamine levels is too simplistic. These scientists also point out that the small number of schizophrenia studies could mean that any difference observed between schizophrenic and nonschizophrenic people could be due to other differences between the individuals, and not necessarily to schizophrenia. A wider circle of critics that includes scientists, doctors, and the Church of Scientology believes that the dopamine hypothesis has been inappropriately advanced for profit motives by the companies that make dopamine-controlling drugs. These critics hold a variety of opinions about the dopamine hypothesis; some believe that it is merely incomplete, while others believe it is completely incorrect.

Addiction, like schizophrenia, has a history of stigmatization. In the past, addiction to alcohol and other drugs was viewed as a personal and moral failing. This STIGMA largely persists today. Evidence of changes in D2 dopamine receptors in addiction have changed the medical understanding of addiction, and the 2000 edition of psychiatry's *DIAGNOSTIC*

AND STATISTICAL MANUAL OF MENTAL DISORDERS classifies addiction as a mental disorder, not a moral failing.

Katherine Randle

Further Reading:

American Psychiatric Association. *Diagnostic and Statistical Manual of Mental Disorders DSM-IV-TR Fourth Edition.* Washington, D.C.: American Psychiatric Association, 2000.

Healy, David. *The Creation of Psychopharmacology.* Cambridge, Mass.: Harvard University Press, 2002.

Swazey, Judith. *Chlorpromazine in Psychiatry: A Revolution in Innovation.* Cambridge, Mass.: Massachusetts Institute of Technology Press, 1974.

Down syndrome

Down syndrome is a chromosomal disorder also known as trisomy 21 because people with Down syndrome have an extra 21st chromosome. Down syndrome is a congenital genetic condition resulting in a DEVELOPMENTAL DISABILITY and varied medical- and health-related conditions. The condition was formerly called mongolism because individuals with Down syndrome were perceived as having "slanted" eyes similar to those commonly found among some Asian peoples. The terms *mongolism* and MONGOLOID have been considered pejorative however, since the 1970s; the condition is named for British doctor John Langdon Down, who first described it in 1866.

Individuals with Down syndrome share similar physical features. As infants, they have small, flattened heads. The ears, mouth, teeth, and nose are smaller than usual, and the nasal bridge may be flatter. People with Down syndrome also have hypotonia, or low muscle tone, which affects movement, strength, and overall development.

There is a wide range of cognitive functioning among people with Down syndrome, with most individuals appearing to fall into the mild to moderate range of COGNITIVE DISABILITY. It is often difficult to gauge the exact level of impairment, however, because associated physical disabilities interfere with speech, vision, hearing, and physical coordination (including the physical ability to write).

In early America most people with Down syndrome lived with their extended FAMILY within the community, but by the 1830s many states had opened training schools and institutions where people with disabilities were to receive specialized instruction. Theoretically, this empowered students with skills to gain EMPLOYMENT and social skills. In actuality, it largely isolated individuals from the broader community and from their families, isolation that often led to ABUSE and mistreatment. Some people with Down syndrome were placed in psychiatric HOSPITALS. Some institutions for

> "I want people to know I'm great. I love myself. I don't like people to make fun of me. It makes me feel bad. I'm not making fun of them. I have Down syndrome and I'm black. You can't say the 'n' word—that's bad."
>
> —Matthew Foster, a 15-year-old, from an interview in the 1990s

developmentally disabled citizens had abysmal conditions where diseases proliferated and untrained staff used force to maintain order in overcrowded facilities. By the turn of the 20th century, the EUGENICS movement had a direct influence on the status of people with Down syndrome: Because Down syndrome is congenital, and possibly heritable, some people with the condition were subject to INVOLUNTARY STERILIZATION. This process was judicially approved in the Supreme Court case of *BUCK V. BELL* in 1927, in which Justice Oliver Wendell Holmes reasoned that since society could call on citizens to sacrifice their lives in times of WAR, it could demand that people "who already sap the strength of society" could be forced to make lesser sacrifices.

By the 1950s and 1960s, the DEINSTITUTIONALIZATION movement vocalized criticism of and opposition to various disability institutions, and by the 1970s, CHILDREN with Down syndrome increasingly remained with their families. Two major U.S. Down syndrome associations also appeared in the 1970s: the National Down Syndrome Congress (1973) and the National Down Syndrome Society (1979). These parent and professional associations also included people with Down syndrome in their membership, especially with the growth of the DISABILITY RIGHTS MOVEMENT that pushed for self-advocacy. The trend toward self-advocacy took longer for those with Down syndrome than for many other disability groups, in part because of general societal attitudes and paternalism toward those with developmental disabilities: Efforts at self-advocacy, however, have now resulted in tangible changes. In the last two decades, people with Down syndrome have become more visible and the COMMUNITY has become more inclusive. Even on TELEVISION, Down syndrome has a more visible presence, as, for instance, with the success of actors like CHRIS BURKE.

Medical research has created new and complex challenges for the community. In 2007 the American College of Obstetricians and Gynecologists recommended that all pregnant women be given a noninvasive first trimester test (nuchal translucency test) to identify fetuses with Down syndrome. In the past only pregnant women over age 35 were generally urged to have testing for Down syndrome in the United States. The majority of babies with Down syndrome, however, are born to mothers under 35, so this advice, if followed, is likely to increase significantly the number of women who are aware that they are carrying a fetus with Down syndrome and will likely result in a greater number of abortions.

While this development may increase the incidence of Down fetus abortions, it may also increase the ability of practitioners to provide medical care at birth for babies with typical Down syndrome complications. As in prenatal testing for other disabilities, there is also the potential for society to decide that parents who intentionally have a disabled child should not depend on public programs to provide assistance for them. Expanded testing will likely increase the need for advocacy groups to dispel stereotypes surrounding Down syndrome so that Americans can understand the potential of people with Down syndrome as well as the challenges they will face in life. Improvements in medical treatments and education and the application of technology have allowed an increasing number of people with Down syndrome to participate more fully in society. For example, computer programs that read aloud scanned documents or can transcribe spoken communication allow people with Down syndrome to communicate even when reading or writing are challenges.

See also AMNIOCENTESIS; ASYLUMS AND INSTITUTIONS; SELF-ADVOCATES AND SELF-ADVOCACY.

David Penna
Vickie D'Andrea-Penna

Further Reading:

Berube, Michael. *Life As We Know It: A Father, a Family, and an Exceptional Child.* New York: Vintage, 1998.

Cohen, William I., Lynn Nadel, and Myra E. Madnick. *Down Syndrome: Visions for the 21st Century.* New York: Wiley-Liss. 2002.

Palmer, Greg. *Adventures in the Mainstream: Coming of Age with Down Syndrome.* Bethesda, Md.: Woodbine House, 2005.

Pueschel, Siegried, ed. *A Parent's Guide to Down Syndrome.* Baltimore: Brookes, 2001.

drama

For most of American history, the stage has been a central source of visual REPRESENTATION in American life, where many of the nation's cultural conversations on issues of the day were quite literally acted out. And so the centrality of disability to American drama has occurred on multiple fronts. Canonical plays are rife with both minor and major disabled characters; these representations serve as metaphors, but also communicate to audiences pervasive and changing beliefs alike about physical difference. Disability has also been an important presence in American drama with a socially activist message. Most recently, with the rise of the DISABILITY RIGHTS MOVEMENT has come a simultaneous increase in dramatic LITERATURE written from within DISABILITY CULTURE, contributing to the creation of a DISABILITY ARTS movement with its own aesthetic.

Most people can readily pinpoint Laura Wingfield in Tennessee Williams's THE GLASS MENAGERIE (1945), or HELEN KELLER in William Gibson's THE MIRACLE WORKER (1959) as examples of disabled characters in American drama, but not many others. From the 19th century onward, however, American PLAYWRIGHTS have been fascinated with disability. They have written about disabilities visible and invisible, as well as conditions closely related to them: TUBERCULOSIS, syphilis, yellow fever, CANCER, amputeeism, alcoholism, blindness, deafness, paralysis, and AIDS, among other bodily impairments. Plays considered benchmarks in the evolution of melodrama such as William Smith's *The Drunkard; or, the Fallen Saved* (1844), the adaptation of Harriet Beecher Stowe's *Uncle Tom's Cabin* (first dramatized in 1852), Charles M. Barras's *The Black Crook* (1866), and Augustin Daly's *Under the Gaslight* (1867) have all featured disabled characters of one kind or another. Just within this short list of plays are represented alcoholism, consumption, hunchback, and amputeeism; most often, these invoke the moral model of disability. As American drama developed in scope and depth, playwrights continued to use disability as a metaphor, but they also brought the consideration of bodily difference to bear on important discussions about difference in American society. From the earliest beginnings of our country, literature has constantly raised questions of belonging: Who *belongs* in America? What makes someone an "American"? And, influenced by the THEATER of European playwrights like Henrik Ibsen and Anton Chekhov at the end of the 19th and beginning of the 20th centuries that took as its focus how social movements played out through the lives of ordinary people, American drama moved these essential questions to stage center as the 20th century progressed. This new place for disability, within a drama seriously interested in exploring new ideas about American IDENTITY and social justice, came into being in the early decades of the 20th century with the THEATER of Eugene O'Neill (*Beyond the Horizon,* 1920), Sophie Treadwell (*Machinal,* 1928), Lillian Hellman (*The Little Foxes,* 1939), Elmer Harris (JOHNNY BELINDA, 1940), Langston Hughes (*Emperor of Haiti,* 1963), and others who would follow them. By midcentury, when more conformist notions about GENDER and SEXUALITY held sway, disability was used to question sharply these mores by playwrights like Tennessee Williams and CARSON MCCULLERS. Through midcentury plays like *The Member of the Wedding*

(1950) and *Cat on a Hot Tin Roof* (1955), McCullers and Williams connected "queerness," nontraditional GENDER roles, and disability as allies in resisting wider political and social domination.

An even more open use of similarly complex disability images emerged in theater in the late 20th and early 21st centuries. At times these images have been powerfully allied with an activist message. Plays about the DEAF COMMUNITY (Mark Medoff's CHILDREN OF A LESSER GOD, 1980) and the AIDS crisis (Larry Kramer's *The Normal Heart*, 1985) have, for example, demanded that attention be paid to the deaf and HIV-positive communities, and the lives at their center, as vital and important. At other times, the use of disability has transitioned from metaphorizing the "defect" of non-normative RACE, gender, or sexuality to, conversely, symbolizing the pathology of oppression. In such a case, disability was, ironically, turned from the cause of deviance to the tangible evidence of oppression, and therefore still inscribed as DEFECTIVE and deleterious. There are, however, examples of plays in which disability's presence, in concert with other "othered" identities, works to enhance the spectator's understanding of the larger social forces at play that enforce normalcy; examples of such plays include Cherrie Moraga's *Heroes and Saints* (1992) and Tony Kushner's ANGELS IN AMERICA (1992). Even so, disability can still be invoked by contemporary playwrights in conventional ways, for comic or melodramatic effect with examples such as *WIT* (1998) and *Fuddy Meers* (1999).

Perhaps the most significant presence of disability in drama today is that of disabled artists who are creating theater from within disability culture, art as multifaceted as the disability community itself. There are artists whose approaches to theater run the gamut from writing plays (JOHN BELLUSO, Susan Nussbaum, Mike Ervin) to conducting performance workshops (the OTHER VOICES PROJECT, The DisAbility Project, Actual Lives) to creating solo performance work (LYNN MANNING, David Roche, Ann Stocking). Whether more subtly or more overtly, drama from within disability culture also has multiple effects: It can expose and subvert stereotype, historicize and valorize disability and the presence of the disabled body on stage, and show the ways in which disability is both a socially constructed IDENTITY and a common human experience.

The dramatic representation of disability, then, is an ongoing, pervasive, and complex part of both dramatic and disability history in the United States, one in which the intersection of the visual representation of disability, disability history, and the evolving nature of metaphor create not static STIGMA but, rather, an ongoing, dynamic site of disability representation.

See also NORMAL AND NORMALCY; STEREOTYPES.

Ann M. Fox

Further Reading:
Lewis, Victoria Ann, ed. *Beyond Victims and Villains: Contemporary Plays by Disabled Playwrights.* New York: Theatre Communications Group, 2006.
Tolan, Kathleen. "We Are Not a Metaphor: A Conversation about Representation." *American Theatre* (April 2001): 17–21, 57–59.

Dr. Strangelove or: How I Learned to Stop Worrying and Love the Bomb

Dr. Strangelove, the title character of Stanley Kubrick's darkly cynical comedy about the improbable events leading to a nuclear apocalypse, repeats several long-standing conventions in the ways mainstream FILMS have represented persons with disabilities. A cult classic originating shortly after the Cuban Missile Crisis of October 1962 and the acute awareness of the threat of nuclear holocaust that followed, *Dr. Strangelove or: How I Learned to Stop Worrying and Love the Bomb* also reflected broader cultural STEREOTYPES of people with disabilities.

Dr. Strangelove, one of three characters played by the actor Peter Sellers, does not appear until slightly after halfway into the film. Confined to a WHEELCHAIR for most of his time on screen, he wears tinted glasses and also sports a black glove on his right arm. The limb at times appears to have a mind of its own, entering into a variety of struggles with the rest of Strangelove's body. At one point Strangelove's hand tries to strangle its owner, drawing attention to the possible pun with "strange" and "strangle," and bringing to mind other malevolent independent hands such as the disembodied hand in the movie *THE BEAST WITH FIVE FINGERS* (1946). Kubrick's film reveals little about Strangelove's past as a Nazi but instead forces assumptions and inferences. While the director never articulates Strangelove's particular conditions, the black glove marks Strangelove as villainous, following in the tradition of Fritz Lang's evil scientist in *Metropolis* (1927), the similarly black-gloved Rotwang. His apparent disabilities reinforce his deviant character.

Strangelove's temporary confinement to a wheelchair (he leaps out of it at the end of the film) suggests several possible readings. Perhaps Strangelove's IMPAIRMENT was psychological, and something about the doomsday scenario has a cathartic effect for him, thereby mocking his INSANITY by suggesting a CURE originating from his sociopathic lust for death. But another possibility is that Strangelove had been faking an impairment for any number of reasons, and in this case the film offers up the familiar scenario in which disability and IMPOSTER conflate to enhance a story line. Strangelove's disabilities function as part of Sellers' slapstick comedy as well as a stereotypical symbol of an inner degeneration, the age-old convention of linking disability with evil.

As a dark comedy, *Dr. Strangelove* mocks the hubris of scientists, politicians, and military leaders, providing pointed social critiques of its time. The use of Strangelove's disability to further the film's satire, though, points to another dark side in the film: the reinforcing of disability stereotypes.

Neil Lerner

Further Reading:

Crowther, Bosley. "Kubrick Film Presents Sellers in 3 Roles," *New York Times,* 30 January 1964, p. 24.

Longmore, Paul K. "Screening Stereotypes: Images of Disabled People." *Social Policy* 16, no. 1 (Summer 1985): 31–37.

Norden, Martin F. *The Cinema of Isolation: A History of Physical Disability in the Movies.* New Brunswick, N.J.: Rutgers University Press, 1994.

Renaker, John. *Dr. Strangelove and the Hideous Epoch: Deterrence in the Nuclear Age.* Claremont, Calif.: Regina Books, 2000.

DSM See *DIAGNOSTIC AND STATISTICAL MANUAL OF MENTAL DISORDERS.*

dwarfs and dwarfism

Dwarfism is extreme short stature caused by one of many different medical conditions. Persons with dwarfism—also called dwarfs or LITTLE PEOPLE—range in height from about 2 feet 8 inches to 4 feet 10 inches (81 to 147 centimeters). Among the many causes of dwarfism present at birth are irregularities in chromosomes and genes, malfunctions in metabolism, and intrauterine growth problems. Dwarfism may also develop later from poor nutrition, certain diseases, or extreme neglect or ABUSE.

Medical authorities often categorize these conditions as "disproportionate" or "proportionate" types. There are more than 200 conditions—also called skeletal dysplasias or chondrodystrophies—that result in disproportionate dwarfism. The torsos of affected individuals may be short relative to their limbs, or the limbs may be short relative to their torsos. These conditions—occurring in approximately 1 of every 4,000 births—result from genetic factors that inhibit the growth of bone, cartilage, and connective tissue. They may be accompanied by arthritic joint deterioration, spinal compression, reduced lung function, or hearing problems. When addressed in a timely fashion, such complications can often be successfully treated. Although some young dwarfs have undergone an arduous procedure called extended-limb lengthening to increase their height, most people with dwarfism reject such radical surgical alternatives, choosing instead to embrace their existing physical identity.

In proportionate dwarfism, the bodies of affected individuals, though smaller overall, appear similar to those of average-statured individuals. Pituitary dwarfism, the best-known proportionate type, is caused by growth hormone deficiency. When young CHILDREN with growth hormone deficiency are given synthetic growth hormone injections, their height and vigor can often increase. Similarly, through early screening, short stature associated with hypothyroidism can be treated with thyroid replacement.

In the past, the causes of dwarfism were unknown, and treatments for related medical problems nonexistent. Currently, however, in the United States and Europe, the advent of genetic mapping, synthetic growth hormone treatment, and improvements in radiological and surgical techniques at specialized medical centers have resulted in dramatic progress in diagnosis and treatment. Further research seeking effective therapies for many dwarfing conditions is currently under way.

Although differing in appearance from average-statured individuals, and confronting unique physical and medical challenges, dwarfs do not differ intellectually, emotionally, or in abilities and interests from persons of average stature. Their families generally include parents, siblings, spouses, and children of both short and ordinary stature. Despite these commonalities with others, dwarfs have historically been subject to extreme prejudice and social exclusion. Until the 18th century, they were retained as entertainers and "playthings" in the royal courts; in later periods, dwarfs were often regarded simply as human oddities and exhibited. Unlike many other disabled people who have been stereotyped as tragic or pathetic figures, dwarfs have tended to be viewed through the equally distorted lens of comedy, as evidenced by FILMS such as *The Terror of Tiny Town* (1938) and *Time Bandits* (1981)

As late as the 1930s, most dwarfs in the United States were either unemployed or employed in various "low-bar" entertainment venues, where they were often exploited. The public's image of them was more likely to have been shaped by the 1937 Disney animated movie *Snow White and the Seven Dwarfs* or the 1939 film classic *The Wizard of Oz* than by personal acquaintance. Until the 2005 publication of Betty M. Adelson's social history *The Lives of Dwarfs: Their Journey from Public Curiosity Toward Social Liberation* the presence of many accomplished individuals with dwarfism in all eras was rarely recognized: Few people (including dwarfs themselves) were familiar with biographical or autobiographical accounts of eminent leaders in their fields, such as American Quaker abolitionist Benjamin Lay (1681–1760), engineer and inventor Charles Proteus Steinmetz (1865–1923), and secretary of labor Robert Reich (1946–).

Today, as a result of disability rights legislation, medical progress, and increased educational opportunity, dwarfs in the United States have become more integrated in society. Thoughtful documentaries about dwarfs as well as the performances in TELEVISION series and movies of skilled professional ACTORS who are dwarfs—notably Danny Woodburn in *Seinfeld* (1994–98), Meredith Eaton in *Family Law* (2001–02), and Peter Dinklage in *The Station Agent* (2003)—have been among the important cultural milestones that have helped dispel the public's ignorance about the lives of dwarfs. Audience familiarity was further enhanced by the appearance of the Roloff family on the popular reality television show *Little People, Big World* (Discovery Health Channel, 2006–08).

Despite many advances, the greatest obstacle still faced by dwarfs is ongoing prejudice and ridicule. Regarded as "other" and inherently amusing, individuals with dwarfism continue to be subjected to relentless taunts in the streets and mocked with impunity in the media. Thus while the history of dwarfs in America presents important markers of progress, it shares with other disability populations the as yet unattained goal of true inclusion and equality.

See also POPULAR CULTURE.

Betty M. Adelson

Further Reading

Adelson, Betty M. *Dwarfism: Medical and Psychosocial Aspects of Profound Short Stature*. Baltimore: Johns Hopkins University Press, 2005.

———. *The Lives of Dwarfs: Their Journey from Public Curiosity toward Social Liberation*. New Brunswick, N.J. and London: Rutgers University Press, 2005.

"Medical Resource Center." LPA Online. Available online. URL: LPAonline.org/resources_library.html.

Parker, James N., and Philip M. Parker, eds. *Dwarfism: A Medical Dictionary, Bibliography, and Annotated Guide to Internet References*. San Diego, Calif.: Icon Health Publications, 2004.

Dybwad, Gunnar (1909–2001) *advocate for people with disabilities*

Gunnar Dybwad was a lifelong advocate for people with disabilities. His advocacy brought international attention to the civil rights of people with mental disabilities. He believed in their right to self-expression and self-determination.

Dybwad was born on July 12, 1909, in Leipzig, Germany. While completing his law degree and a dissertation on the Italian penal system, he met his wife, Rosemary, who was completing her doctorate in sociology. Upon completion of their education in 1934, the couple moved to the United States and began work on the behalf of children. Initially Dybwad worked with adolescents in the criminal justice system, in whom he recognized the occurrence of underlying intellectual disabilities. In light of this awareness, he began a lifetime of work devoted to the recognition of the rights of CHILDREN with disabilities.

He completed a master's degree in social work from the New York School of Social Work in 1939 and directed the child welfare program of the Michigan State Department of Social Welfare from 1943 to 1951. Dybwad subsequently became executive director of the Child Study Association of America and, in 1953, became the executive director of the National Association for Retarded Citizens (NARC). He served in this position for nine years until he and Rosemary became the codirectors of the Mental Retardation Project of the International Union for Child Welfare in Geneva. In 1969 Dybwad worked with leaders of the Pennsylvania Association for Retarded Children (PARC) to sue on behalf of children with cognitive disabilities for a free and equal public education. This case, *PARC v. PENNSYLVANIA*, was followed by more than a dozen cases that set a precedent for equal rights by casting cognitive disabilities in rights-based terms rather than charitable or strictly medical categories. In 1971 the recognition of these rights was documented in the United Nations Declaration of the Rights of the Mentally Retarded, which reflected the growing self-advocacy movement. Although Dybwad did not write this declaration, his international work facilitated its creation as self-advocacy gained international acceptance. The work of the Dybwads, as well as similar leadership emanating from Europe, led to the founding of the International League of Societies for Persons with Mental Handicaps in the 1960s (known today as Inclusion International). Dybwad was president of Inclusion International from 1978 through 1982. Beginning with the administration of President JOHN F. KENNEDY in the early 1960s, Dybwad also served as the first consultant to the President's Panel on Mental Retardation. He continued to serve on the President's Committee on Mental Retardation under Presidents Johnson, Nixon, Ford, Carter, Reagan, Bush, and Clinton.

In 1967 Dybwad moved to Massachusetts and began an academic career at Brandeis University, where he was the first director of the Starr Center on Mental Retardation at the Heller Graduate School. He also taught SPECIAL EDUCATION for 12 years at Syracuse University. In 1977 Dybwad became professor emeritus of human development at Brandeis. He continued working in the field until his death on September 13, 2001.

In his lifetime, Gunnar Dybwad had a profound impact on the REPRESENTATION and understanding of people with cognitive disabilities. As an adviser to eight presidents, he helped shape policies at the highest levels of government, and as an advocate among families and people with cognitive disabilities, he fostered important grassroots ACTIVISM. Dybwad believed that all people have the right to develop to their full potential. He expressed this belief through public speaking, and writing, and by fostering a global COMMUNITY of SELF-ADVOCATES who were finally able to speak for themselves.

See also COGNITIVE AND INTELLECTUAL DISABILITY.

Liza H. Colby

Further Reading:
Allard, Mary Ann, and Gunnar Dybwad. *Ahead of His Time: Selected Speeches of Gunnar Dybwad.* AAMR, 1999.

"The Handicapped—Rights and Prejudices" by Gunnar Dybwad (July 21, 1968)

Gunnar Dybwad (1909–2001) was a leading advocate for people with cognitive disabilities in the United States. As he argues in this presentation on July 21, 1968, at Wesley Church in Melbourne, Australia, Dybwad believed that education could solve most problems. Educating general society, he asserted, would eliminate prejudices against those with disabilities, and educational opportunities for individuals with disabilities would empower them. This message framed much of Dybwad's work and that of many disability advocates.

"The Handicapped—Rights and Prejudices" by Gunnar Dybwad July 21, 1968

In 1924 the Assembly of the League of Nations adopted [the Declaration of the Rights of the Child], but subsequently it became painfully evident that the world was not ready for this forward looking and yet so simple Declaration. Not until 35 years later did it once again come to the forefront when, with some minor editorial alterations, it was adopted on November 20th, 1959, by the Geneva Assembly of the United Nations. And so I would like to take as a motto for my point of departure today Principle 5 of this Declaration; "The child who is physically, mentally or socially handicapped shall be given the special treatment, education and care required by his particular condition."

. . . One of the most frequent weapons of prejudice is segregation, and forever segregation has been rationalized as merely a way of making it possible for people who are alike to stay together. The black ghettos throughout the United States are just one example.

. . . Prejudice typically does not look at *the whole man*; it picks on whatever characteristic makes him different whether it is the color of his skin or his national origin, his religion, his physical or mental condition and—yes—even his pocketbook, because in recent years we have increasingly seen the connection between poverty, discrimination and prejudice.

Prejudice *categorizes* and *stereotypes*. It closes its eyes to the tremendous range of human qualities inherent in the individual because it must focus on the point of weakness. Prejudice is a group *phenomenon,* it derives its strength from the fact that it is shared by the many against the few.

. . . Prejudice must be fought with knowledge; education of the public must be our weapon.

And thus I want to use the opportunity accorded me today by the Wesley Church and the cooperating radio stations to make an urgent plea on behalf of handicapped children and in particular on behalf of the handicapped child's right to receive, in the words of the United Nations' Declaration "the special treatment, education and care required by his particular condition."

It is a fair statement to make. Indeed it is axiomatic, that a sure sign of a civilized country is a scheme of free education, under public auspices, available to all its children. And I wonder how many of the listeners are aware to what extent in this great and wonderful and evermore progressive and affluent country children afflicted with handicaps are deprived of this right to adequate, free education.

. . . Prejudice against children and adults with handicaps is still evident to varying degrees in countries around the world, but strangely the degree of prejudice varies considerably with the nature of the handicap. And it is the child or adult with a mental handicap who is hit most severely.

At the center of this problem rests the long held belief that with the exception of the mildly mentally handicapped, retarded children are indeed ineducable and not entitled to an education. This belief cannot be based on scientific evidence. We deal indeed with a plain example of prejudice—all its earmarks are clearly present—the emphasis on the weakness of the child, on his intellectual limitation rather than on his total needs, the categorization and stereotyping, the insistence on overlooking scientific evidence to the contrary, the protestation that the retarded child must be *protected* from demands he cannot meet.

Source: Gunnar Dybwad. "The Handicapped—Rights and Prejudices." Presented at Wesley Church, Melbourne, Australia, July 21, 1968. Available online. URL: http://www.disability museum.org/lib/docs/2259.htm. Accessed May 26, 2008.

E

Early Intervention See CHILDREN; HEAD START.

Easter Seals

A nonprofit, charitable ORGANIZATION providing community-based care to people with disabilities, Easter Seals delivers rehabilitation and support services, funds medical and rehabilitative research, and advocates for the right of people with disabilities to achieve maximum independence.

The organization known today as Easter Seals began in 1919 when Edgar F. Allen founded the Ohio Society for Crippled Children (OSCC). Until then, medical and support services were available only to CHILDREN with disabilities at state institutions. OSCC brought facilities and treatment to the child and helped eliminate lengthy parent-child separations. Delivering community-based care was revolutionary, because prevailing opinion was that people with disabilities should reside in institutions. As the model for societies created in other states, OSCC became the National Society for Crippled Children (NSCC) in 1921. In addition to medical and rehabilitative services, NSCC advocated for the inclusion of children with disabilities in all aspects of society.

With the Great Depression of the 1930s, charitable donations for humanitarian causes tapered off, and NSCC needed a creative new way to raise funds. In 1934 Paul King, chair of the finance committee, proposed selling decorative seals at Easter. Annual sale of the seals served not only to raise funds but also to raise public awareness of the needs of children with disabilities and of the help available. In soliciting donations, NSCC reasoned that demonstrating the effectiveness of NSCC in real lives would ensure continued financial support, so in 1947 NSCC named its first National Easter Seal Child. This child representative, chosen annually, appeared in fund-raising advertisements and eventually appeared on the NSCC annual TELETHON beginning in 1971.

In the 1950s and 1960s NSCC expanded its services into all 50 states and Canada, changed its name to the National Society for Crippled Children and Adults (NSCCA) to reflect its service to all people with disabilities, and established the Easter Seal Research Foundation. Already known informally as the Easter Seal Society, in 1967 NSCCA officially became the National Easter Seal Society for Crippled Children and Adults (NESSCCA).

With national attention on civil rights in the 1960s and 1970s, disability advocates raised several concerns about how NESSCCA represented people with disabilities. In particular, they criticized the organization's name and its sole use of children in its campaigns. Responding to concerns about the negative connotations of *crippled,* the organization shortened its name to the National Easter Seal Society (NESS) in 1979. In addition, to avoid representing all people with disabilities as childlike and dependent, NESS began to choose both adult and child representatives, and it consciously showed them engaged in work, school, and COMMUNITY contexts. According to some disability activists, these changes have made Easter Seals an acceptable model for others.

Since its inception, NESS, now formally Easter Seals, has served millions of people with disabilities and has actively participated in changing public policies and perceptions of disability. These endeavors have included advocating for the EDUCATION of children with disabilities, funding research to establish accessible building standards, and lobbying in support of legislation that affirms the rights of people with disabilities to live independently and participate in society. Its efforts today remain focused on its three-part mission: direct care, research, and advocacy.

See also ACTIVISM AND ADVOCACY; ASYLUMS AND INSTITUTIONS; CHARITY; ORGANIZATIONS; POSTER CHILD; REPRESENTATION.

Marsha M. Olsen-Wiley

Further Reading:

Boone, Pat. *The Human Touch: The Story of Easter Seals.* New York: Wiesner & Wiesner, 1991.

Easter Seals. "About Us: The Story of Easter Seals," Easter Seals. Available online. URL: http://www.easterseals.com/site/PageServer?pagename=ntl_wwa_we_are&s_esLocation=wwa_. Accessed January 29, 2008.

Riley, Charles A., II. *Disability and the Media: Prescriptions for Change.* Lebanon, N.H.: University Press of New England, 2005.

Rotary Global History Fellowship. "Rotary and Care for Crippled Children," Rotary Global History Fellowship. Available online. URL: http://www.rotaryfirst100.org/history/history/otherorganizations/easterseals/index.htm. Accessed January 24, 2008.

Eastwood, Clint (1930–   ) *actor, film director/producer*

Influential actor and filmmaker Clint Eastwood has drawn the anger of disability rights activists twice: first in 2000 over his attitude about ACCESS by people with disabilities to a resort he owned and again in 2005 over his REPRESENTATION of disability in his FILMS. These controversies reveal important ways in which disability rights sensibilities clash with society's views of disability.

Born on May 31, 1930, in San Francisco, Eastwood moved frequently with his family along the West Coast as his father pursued various job opportunities. He graduated from Oakland Technical High School in 1949 and was drafted into the army in 1950, serving for three years. Friends then encouraged him to pursue work in Hollywood. His career started with bit parts in films in the 1950s, but stardom came with his role in the CBS TELEVISION series *Rawhide* in 1959. Various films followed, including the popular *A Fistful of Dollars* (1964) and his signature role in *Dirty Harry* (1971). Eastwood earned critical acclaim as director in films such as *Unforgiven,* which also won an Academy Award in 1992 for best picture.

In spring 2000 Eastwood waged a public campaign on behalf of a bill introduced by Rep. Mark Foley (R-Fla.) that would have amended the 1990 AMERICANS WITH DISABILITIES ACT (ADA). The bill, known as the ADA Notification Act, sought to require disabled individuals to provide a 90-days advance notice before filing a lawsuit against a business owner who had failed to provide the access required under the 1990 law. Disability activists believed that such an amendment would encourage business owners to put off making access modifications until they were sued. Eastwood was at the time fighting his own ACCESS lawsuit, filed by WHEELCHAIR user Dianne zum Brunnen over what she said were access violations at his Mission Ranch resort in Carmel, California. Eastwood testified in support of Foley's bill in a May 18, 2000, hearing before the House Judiciary Committee's Subcommittee on the Constitution. In the days leading up to the hearing, the actor appeared on many talk shows, including CNN's *Crossfire,* giving his side of the issue, insisting that many charges were exaggerated if not untrue and that trial lawyers unreasonably attacked business own-

ers to further their own selfish interests. Various national news publications covered his statements as well. "We have the same few lawyers that are perpetrating this case," he testified before the House subcommittee, "and in my opinion they are perverting the law by going around and filing these broadside, sand-bagging type suits where they hit you broadside from nowhere, with absolutely no warning." Disability activists spoke against the bill at the hearing, however, and despite the actor's involvement, Foley's bill did not make it out of committee.

Five years later, Eastwood again angered a number of disability rights activists with his movie MILLION DOLLAR BABY. In the movie, which won Eastwood an Academy Award for Best Drama in 2005, boxer Maggie Fitzgerald is paralyzed during a fight and becomes a quadriplegic. She later tells her devoted trainer Frankie Dunn, played by Eastwood, she would rather die than live as a quadriplegic. Sneaking into the hospital after hours, Frankie, in a final act of love, turns off her ventilator and gives her a lethal injection. "I'm saddened but not surprised that [Eastwood] uses the powerful vehicle of film to perpetuate his view that the lives of persons with significant disabilities are not worth living," said Marcie Roth, head of the NATIONAL SPINAL CORD INJURY ASSOCIATION. Protesting at the Chicago Film Critics Association gala, the disability group NOT DEAD YET handed out a flyer that called the film "Eastwood's revenge." "We will not sit by silently while ignorant reviewers further Eastwood's career on our collective backs," said the group. Eastwood strenuously rejected these assertions, claiming his film reveals the fragility of life and focuses on human relationships. "The picture was never made to make any statement for or against anything," Eastwood told *New Mobility's* reporter Jeff Shannon in 2005. "It was just these two people and how they were feeling under these circumstances." Many disabled Americans, however, interpret his actions as the embodiment of ABLEISM, a belief system that discriminates against individuals based on bodily or cognitive differences.

The conflict between Eastwood and disability rights activists highlights the power of media in shaping the status and images of people with disabilities; it also points to the importance of policy and social attitudes toward those deemed different.

See also BACKLASH; EUTHANASIA; PROTEST.

Mary Johnson

Further Reading:

Johnson, Mary. *Make Them Go Away: Clint Eastwood, Christopher Reeve & The Case Against Disability Rights.* Louisville, Ky.: Advocado Press, 2003.

Lee, Chris. "'Baby' Plot Twist Angers Activists: A Group Alleges That the Movie Is Part of a 'Vendetta' by Eastwood," *Los Angeles Times,* 27 January 2005. Available online. URL:

http://8.12.42.31/2005/jan127/news/wk-mdb27. Accessed September 10, 2008.

Shannon, Jeff. "Clint Eastwood Defends His 'Baby'." *New Mobility* (April 2005). Available online. URL: http://newmobility.com/review_article.cfm?id=995&action=browse. Accessed February 10, 2007.

Ederle, Gertrude (1905–2003) *swimmer*

Gertrude Caroline Ederle was the first woman to swim across the English Channel. She was born on October 23, 1905, in New York City, the daughter of German immigrants who ran a delicatessen. A childhood case of measles left Ederle with significant hearing loss, which would intensify throughout her youth and adulthood. Her parents placed strong emphasis on physical fitness, and all six of their children were taught to swim during summers in New Jersey. By age 13, Gertrude was training at the Women's Swimming Association and breaking amateur records. She dropped out of high school to train full-time. By age 18, she held more than a dozen world records and was a local New York City celebrity for her age and skill, with newspaper headlines reading "Another Record for Miss Ederle" and "Miss Ederle Stars in Swim Carnival." Ederle was a triple-medalist at the 1924 Summer Olympics in Paris, including a gold-medal showing as part of the 400-meter relay team.

In 1925 Ederle swam the 21 miles from Manhattan to Sandy Hook, New Jersey, in just over seven hours, faster than any previous swimmer, male or female. In 1926 she succeeded in her second attempt to cross the English Channel, finishing in 14 hours and 31 minutes (though some sources report the time as 14 hours and 39 minutes), more than two hours faster than any man had previously made the crossing. Her time stood as the women's record for decades. While the English Channel is 21 miles wide at its narrowest, the total length of Ederle's swim was approximately 35 miles because rough conditions kept nudging her off the direct route. Upon her return to the United States, Ederle was given a ticker-tape parade in New York City ("I remember the sea of faces, and I could see them all cheering, but I couldn't hear them," recalled Ederle in the 1970s). She toured the United States on the vaudeville circuit. Ederle's feat was cited as an inspiration by the thousands of women earning American Red Cross swimming certificates in the late 1920s, and by colleges that started women's aquatic programs in the same era.

In 1930 she denied a report that swimming had made her DEAF, saying, "I have always had a running ear. My physicians said that the tremendous nervous strain of my Channel swim, the vaudeville engagements which immediately followed and other subsequent events—all without rest—cast all their effect on my ears." She discussed her deafness again in a 1956 interview: "I know that being deaf has made me shy away from the public. When I go to the beach I'm terribly conscious that I won't hear if people come up and talk to me. Because of my hearing I've run away from people, I guess, and run back to my family where I have always felt sheltered."

Ederle's competitive swimming days were short-lived. In 1933 she broke her pelvis and injured her spine in a fall. She spent about four years in orthopedic casts and in time regained the ability to swim, but not at her previous levels nor without chronic PAIN. She worked as an adjuster of instruments at LaGuardia Airport during WORLD WAR II, and afterward taught swimming for many years at the Lexington School for the Deaf in New York City. She said of Lexington, "We're all the same there. They can't hear and I can't hear." Ederle served on the President's Council on Youth Fitness in the 1950s and 1960s.

Gertrude Ederle died in a New Jersey nursing home on November 30, 2003, at the age of 98. Her custom leather-and-rubber goggles, worn on her historic swim across the English Channel, are part of the collection at the Smithsonian Institution. Ederle was a robust model of physical fitness for young women in the 1920s. Her Channel crossing represented not only equality with men but superior performance. But Ederle's deafness and spinal injury became the "tragic aftermath" in many stories afterward, much as she fought that characterization, once warning a reporter, "Don't write any sob stories about me."

Penny L. Richards

Further Reading:

Benjamin, Philip. "Then and Now: Gertrude Ederle, First Woman to Swim the English Channel, Still Gets Fan Mail," *New York Times,* 6 August 1961, SM58.

"Miss Ederle Denies Deaf Report," *New York Times,* 29 July 1930, 44.

Mortimer, Gavin. *The Great Swim.* London: Bloomsbury, 2008.

Severo, Richard. "Gertrude Ederle, the First Woman to Swim Across the English Channel, Dies at 98," *New York Times,* 1 December 2003, B7.

Talese, Gay. "Memories Are Still Golden for Gertrude Ederle: She Has No Regrets about Years Since Her Channel Swim," *New York Times,* 6 August 1958, 32.

Edgerton, Robert   See CLOAK OF COMPETENCE, THE.

education

Today most individuals with disabilities and their families experience education in a formal, bureaucratic context: school systems. With federal law establishing the rights of all students to certain educational services as well as the procedures to obtain those services, public schools in the United States must accept all CHILDREN regardless of the nature or degree of disability and provide an education of some benefit to students with disabilities. The creation of these rights is recent, beginning in the 1960s. But there is a much longer history of education for persons with disabilities, related closely to the histories of residential institutions and the development of school bureaucracies.

In English-speaking North America, teachers have provided formal educational opportunities to persons with disabilities since before the AMERICAN REVOLUTION (1775–83). The earliest such efforts occurred on behalf of persons who were DEAF or BLIND. Methods for instruction of the deaf and the blind had been developed in Europe and followed European colonists to North America, where instructors and tutors used them in private sessions. Such teachers typically were hired by a FAMILY with a member needing formal instruction in literacy and communication skills, including sign language; tutors would work one-on-one with a student or perhaps run a small school with a few pupils. Since then, SPECIAL EDUCATION has become an integral part of public schooling, even as parents and educators continue to debate the definition of who belongs in school and how schools can and should educate students with disabilities.

BUILDING RESIDENTIAL INSTITUTIONS

When early 19th-century reformers visited European institutions for people with sensory IMPAIRMENTS, they brought back two ideas: Individuals with disabilities were teachable, and residential institutions were a logical place to educate students with disabilities. In the early 1800s several prominent American reformers and educators, including THOMAS HOPKINS GALLAUDET and SAMUEL GRIDLEY HOWE, visited various schools and individuals in Europe to study educational methods for deaf as well as blind persons. Back home they advocated both for education and for the creation of residential institutions. The first such institution opened in Hartford, Connecticut, in 1817 as the Connecticut Asylum for the Education and Instruction of Deaf and Dumb Persons, later renamed AMERICAN SCHOOL FOR THE DEAF. Similar institutions soon followed, with New York, Pennsylvania, Kentucky, Ohio, Virginia, and Indiana all at least partially supporting residential facilities by 1843. Institutions for the blind developed at the same time. Howe had a leadership role in creating the New England Asylum for the Blind, which began operations as the Massachusetts Asylum for the Blind in Boston in 1832. New York started a similar institution the same year; between 1833 and 1849 other such facilities commenced in Pennsylvania, Ohio, Tennessee, North Carolina, Kentucky, Indiana, South Carolina, and Virginia (combined with its school for the deaf). By the early 1900s more than

150 residential educational institutions served deaf or blind persons in the United States, some of them combining services for deaf as well as blind students under one roof, with others segregated by RACE.

Residential institutions also became the preferred location for educating individuals who today would likely be labeled mentally retarded or cognitively or developmentally disabled. Advocates of residential institutions for cognitive and developmental disabilities used the existing institutional model not only because other residential institutions were visible models of reform but also because "MENTAL RETARDATION" became visible only after residential institutions had become a model. Involving intellectual, behavioral, and arguably moral dimensions, the concept of mental retardation evolved fitfully throughout the 1800s, gradually separating itself from MENTAL ILLNESS and INSANITY as a cognitive and behavioral disability. Various descriptors emerged as clinically accepted labels for persons with COGNITIVE DISABILITY: Cretin, idiot, imbecile, FEEBLEMINDED, MORON, mentally DEFECTIVE, retarded, backward, borderline, delayed, and developmentally disabled have all been accepted terms at some point in the past two centuries. As with the education of the deaf and of the blind, methods for instruction and treatment of the cognitively disabled were largely imported from Europe. Samuel Gridley Howe once again was involved in importing ideas and generating American interest. The first residential facility was a small private school in Barre, Massachusetts, opened in 1848 by Dr. HERVEY B. WILBUR. Wilbur then became superintendent of a residential institution in Syracuse, New York. Howe lobbied the state of Massachusetts for public support; his efforts led to the Massachusetts Asylum for Feebleminded Youth, authorized by the state legislature in 1848 and opened for instruction in 1851.

The borders between public and private were porous in the mid-19th century. Both public and private facilities often received both public and private support, and they continued to open on a regular basis into the 20th century. By 1917 more than 30 states supported residential institutions for individuals with cognitive and developmental disabilities. These were often but certainly not always segregated by race and GENDER and included persons exhibiting all levels of mental disability. The leading institutions included those in Waltham, Massachusetts; Elwyn, Pennsylvania; Syracuse, New York; and Vineland, New Jersey. For the first decades of their existence, residential institutions for the cognitively disabled typically subscribed to the teaching methodologies of EDOUARD SÉGUIN, a French doctor who emigrated to the United States in 1848 and gained wide respect for his "physiological method" of instruction. By the early 20th century, however, the educational focus of these institutions became supplanted by more custodial functions. This transition occurred as pessimism regarding the educability of the "feebleminded" grew and as contempt toward them strengthened. Institutions thus became more mechanisms for isolating and detaining those identified as mentally retarded than institutions for their education.

The first college openly admitting students with disabilities developed out of residential institution building. GALLAUDET UNIVERSITY was originally the Columbia Institution for the Instruction of the Deaf and Dumb and Blind, founded in 1857 and then rechartered by Congress in 1864 as a college (later renamed Gallaudet College and eventually, in 1986, Gallaudet University). The chartering of Columbia Institution as a college occurred two years after the Morrill Act created land grants for public colleges and three years before Congress chartered Howard University as a federally sponsored institution of higher education for African Americans. The chartering of a residential institution as a college thus melded two mid-19th-century reform trends: the creation of residential institutions for persons with disabilities and the decision of Congress to support colleges in the 1860s.

PUBLIC SCHOOLS AND STUDENTS WITH DISABILITIES

In the last third of the 19th century and the first few decades of the 20th, the public schools of the United States assumed an increasingly strong and significant role in the education of persons with disabilities. The first such initiative was the Horace Mann School for the Deaf, a day school opened in 1869 by the Boston Public Schools. Urban school systems such as those of Cleveland, New York, Boston, Providence, and Indianapolis experimented before 1900 with segregated settings for students exhibiting serious mental, physical, or behavioral disabilities. In 1896 Providence started the first class specifically designated for "feebleminded" children in the United States. Six year later, the National Education Association coined the term "special education" in its 1902 *Proceedings* to refer to programs for teaching students with disabilities. Over the next quarter-century most large urban school systems included small but well-established programs and settings not only for children with mental retardation but also for those who were significantly hearing or vision impaired, "crippled," or "incorrigible." Many systems also offered programs for students with speech defects and CHRONIC ILLNESS as well as for those considered "superior" or gifted. By 1930 dozens of sizable school systems across the country featured a formal, fully acknowledged Department of Special Education. In Boston, for example, more than 6 percent of its public school students participated in SPECIAL EDUCATION programs for disabled students as of the 1920s.

Historians have suggested several explanations for the expansion of special education in public schools. The common explanation is that the creation of compulsory-school laws in the late 19th century brought more children with disabilities into schools. While states did draft compulsory school laws in the same decades as the creation of many special education programs in public schools, most compulsory school laws were weakly enforced. A more satisfactory explanation is tied to the growth of large cities and the increasing immigration from southern and eastern Europe. As urban school enrollments expanded dramatically, school systems became more bureaucratic and developed tools for dividing students, including sending some to the new special education programs. Special education programs also depended on individual educators who pushed for their creation, acting as entrepreneurs within school systems, systems that were responsive to suggestions for new programs; for example, the New York City system heeded teacher Elizabeth Farrell's call for special education at the turn of the century. Farrell's initiative in her own elementary classroom became the model for the city's new ungraded classrooms, with Farrell appointed in 1906 as the head of the new special education program.

Over the next 40 years the education of students with formally identified disabilities became an accepted and important aspect of public schooling in the United States. Smaller urban and even rural districts first piloted and then committed to segregated instruction for disabled children as the administrative, operational, and instructional value of special education gained credence and ultimately acceptance among school leaders as well as the general public. Teacher training institutions developed specific programs for teachers interested or assigned to special education. Special education programs assumed larger budgets as the number and even percentage of public school students designated "handicapped" increased. Special education became in many ways a world of its own, with students, teachers, and administrators who engaged in significant yet separate school operations and classroom instruction on behalf of those identified as disabled. Meanwhile the number of residential institutions for the deaf, blind, or cognitively disabled also increased. Those for the deaf or the blind continued to offer extensive academic as well as vocational educational programs; in contrast, those for the cognitively disabled were mostly custodial and offered little in the way of formal education beyond basic vocational and manual training.

The nature of school programs for children with disabilities varied according to the specific category of disability. For the tens of thousands of students enrolled in "special classes" for mentally disabled children by the 1920s, the curriculum usually consisted of some basic academic instruction and a significant amount of manual, industrial, and VOCATIONAL TRAINING designed to help such students develop functional life skills as well as prepare them for some form of EMPLOYMENT. Students with physical disabilities also

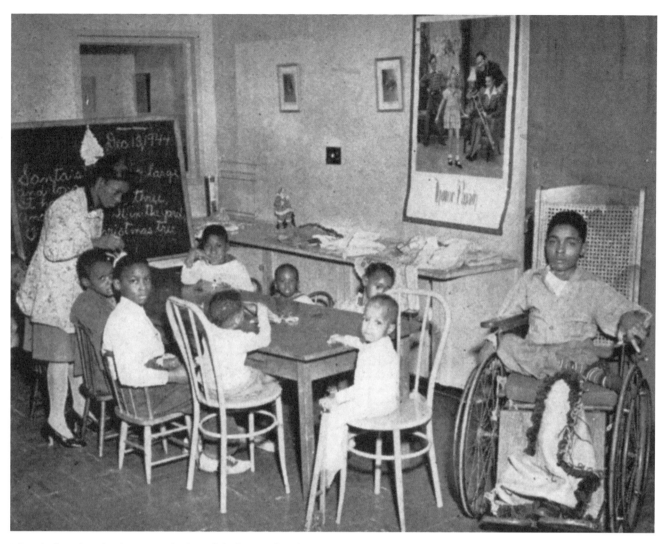

Historically, education has strongly shaped the lives and understanding of people with disabilities. This 1944 photograph of students at the Tuskegee Institute in Alabama embodies diverse disability experiences, including the impact of racial segregation.   *(March of Dimes Foundation)*

encountered primarily vocational training but addressed academic instruction as well, often at an adjusted pace or in a specialized classroom designed to accommodate their specific physical needs. Children with SPEECH DISORDERS were typically "pulled out" of the regular classroom once or twice a week to receive therapeutic instruction for their speech problem. Students with identified behavior problems experienced strict disciplinary environments and the standard manual and vocational training. For most students with disabilities, their formal education took place in separate settings and emphasized skill development that would, it was argued, reduce the students' supposed burden on society. Initially students with disabilities rarely stayed in school beyond the elementary years; during and after the Depression of the 1930s, special education began to extend steadily and more fully into secondary schooling.

EDUCATIONAL RIGHTS

By the late 1960s the development and nature of special education as a separate system came under increasing scrutiny and critique. With hundreds of thousands of students enrolled in special education by 1970—and with frequently stated claims that so many more needed special education services but were not getting them—the rationales, structures, methods, and assumptions driving special education began to generate greater skepticism from those affected by special education's extended reach. Scholars, parents, advocates for people with disabilities, and even many teachers in the special classrooms openly questioned the value and consequences of labeling students as "handicapped" and segregating them from their "NORMAL" peers. In 1968 special education researcher Lloyd Dunn openly challenged the legitimacy of special education for children labeled as mildly retarded, and others criticized special education for having become a separate empire within school systems. At the same time, other critics pointed out that thousands of other children were denied education entirely, excluded because of disabilities. Consequently, legal and public policy initiatives addressing the rights, status, and concerns of special education and its students brought to public attention practices related to identification, placement, and treatment of students with disabilities in public schools. In particular, the practices of identifying and labeling handicapped students through questionable, biased, and often uncertain methods and then segregating such students in separate classes or schools full-time faced significant challenges. Lawsuits in the early 1970s challenged exclusion of children with disabilities from schools in Pennsylvania and the District of Columbia, and settlements in those cases led to several other dozen right-to-education cases filed in federal courts. These in turn led to the passage of state special education guarantees in Massachusetts and Tennessee and a federal law, Public Law 94-142, the Education for All Handicapped Children Act, signed by President Gerald Ford in November 1975.

The growth of educational rights for children with disabilities is a consequence of efforts to end racial segregation. The Supreme Court's *Brown v. Board of Education* (1954) decision striking down segregation laws established both legal precedents and also a language of rights that others used in the post–WORLD WAR II era. One such use was in the postwar DISABILITY RIGHTS MOVEMENT, which resulted in passage of Public Law 94-142. The creation of new educational rights for children with disabilities both came from and fed into that larger movement. Children who received special education services or otherwise learned a philosophy of equal rights became adults who could then advocate for disability rights in the broader society. Adults with disabilities could become models for children with disabilities and their families. This borrowing of language extended to laws and policies; for example, when Title VI of the Civil Rights

Act of 1964 forbade racial discrimination in federally funded programs, that language became a model for SECTION 504 of the Rehabilitation Act of 1973, which forbade disability discrimination in programs funded under the act.

Since the passage of Public Law 94-142, the education of persons with disabilities in the United States has become much more integrated into the mainstream of schools and communities. The LAW has been reauthorized several times and is now known as the INDIVIDUALS WITH DISABILITIES EDUCATION ACT (IDEA). It currently recognizes 13 categories of disability and mandates free appropriate educational services for persons from birth to age 22. The law directs public schools to pursue reasonable and appropriate accommodations for any student with an identified disability and to assure that rights of such students are respected and upheld. Over the past 30 years all students with disabilities thus have gained guaranteed access to a free and appropriate education in a public school environment. The language of the law emphasizes far more inclusion than existed before 1975, and the majority of students with disabilities spend at least part of the school day with NONDISABLED peers.

Even with those changes, controversy continues to surround the legal, practical, and ethical implications of special education. Immediately after 1975, implementation of the newly won rights faced several obstacles. As with desegregation, local school districts in many places resisted the new obligations to educate *all* children and to follow the procedural requirements of the federal law. The federal government did not release implementing regulations until 1977, two years after the passage of Public Law 94-142. Parents and their lawyers could then contest school decisions through two mechanisms: quasi-judicial hearings that could be appealed to courts and complaints to the federal Office of Civil Rights. These mechanisms were sufficient for the clearer mandates of the law, including opening up ACCESS to schools, making eligibility decisions within the law's deadlines, and planning individual educational programs every year. But the most substantive conflicts still required interpretation. In 1982 the Supreme Court established the standard for what type of education schools had to provide. In *BOARD OF EDUCATION v. ROWLEY*, the court ruled that schools had to provide a program reasonably calculated to provide *some* educational benefits commensurate with opportunities available to children without disabilities. In 1988 the court ruled in *Doe v. Honig* that schools could not suspend students with disabilities for more than 10 days if the violation of school rules was related to the child's disability (or disabilities) and if the parents had not agreed to a longer suspension.

In the long term, the legal rights of students with disabilities redefined the community of schools, with a common acceptance of the rights of individuals with sensory, mobility, and mild or moderate cognitive disabilities and some

> "Before Mom found an opportunity to go down to the grade school office to register me, three members of the school board came to visit us. . . . 'It has been brought to my attention that you folks have a son in a wheelchair. It is our duty to inform you he will be unable to attend school. . . .'"
>
> — Don Kirkendall, recalling barriers to his education, 1973

acceptance of the rights of individuals with more severe cognitive disabilities. Over time educators discovered that the majority of students with disabilities either had sensory or MOBILITY impairments, relatively mild speech and language problems (concentrated among younger students in elementary schools), or demonstrated real academic difficulties but no severe cognitive problems (typically labeled as learning-disabled). Because many local public school districts received some minimum subsidies from the federal government in exchange for providing these services, within a few years educators in many districts welcomed most of these children as proper members of school communities. While there are still fights over how schools may discipline students with disabilities and where schools can place students with disabilities, much of the structure of special education law is an established fact of educational politics with robust constituencies.

In the 1990s the issues of inclusion and full inclusion split advocates, a split that had begun after the 1970s victories. When signed in 1975, Public Law 94-142 provided an ambiguous mandate: Students must be in the "least restrictive environment," with as much contact with nondisabled peers as was consistent with an appropriate education. There was some controversy about the appropriate extent of "MAINSTREAMING" students (the term used at the time), but little among advocates for special-education rights. In the early 1970s the primary concerns were basic: access to school for those who had been excluded before, fair assessment, the inclusion of parents in individualized educational planning, and due-process protections. While the statistics from the 1960s and early 1970s are sketchy, parents and advocates observed that hundreds of thousands of students with sensory impairments and mild cognitive disabilities were unnecessarily separated from nondisabled peers in self-contained classes and that tens of thousands of students with more involved cognitive disabilities were in separate schools with no possibility of contact with nondisabled peers. While there was resistance from some educators, most advocates were firmly convinced that the vast majority of students with disabilities needed and had a right to more contact with nondisabled peers.

By the early 1990s the majority of students receiving special education services *did* have meaningful, frequent contact with nondisabled peers in school; for all students aged 6–17 receiving special education services in 1990–91, 69 percent spent at least 40 percent of their time in the general-education setting, with nondisabled peers. A plurality received services in "resource rooms" and other part-time settings where special education teachers juggled responsibilities for groups of students who shuttled in and out for "pull-out" academic instruction during the day. Other students had very limited social contact with nondisabled peers, outside academic instruction—a more common routine for interaction between nondisabled peers and students with more severe cognitive disabilities.

This dramatic change in the placement pattern of special education helped ignite additional debate about moving students more systematically into general-education settings—what educators and parents began to call inclusion (see INCLUSION EDUCATION) in the 1980s. Having some success in changing where schools placed students, some advocates pushed for more inclusion. They had an ally in U.S. assistant secretary of education Madeleine Will, who launched what she called the Regular Education Initiative in 1984, including focusing millions of federal grant dollars on research to improve the support of students with disabilities in general classroom settings. Beginning in the late 1980s, some parents, researchers, students, educators, and advocates for children with the most severe cognitive disabilities argued that *any* separation from a general education classroom was inappropriate, and they began to argue for the full inclusion of all students with disabilities in classrooms with nondisabled peers.

Very quickly, other parents, researchers, students, educators, and advocates within special education argued against full inclusion and against some other inclusion proposals. The most visible advocates of full inclusion were tied to the education of individuals with severe cognitive disabilities, an area still on the margins of many schools more than a decade after Public Law 94-142. For these students, their appropriate curriculum stressed learning the social and survival skills necessarily to live as adults with cognitive disabilities. While advocates of adults with developmental disabilities were some of the key proponents of full inclusion, many of the most visible opponents of full inclusion were tied to the education of individuals with relatively mild cognitive disabilities, whose most urgent concerns were effective academic instruction, not social contact with nondisabled peers. Parents, students, researchers, educators, and advocates closely tied to other areas of special education had their own particular concerns that they used to judge inclusion proposals, whether concerns that most general classroom teachers did not have the skills or time to reward good behavior for students with severe behavior problems or concerns that full inclusion (or something close to it) might endanger the ties between students with hearing impairments and the Deaf COMMUNITY, a community that many adults with hearing impairments have remained connected to and identified with long after formal schooling ended. As the example of the Deaf community suggests, it is important to recognize the immense complexity of what has been called "the inclusion debate": Beliefs and attitudes vary widely within and among groups of persons with and without disabilities, depending on ideological, political, educational, and ethical priorities, values, and perspectives.

At the end of the 20th century and beginning of the 21st, the policy debate around the rights of children with disabilities began to intersect with the policy debate about educational accountability. Beginning with the 1997 reauthorization of the Individuals with Disabilities Education Act, the federal government began to require that states include students with disabilities in state assessment programs, establish an alternative system for students whose educational goals did not overlap with the standard academic curriculum, and report the achievement of students with disabilities at the same time they reported achievement data of students more generally. When Congress wrote the No Child Left Behind Act, signed by President George W. Bush in January 2002, the federal government included students with disabilities in the new federal accountability requirement for annual testing in grades 3–8, and states began having to report whether students with disabilities were meeting the state requirement for the proportions of students who are proficient in reading and math. Together with the reporting of achievement separately for English-language learners, the responsibility of schools for the academic achievement of students with disabilities became one of the most controversial aspects of how Congress had defined "adequate yearly progress" in the No Child Left Behind Act.

The expansion of special education and passage of the AMERICANS WITH DISABILITIES ACT of 1990 have shifted upward the age at which students can request accommodation of their disabilities. As more students with disabilities have graduated from high school and wished to attend college, colleges have faced increasing legal obligations to accommodate students with disabilities. Unlike in elementary and secondary schools, where federal law guarantees individualization, accommodation of disabilities in colleges has been more limited. Colleges have not had to accommodate students who disrupt the classroom environment, nor have they needed to craft modified curricula. Because a right to elementary and secondary education is a political value tied to citizenship, the protections for students in public K–12 schools are greater than for students in college.

ISSUES IN CURRICULUM AND INSTRUCTION

As residential institutions and then schools became responsible for the education of students with disabilities, teachers and administrators have wrestled with what to teach students and how to teach them. Within the general structures and operations of education for persons with disabilities, a host of approaches to developing appropriate curricula for and teaching disabled students have been attempted and practiced. These efforts also have generated a great deal of discussion and controversy, even since the beginning of educational programs developed in residential institutions in the 1800s. Psychological, cultural, and ideological concerns have generated rich and often contentious conversations across generations regarding what and how to teach persons with disabilities. In almost all cases, the controversies are about both the effectiveness of an approach and also the symbolic values tied to a curricular or instructional approach. These observations apply to approaches to teaching all kinds of content to students with every kind of disability.

For individuals with sensory disabilities, an academic curriculum has often been accepted as appropriate. Since the mid-1800s there has been a stable consensus that deaf persons can master the traditional scope of academic content at all levels of instruction. However, the education of deaf students has featured strenuous controversy over appropriate methods of teaching that content. The initial method imported from Europe and championed by the founding residential institutions, tutors, and private schools involved the use of sign language as the sole mode of communication among deaf persons—a method known as manualism. In the 1860s an approach called ORALISM gained significant support among educators and others interested in deaf education. Supporters of oralism, or oralists, dismissed manualism as a crude and isolating approach to teaching and communication that inhibited full participation in society by deaf persons while stigmatizing them as outsiders. Oralists thus argued for abandoning manualism in favor of relying on reading lips and learning to speak aloud, not only with hearing persons but also with the deaf. Supporters of manualism expressed great pride in Deafness and in participating in Deaf culture and communities, whereas oralists considered deafness to be a defect that should be suppressed, hidden, and eventually extinguished. Others have since forged a compromise combining both approaches. Known as total communication, this approach also claims its own avid supporters and strong detractors. These characteristics and differences among methods exist to this day, with schools and institutions typically using one method over the others in their instruction.

The manualism-oralism controversy (also known as the COMMUNICATION DEBATES) has had no parallel in the education for blind students. Some contention did exist over the best finger-reading system for texts—a contest that the BRAILLE system eventually "won." Even so, most of those involved in the education of the blind agreed that blind students exhibited normal ranges of intelligence and that they required a combination of academic and vocational instruction. For students who had vision impairments but were not totally blind, environmental adjustments concerning color and light constituted accepted procedure in most classrooms, whether in institutions or in public schools. There have been two significant developments in the education of students with visual impairments in the past 50 years. In the 1960s the research of Natalie Barraga documented that students with low vision would not degrade their sight by using it, and so-called sight-saving techniques that emphasized Braille slowly gave way to instruction that encouraged the use of sight and taught the use of optical equipment for students with low vision. More recently, with the development of text-to-speech software, text-reading systems such as JAWS, and most recently MP3 players, students with visual impairments have had a variety of tools to access text without braille versions, even while programs that translate electronic text to Braille are making blind individuals less reliant on printed braille books.

While students with single sensory impairments have generally been accepted as academic students, individuals with cognitive and developmental disabilities have been the targets of both instructional and curricular idiosyncrasies. For most of the past two centuries, the primary controversy has been whether individuals identified as mentally retarded were educable. For those places and times when institutions or schools have accepted responsibility to educate students with cognitive and developmental disabilities, there has been little consensus on the primary emphasis of education. Until recently, relatively few students with cognitive and developmental disabilities were provided access to an academic curriculum. For most of the 20th century, educators described almost any goal for such students as vocational in nature, though such vocational activities have ranged from screwing plastic bolts onto plastic nuts to introduction to paid work environments, either in sheltered or competitive employment. Historically, "vocational" has been a residual category that educators have used to justify a variety of nonacademic instruction.

In the past few decades, educators of and advocates for students with cognitive and developmental disabilities have worked to provide academic opportunities at some level for many individual students. They have also pushed school systems to create programs in and support teaching of functional daily living and social skills. In the 1970s Lou Brown argued that students with the most severe cognitive disabilities required and had a right to functional instruction targeted at improving their immediate lives. To Brown, a well-known advocate whose views have generated significant controversy concerning the appropriate education of persons with severe disabilities, much functional instruction had to be conducted in the environment in which the student would have to perform the skill. To students who would not generalize from a classroom to a street, learning to recognize "Walk" and "Don't Walk" signs on flashcards was far less valuable than learning safe street crossing on a street. Adding to such a functional curriculum, many educators and parents have also argued for explicit instruction of social skills. Such skills have become more important with requirements that individual education plans include goals for transitions to adulthood and post-school lives.

Part of the debates over curriculum are intimately tied to instructional debates over the relative effectiveness of teaching task-specific skills, learning strategies that one might call metaskills, and general mental discipline or process training. Much of education specifically targeted at students with disabilities has depended on the teaching of specific skills: how to read Braille or communicate in AMERICAN SIGN LANGUAGE; how to answer math problems; how to operate a drill press; how to dress; how to ask someone for help. There has also been research in metacognitive strategies, teaching students when they can create their own mnemonic memory aids or use other strategies to help themselves learn a skill or subject-specific content. Finally, there is a long history of so-called process training, whose advocates have argued that one can teach the body or brain to learn better in general. One example of such process-training advocates is the Institutes for the Achievement of Human Potential, founded in 1955 by Glenn Doman and Carl Delacato, who claimed in 1960 that by teaching children with developmental disabilities to crawl, creep, and engage in other physical activities, the children would recapitulate normal development and learn better. This "patterning" technique has been the target of widespread criticism among pediatricians and psychologists, who point out the lack of controlled evidence for the effectiveness of patterning. Patterning is one of many claims over the past century and more that one could train the brain to learn better without engaging in a curriculum.

These curricular debates have been overlaid with cultural and ideological values held about disability and dependence. Widespread disagreements as to just how much benefit cognitively disabled individuals might derive from formal instruction and how best to teach students with cognitive disabilities have reflected the vastly ambivalent attitudes toward and beliefs about mental disability itself. To those who assumed intelligence was an inherited, immutable trait, the need for or advisability of formal instruction seemed limited to basic instruction in developing personal functional skills, basic vocational skills, and essential social skills to the maximum extent possible, depending on the severity of the disability. For those who argued mental ability could be improved through education, academic instruction seemed a more reasonable approach, one that could be combined with vocational, functional, and social components. Thus, the severity of the ascribed disability and beliefs about disability's fixed or fluid nature has led to a range of curriculum and instructional variations for students in the institutions as well as the public schools.

CONSTRUCTING DISABILITY IN SCHOOLS

If people have acted on their beliefs about the educability of children, those beliefs in turn depend on the ways that society structures childhood. The growing age segregation of childhood within schools over the past two centuries has helped define the education of children with disabilities. While physical disabilities have been recognized as part of the human condition outside schools, many children have been identified as disabled only within a school context. In some measure, this school-specific construction of disability is a legacy of clinical psychological definitions, what noted child psychologist Jane Mercer described in the 1970s as the "eight-hour retardate" who was a perfectly functioning person outside school hours. But the school-specific construction of disability is also a matter of how and where society defines deviance from normality. After most education shifted to schools with an age-graded curriculum, one could identify a nonreading eight-year-old as outside the established norm, a norm established only when a nonreader is compared to a majority of eight-year-old children who can read.

The organizational life of schooling has helped construct disability in other ways. Schools have often accommodated a number of pressures by creating additions to the existing curriculum and structure rather than dramatically changing prior practices. School systems accommodated federal special education guarantees in a similar fashion, by hiring specially certified teachers and specialists and by creating new programs for students. They have accommodated inclusion of students with disabilities in a piecemeal fashion and where teachers have tolerated it, most commonly with students who behave well and whose disabilities do not prohibit participation in an academic curriculum. Even the individualized education programming required by federal law has often become subsumed into bureaucratic procedures, with some critics describing school responses as largely compliance-oriented. While parents and other advocates have successfully expanded the education rights of students with disabilities, most education of persons with disabilities occurs in a bureaucratic context. Consequently, many special educators—most notably Douglas Biklen, Tom Skrtic, Susan and William Stainback, Allan Gartner, and Dorothy Lipsky—have argued for a complete restructuring of schools to integrate children with disabilities fully and authentically.

The education of persons with disabilities in the United States has always reflected the complex and controversial constructions—and discussions—of disability that has characterized this nation from colonial times. Public and professional discourse regarding identification and placement; instructional purposes, settings, and methodologies; status, power, and prejudice; and the role of persons with disabilities in society tell us much about ourselves and our relations with one another. As formal education for persons with disabilities looks to the future, it is imperative to keep our past, as well as our sense of selves, fully in mind.

See also ACCESS AND ACCESSIBILITY; ACTIVISM AND ADVOCACY; COGNITIVE AND INTELLECTUAL DISABILITY; DEVELOPMENTAL DISABILITY; HANDICAP; INCLUSION EDUCATION; LAW AND POLICY; LEARNING DISABILITY; RESIDENTIAL SCHOOLS; VOCATIONAL REHABILITATION ACT.

Sherman Dorn
Robert L. Osgood

Further Reading:

Osgood, Robert L. *The History of Inclusion in the United States.* Washington, D.C.: Gallaudet University Press, 2005.

Sarason, Seymour, and John Doris. *Educational Handicap, Public Policy, and Social History: A Broadened Perspective on Mental Retardation.* New York: Free Press, 1979.

Trent, James W., Jr. *Inventing the Feeble Mind: A History of Mental Retardation in the United States.* Berkeley: University of California Press, 1994.

Van Cleve, John Vickrey, and Barry Crouch. *A Place of Their Own: Creating the Deaf Community in America.* Washington, D.C.: Gallaudet University Press, 1989.

"Educational Facilities Available for Physically Handicapped Negro Children" by James Scott (1937)

Education is one of the most important features in American disability history. Who should be educated, and how, are among the many issues parents, children, teachers, and policymakers have faced since the colonial period. In this 1937 article, author James Scott notes powerful complications in educating children with physical disabilities: race and social stigma. In the era of segregation, racial disparity further limited the options for all children with disabilities to achieve a meaningful education. Although desegregation gained legal and social support in the 1950s, negative social attitudes toward people with disabilities of all races, and educational options for those who have disabilities, still present significant challenges in the 21st century.

"Educational Facilities Available for Physically Handicapped Negro Children" by James Scott July 1937

Several further problems involving the welfare of physically subnormal children as a class are receiving careful study by workers with them. One is the rationalization of parental anxiety so that it will militate for rather than, as it now so often does, against the child. This means enlightenment of the parent so that he will know what is to the ultimate health interests of his boy or girl and motivating him to act accordingly. Evidence of the direct results of past efforts in this direction is seen in the vastly improved bodily formation of children in Negro schools of today as compared with those of twenty-five years ago—their parents have received and followed expert hygienic advice. A second problem is provision of worthwhile recreational opportunities for the deviating individual by affording him a physical and psychological setting for wholesome, health-building, unselfconscious play free from embarrassment consequent upon his deficiency and leading to his happy integration into the leisure-time life of his normal environment. A third is the problem of mental hygiene—the cultivation in the child of a positive, healthful, matter-of-fact attitude towards his handicap and towards other people's attitudes towards that handicap. Finally—and most far-reaching of all—is the task of educating the public to an appreciation of the real capacities of the physically handicapped—an understanding which will eventuate in its more enthusiastic demand for the contributions they are demonstrably capable of making. Such an understanding, moreover, will exercise a wholesome, invigorating influence upon the deviates themselves, for it is a socio-psychic truism that one tends to live up or down to the expectations of those about him.

. . . According to the findings of this Committee there were in the United States:

14,400	blind children under twenty years of age
6,000	of whom were being educated in state, private, or public day schools or classes
50,000	partially seeing children who should be in sight-saving classes
5,000	or less of whom were so enrolled
3,000,000	children with hearing impaired in various degrees with
18,212	deaf children enrolled in schools and classes for the deaf
1,000,000	children so defective in speech as to require remedial speech and training
60,000	of whom were receiving such training
100,000	crippled children in need of special education,
10,110	of whom were enrolled in special public schools and
1,480	in state hospitals and schools
382,000	children who were tuberculous
850,000	children who were tuberculous suspects
1,000,000	children who had weak or damaged hearts,
375,000	of whom had serious organic heart disease
6,000,000	children of school age who were malnourished. Less than
40,000	of these enrolled in open-air and open-window schools and classes

The foregoing comparison between the number of physically handicapped children in need of special education and the number actually receiving it tells a tragic story of wholesale denial of educational opportunity to millions of our future citizens.

. . . The following points give a composite picture of the status of care for such Negro children by the eighteen Southern states.

1. Eight states—Alabama, Kentucky, Maryland, North Carolina, Tennessee, Texas, Virginia, and West Virginia—maintain separate schools for deaf Negroes. In six other states—Arkansas, Florida, Georgia, Mississippi, South Carolina, and Missouri—separate departments for Negroes are conducted as integral parts of the respective institutions.

2. Nine states—Alabama, Arkansas, Louisiana, Maryland, North Carolina, Tennessee, Texas, Virginia, and West Virginia—maintain separate schools for blind Negroes. Five other states—Florida, Georgia, Kentucky, South Carolina, and Missouri—conduct separate departments for Negro and white pupils in the same school.

3. All of the Southern states maintain residential schools for both deaf and blind white children.

4. The quality of instruction in institutions and departments for Negroes is distinctly inferior to that in institutions and departments for whites. In the former antiquated methods of teaching are employed to a greater extent and a different course is frequently offered. This is in line with the discriminatory practice of a section which spends $49.30 per white child enrolled in its public schools and $15.14 per Negro child.

5. Practically no effort is made to enforce compulsory attendance laws for either Negro blind or deaf pupils. Educators acquainted with the situation are of the opinion that if more than

a small fraction of those who should be in these state institutions were enrolled, there would be no room to house them.

. . . Since 6,697,230 Negroes or 56.3 per cent of the population of the race, including 2,547,072 children between 5 and 19 years of age, live in rural areas of the United States, it is pertinent to inquire to what extent facilities for physically handicapped children have been initiated in these sections. Despite the fact that some promising study and experimentation of this phase of the problem is in progress in several states, it is safe to say that such provisions are virtually non-existent—even in the North. Of 113 cities reporting special classes for blind and partially-seeing children in the Biennial Survey of Education, 1930–1932, only one was a community of less than 10,000 population. Of the 144 cities reporting classes for the deaf and hard-of-hearing, five were communities of less than 10,000 in population. It is significant to note that not one city of less than 10,000 which reported special classes for any of the above types of handicapped children was in the South—all of them were Northern. While more or less satisfactory ways of handling physical deviates have been worked out by several small communities, the fact remains that no educational opportunities of this kind are available to the thousands of Negro and white children of the rural South.

Our analysis has thus far shown the serious disadvantage under which the handicapped group of three million Negro children of school age in the area of segregated education must labor. Approximately three quarters of a million Negro children live in the North. How does the handicapped element of their number fare? Since most of the advances made in special education for the physical deviate have been made in the Northern cities, and since Negro pupils in these cities are entitled by law to unrestricted admission to public schools, the natural assumption is that they share fully whatever opportunities may be afforded. Without question they do enjoy advantages greatly superior to those of their race in the South. But even here, there is sufficient evidence that Negro children are not admitted as freely to classes for the handicapped as whites to cause the White House Committee to raise a serious question in regard to it. This is a topic which calls for additional study and investigation.

The foregoing review of the availability of educational facilities to physically handicapped children in the United States may, then, be generalized in the following theses:

1. Physically handicapped children in the aggregate—white and colored—are the most educationally neglected element of our school population. Provisions for proper training are made for but an extremely small fraction of their number.

2. The apparently best cared for Negro group are the blind and deaf; but for these care is inadequate, because of the lack of facilities sufficient to accommodate all of them, non-enforcement of compulsory attendance laws in the case of Negro children in the majority of Southern states, and the inferior quality of instruction that is given in the segregated residential schools maintained for them.

3. In the South, public school care for physically handicapped white children is practically non-existent; for physically handicapped Negro children, it is—with one or two brilliant exceptions—non-existent.

4. Both Negro and white handicapped children in rural areas—especially in the South—are woefully underprivileged.

5. Even in the North there is some evidence of racial discrimination in admissions to schools for the handicapped.

Source: James Scott. "Educational Facilities Available for Physically Handicapped Negro Children." *Journal of Negro Education* 6, no. 3 (July 1937): 455–467.

Education for All Handicapped Children Act
See INDIVIDUALS WITH DISABILITIES EDUCATION ACT.

Eigner, Larry (1926–1996) *poet*
Larry Eigner was a poet and writer often connected with the New American Poets of the 1950s and 1960s. Born on August 6, 1926, in Lynn, Massachusetts, Eigner developed CEREBRAL PALSY at birth and remained severely disabled throughout his life, spending his early days in the glassed-in porch of his parents' home in nearby Swamscott. In a brief MEMOIR Eigner speaks of his need as a child to focus and concentrate: "in order to relax at all I *had* to keep my attention away from myself, *had* to seek a home, coziness in the world." To some extent these remarks speak as much for the values of his POETRY as they do for his physical condition. The administration at age 35 of cryosurgery, a procedure that froze his

left side in order to control his spastic movements, offered him a greater degree of control over his body. Following the death of his father in 1978, Eigner moved to BERKELEY, CALIFORNIA, where he participated, briefly, in the city's INDEPENDENT LIVING MOVEMENT. He became dissatisfied with aspects of communal living and subsequently moved into his own home along with the poets Robert Grenier and Kathleen Frumkin, who served as his aides and companions until close to his death on February 3, 1996. During his time in Berkeley, he maintained an active relationship to the burgeoning West Coast poetry scene and was a familiar figure at local readings and talks.

Eigner is usually associated with the New American Poets, a postwar group of writers whose poetics stressed the immediacy of perceptual and cognitive responses. Eigner encountered some of these poets in 1949 through Cid Corman's *This Is Poetry* radio program in Boston and began an active correspondence with Charles Olson, Allen Ginsberg, Robert Duncan, and others. His first book, *From the Sustaining Air* (1953), was published by Robert Creeley's Divers Press; Robert Duncan wrote one of the first appreciations of his work; and many of his poems were printed in avant-garde journals of the day—*Yugen, The Black Mountain Review,* and *Origin.* Despite his limited access to a larger public world, Eigner maintained a regular pattern of publishing, correspondence, and literary debate.

Eigner's particular contribution to the poetics of the New American Poetry was his perceptual immediacy—his attention to the immediacy of his surroundings, the changing texture of light and shade, recording of sounds and speech. Eigner used his limited MOBILITY to create a highly distinctive organization of lines on the page, determined very much by the physical limitations imposed on him by cerebral palsy. His lines tend to slant gradually across the page, each line indented a few spaces farther toward the right to indicate both the onrushing force of his perceptual awareness and his physical difficulty in returning the carriage to the left margin. Because his typing was limited to his right index finger, he painstakingly measured each word and phrase, often isolating individual words on a single line or using the space bar to mark changes of attention. And to avoid having to put a new piece of paper into the typewriter, he often continued the poem in the space vacated by his rightward-tending lines. In short, Eigner's material page became a cognitive map of his relationship to space, phenomena, and bodily processes.

Although Eigner did not self-consciously identify with the DISABILITY RIGHTS MOVEMENT, he nevertheless embodied its political activism and its belief in independent living and human rights. Furthermore, many of his short stories, memoirs, and poems record his life growing up as a child with a disability—attending summer camps, engaging in regimes of physical therapy, and confronting the limits of an ableist (see ABLEISM) world. Although his work is not well known in the disability community, some of his poems have appeared in disability-themed collections, including Kenny Fries's anthology, *Staring Back.* The forthcoming two-volume edition of his *Collected Poems* from Stanford University Press will bring him a larger readership, both within and without the disability COMMUNITY.

Michael Davidson

Further Reading

Davidson, Michael. "Missing Larry: The Disabilities Rights Movement and the Work of Larry Eigner." *Sagetrieb* 18, no.1 (Spring 1999): 5–38.

Friedlander, Benjamin. "Larry Eigner." *Dictionary of Literary Biography* 193.

Forrest, Seth. "The Body of the Text: Cerebral Palsy, Projective Verse and Prosthetics in Larry Eigner's Poetry." *Jacket Magazine* 36 (2008). Available online. URL: http://jacketmagazine.com/36/forrest-eigner.shtml. Accessed November 20, 2008.

electric shock therapy   See ELECTROCONVULSIVE THERAPY.

electroconvulsive therapy

Often referred to by its earlier name "electroshock therapy," electroconvulsive therapy (ECT) is a controversial procedure used to treat severely depressed people whose symptoms are considered by physicians to be life threatening and resistant to or intolerant of drug therapies. Electricity is used to shock a person's brain to induce a seizure. As a radical form of "treatment" for mental illnesses, ECT demonstrates the controversy between medical views of disability and social interpretations of disability.

ECT was first used by Italian neuroscientists Ugo Cerletti and Lucio Bini in 1938. Over the years, changes in protocols have attempted to lessen the pain and trauma experienced by the recipient; these changes include administering succinycholine (a muscle paralyzer) to prevent bone fractures during the convulsions, and anesthesia to lessen PAIN. Originally, high levels of electricity were applied by sine-wave devices, but since the 1980s those have been replaced by machines that administer brief pulses, sometimes of lower (and sometimes higher) voltage electricity. Former therapies also passed electricity through the whole brain, while some newer techniques only shock the "nondominant" side of the brain. Scholars have been unable to track the specific number of Americans who have received this treatment, in part because most states do not require medical facilities to report these data.

Physicians and scientists are still unable to explain fully why, how, or to what extent, ECT benefits the patient. ECT has been modified since its introduction in attempts to lessen its destructiveness, and treatments vary in strength, length, and placement of the electrodes. The effects of ECT generally include short-term confusion and memory loss, as well as a sense of well-being. In the longer term, people often experience amnesia and other symptoms of brain damage, and many eventually relapse into DEPRESSION.

The strongest proponents of ECT have been psychiatrists. They have argued that negative REPRESENTATIONS of the therapy have created unfair skepticism. Kitty Dukakis, wife of 1988 presidential candidate Michael Dukakis, reported positive effects from ECT, and viewed her memory loss as an acceptable trade-off for relief from depression. Opponents of ECT, many of them members of the PSYCHIATRIC SURVIVORS movement founded in the mid-1980s, note that it often causes permanent brain damage and amnesia, while rarely providing relief for patients. Another contentious issue has been that many people were forced to undergo the procedure, either as treatment for depression or other disorders (including SCHIZOPHRENIA) or in order to more easily control them within psychiatric facilities. Furthermore, there have been serious questions about whether or not severely depressed (and often drugged) patients are capable of informed consent. They claim that many are pressured to sign consent forms when their symptoms are acute and they are already being treated with pharmaceuticals that may affect their judgment and competency.

Other well-known recipients of ECT include poet Sylvia Plath, author Ernest Hemingway, and musician Lou Reed. Perhaps the most dramatic depiction of the treatment was by KEN KESEY in his 1962 novel ONE FLEW OVER THE CUCKOO'S NEST, and in 1975 produced as a FILM. The notoriety of these instances of ECT helped to raise awareness about the severity of the treatment, which in turn opened the door for questions about its use.

The example of ECT illustrates the lengths to which medical experts have been willing to go to "fix" disabilities. Although drugs have since replaced ECT as a common form of treatment, the patient's experience is still largely secondary to society's need to "CURE" people.

Laurel A. Clark

Further Reading:

Ayd, F. J., Jr. "Ugo Cerletti, M.D. (1877–1963)." *Psychosomatics* 4 (1963): A6–A7.

Frank, Leonard R., ed. *The History of Shock Treatment.* San Francisco: Frank Publishing, 1978.

Kesey, Ken. *One Flew Over the Cuckoo's Nest.* New York: Viking Press, 1962.

"Advantages Noted on Shock Therapy" by Lucy Freeman, *New York Times* (December 18, 1949)

First used in 1938, electroconvulsive therapy (ECT), also known as electric shock therapy, sought to treat mental illness by shocking an individual's brain with electricity, which caused seizures. It is not known how many people experienced this radical and controversial "treatment," but its damaging effects and testimony by those who received it have contributed to ECT's decreased application since the late 20th century. As this 1949 New York Times article proclaims, many medical professionals resolutely supported this measure for dealing with various forms of mental illness. Positive, unquestioning representations of medical approaches to disabilities historically have dominated the media, and thus this article also serves as a reminder of the complex and shifting understanding of disability and status of people with disabilities.

"Advantages Noted on Shock Therapy" by Lucy Freeman *New York Times,* December 18, 1949

Most criticism of electric shock therapy, which has been "an extremely valuable tool" in the treatment of psychotic patients, result from its "indiscriminate use" in the psychoneuroses, and "it cannot be emphasized enough that, contrary to psychotics, some neurotics may be harmed by it."

This was reported by Dr. Lothar B. Kalinowsky, a leading authority on electric shock therapy, in an article entitled "Present Status of Electric Shock Therapy" in the New York Academy of Medicine bulletin, which summarizes ten years of personal experience with electric convulsive therapy.

The largest group of psychiatric patients not responsive to electric shock are the psychoneurotic patients, and anxiety the most frequent symptom in neurotics, is often aggravated by the treatments, said Dr. Kalinowsky, research associate in psychiatry, College of Physicians and Surgeons, Columbia University. He added, however, that psychoneurotics who were very depressed were helped by the treatments.

Side-Effects are Noted

"Many neurotics react badly to the memory impairment and complain of it long after psychological tests have shown that actually no impairment persists," the article said. Often side-effects, such as headache and muscle pain, are added to the patient's complaints, it noted.

The question of when electric shock should be applied is a controversial one among psychiatrists. At the recent annual meeting of the American Psychiatric Association several sessions were devoted to discussion of its use both inside and outside mental hospitals.

In the article Dr. Kalinowsky said that electric shock treatment's "great value cannot be questioned when we realize how much human suffering is prevented by shortening depressions and preventing suicides and mental deterioration." He held that it was "frequently overlooked that moderate depressions are a much greater suicidal risk than advanced cases with no initiative left."

Use in Chronic Wards Urged

He suggested that electric shock treatments be applied in all chronic wards of mental hospitals, predicting they would do away with restraint, tube feeding, continuous baths and similar measures, and completely change the appearance of the "back wards" of the mental institutions.

"The reluctance on the part of some psychiatrists to apply electric shock therapy even in those case where a favorable result is clearly predictable is based primarily on theoretical objections," Dr. Kalinowsky said. "It is true that the shock treatments have no foundation in psychological theories; on the other hand, those thinking in organic terms are as much at a loss to understand their action.

"As treating physicians we cannot wait for satisfactory theories. As psychiatry begins to enlarge its therapeutic armentarium, we psychiatrists, like other physicians, will learn to select the right therapeutic techniques for the right type of patient. If this is done, electric shock therapy, applied with discrimination, will be helpful to many psychiatric patients."

Source: Lucy Freeman. "Advantages Noted on Shock Therapy." *New York Times,* 18 December 1949, p. 63.

Elkin, Stanley (1930–1995) *writer and university professor*

Stanley Elkin was a novelist and writer whose themes often focused on disability and illness. He was born on May 11, 1930, in New York City, the son of Russian immigrants. During the Depression, the Elkins relocated to Chicago, where the writer spent most of his childhood. He earned bachelor's and master's degrees in English literature at the University of Illinois, and in 1953 he married Joan Jacobson, an artist. They had three children together. He was drafted into the army in 1955, but returned to the University of Illinois to complete a Ph.D. in 1961. Elkin's academic career was spent mainly as a professor in the English department at Washington University in St. Louis. In 1972 he was diagnosed with MULTIPLE SCLEROSIS (MS); from the mid-1970s, he used a WHEELCHAIR or a walker.

Elkin's experience as a disabled person was reflected in his critically acclaimed fiction, which had long tended toward dark, comic observations, inventive language, and complicated plots centered on deeply flawed characters. Most pointedly, the hero of *The Franchiser* (1976) was named Ben Flesh and has MS; his adoptive FAMILY, the Finsbergs, were all affected by various rare disorders. Flesh was a small businessman, an entrepreneur in the midst of the energy crisis of the mid-1970s. Flesh faced both external and internal disruptions and deteriorations, including brownouts he called "civilization's demyelination," a reference to the neurological process that characterizes MS. *Magic Kingdom* (1985) centered on seven terminally ill CHILDREN who are treated to a Disney World vacation by a wish-granting CHARITY. The children resent being made into pitiful spectacles by the charity's publicity, and wish only to be left alone together to share as peers. In his novella "Her Sense of Timing" (1993), the main character is Professor Schiff, a political geographer with MS who uses a wheelchair and must prepare and host a party without the expected help of his wife. His last novel, *Mrs. Ted Bliss* (published posthumously in 1995), followed an octogenarian widow in Miami, dealing with a literal hurricane and some figurative whirlwinds as well; in a passage on ageism, Elkin wrote, "there ought to be a law, she thought, against all the song and dance they foist on you if you live past sixty. The victims they turn you into, the scams they run." *Mrs. Ted Bliss* won the National Book Critics Circle Award for fiction.

In 1993 *Harper's Magazine* published "Out of One's Tree: My Bout with Temporary Insanity," in which Elkin described a two-week, prednisone-induced psychosis he experienced from prescription medication for his MS. Of his own writing about these themes, Elkin said in a 1995 interview, "There's no way in the world I could ever take revenge on the disease that has disabled me. It just seems to me that disease, because it flirts with death, is a rather important subject to write about." Stanley Elkin died on May 31, 1995, at the age of 65, from complications following heart surgery. His papers are archived in the Department of Special Collections, Washington University in St. Louis.

See also AGE AND AGEISM; LITERATURE.

Penny L. Richards

Further Reading:

Bailey, Peter J. "'A Hat Where There Was Never a Hat': Stanley Elkin's Fifteenth Interview." *Review of Contemporary Fiction* 15, no. 2 (Summer 1995): 15.

———. *Reading Stanley Elkin.* Urbana: University of Illinois Press 1985.

Dougherty, David. "A Conversation with Stanley Elkin." In *The Muse Upon My Shoulder: Discussions of the Creative Process,* edited by Sylvia Skaggs McTague. Madison N.J.: Fairleigh Dickinson University Press 2004.

Elkin, Stanley. "Out of One's Tree." *Harper's Magazine* (January 1993).

Emerson, Ken. "The Indecorous, Rabelaisian, Convoluted Righteousness of Stanley Elkin," *New York Times,* 3 March 1991.

employment and labor

Work is a defining feature in the history of the United States. Not only has work been a means of sustaining life by meeting basic needs and providing stability to family and society, it also represents an activity through which individuals affirm their own IDENTITY and self-esteem. Successful employment has played a central role in the full inclusion of people with disabilities in mainstream society.

PRE-INDUSTRIALIZATION TO THE 20TH CENTURY

While people with disabilities have been excluded from the labor market throughout history, before U.S. INDUSTRIALIZATION in the early 1800s, individuals with disabilities were generally integrated into the COMMUNITY and protected by ties of kinship and participation in wider social networks. There was no need for specific employment interventions. Agriculture and manufacturing supplied most jobs, and the FAMILY social structure furnished basic security. Thus, people with disabilities were accommodated in families where the self-sufficient economic pattern provided a wide range of tasks that could be performed at a pace feasible for each individual. However, those with disabilities whose families could not care for them were left to the mercy of their community.

Nonetheless, in the American colonies disability often was viewed as a moral issue. Community assistance was limited and dependent on economic conditions and the attitude of its members. Occasionally a colonial General Assembly would find it necessary to order the community to take responsibility for its indigent residents to prevent their wandering into neighboring towns or counties seeking sustenance. Yet even when the colony took up this responsibility, it likely was carried out in an inappropriate manner. Persons with MENTAL ILLNESS or intellectual disabilities such as MENTAL RETARDATION were frequently placed and cared for in special town council appropriations or jails. Other communities solved their problems involving dependency by "auctioning off" persons with disabilities into SLAVERY.

As industrialization began taking hold in the early 19th century, a gradual exodus of workers from the countryside to the city contributed to the dissolution of extended family networks. ASYLUMS and workhouses were established to meet the growing indigent population and others labeled "idiots"—individuals with disabilities who could not sustain a living in the community within the context of individualized or nuclear family units.

In addition, the Industrial Revolution caused increased accidents and deaths from the new machinery and exposure to toxic materials. Rapid technological progress led to crowded, unsanitary working and living conditions and had a profound impact on the onset of work-related disabilities and occupational DISEASES. The introduction of power machinery into mines, stone-working facilities, and foundries gave rise to epidemics of silicosis and BLACK LUNG DISEASE among workers. Factory conditions commonly disabled workers, burning skin, damaging or destroying limbs, hearing, and sight, or impairing other physical and mental functions. Nevertheless, in no occupation (aside from mining and lumberjacking) did workers experience death and disability as frequently as they did in the U.S. rail trades. Despite gains in railroad safety, the catastrophic injury of losing an arm or a leg could not be entirely avoided, and railroaders and their families often found themselves without their basic economic needs being met.

Social justice came to be a key concern in the 19th century, particularly at its end in the burgeoning progressive political movement. Many forward-looking VOCATIONAL REHABILITATION organizations were established during this era. The first of these was the New England Asylum for the Blind (later renamed the PERKINS SCHOOL FOR THE BLIND), incorporated in Boston in 1829 to train blind individuals for manufacturing jobs. Some programs evolved under the sponsorship of religious ORGANIZATIONS, such as GOODWILL INDUSTRIES, the Salvation Army, and the Jewish Vocational Service Agencies. Others were the result of more secular private philanthropy, such as the Sunbeam Circle and the Red Cross Institution for Crippled and Disabled Men. The first American school for crippled children, the Industrial School for Crippled and Deformed Children, was established in Boston in 1893 to train children with physical impairments in the skills necessary to earn a living. Yet such efforts were few and far between.

The first comprehensive federal initiatives addressing individuals with disabilities date back to the CIVIL WAR (1861–65). In 1862 Congress implemented a pension program for Union Army VETERANS with disabilities unable to work. Program eligibility was based on a medically-diagnosed "incapacity to perform manual labor," which by linking the definition of disability to an inability to work began to institutionalize the MEDICAL MODEL OF DISABILITY. This model viewed disability as personal tragedy, hampering equal participation in society, and thereby leading to social welfare policies addressing the needs of people with disabilities as a form of CHARITY. Moreover, this model would influence American societal views regarding the place of individuals with disabilities in the labor market for over a century.

By the end of the 19th century there was a growing awareness of another group of people with disabilities: those with work-related injuries or occupational diseases. The growing number of workers who became ill or disabled as a consequence of their work tasks had no recourse other than to sue their employers under common law, an expensive and time-consuming process. The crowded court system caused long delays. Compensation for injuries was usually insufficient and uncertain. Employees were sometimes forced to bear the expense of injury themselves or throw themselves upon the mercy of others.

THE EARLY 20TH CENTURY

The first WORKERS' COMPENSATION law was passed in Maryland in 1902, and the first such law covering federal employees was passed in 1906. These laws were enacted to provide workers injured on the job with prompt, equitable, and guaranteed benefits. Employers, in turn, were protected from potentially catastrophic loss by a stated amount of specific benefits for the injuries suffered by the employee. Under workers' compensation statutes employers are required to make provisions such that workers injured in accidents arising "out of or in the course of employment" receive medical treatment and receive payments to replace lost income. By 1949 all states had enacted some kind of workers' compensation program.

THE FEDERAL VOCATIONAL
REHABILITATION PROGRAM

Before the 1920s, training and vocational rehabilitation were provided only by private and religious groups. This course changed after WORLD WAR I, when the influx of veterans with disabilities from overseas battlefields proved too much for private institutions to serve. In this pre-public welfare era, there was an urgent need for federal intervention to give veterans with disabilities opportunities to return to work and productivity. The first federal vocational rehabilitation program for veterans with disabilities, the Smith-Sears Act of 1918, aimed to return them to civil employment. In 1920 the SMITH-FESS ACT extended these vocational rehabilitation principles to civilians with physical impairments. In 1954 MARY SWITZER (1900–71), as the director of the Vocational Rehabilitation Program, shaped amendments to this act that

tripled federal funding for programs and services specifically addressing the integration of individuals with physical disabilities into employment.

Funds were appropriated for vocational guidance and training, occupational adjustment, PROSTHETICS, and job placement services for people with physical disabilities. Federal expenditures increased between the 1930s and 1960s, and eligibility criteria were expanded during this period to include people with developmental and mental impairments. In 1923 the U.S. Department of Labor and Printing founded the Bureau of Labor for the Deaf whose aim was to study and promote methods of EDUCATION for the DEAF and to encourage appropriate employment for deaf persons.

These early vocational laws aimed to "CURE and restore." Their premise was that people with physical and mental impairments were maladjusted and could achieve acceptance in the labor market only by "overcoming" their impairments. Physicians and policymakers required persons with disabilities to pursue "normalcy," particularly in the workplace. An interdisciplinary team, including a psychiatrist, a physician, social workers, occupational and physical therapists, vocational rehabilitation experts, and on occasion an anthropologist, would assess the individual and provide a diagnosis. If the person was determined to be capable of integration into the labor market, after the "right" training, the individual would be referred to a "sheltered (nonintegrated) workshop." Consequently, these programs accepted only people with disabilities who were perceived as capable of being "cured," in effect, only those workers with the greatest chance of securing a job; for instance, from 1920 to 1943, the vocational rehabilitation program served only 12,000 people, while approximately 250,000 became disabled every year. Additionally, in the 1920s and 1930s selection favored rehabilitating young white men.

THE GREAT DEPRESSION

On October 29, 1929, the U.S. stock market crashed. This day, known as Black Tuesday, marked the beginning of the Great Depression in the United States. The Depression had devastating effects. Personal incomes, tax revenues, prices, and profits declined sharply. Facing plummeting demand with few alternate sources of jobs, areas dependent on primary-sector industries such as farming, mining, and logging suffered the most.

Between 1933 and 1938 President FRANKLIN D. ROOSEVELT initiated the NEW DEAL—a series of programs with the goal of giving relief to the people and economy of the United States, and putting as many persons as possible back to work. Federal employment programs such as the Works Progress Administration (WPA), National Recovery Administration (NRA), and Civilian Conservation Corps (CCC) exemplify the variability and sometimes socially constructed nature of disability. Initially people with disabilities were classified as "unemployable" and were denied access to the jobs and resources available through the various New Deal programs.

This discriminatory categorizing was challenged in May 1935 when members of the League of the Physically Handicapped (LPH) picketed in front of the New York headquarters of the WPA, one of the primary New Deal agencies for employment. They demanded that "handicapped people receive a just share of the millions of jobs being given out by the government." Joined by the League for the Advancement of the Deaf, the LPH obtained a commitment that, in the future, workers with disabilities would receive at least 7 percent of WPA jobs in New York. This resulted in 1,500 jobs for people with disabilities, although more than 600 of those were lost to layoffs in the following spring.

The LPH's experience with New York's WPA was indicative of both its successes and failures. Although the LPH's actions did not alter federal policies toward people with disabilities, its efforts got a number of people jobs and opened the public sector to some workers with disabilities.

WORLD WAR II AND THE 1950S

The notion that people with disabilities can be a productive and vital part of the labor market was further shown during World War II, when competition for jobs disappeared. Desperate for workers, employers were willing to hire anyone who could do the work in their plants and shops. People with disabilities by the tens of thousands were engaged in gainful employment, but the labor market returned to the prior status quo when the economy shifted from war to peace in 1945. Millions of veterans came back to enter the labor market, and many of them were assured under the mobilization laws that they could displace anyone who had taken their jobs. This series of events epitomized the proposition that people with disabilities are the last hired and the first fired.

SHELTERED WORKSHOPS

The original concept of sheltered workshops was to promote a protected environment in which the individual with a disability could experience the stimulation and learning required for work without the elements of competitive employment. The workshop was an effort to allow the individual the opportunity to work without having to risk failure, which, it was assumed, would occur in mainstream work environments. Rather than provide normalization, the workshop sheltered the individual from standard frustrations, problems, and risks while allowing him or her to experience a form of normal job requirements, such as paychecks, time clocks, work hours, supervision, and production schedules. These workshops were aimed at training the person but ignored societal barriers and attitudes generally prohibit-

"There's an old man, he pulls hot fat. . . . He's been on the killing floor for thirty years, and been stone blind for twenty years. He can get around on that floor as well as anyone of us with eyesight. Knows every man on the floor by the sound of his voice. He does his full share of work, and better than most, at that. . . . Guess after you been working thirty years at one job you don't need much else except habit to keep going."

—Elmer Thomas, a Chicago packinghouse worker, in an interview describing his blind colleague, May 10, 1939

ing the inclusion of individuals with disabilities in the labor market. Rarely has this "train and place" approach led to the integration of individuals with disabilities into the competitive workforce.

THE SOCIAL SECURITY ACT

As the 20th century progressed, American society addressed the economic needs of individuals with disabilities in other ways. Congress enacted laws providing health and welfare benefits to different groups of individuals with disabilities. The Social Security Act of 1935 established a federal and state system of health services for "crippled" children. In 1954, the act was amended to provide monthly benefits for "eligible" workers who had become disabled. This act was again amended in 1972 to provide benefits to limited groups of poor individuals with disabilities.

The Social Security Administration (SSA) ran two federal programs: Social Security Disability Insurance (SSDI) for individuals who had a work history and paid taxes, and Supplemental Security Income (SSI) to assist individuals who had never been in the labor market and with income and assets below set thresholds. Eligibility for these programs was based on a medical model of disability, viewing disability as a long-term or permanent excuse from any obligation to work. These social welfare programs were designed to serve only the "truly needy." Earning more than the set threshold would render those covered no longer eligible, and they would lose their benefits.

THE EMERGENT DISABILITY ANTIDISCRIMINATION MOVEMENT, 1960S–1980S

During the civil rights era of the 1960s, minority groups began to view equal access to society as a fundamental right, and some within the disability community started to view disability rights as a part of this larger struggle. A growing DISABILITY RIGHTS MOVEMENT fought for federal protections from the social and economic inequalities individuals with disabilities encounter. Activists such as ED ROBERTS in California and JUDY HEUMANN in New York took further the conception that individuals with disabilities are not disabled by their individual capacities, but by the ideas, attitudes, and misconceptions of an able-bodied society, perpetuating prejudice, exclusion, discrimination, and inequality.

In this struggle individuals with disabilities started to challenge the medical model as expressed in rehabilitation services. An alternative model of supported employment was developed, based on the idea that individuals with significant disabilities learn better if trained in the integrated work settings of their choice and provided with ongoing support. This "place and train" model was based on the premise that even individuals with significant disabilities, given the right support, can be integrated into inclusive and normative settings.

The disability civil rights movement had its first major victory with Congress's passage of the Rehabilitation Act of 1973, which established a critical bridge between disability and antidiscrimination LAW AND POLICY. SECTION 504 of this act, ratified first in 1977 after a national 28-day sit-in staged by FRANK BOWE (1947–2007), prohibits discrimination by recipients of federal funding on the basis of a disability toward otherwise qualified individuals with disabilities.

Despite the rights and protections provided by the Rehabilitation Act of 1973, research and practice found that discrimination and exclusion from the mainstream labor market remained widespread. In the mid-1980s, the disability community and policymakers recognized the need for more comprehensive civil rights protections while addressing the responsibilities and obligations of employers, state and local governments, and public entities. A response to this need came with passage of the AMERICANS WITH DISABILITIES ACT (ADA), the hallmark of the disability civil rights movement, signed into law on July 26, 1990. The ADA provides a comprehensive national mandate for eliminating discrimination against persons with disabilities and serves as a model of antidiscrimination law for the world.

THE CIVIL RIGHTS MODEL OF THE 1990S
The ADA, consisting of five main sections known as "Titles," articulates the nation's goals for assuring "equality of opportunity, full participation, independent living, and economic self-sufficiency" for individuals with disabilities. Title I specifically prohibits discrimination in employment practices. Section 504 of the Rehabilitation Act of 1973 helped model the protections of the ADA's employment provisions, but the ADA extended these protections to employees with disabilities of both private employers and state and local government employers.

The ADA did not take immediate effect upon its signing into law. Rather, it directed federal agencies to develop regulations for implementing and enforcing the different titles. The Equal Employment Opportunity Commission (EEOC) was charged with issuing regulations interpreting and implementing the employment provisions under Title I within one year of the ADA's enactment. The General Counsel of the EEOC is responsible for conducting enforcement litigation under the ADA and enforcing antidiscrimination employment policy for other marginalized groups, based on AGE, RACE, color, RELIGION, GENDER, and national origin.

Shortly after the ADA's enactment, individuals with disabilities were quick to assert their new rights. Employment discrimination claims were made to the EEOC and, in turn, taken to court in record numbers. Private employers were equally motivated to question their obligations under the ADA. Research shows that private employers' response largely arose and continues to do so from concerns (often not justified in fact) about the costs of providing reasonable accommodations.

Challenges for workers with disabilities have continued as the medical model of disability infiltrated the ADA's civil rights framework. In contrast to race- and gender-based employment discrimination cases, courts began applying highly scrutinizing tests to determine whether the employee was a qualified individual with a disability. Courts analyzed whether the employee was substantially limited in a major life activity often using exclusively medical data, records, testimony, and evaluations. Additionally, the U.S. Supreme Court announced the "mitigation doctrine" in the case of *Sutton v. United Airlines,* which requires courts to analyze the employee's claimed substantial limitation with the use of his or her medications, assistive hearing devices, and prosthetics, for instance. Without these tools, many individuals with disabilities would not be able to perform their jobs or function in daily life, and yet by using them they lose their ADA protection as a person with a disability under the law. In other words, in some cases individuals with disabilities are either not disabled enough to be covered by the ADA or they are too disabled to work and therefore not qualified for ADA protections.

Since 1990 there has been an ongoing debate around the ADA's impact on employment opportunities and economic independence for individuals with disabilities. Research attempting to determine the effects of Title I is not conclusive. Some studies show a decline in employment rates for individuals with disabilities, while others point to an increase. This difference in reported outcomes depends to a large extent on how disability is measured. While employment of people who report a work-limiting impairment or health condition decreased in the 1990s, the employment rate rose among those with more severe functional limitations. Additionally, researchers focusing on the outcomes of employment complaints filed under the ADA found that only 15.7 percent resulted in some benefit to the individual with a disability. Only 1.7 percent of all claims resulted in job reinstatement or new hires.

The ADA alone has not brought about the anticipated increase of individuals with disabilities in the labor market. This outcome, however, cannot be attributed solely to the ADA. Part of the explanation is found in the ongoing tension between the medical and civil rights models still affecting and coexisting in different segments of disability policy. Although the ADA's goal was to remove discriminatory barriers facing individuals with disabilities, recognition of the civil rights model has not caused a complete overhaul of disability policy. Instead, recent policy instruments embedded in the civil rights model have been added to existing and older instruments, such as long-established Social Security schemes.

As a result, prominent barriers remain in federal and state government programs, including economic disincentives to work as reflected in the SSDI and SSI programs. Because medically based welfare programs link eligibility to the inability to work, an individual with a disability risks losing his or her benefits and health insurance when becoming gainfully employed. Recent national policy initiatives, such as the MEDICAID Buy-In program, target this flawed interaction and aim to diminish economic barriers to work for individuals with disabilities.

1998–PRESENT: STRIVING FOR AN INTEGRATIVE DISABILITY POLICY

In the late 1990s, as a complement to the ADA, Congress amended several key policies and programs. Some extend benefit eligibility for individuals with disabilities engaged in gainful employment; others emphasize information and coordination among different employment services to facilitate a smoother transition into the labor market.

In 1998 Congress passed the Work Investment Act (WIA), establishing state and local Workforce Investment Boards responsible for developing a "one stop" delivery system of accessible, innovative, and comprehensive employment services. One-Stop centers provide assistance in job search activities, career planning, job skill assessments and training, and child care resources. One-Stops also provide resources for job and entrepreneurial training, TRANSPORTATION and housing assistance, and ACCESS to affordable health coverage.

WIA further provided the means for states to enter into cooperative agreements with the U.S. Department of Labor and the Social Security Administration to create the Disability Program Navigator (DPN) demonstration initiative. DPNs are located in One-Stop centers (currently in 45 states).

The Disability Program Navigator initiative is designed to increase employment and self-sufficiency for Social Security beneficiaries and others with disabilities, facilitate access to federal and state employment training programs and services, and enhance access to the private employer community. Navigators possess a skill set that uniquely qualifies them to strengthen systems and serve individuals with disabilities.

In 1999 Congress passed the Ticket to Work and Work Incentives Improvement Act (TWWIIA), extending benefit eligibility to individuals with disabilities working in competitive employment and earning more than the benefit threshold. The intent of the act was to provide recipients of SSDI and SSI with more support from the programs during a lengthier period of reentry to employment; make it easier to return to the benefit programs if work efforts ultimately fall short of self-sufficiency; and extend health insurance for a longer period after termination of cash benefits.

TWWIIA also established the Ticket to Work and Self-Sufficiency Program (Ticket Program). The purpose of the Ticket Program is to ensure that individuals with disabilities have access to job-related training and placement assistance from an approved provider of their choice. SSDI and SSI recipients may use a "ticket" to obtain employment services from employment networks (ENs). ENs are public or private entities that provide services such as workplace accommodations, peer mentoring, job training, and transportation assistance to Ticket participants seeking employment. The goal of the Ticket Program is to give beneficiaries choice and control over their employment services and foster competition and innovation among employment service providers.

The Ticket Program and the ADA reflect the disability policy framework that endorses the civil rights of qualified individuals with disabilities to work and be free from discrimination on the basis of disability. These initiatives, along with other policy changes, are designed to assist individuals in obtaining and retaining employment through the integration of job-related supports, enhancement of work incentives, and access to affordable HEALTH CARE benefits.

DISABILITY AND EMPLOYMENT FROM A SOCIETAL VIEW

In this first decade of the 21st century, there has been an increasing awareness that ensuring employment opportunities for people with disabilities is important not just for those individuals, but also for employers, government, and society as a whole. Social, political, and economic research had shown that there are societal benefits from greater inclusion in mainstream society as the barriers facing people with disabilities are dismantled.

For instance, assistive technologies (e.g., voice-activated and screen-reader computer software) specifically designed to meet the needs of people with disabilities have proven useful for persons without disabilities, such as the elderly and second language learners. Making the social and physical environment accessible for people with various disabilities is also beneficial for the general population, such as CURB CUTS for parents pushing strollers and electronic door openers for persons delivering oversize packages. In addition, a variety of products and services have arisen specifically to meet the needs of people with disabilities like Tele-care, personal assistant services, and the home health industry supplying tens of thousands of jobs to persons with and without disabilities.

PAST, PRESENT, AND FUTURE

In the last two centuries a significant change has taken place in how disability is understood in American society and its impact on employment policies and opportunities for individuals with disabilities. The medical model of disability informed societal attitudes and governmental policies for a century before a civil rights approach received significant attention. Passage of the Americans with Disabilities Act in 1990 embraced the civil rights model and promised a level playing field for workers with disabilities.

However, the medical and civil rights models of disability continue competing in the realm of labor and employment law and policy. This is due largely to the competing purposes of varying federal policies, the role of medical professionals in diagnosis and treatment, and the restrictive view taken by the courts about who meets the ADA's definition of disability in order to invoke it protections. The evolving disability policy also provides an intriguing perspective on how people with disabilities refer to themselves and others. For instance, in the first half of the 20th century when federal policies aimed at identifying and separating the able-bodied from the crippled and sick tied benefit eligibility to the inability to work, different individuals and groups with disabilities distanced themselves from the disability community, perhaps to avoid STIGMA, yet at the expense of garnering community support. As the policy orientation has become framed around civil rights protection and antidiscrimination, many more individuals with various impairments and health conditions are seeking inclusion in the disability community for its protections against employment discrimination.

Despite these advances, Americans with disabilities remain employed at significantly lower rates than those without disabilities. A national study from 2006 shows that there was a 42.0 percentage point gap between the employment rates of working-age people with (37.7 percent) and without (79.7 percent) disabilities. The mean annual earnings of workers with disabilities were just 58 percent of the mean annual earnings of workers without disabilities. Policymakers and disability advocates realize that to close these gaps, there is a need for further and continuous dialogue among employers, government, and individuals with disabilities about the economic and social implications of hiring, advancing, and retaining qualified workers with disabilities. This dialogue is necessary to appreciate employers' needs while shifting their attitudes toward hiring and accommodating qualified individuals with disabilities, and to create new opportunities for individuals with disabilities to achieve economic independence and social inclusion.

In American history, employment has been the major criterion for whether a physical or mental impairment was disabling, whether it led to the self-fulfilling label of "disabled" that characterizes an individual as incapable of self-sufficiency and reliant on private CHARITY or government support to survive. If people with impairments have been employed in nonsegregated jobs, they have not faced the same overall degree of exclusion and stigma. Knowledge of the participation of people with disabilities in employment is key to understanding the general significance of disability. It is important to note the progress that has been attained in the integration of disabled people into the workforce through changing attitudes and governmental actions, but many people with disabilities still live on the margins of society due to economic and social environments that exclude rather than accommodate and support.

See also ACCESS AND ACCESSIBILITY; ASSISTIVE TECHNOLOGY AND ADAPTIVE DEVICES; CARPAL TUNNEL SYNDROME; DEPENDENT AND DEPENDENCE; FORD MOTOR COMPANY; FREAK SHOWS; IMPAIRMENT/IMPAIRED; INDEPENDENT LIVING MOVEMENT; LABOR BUREAUS FOR THE DEAF; OVERCOME AND OVERCOMING; RAILROAD SPINE.

Tal Araten-Bergman
Janikke Solstad Vedeler
William N. Myhill
Peter Blanck

Further Reading:

Blanck, P. "Americans with Disabilities and Their Civil Rights: Past, Present, and Future." *University of Pittsburgh Law Review* 66 (2006): 687–719.

Blanck, P., E. Hill, C. Siegal, and M. Waterstone. *Disability Civil Rights Law and Policy: Cases and Materials.* Eagan, Minn.: Thomson/West, 2005.

Blanck, P., L. Schur, D. Kruse, S. Schwochau, and C. Song. "Calibrating the Impact of the ADA's Employment Provisions." *Stanford Law and Policy Review* 14, no. 2 (2003): 267–290.

Longmore, Paul K., and David Goldberger. "The League of the Physically Handicapped and the Great Depression: A Case Study in the New Disability History." *Journal of American History* 87, no. 3 (Dec. 2000): 888–922.

National Council on Disability. *Empowerment for Americans with Disabilities: Breaking Barriers to Careers and Full*

Employment. Washington, D.C.: National Council on Disability, 2007.

Obermann, C. Esco. *A History of Vocational Rehabilitation in America.* New York: Arno Press, 1980.

O'Brien, R. *Crippled Justice: The History of Modern Disability Policy in the Workplace.* Chicago: University of Chicago Press, 2001.

empowerment

The term *empowerment* refers to the goal and process of increasing the political, social, or economic power of individuals, groups, classes, and communities. Empowerment is a process of increasing the control that individuals or groups have over their lives. Empowerment implies creating or acquiring power, often by taking it from someone else, and the capacity for self-determination at the individual and group level, typically represented in political activity, public discourse, and, where successful, government policies. For American disability history, empowerment is of vital importance.

Throughout American history there are many examples of people with disabilities attempting to gain empowerment for themselves and their peers, but a more formalized demand for empowerment determination by Americans with disabilities emerged especially with the growth of the disability rights and INDEPENDENT LIVING MOVEMENTS during the 1960s and 1970s. At that time many excluded and marginalized groups, including people with disabilities, borrowed ideas, rhetoric, and social and political goals from the civil rights movement. Inclusion and political participation were primary goals of this effort. Beginning in that era (and building on previous political action by disability activists), a critical mass of people with disabilities experienced a social transformation, developing a new form of consciousness that focused on empowerment.

While there had been previous political advocacy by individuals with physical, sensory, and cognitive impairments, in the 1960s and 1970s a broad spectrum of disability activists began to question and resist prevailing ideas about disability, and a new collective consciousness concerning disability emerged. This consciousness was as much political as it was psychological (although it is hard to identify where one ends and the other begins), and led, over time, to a new identity politics that emphasized organizing dispersed communities of people with disabilities, combating self-doubt and disempowering attitudes, and building and promoting a DISABILITY CULTURE that undermines oppression and increases awareness.

By the late 1970s a broad social movement had emerged that expressed and was an expression of the new political consciousness, speaking to the needs and aspirations of disabled

A central goal of the disability rights movement, which gained force in the 1960s, is empowerment. The slogan in this poster by Mark Morris contrasts disabled people's status as objects of charity with their desired aim to be equal and accepted full citizens.   *(The Center on Human Policy at Syracuse University)*

people. This consciousness was rooted in the interconnected principles of inclusion, independence, self-help, self-determination, and human rights. The application of these principles varied but included such divergent actions as street PROTESTS by DISABLED IN ACTION in New York, student activism by the ROLLING QUADS in BERKELEY, CALIFORNIA, legislative advocacy by the NATIONAL FEDERATION OF THE BLIND, the SIT-IN PROTEST AT THE HEALTH, EDUCATION AND WELFARE DEPARTMENT in San Francisco (1977), the DEAF PRESIDENT NOW! movement in 1988, as well as through lawsuits by such advocacy centers as the Public Interest Law Center of Philadelphia and the DISABILITY RIGHTS EDUCATION AND DEFENSE FUND that helped establish the rights of people residing in state facilities and of CHILDREN excluded from public schools because of their disabilities.

In the midst of other civil rights ACTIVISM, American disability advocates joined forces across the lines of impairment to build a cross-disability movement, including the Berkeley (California) Center for Independent Living, and the AMERICAN COALITION OF CITIZENS WITH DISABILITIES;

subsequently nationally organized groups such as ADAPT, NOT DEAD YET, and the SOCIETY FOR DISABILITY STUDIES joined the effort to achieve full civil rights. These disability rights advocates went on to build cross-national alliances and ORGANIZATIONS such as Disabled People International. Relationships and coalitions also developed with other oppressed groups at the local, national, and global levels in pursuit of common goals. The social movement of people with disabilities has spread globally over the last three decades, in both advanced industrial nations such as Canada, the United Kingdom, and Japan, and in developing nations around the world.

The desire of people with disabilities to take control of their lives and to live freely in the community is rooted in a politics of empowerment that advocates the independence and inclusion of people with disabilities, although its philosophical tenets are differentiated by politics and place. While the disability movement's center of gravity has been anchored by the idea of empowerment, it often is an indistinct empowerment having something to do with individuals with disabilities "gaining" more capacity or options, or the ability to seek equal opportunities. The diversity of objectives sought by people with disabilities reflects the diversity of their impairments and experiences, but this diversity also obscures the systemic oppression experienced by people with disabilities.

Many activists have asserted that the only pathway to true empowerment for people with disabilities has been through their own conscious political activity. The politics and philosophy of the disability rights movement have evolved out of an emerging consciousness of political activists worldwide as they incorporated principles such as empowerment, inclusion, and self-determination. Out of both similar and divergent experiences, people with disabilities have acquired a consciousness about themselves and the world around them that has affected their aspirations. They have come to a raised consciousness of themselves not only as people with disabilities but also as oppressed people.

Moreover, people with disabilities have become political activists because their raised consciousness has become empowered. They are no longer interested in the "welfare of the handicapped," in which disability represents a pitiful, medical condition. Empowered consciousness develops through collective political action, and is an experientially evolved awareness of self, in which the (false) medical notion of disability has been replaced by the (true) awareness of disability as a social condition shaped by an environment that can accommodate people's impairments or segregate and constrain them. Disability activists thus approach the problems of people with disabilities in terms of human rights.

Empowered consciousness means acting collectively to challenge the oppressive values, images, and meanings of the dominant culture and to empower others. This may mean educating people, creating disturbances, confronting institutions, and seeking group power in communities, schools, churches, and medical and rehabilitation facilities. Empowered consciousness insists on the active, collective contestation for control over the necessities of life and over every other facet of life, as represented by the demand "Nothing about us without us!"

Persons with empowered consciousness may still see only part of the larger world but understand that they can and should influence it. These people see the connections between themselves and others and begin to recognize a level of universality that was obscured in their previous consciousness. They begin to speak of "we" instead of "I" or "they."

This new consciousness is profoundly liberating. It allows individuals to recognize themselves in the context of something bigger than themselves and enables them to appreciate the commonalities they have with others. Isolation and estrangement are replaced by association and connection.

The empowerment of disabled persons has yielded a variety of disability-related human rights and civil rights laws. Beginning in the 1960s, many cities, states, and nongovernmental organizations have adopted statutes and policies prohibiting discrimination on the basis of disability. Nationally, the empowerment of people with disabilities is represented in the 1975 INDIVIDUALS WITH DISABILITIES EDUCATION ACT (IDEA) and the AMERICANS WITH DISABILITIES ACT of 1990 (ADA), as well as other laws that address disability discrimination. Globally, many nations have adopted laws prohibiting disability discrimination that were influenced by the ADA. In December 2006 the United Nations approved the INTERNATIONAL CONVENTION ON THE RIGHTS OF PERSONS WITH DISABILITIES.

Empowerment continues to be a central aspect of the DISABILITY RIGHTS MOVEMENT. The different interpretations, strategies to achieve it, and results from the efforts likewise continue to shed light on the evolving meaning of disability and citizenship in America.

See also ACTIVISM AND ADVOCACY; LAW AND POLICY; SELF-ADVOCATES AND SELF-ADVOCACY.

James Charlton
Richard K. Scotch

Further Reading:

Barnes, C., G. Mercer, and T. Shakespeare. *Exploring Disability: A Social Introduction.* Cambridge, Eng.: Polity Press, 1999.

Charlton, James. *Nothing About Us Without Us: Disability Oppression and Empowerment.* Berkeley: University of California Press, 1998.

Driedger, Diane. *The Last Civil Rights Movement: Disabled Peoples' International.* New York: St. Martin's Press, 1989.

Gannon, Jack. *The Week the World Heard Gallaudet.* Washington, D.C.: Gallaudet University Press, 1989.

Linton, Simi. *Claiming Disability: Knowledge and Identity.* New York: New York University Press, 1998.

Oliver, Michael. *The Politics of Disablement.* New York: St. Martin's Press, 1990.

endocrine therapy   See ENDOCRINOLOGY.

endocrinology

Endocrinology, the study of hormones and the glands that secrete them, occupies an important though neglected place in the history of disability in the United States.

Chemists in the 19th century discovered that hormonal substances originated with particular glands, and by the early 20th century physiologists had thoroughly identified each of the major glands in the body—pituitary, thalamus, thyroid, adrenals, ovaries, and testes. As each gland held a discrete function, physiologists linked the origins of certain physical conditions and chronic illnesses to glandular function or dysfunction. Individuals born with restricted growth (so-called DWARFISM), for example, became associated with a deficit of growth hormone from the pituitary, while those with hirsutism ("excessive" body hair) became associated with a surfeit of androgen, the male hormone.

These discoveries were both a relief and a curse for people with disabilities. On one hand, as information about glandular diseases circulated, popular freak and CIRCUS sideshows that exhibited individuals with bodily differences—"fat ladies," "midgets," "pygmies," "pinheads," and so forth—were criticized for exploiting those with hormonal imbalances. On the other hand, as scientists and physicians argued that proper hormone balance was an essential precondition for a "NORMAL" body, they advocated medical interventions for those believed to be too short or too stout, with too much or too little pigment, or who were too masculine or too feminine or who were not masculine or feminine enough. Endocrinologists believed that such individuals, characterized as embodying a "primitive" state of physical development, could be corrected through modern endocrine science. From the 1890s through the 1930s, nonreproductive hormones were regularly administered through "organotherapy" and "pluriglandular" therapy, common terms for the injection of animal gland extracts to human bodies. Writing in 1916, for instance, physician Frank R. Starkey announced that pluriglandular therapy had brought about "brilliant results" "in children who are backward in either mental or physical development."

Early hormone therapies were often prohibitively expensive, as glandular essences required the distillation of literally tons of animal glands. By the early 1940s, however, pluriglandular extracts gave way to the commercial development of synthetic steroid hormones, such as cortisone, which were quickly identified as medical "miracles" for their capacity to treat a range of CHRONIC ILLNESSES, from Addison's disease to ARTHRITIS. Some older attitudes toward those with glandular imbalances persisted, however. In 1945, for example, New York attorney William Wolf regarded violent criminals, people with MENTAL ILLNESS, and those with GENDER or sexual differences as "endocrinopaths" and advocated treating their behavioral problems through hormone therapy.

The idea that hormonal balance was an "objective" measure of bodily health and physical normalcy held sway for much of the 20th century and anticipated the ways in which genetics in the 1980s and 1990s would come to be perceived as a reliable indicator of the "truth" of the body. In the 21st century endocrinology is often regarded as a relatively conservative medical practice. Still, some recent controversies, such as the correlation between hormone replacement therapy for pre- and postmenopausal women and rising incidents of osteoporosis and breast cancer, or the appropriation of the category "disabled" by some transgender individuals seeking hormone treatments, remain points of contention among many disability rights activists.

David Serlin

Further Reading:

Serlin, David. *Replaceable You: Engineering the Body in Postwar America.* Chicago: University of Chicago Press, 2004.

epilepsy

Derived from the Greek *epilepsia,* epilepsy is a chronic neurological disorder, or group of disorders, characterized by recurrent seizures. In the past, epilepsy has been associated with visionary religious experience, demonic possession, and sacred foresight. Americans with epilepsy historically have been viewed with fear and suspicion and most studies of epileptics emphasize treatment as an indicator of social progress. The history of this condition and of those who have it reflects several important themes in disability history, including medical diagnosis, treatment, and the STIGMA.

In American history, people with epilepsy have been understood and treated in negative terms from the colonial period to the present day. Although the medieval view of epilepsy as a manifestation of demonic possession lost currency during the European Enlightenment, popular CURES, such as the use of blessed rings, continued well into the 18th century. In colonial America, people with epilepsy were perceived as insane or less than human and were often jailed, beaten, or driven from town to town. The belief in the efficacy of popular cures characterized attitudes toward the treatment of epilepsy in colonial America. In an effort to control the epileptic seizures suffered by his stepdaughter Patsy, George Washington followed a common prescription at the time and had an iron ring made for her; usually placed on a finger, it was believed that iron rings had curative powers.

The 19th-century work of American neurologist Hughlings Jackson firmly established epilepsy as a medical disability that could be understood and treated. However, 20th-century advocates of EUGENICS have characterized epileptics as FEEBLEMINDED, individuals adjudged neither severely mentally retarded nor "NORMAL." As a result, epileptics were often unjustly institutionalized with the mentally retarded and criminally insane. Beginning in the 1920s, people with epilepsy were forbidden to marry or have CHILDREN in many states, and were often forcibly sterilized. Institutions, such as the VIRGINIA COLONY OF EPILEPTICS AND FEEBLE MINDED, were established in part to promote the INVOLUNTARY STERILIZATION of people with epilepsy. In *BUCK V. BELL* (1927), the U.S. Supreme Court upheld a Virginia law that gave the state permission to sterilize citizens considered "unfit," among whom were people deemed insane, feebleminded, or epileptic. Although seldom enforced after 1960, laws in some states as late as 1990 continued to forbid people with epilepsy to marry or become parents, while states such as Virginia continued to permit legal sterilization of people with epilepsy as late as the early 1970s.

Although new medications such as potassium bromide and Phenobarbital emerged after the 1920s, diagnosis and treatment of epilepsy in the United States remained inadequate until recent years. Beginning in the 1930s, however, the development of diagnostic tools such as the electroencephalograph (EEG), treatments such as vagal nerve stimulation, surgery, and the ketogenic diet, and new medications such as Neurontin, Keppra, Lamictal, Topamax, and Tegretol have provided more effective control of seizures. Despite these advances, the stigmatization of people with epilepsy continues.

In the aftermath of a legacy of ABUSE, civil rights groups emerged in the 1960s to advance the political, social, and medical interests of people with epilepsy. Founded in 1968, the EPILEPSY FOUNDATION, a national ORGANIZATION composed of state affiliates, has promoted medical research, defended the legal rights of people with epilepsy, and organized such important national programs as the Epilepsy Resource Center, the National Epilepsy Library, and the Jeanne A. Carpenter Epilepsy Legal Defense Fund. For two decades, the EPILEPSY FOUNDATION, together with a host of other advocacy groups, lobbied Congress for a law, or laws, that clearly prohibited discrimination on the basis of disability. This effort led to the passage of the AMERICANS WITH DISABILITIES ACT (ADA) of 1990. In 2000 the Epilepsy Foundation sponsored an important conference, Curing Epilepsy: The Promise and the Challenge, that set national goals for the prevention, treatment, and cure of epilepsy. Since 2000, however, it has become increasingly difficult for people with epilepsy to persuade the courts that they are disabled under the ADA. In 2002, *Toyota v. Williams,* the U.S. Supreme Court held that individuals must be limited in their ability to perform activities both in the workplace and out. Many advocates and scholars have interpreted this decision as a narrowing definition of disability that will make it more difficult for those with epilepsy to claim protections under the ADA. Many stakeholders, including medical professionals, employers, lawyers, politicians, and advocates, continue to debate the meaning of disability and of specific condition in the early 21st century, demonstrating the complexity and multifaceted nature of epilepsy in American society.

See also ASYLUMS AND INSTITUTIONS; REPRODUCTIVE RIGHTS.

Brian W. Refford

Further Reading:

Dwyer, Ellen. "Stigma and Epilepsy." *Transactions and Studies of the College of Physicians of Philadelphia* 13, no 4 (1991): 387–410.

Friedlander, William. *The History of Modern Epilepsy: The Beginning, 1865–1914.* Wesport, Conn.: Greenwood Press, 2001.

Temkin, Owsei. *The Falling Sickness: A History of Epilepsy from the Greeks to the Beginnings of Modern Neurology.* Baltimore: Johns Hopkins University Press, 1994.

Epilepsy Foundation

The Epilepsy Foundation is an organization based in Landover, Maryland, that works as an advocate for people with either the medical diagnosis of EPILEPSY or some other seizure disorder in all areas including EMPLOYMENT, research, and building acceptance by society in general.

The foundation's origins date to January 1965, when three national epilepsy ORGANIZATIONS in the United States—the American Epilepsy Federation of Boston, the National Epilepsy League of Chicago, and the United Epilepsy Association of New York—merged into the Epilepsy Association of America to expand their programming. The new organization was based in New York. A fourth group, the Epilepsy Foundation of Washington, D.C., which was also the largest epilepsy association at the time, declined to join due to disagreements over how the new group would be organized. In 1968, however, the Epilepsy Foundation merged with the Epilepsy Association to form the Epilepsy Foundation of America. The group shortened its name in 1998 to Epilepsy Foundation.

The group's focus on changing social perception of epilepsy bore positive results early in its history; for example, a 1968 Gallup poll showed an improvement in attitudes toward people with epilepsy; seven years later in 1975 Congress passed a LAW that established the Commission for the Control of Epilepsy and its Consequences.

Since the mid-1980s the group has been involved actively in outreach to all people with seizure disorders. It launched its first transcultural project in 1986, and in 1997 the foundation began a national program targeting women called Women and Epilepsy. This led in 2001 to the creation of the Making a Difference Award, an annual award for women with epilepsy. The same year the foundation created the Partnership for Pediatric Epilepsy Research, which works with both individuals and organizations to CURE pediatric epilepsy. In 2001 the foundation launched Entitled to Respect, a program to reach youths. Two years later, Entitled to Respect was expanded the better to include African-American youth. In 2005 the foundation sponsored the first Epilepsy Leadership Conference.

The foundation is involved also in research on seizure disorders; for example, it maintains the National Epilepsy Library, founded in 1982, at its Landover headquarters. It also gives grants to researchers looking for cures and treatments for epilepsy.

The foundation has continued to emphasize social dimensions of disability; for example, it successfully lobbied Congress in 2003 to improve the lives of people with epilepsy by making certain that anticonvulsants are included in the MEDICARE prescription drug benefit. The foundation also helps people on the job with training and counseling. Additionally, it runs the Jeanne A. Carpenter Epilepsy Legal Defense Fund, which works to fight discrimination against people with epilepsy in legal situations. This fund was named in honor of Jeanne A. Carpenter, one of the foundation's trustees, who died in 2003.

By 2009 the foundation had approximately 60 local affiliates. As the leading national organization for people with epilepsy and other seizure disorders, the Epilepsy Foundation reflects a pluralistic approach to disability by funding medical research to alleviate the symptoms of epilepsy and seizure disorders and also directing resources to reduce and end the STIGMA associated with this disability. DISABILITY STUDIES scholars historically have emphasized the limits of a MEDICAL MODEL OF DISABILITY, but the example of the Epilepsy Foundation suggests rich and complex possibilities of understanding treatment, IDENTITY, and EMPOWERMENT.

Scott Sheidlower

Further Reading:

Encyclopedia of Associations: National Organizations of the U.S., 44th ed., s.v. 13721.

Epilepsy Foundation, n.d. Available online. URL: http://www. epilepsyfoundation.org. Accessed March 10, 2008.

Shapiro, J. P. *No Pity: People with Disabilities Forging a New Civil Rights Movement.* New York: Times Books, 1993.

ER

First airing in 1994, NBC's long-running medical melodrama *ER* provided a dramatic space for several recurring characters with disabilities. Its depictions of disability varied from the superficial and narrowly pathological to the complicated and nuanced. As one of the most watched TELEVISION series of the 1990s and early 21st century, *ER* introduced debates about a number of physical and mental issues to a wide viewing public. Its final episode aired in 2009.

The HOSPITAL setting provided rich opportunities to discuss disability, but *ER* distinguished itself from many other medical shows by its often progressive depictions of people with disabilities. The brusque character of Dr. Kerry Weaver went for nearly 10 years without identifying the reason for her limp and iconic forearm crutch, but in the 2005 episode "Just As I Am," Weaver meets her birth mother and the audience finally learns that she had been dealing with congenital hip dysplasia, a condition that would be addressed surgically in a later episode, removing the need for her crutch.

Deafness also figured prominently in the series. In the fall of 1998, the story of surgeon Peter Benton included his anguish at deciding whether or not to have COCHLEAR IMPLANTS for his HEARING IMPAIRED son, Reese. (Reese was played by a hearing impaired actor, Matthew Watkins.) DEAF actress PHYLLIS FRELICH appeared briefly as a doctor in episodes focused on the issue of cochlear implants, and the character played by deaf actress MARLEE MATLIN was a sign language instructor. In one telling episode, Frelich's character contrasts deafness with RACE, challenging Benton's narrowly medical understanding of his son's IDENTITY as deaf. Unlike many parents (and doctors) at the time, Benton ultimately chose not to have his son undergo the implant procedure.

As the series progressed, some of the story arcs involving patients and medical workers at Cook County Hospital in Chicago became increasingly implausible and melodramatic. The deeply sexist surgeon Robert "Rocket" Romano lost an arm to a helicopter blade, and his subsequent rehabilitation emphasized his frustrations over the reattached arm and then a clumsy prosthesis. Although the cause of his amputation was somewhat unrealistic, Dr. Romano's long and frustrating rehabilitation parallels real-life experiences.

Occasionally guest stars provided opportunities to focus on particular conditions. A former teacher of Weaver, Dr. Gabriel Lawrence, was gradually revealed to have ALZHEIMER'S DISEASE, while a medical student played by Don Cheadle grappled with PARKINSON'S DISEASE (his uncontrolled tremors led Romano to refer callously to him as "the martini shaker"). Although Cheadle's character had begun a surgical rotation, his supervising doctor failed him because of his inability to control his body. Both situations drew attention to the risk and STIGMA of revealing medical conditions.

Major pharmaceutical companies sponsored *ER,* which may have influenced some of the show's treatment of disability issues; the show also occasionally used disability simply to further dramatic tension. Some activists have criticized the series for its use of able-bodied ACTORS to play disabled characters; others have praised the show for its diverse group of performers. Many would agree that *ER* put a number of physical and mental disability issues before a mainstream audience. Its characters were often defined by more than just their impairment, and its strong narrative and character development has offered insightful and subtle depictions of disability.

See also POPULAR CULTURE.

Neil Lerner

Further Reading:

Official site available online. URL: www.nbc.com/ER/. Accessed February 7, 2007.

Taylor, Zara Buggs. "Honest Portrayals of Disabilities Drive Popular Television Show." Independent Living Institute. Available online. URL: http://www.independentliving.org/ docs1/taylor.html. Accessed February 15, 2007.

TV Acres: The Web's Ultimate Guide to TV Program Facts. "Physical Impairments." Available online. URL: www. tvacres.com/handicapped_physical_EK.htm. Accessed February 7, 2007.

Ethan Frome   See WHARTON, EDITH.

ethnicity

The term *ethnicity* refers a cluster of cultural attributes that identify individuals as a social group. Language, dress, food, RELIGION, and the observance of certain feasts and holidays are among the most prevalent ethnic markers. The first settlers in the American colonies in the 17th century, white northern European Protestants, early became the country's dominant ethnic group, and although their cultural and political influence has lessened since the 1970s, they remain powerful. During the 20th century, as minority ethnic groups increased in number, they were perceived as a threat to the mainstream culture and pressured to conform to "American" values. This pressure toward Anglo-conformity resulted in some ethnic minorities changing their religions, anglicizing their names, suppressing their native languages, altering

their appearance, and abandoning many other cultural practices. Ethnicity as both a concept of IDENTITY and a historical feature of America shares many connections to disability. Although scholars have yet to explore fully the experiences of many disabled people from various ethnic groups, some have examined the similar experiences of oppression and the ways disability has been used to justify the unequal treatment of minorities in the United States.

Historical evidence from the 19th century embodies these two intertwined themes; for example, in the period following the CIVIL WAR, millions of immigrants entered the United States, and African Americans from the South migrated west and north. Many minorities actively sought to assimilate into mainstream society, yet their actions remained suspect—especially as their numbers grew. A major consequence of this increased presence was the dominant group's attribution of disability to them as a strategy to control their growing influence on the country. This association of disability with ethnic minorities manifested itself in negative cartoons, in the philosophical discussions of mainstream thinkers, in the language of immigration laws, and in the literature written by and about these groups.

Comparing minority ethnic groups to animals was a widespread tactic to instill a perception that they were deformed and disabled. In the late 19th century, American cartoonist Thomas Nast routinely portrayed Irish immigrants with ape-like faces to underline their "bestial" natures. In 1892 the influential author and former editor of the *Atlantic Monthly* Thomas Bailey Aldrich, referred to Irish, Italian, and Jewish immigrants as "human gorillas." Early 20th-century ethnic fiction often noted such portrayals; in "The Free Vacation House," for example, a short story by Jewish immigrant Anzia Yezierska, the narrator recalls that she and other Jewish mothers were treated like "stupid cows," "tagged horses," and misbehaving dogs.

Another technique reflecting the condescension of the dominant group toward ethnic minorities was to associate them with dwarfism, in contrast to the tall, robust Anglo and Nordic citizens of the United States. In THE PASSING OF THE GREAT RACE (1916), Madison Grant singled out Poles as dwarflike, while his contemporary, sociologist E. A. Ross, alluded to Jews as being "undersized and of weak stature." An 1888 cartoon, "The Last Yankee," pictures a member of the dominant group towering over pint-sized, moon-faced ethnic immigrants. The image of people from ethnic minority groups as DWARFS persisted into the late 20th century. The extremely short stature of the recently arrived Puerto Rican protagonist of Nicolasa Mohr's *In Nueva York* causes him to be both figuratively and literally looked down on.

Another physical disability—that of being crippled— was also ascribed to late-19th and early-20th century ethnic immigrants. Richmond Mayo-Smith, professor of political economy and social science at Columbia College, bemoaned that the United States was becoming an "asylum for the paupers, the convicts, and the cripples of all nations." Reflecting this derision, author Mary Gordon makes the young Irish-American protagonist in her short story collection *Temporary Shelter* (1987) a person who was born "with one leg shorter than the other." Although the young woman is bright and ambitious, members of the dominant group spurn her because of her disability and stifle her dreams.

A final disability often ascribed to ethnic minorities in the United States is mental defectiveness. The immigration laws of the early 20th century focused on restricting the entry into the country of "idiots, imbeciles, feeble-minded persons, epileptics, [and] insane persons" (as one 1917 immigration statute noted), too many of whom, it was believed, had already made America their home. Not surprisingly, newcomers, who had had little schooling in their native lands and who did not speak English, performed poorly on recently devised American INTELLIGENCE TESTS. In consequence they were easily branded as having sub-par intelligence. The pseudoscience of EUGENICS exacerbated these stigmatizing REPRESENTATIONS, using the smaller head measurements of southern and eastern Europeans to brand them as mentally DEFECTIVE.

As a result of these attitudes and policies, many members of minority ethnic groups were unfairly labeled with disabilities that they did not have. Many internalized the negative opinions of those in power and saw themselves as deformed or stupid, and were, as a result, unable to function. In reality, they were simply members of different ethnicities trying to adjust to the customs of their new land.

Although most ethnic immigrants arrived in the United States in relatively good mental and physical health, they often became disabled in America because of the overcrowding in the slums where they lived and the unsafe conditions in the factories where they worked. Novelist and social reformer Upton Sinclair chronicles the physical and mental hardships (and subsequent disabilities) of Chicago's stockyard workers in *The Jungle* (1906). In a similar vein, historian Alan Kraut, in his study *Silent Travelers: Germs, Genes, and the "Immigrant Menace"* (1994), details how infectious DISEASES such as cholera, bubonic plague, POLIO, and TUBERCULOSIS were prevalent in the United States among the Irish, Chinese, Italians, and Jews. Because of the crowded and ill-ventilated environments where they lived and worked, these groups were particularly susceptible to contagion. Instead of recognizing their vulnerability, however, the dominant group derided them for being weak and blamed them for infecting the established American population.

See also IMMIGRATION POLICY; STIGMA.

June Dwyer

Further Reading:

Gordon, Mary. *Temporary Shelter*. New York: Random House, 1987.

Grant, Madison. *The Passing of the Great Race*. New York: Scribner, 1916.

Kraut, Alan. *Silent Travelers: Germs, Genes, and the "Immigrant Menace."* New York: Basic Books, 1994.

Sinclair, Upton. *The Jungle*. 1906. New York: Heritage Press, 1965.

Yezierska, Anzia. *Hungry Hearts*. 1920. New York: Signet, 1996.

eugenics

For most of the first half of the 20th century, the movement known as eugenics profoundly influenced attitudes and policies toward people with disabilities in the United States and much of the rest of the world. The term *eugenics* was introduced in 1883 by Charles Darwin's cousin Sir FRANCIS GALTON, who defined it as the science of improving human heredity. That definition, however, left many key issues unresolved: What traits are considered "defects" and what counts as "improvement"? What does hereditary mean? What methods should be used? Who should answer these questions? Support for eugenics remained widespread through the 1930s, including such leading American progressives as President Theodore Roosevelt and birth control crusader Margaret Sanger. However, there was considerable variation over how to define "improvement" and over what methods could produce it. These questions remain fundamental to genetic medicine today.

In the 1910s and 1920s an international elite of mostly professional and managerial experts organized a network of formal institutions, such as the American Eugenics Society and the British Eugenics Education Society. They promulgated an official program of answers to these questions that significantly influenced public policy, despite the relatively small size of their memberships. However, these organizations never monopolized the meaning of eugenics. Public discussions of the term included multiple conflicting alternative answers to each of these questions, with differing implications for defining and responding to people with disabilities.

Eugenicists' diagnoses of what constituted a disability were shaped by the values of their particular cultures, including racial, religious, sexual, and other prejudices. From American immigration restrictions in the 1920s to Nazi genocide in the 1930s and 1940s, eugenics programs often first targeted people with cognitive, psychiatric, sensory, or MOBILITY disabilities, the conditions most widely accepted as constituting "defects," and then expanded the category to include ethnic, religious, and racial groups. The American exclusion of immigrants with physical disabilities was first expanded to those who failed INTELLIGENCE TESTS, and was broadened again in 1924 to limit non-Nordic European nationalities. Similarly, Nazi medical murder began with hospitalized patients who had mental or physical disabilities and then was expanded to Jews and others judged racially impaired. Eugenicists also differed over which disabilities were the most important. While eugenic scientists and intellectuals emphasized what they termed the "menace of the FEEBLEMINDED," in mass culture eugenic popularizers often portrayed an attractive strong body as more important than a high IQ score. Although the subjective basis of these definitions is obvious in hindsight, at the time each was portrayed as an objectively determined diagnosis.

In the late 1800s experiments by German biologist August Weismann demonstrated that heredity was unaffected by environment. But many eugenics supporters still included environmentally caused conditions, from infectious DISEASES to malnutrition, within the scope of their movement. This expansive view of heredity did not result from scientific ignorance. If every human trait had some hereditary component, eliminating such hereditary predispositions could be more efficient and permanent than trying to control the environmental causes. In addition, calling something hereditary often meant simply that "you got it from your parents." Parents' moral responsibility, not the technical method of transmission, was what counted. Any fault in a child that could be blamed on the parents could be seen as a eugenic defect. Eugenics could mean not simply having good genes, but being a good parent. All disabilities, not simply those with a clear genetic cause, could fall within the purview of this sweeping version of eugenics.

Emerging in the late 1800s, the study and movement known as eugenics evaluated people by their perceived genetic worth. In this 1920 photograph, medical professionals and other eugenics advocates stand along with apparent winners of a "fitter families contest," a competition celebrating people who exemplify "superior" genetic stock. *(American Philosophical Society)*

Eugenicists often distinguished between positive and negative methods to achieve their goals. Positive measures aimed at increasing the reproduction of those judged fit, including government subsidies for healthy large families and Better Baby and FITTER FAMILIES CONTESTS modeled on livestock competitions. Negative methods sought to reduce the reproduction of those considered unfit. Negative measures included INVOLUNTARY STERILIZATION, immigration exclusion, INSTITUTIONALIZATION to prevent reproduction, and EUTHANASIA. Perhaps the best known of these policies was compulsory eugenic sterilization, initiated in Indiana in 1909 and upheld by the U.S. Supreme Court in the 1927 case of *BUCK V. BELL*. Eugenic euthanasia was less common and more private, though the case of Chicago surgeon HARRY HAISELDEN shows that as early as 1915, some Americans were publicly permitted to die for their disabilities, and that the practice won wide support.

The terms "positive" and "negative" were not moral evaluations, but arithmetic operations. Positive methods added to the population while negative methods subtracted from it. Although negative measures were often more invasive and more coercive than positive methods, there were government-sponsored measures of positive eugenics, while negative techniques from sterilization to euthanasia were often practiced voluntarily, sometimes in defiance of the law. In addition, positive and negative methods were not mutually exclusive, but complementary tools to reach the same goal.

Support for anything labeled *eugenics* declined in the United States after the 1940s, in reaction to the Nazi use of eugenics to promote genocide, and in recognition of the complexity of genetic science. By the early 1970s, even the American Eugenics Society changed its name to the Society for the Study of Social Biology. But the question of whether or not current medicine bears any similarities to past eugenics remains bitterly controversial. In making such comparisons between past and present, it is important to distinguish the concept of "improving heredity" from the specific goals and specific methods employed, as well as to examine both the similarities and the differences. For example, in the early 1900s ALEXANDER GRAHAM BELL hoped eugenics would help eliminate disabilities like deafness. If a DEAF couple today used genetic testing to have a Deaf baby, would that be eugenics too? What if it became possible to find and eliminate the genetic basis of prejudice? Would such efforts be *eugenics*? Arguably both would be using science to improve heredity, but they would define improvement quite differently from Galton. The questions raised by past eugenics remain vital, even though the answers have changed considerably.

To protect modern genetics from the prejudiced values of past eugenics, many post–WORLD WAR II scholars concluded that medicine should treat only objectively defined disabilities. But others have argued it has never been possible to define ability or disability without employing some values. They argue that the problem with past eugenics was not that it *had* values, but that it had *bad* values under the cloak of objectivity. Well-intentioned efforts to keep modern medicine value-free will not succeed in eliminating values from such diagnoses, but will only obscure and delegitimate the ethical and social analysis needed to make such value judgments wisely.

See also BLACK STORK, THE; COGNITIVE DISABILITIES; DEFECTIVE; ETHNICITY; GENETICS; HUMAN GENOME PROJECT; IMMIGRATION POLICY; LAW AND POLICY; LGBT; NORMAL AND NORMALCY; RACE; REPRODUCTIVE RIGHTS; SEXUALITY.

Martin S. Pernick

Further Reading:

Baynton, Douglas. "Defectives in the Land: Disability and American Immigration Policy, 1882–1924." *Journal of American Ethnic History* 24:1 (Spring 2005):31–44.

Kevles, Daniel. *In the Name of Eugenics: Genetics and the Uses of Human Heredity.* Berkeley: University of California Press, 1985.

Lombardo, Paul A. *Three Generations, No Imbeciles: Eugenics, the Supreme Court, and* Buck v. Bell. Baltimore: Johns Hopkins University Press, 2008.

Paul, Diane B. *Controlling Human Heredity: 1865 to the Present.* Atlantic Highlands, N.J.: Humanities Press, 1995.

Pernick, Martin S. *The Black Stork: Eugenics and the Death of "Defective" Babies in American Medicine and Motion Pictures since 1915.* New York: Oxford University Press, 1996.

———. "Defining the Defective: Eugenics, Aesthetics, and Mass Culture in Early 20th-Century America." In *The Body and Physical Difference: Discourses of Disability,* edited by David T. Mitchell and Sharon Snyder, pp. 89–110. Ann Arbor: University of Michigan Press, 1997),

Stern, Alexandra Minna. *Eugenic Nation: Faults and Frontiers of Better Breeding in Modern America.* Berkeley: University of California Press, 2005.

"The Burden of Feeble-Mindedness" by W. E. Fernald (1912)

Eugenics, the pseudoscience based on the belief of inherent genetic worth and intended to improve the human species, became a dominant feature in American society in the late 19th and early 20th centuries. Its impact strongly shaped the meaning and lived experience of disability. A primary target of eugenicists was "the feebleminded," a broad category that included individuals with (or perceived to have) cognitive or developmental disabilities, the poor, racial and ethnic minorities, and criminals. Considering ways to combat "the burden of feeblemindedness," eugenicist and superintendent of the Massachusetts School for the Feeble-Minded W. E.

Fernald promotes in this 1912 article in the Journal of Psycho-Asthenics *their strict segregation from others and control over their sexual reproduction. This is but one dimension of eugenics's oppressive impact on Americans.*

"The Burden of Feeble-Mindedness" by W. E. Fernald March 1912

The methods of patient research and collective investigation which have led to such brilliant results in the study of various diseases in general medicine and surgery are now beginning to be applied to the study of the causation, extent, significance, treatment and prevention of feeble-mindedness—the synonym of human inefficiency and one of the great sources of human wretchedness and degradation.

The past few years have witnessed a striking awakening of professional and popular consciousness of the widespread prevalence of feeble-mindedness and its influence as a source of wretchedness to the patient himself and to his family, and as a causative factor in the production of crime, prostitution, pauperism, illegitimacy, intemperance and other complex social diseases.

. . . The fact that feeble-mindedness is the result of pathological conditions of the brain, either gross lesions caused by faulty development or by the destructive results of disease, or perhaps numerical deficiency or imperfect evolution of the ultimate cortical cells, makes it obvious that the resulting mental defect is incurable and permanent. If a nerve cell is damaged or destroyed by traumatism or disease, it is gone forever. It is never replace[d] by the multiplication of other similar cells, as may happen in other bodily tissues.

The various known causes of feeble-mindedness occur in two main groups—the hereditary and the accidental. The hereditary cases are those where the person is feeble-minded because his parents, or other ancestors were feeble-minded. The accidental group includes those who are feeble-minded as a result of environmental causes, without hereditary influence.

. . . So far as is known, if both parents are feeble-minded, all the offspring will be feeble-minded. If one parent is feeble-minded, it is probable that some of the offspring will be feeble-minded, and the children who are themselves normal will be likely to beget defectives. These normal persons in tainted families who are potential "carriers" of the defective germ plasm may keep up the sequence. If both parents come from tainted families, the probability of defect in the children is much increased. The normal members of tainted families who mate with healthy individuals with no family taint are not so likely to have defective children; indeed, the tendency may be eradicated by judicious breeding-up for several generations. This tendency may be expressed by one or more cases in every generation, or it may skip one generation to reappear in the next. Inheritance is not merely a question of fathers and mothers, but the family tree goes farther back.

. . . To sum up, there is a large number of feeble-minded persons in our community. The great majority of these persons are feeble-minded because they come from a stock which transmits feeble-mindedness from generation to generation in accordance with the laws of heredity. Many of the members of these families are not defective themselves, but to a certain extent these normal members of tainted families are liable to have a certain number of defectives among their own descendants.

. . . The social and economic burdens of uncomplicated feeble-mindedness are only too well known. The feeble-minded are a parasitic, predatory class, never capable of self-support or of managing their own affairs. The great majority ultimately become public charges in some form. They cause unutterable sorrow at home and are a menace and danger to the community. Feeble-minded women are almost invariably immoral, and if at large usually become carriers of venereal disease or give birth to children who are as defective as themselves. The feeble-minded woman who marries is twice as prolific as the normal woman.

We have only begun to understand the importance of feeble-mindedness as a factor in the causation of pauperism, crime and other social problems. Hereditary pauperism, or pauperism of two or more generations of the same family, generally means hereditary feeble-mindedness. In Massachusetts there are families who have been paupers for many generations. Some of the members were born or even conceived in the poorhouse.

Every feeble-minded person, especially the high-grade imbecile, is a potential criminal, needing only the proper environment and opportunity for the development and expression of his criminal

tendencies. The unrecognized imbecile is a most dangerous element in the community. There are many crimes committed by imbeciles for every one committed by an insane person. The average prison population includes more imbeciles than lunatics. The term "defective delinquent" is applied to this special class of defectives where the mental lack is relatively slight, though unmistakable, and the criminal tendencies are marked and constant.

. . . It has been truly said that feeble-mindedness is the mother of crime, pauperism and degeneracy. It is certain that the feeble-minded and the progeny of the feeble-minded constitute one of the great social and economic burdens of modern times.

. . . In the light of our present knowledge, the only way to reduce the number of the feeble-minded is to prevent their birth. The perpetuation of defective family stocks should be inhibited. This would be possible to a great extent if every feeble-minded person and potential "carrier" of the defective germ plasm could be prevented from parenthood. . . . The segregation of this class should be rapidly extended until all not adequately guarded at home are placed under strict sexual quarantine. Hundreds of known cases of this sort are now at large because the institutions are overcrowded.

. . . The biological, economic and sociological bearings of feeble-mindedness have overshadowed the fact that it is fundamentally and essentially a medical question.

. . . The growing appreciation of the medico-legal bearings of feeble-mindedness, the increasing tendency of the courts to inquire into the mental status of persons accused of crime, and the widespread movement to recognize and treat mental defect in the public schools have created an urgent demand for the services of physicians skilled in the diagnosis of mental defect which cannot be met at the present time. Indeed, the social worker, the charity visitor, the teacher and the court official often recognize cases of feeble-mindedness which they are unable to properly treat and control because they cannot secure the co-operation of suitably qualified physicians. A medical diagnosis of feeble-mindedness is necessary before a case can be properly or legally considered.

. . . The most important point is that feeble-mindedness is highly hereditary, and that each feeble-minded person is a potential source of an endless progeny of defect. No feeble-minded person should be allowed to marry, or to become a parent. The feeble-minded should be guarded or segregated during the child-bearing period.

◆

Source: W. E. Fernald. "The Burden of Feeble-Mindedness." *Journal of Psycho-Asthenics* (March 1912). Available online. URL: http://www.disabilitymuseum.org/lib/docs/1208.htm. Accessed June 26, 2008.

euthanasia

Euthanasia, literally translated as a "good death," and sometimes known as "mercy killing," may have existed throughout history and in many cultures, and its history in America is significantly intertwined with issues of disability. The history of euthanasia in the United States involves important questions about the practice of having physicians or families terminate life-sustaining treatment for those who, because of their AGE, mental status, or disability, have been deemed incompetent. This practice is distinguished from PHYSICIAN-ASSISTED SUICIDE, which can occur when competent adults actively seek out aid in dying.

Throughout American history, euthanasia was seen as an option for people with disabilities. However, the practice gained scientific credibility in the 19th century with the birth of the EUGENICS movement, which sought to improve human heredity and eradicate genetic diseases. One of many eugenicists who advocated for euthanasia was Dr. HARRY J. HAISELDEN, a prominent Chicago surgeon who counseled parents to withhold treatment from their children born with severe abnormalities. He gained notoriety in 1915 by writing about his cases in the *Chicago American* and starring in *THE BLACK STORK*, a film that featured parents of a newborn with a genetic disease who opt not to provide life-saving treatment for their child. Many parents of CHILDREN with disabilities wrote to Haiselden, asking for help ending their own children's lives.

This attitude persisted through at least the 1930s. Historian Janice Brockley has drawn attention to this trend through the stories of Louis Repouille and Jerry Greenfield, two young boys with disabilities who were murdered by their fathers during this decade. The fathers were met with tolerance and support for their actions as juries declared them "not guilty" of murder in part because the boys were viewed as draining influences on their families.

These events from the early decades of the 20th century illustrate common attitudes in American society. Support for euthanasia naturally followed from the broad acceptance of eugenics as scientific truth and from the attitudes about life for people with disabilities. Some parents of children with disabilities welcomed euthanasia as a way to end their children's suffering. Public discussion of the cases in the press commonly assumed that parents had few choices: to care for their children without any societal support, to confine their children to a custodial institution, or to kill them. To date, there is no evidence that any individuals with disabilities participated in these public discussions during this period.

In the 1970s advances in life-sustaining technology and the emergence of both the field of bioethics and a strong movement for disability rights thrust the issue of euthanasia into a public spotlight. Most bioethics literature, legal decisions, and professional practice in recent decades has proceeded from the conviction that impairment reduces the quality of the life being lived. From this conventional perspective, someone with a significant disability has reason to end life-sustaining treatment and to desire death. If people with disabilities are perceived to have few opportunities and to find their lives burdensome, the same logic fosters familial views that ending a disabled person's life is in everyone's interest. Justifications for euthanasia include the physical suffering and PAIN of the potential treatments as well as the IMPAIRMENTs themselves, the conviction that technology is being used to sustain people who will have painful and miserable lives regardless of what is done for them, the anguish for families who watch loved ones die slowly after fruitless procedures, familial stress and burden in their involvement with a disabled person, and the belief that the dollars spent on life-sustaining treatments are better used in other ways. This understanding of disability motivates discussions about withholding treatment from newborn infants, ending life-sustaining treatments for adults with disabilities, and refusing to treat someone with a new condition because of an individual's preexisting, uncorrectable disability.

Members of the DISABILITY RIGHTS MOVEMENT oppose this thinking. They point to cases of persons with disabilities who could live for several years with their conditions, but on whose behalf families make requests to end life-sustaining treatment. Considering euthanasia to be more than an "end of life" issue, the movement lobbies against the denial of potentially lifesaving and life-improving treatments for anyone with disabilities who could live if treatments were given, but who will not be cured of their disabling conditions.

Disability scholars and activists first spoke out on these matters in 1983, when a legal case made headlines in the United States. Baby Jane Doe was an infant born with SPINA BIFIDA whose parents sought to deny life-prolonging surgery on the grounds that without treatment she would die more quickly. A case was brought to court by an independent attorney to argue on behalf of Baby Jane Doe.

During the discussion of this case and subsequent similar cases, many commentators from the disability COMMUNITY contended that even a demonstrably loving and involved FAMILY may be unable to put aside its own view of life with disability to imagine such a life from the vantage point of someone with an impairment. The family's distress about a child's DEVELOPMENTAL DISABILITY, a young man's TRAUMATIC BRAIN INJURY, or a parent's DEMENTIA may prevent them from appreciating life as it is left to their loved one. Consequently, some people with a disability rights perspective are wary of family as decision makers for newborn infants or for conscious, minimally aware, or otherwise cognitively disabled people who appear to enjoy some parts of their lives. Moreover, these scholars believe that physicians and families should ascertain the values and preferences of people with impaired communication and cognition, and that most of those people could express some views about their lives. If family members must decide questions of life and death for relatives whose condition deprives them of the legal authority to assert themselves, some disability rights adherents insist that quality of life should be judged from the patient's current vantage point. The judgment would take account of current activities and satisfactions, rather than evaluating life from the perspective of the nonimpaired family members or the formerly unimpaired individual.

In 2000 NOT DEAD YET and other groups opposed the efforts of Robert Wendland's wife to withdraw food and water from her minimally conscious husband. Robert Wendland was able to engage in some life activities and could communicate on some topics using a "yes-no" communication system. The California Supreme Court upheld the opposition to terminating his life by withdrawing food and water in its 2001 ruling. The court determined that Wendland's wife failed to show by "clear and convincing evidence" that Mr. Wendland would want to die.

Disability advocates did not prevail in the TERRI SCHIAVO case decided in Florida in 2005. In that instance, the court found—and the autopsy subsequently confirmed—that Schiavo was in a persistent vegetative state and not minimally conscious; it also accepted that her husband had provided sufficient evidence of her prior wishes for death as opposed to life in a persistent vegetative state. In 2005, 43 disability groups published a Statement of Common Principles on physician-assisted suicide, euthanasia, and life-ending decisions. A key point of the statement is its view that, in the absence of "clear and convincing evidence" of prior wishes, food and water should never be withdrawn from minimally conscious persons and that medical treatment should continue unless death is imminent and treatment would only prolong the dying process. To do otherwise, in this view, is to commit involuntary euthanasia.

Disability rights opposition to ending life flows from beliefs quite different from the views of many religiously oriented, antiabortion opponents who affirm an unqualified "sanctity of life" stance. The disability rights movement affirms the capacity for self-direction of those with even very severe disabilities and respects their informed decision making, maintaining that only careful exploration of treatment and life alternatives, along with ACCESS to social and health services, assures genuine choice. The movement also believes that much of the frustration and anguish experienced by people with disabilities and their families stems not from disabling conditions but from living in a world that resists accommodating individual differences and thus fails to create environments in which people with disabilities can flourish. The disability rights movement lobbies not for the "sanctity of life" but for making changes in society to enhance the lives of those with disabilities, and its political and social agenda on end-of-life issues must be understood as part of its commitment to broad social transformation to respect the dignity, humanity, and moral equality of people regardless of their disability.

See also BABY DOE CASES.

Adrienne Asch

Further Reading:

Brockley, Janice. "Martyred Mothers and Merciful Fathers: Exploring Disability and Motherhood in the Lives of Jerome Greenfield and Raymond Repouille." In *The New Disability History,* edited by Paul K. Longmore and Lauri Umansky. New York: New York University Press, 2002.

The Center on Human Policy. 2005. *Statement of Common Principles on Life-Sustaining Care and Treatment of People with Disabilities Home Page.* Available online. URL: http://thechp.syr.edu/endorse/. Accessed April 15, 2008.

Not Dead Yet. 2002. Amicae Curiae Brief in the Matter of the Conservatorship of Robert Wendland. Available online. URL: http://www.notdeadyet.org/docs/wendbrief.html. Accessed April 15, 2008.

Pernick, Martin. *The Black Stork: Eugenics and the Death of "Defective" Babies in American Medicine and Motion Pictures Since 1915.* New York: Oxford University press, 1996.

Evans, Dale (Frances Octavia Smith, Dale Evans Rogers) (1912–2001) *author, performer*

Although she was best known for her roles during the 1940s and 1950s in 29 Western films and over 100 television shows with her husband, Roy Rogers, Dale Evans also played an important role in advocacy for CHILDREN with developmental disabilities and their families. Born on October 31, 1912, she grew up as Frances Octavia Smith in Uvalde, Texas, eloped when she was 14, had a son at 15, and was a divorced, single mother at age 17.

In spite of her Texas roots, Evans's career in show business began as a big-band vocalist and radio personality before she moved to Hollywood under contract with a movie studio. After making several other movies, she was cast with rising cowboy star Roy Rogers in *The Cowboy and the Senorita,* a 1944 Western. Rogers and Evans married in 1947 and remained together until his death in 1998.

The couple's only child, Robin Elizabeth Rogers, was born on August 26, 1950, with DOWN SYNDROME. In an era when society stigmatized families of children with intellectual disabilities, Evans and Rogers were counseled to institutionalize their daughter and hide her existence from the public, but they both refused. Sadly, Robin contracted the mumps and died when she was only two years old.

By the early 1950s, a few parents of children with intellectual disabilities had begun to openly tell their stories. When Evans read novelist PEARL BUCK's 1950 article "The Child Who Never Grew," she had a mixed reaction. She was impressed that Buck was finally acknowledging her 30-year-old disabled daughter, but upset that Buck had institutionalized her daughter and hidden her existence for decades. She decided to write her own story about her daughter, Robin. *Angel Unaware* (1953) was written in deeply religious terms, but it expressed a universal maternal pride and asserted that the Rogers FAMILY had benefited from Robin's presence. The book was serialized in newspapers concurrently with its publication, and expected to have a modest readership. In its first nine months of sales, more than 257,000 copies of the story had been purchased. The original price of the hardcover book was $1 and the royalties were donated to the National Association for Retarded Children (later named THE ARC). The book earned $40,000 in royalties during its first year in print, which enabled the organization to open its first national office. The ARC of the United States eventually became a powerful advocacy group for people with intellectual disabilities and their families.

Evans's financial assistance during the organization's early days gave an important boost to its development, but the emotional support she provided for families of disabled children made a much larger impact. At a time when most families of children with developmental disabilities had been shamed, Evans and Rogers became the role models for parental pride. In the years that followed, the rodeos hosted by Evans and Rogers across America became gathering places for parents of children with disabilities.

Although Evans had been warned that speaking out about her daughter's disability would hurt her public image, the publicity generated by telling her family's story actually added to her popularity. The public's acceptance of Evans's and Rogers's commitment to improving the lives of people with intellectual disabilities was also instrumental in getting then-president Dwight D. Eisenhower and other prominent figures of the 1950s to join in the effort.

Seen here in 1950 with her infant daughter Robin, famed Western television and film star Dale Evans (1912–2001) rejected doctors' advice to institutionalize her only child. Instead, Evans spoke positively about her experiences as a parent of a child with cognitive disabilities and helped fund the National Association for Retarded Children (later known as The ARC).   *(The Roy Rogers-Dale Evans Happy Trails Theater & Attraction, Branson, Missouri)*

Evans's experiences as a mother of a disabled child and a disability advocate reflect important changes in the latter half of the 20th century. As parents increasingly challenged stereotypes of disability and initiated activist networks, important organizations and reforms emerged. Even though these members often agitated for, rather than with, disabled individuals, their concerns as family members highlight the broad impact of disability in American society. By the early 21st century, *Angel Unaware* had sold more than 2 million copies worldwide, evidencing Evans's direct contribution to disability awareness. Evans died in her home in California on February 7, 2001.

See also ACTIVISM AND ADVOCACY; COGNITIVE AND INTELLECTUAL DISABILITY; DEVELOPMENTAL DISABILITY; INSTITUTIONALIZATION; PARENT ADVOCACY GROUPS; STIGMA.

Dick Sobsey

Further Reading:

Garrison, Maxine. *The Angel Spreads Her Wings: The Inspiration of* Angel Unaware *and the Influence of the Roy Rogers Family in the American Home.* Westwood, N.J.: Fleming H. Revell, 1956.

Rogers, Roy, and Dale Evans. *Happy Trails: Our Life Story.* New York: Simon & Schuster, 1994.

Sobsey, Dick. "Dale Evans and the Great Rescue: A Parent's View." *Mental Retardation* 39, no. 5 (2001): 401–404.

exhibitions

Exhibitions have played an important role in the history of disability. The exhibition of disabled bodies in the United States has early modern origins in the tradition of English fairs. In the premodern era, the disabled body was often given some supernatural or extra-rational significance, seen as a sign of divine disfavor or selection.

In the United States, exhibitions were common from 1850 to the early 1940s. Business managers oversaw the contracts and work of many of those exhibited. These relationships ranged from beneficial partnerships to EXPLOITATION, bordering on and including captivity.

With the formation of dime museums in the mid to late 19th century, exhibitions moved from itinerant to relatively permanent. This offered performers the benefit of stable EMPLOYMENT without the demands of frequent travel. These exhibitions were also increasingly marked by a move from premodern understanding of disability to one informed by a scientific enthusiasm for classification. Exhibitors often stressed the educational and scientific value of exhibitions in hopes of minimizing criticism from religious and other community organizations. P. T. BARNUM's American Museum, formed in 1841 in New York City, was among the most financially successful. The museum featured a variety of performers with disabilities or congenital anomalies, including CONJOINED TWINS, those of abnormally tall or short stature, and individuals who would now be identified as developmentally delayed. Notable exhibits included the elderly and blind Joice Heth, touted to be the 160-year-old nurse to George Washington. (A later autopsy revealed her to be no more than 80.) The exhibition of the diminutive TOM THUMB (Charles Sherwood Stratton) and LAVINIA WARREN was also especially successful. Barnum also promoted their wedding in 1863 and it became one of the biggest events of the year, attended by thousands.

In addition to being exhibited in dime museums, other locations, including world fairs, featured those with disabilities. Alongside ethnological displays and foreign villages of exotic others displayed at world fairs, managers also featured people with disabled bodies, though they often appeared in "freak shows" and other exhibitions just outside of the fairs'

gates. Until at least the mid 20th century, amusement parks, CIRCUSES, carnivals, and fairs were all also frequent sites of exhibitions of human "oddities."

In the 20th century, the rise of EUGENIC ideology that defined disabilities in strongly stigmatized, pathological terms, as well as increased ACTIVISM by reform groups, among other factors, made exhibitions of people with disabilities increasingly inappropriate to the public. Under increasing cultural pressure and diminishing public interest, exhibitions of people with disabilities became extremely rare by the late 1940s. Public exhibitions of disabled bodies or human "oddities" continue to be extremely rare in the present. Only a handful of itinerant performance groups continue to showcase the disabled body. The oldest permanent "FREAK SHOW" exhibition in America continues in Coney Island, though now largely dominated by sword-swallowers and other "self-made" freaks, rather than genetic human "oddities."

Today a number of disability activist PERFORMANCE ARTISTS explicitly use the history of the exhibition of disabled bodies to analyze and question conceptions of disability in the present. Many disability scholars and historians debate the cultural legacy of the exhibition of people with disabilities, particularly the "freak show." Some believe it represents the worst form of exploitation; others point to examples of how people with disabilities used exhibitions to advance themselves; and others believe the history of the exhibition of disabled bodies may hint at other possible ways to conceive of disability and of the body itself.

See also POPULAR CULTURE; REPRESENTATION; STARING; STEREOTYPE.

Raphael Raphael

Further Reading:

Adams, Rachel. *Sideshow U.S.A., Freaks and the American Cultural Imagination.* Chicago: University of Chicago Press, 2001.

Bogdan, Robert. *Freak Show: Presenting Human Oddities for Amusement and Profit.* Chicago: University of Chicago Press, 1988.

Garland Thomson, Rosemarie. *Extraordinary Bodies: Figuring Physical Disability in American Culture and Literature.* New York: Columbia University Press, 1997.

Rydell, Robert W. *All the World's a Fair: Visions of Empire at American International Expositions, 1876–1916.* Chicago: University of Chicago Press, 1984.

exploitation

Exploitation involves treating a group or individuals unfairly or unjustly for personal, financial, or political gain. Exploitation may occur in a variety of situations and under many circumstances. People with disabilities represent a significant group of individuals who have encountered exploitation throughout different periods of America's history.

The long-held cultural perception that disabled individuals lack intelligence, ability, or control over their faculties has in part served to justify their exploitation. This was particularly evident in the 19th century with the advent of the popular amusement known as the sideshow, or "FREAK SHOW." Associated with carnivals, fairs, and curiosity museums, the sideshow featured both animate and inanimate "oddities" on display for the public's amusement and the manager's profit. Many people with congenital disabilities appeared in sideshows. Not only were they subjected to physical scrutiny by masses of spectators, but many of these individuals failed to receive adequate economic compensation for their participation. Sideshows remained popular through the 1930s until the public began raising objections about the ethics of showcasing individuals who may or may not understand the consequences of their participation in this "entertainment." Few actual accounts by these performers survive, making it impossible to generalize about their treatment and attitudes toward sideshow culture. However, many performers whose life stories are documented spoke favorably of their time working in sideshows, explaining that they did not feel exploited. The sideshow, they argue, provided a means to make a living when labor opportunities for people with disabilities were scarce and helped to create community for people unwanted or abandoned by their families. Scholars like David Gerber, however, point out that many FREAK SHOW performers may have had few other options for EMPLOYMENT and that managers like P. T. BARNUM made fortunes from showcasing these individuals in venues that disregarded their humanity.

The 20th-century CHARITY industry is another entity that many disability scholars and activists believe exploits disabled individuals in an effort to drive fund-raising. Numerous charities employ graphic strategies to raise both awareness and money for their particular cause. Billboards, print advertisements, and TELEVISION appearances on TELE-THONS typically feature the person with disabilities acting as a spokesperson for the charity and representative of the given DISEASE or disability. Historically, children have fulfilled these roles due to the belief that images of suffering children held great emotional impact and would therefore motivate the public to donate. Scholars, disability activists, and social critics have raised objections to the use of such

personalization, arguing it is a practice analogous to the displays of the 19th-century sideshow. In addition, many contend that it unfairly reduces the many complexities of a disabled person's physicality and experience to a portrayal of disability as sentimentalized and pathetic. In the 1990s a backlash against the charity industry occurred when several former poster CHILDREN turned activists began speaking out about their experiences. According to these individuals, the charity industry took advantage of their youthful naïveté to objectify their images unfairly, distorting their experiences to raise money. These types of complaints not only drew attention to the charity industry's fund-raising methods, but they also, in some cases, provoked boycotts and public PROTEST over events such as telethons. Conversely, many disabled children and adults report a positive experience in their involvement with the charity industry. They counter accusations of exploitation by stating that utilizing actual disabled people in charity campaigns helps to educate the public about the disability experience, and provides the disabled individual with a voice.

As evidenced, exploitation is often a subjective issue given to interpretation and influenced by additional factors such as changes in cultural attitudes or new ways of examining historical evidence; for instance, the photographer DIANE ARBUS took many photographs of disabled adults and children with their permission during the 1960s. Twenty-first century critics of her work state that Arbus's photographs exploit people with disabilities in the way that they are objectified and made to seem "freakish" to further Arbus's professional career. Disability rights activists, scholars, historians, and social critics who continue to criticize moments where exploitation may be evident enable a public debate that raises important awareness about the ways in which disabled people are represented and participate in American society.

Sheila C. Moeschen

Further Reading:

Bogdan, Robert. *Freak Show: Presenting Human Oddities for Amusement and Profit.* Chicago: University of Chicago Press, 1988.

Garland Thomson, Rosemarie. *Extraordinary Bodies: Figuring Physical Disability in American Culture and Literature.* New York: Columbia University Press, 1997.

Index

spinal cord injury **3**:856

sports **3**:858

Star Trek **3**:863

Star Wars **3**:863–**3**:864

stereotypes **3**:866, **3**:867

Stratton-Porter, Gene **3**:872

Suddenly, Last Summer **3**:874

TBIs **3**:909

television **3**:888

theater **3**:900

Twitch and Shout **3**:912–**3**:913

ugly laws **3**:914

Unbreakable **3**:914–**3**:915

Veditz, George W. **3**:924

Vetter, David **3**:929

Vietnam War **3**:931

Wait Until Dark **3**:942

Walloch, Greg **3**:944

war **3**:948

Waterdance, The **3**:953–**3**:954

Waterstreet, Edmund, Jr. **3**:954–
      3:955

What's Eating Gilbert Grape **3**:959–
      3:960

Wit **3**:971–**3**:972

X-Men **3**:985

Finding Nemo **1**:livc, **2**:362

Finger, Anne **1**:266, **3**:819

fingerspelling **2**:363, **2**:363–**2**:364

      Breslin, Mary Lou **1**:142

      Carlin, John **1**:160

      deaf-blind **1**:238

      Howard, Petra Fandrem **2**:452

      Howe, Samuel Gridley **2**:453

      Keller, Helen **2**:526

      Macy, Anne Sullivan **2**:583

Fischer, Angeline Fuller **2**:364–**2**:365

Fisher, John D. **2**:453–**2**:455, **2**:712

Fitter Families contests **1**:334, **2**:346,
      2:365, **2**:365–**2**:366

Fjeld, Julianna **2**:366–**2**:367

Flanagan, Bob **1**:268, **1**:270, **2**:711

Flournoy, John **1**:xxvic, **1**:31, **1**:161,
      1:233, **2**:367–**2**:368

Flowers for Algernon (Keyes) **1**:xxxixc,
      2:368–**2**:369

fluoxetine. *See* Prozac

Food and Drug Administration **1**:14,
      1:60, **1**:193, **1**:194, **2**:437, **3**:899

forced sterilization. *See* involuntary
      sterilization

Ford, Gerald **1**:xliiic, **1**:35, **1**:311, **3**:852

Ford, Henry **1**:xxixc, **2**:369, **2**:369–
      2:370

Ford Motor Company **1**:xxixc, **1**:83,
      2:369, **2**:369–**2**:370, **2**:547, **3**:907,
      3:976

Forman, Miloš **2**:486, **2**:535, **2**:675

"for," "of" v. **2**:681, **2**:684

Forrest Gump **1**:56, **1**:57, **2**:370–**2**:371,
      2:700, **2**:730

Foster, Andrew **1**:xxxviic, **2**:371–**2**:372,
      2:394

foster care **2**:372–**2**:374, **3**:777

Foucault, Michel **2**:374

      insanity **2**:485

      LGBT **2**:563

      mental illness **2**:611, **2**:612

      peddlers and peddling **2**:709

      prison **2**:742

      social construction of disability
            3:837–**3**:838

      social control **3**:838

Foundation for Infantile Paralysis. *See*
      March of Dimes

Fourteenth Amendment **2**:400, **2**:701,
      3:848, **3**:896, **3**:937, **3**:989–**3**:990

Fowler, Sophia. *See* Gallaudet, Sophia
      Fowler

Fox, Michael J. **1**:lvc, **2**:374–**2**:375,
      2:704

Frampton, Merle **2**:375–**2**:376

Francis, Thomas **1**:xxxviic, **2**:651, **2**:726

Frank, Morris **1**:xxxiic, **2**:416, **3**:811

Franklin Delano Roosevelt Memorial **1**:
      liic, *2:376,* **2**:376–**2**:377, **2**:655, **2**:750

freakery **1**:132–**1**:133, **1**:248, **2**:377–
      2:379

Freaks (film) **1**:xxxiic, **1**:207, **1**:269,
      2:361, **2**:378, **2**:379–**2**:381, *2:380,*
      3:774

freak shows **1**:xxvic, **1**:xxixc, **2**:381–
      2:383

      ableism **1**:2

      Barnum, P. T. **1**:90, **1**:91

      Bunker, Chang and Eng **1**:149

      circus **1**:178, **1**:179

      community **1**:207

      conjoined twins **1**:212

      deformity **1**:249

      disability culture **1**:269–**1**:270

      disfigurement **1**:294

      exhibitions **1**:340

      exploitation **1**:341

      Midget Cities **2**:615–**2**:616

      photography **2**:718

      popular culture **2**:732

      race **3**:757

      representation **3**:773

South Park **3**:850

staring **3**:860–**3**:861

stereotypes **3**:866

stigma **3**:868

Stratton, Charles Sherwood **3**:870–
      3:871

Swan, Anna Haining **3**:876

television **3**:889

"What Is It?" **3**:958–**3**:959

Freeman, Walter **1**:xxxiic, **2**:573, **2**:613,
      3:865

Frelich, Phyllis **1**:12, **1**:173, **1**:331,
      2:383–**2**:384

Freud, Sigmund **2**:384–**2**:385

      cerebral palsy **1**:164–**1**:165

      depression **1**:256

      hysteria **2**:462

      insanity **2**:484–**2**:485

      melancholy **2**:605

      neurasthenia **2**:659

      OCD **2**:670

Fries, Kenny **1**:liic, **1**:266, **2**:467–**2**:469

frontal lobotomy. *See* lobotomy

Fruchterman, Jim **1**:lvc, **1**:124

funding **1**:xlivc, **1**:74, **1**:198, **2**:481,
      3:790, **3**:916

G

Gage, Phineas **1**:xxvic, **2**:386–**2**:388,
      3:908

Galen **1**:262, **2**:605

Gallagher, Hugh Gregory **1**:63, **1**:64,
      2:352, *2:388,* **2**:388–**2**:389, **2**:700

Gallaudet, Edward Miner **1**:xxviic,
      2:389, **2**:389–**2**:391

      Fay, Edward Allen **2**:350

      Fischer, Angeline Fuller **2**:364

      Gallaudet, Sophia Fowler **2**:391

      Gallaudet University **2**:394–**2**:395

      Kendall, Amos **2**:531

      Stafford, May Martin **3**:860

Gallaudet, Sophia Fowler **1**:43, **2**:389,
      2:391–**2**:392, **2**:393, **2**:394, **2**:531

Gallaudet, Thomas **2**:391, **2**:392

Gallaudet, Thomas Hopkins **1**:xxvc, **1**:
      xxvic, **2**:392–**2**:393

      activism and advocacy **1**:9

      American School for the Deaf
            1:42–**1**:45

      American Sign Language **1**:45

      asylums and institutions **1**:72

      Carlin, John **1**:161

      Clerc, Laurent **1**:186–**1**:188

      Cogswell, Alice **1**:199, **1**:200